Performance Budgeting

Performance Budgeting

Linking Funding and Results

Edited by

Marc Robinson

palgrave
macmillan

INTERNATIONAL MONETARY FUND

Nothing contained in this book should be reported as representing the views of the IMF, its Executive Board, member governments, or any other entity mentioned herein. The views expressed in this book belong solely to the authors.

First published 2007 by
PALGRAVE MACMILLAN
Houndmills, Basingstoke, Hampshire RG21 6XS and
175 Fifth Avenue, New York, N.Y. 10010
Companies and representatives throughout the world

PALGRAVE MACMILLAN is the global academic imprint of the Palgrave Macmillan division of St Martin's Press LLC and of Palgrave Macmillan Ltd.
Macmillan® is a registered trademark in the United States, United Kingdom and other countries. Palgrave is a registered trademark in the European Union and other countries.

ISBN-13 978–0–230–55356–9 hardback
ISBN-10 0–230–55356–7 hardback

This book is printed on paper suitable for recycling and made from fully managed and sustained forest sources. Logging, pulping and manufacturing processes are expected to conform to the environmental regulations of the country of origin.

A catalogue record for this book is available from the British Library.

Library of Congress Cataloging-in-Publication Data
Performance budgeting : linking funding and results / edited by Marc Robinson.
p. cm.
Includes index.
ISBN 0–230–55356–7 (alk. paper)
1. Program budgeting. I. Robinson, Marc, 1953–

HJ2031.P47 2007
658.15'4—dc22 2007021651

10 9 8 7 6 5 4 3 2 1
16 15 14 13 12 11 10 09 08 07

Printed and bound in Great Britain by
Antony Rowe Ltd, Chippenham, Wiltshire

Contents

List of Tables and Figures

Tables

Figures

Notes on Contributors

Kate Ashcroft

Professor Kate Ashcroft has recently returned from two and a half years in Ethiopia as management advisor to the Minister of Education and Acting Director of the Ethiopian Higher Education Strategy Center. During her time in Ethiopia she chaired the National Committee of Enquiry into Governance, Leadership and Management in Ethiopia's Higher Education Institutions, chaired the task force on Private/Public Partnership in Higher Education, undertook a major report on the curriculum, organizational arrangements and financing of the 13 new higher education institutions to be opened in Ethiopia, as well as leading the development of a funding formula for teaching and learning in Ethiopia's higher education system to be operated from next financial year. Before going to Ethiopia, Kate had experience as a senior manager in the Higher Education Funding Council for England and a senior and middle manager in four UK higher education institutions, finishing as the Deputy Vice Chancellor of the University of Wales Institute, Cardiff. Kate has published 11 books and numerous papers and reports on educational issues. She is now working as an independent educational consultant, mainly in Ethiopia and Zambia, and is visiting professor at the University of Northampton and the University of Wales Institute, Cardiff.

Elena Belyanova

Dr. Elena Belyanova is a Managing Partner of ECORYS Nederland BV (successor of the Netherlands Economic Institute (NEI)). Since 1990 Elena has been working as manager and consultant in many projects promoting social and economic reforms in all CIS countries and in Africa. In 1997 she set up the Russian branch of NEI and headed it for ten years. In 2003–06 she managed three subsequent EU-funded projects which supported the RF Ministry of Finance in initiating a multi-year results oriented reform, elaborating its concept and managing its implementation. Her professional activities also encompass research into corporate and public finance, developing and delivering an interactive course on Financial Sector in Transition in the Moscow State University, Economic Department, and running the Economic Analysis Chair there. Elena co-founded the Russian Economic Barometer, an organization which was the first to launch economic surveys in Russia, and co-managed it from 1991 to 1996. At present she chairs the Board of the Economic Development and Civil Society Foundation, a Russian NGO which has been recently established on her initiative.

Jim Brumby

Jim Brumby, an Australian national who joined the IMF in 1999, has been engaged in public management reform at state, national, and international levels for two decades. Prior to moving to the Fund's Office of Budget and Planning in late 2005, he worked in FAD on public expenditure management, providing technical assistance to China, Indonesia, the Slovak Republic, Slovenia, Bulgaria, Malawi, Ghana, and Nigeria. He has also contributed to fiscal transparency reports on Italy, Malawi, and the USA, and played a leading role in assessing public expenditure management systems in the so-called "heavily indebted poor countries." Prior to joining the IMF, he was in charge of the Organization for Economic Co-operation and Development's program on budgeting and management run by the Public Management Service (PUMA), with responsibilities that included coordinating the work of the Senior Budget Officials working party. He worked in the New Zealand Treasury for four years as head of its unit providing advice on public service reform and prior to that at the central finance ministry of the State of Victoria in Australia. He has a Masters degree in public administration from Harvard University.

Benoît Chevauchez
A senior French civil servant, Benoît Chevauchez has dedicated most of his professional career to public finance and public management. A graduate of the Ecole Nationale d'Administration, Benoît held several positions in the Budget Directorate of the Ministry of Finance and was budget advisor to a former Prime Minister. After having spent one year as an advisor to the OECD, Benoît established in 2001 the Public Management Institute—the Ministry of Finance training agency—which he managed until the summer of 2005. Now a "Controleur Général" and consultant, Benoît also teaches public finance at Sciences Po and Paris I La Sorbonne, two leading Paris universities.

Teresa Curristine
Teresa Curristine works for the Budgeting and Public Expenditure division of the OECD Public Governance Directorate. She leads the project on governing for performance and heads the OECD Senior Budget Officials Network on Performance and Results. She manages projects and teams working on accountability and control issues and the OECD database on budget practices and procedures. She planned and coordinated a directorate-wide project on public sector modernization. She edited the book entitled *Modernizing Government: The Way Forward*, which resulted from this project and was the main book for the recent OECD ministerial meeting for ministers of public sector reform. She has also worked as lecturer at Oxford University from where she received her PhD.

Matt Davies
Matt Davies is currently a senior economist in the Asia and Pacific Department of the IMF. He previously worked in the Fiscal Affairs Department on expenditure policy and management issues where the work on his paper for the Performance Budgeting seminar was undertaken. Prior to joining the Fund he worked in the UK government, in the Department for International Development and the Department of Social Security, and for the Government of Papua New Guinea in the Ministry of Finance and Planning.

Michael Di Francesco

Michael Di Francesco is Principal Advisor in Financial Management Policy in NSW Treasury, where his responsibilities include leadership for developing and implementing Results and Services Plans and financial management reform in the General Government sector. Prior to joining the Treasury in 2001, Michael was a Lecturer in Government in the School of Economics and Political Science at the University of Sydney, where he taught public sector management and Australian politics, and directed the graduate program in Public Policy and Policy Studies. He has served as a Councillor with the NSW division of the Institute of Public Administration Australia (IPAA). Michael holds a Bachelor of Economics with first class honors in Government and Public Administration from the University of Sydney, and a PhD in Public Policy from the Australian National University. He has published on performance evaluation and financial management and budgeting reform in the public sector. In 2001 he shared IPAA's prestigious Sam Richardson Prize for the most important/influential article published in the *Australian Journal of Public Administration.*

Jack Diamond

Jack Diamond was, prior to his retirement after a long career with the International Monetary Fund, Division Chief, Public Financial Management Division I, in the Fiscal Affairs Department. Over his career, Jack worked in many countries and made a particularly notable contribution during the transition period in Russia and other parts of the ex-Soviet bloc. He is the author of many IMF Working Papers and other publications, including *Introducing Financial Management Information Systems in Developing Countries* (2005, with Pokar Khemani), *Reforming the Russian Budget System: A Move to More Devolved Budget Management?* (2005), *Establishing a Performance Management Framework for Government* (2005), *From Program to Performance Budgeting: The Challenge for Emerging Economies* (2003), *Performance Budgeting: Managing the Reform Process* (2003), and *Performance Budgeting – Is Accrual Accounting Required?* (2002).

Israel Fainboim Yaker

Since 2004 Israel Fainboim has been a Technical Assistance Advisor with the Public Financial Management Division of the Fiscal Affairs Department, IMF. Before joining the Fund he led the Mission on Institutional Reform of Bogota and was the Secretary of Finance of that city, and a board member of four public utilities. He held the position of Research Associate at Fedesarrollo, a leading think tank on economic policy. Previously he was a member of the Council on Fiscal Policy in the Ministry of Finance and Director of Economic Research in the Corporación Financiera del Valle. At the beginning of his career he worked in the Economic Research Unit of the Banco de la República (Central Bank of Colombia) and was an advisor to the National Planning Department. He has also been a consultant of the World Bank, the Inter-American Development Bank and the Ministry of Finance and professor of Public Economics in the Universidad de los Andes. He has published papers on fiscal sustainability, public investment, decentralization, concession contracts, credit subsidies, contingent liabilities, and regulation of public utilities.

Denise M. Fantone

Denise M. Fantone is Acting Director, Education, Workforce, and Income Security, US Government Accountability Office (GAO). After working for local government and a public utility in California, Ms. Fantone began her federal government career at the Department of Justice in the charter class of the Presidential Management Intern Program. Following her internship, she joined the US Office of Management and Budget's (OMB) Budget Review Division, where she served as an OMB analyst on appropriations issues, was team leader for the budget execution and apportionment unit, and led teams in the annual preparation of the President's Budget. Prior to coming to GAO, she was progressively Budget Director, Deputy Director for Planning and Budget, and Assistant Inspector General for Oversight at the Peace Corps. At GAO, she is primarily responsible for agency budget execution issues. Recent work includes reports on performance integration efforts in the Veterans Health Administration, the Administration for Children and Families, and Nuclear Regulatory Commission; reviews of OMB's Program Assessment Rating Tool (PART); and best practices in state performance budgeting. Ms. Fantone is currently on a rotational assignment as part of GAO's Executive Candidate Development and Assessment Program.

Victoria Gunnarsson

Victoria Gunnarsson is a Research Officer in the Expenditure Policy Division of the Fiscal Affairs Department. She joined the Fund in October, 2005 from the World Bank Institute where she worked on designing and interpreting impact evaluations of the effectiveness of capacity enhancement programs. In the Fund her work has centered on measuring the efficiency and flexibility of health and education expenditure in various country contexts. Her previous research focused on the impact of child labor on educational attainment of young children in developing countries and the effect of school autonomy on schooling outcomes.

Marcela Guzmán

Marcela Guzmán is a principal of Politeia, a consultancy firm based in Santiago de Chile, and was formerly Chief, Performance Monitoring Division, Budget Office, Ministry of Finance in Chile, since 2000. Prior to that, she held a range of other senior positions in the Finance Ministry, including Chief of the Research Department in the Budget Office. From 1997 to 1999, she was Chief, Research and Statistics Department, Ministry of Education. Marcela spent a year on secondment at the Budget and Management Division of the OECD in Paris from October 2002 to September 2003. She has undertaken many consultancies for the World Bank, the Inter-American Development Bank, and other organizations. She holds two degrees from the Universidad de Chile and an MSc. in Economics from ILADES-Georgetown University.

Ole Hovland

Ole Hovland worked in the Norwegian Ministry of Finance from 1980 to 2001 on taxation, macroeconomics, and budget issues, the last ten years as Budget Director. From 2001 to 2005 he worked as IMF Budget and Treasury advisor to the Russian Ministry of Finance, and from 2005 to 2006 as an IMF Macro-Fiscal advisor to the Egyptian Ministry of Finance. Mr. Hovland is presently a director in the European Bank for Reconstruction and Development representing Norway, Finland, and Latvia on the board.

Philip G. Joyce

Philip Joyce is Professor of Public Policy and Public Administration at The George Washington University. His research primarily focuses on the US federal budget and the use of performance information in the budget process. He has 12 years of public sector work experience, including five years each with the US Congressional Budget Office and the Illinois Bureau of the Budget. He has consulted internationally, both as an individual and with the International Monetary Fund and the World Bank, in the People's Republic of China, Latvia, Slovenia, and Mexico. Professor Joyce is a Fellow of the National Academy of Public Administration.

Brice Lannaud

Brice Lannaud has been Manager of the Performance Project within the Directorate of Budgetary Reform at the French Ministry of Economy, Finance and Industry since 2003. In that capacity he has been responsible for organizing and coordinating cross-ministry work on the specification of program objectives and indicators for inclusion in the annual budget. He also oversees the preparation of methodological manuals on these matters. A graduate of the Ecole Nationale d'Administration, his previous civil service positions include that of Chief of the Bureau of Budget and Finance at the Ministry of Culture and Communications.

Alexey Lavrov

Alexey Lavrov is Director of Budget Policy in the Russian Ministry of Finance. He has previously held other senior positions in the Ministry of Finance, including deputy head of intergovernmental financial relations (1999–2002) and advisor to the Minister of Finance (1998–99). Mr. Lavrov was advisor to the Deputy Chairman of the government of Russia in 1998, and served on the staff of the President from 1994 to 1997. He commenced his civil service career with Gosplan, the former ministry for the economy. During 1997–98, he was a visiting expert with the OECD in Paris. He is a graduate of Moscow State University and the University of Birmingham.

Javier Loscos

Javier Loscos is a lecturer in the Department of Applied Economics IV, Universidad Complutense de Madrid. His academic qualifications range from a degree in law from the Universidad Pontificia "Comillas" de Madrid and another in economics from the UNED (the Spanish Open University) to a PhD in applied economics from the Universidad Complutense de Madrid (Department of Applied Economics IV).

He lectured previously at the University of Salamanca. He is also a member of the Department of Governance, Administration and Public Policies at the University Research Institute "Ortega y Gasset" as Director of the postgraduate course on Public Governance and Management. At present, he is carrying out research at the Spanish Institute of Fiscal Studies where he is Deputy Director of Tax Studies.

Elisabeth Paul

Elisabeth Paul received her PhD in management/economics at the University of Liège (Belgium) in 2006, with a thesis on "Improving Public Outcome in Developing Countries—Applications of Incentive Theory to Foreign Aid and Public Finance Management." She is a member of the "GRAP-SWAP," a multidisciplinary research group which studies sector-wide approaches in health, supporting the Belgian cooperation policy. Elisabeth was FNRS (Fonds National de la Recherche Scientifique) Research Fellow in 2002–06 and after that, she became a consultant, notably for the Belgian Co-operation Agency and the European Commission. In 2005, she was a visiting scholar to the International Monetary Fund/Fiscal Affairs Department. Elisabeth has field research experience in a dozen less-developed countries, especially in sub-Saharan Africa. Notably, she has studied the public financial system in Benin, as well as the aid system and sector-wide approaches to health in Benin, Mali, Senegal, and Rwanda. At present, she is technical advisor to the Ministry of Health in Mali.

John Pierce

John Pierce was appointed as Secretary of the Treasury of New South Wales, Australia's largest state, in April 1997. Prior to joining NSW Treasury, John held the position of Chief Economist at Pacific Power. He joined NSW Treasury in 1993 as the Chief Economist and then held a senior executive position responsible for intergovernmental financial relations, tax policy, revenue forecasting, economic analysis, and reform. John also headed the Treasury team responsible for restructuring the NSW electricity industry and the introduction of competition. As Secretary, John is responsible for the strategic direction of NSW Treasury. He advises the government on matters relating to the management of the State's finances and economic policy. He has continuing involvement in the reform of the state's electricity sector. His position as Secretary of Treasury also includes the Chairmanship of NSW Treasury Corporation. John has an honors degree in Economics from the University of NSW and was President of the NSW Branch of the Economic Society of Australia for three years from 1996 to 1999.

Marc Robinson

Marc Robinson is Senior Economist in the Fiscal Affairs Department of the IMF. Since joining the IMF staff in November 2004, he has led and participated in Fund missions on public financial management and fiscal issues to Belarus, Botswana, Bulgaria, Ethiopia, Haiti, Hungary, and Italy. Prior to joining FAD, he was an economics professor in Australia for ten years during which time he published extensively on public financial management, medium-term fiscal policy and government accounting. During this period, he was a frequent public policy commentator, particularly as an op-ed contributor to Australia's leading national business newspaper. Dr. Robinson was Visiting Scholar with FAD from November 2003 to February 2004. Before becoming an academic, Dr. Robinson was a senior civil servant with the government of the Australian State of Victoria, serving, amongst other things, as board member of a number of public enterprises and as director of research of the Economic and Budget Committee of the Victorian parliament. He commenced his career as a civil servant with the Australian national government. Dr. Robinson holds degrees from the Australian National University, the University of Melbourne, and Sydney University.

Jesús Ruiz-Huerta

Jesús Ruiz-Huerta is Professor in Public Economics in the Department of Applied Economics II, at the Universidad Rey Juan Carlos, Madrid. He was a professor in Public Finance at the Universities of Salamanca and Complutense (Madrid). He also worked for eight years in the Institute of Fiscal Studies in Madrid as Deputy Director of Budget and Public Expenditure Studies, and Research Director. At present, he is the General Director of this Institute. Professor Ruiz-Huerta has published different articles and books on public finance, that is, budgeting, fiscal decentralization and economic impact of public expenditure and revenue.

David Shand

David Shand is a public financial management consultant, who prior to his retirement in 2005 worked in the World Bank, the IMF, and the OECD on public sector reform issues, with particular emphasis on performance management. He was convenor of the OECD's 1996 symposium on Performance Auditing and the Modernization of Government. Prior to his work in these international organizations he held senior positions in the Australian government at both federal and state levels, including Chief Director of Audits in the Victorian Auditor-General's Office (1983–86) and First Assistant Secretary for Financial Management in the Australian Department of Finance (1986–90).

Peter C. Smith

Peter C. Smith is Professor of Economics and Director of the Centre for Health Economics at the University of York, UK. His research areas include public finance, regulation, and productivity analysis, both in health care and in the broader public sector, and he has a particular interest in the link between research and policy. Current research includes efficiency measurement, health care payment mechanisms, and the financing of health care, topics on which he has written extensively. Recent books include *Measuring Efficiency in Health Care: Analytic Techniques and Health Policy* (with R. Jacobs and A. Street, Cambridge University Press) and *Formula Funding of Public Services* (Routledge). Peter has sat on numerous UK government advisory committees, and is currently a commissioner at the Audit Commission and chair of the Advisory Board of the UK Centre for the Measurement of Government Activity. He has acted as consultant to a range of national and international agencies, including the World Health Organization, the World Bank, and the OECD, and has a special interest in the methodology of international comparisons.

Tamón Takahashi

Tamón Takahashi is currently studying for a PhD in Government and Public Administration at the Instituto Universitario de Investigación Ortega y Gasset, and collaborating in several research projects with the Instituto de Estudios Fiscales, in Madrid, Spain. He has worked at the Ministry of Finance in Mexico as Director of Budgetary Research since 2002. He graduated Magna Cum Laude in Law from the Universidad de las Américas-Puebla in Mexico in 1999, where he also studied Mathematics. In 2001, he graduated European Master in Law and Economics from the universities Erasmus Rotterdam, Ghent, and Complutense de Madrid; and took part in the III Course in Law and Economics at Harvard Law School in Cambridge, MA. As Director of Budgetary Research, he has studied several issues on budgeting policy and best practices and made some case studies on budgetary issues from different countries, which were used during the formulation of the new Mexican Federal Budget Law. He also participated in the elaboration of the Federal Budget Act from 2002 to 2005. Some of his current research papers are about budgeting in Mexico and about incentives to enhance the efficiency of public expenditure, under a law and economics perspective.

Teresa Ter-Minassian

Mrs. Ter-Minassian holds degrees in Law from the University of Rome, Italy, and in Economics from Harvard University in the United States. From 1967 to 1978, she was on the staff of the Central Bank of Italy, part of the time on secondment to the International Monetary Fund. In the IMF, she was for eight years Chief of the Southern European Division in the European Department (which covered Italy, Spain, and Portugal, among other countries). In this capacity, she negotiated the 1983 IMF Stand-By Agreement with Portugal. From 1988 to 1996, she held the position of Deputy Director of the Fiscal Affairs Department of the Fund. In 1990, she headed the IMF Task Force for the joint study of the Soviet economy, commissioned to the IMF, IBRD, OECD, and EBRD by the G-7. As Deputy Director of the Western Hemisphere Department from 1997, she headed the negotiations of the IMF programs with Brazil and Argentina, and oversaw the department's work on various other countries in the region. Mrs. Ter-Minassian was appointed Director of the Fiscal Affairs Department effective January 2, 2001. Her areas of principal interest and expertise include macroeconomic analysis, fiscal policy, budget management, and intergovernmental fiscal relations. She has published several papers in these areas, including the book entitled *Fiscal Federalism in Theory and Practice*.

Holger van Eden

Holger van Eden is a senior economist in the Public Financial Management Division II of the Fiscal Affairs Department of the IMF. He has worked extensively with Ministries of Finance in Eastern Europe, China, and the Caribbean. His areas of focus are budget preparation—including program budgeting and medium-term budgetary frameworks—institutional restructuring, budget law, and government cash management. Before joining the Fund, Mr. van Eden worked as team leader and project coordinator on major EU- and Dutch government-funded projects in the public financial management field. He has also worked as economic journalist and editor for a nationally circulated magazine in the Netherlands, and as a government financial consultant for one of the major global accounting/consultancy firms. Mr. van Eden started his career in the Dutch Ministry of Finance.

Marijn Verhoeven
Marijn Verhoeven is a Deputy Division Chief in the Expenditure Policy Division of the IMF's Fiscal Affairs Department. He holds a Masters and postgraduate degrees in economics from Tilburg University in the Netherlands. Mr. Verhoeven joined the Fund in 1994, where he has spent most of his time in the Fiscal Affairs Department. He was also the Fund's resident representative in Bangladesh during 2001–04. His research interests focus on expenditure policy questions, including the efficiency and flexibility of government spending, public spending and addressing human development issues in low-income countries, social protection issues, and the economics of pensions.

Eduardo Zapico
Eduardo Zapico is advisor in the Evaluation Unit of the Directorate General of the Budget of the European Commission. Previously he worked as a Deputy Director of Policy Analysis, in the DG Budget at the Ministry of Finances in Spain. He has worked in the National Audit Office of the Spanish central government, in the fields of public expenditure control and program evaluation. He has collaborated on budgeting and PEM capacity development projects with the OECD/SIGMA department, for Central and Eastern Europe, and with the World Bank financial management team for Latin America. Previously he worked at the European Institute of Public Administration in Maastricht, teaching and researching on public management and budgeting, and was a part-time associate professor on public management and budgeting at the Universidad Autonoma de Madrid. His publications include *The Symbolic Modernization of Public Budgeting in Spain* (IVAP, 1989); with Aaron Wildavsky, *National Budgeting for Economic and Monetary Union* (EIPA, 1993) and, with John Mayne, *Monitoring Performance in the Public Sector* (Transaction Publishers, 1997).

Preface

The Fiscal Affairs Department of the International Monetary Fund (IMF) has seen in recent years a marked upsurge in demand for technical assistance on the design and implementation of performance budgeting systems. This upsurge reflects a broader wave of international interest in performance budgeting. Leaders in the field such as the United Kingdom, the United States, and Australia have, over the past decade, implemented new performance budgeting systems with strikingly novel features. Nations as diverse as France, India, South Africa, Ethiopia, Brazil, Belarus, and Colombia—to name just a few—have also implemented, or are in the process of implementing, performance budgeting.

This volume is part of the IMF response to these developments. Performance budgeting is about expenditure efficiency, and the IMF views expenditure efficiency as not only important in its own right, but also as having an important connection with fiscal discipline and, therefore, macroeconomic stability.

Performance budgeting seeks to improve expenditure efficiency by systematically linking funding to results, making use of performance information to achieve that linkage. It aims to redesign the budget process so as to improve the allocation of public expenditure—so that it is directed towards services of greatest social value—and also to increase the efficiency of the production process. In the language of economists, it aims to boost both allocative and technical efficiency. There are, as this volume stresses, different forms of performance budgeting. One major strand of performance budgeting practice—of which "program budgeting" is representative—places primary emphasis upon allocative efficiency and, more specifically, upon improving expenditure prioritization in the budget preparation process. Governments have not always been good at prioritizing expenditure. They have often been much better at identifying priorities for new or increased spending than at identifying and cutting out low priority or ineffective spending. This suggests that there are great welfare gains which can be made by improving prioritization processes.

Good expenditure prioritization is particularly essential when governments face new and unexpected challenges which require substantial expenditure responses. We are all well aware, for example, of the enormity of the fiscal challenge which the AIDS pandemic has posed for many countries over recent decades. Finding the funds to meet these and other emerging challenges is never an easy matter.

It is not an option to respond to emerging new fiscal priorities by continually increasing aggregate expenditure. Rising expenditure has to be financed, and this can only be through deficits or higher taxes—both of which are costly in resource and social terms. Budgeting is therefore necessarily about expenditure choices. And these choices are often tough. The tighter the aggregate expenditure constraints facing governments, the more important it is to be able to prioritize expenditure well.

A distinguishing characteristic of some of the new performance budgeting systems which have emerged over the past decade has been the idea of using the funding process as a means of putting pressure on government agencies to perform better, either or both by improving technical efficiency and by improving the design and management of programs. In some countries, this has been done by setting demanding performance targets as part of the budget process. In other countries, the funding process has been transformed in something like a "purchaser-provider" transaction. In general, the idea is to build even tighter links between funding and results than classic forms of performance budgeting sought to build. Closely linked to this has been the idea that budgeting mechanisms—and public management systems more generally—should be stripped of unnecessary controls and restrictions which inhibit managers from performing effectively.

Whether achieved through better expenditure prioritization, or through improved efficiency and effectiveness at the agency level, the social benefits of increased expenditure efficiency are clear. There is also good reason to believe that expenditure efficiency can contribute to aggregate fiscal discipline. If performance budgeting contributes to rising public sector productivity, agencies are able to do more with less and this will help to some extent to reduce the upward pressure on public expenditure over time. Good expenditure prioritization should also have the same effect of facilitating aggregate expenditure restraint over the medium and long term by helping to finance new priorities by cuts in low-priority existing programs. In the short run, moreover, improved expenditure prioritization should contribute to aggregate fiscal discipline under circumstances where fiscal consolidation is required. This is because if expenditure reductions target the least useful areas of expenditure and preserve higher-priority social spending, fiscal adjustment is more likely to be sustainable.

The inherent importance of expenditure efficiency and its close link with fiscal discipline are key reasons for the current wave of interest in performance budgeting. It is not accidental that countries facing particularly significant structural fiscal pressures tend to be those most interested in implementing performance budgeting systems.

This volume aims to help governments and their advisors assess the most appropriate way of reforming their budget and funding processes to boost expenditure efficiency. Because there are today a number of forms of performance budgeting, the starting point for this has to be the development of a clear taxonomy of performance budgeting systems. What are the key forms of performance budgeting? In what specific and different ways do they seek to link results and funding? How do they differ in their approach to the use of performance information? To what extent are they alternatives, and to what extent are they complementary?

Against this background, this volume aims to significantly improve our understanding of what forms of performance budgeting work, and under what circumstances. This is not an area where we are able to easily reach conclusions with scientific rigor. The complex causality of public budgeting and management systems makes that exceedingly difficult. Nevertheless, international experience and theoretical analysis can and do provide substantial guidance on the efficacy of alternative approaches to linking funding and results. It can, moreover, be of as much value to identify what has not worked well—and to understand why—as to identify the apparent success stories. To paraphrase the famous adage, those who do not understand the lessons of failed budgeting experiments are fated to repeat them. This underlines the importance of frankness in the review of national experiences with performance budgeting.

There are many important questions which arise in any systematic assessment of performance budgeting. To give some flavor of the issues addressed in this volume, let me identify just a couple:

1. *What type of performance information is most useful for performance budgeting?* This is a question on which opinion and practice diverge to some degree. For example, some countries place primary emphasis on performance measures, while others place considerable stress on program evaluation. Some believe that accrual budgeting is essential if proper allocative decisions are to be made. Others disagree. The answer to this question is, clearly, closely linked to the choice of the type of performance budgeting. For example, the newer forms of performance budgeting have more demanding information requirements because they seek to build tighter links between results and funding. But performance information is not costless. The more sophisticated the performance information system, the more costly it will be. This makes it essential that choices about information systems be made carefully, as part of a broader decision on what model of performance budgeting is most suitable for the circumstances of each country, based on a judgment of whether the expected benefits are likely to justify the cost.
2. *How do we make sure that performance information is actually used in the budget process as performance budgeting intends that it be used?* It is not uncommon to hear that great efforts have been made in particular countries to develop performance information but that this information is not actually being used in the budget process. There are, for example, a number of countries where the budget classification has been subject to a detailed overhaul to put it on a program basis, but no use has been made of this new budget classification as a tool to improve expenditure prioritization. In other countries, performance indicators have been developed and then used for no other purpose than filling in reports. What is the problem here? Does it indicate a need to pay more attention to the mechanisms and processes for the systematic use of that information? Or are there, in the case of at least some countries, more fundamental problems which raise questions about the appropriateness of introducing performance budgeting prior to other reforms?
3. *To what extent, and under what circumstances, is it possible to give agencies and managers greater budgetary freedom without compromising aggregate fiscal discipline?* In a budgeting context, greater managerial freedom means, in particular, the reduction or elimination of appropriation controls based on input types. The idea is that managers should be held responsible for the results they deliver—and not controlled in the manner in which they produce those results. This sounds

very appealing. Are there not, however, risks that this freedom will be abused to enter commitments (such as increased employment) which will reduce longer-term fiscal flexibility? What are the preconditions which should be met for such deregulatory moves?

These questions point to a key theme of this volume: in performance budgeting, one size definitely does not fit all.

For example, more complex forms of performance budgeting may not suit countries with greater financial and human capacity constraints. The cost of the necessary information requirements may be simply unjustifiable. Or budgetary institutions may not be robust enough to make use of that information. It is always a mistake to simply copy the management systems of advanced nation without explicitly considering local circumstances and capacity.

For some countries, performance budgeting may actually be inappropriate in any form. There are, for example, a minimum set of basic elements of good public financial management which any country should have in place before it contemplates moving to performance budgeting.

Performance budgeting systems need also to take into account national characteristics in other ways. For example, the type of political system can have major consequences for the appropriate form of performance budgeting, and its probability of success. In a parliamentary system, the executive branch may be in a strong position to impose a single set of expenditure priorities. By contrast, in some presidential systems, both the executive branch and the legislature possess strong independent budgetary power. Priorities have to be negotiated.

All of these, and many other, questions are explored in this volume. They are examined partly from the perspective of national experience, in case studies which cover countries ranging from Ethiopia to the United States. And they are examined also through the prism of thematic chapters focused on, for example, the information requirements of performance budgeting and specific models such as formula funding and the purchaser-provider mechanism.

It is important that performance budgeting be seen in a broader context. It is a tool to address the basic performance problems which often characterize the public sector. In the public sector, there is no mechanism of consumer choice which directs resources to the production of the goods and services which society needs most. Competition is usually weak or entirely absent. The result is a lack of competitive pressure to be efficient.

Performance budgeting is, however, only one among a number of tools with which to address these problems. For example, many governments have been working hard to increase the degree of consumer choice in publicly financed services. Others have harnessed competitive forces by outsourcing, where appropriate, the production of such services. Moreover, as made clear in this volume, many contemporary forms of performance budgeting are part of a broader *managing-for-results* movement which calls for reforms on multiple fronts, ranging from human resource management through to organizational design, and including budgeting.

In the final analysis, all of these tools—including performance budgeting—have limitations. All too often, management reforms, including budget management reform, are oversold by their advocates. Exaggerated expectations inevitably produce subsequent disillusion. So in assessing performance budgeting, we need to take a dispassionate and critical perspective in order to identify its limitations as well as its potential benefits.

Precisely because of the limitations of reforms in the management of the public sector, it is also crucial to continually keep under review the boundaries of the state. If there is no good reason why a service should be provided by government, it is far better to leave it to private production and provision.

Although performance budgeting should not be seen as a solution to all of the performance problems of the public sector, it is my belief that well-designed performance budgeting systems which are appropriate to relevant national circumstances can do much to improve the efficiency of public expenditure. It is for this reason that the IMF is pleased to be able to offer this volume as a contribution to the work of improving the design and implementation of performance budgeting around the world.

Teresa Ter-Minassian
Director
Fiscal Affairs Department

Glossary

Accrual Output Budgeting	Widely used to refer to government-wide budgeting systems, inspired by the *purchaser-provider model,* which were introduced, most notably, in New Zealand in the mid-1990s and in Australia in the late 1990s.
Activities	Types or categories of work undertaken in the production and delivery of outputs. The term is also often used to refer to lower-level components of the *program hierarchy* (see below).
Activity-based budgeting	The use in budget preparation of information on activity costs derived from *activity-based costing.*
Activity-based costing	A costing methodology in which input costs are allocated to categories of activity, using an allocation basis which as closely as possible reflects the real consumption of resources by those activity categories.
Administration programs	Programs which cover overhead costs of a ministry or agency, such as central management and personnel services.
Allocation basis	Formula or principle used to allocate a specific indirect cost between two or more "cost objects"—in the context of program costing, between two or more programs.
Allocative efficiency	The delivery by government of the mix of different types of services which most closely reflects social priorities, based on society's valuations of output choices.
Alternative budgeting	A variation of *zero-base budgeting* in which decisions are focused not on a zero base but on the margins near the current budget base. Usually three or more alternative budgets have to be submitted for each program. Generally, at least one of the alternatives has to be less than the current budget. Often a specific percentage reduction is mandated.
Appropriateness	The extent to which a policy or program is consistent with current government priorities. Also known as "relevance."
Capitation payment	Funding on a per-head basis or some similar proxy for expected output.
Case payments	Funding based on actual output.
Contingent capacity services	Services for which the demand is unpredictably variable, which must be supplied immediately when the demand arises, and for which it is necessary to have pre-existing production capacity if demand is to be quickly met. Emergency services (fire, ambulance) are examples.

Cost-effectiveness	The achievement of intended outcomes at the lowest possible cost.
Cost function	Functional relationship between outputs and cost, assuming technical efficiency.
Cream-skimming	The deliberate avoidance by providers of complex, and therefore high-cost, clients/cases. May be used as a strategy to maximize profits or avoid losses under an output-based payment systems where there is significant client/case *heterogeneity*.
Diagnosis related group	A system for classifying hospital services (outputs) originally introduced for performance measurement purposes, which has subsequently been used as the basis for output-based funding systems.
Economy	The acquisition of inputs at appropriate prices. An element of (technical) efficiency.
Effectiveness	The degree of success of an output in delivering its intended outcomes.
Efficiency	See *technical efficiency*, for which it is an equivalent term in the public administration literature.
Evaluation	Analytic assessments typically addressing the cost-effectiveness or appropriateness of public policies, organizations, or programs.
External factors	Factors outside the control of government which influence the outcomes achieved by public programs—that is, which impact on the effectiveness of programs. External factors may be either client/case characteristics or aspects of the context in which the program is delivered. Sometimes these are also referred to as "contextual factors."
Formula funding	When used as a performance budgeting tool, formula funding is a system in which funding provided by government to a public sector agency is an explicit (that is, algebraic) function of measures of expected and/or actual results—that is, of measures of outputs and/or outcomes.
Forward estimates	Projections by a central budget agency of aggregate expenditures over a fixed term (usually budget plus three years) on a no policy change basis. Forward estimates are the basis for medium-term fiscal planning and may also be used as the basis for imposing expenditure limits.
Heterogeneity (of an output)	The deliberate variation in the amount and/or types of activities delivered to different clients/cases receiving the "same" service, particularly in response to difference in client/case characteristics. For example, more intensive teaching activity directed to students with disabilities.

High-powered incentives	Incentives are more "high-powered" the more strongly and more directly they are linked to measured results and conversely more "low-powered" the weaker and more indirect that link.
Higher-level outcomes	The more indirect outcomes of outputs, which arise as a consequence of the achievement of proximate outcomes. For example, in education, the proximate outcome of higher numeracy and literacy contributes to the higher-level outcome of better economic performance. Also sometimes known as "end" or "ultimate" outcomes.
Impact	Term used by some to refer to outcomes, or to higher-level outcomes.
Incentives	Material rewards and sanctions linked to desired behaviors.
Incrementalism	Budgeting that is characterized by "inattentiveness to the (budgetary) base"—in other words, that budgetary decision-makers take the budgetary base more or less for granted as the starting point in budget formulation, and focus their attention primarily on the size of the increment (or, occasionally, decrement) in agency or program budgets, mainly by a process of adjusting budgets for cost changes.
Indirect cost	In the context of costing programs, costs of inputs or activities which contribute to more than one program. More generally, shared costs which need to be allocated between a number of "cost objects."
Input controls	Controls imposed either in the appropriation legislation, or by regulation on the part of the Ministry of Finance, over the manner in which a line agency's expenditure is to be allocated between different input types (setting, for example, a limit for expenditure on salaries).
Inputs	Resources used in the carrying out of activities to produce outputs (for example, labor, equipment, buildings).
Intermediate outcome	See *proximate outcomes*.
Intermediate output	Goods or services which are supplied to an internal user rather than to the external client/customer. For example, IT support services delivered by ministry IT staff to staff of the ministry.
Internal motivation	Behavioral motivation independent of any immediate external pressure or inducement. Can be of two types—moral motivation and intrinsic motivation.
Intervention logic	A planning methodology that uses "cause and effect" hierarchies to map logic links between outputs, proximate outcomes, and outcomes.

Intrinsic motivation	Motivation which derives from the enjoyment of work—that is, from pleasure in undertaking work activities one enjoys or producing results in which one takes pleasure or pride.
Line-item budgeting	Budgeting in which agencies are provided with budget appropriations specified in terms of input categories (that is, by economic classification).
Managing-for-results	The use of formal performance information to improve public sector performance across the board, including in human resource management, in strategic planning and budgeting. Sometimes also referred to as "performance management."
Mandatory expenditure	Expenditure which occurs by virtue of standing legislative provision ("standing appropriation"), as opposed to allocation in the annual budget. Most social security expenditure is usually of this type.
Moral motivation	Internal motivation driven by a desire to behave in accordance with one's moral beliefs and values.
Outcome	Changes brought about by public interventions upon individuals, social structures, or the physical environment. Expressed differently, the impacts of public services.
Output	A good or service provided by an agency to or for an external party.
Performance auditing	Audit of the efficiency and effectiveness of public expenditure.
Performance budgeting	Public sector funding mechanisms and processes designed to strengthen the linkage between funding and results (outputs and outcomes), through the systematic use of formal performance information, with the objective of improving the allocative and technical efficiency of public expenditure.
Performance indicator	See *performance measure*.
Performance information	Information on results achieved by public expenditure and/or on the costs of achieving those results.
Performance measure	Ratings or quantitative measures which provide information on the effectiveness and efficiency of public programs.
Performance targets	Quantitative statements of the output and/or outcome an agency or subordinate unit is expected to deliver.
Planning, Programming, and Budgeting System	The original form of program budgeting introduced in the United States in the 1960s.
Processes	The means by which inputs are transformed into outputs.
Productivity	The degree of technical efficiency.

Program appropriation	The appropriation of funds in the budget on the basis of programs.
Program Assessment Rating Tool	Technique developed by the US Office of Management and Budget from 2004 in order to rate program performance for use in the budget process. Programs rated in five categories ranging from "effective" down to "ineffective" and "results not demonstrated."
Program budgeting	The systematic use of performance information to inform decisions about budgetary priorities between competing programs, based on the program classification of expenditure (see *programs*).
Program hierarchy	Classification which breaks programs into component sub-programs, and in turn breaks these into lower-level components. In one common version of the program hierarchy, programs are broken into sub-programs, which are in turn broken into activities.
Program structure	The manner in which an agency classifies its expenditures into objective-based programs and other elements (sub-programs, and so on) of its *program hierarchy*.
Programs	Objective-based categories of expenditure, where objectives should generally refer to the intended outcomes of the expenditure. As used in this book, generally refers to the highest level of the program hierarchy.
Proximate outcomes	The more direct or immediate impacts of outputs. For example, in education, student knowledge (such as, higher numeracy and literacy) is a key proximate outcome.
Public Service Agreements	System developed in the United Kingdom from the late 1990s, under which high-level performance targets are set for each ministry as part of a biennial spending review process which defines multi-year agency budgets. Targets have evolved over time from being primarily output focused to primarily outcome focused.
Public service motivation	An altruistic motivation to serve the interests of the community, as perceived by public employees.
Purchaser-provider systems	Funding systems under which government agencies are paid "prices" for the results (usually outputs) which they deliver.
Quality	The extent to which the characteristics of an output—in the case of a service output, the activities delivered and their timeliness—are such as to increase its potential capacity to achieve its intended outcome. Not to be confused with the outcome itself.

Risk adjustment	Fine-tuning a case payment or capitation payment system so that funding more closely reflects the variability of client/case costs due, in particular, to *heterogeneity*.
Scissors approach	Implementation strategy which combines pressure from above to encourage managers to change, with action from below to increase their capacity to change.
Skimping	Deliberate underservicing of more complex clients/cases; for example, as a response to an output-based payment system in which the quality of the output delivered is imperfectly measured.
Social motivation	Behavior motivated by the desire of individuals to build certain types of social relationship (in the context of this book, in the workplace), such as the acceptance and approval of others, or power and status.
Substantive performance auditing	Audit to assess the efficiency and effectiveness of a program or agency.
Systemic performance auditing	Auditing of management systems to gauge their capacity to contribute to the efficiency and effectiveness of public expenditure.
Technical efficiency	Production of an output at minimum cost while holding quality constant, given prevailing input prices. Requires both the avoidance of waste and the choice of the least-cost combination of inputs.
Unit costs	Cost per unit of output. Can refer to average cost or average variable cost.
Virement	Shifting of funds between appropriation categories.
Zero-base budgeting	A system of performance budgeting in which expenditure is broken down into, and analyzed in terms of, "decision packages" (also known as "service increments") which constitute a series of optional funding levels from the presumed base of zero to and beyond the current level of service. Priority rankings are attached to these decision packages, and these rankings are used to ensure that the available level of revenue funded those decision packages which are of highest priority.

1
Performance Budgeting Models and Mechanisms

Marc Robinson[1]

This chapter aims to achieve two tasks. The first is to provide a clear definition of performance budgeting. The second is to provide a taxonomy of forms of performance budgeting.

The definition of performance budgeting put forward is a broad one. It refers to public sector funding mechanisms and processes designed to strengthen the linkage between funding and results (outputs and outcomes), through the systematic use of formal performance information, with the objective of improving the allocative and technical efficiency of public expenditure. "Performance information" in this context refers, first, to information on results achieved by public expenditure and, second, to information on the costs of achieving those results. In what follows, this definition is contrasted with some alternative views of what performance budgeting means.

Providing a taxonomy of performance budgeting is important because there are a range of performance budgeting models, which differ to varying degrees in respect to the objectives which they emphasize, the manner in which they aim to link results and funding, and the type of performance information upon which they rely. If the efficacy of these alternative models is to be analyzed with any precision, it is necessary to make clear their component elements. For this purpose, the chapter identifies the following four fundamental mechanisms used in performance budgeting systems:

- *Program budgeting*, which uses information about the costs and benefits of the objective-based ("program") expenditure categories for expenditure prioritization.
- *Funding-linked performance targets*, which seek to link the level of funding to results targets—that is, to quantitative statements of the output and/or outcome the agency is expected to deliver.

- *Agency-level budgetary performance incentives*, which aim to motivate agencies to perform better by rewarding agencies financially for good performance (and possibly also by financially sanctioning unsatisfactory performance).
- *Formula funding*, in which funding provided is made an explicit function of measures of expected and/or actual results (usually outputs, but sometimes outcomes).

Each of these mechanisms may be sub-classified further. It is particularly important to distinguish between models of formula funding which are *cost-based* and those which are not. (In its simplest form, cost-based formula funding is funding calculated by multiplying expected/planned output quantity by unit output costs.)

This chapter suggests that each of the diverse range of performance budgeting systems which may be observed across the world at the present time, or which have existed historically, are based on one or more of these four fundamental mechanisms. For example:

- Contemporary *target-based performance budgeting systems*, of which the UK Public Service Agreement system is perhaps the most important example, typically combine funding-linked performance targets with a program budgeting mechanism.
- *Purchaser-provider performance budgeting*—under which agencies are paid "prices" for the results (usually outputs) which they deliver—combine cost-based formula funding with agency-level budgetary performance incentives.

Performance budgeting and its relation to "managing-for-results"

The definition of performance budgeting advanced above embodies a quite general notion of performance budgeting which encompasses a diverse range of specific performance budgeting systems. It is also quite close to the definitions put forward by others including, for example, the OECD ("a form of budgeting that relates funds allocated to measurable results" (OECD, 2003, p. 7)) and the US General Accounting Office ("the concept of linking performance information with the budget" (GAO, 1999, p. 4)).

It is a definition which needs to be supplemented by noting that almost all forms of performance budgeting have one additional point in common—an emphasis on the importance of managerial freedom in budget management. Concretely, this manifests itself in hostility to the traditional budgeting practice of appropriating agency budgets by detailed input categories (wages, supplies, travel, and so on) and banning agencies from shifting money between those input categories (a practice widely known as "line-item" budgeting). Such controls are viewed by performance budgeting proponents as barriers to good performance. The performance budgeting focus is upon accountability for results produced, rather than on control of how those results are produced.

A crucial feature of the way performance budgeting is defined in this book is that it focuses on the use of performance information *in budgeting and funding*, rather than in public management more generally. In recent decades, performance budgeting has often been adopted as part of a broader set of management and budgetary reforms designed to improve the efficiency and effectiveness of the public sector and/or to facilitate the achievement of fiscal sustainability. Many of these reforms fall into the category of what has often been referred to as *managing-for-results* (Poocharoen and Ingraham, 2003), while others take focus in different but complementary directions (for example, introducing increased consumer choice and competition). Managing-for-results—also sometimes referred to as "performance management"—can be defined as the use of formal performance information to improve public sector performance. Its fundamental starting point is maximum clarity about the outcomes which government is attempting to achieve, and about the relationship of outputs and activities to those desired outcomes. Often, this is linked with broader strategic planning models incorporating significant elements of private sector corporate planning practices. Managing-for-results also tends to emphasize the ex-ante stipulation of performance expectations for agencies, work units and individuals through the use of performance targets and standards. A standard element of the "strategic human resources management" component of managing-for-results is the introduction of stronger performance-based extrinsic incentives (rewards and sanctions) for public officials. The other crucial element is the call to "let the managers manage"—to strip away procedural controls which are seen as having encumbered management in the past. This calls, in the recent words of the British Chancellor of the Exchequer, for "a bonfire of the old input, interventionist, departmentalist controls over front line public service managers—which is too often what they still find frustrating" (Brown, 2003).

The close relationship between managing-for-results and performance budgeting is obvious. The performance budgeting demand for freedom from detailed budgetary line-item controls is, for example, one element of the broader "let the managers manage" theme. Similarly, the notion of funding-linked targets for agency outputs/outcomes is a specific budgetary application of the broader managing-for-results notion of using target-setting to improve public management.

It is therefore not surprising that some have defined performance budgeting in such a way as to equate it to the overall managing-for-results package of reforms. However, much of the managing-for-results package is not concerned with budgeting at all (for example, the use of non-financial rewards and sanctions for measured agency performance, and the use of performance targets in human resource management). If defined this way, performance budgeting ends up being seen as something which is not integrally about budgeting, or perhaps not even about budgeting at all.[2]

The view taken here is that, despite the close relationship between contemporary approaches to performance budgeting and the broader managing-for-results package, performance budgeting should be seen as a distinct element within the broader picture, the defining characteristic of which is that it is concerned with the *budgetary* use of performance information—that is, its use in budget formulation and execution.

Two other features of the definition of performance budgeting employed here are worth mentioning. The first is that it is a definition which is wider than that employed by those who consider performance budgeting to be concerned only with the use of performance *measures* in the budget. It is true that performance measures are a necessary and fundamental element of the performance information required by any performance budgeting system. However, the type of "performance information" used in performance budgeting systems in many cases goes beyond performance measures to include, for example, program evaluations and other analytic techniques (for example, cost-benefit analysis). In many contexts, performance measures can provide a starting point in making decisions, and need to be used in conjunction with other types of performance information. Thinking of performance budgeting simply in terms of the use of performance measures in budgeting has perhaps led some analysts to look for a direct or even mechanical link between measures and budget decisions which it is not always reasonable to expect.

The final point is that the definition put forward is one that does not restrict the performance budgeting concept to resource allocation decisions made in the formulation of the government-wide budget. Rather, it is relevant also to the way in which agencies execute their budgets—either when allocating resources internally or when distributing funding to lower-level public sector entities which they supervise.

Against this background, we can proceed to delineate the key performance budgeting mechanisms.

Program budgeting and expenditure prioritization

Program budgeting is the performance budgeting mechanism which has had the most enduring influence. As the term will be used in this volume, program budgeting comprises (a) the objective-based ("program") classification of expenditure and (b) the systematic use of performance information to inform decisions about budgetary priorities between competing programs. Program budgeting made its true debut with the Planning, Programming and Budgeting System (PPBS) introduced in the US federal government in the 1960s, although its core themes had much in common with other earlier strands of performance budgeting.[3] The primary objective of program budgeting was improved allocative efficiency through better expenditure prioritization. The driving concern was a belief that expenditure allocation in the public sector was insufficiently responsive to changing social needs and priorities, and that money could keep flowing year after year to ineffective programs because of a lack of proper expenditure planning processes or of accountability for results linked to the budget process. Program budgeting exponents viewed traditional "line-item" budgeting (see above) as a key part of the problem. More generally, they viewed traditional budgetary processes as inherently "incrementalist"—that is, as characterized by a tendency for the "base" funding of established agencies and programs to be unthinkingly renewed year after year.

Program budgeting aimed to change all this through a system in which expenditure would be planned and controlled by objective. The basic building block of this system was the classification of expenditure into *programs*—"objective-oriented classifications so that programs with common objectives...are considered together"

(Carlson, 1969, p. 617)[4]—with the objectives of of each program being explicitly defined. The program classification of expenditure is intended to facilitate "major allocative decisions" such as "should more resources be employed in national security in the future, or in national health programs, or in the preservation and development of natural resources" (Fisher,[5] 1967, p. 63).

As its name indicates, PPBS went well beyond the core elements of program budgeting defined above. It was, indeed, much more than a budgeting system: it aimed to be an integrated expenditure management system in which systematic policy and expenditure planning would be developed and closely integrated with the budget. PPBS aimed, as Schick (1971, p. 212) put it, "to move planning from the periphery to the center of budget operations." Expenditure planning under PPBS was also intended to be multi-year in nature (usually based on a five-year plan) (McKean and Ashen, 1967). The emphasis upon planning within the PPBS system reflected the mood of the time, in which indicative economic planning enjoyed considerable international popularity. PPBS also placed great emphasis upon systematic, in-depth analysis of the costs and benefits of programs as the basis for expenditure decisions.

Particularly after the introduction of PPBS in the US, program budgeting enjoyed almost immediate international popularity and was over time adopted by many other advanced and developing countries (Axelrod, 1988, pp. 272–3; Premchand, 1977). In France, for example, it was adopted enthusiastically—reflecting its resonance with the traditions of state economic planning and *calcul économique*—in the form of *Rationalisation des Choix Budgétaires* (Huet, 1971; Toulemonde and Rochaix, 1994, p. 38). Its spread through the developing world was encouraged by the advice of international organizations such the United Nations (UN, 1965), the World Bank, and the IMF. Even today, there are many governments which use the "program budgeting" label for their performance budgeting systems.[6] The contemporary influence of the basic program budgeting idea is, however, much wider than the continuing use of the label. If defined in terms of the two core elements identified above, program budgeting is an element of many contemporary performance budgeting systems which also make use of other mechanisms for linking funding and results (such as funding-linked performance targets). The extent of the ongoing influence of program budgeting is partly obscured by the wide variety of terminology used today to refer to programs—such as "outcomes" or "output groups" (Australia) and "Requests for Resources" (UK) (see the discussion of program classification in Chapter 5).

The core informational requirements of program budgeting are information on (a) the results achieved by programs and (b) the resources consumed to deliver the program. From the outset, a diversity of approaches to the performance information existed. One approach—represented, for example, by the UN *Manual for Programme and Performance Budgeting*—placed overwhelming emphasis upon performance measurement. In this view, "the primary objectives are to obtain physical measures of work effort and results, and to establish pertinent relationships with the use of resources, so as to provide data that will help in developing and presenting budget proposals" (UN, 1965, p. 48). By contrast, PPBS and its derivatives went much further in emphasizing "scientific decision-making for allocating public funds" (Toulemonde and Rochaix, 1994, p. 38). This meant that systematic and formal "analytic processes" such as cost-benefit analysis, cost-effectiveness analysis, systems analysis and operations research were to be used for this purpose (Steiner, 1967, p. 311). PPBS, as a senior US budget official put it at the time, was "premised on the belief that the expansion of our knowledge in the social and physical sciences and of the sophistication and quality of data holds great promise for improving specific decisions of Government" (Carlson, 1969, p. 615). This highly formal PPBS approach to program performance analysis—to what will be referred to in this volume as *evaluation*—has not generally survived. As discussed in Chapter 3, there has been a loss of faith in the "scientific" approach to evaluation. Beyond that, however, approaches to the assessment of program performance have varied over time and between countries. During the 1980s, for example, program evaluation enjoyed renewed popularity in a many countries, albeit in a rather different form from the PPBS. From the mid-1990s, performance measures rather than broader evaluation became the main focus in most countries. However, as noted in Chapter 3, there are now signs of a new resurgence of interest in program evaluation as an important element of the budget process.

Another area where contemporary program budgeting practice often differs from the PPBS model is in respect to the nature and role of planning. Support for comprehensive strategic planning based on highly formalized processes also tends to wax and wane. It has probably enjoyed the most consistent support in the United States, where strategic planning essentially based on the so-called Harvard policy model (Bryson, 1988) is a core part of the Government Performance and Results Act (GPRA) 1993, which sets the framework of contemporary performance management in the US federal government (see below and Chapter 10). As mentioned above, there are some who view strategic planning as a defining element of performance budgeting. However, such a view is not consistent with the diversity of international performance budgeting practice and opinion. Thus, for example, Australia moved from imposing compulsory prescriptive strategic planning procedures upon agencies in the 1980s and early 1990s, to an approach which left strategic planning largely up to the agencies (in line with a new "purchaser-provider" model of performance budgeting which tended to conceptualize agencies as more like stand-alone businesses).

Views on the usefulness of formal strategic planning in government tend to be rather polarized. Some take the view that in practice it is usually a resource-intensive exercise with little impact on actual practice. Such views reflect, in part, the skepticism of certain key contributors to the debate on corporate planning in the private sector (for example, Mintzberg, 1993). Others would, however, argue that some form of strategic planning is essential in order to promote both a focus on objectives and a longer-term perspective. Whatever one's view of the desirability and appropriate form of strategic planning, however, it would be a mistake to view it as a defining and essential element of performance budgeting.

Expenditure prioritization at the margin

Budgetary decision-making is usually much more focused on whether to increase or reduce program expenditures than on whether to abolish programs altogether. Expenditure prioritization decisions are, in other words, generally made at the margins. Basic microeconomics teaches that allocative efficiency is realized by equating the marginal utility per dollar (in a public sector context, the marginal social benefit/marginal social cost) of every product. Program budgeting does not, however, incorporate any formal methodology for marginal decision-making. It is therefore not surprising that a number of forms of performance budgeting emerged which attempted to remedy this perceived defect by proposing formal methodologies for expenditure prioritization at the margin.

There are a number of forms of what might be called *marginal prioritization techniques*. The most well-known of these is zero-base budgeting (ZBB)—a budgeting methodology with private sector roots (Phyrr, 1973) which was formally adopted by the US federal government under President Carter in the late 1970s, and subsequently by governments elsewhere in the world. As initially applied within the public sector, it called for all programs to be decomposed into "decision packages" (also known as "service increments") which would constitute "a series of optional funding levels from the presumed base of zero to and beyond the current level of service" (Cleaveland, 1979, p. 15). Priority rankings would be attached to these decision packages, and these rankings would then be used to ensure that the available level of revenue funded those decision packages which were of highest priority. In this way, ZBB would enable "rational shifting of funds from one program to another on the basis of relative priorities" (Cleaveland, 1979, p. 20),[7] based upon "the systematic application of marginal analysis techniques to budget formulation" (Taylor, 1977, p. 3).

In its pure form, ZBB—as its name suggests—required the review and justification of *all* public expenditure *every year*. However, reflecting the practical difficulty of undertaking a task of this magnitude annually, in practice ZBB tended to evolve into what has been referred to as "alternative budgeting" (Axelrod, 1988, p. 300). As Lewis (1988, p. 14) put it, this

> focused not on a zero base but on the margins near the current budget base. Usually three or more alternative budgets have to be submitted for each program ("decision packages" in ZBB terminology). Generally, at least one of the alternatives has to be less than the current budget. Often a specific percentage reduction is mandated.

A very similar methodology—so-called "program budgeting and marginal analysis" (PBMA)—remains in active use as a priority-setting framework (particularly at the regional level) in the health sector in certain countries, having been originally developed in the mid-1970s (Mitton and Donaldson, 2001). However, at the level of government-wide budgeting marginal prioritization techniques have for the most part fallen into disuse over recent decades.

As is made explicit in the case of PBMA, these marginal prioritization techniques may be viewed, in a public sector context, as variants of program budgeting because, in the main, they envisage that the "decision packages" for marginal analysis would be identified *within* program (that is, objective-based) expenditure categories. For this reason, marginal prioritization techniques are viewed in this chapter not as a fundamental mechanism of performance budgeting, but as a refinement (and therefore a sub-category) of program budgeting.

The minimum performance information requirements for the application of marginal prioritization techniques exceed those of mainstream program budgeting (at least in its usual contemporary form) because they require information not only on the benefits and costs of the program as a whole, but on the marginal changes in benefits and costs associated with the various "decision packages" under consideration.

Budget-linked performance targets

As noted at the outset of this chapter, the setting of performance targets—that is, explicit (mainly quantitative) stipulations of expected levels of performance—has for some time been an influential *managing-for-results* theme. Target-setting can aim to improve either or both effectiveness (through outcome targets) and efficiency (through output targets). The roots of the current popularity of target-setting go back at least to the influence of "Management by Objectives" in the 1970s. In recent times, the US GPRA (see Box 1.1) has been particularly influential internationally in spreading the idea of target-setting, together with a range of other performance management techniques. Another influential contemporary theme has been the use of so-called "contracts"—whether between agencies and ministers, between ministers and chief executives, or between civil service managers and their staff—to formalize performance targets.

The setting of performance targets does not, however, in itself constitute performance budgeting. Performance budgeting is about linking funding and

Box 1.1 The Government Performance and Results Act (GPRA), 1993

Under the US federal "Results" Act, agencies are required to prepare:

- A **strategic plan**, usually on a five-year timeframe, which states mission, goals, and objectives, and the strategy for achieving those goals and objectives. Detailed procedural guidelines govern the way in which this strategic plan is to be prepared, setting out such matters as requirements for consultation with "stakeholders." The agency must also indicate their plans for program evaluation.
- An **annual performance plan**, which must set measurable performance targets, and outline the managerial approaches to be taken to realizing objectives and goals with the annual timeframe.
- An **annual performance report**, comparing actual performance to targets, explaining any failures to achieve target levels of performance, and outlining actions to be taken to prevent further failure in the future.

results. Advocates of target-based performance budgeting focus on *the integration of budgeting and target-setting*—that is, on the calibration of performance targets to the level of funding. The need for such integration has been a major theme of the "budget and performance integration" initiative of the Bush administration in the United States. It had been an express objective of GPRA at the time of its inception that target-setting and other GPRA performance management processes would be integrated with budgeting. It is widely agreed, however, that this happened only to a very limited degree (GAO, 1999) and that, in particular, performance targets under GPRA tended to be set without much relationship to the level of budgetary resourcing provided. Addressing this perceived problem, President Bush's first budget stated that, in order "to strengthen the linkage between budget decisions making and program performance," performance targets "compatible with funding levels" would henceforth be set as part of the budget process (US Government, 2002, p. 12). (The way in which the administration attempted to do this, and the extent to which it succeeded, are the subject of one of the case studies in this volume.) The budget and performance integration initiative followed the approach introduced in a number of US states in the 1990s. In the Florida "performance-based program budgeting" system of the late 1990s, for example, the intention was that "appropriations acts [would]...set performance standards [that is, targets] for each output and outcome measure" which "describe the level of performance the Legislature expects programs to attain with the resources it provides to them" (OPPAGA, 1999, p. 2).

Internationally, the British Public Service Agreement (PSA) system—discussed by Peter Smith in Chapter 12—is today perhaps the most large-scale exercise in target-setting broadly linked to the budget process. The PSAs are documents which set out for each agency key objectives and a number of targets. These "headline" targets are relatively small in number (110 in total for the 2005–08 PSAs), and the great majority of the targets are outcome targets. For example, there are numerical targets for improving the literacy and numeracy outcomes of school children, halting the rise in child obesity rates, and reducing mortality rates from heart disease and cancer (HM Treasury, 2004). The process of PSA target-setting is closely linked with the (multi-year) budgeting process (see Box 1.2). The context of the introduction of the

Box 1.2 Target-setting and the budget process in the British PSA system

- "...decisions on budgets and targets are made alongside each other and are considered by the same Cabinet committee. So the negotiation of outcome measures is part of the budgeting process."
- "To inform the discussions of the Cabinet committee, departments are asked to provide information on the outputs or improvements in outcomes that any additional money requested would buy."
- "The White Papers which announce the new expenditure plans and the new PSAs are published as part of the same budget announcement."
- "The progress against targets provides a background to decisions on resources in the following budgeting round."

Source: HM Treasury (2000, pp. 10–11).

PSA system helps shed light on this linkage. Upon coming to office in 1997, the Blair government took the view that significant expenditure increases in certain areas of public services, including health, education, were necessary. It was concerned, however, about the danger of sinking extra funds in without achieving the necessary service improvements. PSA targets were therefore introduced in 1998 as a means of, in the words of the Chancellor of the Exchequer (finance minister), "tying new resources to new reform and results" (HM Treasury, 2002, p. i).

Agency-level budgetary performance incentives

One widely-held notion of performance budgeting emphasizes budgetary rewards (or sanctions) for performance—in other words, mechanisms whereby strongly performing programs or agencies receive additional budget funding, and poor performers lose money. The defining characteristics of such agency-level budgetary performance incentives are, first, that the results/funding linkage is retrospective—it flows from actual past performance to future funding—and, second, that the assumption is that the link between agency funding and performance will act as a strong motivator for better performance. The second point is particularly crucial. Program budgeting, for example, aims to link past performance and future funding, because it uses information on past performance (together with other information) to make judgments on future program funding. However, this type of linkage between past performance and future funding is not about creating incentives, but is rather entirely about allocative efficiency through better expenditure prioritization. By contrast, the newer idea of agency-level budgetary performance incentives is part of the broader contemporary emphasis on sharper financial incentives for performance in the public sector, and in a sense represents an application at the agency level of the notion of individual performance pay.

Financial incentives of this type have been widely used in sectoral formula funding systems. For example, funding systems for public universities in a number of countries have incorporated formularized funding rewards based on measures of outcomes achieved, such as graduate employment rates, graduate salaries, as well as for certain outputs such as research (Wellman, 2001; Carnevale et al., 1998). In this and similar schemes which have operated in other sectors, such incentive funding takes the form of "bonus" funding which is a supplement to core funding.

Attempts have been made to apply the performance bonus approach at the level of the government-wide budget. Thus, for example, a handful of US states have legislated provisions for performance-based financial incentives for budget sector government agencies (see Box 1.3).

The Canadian province of Ontario recently experimented with a somewhat different approach to performance bonus funding, starting with a cabinet-level assessment of the performance of the government as a whole, and then a judgment as to how good each department's performance had been—leading to an award of a performance bonus to each department (GAO, 2002, p. 20). These types of system aim to provide performance incentives which are discretionary rather than formula-based.[8]

Box 1.3 Performance rewards and incentives in the Florida performance budgeting system

Under the Florida Performance-Based Program Budgeting system, the Governor may (Section 216.163(4), Florida Statute) recommend to the Legislature the following rewards and sanctions for measured performance:

Incentives

- Additional flexibility in budget management
- Additional flexibility in salary rate and position management
- Retention of up to 50% of unexpended and unencumbered balances of appropriations
- Additional funds

Disincentives

- Mandatory quarterly reports to the EOG and the Legislature on the agency's progress in meeting performance standards
- Mandatory quarterly appearances before the Legislature, the Governor, or the Governor and Cabinet to report on the agency's progress in meeting performance standards
- Elimination or restructuring of the program
- Reduction of total positions for the program
- Restriction on or reduction of spending authority
- Reduction of managerial salaries

Source: Florida Government Performance and Accountability Act, 1994.

Performance budgeting based on formula funding

Another instrument of performance budgeting is *formula funding*. As is made clear in Chapter 15, formula funding is a tool with a number of public sector applications, some of which have nothing to do with performance budgeting. When used as a performance budgeting instrument, however, formula funding may be defined as intra-public sector funding arrangements in which:

- funding provided is an explicit (that is, algebraic) function of measures of expected and/or actual results—that is, of measures of outputs and/or outcomes, and
- the objective of this linkage is to boost performance and/or improve allocative efficiency.[9]

It is possible to determine either the totality, or only part, of the funding of agencies on a formula basis. Formula funding may, moreover, be based upon either the *expected* or the *actual* results of the agency concerned. To base funding upon *expected* results means setting an agency's funding as a function of the results it is considered that the agency should be able to deliver with that funding in the coming budget year (without there necessarily being any attempt to adjust the agency's funding after the event if actual results differ from what is expected). This is equivalent to setting a performance target closely linked to the funding level. By contrast, to base formula funding upon *actual* results means determining some part of an agency's funding on a retrospective basis reflecting the results which it actually delivered in the previous year—which takes one into the realm of financial incentives for performance, discussed further below.

As mentioned at the outset of the chapter, it is important to distinguish between funding formulas which are cost-based and those which are not.

Funding formulas for the purpose of linking funding to *expected* results are in general based upon measures of the costs of delivering those results.[10] Commonly, the focus is upon the use of "*unit cost* information...to determine the relationship between changes in the cost of program services and the outcomes [or outputs] obtained from these services" (OPPGA, 1999, 2001). The unit cost budgeting idea, in its simplest form, is to use the identity *average cost* • *quantity* = *total cost* as the basis for predicting the funding required to deliver any targeted level of results. Cost-based formula funding need not, however, be based on unit costs—more complex funding formulas (for example, based on marginal cost) are possible.

This approach has most commonly been applied to outputs, and rather less to outcomes. For example, the forward budgetary funding requirements of school education have been estimated as a function of projected school age population multiplied by cost per student year (perhaps with various adjustments for the differential costs of different age cohorts and other cost factors). Unit costs have also been used for funding models which distribute funding *within* sectors. Thus in quite a few jurisdictions (for example, Denmark) the bulk of funding to schools is based on per-student funding (Serritzlew, 2003). The same approach has been widely applied to universities, with core funding set as a function of planned student admissions by course type (with differentiation between courses at various cost levels). Thus, the enrollment of a law student might attract a university $30,000 per year, and that of a medical or science student $90,000, with these figures being based on estimates of the cost of providing these courses. (The introduction of a system broadly along these lines in Ethiopia is discussed in Chapter 24.)

It will be obvious that the informational requirements of cost-based formula funding are considerably greater than those of program budgeting. Information is needed not only on the costs of individual services, but also on the relationship between costs and the result concerned.

Not all formula funding is, however, cost-based. For example, bonus funding based on outcomes achieved—such as the funding supplements to universities based on variables such as graduate employment rates which were mentioned above—are generally not based on cost estimates (because, among other things, the costs of achieving most of the outcomes upon which performance bonuses are based cannot be measured).

There are essentially three ways in which formula funding may be used as an instrument of performance budgeting:

- *To put pressure on the agency to deliver the results upon which funding is based.* If, for example, one uses unit costs to determine the budget necessary to deliver certain results, with the expectation that those results would be delivered, one is in effect setting the level of expected performance which the agency should achieve with those funds.
- *As the basis for a "purchaser-provider" model* (see below).
- *To improve allocative efficiency by linking overall budget allocation more effectively to demand for public services.* For example, knowledge of the unit costs of school education enables one to use demographic projections to estimate forward budget requirements, thus improving the quality of medium-term budgeting.

The purchaser-provider model

The most thoroughgoing approach to financial rewards and sanctions for performance—one which goes well beyond performance bonus payments—is that taken by the purchaser-provider budgeting model. Usually based upon outputs, the purchaser-provider model seeks to build upon the principle of cost-based formula funding to create incentives both for delivering targeted results and also for technical efficiency. The aim is to place agencies on a business footing, introducing strong profit/loss incentives for efficiency. There are two key elements to this approach:

- Payment of a *"price"* per unit for the agency's outputs, with the agency retaining any profit made by producing at a cost below the price which it is paid (but, conversely, losing money if its cost exceeds that price).
- *Payment-for-results*: the per-unit "price" is only paid to agencies for the outputs they *actually produce*. Producing less therefore results in less funding. This applies the usual practice of the market, where businesses generally do not get paid for products they do not supply. It contrasts with the usual public sector budgeting and funding practice that agencies receive funds which are essentially an expenditure allowance—there is no requirement to return funds if output and/or outcome expectations are not met.

This model was first applied on a sectoral basis, most notably as the basis for the funding of public hospitals in a number of countries under the so-called "diagnosis related group" (or "casemix") funding model. Simplifying for the sake of exposition, it meant that each hospital is paid \$x for, say, every hip fracture patient treated, irrespective of whether it actually cost that hospital \$(x + y) to treat the patient, or \$(x – y) dollars. Commonly, in this type of system, the price paid (the \$x) would be determined either by the average cost of treating that type of patient or, to increase the pressure for efficiency further, on something closer to the average costs of treatment of the more efficient hospitals in the system (Palmer and Reid, 2001; Newhouse, 2002). This system was originally introduced in the US for government funding of private hospitals under Medicare and Medicaid. It was, however, later adopted for the funding of *public* hospitals in a number of countries, including

Portugal (1990), Australia (from 1993), Norway (1997), Singapore (1997), and the United Kingdom (2004).

Another early application of the purchaser-provider model occurred within the US defense establishment, where it is referred to as "unit cost resourcing" (US Defense Resource Management Institute, 1998), and was applied to internal supplies and a number of defense business areas (Harr and Godfrey, 1992). From there the idea spread to internal supplies in a number of other departments such as Energy (US Department of Energy, 2003), in the form of the "Working Capital Fund" model (see Box 1.4).

Box 1.4 US Defense Working Capital Fund system

"Once Congress appropriates resources to the Department of Defense, the Office of the Secretary of Defense (OSD) and the Component [that is, organizational units with Working Capital Funds] establish Unit Cost Goals (UCGs) for the individual business areas, and issues these in individual Annual Operating Budgets (AOBs). The AOBs contain the approved unit cost goals and the projected workload for the business area. These AOBs are based on the business areas' submitted budget estimates and adjustments made by the individual Component and the OSD. As the Defense Working Capital Fund (DWCF) business area sells goods and services, it receives revenue. The difference between the revenue from sales and actual costs incurred is the Net Operating Result (NOR). Operating to break even is the goal of each DWCF business area manager—to achieve an annual NOR equal to zero. The goal for all years and for all divisions of the fund is an accumulated operating result (AOR) equal to zero."

Source: *DCWF Planning, Programming and Budgeting*, <www.picosearch.com/cgi-bin/ts.pl> (accessed August 1, 2005).

In the mid and late 1990s respectively, New Zealand and Australia introduced an "accrual output budgeting" system which was—at least as originally conceived by its key proponents—intended to place the whole government budget on a purchaser-provider footing. In these models, government recast itself as a purchaser of services from each of its ministries on behalf of the public, and distinguished between this purchaser role and its "ownership" role vis-à-vis these bodies. The principal budget appropriation received by agencies was a "payment for outputs" which would be treated as revenue earned in the business-style accrual accounts of the recipient agency. The original intention was to apply the principle of payment-for-results (that is, that money is only paid for outputs actually produced) in such a manner that "recognition of Departmental output appropriations" would "reflect agencies [sic] delivery of their outputs" (DOFA, 1999, p. 43). This meant that if an agency did not fully deliver all the outputs expected of it, it would record an operating loss. It was also planned that the prices paid for outputs would be based upon an estimate of the *efficient* cost of producing the output, which was naturally expected to be as a rule below actual prevailing average costs. As the Australian finance ministry put it, "departmental output appropriations will progressively be based on market (or benchmark) prices, rather than...input costs" (DOFA, 1999, p. 27). The implication of this was that inefficiency would also be reflected in operating losses.

Purchaser-provider models require all the information needed by cost-based formula funding systems in general. Insofar as these models seek, however, to apply the principle of payment on the basis of efficient cost, they also require the use of *comparative cost information* to determine what expected efficiency gains to factor into the "prices" paid for agency outputs. Concretely, the aim is to use information on the costs at which others—that is, organizations delivering similar services—produce results, through cost benchmarking or market price comparisons.

Purchaser-provider models are discussed in greater detail in Chapter 16.

Conclusions

Performance budgeting seeks to link the funding provided to government agencies to the results they deliver, in order to increase the efficiency and effectiveness of public expenditure. For this purpose, it makes systematic use of performance information in the budgeting/funding process. It is important to distinguish performance budgeting from "managing-for-results," which is about the use of performance information in public management more generally. In many of its contemporary incarnations, performance budgeting is part of a broader "managing-for-results" set of reforms. It is, however, a distinct component of those reforms, focused on the budgeting/funding process.

There is no single form of performance budgeting. Different forms of performance budgeting seek to link results and funding in different ways, and with somewhat differing objectives. Some place primary emphasis on improved expenditure prioritization, whereas others place stronger emphasis upon improved program/service effectiveness or upon (technical) efficiency. Certain models seek to link funding to *future* expected results, whereas others seek instead (or in addition) to build a link between *past* results and future funding. Some incorporate the idea of funding "incentives" for performance, whereas others do not. Outputs are the main focus of attention in some, whereas in others it is outcomes. While measures of results achieved are important in all cases, the performance information needs of the different performance budgeting models vary—on the cost side, for example, some require detailed information on the unit costs of specific services, whereas others require "only" program costing. Any discussion of performance budgeting—and, in particular, any assessment of its efficacy—must pay attention to the diversity of forms of performance budgeting, and avoid inappropriate generalization.

This chapter has identified four fundamental mechanisms used by performance budgeting: program budgeting, funding-linked performance targets, agency-level budgetary performance incentives, and formula funding. It has also distinguished between formula-funding mechanisms which are cost-based, and those which are not. Both the case studies and theoretical analysis in this book are intended to shed light on the modus operandi and efficacy of each of these performance budgeting mechanisms.

Notes

1. The author would like to thank Philip Joyce and Eivind Tandberg for their valuable comments and suggestions on a draft of this chapter.
2. Thus Melkers and Willoughby (2001, p. 54) define performance budgeting as "requiring strategic planning regarding agency mission, goals and objectives, and a process that requests quantifiable data that provides meaningful information about program outcomes." This effectively equates performance budgeting with the particular approach to managing-for-results reform which has dominated the United States in recent years, particularly the Government Performance and Results Act (GPRA) (see, for example, Radin, 1998).
3. Including the "performance budgeting" system advocated by the 1949 Hoover Commission (see Hoover, 1949). On the similarities and contrast, see Schick (1966).
4. Or as the UN *Manual for Programme and Performance Budgeting* (1965, p. 91) put it, "programmes identify end products of the departments and agencies and enable evaluation of the achievement of functional objectives."
5. Fisher (one of the RAND Corporation staff who developed PPBS) defined programs as "a set of categories oriented primarily toward 'end-product' of 'end-objective' activities that are meaningful from a long-range planning point of view" (Fisher, 1967, p. 61).
6. Thus, for example, Georgia in the United States has a system of so-called "Prioritized Program Budgeting," Bulgaria is in the process of introducing a program budgeting system, and the British Department of Health has an internal program budgeting system for prioritizing health expenditures.
7. This should not be taken to imply that public sector ZBB exponents viewed ZBB only as an expenditure prioritization tool. To the contrary, it was viewed as also serving a range of other purposes, including the identification of efficiency savings.
8. One can measure the relative performance of, say, different universities, or different schools, because they are delivering the same type of service. One cannot, by contrast, measure the performance of a health department relative to that of a defense department. Consequently, no financial performance bonus system at a government-wide level could ever operate in a formularized manner based entirely upon "objective" performance measures but must, instead, depend upon more subjective approach to performance assessments.
9. Formula funding which does not involve any degree of pressure to deliver the results upon which funding is based cannot be considered performance budgeting. For example, formulas based upon the cost of providing a range of services (outputs) at certain minimum or standard levels are used in a number of countries for determining the sharing of central government grants between sub-national governments. However, if the sub-national governments retain total freedom to spend such grants in any way, and for any purpose they wish, this does not constitute performance budgeting. More generally, formulas are often used as a means of achieving a transparent form of equity in the sharing of funding, rather than for the purpose of promoting improved performance. Formula-based performance budgeting is, therefore, only one form of the more general category of formula funding.
10. As the US Federal Accounting Standards Advisory Board puts it (using the term "activities" somewhat imprecisely), they use "information on the costs of program activities...as a basis to estimate future costs in preparing and reviewing budgets" (FASAB, 1995).

References

Axelrod, D., 1988, *Budgeting for Modern Government* (New York: St. Martin's Press).

Brown, G., 2003, "A Modern Agenda for Prosperity and Social Reform." Speech made by the Chancellor of the Exchequer, Gordon Brown, to the Social Market Foundation at the Cass

Business School, London, February 3, <www.smf.co.uk/site/smf/speeches/brown20030203/pdfFile> (accessed August 1, 2005).
Bryson, J., 1988, *Strategic Planning for Public and Nonprofit Organizations* (San Francisco: Jossey-Bass).
Carlson, J., 1969, "The Status and Next Steps for Planning, Programming, and Budgeting," in *Joint Economic Committee. The Analysis and Evaluation of Public Expenditures: The PPB System, A Compendium of Papers*, Volume 2 (Washington: US Congress).
Carnevale, A.P., N.C. Johnson, and A.R. Edwards, 1998, "Performance-Based Appropriations: Fad or Wave of the Future," *Chronicle of Higher Education*, April 10, pp. B6–B7.
Cleaveland, J.R., 1979, "Zero-Base Budgeting in Local Government," in *Zero-Base Budgeting in State and Local Government: Current Experiences and Cases*, ed. J.A. Worthley and W.G. Ludwin (New York: Praeger).
DOFA (Department of Finance and Administration), 1999, *Commonwealth Accrual Budgeting Guidelines* (Canberra: DOFA).
FASAB (Federal Accounting Standards Advisory Board), 1995, *Statement of Federal Financial Accounting Standards No. 4: Managerial Cost Accounting Standards and Concepts*, <www.fasab.gov/pdffiles/vol1v4.pdf> (accessed August 1, 2005).
Fisher, G.H., 1967, "The Role of Cost-Utility Analysis in Program Budgeting," in *Program Budgeting: Program Analysis and the Federal Budget*, ed. D. Novick (Cambridge, Mass.: Harvard University Press).
GAO (General Accounting Office), 1999, *Performance Budgeting: Initial Experiences Under the Results Act in Linking Plans with Budgets*, GAO/AIMD/GGD-99–67 (Washington: GAO).
——, 2002, *Results-Oriented Cultures: Insights for US Agencies from Other Countries' Performance Management Initiatives*, GAO-02–862 (Washington: GAO).
Harr, D.J., and J.T. Godfrey, 1992, "The Total Unit Cost Approach to Government Financial Management," *Government Accountants Journal*, Vol. 40(4), pp. 15–20.
HM Treasury, 2000, *Outcome Focused Management in the United Kingdom*, <www.hmtreasury.gov.uk/Documents/Public_Spending_and_Services/publicservice_performance/pss_perf_index.cfm> (accessed August 1, 2005).
——, 2002, *Public Service Agreements, 2002*, <www.hm-treasury.gov.uk./Spending_Review/spend_sr02/psa/spend_sr02_psaindex.cfm> (accessed August 1, 2005).
——, 2004, *Public Service Agreements, 2005–08*, <www.hm-treasury.gov.uk/spending_review/spend_sr04/psa/spend_sr04_psaindex.cfm> (accessed August 1, 2005).
Hoover, H., 1949, *The Hoover Commission Report on Organization of the Executive Branch of the Government* (New York: McGraw-Hill).
Huet, P., 1971, "Présentation de la Rationalisation des Choix Budgétaires en France," in *Rationalisation des Choix Budgétaires: Vers Une Nouvelle Raison d'État*, ed. P. Huet et al. (Paris: La Documentation Française).
Lewis, V., 1988, "Reflections on Budget Systems," *Public Budgeting & Finance*, Vol. 8(1), pp. 4–19.
McKean, R.N., and M. Ashen, 1967, "Limitations, Risks and Problems," in *Program Budgeting: Program Analysis and the Federal Budget*, ed. D. Novick (Cambridge, Mass.: Harvard University Press).
Melkers, J.E., and K.G. Willoughby, 2001, "Budgeters' Views of State Performance-budgeting Systems: Distinctions across Branches," *Public Administration Review*, Vol. 61(1), pp. 54–64.
Mintzberg, H., 1993, "The Pitfalls of Strategic Planning," *California Management Review*, Vol. 36(1), pp. 32–47.
Mitton, C., and C. Donaldson, 2001, "Twenty-five Years of Programme Budgeting and Marginal Analysis in the Health Sector," *Journal of Health Services Resources Policy*, Vol. 6(4), pp. 239–48.
Newhouse, J.P., 2002, *Pricing the Priceless: A Health Care Conundrum* (Boston: MIT Press).
OECD (Organization for Economic Cooperation and Development), 2003, *Public Sector Modernization: Governing for Performance*, GOV/PUMA(2003)20.

OPPAGA (Office of Program Policy Analysis and Government Accountability, Florida Legislature), 1999, *PB² Status Report Fiscal Year 1998–99*, Report No. 98–45, <www.oppaga.state.fl.us/budget/r98–45s.html> (accessed August 1, 2005).

——, 2001, *PB² Commentary: Florida's Unit Cost Initiative Shows Promise, but Needs Further Development*, <www.oppaga.state.fl.us/budget/r01–05s.html> (accessed August 1, 2005).

Palmer, G., and B. Reid, 2001, "Evaluation of the Performance of Diagnosis-Related Groups and Similar Casemix Systems: Methodological Issues," *Health Services Management Research*, Vol. 14, pp. 71–81.

Phyrr, P., 1973, *Zero-Base Budgeting* (New York: Wiley).

Poocharoen, O.-O., and P. Ingraham, 2003, "Integration of Management Systems in Government Performance Project," *Paths to Performance in State and Local Government: A Final Assessment from the Maxwell School of Citizenship and Public Affairs* (Syracuse: Maxwell School).

Premchand, A., 1977, "Restructuring Budgetary Systems in Developing Countries: Relevance of PPBS Systems," in *National Budgeting and Planning for Development: Selected Readings*, Vol. 1, ed. M.L Hensley, M.H. Martens, and W.W. Jourdin (Washington: International Law Institute).

Radin, B., 1998, "The Government Performance and Results Act (GPRA): Hydra-headed Monster or Flexible Management Tool," *Public Administration Review*, Vol. 58(4), pp. 307–16.

Schick, A., 1966, "The Road to PPB: The Stages of Budget Reform," *Public Administration Journal*, Vol. 26(4), pp. 243–58.

Schick, A., 1971, *Budget Innovation in the States* (Washington: Brookings Institution).

Serritzlew, S., 2003, "Linking Budgets to Activity: A Test of the Effect of Output-purchase Budgeting." Unpublished, Institut for Statskundskab, Århus, Denmark.

Steiner, G.A., 1967, "Problems in Implementing Program Budgeting," in *Program Budgeting: Program Analysis and the Federal Budget*, ed. D. Novick (Cambridge, Mass.: Harvard University Press).

Taylor, G.M., 1977, "Introduction to Zero-Base Budgeting," in *Experiences in Zero-Base Budgeting*, ed. J.L. Herbert (New York: PBI).

Toulemonde, J., and L. Rochaix, 1994, "Rational Decision-Making through Project Appraisal: A Presentation of French Attempts," *International Review of Administrative Sciences*, Vol. 60, pp. 37–53.

UN (United Nations), 1965, *A Manual for Programme and Performance Budgeting* (New York: United Nations).

US Defense Resource Management Institute, 1998, *Unit Cost Handbook*, <www.nps.navy.mil/drmi/98handbookds.htm> (accessed August 1, 2005).

US Department of Energy, 2003, *Working Capital Fund: Guidebook for Creating and Managing a Working Capital Fund Business*, <www.wcf.doe.gov/guides/GrayGuidebook.pdf> (accessed August 1, 2003).

US Government, 2002, *Budget: Fiscal Year 2002*, <www.gpoaccess.gov/usbudget/fy02/pdf/budget.pdf> (accessed August 1, 2005).

Wellman, J., 2001, "Assessing State Accountability Systems," *Change*, March/April, pp. 46–52.

Part One

Performance Information Foundations

2
Informing Performance Budgeting

Marc Robinson[1]

Part One of this volume focuses upon performance information. "Performance information" has been defined in this volume as referring to information first on the results achieved by public expenditure, and second on the costs of achieving those results. Since performance budgeting is about the use of performance information in budgeting/funding decisions, the development of the right type of performance information is clearly a crucial prerequisite for its success. The first key objective of Part One is, accordingly, to identify the type of performance information required to underpin performance budgeting systems, and the criteria and principles which should govern the selection and development of that information. A further objective is to delimit the potential value of performance information for budgeting purposes. This is one important element in establishing realistic expectations about the efficacy of performance budgeting.

There are a number of overarching considerations relevant to performance information strategy for performance budgeting. The literature has articulated a number of well-developed, and largely overlapping, sets of criteria for the development of performance information (see HM Treasury et al., 2001; Morley et al., 2001; Poister, 2003). Two criteria deserve special emphasis here. One is *relevance*, which means that the choice of performance information should be guided by explicitly-identified uses. In the present context, it is relevance to *budgetary* decisions and processes which is of concern. Different approaches to performance budgeting have, as noted in Chapter 1, different information requirements. For example, on the cost side, program budgeting requires a capacity to measure the costs of programs, whereas performance budgeting systems which aim to more tightly link results and funding have correspondingly more demanding cost information requirements (unit costs, comparative cost information, and so on). Performance information strategy should therefore be developed in light of the type of performance budgeting mechanisms which it is desired to introduce.

The other particularly relevant criterion is *cost-effectiveness*. In the textbook world of traditional public finance theory, allocative efficiency is achieved by equalizing the ratio of marginal social benefit/marginal social cost of each individual type of output produced. Information is assumed in this context to be perfect and costless. The real world is, of course, fundamentally different. Performance information is not free, and the marginal cost of additional performance information can be substantial, both in terms of financial cost and in terms of the use of scarce human capital. Performance measurement is no different from any other activity—it should not be pursued beyond the point where its marginal cost equals its marginal benefit. This is true even in the most affluent countries, but is particularly true in developing countries where financial resources and skilled personnel are in much shorter supply and therefore have a higher opportunity cost.

Even if money were no object, performance information would nevertheless remain imperfect—and in many cases highly imperfect—because of intrinsic measurement difficulties. There are, for example, a set of fundamental problems which often arise in seeking to measure outcomes, and even the measurement of outputs is problematic in certain respects. Particularly important from the point of view of expenditure prioritization is the absence of a metric for comparing the social utility of expenditures with very different objectives (for example, comparing a defense program with a health program)—marginal social utility being, regrettably, largely unmeasurable.

Not only is information costly and necessarily imperfect, but it is held asymmetrically. Some players have more information (or, expressed differently, are less badly informed) than others. In particular, "line" agencies will in general be somewhat better informed about their own operations—including the effectiveness of their programs, and the relationship between costs and results—than central decision-makers, including the Ministry of Finance. Information is a valuable commodity, and will not be readily shared, particularly if the center may use it to what the agency perceives as its detriment. In this context, the response to central demands for information may be strategic game-playing. This is, for example, said to have been what happened when agencies were invited, as part of the ZBB-related *marginal prioritization* performance budgeting mechanisms outlined in Chapter 1, to identify and rank options at the margin for program expenditure reductions. Agencies in many cases responded by identifying programs which they knew would never be cut because they were regarded as too important, for political or other reasons, by the center. By contrast, when in some other countries the agencies were offered the incentive that any savings they identified might be applied to increasing their spending elsewhere, the response was very different.

In terms of information strategy, one of the issues which this raises is the extent to which the center—the political leadership of executive government, the finance ministry, and other relevant central agencies—must itself be involved in defining what performance information is to be gathered by line agencies, and perhaps also in directly gathering that information.

All of this suggests it is essential that a highly selective approach is adopted to choosing what performance information will be gathered to support performance budgeting. The importance of selectiveness is further reinforced by so-called "bounded rationality." Bounded rationality refers to the limits on the human capacity to process information in order to take it into account in decision-making. If performance information were costless and complete, much of it would nevertheless remain unused because of bounded rationality. The importance of bounded rationality has been borne out time and time again in the history of performance budgeting. Thus, for example, the US PPBS system in the 1960s generated a massive quantity of analytic paperwork—particularly program evaluations—much of which did not influence (and was not even looked at by) decision-makers precisely because there was too much of it for busy people to absorb and process.

The other implication is that the cost-effectiveness of performance information must be an important consideration in deciding in what manner to seek to link results and funding—that is, what form of performance budgeting to adopt. It is, in particular, important to ask to what extent and under what circumstances the substantially higher information costs of more "sophisticated" performance budgeting systems are justifiable in terms of likely benefits. In this context, it is important for there to be a clear understanding of the nature and order of magnitude of cost of the requisite information. It is also necessary to consider under what circumstances information on the cost of delivering results will have a sufficiently strong predictive value so as to be able to serve as the basis for linking results and funding.

Against this background, Chapter 3 focuses upon results information. The literature on methodology for measuring and evaluating the results achieved by public services is quite extensive, and there is no need to duplicate its contents here. It is for these reasons that this chapter focuses primarily on three areas—the clarification of key performance concepts (outcomes, outputs, and so on) which are fundamental to the discussion of performance budgeting; the limits of results information; and the identification of a number of issues in the measurement of outcomes and outputs which are of particular relevance to efforts to link results to funding.

Chapter 4 focuses on the costing of results. The literature in this area is somewhat less well-developed than that on the measurement of results. In particular, there are a set of issues in this area which have considerable practical relevance for performance budgeting and which are the subject of divergent practice and opinion (for example, the relationship of accrual accounting to performance budgeting). There are also certain other costing issues highly relevant to performance budgeting which require a somewhat more analytical treatment than is available in the present performance budgeting literature. These are addressed in that chapter.

Chapter 5 focuses upon the specific informational requirements of the most basic form of performance budgeting—namely, program budgeting. While the informational requirements of program budgeting on the costing side may not be as great as those of systems which attempt to link funding and results more tightly, this does not mean that these informational requirements are in any sense trivial. It requires considerable resources and effort to systematically gather useful information on program effectiveness. There is, moreover, the crucial threshold requirement that programs be defined in a way which serves the purpose of program budgeting—which is to facilitate better allocative decision-making. Programs must, in other words, be defined in a way which is relevant to the priority-setting challenges which policy-makers deem to be of the highest social significance. Too often, program structures have been designed without sufficient regard to their purpose. However, even when the allocative relevance of programs serves—as it should do—as the starting point for the design of a program classification system, a set of important issues and trade-offs arise. What, for example, should be the relationship between program structure and organizational structure? If programs are supposed to be defined in terms of relevance to allocative choices, does that mean that overhead cost ("corporate services") type programs should be avoided? Should expenditure be appropriated by programs, or should programs be used as a planning rather than appropriation tool? These and a number of other issues arise time after time, yet have not always been subject to systematic analysis.

The final chapter in this part turns to the question of performance auditing. This is an area in which supreme audit authorities in many countries have become increasingly involved over recent decades. As David Shand explains in Chapter 6, there are a range of approaches taken to performance auditing. Shand reviews in detail the approaches taken to performance auditing in nine countries. In some of these countries, performance auditing focuses on reviewing the efficiency and effectiveness of programs, and therefore amounts to a form of program evaluation which can potentially provide a significant direct information input into budget decision-making. In other countries, the focus of performance auditing is primarily on the verification of performance indicators—although often not by attesting individual indicators, but by assessing the systems which generate the data. The independent status of supreme audit authorities makes their role in such verification of performance information a particularly valuable contribution to the broader "managing-for-results" enterprise, and in particular to the soundness of the information base for performance budgeting.

The focus of Part One, it should be stressed, is not upon performance information strategy in general, but rather upon the more specific information requirements of budgeting. When a government or a specific agency embarks upon the development of a performance information strategy, it should of course be guided not only by what will be of value in budget processes, but by a broader set of performance management and accountability purposes. Thus, for example, there will be a need for information on individual or internal work unit performance for human resources and internal management. These are not, however, of concern here.

Nevertheless, it is important to emphasize that developing performance information takes time. It is not uncommon to find countries that wish to introduce performance budgeting (and managing-for-results more generally) drawing up implementation plans which envisage the development of performance measures within a one- or two-year timeframe. All experience in countries which have to date developed successful performance measurement systems indicates that this is completely unrealistic.

Equally, however, it should not be assumed that performance information needs to be perfect before it can be put to work to improve budgeting, and to help in other areas of public management. Particularly because of an awareness of the risks of "perverse effects" arising from the use of flawed performance measures (discussed in Chapter 18), there are many who believe that measures should be developed over several years before being put to use. However, experience has indicated that even quite imperfect measures may be used to considerable benefit—while, of course, still being improved over time. A striking example of this is the use of very imperfect output measures and output costing in the early days of the diagnosis related group (output)-based payment system in the hospital sector, where "even with seemingly inadequate databases," the system had "profound [positive] effects" (Coffey, 1999).

Note

1. The quthor would like to thank Peter C. Smith for his valuable comments on an earlier draft of this chapter

References

Coffey, R.M., 1999, "Casemix Information in the United States: Fifteen Years of Management and Clinical Experience," *Casemix Quarterly*, Vol. 1(1).

HM Treasury et al., 2001, *Choosing the Right Fabric: A Framework for Performance Information* (London: HM Treasury).

Morley, E., S.P. Bryant, and H.P. Hatry, 2001, *Comparative Performance Information* (Washington: Urban Institute).

Poister, T.H., 2003, *Measuring Performance in Public and Non-Profit Organizations* (San Francisco: Jossey-Bass).

3
Results Information

Marc Robinson[1]

This chapter focuses on performance information on the results delivered by public expenditure. It commences with a primer on performance concepts. The chapter then examines certain aspects of the public sector production chain which can create uncertainty in the results which public expenditures might be expected to deliver. Following this, the limitations of performance measurement are discussed, and this leads into the role of program evaluation in adding important performance information which cannot be provided by performance measures alone. Finally, a number of key principles of implementation strategy are identified.

This chapter does not aim to provide detailed hands-on guidance on the design and implementation of performance information systems. This is because, as mentioned in Chapter 2, there is an abundance of literature on this topic, and also because performance information systems should be designed with multiple uses, and not only budgeting applications, in mind.

Core performance concepts

A review of core performance concepts is important because an analytic discussion of performance budgeting requires a clear conceptual framework. All too often, discussions of performance budgeting and management have been conducted at cross-purposes because of terminological misunderstandings and confusion.

The most fundamental concepts in the conceptual framework of performance management and budgeting are outcomes, outputs, activities, and inputs. An *output* is a good or service provided by an agency to or for an external party. *Outcomes* are the intended impacts of those outputs. Thus, for example, the medical treatment received by a road accident victim is an output, the intended outcomes of which are the preservation of the patient's life and the minimization of any disability resulting from the accident. Similarly, investigations of crimes are a police output, and reduced crime the intended outcome of that output. *Activities* are types of work task undertaken in the production of outputs. The delivery of an output generally requires a set of coordinated activities of different types and in different quantities. (The term "process" is often used more or less synonymously with "activity," and differences between the two terms are too subtle to be worth dissecting here.) Thus the treatment of the road accident victim may involve a combination of direct treatment activities such as surgery, nursing, and anesthesia, as well as supporting activities such as supplies and facility management.[2] *Inputs* are resources used in the carrying out of activities to produce outputs (for example, labor, equipment, buildings).

Outcomes—to define the concept more precisely—are changes brought about by public interventions upon individuals, social structures, or the physical environment. It is common for an output to have more than one intended outcome. For example, the intended outcomes of school education include increased knowledge (the "student learning outcome"), a stronger economy, and a more harmonious society (through, for example, greater respect for the rights of others and for the law). This example also highlights the important distinction between *high-level* and *proximate* outcomes. Proximate outcomes are the more direct or immediate impacts of the output, whereas high-level outcomes refer to the ultimate objective or purpose of providing the output. The former are means of achieving the latter. In the case of school education, knowledge is a proximate outcome, whereas a stronger economy is a high-level outcome.[3] Utility—the concept used in microeconomics to refer to the satisfaction or well-being derived from outputs—can be regarded as the highest-level outcome of all.

Although the use of the term "outcomes" to refer to *all* impacts of public interventions is predominant practice, there are some who seek to distinguish between "outcomes" and "impacts"—usually with something like the distinction between proximate and high-level outcomes in mind.[4] This usage is not employed here.

This set of widely-understood and largely standardized concepts is referred to as the "logical (results) framework," the interrelationships of which may be thought of as representing a *public sector production chain* (Figure 3.1).

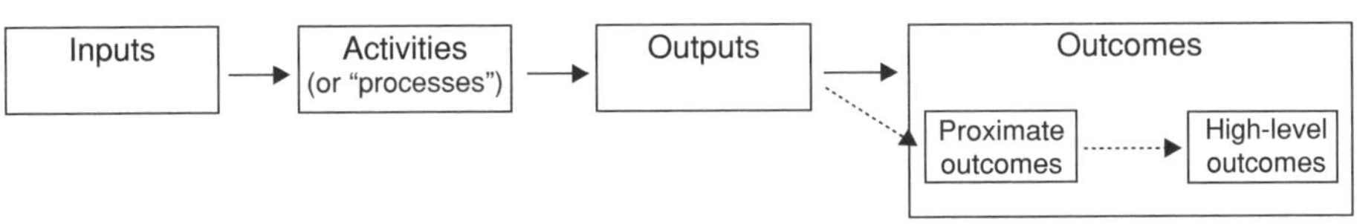

Figure 3.1 Public sector production chain

Having defined the key concepts in broad terms, it is useful to pin them down more precisely. Outputs are the "products" supplied by government, although in using this term it must always be borne in mind that most government outputs are services rather than physical goods. Products—outputs—can only be said to have been produced when the production process is complete. One would not consider a car which was pulled off the production line before the engine was installed and wheels attached to be a "product." The same applies to service outputs—if the medical team walks out in the middle of an emergency operation on the road accident victim, making it impossible to achieve the intended outcome of saving the patient's life, no output has been delivered. Expressed differently, if it is to be considered an output, a service (or good) must be *potentially capable of producing its intended outcome.*

This sheds important light on the relationship between outputs and outcomes. In stating that a completed unit of output must be potentially capable of producing its intended outcome, the word "potentially" is important because there are many services where there is uncertainty about whether the intended outcomes will be achieved in each individual case. There may, for example, be considerable uncertainty about whether even the best emergency treatment of a severely injured road accident victim will succeed in saving the patient's life. For such outputs, all that can be said is that the *expected* outcome is positive. It follows from this that it is inappropriate, for some types of services, to define the completion of the production of the output in terms of the achievement of the desired proximate outcome. In other words, outputs do not necessarily produce their desired outcomes.

This also helps clarify the distinction between activities and outputs, which is a matter in respect to which confusion is common. As noted above, service outputs generally involve bundles of activities. These constituent activities cannot normally be considered to be outputs in their own right because it is only when they are combined with the other activities that an intended outcome can potentially be achieved. Anesthesia, for example, may be of no potential benefit to a patient unless combined with other treatment activities such as surgery (likewise surgery cannot be delivered without appropriate anesthesia). Another reason why the distinction between activities and outputs is important is that in the case of collective services,[5] a single activity or set of activities may deliver multiple outputs. For example, teaching is an activity rather than an output because the teaching activity of one teacher delivers a service to multiple students in that teacher's class.[6] The educational output is therefore students taught, rather than the teaching itself.

As noted above, the usual definition of an output refers to products delivered by agencies to or for *external parties*. The most important implication of this is that services provided *within* an agency to *internal* clients—such as the services provided by an agency's human resources unit to its line divisions—are not in the performance budgeting literature generally considered to be outputs. The logic of this is that to, say, a car manufacturer, the services provided by the internal marketing department, or the finance department, are not products—cars are the product.[7] Confusion may best be avoided by referring to the services (or goods) produced for internal clients as "intermediate" outputs—with the understanding that when the term "outputs" is used alone, it refers to services provided to external, and not internal, parties.

The concept of output *quality* is a particularly slippery one, about which there is no general consensus. It is, unfortunately, not possible to review the issues involved here. Output quality may, however, be defined as the extent to which the characteristics of the product are such as to increase its potential capacity to generate its intended outcomes. For *goods*, the "characteristics" of the product refer principally to physical characteristics. For *services*, product characteristics refer to the nature, quantity, and mix of the activities which comprise the service output, as well as to the timeliness of the delivery of the overall service output. For example, high-quality treatment of a road accident victim means that the victim expeditiously receives the appropriate medical interventions. A crucial point about this definition is that it distinguishes between the quality of an output and the actual outcome which it achieves: in this usage, output quality increases the probability that the outcome will be achieved, but does not guarantee it.[8] It is regrettable that the term "quality" is all too often used in a manner which equates it with outcomes.

Effectiveness, efficiency, economy, and equity

Performance management and budgeting distinguish between *efficiency* and *effectiveness*—concepts which are drawn from the public administration literature, and which are different in meaning from the terminology used by economists. Effectiveness pertains to outcomes, whereas efficiency relates to outputs. More specifically, efficiency refers to the degree of success in delivering a defined output at minimum cost while holding quality constant, given prevailing input prices.[9] To cut the costs of issuing a certain regulatory approval by redesigning the relevant work process would, for example, improve the efficiency of that service (so long as quality is maintained).

Effectiveness, on the other hand, refers to the degree of success of a particular output or program in achieving its intended outcomes (thus a road safety awareness program is effective if it reduces road deaths). *Cost-effectiveness* increases if the same outcomes are produced at lower cost, given prevailing input prices. Cost-effectiveness may be improved either through more efficient delivery of existing services, or by changing the nature of the service. It is possible for an output to be efficiently produced but ineffective.

How do these terms relate to concepts used by economists? The term "effectiveness" is not used in the professional terminology of economics. Economists instead use the term "efficiency," although this is a term which they use in two distinct senses.

The first of these is *technical efficiency*, which corresponds to the public administration concept of efficiency. Technical efficiency refers to the choice of the least-cost combination of inputs for the production of the good or service concerned, for given input prices. There are two prerequisites for technical efficiency. One is the absence of waste (which economists sometimes refer to, following Leibenstein (1966) as X-inefficiency[10]). The other is that the right mix of inputs is used.[11] Technical efficiency is sometimes also referred to as *productive efficiency* or *operational efficiency*, and is also what the less formal term *productivity* usually connotes.

The other relevant economic concept is *allocative efficiency*. This subsumes, but is also broader than, the public adminstration concept of effectiveness. A standard definition of allocative efficiency is the production of the best or optimal combination of outputs given society's valuation of those outputs. Allocative efficiency thus defined requires and subsumes technical efficiency. However, at the heart of the concept of allocative efficiency is the requirement that the overall mix of goods and services is such as to maximize social well-being (utility). The degree of allocative efficiency of government expenditure therefore depends not only on the effectiveness of government expenditures in achieving their intended outcomes, but also upon the extent to which (a) those outcomes are beneficial to society and (b) it might be possible to deliver even greater benefit to society by changing the output mix.[12]

Equity is not an outcome, at least in the sense defined in this chapter. It is, rather, a property of the *distribution* of outcomes, outputs, or expenditures. Society may have different notions of what constitutes equity in relation to different government services, depending on the relevant concept of what Sen (1992) calls "basal equality." For some services, it might be thought that equity requires that each client receives the same level of service—that is, that there be an equal distribution of *outputs*. For other services, however, it may be considered that equity demands either equal *outcomes*, or at least that the dispersion of outcomes be contained within some acceptable range. For yet other services, an equal distribution of *expenditure* may be desired. These concepts of equity are often mutually exclusive. In school education, for example, the delivery of the same education to all students of a particular cohort (equality of *outputs*) will yield widely different student learning outcomes. If one wishes to reduce the degree of divergence of these outcomes, it is necessary to accept greater inequality of outputs (through, for example, additional services for disadvantaged students). Another example of the conflict between different concepts of equity is that equality of *expenditure* per student will not deliver equality of outputs (let alone of outcomes) for a range of reasons, including the fact that some students live in more remote areas where it costs more to deliver education services. A choice therefore needs to be made as to which concept of equity—or rather, what compromise between these competing concepts of equity—will guide the provision of education.

Controllability and predictability in producing results

In the public sector production chain, money is spent on acquiring inputs which are used to carry out activities, in order to produce outputs, and these outputs are in turn intended to generate outcomes. Performance budgeting seeks to strengthen the linkage between the starting point of this production chain (the money) and the end points (outputs and/or expected outcomes). In considering how far, and in what way, it is possible to link funding and results, an important consideration is the extent to which the results delivered via the production chain are controllable and predictable. There are, in this context, two important sources of uncertainty which need to be taken into account. One concerns the link between outputs and outcomes and the other the link between activities and outputs.

The link between outputs and outcomes

The characteristics of individuals, social structures, or the physical environment which public interventions seek to change are almost always subject to multiple influences outside the control of the unit of public administration, the performance of which is being examined. These influences are often referred to as *external factors*.[13] External factors may be characteristics of the client—a familiar example of which is the impact of student characteristics (intelligence, motivation, parental and social support, and encouragement) on knowledge outcomes in education. Or they can be aspects of the context in which the public program is being delivered. Thus, for example, a labor market program, the intended outcome of which is to increase the rate of reintegration into the workforce of workers who have suffered an industrial injury, will need to recognize that hiring rates for the program's target group are subject to the overarching influence of the state of the macroeconomy.

What constitutes an external factor varies depending upon the institutional focus. From the perspective of individual government agencies, external factors commonly include the actions and performance of other government agencies. For example, the educational effectiveness of individual schools will be influenced by the regulatory regime imposed upon them by the national or regional education ministry. Similarly, the effectiveness of the educational system as a whole will tend to be affected by the quality of anti-poverty policies (for example, are steps being taken to ensure that all children arrive at school with a full belly?). But from the perspective of the government as a whole, such influences are controllable and are therefore not external factors at all.

The consequence of external factors is that the "same" output may deliver different outcomes at different times, in different contexts, or when delivered to different clients. Moreover, to the extent that the impact of external factors is unpredictable, it may be difficult to specify ex ante what outcomes a service should be capable of delivering. External factors may also make the timeframe in which outcomes may be expected to be achieved uncertain. In some cases, the degree of such unpredictability in the relationship between outputs and outcomes may be high. To take an extreme example, there tends to be enormous ex-ante uncertainty about the outcomes (whether the perpetrator will be caught and punished) which can be expected from murder investigations. Similarly, it is very hard to predict in advance how much impact, and over what time horizons, to expect of public health programs which aim to reduce rates of cardiac and other disease arising from poor lifestyle habits. In general, high-level outcomes are more subject to the impact of external factors than proximate outcomes.

The link between activities and outputs

Most textbook microeconomic analysis focuses on homogeneous (standardized) products. For physical goods, homogeneity means that the physical characteristics of each unit of the product are essentially identical, as is the case for mass-manufactured commodities. A homogeneous (standardized) service may, equivalently, be defined as one where the set of activities delivered to each client are the same.[14] In the public sector, motor license testing is an example of a highly standardized service—the activities required to administer a motor license test (administration of a written test, followed by observation of the candidate carrying out a pre-specified set of driving activities) are usually both precisely prescribed in regulation and essentially the same for all would-be drivers.

Very few public sector services are as standardized as mass-produced goods, but a significant number are (or are intended to be) quite standardized. Thus in many countries the *aim* is that government-supplied school education should be essentially the same for the bulk of students of each cohort—with, say, nearly all third-graders in public schools receiving pretty much the same education. By contrast, however, many public services are intended to be *heterogeneous*. Outputs are heterogeneous when there is a *deliberate* variation in the amount and/or types of activities received by each client/case of the "same" service, particularly in response to differences in client or case characteristics. An extreme example is police murder investigations. Differing circumstances make some murders easy to solve, while others are difficult or even impossible, and this leads to great variations in the activity devoted to investigating them. In acute medical care the treatment accorded to two different patients receiving treatment for the same condition—whether it be a heart attack or a broken hip—will often vary because of other factors such as the age and general condition of health of the patient. Some degree of heterogeneity often affects even relatively standardized services. Thus even if a national education system aims to deliver essentially the same education to the bulk of students, it is commonly also the intention that certain categories of the student population—such as children with disabilities—should be the beneficiaries of more intensive teaching and other services which are tailored to their specific needs. As this example suggests, the degree of heterogeneity in public service delivery depends not only on the degree to which client or case characteristics vary, but also on the extent to which policy-makers and the community decide that they wish to tailor services according to those characteristics.

Heterogeneity is the *deliberate* variation in the level of service activity delivered to different clients/cases because there is a conscious objective behind the targeting of some clients/cases for greater activity than others. Very often—as in the provision of more intensive education for children with disabilities—the objective is to reduce the disparity of outcomes relative to that which would result if all clients received the same service. Reduced inequality of outcomes is, however, not the only motive for heterogeneity.[15]

Heterogeneity is relevant to performance budgeting because the greater the degree of heterogeneity affecting a particular service, the more uncertainty may arise in the relationship between activities and outputs (as well as between inputs and outputs). Consider, for example, a program aimed at providing emergency accommodation (for example, in foster care) for children who cannot, for some reason, be cared for by their own family. The duration (and type) of placements for such children can be expected to vary enormously—and in a way which is not usually unpredictable in advance—depending on the reason why their parents are unable to take care of them (for example, temporary illness, death, domestic abuse), and upon a range of other factors such as whether there are other family members who can be located and who can care for the child. (Moreover, an integrated approach to service delivery would treat as part of the same service the delivery of other support activities such as psychological support services, the need for which would also vary greatly been clients.)

Heterogeneity has another important implication—that for heterogeneous services, the concept of an output "type" (that is, the type of product) may be

Box 3.1 Heterogeneity and the definition of outputs

The heterogeneity problem may be reduced if, and to the extent that, it is possible to pre-classify clients or cases with greater precision in such a manner as to provide greater predictability about the type and extent of activity which each will require. What this involves, in essence, is the development of a more "fine-grained" classification of product types (that is, of outputs). A good example of this can be found in the so-called "diagnosis related group" (DRG) health output classification system. As outlined in Chapter 1, DRG output categories—originally designed as a performance measurement tool—are now used in many countries as the basis for a "purchaser-provider" form of performance budgeting. Patients are classified into groups (DRGs) depending primarily upon the type of medical problem for which they are being treated, and a price is determined for each DRG category. Thus, for example, hospitals might receive $x for every hip fracture patient they treat, and $y for every hernia patient. The DRG classification system became progressively more detailed over the years following its inception precisely in order to reduce the degree of heterogeneity within each DRG (output) category. Thus, for example, in the earliest versions of DRG classifications, all hip fracture patients were categorized under the same DRG. However, because there was great variability in the extent and nature of the treatment required by different hip fracture patients, research was undertaken to identify patient characteristics which were good predictors of a more intensive treatment requirement. It was established that the two most important predictors were (a) whether the patient was an aged person or not and (b) whether the patient had other significant acute health problems. As a result of this, the single hip fracture DRG was, in later versions of the DRG output classification systems, broken into three different DRGs—one for aged hip fracture patients, one for hip fracture patients with secondary complications, and a third group for all remaining hip fracture patients. This reduced the heterogeneity problem greatly, although it did not eliminate it entirely. Unfortunately, however, there are limits to how far this approach can be applied across the public sector. One limitation is information costs—the more fine-grained the classification of outputs, the more costly it is to obtain reasonably accurate output costing (see Chapter 4). The other limitation arises from the fact that it is sometimes very difficult to distinguish in advance case/client characteristics which will lead to differing required levels of activity.

inherently ambiguous. For mass-manufactured products, there is no ambiguity, because a product type is defined as a class of physically identical products. The same is true for a standardized service such as motor license testing, because the prescribed activities are the same for each client. In the case of a highly heterogeneous service, however, the activity content of the outputs delivered may vary so much between clients/cases that it may be impossible or impracticable to define output groups for which the activity content is identical. In the DRG system, for example, even when output types (DRGs) are defined more narrowly—as in the hip fracture example—a degree of heterogeneity remains. For such types of services, whatever definition of output types is adopted, output quantity measures will inevitably be affected to some extent by an additivity problem—a problem, in other words, of adding apples and pears.

There is, in addition to heterogeneity, another source of uncertainty in the relationship between activities and the outputs produced by that activity which is worth specific mention in a government context. This concerns collective services where, as noted above, a single set of activities delivers outputs to multiple recipients (recall that, as noted above, it is the receipt of the service by the client, and not the delivery of the activities by the producers, which constitutes an output). The extreme case of this is services which possess the pure "public good" characteristic that the marginal cost of supplying the service to an additional client is zero. A classic example of this is the service provided by a free-to-air public (or private, for that matter) radio or television channel. Clearly if the marginal cost of additional output is zero, the relationship between the level of funding provided and the quantity of output delivered is completely indeterminate.

Measuring results

Performance measures may be defined as *ratings or quantitative measures which provide information on the effectiveness and efficiency of public programs*. It should be emphasized that, for reasons explained below, the terms "performance measures" and "performance indicators" are used interchangeably in this volume. Like performance information in general, performance measures fall into two categories—those which provide information about the results achieved, and those which provide information on the costs of achieving those results. Here the focus is principally upon the former (costing issues are considered in Chapter 4).

Great progress has been made in output and outcome measurement in many countries over recent decades. A recent survey of OECD countries[16] (OECD, 2005) reported that 77 percent of (27) respondent nations had taken their first government-wide output measurement initiative less than five years ago, and that half of respondents claimed to have developed a combination of output and outcome measures. There exist a number of impressive examples of best practice in performance measurement. One is the system of local government performance measurement and reporting which has been developed in Britain since the early 1980s. Under this system—managed primarily by the Audit Commission—a standardized set of performance measures for the full range of services delivered by local government (education, police, housing, waste management, social services, and so on) has been developed and is publicly reported.[17] More recently, under the "Comprehensive Performance Assessment" initiative, these performance measures and other information have been used to develop a composite performance ranking system under which each local government is rated on a five-point scale from "poor" through to "excellent,"[18] with this rating being made public. (This illustrates, incidentally, what is meant by "ratings"—as opposed to quantitative measures—in the definition of performance measures above.) Another outstanding example of how far performance measurement can be taken can be found in the annual New York City Mayor's Management Report.[19] In light of this type of success in developing quality performance measures, there is today little scope for arguing—as some have done in the past—that the measurement of results is too difficult and imperfect to be of significant managerial value.

Performance measurement is, nevertheless, a very imperfect science, and it is important to any systematic study of performance budgeting to appreciate its limits as well its possibilities. The following paragraphs therefore briefly survey some of the most important constraints which limit our capacity to measure outcomes and outputs.

Outcome measurement

Three key difficulties arise in the measurement of outcomes. The first is that it is often difficult to distinguish the impact of a public program from that of external factors. Thus, for example, if the crime rate falls from one year to the next, it may be very hard to tell how far (if at all) this is due to better policing and how far to, say, broader social or economic factors outside the control of the police. For this reason, many outcome measures—such as crime rate statistics—do not even attempt to distinguish program outcomes from the impact of external factors. Another way of viewing this problem is that measuring outcomes requires knowledge of a "counterfactual"—namely, of what would have happened had the government not intervened. In some cases, one can only speculate about such counterfactuals. For example, who could say whether, in the absence of the presence of a strong army, a nation might have been subject to military aggression?

There are, however, measurement techniques which enable us in some cases to adjust to at least some degree for the impact of external factors. In the educational sphere, for example, the importance of student characteristics in determining knowledge outcomes has led to the development of so-called "value-added" measures which disaggregate student knowledge outcomes by relevant student type, on the basis of research which identifies key socioeconomic and other determinants of educational success. The idea is that by permitting, for example, comparisons of the performance of *similar students* in different schools, one will obtain a much better idea of the relative performance of those schools than if one compared unadjusted results.[20]

The second, closely-related, difficulty is that it can be difficult to distinguish the impacts of multiple programs which have common intended outcomes. Consider, as an extreme example, the difficulties which would arise in seeking to determine the respective impact on the promotion of economic growth of the multiplicity of government services with that objective (for example, education and training, scientific research, macroeconomic policy). As this example illustrates, this problem tends to be particularly severe for high-level outcomes.

Sometimes, it is possible to use regression analysis to get a better sense of the outcomes achieved by public expenditures. The minimum prerequisite for this is a database of considerable size and (for time series analysis purposes) time duration. However, as Pradhan (1996, p. 12) notes, there is often "a lack of consensus among these studies even about the direction of impact of key expenditure categories (for example, positive or negative impact of the share of health, education and transport spending)...[as well as] uncertainty about its magnitude." Rarely, moreover, is it possible to use such statistical analysis to disentangle the separate contributions of distinct public programs with a broad category of expenditure.

The third key outcome measurement challenge is that some outcomes—particularly high-level outcomes—relate to social variables for which there does not exist, even in principle, a good measure. Consider, for example, the contrast between the outcomes sought by anti-pollution programs—where pollution levels are in principle perfectly measurable—with those of public programs designed to build greater interracial tolerance. There is no good metric for the degree of interracial tolerance in a society. For variables of this type, one is required to use inherently imperfect (and sometimes highly imperfect) proxy measures—such as, in this case, measures of the incidence of race-related crime.

As noted above, utility—well-being or satisfaction—is the highest-level outcome. If we were able to measure the utility which is, or would be, generated by alternative mixes of public outputs, the problem of allocative optimization would be solved. The aim of cost-benefit analysis is, in principle, to develop benefit measures which are proxies for utility, with benefit being measured in terms of willingness to pay. Cost-benefit analysis can, at its best, yield valuable performance measures which can be a useful part of the overall performance information base of a good performance budgeting system. Unfortunately, however, benefit measures often range considerably and are for this and other reasons of questionable reliability. Moreover, cost-benefit analysis is an expensive process which cannot be cost-effectively applied on other than a highly selective basis.

The inability to measure, or obtain good proxies for, the utility of public expenditure in a single metric has far-reaching consequences. It means that there is in general no common yardstick for comparing the allocative merits of alternative expenditure options with significantly different intended outcomes. Thus the outcome measures one might be able to derive for, say, police services (based on crime statistics) and education services (student knowledge outcomes) may enable us to assess the effectiveness of those services, but they do not provide us with a means of determining their relative value to society. In general, in making allocative decisions, it is necessary to make highly subjective and informal judgments. This remains as true today as it was 40 years ago when one of the originators of program budgeting observed that "at the current state of analytic art, no one really knows with any precision how the 'grand optimum' [of public expenditure] might be attained...Intuition and judgment are paramount" (Fisher, 1967, p. 63). This informational problem is in fact one of the key reasons why market economies are superior to centrally planned economies[21] (which is, of course, not to say that there are not, within the framework of a market economy, major areas where the market fails to various degrees, requiring government intervention in various forms).

In addition to the inherent problems of outcome measurement, measuring outcomes is often made more difficult by the ambiguous manner in which some public sector objectives are specified. It is, as noted previously, a key managing-for-results theme that intended outcomes should be made explicit. Sometimes, however, objectives are kept deliberately fuzzy because there is political and/or ideological conflict about what the objectives of the organization should be (Tankersley and Grizzle, 1994), and it is not desired to aggravate the conflict by going through a process of goal clarification.[22]

Output measurement

Outputs are in general less difficult to measure than outcomes. It is, in particular, usually possible to measure output *quantity* (although the greater the degree of heterogeneity, the less meaningful quantity measures will be). The greatest difficulties in output measurement tend to arise in respect to output *quality*. One reason for this is that so many public sector outputs are services rather than goods. The quality of services is a property of their constituent activities, and activities can only be observed at the time they are carried out—not, like the physical properties of goods, after the event. Heterogeneity also creates further measurement difficulties. For standardized outputs, it is possible to apply what the quality literature refers to as the "conformance to specifications" concept of quality. For a mass-manufactured homogeneous physical good, the application of this concept of quality means testing whether the physical characteristics of (a sample of) the product match the product's intended specifications. For a standardized service, it means checking whether the activities carried out in dealing with each case/client were the prescribed ones. (Thus, if there is a "treatment protocol" which defines the best form of treatment for patients with a certain medical condition, the quality of treatment can be—at least in part—assessed by determining how far the treatment provided in any particular case accorded with what is laid down in the protocol.) However, the more heterogeneous a service—that is, the more the activities delivered are tailored to the specific needs of the client/case—the less relevant such an approach becomes, and the more difficult it is to measure quality. For many heterogeneous public services it is, indeed, less difficult to develop outcome measures than output quality measures.

The difficulty of measuring quality presents a particular problem for output *quantity* measurement in respect to the sub-set of public services for which (a) demand is unpredictably variable and (b) the response to demand fluctuations is, at least in part, to vary the amount of activity devoted to each client or case. Consider the example of police investigations of burglaries. The incidence of burglaries in a big city may be expected to vary unpredictably from month to month, and in a month with a particularly high burglary rate, the police might find their investigative resources very stretched. They may respond by working more overtime, but part of the response would almost inevitably be to spend less investigative activity on each burglary than they would in quieter times. What this means is that the quality of each investigation is being varied as a rationing technique. This type of variation of the level of service as a rationing technique—what might be called quality rationing—makes output quantity measures a less meaningful indicator of performance than they might otherwise be.

Quality measurement problems are one reason why activity measures can play an important role as proxies for, or supplements to, output measures for many public services. In the context of police criminal investigations work, for example, this would mean accompanying measures of the numbers of each type of crime which were investigated (an output measure) with measures of the amount of investigative activity per investigation (an activity measure).

The above summarizes only the most important overarching limits on performance measurement. The key point is that performance measures are by their nature imperfect. It is precisely for this reason that it was suggested earlier that the distinction which some draw between performance *measures* and performance *indicators*—a distinction in which the latter term refers to imperfect proxies for the former—is not very useful (HM Treasury, 2001, pp. 29–30). For this reason, the terms are used synonymously in this volume. The imperfection of measurement means that performance measures often do not provide conclusive evidence of whether an organization is performing well or badly. Suppose, for example, that an agency's outputs increase this year even though its budget has not increased. This might be because it has become more efficient. But it might be because it has this year had cases/clients which are on average less complex than last year, or because it has reduced the level of service being provided to clients. Further investigation—desirably involving supplementary performance measures—will be necessary to determine the explanation.

It is often said, correctly, that performance measurement tends to be more difficult in the public sector than in the private sector. The above analysis indicates many of the reasons why this is the case: the general government sector produces mainly services rather than physical goods. Many of the services it provides are heterogeneous, or are contingent capacity in nature. Indeed, it can be argued that these characteristics are fundamental reasons—not fully captured in the traditional textbook taxonomy of market failures—why many public services are provided by the government and not by the market. And of course non-market provision of services means that there are no financial performance measures such as profit/loss and share price.

The degree of performance measurement difficulty does, however, vary enormously between different types of government agency depending on the types of outputs being produced and the types of outcomes being pursued. Similar variations are also to be found in the private sector, from producers of standardized mass-manufactured products at one end of the spectrum to producers of complex and heterogeneous services (for example, consulting, legal services) at the other end of the spectrum.

Evaluation

The limits of performance measurement, and of what performance measures can tell us in isolation, means that assessing the effectiveness and efficiency of programs requires that performance measures be combined with analysis. Analysis is required both in the interpretation of performance measures, and in extending the assessment of program performance beyond the limits of the information which measures alone can provide. Systematic, formal analysis of this type is commonly referred to as *evaluation*. A broad definition of evaluation is that offered by the OECD: "evaluations are analytical assessments addressing results of public policies, organizations or programmes, that emphasize reliability and usefulness of findings." This definition covers both ex-post evaluations of the performance of actual programs, and analysis to develop new programs ("ex-ante evaluations") (OECD, 1998, p. 5). Others, however, reserve the term "evaluation" exclusively for ex-post assessments.[23]

Evaluation necessarily makes use of performance measures, and *good* evaluation requires good performance measures. The role of analysis is, however, fundamental. Thus a key part of evaluation is consideration of the policy logic of the program in the light of relevant theory—in other words, an assessment of whether theory suggests that one should expect the program to achieve its intended outcomes. For example, the evaluation of an anti-smoking health promotion program should make use of the insights of psychology and marketing theory about what works (and what does not) in changing human behavior. The greater the degree to which outcome measures are ambiguous or lacking, the greater the importance of the analysis of policy logic. Part of such analysis should be consideration of whether there is a compelling theoretical rationale for government to provide a particular service, rather than leaving it to the market (in particular, by reference to the well-developed market failure criteria of economic theory).

Analysis is also used in evaluation to *interpret* performance measures. This is true in dealing with the common outcome measurement problem mentioned above: that available outcome measures do a poor job of distinguishing the actual outcome of the program from the impact of "external" factors. When this is the case, analysis, using data on what is happening to the relevant external factors, is likely to be an essential tool for forming a judgment about the effectiveness of the program concerned.

Over the post-war period, enthusiasm for evaluation has waxed and waned, and the approach to evaluation has changed significantly. From the 1960s into the 1970s, the worldwide influence of the original US program budgeting system (PPBS) led to enthusiasm for systematic and comprehensive "scientific" evaluation. The idea, as mentioned in Chapter 1, was to make full use of all the tools of economic and social research—cost-benefit analysis, cost-effectiveness analysis, and information science generally. In 1978 one US observer noted that "over the past 15 years, a new industry has been created to evaluate the performance of government programs," with the federal government alone spending $200 million a year on evaluations (Wholey, 1978, p. 52). By that time, however, there was already a "growing disillusionment with social science evaluation" in government (Floden and Weiner, 1978, p. 367). In part, this was because it became clear that the claims made for scientific evaluation were exaggerated because, for example, it was difficult to handle uncertainty and intangible costs and benefits (Toulemonde and Rochaix, 1994, p. 49). In addition, precisely because of their thorough, "scientific" quality, evaluation reports often took so long to produce that they lost their timeliness and were "too costly and time-consuming compared to their real use and effect" (OECD, 1998, p. 3). Bounded rationality was the other key problem—the mass of analytic paperwork produced under PPBS was far too great for decision-makers to use. As a result, support for program evaluation fell, and by the 1980s in the US the large "program evaluations divisions" which had existed in every government department had "all but vanished" (Weinstock, 2003).

Evaluation has enjoyed subsequent waves of popularity in certain countries. In the US, evaluation requirements were part of the Government Performance and Results Act of 1993, leading to some renewal of evaluation activity, although not on the scale of the PPBS era. In Australia, a system of mandatory evaluation, in which departments were required to evaluate all their programs over a five-year cycle, was introduced in the mid-1980s, as part of a program budgeting system, and lasted till the mid-1990s (Mackay, 2004; Johnston, 1998; Department of Finance and Australian Public Service Board, 1987; Department of Finance, 1994). In Chile, program evaluation has been a core part of the performance budgeting systems in recent years (see Chapter 13). More recently, Canada embarked in 2006 on a project to re-engineer its budgetary expenditure priority-setting processes, and to make a revitalized system of program evaluation a central part of the new system. In these and other countries, however, the type of evaluation being employed tends to differ greatly from the practices of the earlier PPBS period. The contemporary emphasis is more on timeliness, relevance and cost-effectiveness in evaluation methodology, and less on comprehensive "scientific" methodology.

A key informational issue for performance budgeting remains, therefore, that of the appropriate role of program evaluation in budget decision-making, and of the nature of that evaluation. There are those today who think of performance budgeting as being exclusively concerned with the use of performance measures in budgeting. However, given the limits on performance measures in isolation, there is a strong argument for viewing measures as one element of a broader set of performance information which also includes program evaluation. A key challenge is then to ensure that evaluation is practical, useful and cost-effective.

Implementing performance information systems

As indicated at the outset, this chapter is not intended to serve as a manual for building a performance information system to support the introduction of performance budgeting. Nevertheless, some key points about implementation strategy may usefully be made.

The essential first step, before any attempt is made to identify indicators to be measured or to establish evaluation processes, must always be the explicit specification of the key objectives which the government is seeking to achieve. Expressed differently, it is necessary to clearly state the desired outcomes for each of the major categories of government outputs. The articulation of intended outcomes is an exercise which can usefully be combined with the development of a draft program structure for each ministry/agency.

It is necessary to be realistic both about how much information is to be provided, and about the timeframe for the development of the performance information system. The costs of performance information make it essential that, even in the most fully developed performance information system, there be *selectivity* in the choice of performance data which are to be gathered.[24] When embarking for the first time upon the development of performance indicators, even greater selectivity is necessary. It is better initially to identify a small number of indicators which each agency will measure, than to develop long wish-lists of potentially useful indicators. Once experience is gained with a small number of key indicators, the number of measures can be expanded. Selectiveness is even more important in countries with greater-than-normal capacity and resource constraints. As for timing, it is essential to recognize that building even a simple performance information system is a project which will take some years.

There are a range of sources for performance data. The most readily accessible tend to be agency records. Such records will, as a rule, predominantly relate to the volumes of activities carried out and outputs delivered. National statistics, depending upon their scope, can be of considerable value. However, measuring outcomes and output quality is, in general, a more demanding task which cannot be based upon agency records and will require the use of more sophisticated and costly techniques (such as consumer satisfaction surveys). It is therefore entirely appropriate to focus, in the first stage of the development of performance indicators, mainly upon the development of good measures of output quantity and activity. The second stage will generally focus upon the bringing together of results information and accounting systems in order to develop measures of the costs of programs and key outputs (see the next chapter), while recognizing that cost measures will inevitably be very approximate to start with. Only after these stages is it appropriate to make a systematic attack on the more challenging areas of outcomes and output quality.

A key part of any performance information system—no matter how limited or ambitious its scope—is the existence of appropriate mechanisms for the verification and attestation of that information. If performance indicators are not subject to external checks, data manipulation will be the inevitable result. Verification and attestation require appropriate internal control procedures, and also good external audit. The role of external audit in relation to performance budgeting is discussed in Chapter 6.

The development of performance information systems requires significant resourcing and technical support. Collection and processing of data must be computer-based. Appropriately trained professional staff are also essential. Over time, as the scope of the performance information system expands, the capacity requirements to underpin the system will also increase. The quality of professional staff necessary to develop output costing or to develop outcome and output quality measures is, for example, considerably greater than that required for the measurement of output and activity quantities. The conduct of program evaluations also requires adequately trained staff.

Performance budgeting in the government-wide budget requires that the Ministry of Finance and key political leaders receive performance information which is relevant and useful to them in making budgetary decisions. Given this, the selection of performance measures should not be left to the line agencies alone—the result is likely to be the development of a set of uninformative measures which protect the agency from scrutiny rather than facilitating scrutiny. So the center must involve itself intimately in the process of defining what type of performance information it is to be provided with. Indeed, close central involvement must precede this, and start with the process of defining the intended outcomes of key government outputs. At the same time, it is quite inappropriate for the Ministry of Finance to simply dictate to agencies what indicators will be developed. It may sound like a platitude, but it is essential that agencies and the individuals who work within them "own" the performance indicators which are used—that is, that they accept the relevance of them as measures of the results which they achieve. As discussed in Chapter 18, the motivational power of performance information depends in part on such an acceptance and recognition of its validity.

Conclusions

Performance information on the results achieved by public programs is a fundamental prerequisite of performance budgeting, and also of performance management more generally. Clarity about the basic performance concepts is important to avoid unnecessary analytic confusion. Because performance budgeting aims to link funding and results, an understanding of key features of the production chain is important. Three particularly relevant aspects of the production chain for performance budgeting are the impact of external factors for outcomes, the unpredictable time lags which characterize many outcomes, and the heterogeneous nature of many public sector outputs. Performance measurement has advanced far over recent decades in many countries, as has the use of performance measures for a range of purposes. There are, however, major limits to what may be measured. One of the functions of evaluation is to apply a range of analytic techniques to improve on the performance information offered by measures alone.

In the development of a performance information system, it is essential to take a staged approach, starting with the explicit delineation of the intended outcomes of key government services. Initially, performance measurement should focus on the development of a small set of activity and output quantity measures, and only over time should governments go beyond that to output costing measures, program evaluation, and outcome and quality measures. Above all, it is essential to recognize that it is impossible to build performance information systems in a year or two. By its nature, the development of performance information for performance budgeting—and for other "managing-for-results" uses—is a medium- to long-term project. It is, however, a project which can yield some benefits relatively quickly, and others progressively over time.

Notes

1. The author would like to thank Peter C. Smith for his valuable comments on an earlier draft of this chapter.
2. The activity concept is the basis for "activity-based costing" (ABC), which is briefly discussed in Chapter 4.
3. Other terminology is often used to make the same distinction—proximate outcomes have sometimes been referred to as "intermediate" outcomes, and high-level outcomes as "final," "ultimate," or "end" outcomes. The distinction between high-level and proximate outcomes is, however, often a matter of degree, and it is better to think not of a clear-cut categorization of outcomes but of a continuum of outcomes ranging from the most proximate to the most high-level.
4. See, for example, UNDP Evaluation Office (2002), USAID (1983). The problem with this is that it can be difficult, at the margins, to distinguish between impacts and outcomes.

5. The extreme case of which are pure public goods with the property of non-rivalness (zero marginal cost for additional outputs).
6. And also because the teaching activity requires other support activities to be capable of achieving the intended knowledge outcome.
7. It should be noted that in this definition of outputs, "external" parties generally means external to the agency rather than external to the government as a whole. The implication of this is to classify as outputs not only services provided to the public, but also services provided by one government agency to another government agency. The services which a finance ministry provides when regulating and oversighting the fiscal management of other ministries are, for example, considered to be an output, even though no direct service is being provided to the public.
8. If the distinction between outcomes and output quality is not made, one is forced, for example, to brand as "low quality" the treatment received by any road accident patient who dies, even if everything possible was done promptly to save the patient.
9. For completeness, some add a third concept of "economy," which reflects "whether the right price was paid to acquire the necessary inputs" (HM Treasury, 2001).
10. If it is possible to produce the same output with less of one input, while holding constant the amount of other inputs, there is X-inefficiency.
11. Formally, that the marginal rate of substitution between inputs equals the ratio of input prices.
12. Allocative efficiency in public expenditure can also be construed more broadly to embrace in addition establishing the balance between publicly and privately-provided outputs most likely to maximize well-being.
13. Sometimes also known as "contextual" or "confounding" factors.
14. Holding the technology and degree of efficiency constant.
15. In fact, in some cases heterogeneity may reflect objectives which imply increased outcome disparity. This is the case, for example, in respect of educational programs which give additional attention to *gifted* students.
16. Plus two observer countries, Israel and Chile.
17. See <www.local-pi-library.gov.uk/library.asp>.
18. See <www.audit-commission.gov.uk/cpa/index.asp?page=index.asp&area=hpcpa>.
19. See <www.nyc.gov/html/ops/html/mmr/mmr.shtml>.
20. More generally, Jacobs et al. (2006) distinguish three principal methodologies for taking into account the impact of external factors. The first is to compare outcomes of organizations which are confronted with the same, or a very similar, external context. The second is to model the external factors explicitly, analogously to factors in the production process (for example, through regression analysis applied to substantial datasets). The third is "risk adjustment," a term which they use to refer to the process of defining output categories in a more detailed way to reduce heterogeneity.
21. There is no need to conduct cost-benefit analysis of products delivered by the market (serious market imperfections aside), because these judgments are in effect made by consumers and other decentralized decision-makers. During the first half of the twentieth century, a number of economists of the "socialist calculation" school (including, most notably, Oskar Lange) argued that a centrally planned economy could be at least as allocatively efficient as a market economy—as well as having other advantages (particularly in macroeconomic stability)—if government planners solved the allocative optimization problem mathematically. This school was so influential that these techniques (especially linear programming) eventually became the centerpiece of Soviet economic planning. As Friedrich von Hayek in particular pointed out, the most fundamental defect with this line of argument was that it is in practice impossible for central planners to obtain (or, even if they could obtain it, to use) the vast amount of information which such planning would require.
22. This is part of a broader issue of "goal ambiguity" which has received some attention among public administration scholars (see, for example, Rainey, 1993).

23. For example, the British Treasury defines evaluation as "retrospective analysis of a project, program, or policy to assess how successful or otherwise it has been, and what lessons can be learnt for the future" (HM Treasury, 1997, p. 97).
24. As Mackay (2004, p. 17) notes, "Another common mistake when designing a performance system is to over-engineer the information—in terms of both quantity and quality—which it will provide. This mistake can be made by having an overly-comprehensive system of performance indicators, or by commissioning a large and costly number of sophisticated evaluations. In many countries this has proved not only wasteful but also counterproductive. Those responsible for providing the M&E information will have no incentive to produce quality information of a timely nature if they perceive the information is not being fully used. And if the quality of information starts to decline, this can further undermine the demand for it."

References

Department of Finance, 1994, *The Use of Evaluation in the 1994–95 Budget—Issues for Discussion* (Canberra: Australian Government Publishing Service).

Department of Finance and Australian Public Service Board, 1987, *Evaluating Government Programs: Financial Management Improvement Program* (Canberra: Australian Government Publishing Service).

Fisher, G.H., 1967, "The Role of Cost-Utility Analysis in Program Budgeting," in *Program Budgeting: Program Analysis and the Federal Budget*, ed. D. Novick (Cambridge, Mass.: Harvard University Press).

Floden, R.E., and S.S. Weiner, 1978, "Rationality to Ritual: The Multiple Roles of Evaluation in Government Processes," reprinted in *Public Budgeting*, 1982, ed. F.J. Lynden and E.G Miller, 4th edition (Englewood Cliffs, NJ: Prentice-Hall), pp. 366–80.

HM Treasury, 1997, *Appraisal and Evaluation in Central Government: Treasury Guidance* (London: Stationery Office).

——, 2001. *Choosing the Right Fabric: A Framework for Performance Information* (London: HM Treasury).

Jacobs, R., P. Smith, and A. Street, 2006, *Measuring Efficiency in Health Care: Analytic Techniques and Health Policy* (Cambridge: Cambridge University Press).

Johnston, J., 1998, "Strategy, Planning, Leadership, and the Financial Management Improvement Plan: The Australian Public Service 1983–1996," *Public Productivity & Management Review*, Vol. 21(4) (June), pp. 352–69.

Leibenstein, H., 1966, "Allocative Efficiency vs. 'X-Efficiency'," *American Economic Review*, Vol. 56 (June), pp. 392–415.

OECD (Organization for Economic Cooperation and Development), 1998, *Best Practice Guidelines for Evaluation*, PUMA Policy Brief No. 5 (Paris: OECD).

——, 2005, *Performance Information in the Budget Process: Results of OECD 2005 Questionnaire*, GOV/PGC/SBO(2005)6.

Pradhan, S., 1996, *Evaluating Public Expenditure: A Framework for Public Expenditure Reviews*, World Bank Discussion Paper 323 (Washington: World Bank).

Mackay, K., 2004, *Two Generations of Performance Evaluation and Management System in Australia*, ECD Working Paper Series, No. 11 (Washington: World Bank).

Rainey, H.G., 1993, "Toward a Theory of Goal Ambiguity in Public Organizations," pp. 121–66 in *Research in Public Administration*, ed. by J.L. Perry, Vol. 2 (Greenwich, Conn.: JAI Press).

Sen, A., 1992, *Inequality Reexamined* (Oxford: Clarendon Press).

Tankersley, W., and G. Grizzle, 1994, "Control Options for the Public Manager: An Analytic Model for Designing Appropriate Control Strategies," *Public Productivity and Management Review*, Vol. 18(1), pp. 1–17.

Toulemonde, J., and L. Rochaix, 1994, "Rational Decision-Making through Project Appraisal: A Presentation of French Attempts," *International Review of Administrative Sciences*, Vol. 60, pp. 37–53.

UNDP (United Nations Development Programme) Evaluation Office, 2002, *Handbook on Monitoring and Evaluating for Results* (New York: United Nations).

USAID (United States Agency for International Development), 1983, *The Logical Framework: Modifications Based on Experience*, Program Methods and Evaluation Division, Bureau for Program and Policy Coordination (Washington: USAID).

Weinstock, M., 2003, "Under the Microscope", *Government Executive*, January, pp. 37–40.

Wholey, J.S., 1978, *Zero-Base Budgeting and Program Evaluation* (Lexington, Mass.: Lexington Books).

4
Cost Information

Marc Robinson[1]

This chapter focuses on the cost information requirements of performance budgeting, and more generally on the relationship between results and costs. Its objectives are to identify the type of cost information which is of the greatest potential relevance to performance budgeting, to note and discuss some of the key challenges which arise in seeking to obtain that information, and to identify certain significant limits on the potential utility of cost information for performance budgeting purposes.

Because different performance budgeting models seek to link results and funding in different ways, and with somewhat varying objectives, the cost information requirements of those models vary. For expenditure prioritization purposes, it is *program* costing which is usually seen as of primary importance. In other words, with expenditure prioritization decisions viewed as a matter of deciding how to allocate money between programs, the starting point is to measure program costs so as to permit a comparison—be it informal or more systematic—between program costs and benefits. The approach is based upon the widely-held assumption that at the level of the government-wide budget, it is in general only practical to set priorities in terms of the broad categories of expenditure which programs represent. From this perspective, the appropriate place for more detailed expenditure prioritization is internally within agencies, and it follows that for this purpose agencies will require cost information for more disaggregated program components (for example, sub-programs).

What might be called *cost function* information is, by contrast, viewed by many as an important tool for building a tighter relationship between funding and performance through formula funding, or budget-related performance targets. The most common version of this idea, as mentioned in Chapter 1, focuses upon *unit cost* information. As noted there, the idea, in its simplest form, is to use the identity *average cost • quantity = total cost* as the basis for predicting the results an agency should be expected to deliver with any given level of funding or, equivalently, the funding required to deliver any targeted level of results. This approach has usually been applied to outputs, although it is sometimes applied to outcomes.

The notion of linking funding and results through unit costs is, as discussed below, somewhat simplistic, and it is better therefore to express the underlying idea in a more general form: namely as the proposition that cost functions—that is, the functional relationships between cost and any given result (output or outcome)—can be used to set targets or funding formulas.

The role of *comparative cost* information tends to be stressed by performance budgeting models which aim to boost efficiency and cost-effectiveness by factoring savings targets into performance targets or funding formulas. The principal theme is that measures of the costs at which others—that is, organizations delivering similar services—deliver outputs or outcomes can provide an indication of the magnitude of potential efficiency gain. Such information might, in principle, be obtained by market prices for similar products, by cost benchmarking or by market testing. Time series data on an agency's own past costs of delivering results may also potentially serve as a source of comparative cost information.

As with all performance information, cost information is unavoidably costly to obtain, in terms of the expense not only of setting up costing systems, but also of the ongoing collection and verification of data. One of the factors contributing to these information costs is the fact that those at the "coal face" who have easier actual or potential access to cost information can be reluctant to provide this information to central decision-makers who may use it to their disadvantage. But even setting aside such strategic and "asymmetric information" considerations, cost information is not usually cheap or easy to obtain.

Because the cost information requirements of each performance budgeting model differ, so also does the expense of obtaining the cost information which each requires. Unit cost information (more generally, cost function information) is, for example, generally significantly more costly than program costing. It follows that the cost of cost information is an important consideration which should be taken into account in deciding what types of performance budgeting model to adopt, and then in deciding whether to adopt these models across the board or on a more selective basis for certain areas of public expenditure.

It is also necessary to strike a balance between accuracy and information costs in the design of the costing system to support performance budgeting. The more accurate information on the costs of delivering results becomes, the better the linkage between results and funding it is likely to permit. However, the marginal cost of more accurate cost information can be high. And even if a great deal of money is spent on sophisticated cost accounting, cost information will generally remain far from perfect. One of the implications of these information cost considerations is that particular caution should be taken in deciding how much money to invest in costing systems in countries with very limited financial resources and shortages of appropriately trained accountants. (This in turn has implications for the choice of performance budgeting model in such countries.) However, as discussed below, it should not be thought that effective performance budgeting requires *perfect* cost information. Much can be achieved with approximate costing, whether it is for expenditure prioritization purposes, or for more sophisticated forms of performance budgeting such as formula funding and target-setting.

The recognition that cost information does not come free should not lead one to take a negative view towards the role of cost accounting in the public sector. The potential value of results cost information as a tool for improving the efficiency and effectiveness of public expenditure is quite considerable. Traditional government budgeting and financial management systems have made far too little use of such information.

Program costing and expenditure prioritization for allocative efficiency

Programs should, in principle, group together expenditures on services which share common public policy objectives—common intended outcomes—in such a manner that decisions about how much to spend upon competing programs capture the choices which are most central to allocative efficiency. This means choices such as how much to spend on health treatment versus health prevention, or upon primary education versus tertiary education. Budget funding is, however, spent on inputs (or, to be more precise, inputs and transfers), so the costing of programs requires that expenditure on inputs be allocated in accordance with the objectives for which those inputs are used. Expenditure prioritization requires, moreover, not only ex-post information about program costs, but also a capacity to *control* expenditure by program. It is therefore necessary that the program classification of expenditure be an integral part of the budgetary classification system and of the underlying chart of accounts. The allocation and control of expenditure by objectives is, however, not part of traditional government budgeting and accounting systems.[2] For program-based expenditure prioritization, it is therefore necessary to build robust costing and cost control systems based upon the objectives of expenditure.

The next chapter in this part examines the full range of issues which arise in establishing and using a program classification of expenditure. Here the focus is exclusively on one issue—the costing of programs. One of the more important challenges in costing programs is the attribution of *indirect costs*. In the context of costing programs, indirect costs refer to the costs of inputs or activities which contribute to more than one program. What constitutes an indirect cost depends upon how programs are defined. Suppose that all programs are defined in terms of outputs and outcomes—that is, as groups of services to external parties[3] with common intended outcomes. If this is the case, then all ministry-wide support services and infrastructure (such as human resource management, internal financial management, and the IT network)—together with other "overhead" items such as the salaries of the chief executive and other top ministry-wide managers and the costs of ministry-wide (non-program-specific) policy development—will be indirect costs which will need to be allocated between programs.

Accountants use the term "allocation basis" to refer to the formula or principle used to allocate a specific indirect cost between two or more "cost objects" (in this case, programs). Ideally, the allocation basis used for each indirect cost should accurately reflect that indirect cost's contribution to each program. But in the case of some indirect costs this may not be easy to determine. In practice, the cost and effort of accurate cost attribution means that approximate, or sometimes even quite arbitrary, allocation bases are often used, particularly for those indirect costs which are most difficult or costly to allocate accurately. It is, for example, not uncommon for many support service costs to be allocated between programs on the basis of the proportion of the total ministry staffing accounted for by each program, without any attempt to actually measure the usage of those support services by each program. In the extreme, measures of the "full" cost of programs derived by such arbitrary cost allocations may be less useful than measures of direct program costs alone.

There are many who see the solution to the indirect cost allocation problem as lying in the general application to the general government sector of activity-based costing (ABC), which aims to develop a much more accurate two-stage costing process. ABC is discussed further later in this chapter. The key point to be made at this stage is, however, that the level of costing sophistication called for by ABC is expensive and demanding of skilled human resources—which helps to explain why, even in the richest countries, ABC tends to be used selectively rather than across the board. Program costing obtained using less accurate, but also much less costly, costing methodologies may be quite adequate to meet the needs of government expenditure planning.

The indirect cost allocation challenge has other important implications—in particular, for choices about how programs are defined. It is particularly relevant to the question of whether or not to have "corporate services" programs which group together ministry-wide support services, infrastructure, and other overheads. The fundamental objective of program classification—the facilitation of expenditure prioritization choices which are relevant to allocative efficiency—would seem to suggest that the answer should be "no," and that programs ought to be defined in terms of outputs and outcomes, and not in terms of support services and overheads. Support services and overheads are, after all, not incurred for their own sake, but simply in order to facilitate the production of services which are of direct benefit to the community. This implies that the decision on what types of support services are needed and how much money to spend on them should be *derived from* choices about outputs and outcomes, rather than viewed as a program prioritization choice in its own right.

Reflecting this view, the program classification of expenditure in countries such as Australia[4] and the UK does not include corporate service or other overhead costs programs. In these countries, the program structure of, say, an education ministry is comprised exclusively of programs such as primary education, tertiary education, and technical education, with all corporate services and other support services costs attributed to those programs rather than themselves forming a program. There are, however, many other countries (for example, South Africa and Canada) which do have "corporate services" programs—as had, formerly, some of the countries which now have only output- and outcome-based programs.

It is possible to view the decision to make use of corporate services programs as, at least in some cases, a reasonable pragmatic response to the indirect cost allocation challenge. In the early stages of the adoption of program budgeting, any allocation of indirect costs is likely to be particularly arbitrary. Under these circumstances, there are essentially two options:

- to move immediately to programs based exclusively on outputs and outcomes, accepting that the costing of these programs may be highly inaccurate
- to begin by assigning many support service and other overhead costs to corporate services programs, and then progressively move over time to attribute many of these costs to output- and outcome-based programs. In countries with very limited financial and skilled accounting resources, it may make sense to view this process as a gradual one.

It should not, moreover, be assumed that the ultimate objective need necessarily be the full allocation of *all* indirect costs. Some indirect program costs (for example, employment costs of top agency management) are *joint costs*, meaning that they are costs *which would not change even if one of those programs were closed down.* It is a conventional principle of management accounting that joint costs are not decision-relevant and should therefore not be allocated to products. Specifically, in the context of program costing, to allocate joint costs to a program is to give a misleading impression of the costs which are at stake in decisions about program expenditure priorities. This suggests that there is nothing wrong in principle with maintaining, within a program structure which is generally output- and outcome-based, a small unallocated "joint cost" program. This issue will be further discussed at the conclusion of this chapter, as will the related issue of the treatment in program costing of so-called *sunk costs*, which is in turn linked to the choice between accrual and "cash" accounting.

Setting performance expectation using cost information

The idea of using cost information to link funding to results is a very important theme in performance budgeting theory and practice. As a simplified illustration of the idea, suppose that an African government decides to scale-up substantially the effort to vaccinate the population against yellow fever. If at present it costs, say, \$3 per person for such vaccinations, this could be taken to suggest that an additional \$1.5 million should permit 500,000 more people to be vaccinated. Such an expectation could be formalized in an explicit performance target set for the government agency managing the vaccination program. Target-setting of this type can serve as a means of helping to safeguard against the ever-present danger that increased funding can be partially wasted (through, for example, disproportionate wage increases or reduced levels of work effort by staff of the agency concerned).

The same government could in principle go further and use comparative cost information to set performance targets in such a way as to create pressure for improvements in the efficiency of service delivery. Imagine that the vaccination effort is handled by a number of regional units within the country concerned, and that it is established that the most efficient of these deliver vaccinations for, say, \$2.70 per unit. This information could be used to set targets for expected cost reductions to be achieved, over an appropriate interval of time, by the less efficient regional units. This is an example of *cross-sectional cost benchmarking,* which may be defined as the process of comparing the costs of producing services with other similar producers, in order to obtain an indication of the scope for savings from improved efficiency. As discussed elsewhere in this volume, such a use of cross-sectional cost benchmarking is at the heart of the incentives for improved efficiency which can be created by well-designed purchaser-provider funding systems. Under such systems, a service delivery unit which delivers a particular service (output) relatively inefficiently will find itself losing money because the price it receives for the service will be less than its costs.

More generally, as outlined in Chapter 1, cost information can be used to link funding to results in order to improve allocative and/or technical efficiency in the following ways:

- for medium-term expenditure forward estimates
- in the formulation of performance targets
- as the basis for formula funding
- as the basis for the "purchaser-provider" version of formula funding.

If cost information is to be used in such ways, it must be at the level of specific services (output types), rather that at the level of the broad program. Expenditure on vaccinations might, for example, be part of a "preventative health" program in the health ministry's budget, together with many other services such as health awareness information provision, eradication of breeding grounds for malaria-carrying mosquitoes, and free provision of items such as syringes and condoms to high-risk populations. Because most programs are like this, and comprise "apples and pears" baskets of different services, the costs of each service within the program basket will need to be considered separately if the aim is to use the cost information for target-setting or formula funding. Even when dealing with a group of quite similar outputs, there are benefits in differentiating as far as possible between products with different costs. For example, in a formula funding system for undergraduate education in public universities, it is usual to differentiate between different categories of course based on cost. High-cost courses such as medicine would, for example, attract a higher level of funding per student-year than a low-cost course such as law or liberal arts. The logic of this is that if all courses attracted the same rate of funding, universities would be given a financial incentive to shift their course offering away from high-cost course offerings to low-cost course offerings.

The need to undertake costing at the individual product level means that the indirect cost allocation task will be considerably larger than in the case of program costing.

There are two important practical challenges which arise in seeking to use cost information to link performance and funding. One concerns the nature of the underlying cost/results relationship. The other pertains to the degree to which comparative cost differentials can reflect factors other than differences in efficiency.

In respect to first of these issues, to talk about using *unit costs* to link funding and results is to simplify the challenge involved. Unit costs normally mean average costs. To measure the average cost of delivering a service at a given time and use this (perhaps with some downward adjustment to promote improved technical efficiency) for target-setting, or any of the other applications identified above, is in effect to assume that average cost is constant. It is, however, basic economics that average cost is not necessarily constant, but may rise or fall with changes in the volume of production. In the short run, for example, if marginal cost is constant, average cost will fall as production increases due to the spreading of fixed costs[5] over the increased output.[6] In the long run, moreover, average costs may also change with increased production volumes as a result of changing economies of scale. Under these circumstances, using average costs can lead to the setting of performance targets which are insufficiently demanding (or, equivalently in formula funding systems, prices which are too high). Thus, in the example given above, the $3 average cost per vaccination will include program overhead costs and some other costs which do not need to be increased commensurately with any increase in the volume of vaccinations delivered. Performance targets associated with the scaling-up of the program should therefore be set with the expectation that an extra $1.5 million of funding should result in the vaccination of significantly more that 500,000 people.

In principle, inappropriate target- or price-setting of this sort may be entirely avoided by basing the funding/results link on the true underlying relationship between costs and output implicit in the agency's production processes—that is, on what economists call the "cost function"[7]—rather than upon arbitrary assumptions (such as the assumption that average costs are constant). In practice, however, it tends to be costly and difficult (if not impossible) to obtain precise information on the underlying cost function, even if a good deal of money is spent on sophisticated cost accounting.

Fortunately, however, it is not necessary to have perfect information on the cost function in order to use cost information to link funding to results. In many contexts, target-setting, formula funding, or "prices" based on approximate cost information can serve to create very positive incentives for improved efficiency. It can, for example, often make sense to use average variable cost measure instead of average cost for funding formula/target purposes.[8] Thus, for example, it might be established that, after having netted out the program overhead costs and the like, the unit cost of delivering yellow fever vaccinations is $2.50. On this basis, one could set a target of an additional 600,000 vaccinations to be delivered with an extra $1.5 million funding. It may, of course, be objected that such an approach merely substitutes one arbitrary assumption about costs for another, because it assumes that average variable cost is constant. The point, however, is that an approximate cost model of this type may serve the policy objective well (and certainly much better than a model which assumes average cost to be constant), while not requiring huge levels of effort and expense on complex cost accounting. This has been, broadly, the approach taken in the output-based funding in the hospital sector, and the evidence suggests that it has worked quite well despite the imperfect costing model (Newhouse, 2002, p. 30; Robinson and Brumby, 2005).

In respect to the use of *comparative* cost information, the additional problem which must be faced is that cost differentials between different production units may reflect factors other than differences in efficiency. For example, schools or hospitals in rural or remote areas may have intrinsically higher cost structures than their metropolitan counterparts due to a lack of scale economies and other factors such as a need to pay higher salaries to staff to retain their services. It would therefore be inappropriate to use the metropolitan cost levels in setting targets or prices for rural services. Methodologies are therefore needed to make use of comparative cost information in such a way as to remove cost differences unrelated to efficiency differentials. The most obvious way of doing this is to confine cross-sectional cost benchmarking to production units which face similar cost conditions—for example, to comparisons of the relative cost levels of different rural hospitals. The scope for doing this depends on the availability of suitable "benchmarking partners"—organizations sufficiently similar for meaningful cost comparisons to be made. It is not, however, necessary that only service units which face *exactly* the same cost conditions be used as benchmarking partners for costing purposes. As with cost function information, comparative costing methodologies based on approximate data can serve very well to achieve an effective linkage between funding and results.

Cost function information is generally not used to link *outcomes* to funding for two principal and related reasons: one is outcome measurement difficulties; the other is the impact of so-called "external factors" discussed in Chapter 3. These exogenous characteristics of the service delivery environment or of clients/cases give rise to an intrinsic uncontrollability and uncertainty about the outcomes which can be delivered with any given level of funding. The degree of this uncontrollability and uncertainty varies, and tends to be greater for high-level outcomes than it is for lower-level outcomes. In general, however, it is inappropriate to think in terms of a tight "functional" relationship between costs and outcomes.

It is for this reason that cost-based formula funding and target-setting tends to be advocated much more for *outputs* than outcomes. There are quite a few public sector services for which a reasonably stable relationship between costs and outputs[9] exists—even if that relationship (the "cost function") may not be easy to determine. It is, however, also true that there are also many public sector services which are characterized by intrinsic uncertainty in the cost/output relationship.

The most important source of uncertainty in the cost/output relationship is *heterogeneity*. As discussed in Chapter 3, outputs are heterogeneous when the amount and types of activities required to deliver the "same" service varies due to client or case characteristics. Variability in the activities which comprise units of the "same" output gives rise to cost variability, and therefore creates uncertainty about the level of output which can be produced with any given level of funding. For highly heterogeneous services, the use of cost-based formula funding or target-setting is quite impossible. For criminal investigations, for example, it is quite impossible to say in advance how many investigations a particular level of funding will allow the police to handle. Milder heterogeneity may, however, be manageable—methods have, for example, been found to deal with a certain degree of heterogeneity within the context of the DRG funding system for hospitals.

Heterogeneity is not the only factor which can introduce significant uncertainty into the relationship between costs and outputs. Uncertainty also arises in the case of what may be termed *contingent capacity services*. Contingent capacity services are services the demand for which is unpredictably variable, and for which there is an *essentiality* and *immediacy* to supply—in other words, it is considered important that when a demand for the service arises, the service be supplied promptly.[10] Fire services are an example. The funding of fire services typically bears only a loose relationship to the actual level of fire-fighting (the output) they normally carry out. The level of funding is, rather, designed to give the fire service a margin of response capacity to deal with more exceptional and unlikely circumstances. In general, for contingent capacity services, it is inappropriate to expect anything other than the loosest relationship between funding and actual levels of output.

There are quite a few public sector services which have the contingent capacity characteristic to a greater or lesser extent. All emergency services—ambulances, rescue services, and the like—fall into this category. Health systems maintain capacity to fight epidemics and outbreaks of new virulent diseases, and agriculture departments maintain a similar capacity in relation to exotic plant and animal diseases and similar problems. Perhaps the extreme example is the military, the principal "output" of which is the fighting of wars. For most countries, the principal purpose of having a well-funded military is to deter potential attackers and thus avoid having to produce the "output" at all.

Activity-based costing and budgeting

Over approximately the past 15 years, there has been considerable interest within the public sector in a number of countries in the use of activity-based costing (ABC) as the basis for costing and budgeting. ABC is an accounting methodology which seeks to develop a "model of organizational resource consumption" (Kaplan and Cooper, 1991, p. 275) to provide accurate allocation bases through which indirect costs can be allocated to products. In a public sector context, ABC can be applied to costing at the program level, or it can be taken further to cost individual services (outputs). It involves a two-stage costing process in which the first stage is the costing of broadly-defined activities,[11] and the second stage is the allocation of the costs of these activities to programs and possibly also (depending upon the form of performance budgeting which this costing information is intended to support) to more specific outputs within those programs. Human resource management might, for example, be a cost center, in which case the first stage of the process is the accurate measurement of the overall cost of human resource management, and the second stage is the development of accurate "cost drivers" for attributing human resource management costs between the programs or individual outputs which it supports. To ensure accuracy, the cost drivers used in the second stage would be based upon measures of the quantity, number, and relative resource-intensiveness of each type of service (recruitments, promotional processes, disciplinary processes, separations, and so on) which human resource management provides to each program/output.

Public sector proponents of ABC often argue that it is essential for performance budgeting—that, in the words of one US official, "you can't have performance and budget integration unless you actually have ABC" (quoted in Peckenpaugh, 2002a, p. 11). There is, however, a dearth of systematic analysis of actual experience with ABC, and there is no consensus in the (largely anecdotal) available literature that it has been a success in the public sector. In the US, for example, it has been said that "ABC has proved exceedingly difficult to implement," and that many organizations which experimented at the beginning of the current wave of interest have not continued with it (Peckenpaugh, 2002b, p. 42).

Proponents see ABC as relevant to performance budgeting in two ways. The first is as a tool for better expenditure prioritization. The second is as a means of developing a tighter linkage between planned outputs and funding.

In respect to expenditure prioritization, the core argument is that mentioned earlier—that ABC permits much improved program costing and, more generally, that it provides a "systematic way of determining how to apply limited resources to the right activities to produce the right results" (Williams and Melhuish, 1999, p. 36). As noted earlier, it is easy to accept that more accurate program costing can improve the quality of expenditure prioritization choices. ABC is, however, a very high-cost accounting technology. As Brown et al. (1999, p. 18) put it, "installing an ABC system is technically complex, requiring talented personnel and a considerable amount of time and mean dollars." The question is therefore how far, even in rich countries, the benefits of ABC justify the very considerable cost of the system. The answer to this question is not entirely clear.

For the purposes of linking planned outputs and funding, proponents call for the application of activity-based budgeting (ABB). In ABB, the ABC costing process is reversed, and one goes from planned outputs to the activities required to produce those outputs and then to the cost required to carry out those activities (Cooper and Slagmulder, 2000). What is being suggested is, in essence, that the two-stage process offers a better means for working out the true output cost functions. There is not much evidence on how well this works in practice, but it would seem to make sense for appropriate services. However, it should be emphasized that the use of ABB does not in any way circumvent the problems identified above as limiting the scope for using cost function information in budgeting.[12]

Reflecting these problems, it has been argued that "in most instances ABC is not appropriate for public sector applications" (Mullins and Zorn, 1999, p. 54). This may be taking the argument a little too far. It seems more plausible to argue that ABC may be best viewed as a tool for selective application to relatively standardized services, the greatest concentration of which will in general be found at the lowest level of government (including local government).

Decision-relevant costs and performance budgeting

As mentioned earlier, standard managerial accounting theory suggests that joint costs should not be attributed to programs because they are costs which will not change as a result of decisions taken about the program, even if the programs concerned were to be closed down. This argument is consistent with the basic economic principle that decisions should be based upon opportunity costs.

Closely analogous to this is the question of how to treat fixed costs—essentially the costs of using capital—in costing of programs or individual services for performance budgeting purposes. It is clear that all *variable* costs should be taken into account, because these will change not only if a program or output is discontinued, but also if the level of production changes. By contrast, *fixed* costs do not, by definition, change if the volume of production is changed. They are therefore not relevant to decisions about whether to increase or decrease programs at the margin, or, in principle, to formula funding or cost-based performance targets. Fixed costs can, however, be relevant in part to decisions about whether or not to close programs down. This is because, if a program is discontinued, is it often possible to recover some of the fixed cost by selling the capital assets used by the program. But to the extent that fixed costs cannot be avoided in this manner, it is a mistake to consider them in determining whether to continue to program because there is no point crying over spilt milk.[13]

Stated in a more general form, the economic principle is that *sunk costs* (costs which cannot be recovered whatever one does) are never decision-relevant. What is decision-relevant is variable cost and, depending upon the nature of the decision, *avoidable cost* (that is, variable costs plus the avoidable portion of fixed costs).

Notwithstanding this, many accountants favor "full-cost" accounting for both product costing in the private sector and, in the public sector, for program or output costing. Full-cost accounting (also known as "full absorption" costing) calls for the attribution of *all* costs, even if they are joint costs or sunk costs, to products. The naïve version of the argument for full cost accounting simply takes it as self-evident that proper decisions cannot be made unless all costs are taken into account. The more sophisticated version argues that "all costs are variable in the long run—and thus subject to managerial action" (Sharp and Christensen, 1991, p. 32), and that taking all costs into account therefore promotes an appropriately longer-term perspective on decision-making.

The question of the treatment of fixed costs is inextricably linked with the accounting basis chosen for the budget. This points to the issue of the relationship between accrual accounting and performance budgeting.

Accrual accounting and performance budgeting

Does performance budgeting require accrual accounting? Or can it at least be said that accrual accounting supports performance budgeting better than traditional cash accounting?

Applying accrual accounting to performance budgeting means that in linking funding to results, funding is measured using the accrual concept of *expenses*[14] rather than in terms of the *expenditure*.[15] Because this requires the use of the accrual concept of expenses to express the budget authorizations or other funding provided to agencies, it means going beyond the use of accrual accounting for financial reporting purposes to a form of *accrual budgeting*.

As noted earlier, in making expenditure prioritization decisions, all *variable* and *avoidable* costs are relevant. Accrual accounting can facilitate better prioritization between programs by making sure that relevant avoidable costs are not omitted when program costs are measured—and, conversely, that certain irrelevant expenditures are not included. This is because accrual accounting includes in its measure of expenses any costs of production for which payment is deferred to future years. For example, when government employs people, part of the costs of the services which those people deliver to the public in any given year takes the form of entitlements to pension payments in future. These pension costs are clearly a variable cost. An accrual measure of program costs will include these deferred employment costs, whereas a cash accounting measure will not. Failing to take such deferred costs into account may make programs look cheaper than they actually are, and this effect will be greater for those programs which are most public employment intensive. Because such omission can distort program choices, it is desirable that these and other deferred costs be taken into account when making decisions about program priorities.

The use of a cost measure which does not distinguish between costs of production on the basis of whether they are paid this year or in the future is also better for the purposes of performance budgeting systems which seek to develop tighter cost-based links between funding and results. The cash *expenditure* on delivering a service can, for example, be manipulated by expenditure timing shifts which have nothing to do with changes in the cost of delivering services. Such timing shifts can result from the bringing forward or deferral ("leading and lagging") of the payment of accounts, from deferred-payment lease arrangements for equipment or other supplies, or from a range of other transactions.[16]

These clear benefits of accrual accounting for performance budgeting can be realized by placing budgeting on a *partial* accruals basis. Partial accrual budgeting means giving agencies expense budgets which are intended to cover all expenses of current production *which involve payments in either the present or future years*. By contrast, under *full* accrual budgeting, agencies would be given expense budgets from which they would have to cover *all* expenses—which means not only expenses requiring payments in the present or future years, but also expenses arising from expenditures made in the past. By far and away the most important expense arising from expenditure in the past is depreciation. In essence, therefore, the difference between partial and full accrual budgeting is that only under the latter are agencies required to cover depreciation from their expense budgets.

The question then is whether there are gains to performance budgeting from going beyond partial accrual budgeting to place budgeting on a full accrual basis, including depreciation in agency budgets. This is more debatable. For those who take the view that sunk costs should be disregarded for decision-making purposes, full accrual *budgeting* is problematic insofar as depreciation represents a sunk cost,[17] the inclusion of which will, as discussed, give an exaggerated impression of potential savings which could be realized if the program were closed down. From this perspective, it can be argued that it is better for performance budgeting purposes to budget on a partial accrual basis, and that the appropriate time to consider capital costs for budgetary control purposes is when evaluating potential capital projects in the capital budgeting process. In further support for this position, it might also be argued that most expenditure prioritization decisions are about reducing or increasing the size of programs, rather than eliminating them altogether. This implies that for most budgetary decisions, it is only variable cost—information on which requires only partial accrual accounting—which is relevant. When a program is identified as a potential candidate for complete closure, a special ad hoc study can be undertaken to identify avoidable fixed costs.

The contrary position could be argued on two principal grounds. The first is that, as mentioned above, taking all costs into consideration encourages a long-term rather than short-term approach to decision-making. The other is that while some portion of depreciation is a sunk cost, the rest is avoidable cost. In practice, the degree to which depreciation is an avoidable cost varies considerably between different types of programs and services—depending on the "recoverable value" of the assets concerned. There are certainly some instances where depreciation is predominantly an avoidable cost.[18]

There is one other argument which is relevant here. This is the proposition that budgeting on a full accruals base is necessary to support a particular form of performance budgeting—the "purchaser-provider" model, which seeks to extend the principle of formula funding to simulate the market process whereby purchasers pay "prices" to buy products from arm's-length producers. Exponents of the purchaser-provider model argue for the inclusion of depreciation because it is necessary for producers to aim to recover the full costs of production (including depreciation) through sales revenue. The merits of the purchaser-provider model are examined in Chapter 16.

With this one caveat, it can therefore be concluded that budgeting on a partial accrual basis certainly assists performance budgeting, but that the merits for performance budgeting purposes of budgeting on a full accrual basis are less clear-cut. (Note that these comments pertain only to *budgeting*, and not to financial reporting. It is perfectly possible to have full accrual financial reporting while budgeting on a partial accrual basis.)

The conclusion that accrual budgeting—at least in a partial form—assists performance budgeting should not, however, be interpreted as meaning that accrual accounting is a prerequisite for the introduction of performance budgeting. The distortions in the measurement of variable costs which result from the use of cash accounting—or at least from "modified" cash accounting—are probably often not large. There is, moreover, a long history of performance budgeting—particularly program budgeting and variants thereof—operating in the context of cash-based accounting and budgeting systems.

It should therefore not be assumed that performance budgeting and accrual accounting need to be introduced simultaneously. Decisions about the introduction and sequencing of accrual accounting need to be taken carefully, bearing in mind a range of considerations apart from any moves to performance budgeting (Diamond, 2002). These include the substantial resource implications of accrual accounting, whether basic public expenditure systems (for example, enforcement of budgetary spending limits and commitments control) are working well, and a number of other potential uses for accrual accounting information (for example, for aggregate fiscal policy). It should also be noted that accrual budgeting arguably creates some financial control risks of its own, although it is not possible to discuss these here.

Conclusions

Developing cost information to underpin performance budgeting is not a matter of simply seeking the fullest range of information on the costs of achieving results, using the most sophisticated and accurate accounting methodologies. Cost information strategy must, rather, be guided by choices about the form of performance budgeting being implemented, because different forms of performance budgeting have different information requirements. It must also be guided by recognition of the high marginal cost of better cost information and the consequent need to strike a balance between these costs and the decision-making benefits of better-quality information.

For performance budgeting which focuses upon improved expenditure prioritization through program choices, the challenge is to develop acceptably accurate measures of the decision-relevant costs of programs. Indirect cost attribution is one of the more important challenges which need to be addressed for this purpose. Careful thought needs to be given to the degree of precision being sought in indirect cost allocation, as well as to the implications of the design of the program structure for the magnitude of the indirect cost allocation task.

If the aim is to use cost information as the basis for linking results and funding more tightly, through formula funding or cost-based performance targets, considerably more cost information will be required. This is particularly true if it also desired to use comparative cost information to set efficiency targets. Given these high information costs, careful consideration will need to be given on a service-by-service basis as to whether the potential benefits are likely to outweigh these costs. It will also need to be recognized that in many cases the relationship between results and costs is not a tight functional one but is, rather, quite loose. This is particularly true for outcomes. However, it is also true for many public sector outputs, particularly those of a highly "heterogeneous" or "contingent capacity" nature.

Accrual accounting is a useful tool for better performance budgeting. However, it is not a prerequisite for performance budgeting, and it is perfectly possible to introduce performance budgeting in a cash (or modified cash) accounting and budgeting context.

Appendix: the cost–results relationship

Assume that for a particular "result" (output or outcome), there is what might be called a "prevailing (short-run) cost function" $C = f_P(Q)$ which indicates the quantity of results (Q) which the agency receiving funding is capable of producing with funding C. For this purpose, it is assumed that input prices and the level of fixed costs are constant, as is the case for standard cost functions. However, this cost function assumes a given (prevailing) level of technical efficiency (measured by a hypothetical index measuring the degree of technical inefficiency with which the entity concerned produces the result). (By contrast, of course, conventional cost functions assume there is no technical inefficiency.) If the result concerned is, as is usually the case, an output rather than an outcome, then it is assumed that Q measures the quantity of output *of a defined level of quality*. If such a cost function exists, then the starting point of a target-setting regime is that with funding of C^* the agency could be expected to deliver a level of results of at least $f_P^{-1}(C^*)$. This amounts to demanding that if the agency receives, say, an increase in funding, it should be expected to maintain at least its prevailing level of efficiency, and not to allow some portion of the funding increase to be absorbed in extra "slack." The results target could be tightened further to put pressure on the agency to increase its level of technical efficiency—for example, by stipulating an expectation that gains in efficiency should produce additional results of α, in which case the performance target would be $f_P^{-1}(C^*) + \alpha$. Equivalently, formula funding could be based on the prevailing cost function $C = f_P(Q)$, with C being the amount of funding provided to deliver results Q.

Basing targets or formula funding on unit costs (average costs) implicitly assumes that $C = f_P(Q)$ takes the form $b.Q = C$, which requires, improbably, that there are no fixed costs. Assume instead that there are fixed costs a, and that the prevailing production function takes the simple linear form $a + b.Q = C$ (in other words, marginal cost is constant). Suppose that in this context, it is decided to base a funding formula or output target on average cost. Then suppose that in year 1, Q_1 is produced at total cost C_1, so that average cost in that time period is C_1/Q_1, and this average cost measure is used to link funding and outputs for year 2. Suppose that the target output in time period 2 is Q_2. Funding provided would then be $a.(Q_2/Q_1) + b.Q_2$, whereas it "should" be $a + b.Q_2$. The error built into the formula will be $a.((Q_2 - Q_1)/Q_1)$, which will be positive if target output is increasing, and negative if it is falling. If marginal cost is falling, rather than constant—which is what the cost curves employed in basic microeconomics assume within a certain range—then the funding error will be even greater.

If the cost function proper—that is, the conventional cost function assuming no technical inefficiency—is symbolized by $C = f(Q)$, then the prevailing degree of technical inefficiency is measured by the excess cost of production, which is $f_P(Q) - f(Q)$. The practical informational challenge is to derive some approximate measurement of this. There is a large productivity literature that seeks to quantify technical inefficiency using parametric and non-parametric methods (see the survey in Jacobs et al., 2006).

Notes

1. The author would like to thank Peter C. Smith for his valuable comments on an earlier draft of this chapter.
2. In a traditional system, the only thing coming close to this is the functional classification of expenditure under the standardized international Classification of the Functions of Government (COFOG). This is, however, an ex-post expenditure classification for information analysis purposes, rather than expenditure control.

3. Or transfers.
4. As indicated in Chapter 2, in most of the countries referred to in this paragraph, programs go by some other name—for example, "outcomes" or "output groups" in Australia and "Requests for Resources" in the UK.
5. And indirect variable costs.
6. See this chapter's appendix for a formalization of these and related points.
7. Economic theory distinguishes, of course, between short-run and long-run cost functions. In principle, if one is using the cost function for formula-funding or short-run target-setting, the short-run production function would be appropriate. By contrast, for long-term expenditure projections, the long-run cost function would be appropriate.
8. In other words, to base the formula on *average variable cost • quantity + fixed costs = total cost.*
9. At least if one holds constant a set of relevant variables, as discussed in the appendix.
10. To be precise, contingent capacity services also have a third characteristic—that the time lags involved in adding to production capacity (arising from factors such as the specialized nature of the human/physical capital used) exceed the desired service response time.
11. For the purposes of ABC, activities are defined into grouping of work tasks of a similar type. Thus ABC might employ the broad "activity" of human resource management, rather than distinguishing between the multiple specific types of human resource management activity, such as the processing of job applications.
12. Crucially, ABC/B involves a homogeneity assumption (Lathshaw and Cortese-Danile, 2002, pp. 31–2; Brimson, 1991, pp. 109–10), and is therefore only appropriate for standardized products (Mullins and Zorn, 1999, pp. 41–2). As discussed above, many public sector services are heterogeneous in nature, with the activity content of the service delivered varying between clients/cases. Similarly, ABB cannot deal with costs which are driven by capacity requirements rather than actual production volumes (Cooper and Slagmulder, 2000, pp. 85–6). Contingent capacity services, discussed above, are an extreme example of the role of such costs.
13. It should go without saying that this only applies after the point at which capital expenditure has been undertaken and the relevant production asset has been constructed. Prior to that point, all costs are avoidable and need to be assessed in project investment appraisal.
14. Expenses are, approximately speaking, the total costs to the inputs used to produce services in the current financial year irrespective of whether those inputs are paid for in the current year, were paid for in past years (for example, capital) or will be paid for in future years (deferred expenses).
15. Money paid out this year. Under "modified" cash accounting, funding is measured in terms of a mix of expenditure and *commitments* (obligations to make future payments).
16. The scope for such manipulation is reduced significantly by accounting for such items on a commitments basis, although this introduces some other distortions.
17. Accounting depreciation does not seek to measure the avoidable component of capital costs. If one wished to measure the avoidable cost associated with holding physical assets, one would have to base depreciation upon year-to-year changes in "net recoverable value" (NRV). This is quite different from standard accounting depreciation measures, even if based upon current cost accounting and its variants (for example, "deprival value," "fair value," and so on).
18. It also depends to some extent on which accounting methodology is used to calculate depreciation.

References

Brimson, J.A., 1991, *Activity Accounting: An Activity-Based Costing Approach* (New York: John Wiley and Sons).

Brown, R.E., M.J. Myring, and C.G. Gard, 1999, "Activity-Based Costing in Government: Possibilities and Pitfalls," *Public Budgeting and Finance*, Vol. 19(2), pp. 3–21.
Cooper, R., and R. Slagmulder, 2000, "Activity-Based Budgeting—Part 1," *Strategic Finance*, September, pp. 85–6.
Diamond, J., 2002, *Performance Budgeting—Is Accrual Accounting Required*? IMF Working Paper, WP/02/240 (Washington: IMF).
Jacobs, R., P. Smith, and A. Street, 2006, *Measuring Efficiency in Health Care: Analytic Techniques and Health Policy* (Cambridge: Cambridge University Press).
Kaplan, R., and S. Cooper, 1991, *The Design of Cost Management Systems* (Englewood Cliffs, NJ: Prentice-Hall).
Lathshaw, C.A. and A. Cortese-Danile, 2002, "Activity-Based Costing: Usage and Pitfalls," *Review of Business*, Winter, pp. 30–2.
Mullins, D., and C. Kurt Zorn, 1999, "Is Activity-Based Costing up to the Challenge when it Comes to Privatization of Local Government Services?" *Public Budgeting and Finance*, Vol. 19(2), pp. 37–58.
Newhouse, J.P., 2002, *Pricing the Priceless: A Health Care Conundrum* (Cambridge, Mass.: MIT Press).
Peckenpaugh, J., 2002a, "The Money Trail," *Government Executive*, Vol. 34(5), p. 11.
——, 2002b, "Teaching the ABCs," *Government Executive*, Vol. 34(4), pp. 41–6.
Robinson, M., and J. Brumby, 2005, *Does Performance Budgeting Work: An Analytical Review of the Empirical Literature*, IMF Working Paper, WP05/210 (Washington: IMF).
Sharp, D., and L.F. Christensen, 1991, "A New View of Activity-Based Costing," *Management Accounting*, Vol. 73(3), pp. 32–4.
Williams, C., and W. Melhuish, 1999, "Is ABCM Destined for Success or Failure in the Federal Government?" *Public Budgeting and Finance*, Vol. 19(2), pp. 22–36.

5
Program Classification

Marc Robinson and Holger van Eden[1]

The programmatic classification of expenditure—that is, the grouping of expenditure by common objective for budgeting purposes—is a basic information tool used by most contemporary performance budgeting systems. The program classification of expenditure is intended to introduce clarity about the objectives being pursued through public expenditure, the government activities aimed at achieving these, and about amounts being spent on them. Expenditure objectives would usually, at the program level, be defined by the intended results expected for society, or outcome. To borrow the words of the French legislation of 2001 which established the framework for the new performance budgeting system in that country, a program "groups together expenditures which finance actions or coherent groups of actions...[and] which have precise objectives defined in terms of outcomes of relevance to the public."[2]

As noted in Chapter 1, the continued prevalence of the idea of classifying expenditure by objective is obscured by wide differences of contemporary program terminology: while some countries still use the word "programs," others have adopted a confusing array of other terms (for example, output classes, requests for resources, business lines, key result areas,[3] *beleidsartikelen*[4]) to mean essentially the same thing. Whatever the terminology, the basic requirement for the programmatic classification of expenditure is always that programs are clearly defined by reference to their policy objective or, more precisely, that they are coherent groups of outputs (together with their supporting activities) which are aimed at a certain outcome. Program classifications involve the development of a program "hierarchy" classifying programs into constituent components (sub-programs, activities, and so on). In some countries, programs are the highest level of the program hierarchy, but in quite a few others programs are the second level of the hierarchy. The highest level of the hierarchy then encompasses groups of programs aimed at achieving outcomes in a certain policy area. This highest level of the program hierarchy is then referred to as key result area, main policy area, or high-level program. In this chapter, the term "program" is used to mean the highest level of the program hierarchy.

The classification of expenditure by objectives is not intended only for budgetary planning and reporting purposes. The aim is, rather, that it should serve to promote budgetary decision-making which more closely aligns government activities with political priorities, and contributes to better public sector performance. Budgeting in terms of programs is intended to facilitate good allocative decision-making, and is (as discussed in Chapter 1) intrinsically more suitable for this purpose than traditional budgeting in terms of so-called "line-items" ("object classes" in the terminology of the US national government) such as employment costs, supplies, and travel expenses.

It is when the programmatic classification of expenditure is *combined with good information about the results delivered by programs* (performance measures, evaluations, and so on) that it is of greatest use in assisting decision-makers at both central and line-agency levels to make more informed judgments about whether to increase or reduce the amounts spent in the pursuit of competing public policy objectives. However, not many countries have progressed to the stage of actually using performance information in the budget process *in a systematic way*. Defining a program structure of expenditure already provides a major step in reaping the benefits of program budgeting.

In addition to its core role in facilitating improved expenditure prioritization, the program classification of expenditure is also widely seen as contributing to improved technical efficiency. There is, in particular, a strong contemporary consensus that the relaxation of line-item controls is the natural concomitant of the increased used of programmatic controls on expenditure. The relaxation of line-item controls gives managers greater flexibility in the choice of the mix of inputs used to produce outputs, which can potentially result in substantially improved productivity. This increased freedom to function without externally imposed line-item controls, however, carries with it an obligation by these managers to track accurately the costs associated with pursuing various outcomes and outputs.

The use of program classification for budgeting purposes commonly involves all or most of the following:

- The legislative body appropriating expenditure by programs, that is, programs being used in the annual budget law as appropriation items.
- The use of the program format in the supporting budget information papers presented to the legislature (and made available to the public) as the basis for the exposition of expenditure plans. Typically, this involves for each program a statement of the program objective, a description of the key program activities and associated outputs by which the program objective is to be achieved, a short narrative discussion of past and planned program strategies, major investments, and selected measures of program performance. In more sophisticated systems, such a description can be augmented by an overview of past and expected future performance (including possibly performance targets, if the country concerned has decided to engage in target-setting).
- A requirement that line agencies present their budget "bids" by program categories, and, in more sophisticated systems, that these bids be accompanied

by supporting program performance information and sometimes also by proposed performance targets.
- The formulation of forward expenditure estimates according to the program classification—in other words, the preparation of bottom-up costed multi-year estimates of ongoing/approved expenditure agreed between Ministry of Finance and line ministry in terms of program categories.

In essence, the program classification of expenditure becomes the main budget classification under program budgeting.

The objective of this chapter is to articulate key principles of a good program classification—that is, to identify the principles and practical considerations which should determine how programs and their component elements are defined. The chapter will argue that a solid program classification facilitates the budget process immensely. It is not the objective of this chapter to prescribe the manner in which program expenditure information may be *used* to best effect in budgeting and management—this is part of the subject matter of Part Two of this volume. However, the manner in which program information is to be used has a very important bearing on how programs should be defined, and for this reason certain key issues concerning the use of program information are covered in this chapter.

An important practical consideration affecting a number of program classification choices is the need to attribute costs between programs in a reasonably accurate manner. Cost attribution between programs was treated in detail in Chapter 4 on cost information for performance budgeting. This chapter will draw on the information in Chapter 4 where it is relevant to issues such as the role of administration programs and the expenditure coverage of programs.

Key program classification issues

There are a number of recurring issues which arise when governments embark on the program classification of expenditure, and which this chapter explores. These are:

- How should program objectives be defined, and what relation does this have to the way in which programs themselves are defined?
- Is it appropriate that there be "administration" programs or other programs based on support services, or should the costs of these support programs be allocated to programs with a common intended outcome?
- What expenditures (or transactions more generally) should be included in the program structure?
- What should be the size, scope, and number of programs? What would constitute too many programs, or too few?
- How do the various layers of the program's structure connect? Is there a logical relation between programs and the lowers levels of the program structure?
- How should the center of government, that is, usually the Ministry of Finance and the chief executive's (Prime Minister or President) office, guide the

decision-making process on the allocation of expenditure between competing purposes, using the programmatic classification of expenditure? What form should central guidance take, that is, how directive should it be?

- To what extent should the budget law lock in the allocation of expenditure between programs during budget execution? Put differently, what scope should the executive have for reallocating expenditure over programs or over lower levels of the program classification?
- In the context of program-based expenditure control, how far can and should the relaxation of input ("line-item") controls go?
- How should the program classification relate to the organizational structure of government? Should programs be permitted to cross ministry/agency boundaries? And what should be the relationship of program structure to the internal organizational structure within agencies?

Outcome-focused programs

It is fundamental to good program classification that the objective of each program should be clearly articulated. In practice, program objectives are often specified poorly, and this is frequently the result of misunderstandings about the principles which should guide the definition of the programs themselves. It is therefore important to emphasize and elaborate on the point that program objectives should be aligned with the strategic policy objectives of government. Strategic objectives are, mostly, best formulated in outcome terms. As discussed in detail in Chapter 3, outcomes are the intended impacts of the services which government delivers. More precisely, they are changes brought about by public interventions upon individuals, social structures or the physical environment. It is only possible to state the objectives of a program in outcome terms if the constituting parts of the programs, its concrete outputs and activities, are all focused on a common intended outcome. The following are examples of good practice in the specification of program objectives:

- The "Nature" program ("business line") of the Canadian Department of Environment (2004–05 fiscal year), the stated objective of which was "the conservation of biological diversity in healthy ecosystems."
- "Outcome 1" (effectively the school education program)[5] of the Australian Department of Education, Science and Training (2006–07 fiscal year), the objective of which was that "individuals achieve high quality foundation skills and learning outcomes from schools and other providers."

It is as a rule inappropriate to specify program objectives in a way which does not indicate the intended outcome of the program or, more fundamentally, to create programs which are not outcome-based. It is, in particular, important to avoid describing program objectives in terms of *activities* (that is, in terms of the type of work task[6]). This occurred, for example, when one African country relatively new to program budgeting recently specified the objective of a newly-established "general education" program as being to "manage the development, implementation, evaluation and maintenance of national policy, programs and systems for general education and quality assurance." While programs can and should be looked at regularly from an activity perspective, an organizational perspective, and even from an input perspective, when defining programs it is essential to look at them from the perspective of government strategic objectives, which in most cases would be specified by a outcome.[7] Defining programs by the nature of activities performed or, worse yet, by the organizational entity implementing these activities, runs counter to the essential theme of performance budgeting (and "managing-for-results" more generally), which is that budgeting and management should be oriented towards results delivered to the community.

To say that programs should be outcome-focused does not mean that programs can or should always be defined *only* by reference to the common intended outcome of the outputs which they group together. In many cases, program outputs share not only a common intended outcome, but also other defining characteristics. They may, for example, have a common *mode of intervention*. Thus, for example, a "Preventative Health Care" program is defined by reference not only to its intended outcome (lower morbidity and mortality), but also by the fact that all program services aim to achieve that outcome by preventing, rather than treating, disease and injury, that is, a type of activity.

Program objectives are sometimes specified by reference to the intended *proximate* outcome of the program, rather than its intended higher-level outcome(s).[8] This will also depend on where programs are positioned in the program hierarchy, that is, at the first or the second level of the program structure. For example, the objectives of school education programs are (as in the Australian example above) best specified in terms of student educational outcomes, rather than by reference to higher-level outcomes such as a better-educated labor force or a more competitive economy. As this example indicates, stipulating the proximate outcome tends to make clear the program's client or target group,[9] in a way which the high-level outcome often will not, thus defining the program more clearly. High-level outcomes are often served by a wide range of very different types of government services and organizations,[10] so that programs based on high-level outcomes would tend to be large and diffuse.

Precisely because program objectives tend to be specified in terms of proximate outcomes, a number of countries take the additional step of explicitly identifying the high-level outcomes to which each program is intended to contribute. For this purpose, they define, either across government or per ministry, a list of key result areas (alternatively known as main policy areas, or high-level programs). These key result areas would encompass all line ministry programs and would be defined by high-level outcomes. In this way the program level becomes the second-level in the program hierarchy.

Arguably, one contributing factor in the bad practice which may be observed in many countries in respect to the specification of program objectives (and in the underlying definition of programs) is a specific conceptual framework which is sometimes used in public sector strategic planning, which demands that strategic plans be structured around the concepts of missions, values, goals, objectives, and so on. The problem with the use of this framework in program and performance budgeting is that the concepts upon which it is based are much less well-defined than the standard international "logical framework" based on the concepts of inputs, activities, outputs, and outcomes. For example, it is often not at all clear what exactly constitutes a "goal" and an "objective," how (if at all) goals and objectives differ, and, most importantly, how they relate to outcomes.

Administration programs

Having stipulated the principle that programs should be defined by their objectives, and that these objectives should be specified in outcome terms, it is necessary immediately to acknowledge that there is one widely—although not universally—accepted exception to this principle: "administration" ("corporate services") programs. In many countries, program structures have been designed which include an administration program within each ministry. Such programs typically cover the costs of central directorates of the ministry such as personnel, legal services, IT, and security, as well as top management (the expenditures of the minister's office and top ministry-wide civil service management). Administration programs thus bring together a range of activities which do not deliver services directly to external parties, but which support those areas of the ministry which do deliver such services. These are, in other words, programs not focused on own outcomes, but on supporting those of other programs.

The rationale for administration programs is a pragmatic one, and reflects program costing considerations. The issue is discussed in detail in Chapter 4, and the key points are only briefly summarized here: it is quite possible to avoid administration programs in order to maintain uncompromised the basic principle that all programs should be outcome-based. A small number of countries (Australia, for example) do precisely this. However, if one is to adopt this approach, it is necessary to allocate with an acceptable degree of accuracy all of the "indirect" costs of support services to a set of outcome-based programs. To do this requires accounting systems and personnel capable of carrying out the task of indirect cost allocation. Good cost allocation is a quite demanding and resource-intensive task and, even in the most sophisticated systems, always requires a number of "rules of thumb," that is, some imperfect decisions on cost attribution. In practice, proper cost allocation is often beyond the capacity and/or affordability of many countries. There is therefore a good pragmatic case for the use of administration programs in many countries, particularly in the early years of the implementation of a program budgeting system in countries where cost accounting is not yet well developed. If administration programs are used, it is necessary to specify their objectives in terms not of intended outcomes, but of their expected outputs supporting the implementation of other programs. There remains, however, a strong case for moving progressively over time, subject to the availability of resources, to reduce the size of administration programs by allocating more and more support services to outcome-based programs (starting, of course, with those support services which are least difficult to attribute, such as training). Ministries of Finance should be vigilant in pushing line ministries to improve cost attribution. Care should also be taken not to allow line ministries to differ too much in the extent to which they make use of "administration" programs.

Similar considerations apply to programs of the handful of central agencies (such as Ministries of Finance, public service commissions, and departments/offices of the President or Prime Minister) which do not deliver services to the public, but which rather regulate and support the activities of service delivery ministries. The objectives of such programs cannot usually be clearly defined in terms of specific intended outcomes. Rather it is more useful to define them in terms of the specific contribution they aim to make to good governance. For example, a Ministry of Finance might legitimately define the objectives of a "budget management" program as "the maintenance of fiscal discipline and the efficient allocation of public expenditure," notwithstanding that this is not, properly speaking, an outcome.

In addition to administrative programs some countries have also chosen to identify "policy" programs to cover staff activities within line ministries aimed at policy preparation. This approach often reflects internal organizational structures where there are separate policy and operational divisions, with the policy division responsible for policy preparation for multiple program areas. Under such circumstances, it might be argued that cost attribution considerations justify a separate policy program in the same way that they may be used to justify administration programs. The case for this approach is again dependent on the practicality of cost attribution. Often, however, it is less persuasive than for administration programs. The reason for this is that much policy development work is a specialist activity performed by individuals who are specialists in certain subject areas, and who would therefore spend all of their time on policy development related to particular service delivery areas. To the extent that this is not the case, and there are individuals who are involved in policy-making across multiple program areas, a first-best solution is to use a time-recording system to allocate the costs of their work to the relevant program. A further alternative to this is to include the "overhead" component of policy-making in an administration program. Certainly, with time recording of staff becoming more common in bureaucracies in developed countries, the case for policy programs will become less in the coming years.

Which expenditures should be covered

Countries with mature program structures generally try to allocate all or most government expenditure to programs. That implies that the central government's budget can be seen as a collection of programs encompassing all of the central government's expenditure. These programs in turn reflect all the government's policy objectives, all the activities geared to these objectives, and their associated cost, that is, the total of budgetary expenditure.

Developing and transition countries introducing program budgeting often are unable to include all expenditures under the program format—even those that are in principle attributable. For example, personnel costs of programs are sometimes omitted, even for staff working exclusively for specific programs. The reasons for such a stance can be that the accounting department has not made the necessary steps to allocate personnel or other administrative expenditure to programs. As accountancy units are usually not organized according to program expenditure, the easiest category to attribute initially to programs is often so-called external expenditure, that is, transfers and other payments to third parties. By determining the objective of these expenditures, these expenditures can usually be easily attributed to programs. In such cases the program structure omits all internal expenditure within the line ministry. This was and is the practice in a number of transition countries. Internal expenditure is often in such cases still budgeted on the traditional line-item basis.

Another way that developing and transition countries sometimes limit the comprehensiveness of program expenditure is by only identifying expenditure on explicit policy priorities under a program structure. The ongoing activities of government then remain classified under normal input-oriented budget lines. Sometimes, only new expenditure initiatives put in place by the present government are identified as programs. Alternatively, programs are sometimes defined as all government activities of finite duration, with all permanent expenditure classified under the traditional input budget.

Any partial coverage of expenditure in the program structure has a detrimental effect on allocative decision-making. By not fully attributing all expenditures to programs the full costs of programs cannot be compared. This means government cannot compare the cost of pursuing different societal outcomes. Not including personnel costs of the civil service staff would obviously bias expenditure towards programs executed by the civil service, rather than by, for example, lower levels of government or through outsourcing to third parties, even though the latter two options may be more cost-effective for society as a whole.

The non-inclusion of ongoing, or permanent, expenditure in the program structure is detrimental for a similar reason. Expenditure that maintains the basic functions of government will serve particular government objectives. Just because certain functions have been part of government for a long time does not mean they should not be considered as candidates for increased expenditure, or that they should never be cut back. By leaving permanent expenditure outside the allocation mechanism that program budgeting allows, permanent expenditure is, on the one hand, protected against cutbacks, but also, on the other hand, not eligible for increase of expenditure.

A third issue that needs to be tackled in defining program coverage is whether programs should encompass gross expenditure or net expenditure, the latter being defined as gross-expenditure minus own-source revenues attributable to the program in question. A reason for the latter position might be that a program that finances itself through user charges can be seen as cheap, and thus in allocative decision-making government could have a preference for such programs. There are two reasons for not endorsing this position. First of all, user charges can be unrelated to the actual costs incurred by public sector providers and may also be compulsory, so that it has more the character of a quasi-tax than a market price for a service in a competitive market. Second, for transparency reasons it is important to see the full extent of the resources being channeled through government. Without encompassing gross expenditures, a program may look to be very cost-effective, while in reality a lot of public resources are channeled to it. For this reason most countries favor encompassing gross expenditures in their program definitions.

A final issue to note on the coverage of programs, discussed in more detail in Chapter 4, is that mature program budgeting systems integrate current and capital expenditure related to the same policy objective in one program. The reason for this is that if, for example, only the current costs of programs are compared during allocative decision-making, then the capital investment needed to keep the program effective would be seen as a free resource and there would be a bias for more capital intensive programs. In many developing countries, programs have been defined as only covering recurrent expenditure, with capital projects, which are mainly funded by donors, not being linked to recurrent programs. This has led to recurrent expenditures not being aligned with capital expenditure, and has cast in doubt the long-term sustainability of certain public investments. Integration of current and capital expenditure helps present more accurately the true costs of the policy objective a program is pursuing, and provides an opportunity for balancing recurrent costs with capital expenditure, thereby improving the overall effectiveness of government expenditure.[11]

Design, size, and scope of programs

The development of any good system of program classification requires that the center of government (generally the Ministry of Finance (MoF)) provides guidance to line ministries about the appropriate size and scope of programs. This guidance should be consistent with an appropriate balance between centralized and decentralized use of program budgeting in allocative decision-making, reflecting the fact that the program classification should serve as a tool for budget management both for the center of government and for line ministries and agencies.

The development of line ministry program structures should be a collaborative endeavor between line ministries and the MoF. In general, it is advisable that each line ministry start the process by developing a proposed program structure based on the strategic objectives of the ministry. Thus developing a program structure should be intimately linked to a ministry's strategic planning. The main difference is often that strategic planning tends to focus insufficiently on ongoing objectives and activities. In developing a program structure line ministries should make sure that all ongoing policies and activities are adequately encapsulated in the program classification. Also, future strategic objectives and polices which have not yet been approved by cabinet would usually only be incorporated in the program structure once budget resources have been allocated to them.

It is very important for the MoF to provide guidelines to line ministries which specify a clear methodology and uniform approach to developing a program classification. These guidelines should, first, provide a clear statement of the fundamental principles of the definition of programs (for example, that programs should be outcome- and output-based) and, second, indicate a clear position on matters where international practice in program classification may otherwise vary (for example, the level of detail in which outcomes are specified, whether there are to be administrative cost programs, the size and numbers of programs). In some countries with a strong culture of decentralized budget management, such as the Netherlands, line ministry program structures have to some extent developed without sufficient uniformity across ministries, making the program budget less effective for allocative decision-making between ministries than it might otherwise have been.

The importance of ensuring appropriate uniformity of program structures between ministries should not be taken as advice that the MoF should dictate the program structure of ministries. The experience is that, in most countries in which the MoF has unilaterally determined the program structure without substantive input and concurrence from line ministries, those ministries do not really "own" the new program structure. This may lead to a situation where line ministries largely retain their input or organizationally driven budget for internal budget management purposes. To assure use of the common methodology, and to balance usefulness of the program classification between the needs of line ministries themselves and the center of government, it can be a good development strategy to have joint line ministry-MoF working groups develop the program structure at the technical level.[12] Once the line ministries have developed concrete proposals, the MoF should review these on uniformity across ministries and appropriate application of the agreed methodology. Final negotiations with ministries to resolve remaining issues may be necessary. It should be a prerogative of the MoF to give final approval to the program structure for each line ministry, just as it approves economic and functional classifications of the budget as part of its responsibility for coordinating budget management.

One of the seemingly simple, but crucial practical issues that development of a program structure must address is how many programs each ministry should have. Often line ministries will initially take quite extreme positions. For example, a Ministry of Agriculture might take the position that "our activities are all about improving the agriculture sector," and that there should therefore be only one program called "Improving agriculture." At the other extreme, the same ministry may take the position that each of a myriad of services, such as advice to farmers, drought relief, an agricultural research institute, and the like, are all so important that they should be recognized as programs in their own right, rather than being relegated to lower levels of the program hierarchy—with the result that the program structure may comprise 50 or more programs.

Obviously, for allocative decision-making such extreme positions are not helpful. MoFs have often sought to avoid a profusion of small programs, by indicating minimum sizes for programs, or suggesting the approximate numbers of programs that line ministries or agencies should develop. This reflects the desire to keep allocative decision-making of cabinet and parliament—which, as we will see, is often focused on the program level—at a fairly strategic level, and avoid getting these two institutions too involved in details which can, for the most part, be better left to the line ministry itself. There are other reasons for avoiding too many small programs. First, as discussed below, it reduces the flexibility available (given the prevailing virement rules[13]) for line ministries and their agencies to deal with unexpected changes in the demand for services by switching expenditure allocations on their own authority. Second, the magnitude of the task of cost attribution between programs increases more than proportionately as the size of programs falls (see Chapter 4). Third, a structure with too many small programs can make intra-ministry allocations more problematic. As the program level is usually the level at which expenditure is appropriated by parliament, programs and/or agencies described as programs can be insulated from intra-line ministry reallocation through the action of sympathetic parliamentarians.[14]

A further consideration is that a certain stability in the program structure at the higher levels is advisable. This reflects the fact that strategic priorities of government do not usually change much from year to year. It also allows for better tracking and evaluation of expenditure programs over the medium term. A program structure with too much detail at the higher level will not show this stability. Stability is, however, not something which can usually be expected to be achieved in the early years after introducing a program classification. Rather, it is often sensible to let line ministries have the opportunity in the first couple of years to make adjustments to their program classification to let it better reflect their strategic objectives. However, after the early years of implementation, the program structure at the higher level should solidify and only then be changed to reflect important changes in strategic priorities.

Although it is important that the MoF provides guidance on the desirable number of programs per line ministry, and therefore implicitly the minimum program size, there is a case to be made against any excessively *rigid* minimum size requirements. To insist that no program should ever fall below some arbitrary expenditure level could lead to the creation of incoherent programs, grouping together services with different objectives, simply because those services individually account for relatively small portions of the line agency's expenditure. Programs which lack coherence are not of great value for decision-making about expenditure priorities. There is much to be said for the view expressed by the French parliamentary budget commission that

> The coherence of programs is fundamental to the success of (performance budgeting) reform...The need to attain a critical size is often put forward to justify programs which mix activities with little in common. Such an argument is difficult to accept: the coherence of programs is more important than their size. (Commission des Finances, 2004)

It is equally important from the point of view of central decision-makers that programs do not become too big relative to the size of the line ministry budget, because if they do so, they tend to cease to be useful to the government for prioritizing expenditures. Excessive size also tends to produce incoherent programs. In the extreme, for example, if each ministry were to have only one program, many allocative decisions of great interest to the cabinet and parliament would be beyond its reach. This has at various stages been an issue in a number of countries.

For example, under the "accrual output budgeting" system developed in Australia during the late 1990s, ministries greatly reduced the number of programs (now called "outcomes") they had relative to the previous "program budgeting and management" systems which had operated from the 1980s. The concentration was such that the Department of Defense had only a single outcome, which grouped all of the department's services under the common intended objective of "the prevention or defeat of armed force against Australia or its interests." After a few years' experience with this approach, a strong feeling developed among politicians that such highly aggregated programs gave them too little capacity to influence the allocation of resources to more specific objectives when they felt the need to do so. The result was a deliberate move to increase the number of programs so that, for example, in 2005–06 the defense department had seven programs (including separate outcomes for navy capability, army capability and air force capability).[15]

The same concerns arose in France after ministries made their initial attempt to define the program structures required by the new reforms flowing from the new organic budget law (LOLF) of 2001. The parliamentary budget commission complained that too many ministries where suggesting structures which gave them either only one *mission,* or only one *programme* within each mission (Commission des Finance, 2004). Noting that fully two-thirds of ministries proposed single-mission program structures, the Commission posed the rhetorical question of whether one could really reduce the wide-ranging activities of, say, the mega-Ministry of Economy, Finance, and Industry to one single mission.[16]

As a very rough rule of thumb, taking into account the need for coherence in programs, and depending on the number of line ministries and agencies which receive direct allocations in the budget, the number of programs (that is, expenditure classes at the highest levels of the program classification) should generally be between 5 and 15 per line ministry. This indication reflects the importance of line ministries focusing on a limited number of related strategic objectives.[17]

In addition to the overall number of programs, line ministries also often need guidance on the differences in size of the various programs. It has proven not very useful to have one or two huge programs and ten very minuscule ones in the first level of the program structure. While here rules of thumb are even harder to give than for the number of programs, it should be clear that program structures with vastly different program sizes are not very efficient for allocative decision-making, as reallocations in the smaller programs usually have almost no impact on the amount of fiscal space. Decisions about reallocation between minor programs would require the cabinet to spend inordinate time and resources on relatively unimportant government objectives and activities.

Logic of the program structure

We have seen that the program structure consists of various layers. While the names of items in these layers will differ from country to country, the most common program structure consists of three layers that in this chapter will be referred to as: programs, sub-programs, activities. (There are, however, variations on this—for example, in some countries, high-level programs are defined above the program level, while in others a "measure" level is inserted between sub-programs and activities, and in yet others the activity level is further broken down into sub-activities.) Sub-programs typically pursue the same overall policy goal as the program to which they belong but do this by either producing slightly different outputs (resulting in the same societal outcome) or producing similar outputs in different ways, that is, through different public policy instruments. Like the program, the sub-program should be defined by objective, related activities, and amount of resources spent. In contrast to the program, sub-program objectives would be defined by outputs rather than outcomes. Outputs of sub-programs would contribute to the realization of the desired outcome of the program to which they belong.

Beneath the sub-program level, activities will usually represent discrete measures, initiatives, or operations, or projects (geographically or with respect to time, or in some other way distinct) that together form the sub-program. Again the items at the activity level should be connected to well-definable objectives, as all parts of the program structure have the some basic configuration, that is, are based on an objective, encompass certain activities of government, and require a certain amount of resources. The objectives at the activity level would probably be defined as sub-outputs of the output of the encompassing sub-program. Thus, objectives in the program hierarchy generally become more operational the further down one goes; the targeted results tend to become more concrete. At the program level the objectives generally point to outcomes, while at the lower levels of the hierarchy the objectives relate more and more to concrete outputs for which government can be held accountable. Box 5.1 presents the program structure of the Dutch Ministry of Agriculture as an illustration of the relationship between program levels.

Most countries with mature program structures use the first level of the program hierarchy as the basis of allocative decision-making by cabinet. Cabinet and other central executive government decision-makers do not in general concern themselves with the lower levels of the program hierarchy. This is largely left to the line ministries and MoF to discuss in the agreement of the more detailed planning of the budget. In addition to looking at activity and sub-activity levels, MoFs generally would want information on the use of inputs at all levels of the program structure, to verify costing assumptions. The input information would not necessarily need to be detailed, and certainly would be less detailed than under input budgeting systems. It could be limited, for example, to the first layer or layers of the economic classification.

At the line ministry level, more detailed planning of expenditure at the lower levels of the program structure is usually required by the finance department of the line ministry itself. Finance departments would also require input costing of program items. This planning could take place either before or after the approval of the line ministry budget and would be binding to a certain extent for, for example, lower levels of managers in the line ministry. However, this detailed planning under program budgeting should provide more managerial freedom than the very detailed input control that many countries employed under input budgeting. Any mistaken perception that program budgeting does not involve detailed planning and costing of expenditure should, however, be dispelled.

Box 5.1 Budget structure of the Netherlands Ministry of Agriculture & Nature in 2004

Below we present part of the program structure of the Ministry of Agriculture in the Netherlands as it was used for the 2004 State Budget. The first level consists of 11 programs, or *beleidsartikelen* (policy articles) as they are called in Dutch. We then go deeper into the program structure by looking at the program "Promoting Sustainable Production" (program 5, emboldened below), and look at the sub-programs of that program. We then repeat that process by looking at the sub-program "Eco-friendly fishing" (sub-program 5.5, emboldened below) to see its components at the activity level, which is the final level of the ministry's budget.

The budget structure below clearly shows the logical connection between the three levels. The sub-programs and activities all fall within the overall policy objective of promoting sustainable (agricultural) production. However, the objectives of the lower levels are more focused and concrete, and at the activity level more time-limited.

Level 1:

Programs		Budget (€ millions)
1.	Strengthening Rural Areas	256.4
2.	Nature Realization.[a]	176.5
3.	Nature Maintenance	164.3
4.	Economically Viable Agricultural	71.0
5.	Promoting Sustainable Production	121.8
6.	Food Safety, Quality, and Animal Health	90.3
7.	Research & Development	294.8
8.	Training	440.9
9.	Informational Activities	62.1
10.	Nominal and Contingency	–8.4
11.	Administration	245.3
Total expenditure		1,915.1

The presented program structure is by no means perfect. It is obvious that the programs at the first level of the budget structure relate only partially to policy objectives. The ministry seems to have chosen a sizeable Administration program with an unspecified objective, as well as R&D, Training, and Informational Activities programs that seem to reflect support activities of the ministry rather than specific objectives. The Netherlands only introduced program budgeting in 2002 (after a trial period of three years) and to some extent the Ministry of Agriculture's budget shows that a substantial part of the ministry's expenditure is not yet being attributed to policy objectives. In the future the three activity-based programs may be further attributed to specific policy objectives.

Level 2 of program 5:

Program 5	Budget (€ millions)
5. Promoting Sustainable Production	**121.8**
Sub-programs	
5.1 Promoting organic farming	8.8
5.2 Decreasing use chemical fertilizers	7.3
5.3 Protection of crop safety	7.6
5.4 Improved animal welfare	1.1
5.5 Eco-friendly fishing	**15.4**
5.6 Administration	81.7

▶

The second level of the program structure shows that the program "Promoting Sustainable Production" has within it six sub-programs, including again a very substantial Administration sub-program. Obviously, it would be better for allocation purposes if this Administration sub-program within program 5 could be allocated to the five more output-oriented sub-programs. Given that the ministry has administration budgets both at the program and at the sub-program level, a substantial part of the overall budget is not really covered in the program structure, making it less usable for allocative decision-making.

Level 3 of sub-program 5.5:

Sub-program 5.5	
5.5 Eco-friendly fishing	**15.4**
Activities	
5.5.1 International coordination	2.8
5.5.2 Improvement of domestic fishing	1.0
5.5.3 Innovation projects	5.0
5.5.4 Technical measures & research	4.7
5.5.5 Various	1.9

Level 3 further divides the sub-program "Eco-friendly fishing" into five activities. It could be noted at this level that the identified classification items are often described in activity terms. In a well-developed program budgeting structure items at all levels should, however, remain linked to desired results at varying levels of concreteness. Without the link to performance targets, program budgeting reverts to activity-based budgeting. An activity item called "various," while understandable from a practical point of view, is not acceptable from a program budgeting point of view. Activities, like any level of the program structure, should be linked to an encompassing objective. This objective should be the designation of the activity in question.

[a] In a country such as the Netherlands the government has a policy to increase the total land area that could be designated as "nature." Land is purchased from private landowners and then actively turned into nature reserves. As it is a densely populated country it then needs to be maintained.

Role of the legislature: programs and appropriations

In many countries with program budgets, expenditure is *appropriated* by, and at the level of, programs. In other words, the annual budget law passed by the legislative body specifies the allocation of expenditure between programs, but is silent on the allocation of expenditure *within* programs. There are quite a few exceptions to this generalization, however. In Australia, for example, allocation of program expenditure is left to the executive under a system of so-called "global" appropriations under which parliament appropriates an aggregate amount to each ministry and is only informed of the planned program allocation of that aggregate. Conversely, in a country like the Netherlands, parliament has taken the view that the program level of expenditure does not always provide it with sufficient scope for political direction. As a consequence, the government conceded during the introduction of program budgeting that although programs (*beleidsartikelen*) would remain at the level of appropriation, parliament would retain the right to demand changes at lower levels of the program hierarchy when approving the budget.

A key issue which arises in systems where the legislature appropriates expenditure by program is whether the legislature has the power to vary the program appropriations proposed in the budget presented by the executive. There is considerable variation in international practice on this point. In the United Kingdom, at one extreme, the legislature has no power to alter the allocation of expenditure between "Requests for Resources" contained in the budget proposed by the Chancellor of the Exchequer. At the opposite end of the spectrum, the United States Congress has essentially unconstrained power to alter the program allocations suggested in the President's budget. In France, the position under the new performance budgeting system lies somewhere between these two poles. In that country, parliament appropriates expenditure by both the higher-level *missions* and by the second-layer *programs*. However, the parliament may only alter the allocation of funds between programs—and not between missions.

There is no correct answer to the question of how power over program allocations should be shared between the legislature and the executive. The approach taken depends very much on the political system and on social preferences concerning the more general relationship between legislature and executive. The US approach, for example, is a natural expression of a system based upon the deliberate separation of executive and legislative powers as a safeguard against the undue concentration of powers. The greater concentration of powers in the hands of the executive under Westminster-style systems, by contrast, is often justified by a view that efficient government demands strong executive leadership. As noted in Chapter 20, the provisions permitting the French parliament to reallocate between programs are part of a quite deliberate broader effort on the part of the parliament to claim a greater role in budgeting, in a context where traditionally the parliament had very little capacity to influence the executive budget.

Within-year flexibility in program allocations

In countries where expenditure is appropriated by program, the question arises whether changes in legislated program allocations are permitted, and, if so, by what mechanism. It is not uncommon, both in developed and developing countries, that there are unanticipated within-year changes in the demand for certain types of public services. Also, it is not uncommon for program costs to be incorrectly calculated, or for foreseeable circumstances not to have been taken into account, in budget planning. In many countries, a degree of flexibility is given to the executive to change the program allocations determined by the parliament. The main way of providing such flexibility is through provisions allowing line agencies to transfer (vire) funds between programs and within programs with the approval of a suitable authority (usually depending on the scope of the reallocation: the line minister, the finance minister, or cabinet). Any such virement provisions need to be specified in law—usually in the organic budget law. For virements within programs, which we will also describe below, the organic budget law usually authorizes the Minister of Finance to regulate these in financial regulations.

Because virement between programs clearly reduces the degree of legislative control of expenditure priorities, the extent of such virement authority is usually limited (for example, in both France and New Zealand to a maximum of 5 percent of the amount of any program appropriation (Lienart, 2004, p. 334)). The argument usually made for virement provisions is that it would be too slow and cumbersome to require that any and all changes to program allocations be authorized by parliament through supplementary budget legislation. By contrast, however, no virement of funds between Requests for Resources is permitted the UK, and all reallocations of money between programs must be taken back to the parliament. In defense of such an approach, it may be argued that other means do exist with which to deal with sudden and unexpected changes in expenditure requirements—in particular, the Minister of Finance's contingency reserve. Many countries have judged, however, that on balance some recourse to virement is expedient. Virements do, however, in general need to be reported on in budget execution reports and/or supplementary budgets.

Aside from the legal possibility of virement between programs, the question arises to what extent the center—the Ministry of Finance—should use the program structure as the basis for budget execution control. That is, should it control the reallocation of funds between and within programs by line agencies during the budget year, so as to make it conform to planned allocations? Or should the lower levels of the program allocation of expenditure be seen merely as an expenditure planning tool, with agencies free to vary the actual allocation of expenditure during the year as they see fit? Universally, the answer given to this question is that the program structure should be used for expenditure control. For the first layer of the program structure, that is, the programs themselves, there is the classic principle of budgeting that any legislative appropriation should only be amended by another legislative action as otherwise the authorization function—or legislative "power of the purse"—would be negated. As indicated, the organic budget law of some countries has softened this principle to some extent by allowing the MoF to approve requested changes in the budget appropriations up to a certain limit. Such changes are usually only allowed within a line ministry budget, that is, the resources cannot be vired to another ministry's program, and the virement can only take place on request of the line minister in question. For control of fiscal policy, the Minister of Finance also usually has the right, most often only with approval of cabinet, to cut expenditure to below appropriation levels by program if macro-fiscal circumstances require this. Such budget cutbacks should, it is often specified, not invalidate the relative allocative choices authorized by the legislature.[18]

Below the appropriation level—the level in the program hierarchy at which the parliament appropriates money in the annual budget—the degree of allocative flexibility accorded to line ministries differs considerably internationally. In some of the more advanced countries, there is no central control over the manner in which line ministries allocate funds between sub-programs and activities. In other countries that have just introduced program budgeting, line ministries will in general have some, but not full, flexibility to make changes within lower levels of the program classification. Compared to the line-item control imposed by MoFs under input budgeting the amount of flexibility for line ministries has generally increased greatly. A certain level of control by the MoF is deemed necessary in countries with weak decentralized budget management in order to maintain the integrity of the budget, since the budget is the product of allocative decision-making by cabinet and costing review by the MoF, based on detailed justification of program expenditure. If line ministries were able to make unlimited changes to the constituting parts of programs, this would invalidate the screening and approval process of both the MoF and the cabinet.

Virements frameworks will vary from country to country, and, as a general rule, the stronger the planning, financial management, and accountability mechanisms, the more room line ministries can be given to make changes to their budget within the appropriation limits set by parliament.

With respect to the breakdown of program expenditure between inputs, performance budgeting in general calls for the relaxation of central input controls so as to accord line agencies greater managerial freedom to produce services efficiently (see Box 5.2). This does not mean, however, that all input controls should be abolished—that is, that countries should in general not allow for unlimited substitution between elements of the economic classification. Virement rules usually place some restrictions on the reallocation by the line ministry from one main economic category to the other. For example, there are almost always limitations on the extent that line ministries can vire into personnel expenditure and away from capital expenditure. The rationale for these rules, especially in developing countries is, on the one hand, to avoid turning government into an employment vehicle, and, on the other hand, to protect capital expenditure against the ever-present danger that it will be cut particularly severely as a short-sighted response to fiscal pressures.

Above the level of autonomy for line ministries, the Ministry of Finance will have to approve within-year budget amendments. One of the desirable effects of program budgeting is that the number of such approvals has been reduced substantially compared to a systems of input based budgeting. A framework for line ministry autonomy as described above would lead perhaps to one-tenth or even one-hundredth of the approvals by the MoF compared to a system of input budgeting where the MoF has to give approval for any budget change at the lowest level of the line-item classification. (See Box 5.2 for further information on the trend of reducing input controls and replacing them with control on outputs.)

Under program budgeting an interesting development has been that virement powers of line ministries have in general been increased to allow more scope for line ministries to allocate resources so as to maximize desired outcomes. The thinking behind this increase in powers and flexibility was that accountability of ministers should be based on the achievement of stated objectives, not on the mix of resources used for attaining those objectives. However, to avoid invalidating the screening and costing of proposals and to attain some measure of quality in the planning of budget execution, governments have, in general, even under program budgeting, limited the extent to which in-year changes to budget planning can be made.

Box 5.2 Loosening input controls without losing control

When introducing program budgeting, governments are faced with the option of removing or loosening input controls. In many countries, input controls are extensive. The Ministry of Finance in Greece, for example, controls expenditures up to the lowest level of the four-level economic/line-item classification. This means that office supplies need to be planned by type (paper, pens, furniture, and so on), and that any reallocation of funds of a line ministry or agency during the year has to be approved by the MoF. In a country like the Dominican Republic many reallocations even need to be approved by Congress. In practice, countries with input controls can have thousands of virement approvals by the MoF and hundreds of supplementary budget approvals per year.

Not only is such a system of input controls costly, time consuming, and disruptive for budget execution, it is also often ineffective in what it wants to achieve. Input controls have generally been used to maintain appropriate expenditure allocations, to combat fraud, and to achieve fiscal discipline. In effect, very tight input control has often made budget execution inefficient, as it does not allow for government managers to allocate resource to the best of their abilities. Especially in countries where the government budget is prepared by budget analysts on an incremental basis without much input from government managers, input control can lead to large inefficiencies, and/or a process of systematic alteration of the budget during the year. In Greece, for example, line ministries have indicated that they tend to start preparing virement proposals as soon as the budget is published.

Input controls have often proven to be unreliable or insufficient in stopping fraud as they are based largely on a process dominated by paperwork, and not on the physical, financial, or system controls used in audit processes. In developed countries internal and external audit processes have largely replaced input controls as mechanisms much better attuned to ward against fraudulent use of funds.

While input controls may play a role in limiting aggregate expenditure, there seems to be not much reason for the very detailed controls seen in many countries. Controlling overall expenditure can also be done by controlling expenditure at somewhat higher levels of the economic/line-item classification.

In loosening input controls in the context of introducing program budgeting governments generally choose to substitute input controls with outputs controls based on agreed outputs at the subprogram and activity level. Thus while line ministries will be allowed to vire expenditure over different items of the economic classification, outputs achieved by the line ministry will need to be reported on, and ministries are held to those outputs. Thus while the input accountability under program budgeting decreases, the accountability for that which really matters, namely government outputs, increases.

It should also be noted that program budgeting does not exclude some input controls. As indicated, spending on items in the lower levels of the program classification is not fully free. MoFs and finance departments usually impose virement limits for the sub-program and activity levels on line ministry managers. Many countries have also chosen to impose control on aggregate input categories parallel to the program or sub-program level. In such a system the input reallocation is then limited to within the identified main economic categories. A more simple combination of input controls and program budgeting is a system where personnel expenditure and capital expenditure are controlled within the program structure.

One aspect of the increase in budget flexibility under program budgeting is the increased scope for budget planning and for in-year virement by program managers. Line ministries have not only seen their powers increase, they have to some extent also decentralized their powers to program managers and managers responsible for items in the lower levels of the program classification. The reason for decentralizing these powers is the same as for the shift of these powers from MoF to line ministries: individual managers of programs or sub-programs are better aware of which resource mix will optimize their outputs. Given enough accountability for results, such freedoms should be warranted.

However, the experience with providing more budget flexibility to program managers in developing and transition countries has not always been unanimously positive. Loosening of expenditure control has been associated with larger wage increases, especially at the managerial level, and more expenditure on luxury overheads such as cars and office space. In this sense a consensus has grown that control of program expenditure needs accountability for both outputs and program inputs at an aggregated level.

Relationship of program structures to organizational structure

As noted above, it is widely agreed that it is desirable that programs should to the greatest possible degree be defined by a government's strategic objectives defined as outcomes. The sub-components of a program can then be seen providing outputs and sub-output contributing to this societal outcome. This approach poses a number of problems, one of which is that a program structure based on desired outcomes would tend to differ in important ways from the existing organizational structures in government. The question therefore arises whether it is appropriate to seek to align program and organizational structures, and, if so, whether this should be done either by designing program structures in such a way as to respect organizational boundaries or by modifying organizational structure so as to reflect more closely the outcomes being pursued.

Programs and ministry/agency boundaries

Many countries confine programs to ministry boundaries. In other words, programs are not permitted to group together expenditures from different ministries. The Netherlands, Australia, and the United Kingdom are cases in point—although, as discussed further below, some of these countries permit programs to cross agency boundaries within the same ministry.[19]

There are, by contrast, some countries which make selective use of interministerial programs. Sweden and France are examples of this approach, and concrete examples of such programs are given in Chapter 20. The argument for permitting programs which cross ministerial (or agency) boundaries is that this facilitates better central allocative choice, by recognizing that in important cases high-priority government objectives will be the shared responsibility of a number of different agencies. As a 2001 report to the New Zealand government put it:

> Outputs produced by different agencies can constitute related services and having them funding from separate votes [that is, separate appropriations] makes reallocating resources across agencies but within related interventions more difficult...Reducing the number of votes by allowing more than one department and portfolio to draw money from a single vote should provide greater scope to enhance coordination between agencies, make resource allocation decisions across agencies, focus on intended outcomes, and reduce compliance costs. (Advisory Group on the Review of the Centre, 2001, p. 41)

The proponents of such interministerial or interagency programs see this as an important means of counteracting the tendency of agencies to pursue their own objectives with insufficient regard to the broader objectives of the government and the related activities of other agencies—what has sometimes been referred to as "silo" behavior. It has been something of a trend in public administration over the past decade to emphasize the need for mechanisms to build a strong "whole-of-government" or "cross-portfolio" perspective to public administration, by encouraging and compelling ministries and agencies to work collaboratively. (See Box 5.3 for a Swedish cross-ministry example.)

Box 5.3 Cross-ministry budget planning in Sweden

Sweden introduced its present form of program budgeting in the mid-1990s. The highest level of its program structure encompasses 27 expenditure areas which can overlap one or more ministry in the total of 13 ministries. If appropriations are planned for an expenditure area, relevant ministers will discuss the interministerial allocation jointly with the Ministry of Finance. Also during budget execution and evaluation of performance, line ministries need to coordinate their activities. At the ministry level, 48 programs (policy areas) are identified and below that sub-programs and activities (activity areas and activity branches). Parliament allocates at the expenditure area level, and then at the level of individual agencies, and for special investments, grants ands transfers. The lower levels of the program structure are not used for expenditure planning and control, but for managing outputs. In total Sweden has around 500 financial appropriation items spread out over 13 ministries. While most performance budgeting systems would have an explicit link between financial allocations and performance, that is not fully the case in Sweden. The Swedish authorities have indicated that they do not find the coordination requirements of this system overly burdensome.

It might be argued that the case for creating programs crossing ministry (or perhaps even agency) boundaries would disappear if the responsibilities of ministries were properly defined in the first place, so as not to overlap. A moment's thought will, however, make it clear that this would be a simplistic position, and that there are often good reasons why services aimed at the same problem are spread over multiple agencies or ministries. For example, the Ministry of the Interior and the Ministry of Justice in many countries may have parallel aims to ensure the rule of law in society. Most countries have found it sensible, however, to separate law enforcement from the criminal justice system. Organizational structures need to take into account not only the intended outcomes of public services, but also a range of other factors including economies of scale and scope in the production of those services. In the example of the two ministries above, balance of powers and protection of civil rights would be seen as more important considerations than efficient allocation of resources. Also, advocates of cross-ministry programs argue that ignoring institutional boundaries has the advantage of putting the spotlight on existing societal problems and the organizational structures available to address them. Thus such an approach would encourage organizational restructuring on a more results-oriented basis where appropriate.

The main reason why cross-ministry programs exist in only a handful of countries is probably a view that the practical problems which arise are too great to make the exercise worthwhile. Agencies, and ministries as a whole, need clearly defined *organizational* budgets. The existence of pools of "shared" funds without clear ownership rights can be expected to be a source of interagency conflict and also to reduce accountability for the results achieved with those funds. This line of thinking leads to the view that it is wise to temper the principle of outcome-based program classification to reflect the realities of ministerial (and possibly also agency) organizational boundaries.

The need for agencies to have clear budgets suggests that if there are to be cross-ministry programs, it is necessary that the ministry shares of these program expenditures be clearly specified in advance. The most straightforward way of doing this is to specify this allocation at the sub-program level—such as is done in France where the budgets of both the *missions* (effectively programs) and *programs* (effectively sub-programs, which are confined to ministry boundaries) are centrally specified.

The same issues arise in respect to cross-agency programs within ministries. However, one means of facilitating the construction of programs across agency boundaries within the same ministry is for the center to focus primarily on funding ministries, rather than agencies. Under this approach, the center delegates to ministries a large measure of authority over the allocation of the ministry budget between agencies within the ministry. Such an option requires the development of significant ministry-wide budgeting capacity within the core finance department of the ministry.

Programs and the internal organizational structures of agencies

The same type of tension between the program classification principle and organizational structures arises within individual agencies. Here again, it is a mistake to believe that the problem can be resolved by basing organizational structure solely upon the program principle. This would involve defining the "divisional"[20] structure within the agency solely upon product lines—or, to use language more appropriate to the public sector, upon groupings of services delivered to external parties with common outcomes. If the divisional structure were to be based solely upon programs, there could be no regional offices delivering more than one program but managed as a single unit for locational reasons. In addition, there could not be organizational units delivering support or corporate overhead services such as finance and human resource management—because support services are not products/outputs (see Chapter 3). It would be necessary instead for each internal product-based division to provide all of its own support services from separate units within the division. Although it is often the case that support/overhead services tend to be unduly centralized in public sector organizations (and indeed to become ends in themselves), there are good reasons why it does not make sense to totally decentralize all such support services.

It is therefore a mistake, inconsistent with the basic results-oriented principle of budgeting by programs, to assert that the program structure of each ministry should be made to fit its organizational structure.

Managing programs coherently across organizational boundaries

Managerial systems are not within the scope of this chapter. However, it is useful to make a few comments about management issues which arise as a result of inevitable differences between program structure and organizational structure, whether within or between agencies. One common solution to this tension is to operate two cross-cutting layers of management—one for management of the organizational unit, and one for management of the program. This is sometimes referred to as the principle of *matrix management.* A contemporary example of this is the creation under the new French reforms of the position of program manager (*responsable du programme*), which may in many cases require the person concerned to oversee the work of several agencies within the same ministry (see Chapter 20). Such an approach can clearly raise difficult questions about the power relationship of the program manager and the organizational manager—in particular, that of how to endow the program manager with enough real power to make the organizational manager take his or her authority seriously. One response to this question taken by some jurisdictions has been to endow the program manager with significant power over the use of the program budget—possibly even to the extent of creating something analogous to a "purchaser-provider" division. A very similar approach has sometimes been applied to the supply of support services. Thus, for example, in the US Department of Defense (and within certain other departments), many support services are provided on an internal "purchase" basis under what are known as "Working Capital Funds" (see Chapter 1). Whatever approach is taken, it is an important part of managing-for-results that public sector organizations reorient themselves toward external service delivery, rather than internal processes.

Conclusion

The program classification of expenditure is the most important financial management tool that countries have to get right when introducing program budgeting. A program classification should be based on a hierarchy of outcome- and output-oriented programs, sub-programs, and activities. A program classification will clarify the policy debate in cabinet and the legislature and should result in much improved expenditure allocation. Line ministries will also use the lower levels of the program classification to steer internal operations to more effective and efficient service delivery. The MoF should ensure that while line ministry strategic priorities are fully reflected in line ministry program structures, there is an adequate level of homogeneity in defining the program structure across line ministries. Line ministries should not only adhere to the specific guidelines on how programs and lower levels should be defined, but also take into account more practical guidelines on number of programs, relative size, and number of layers in the classification.

Countries should be encouraged to use the program classification as the main presentational format for expenditures in the budget, while the legislature should appropriate spending by programs, or larger parts of the program structure. In introducing a program structure, at least initially compromises should be accepted with regard to the use of administration programs, and keeping programs within line ministry boundaries. While a program structure provides much more flexibility to line ministries and their managers in changing inputs to best achieve desired outcomes and output, program structures should be used to control expenditures. A virement framework should define to what extent line ministries and the MoF are allowed to change allocation, and to what extent parliament has that prerogative. While cabinet and the legislative body would control expenditure allocation at a fairly high level, the lower levels of the program structure would be the instrument with which MoF and finance departments in line ministries monitor and control expenditure.

Notes

1. The authors would like to thank Philip Joyce for his valuable comments on a draft of this chapter.
2. Article 7(I), Loi Organique relative aux Lois de Finances (LOLF) no. 2001–692.
3. KRAs are part of the terminology often used in forms of strategic planning, but they have also been used as labels for groups of expenditure programs.
4. Terminology used in, respectively, the Australian, the British, the Canadian, the Swedish, and the Dutch budget systems.
5. Note, however, that it is not good practice to leave programs without a summary title in this manner. For most programs, it is both possible and desirable that the short title of the program should give an indication of its objectives.
6. See Chapter 3 for more detail on the concept of "activities" within the standard "logical framework."
7. In the Netherlands program budgeting has been communicated to line ministries as the three "W's" system: "What do we want to achieve? What are we going to do to achieve this? What is it going to cost?" The second, instrumental question on activities being carried out is one line ministries are familiar with even under input budgeting. This logical structure of questions allows program budgeting to provide an opportunity for line ministries to better align activities (and organizational structures) to objectives.
8. See Chapter 3 for the distinction between proximate and high-level outcomes.
9. More generally, it tends to make clear *who* or *what* the program directly targets in order to achieve its intended higher-level outcomes.
10. The high-level outcome of a strong economy is, for example, served not only by education, but also by macroeconomic policy, physical infrastructure provision, and a wide range of other government services.
11. This does not necessarily mean that this allocation can be changed without limit during the budget year, as this would undermine the stimulus to plan government expenditure in the pre-budget year conscientiously.

12. Consultants, or an independent third party, can play a useful role in arbitrating in these technical discussions.
13. Virement refers to the authority to change allocations of expenditure authorized by parliament or the executive during the budget year.
14. For this reason the development of the program classification in line ministries often starts with the proposal by line ministry policy departments and agencies for a multitude of programs, to safeguard their own interests.
15. Defining organizational entities as programs is usually not appropriate in the program budgeting framework, as we will discuss further on in this chapter.
16. From parliament's perspective, the development of mono-program missions was also of particular concern. As discussed in Chapter 20, the LOLF represented an attempt by parliament to reassert a role in expenditure prioritization which it had for decades been denied. To this end, the LOLF asserted the power of parliament to reallocate funds *between programs in the same mission* (but not to change the allocations to missions, which would remain the prerogative of executive government). If, however, missions were to have only one program, parliament would remain powerless in respect to expenditure prioritization.
17. As indicated, in some countries the highest level of the program structure is equated with the program level, in others this level is that of key result areas or high-level programs. Further distinctions in sub-objectives and activities of line ministry expenditure should be made at lower levels of the program classification so as not to overload the strategic allocation process at the center of government.
18. In some countries, notably the United States and China, the budget appropriation is both a maximum and a minimum. This implies that appropriations cannot be cut by the executive without supplementary budget approval of the legislature. Exceptions to this can, in principle, only be made if program execution has been delayed for reasons outside the control of the executive.
19. An "agency" is defined here as an organizational unit which has day-to-day management autonomy (so that, for example, its chief executive is not subject to direction and supervision by the chief executive of another agency). A "ministry" is defined here as a group of one or more agencies under the responsibility of a single minister. In many systems, each ministry will have a core department, and a number of other non-core agencies. The core department will tend to have principal policy responsibility for the issues covered by the ministry, and may have some ministry-wide coordination or control function (including usually over the approval of the budgets of the non-core agencies, that is, the core ministry often plays the role of finance ministry of its sector).
20. Using the term to refer to the highest level of organizational unit within the agency.

References

Advisory Group on the Review of the Centre, 2001, *Report of the Advisory Group on the Review of the Centre Presented to the Ministers of State Services and Finance*, New Zealand, November.

Commission des Finance, 2004, *Note D'étape sur La Mise En Œuvre De La Réforme Organique*, January 15, 2004, <www.assemblee-nationale.fr/12/budget/loi-organique.asp> (accessed December 10, 2004).

Lienart, I., 2004, *The Legal Framework for Budget Systems: An International Comparison* (Paris: OECD).

6
Performance Auditing and Performance Budgeting

David Shand

Performance auditing is now a well-established part of the work of national audit institutions in many OECD and other countries. As such it is part of the overall approach to performance management in the public sector of those countries. Its relationship to performance budgeting, as is discussed below, varies between countries, based on the scope and nature of the both the performance auditing function and performance budgeting. In some cases the link between performance auditing and performance budgeting is clear; in others it is less clear.

This chapter first sets the scene by examining a possible taxonomy of performance auditing. It then discusses the historical development of performance auditing, and the possible value added of performance auditing, its impact on the traditional staffing and independence of audit institutions, and then develops links with performance budgeting. Nine countries are used as the basis for this analysis, with a description of the performance auditing approach of each country being set out in an appendix. The analysis is based both on desk research and on discussions with audit officials in most of the nine countries surveyed.

Nature and boundaries of performance auditing

The International Organization of Supreme Audit Institutions (INTOSAI)[1] defines performance auditing as being concerned with the audit of economy, efficiency, and effectiveness, and embracing:

- audit of the economy of administrative policies in accordance with sound administrative principles and practices, and management policies
- audit of the efficiency of utilization of human, financial, and other resources, including examination of information systems, performance measures, and

monitoring arrangements, and procedures followed by audited entities for remedying identified deficiencies
- audit of the effectiveness of performance in relation to the achievement of the objectives of the audited entity, and the audit of the actual impact of the activities compared with the intended impact (INTOSAI, 1992, Basic Principle 1.0.40).

The broad nature of the work covered by this definition reflects the fact that there is no unique concept of performance auditing. It can be regarded as a product line rather than a single product (see Barzelay, 1996a, p. 22) and as such it is difficult to generalize about either its form or impact. A major symposium on performance auditing convened by the OECD in 1995 noted then a substantial variety of different approaches between countries in terms of origin, scope, objectives, and processes (OECD, 1996a).

It can be seen from this definition and the individual country practices outlined in the appendix at the end of this chapter, that a taxonomy of performance auditing can be developed based on two major issues:

1. The scope of the performance auditing mandate, that is, whether it covers only economy and efficiency or also extends to effectiveness.[2]
2. The form of the performance audit. The audit may be a *substantive* review of the level of performance achieved in effect using results standards or targets, or it may be a *systemic* review—of the organizational *management systems* insofar as they will impact on performance, which may be described as based on process standards. Both of these types of audits may include evaluating the adequacy of systems to measure performance, which in a number of countries extends to the review and sometimes formal attestation of reported performance indicators through a short form audit report expressing a formal opinion on the appropriateness and reliability of the indicators.

The performance audit may also cover both approaches, and mixed arrangements may also exist. For example, the comprehensive auditing approach developed in the 1970s by the Canadian Comprehensive Auditing Foundation (CCAF) and implemented by the Canadian Auditor-General's office involves substantive studies of (economy and) efficiency as well as reviewing the adequacy of systems to measure and promote efficiency but focuses only on the review of systems to measure effectiveness, that is, there is no substantive measurement of effectiveness.

It is perhaps useful to clarify this "product range" by looking at the way the public sector production chain is often portrayed, as set out similarly in Chapter 3:

$$\text{Inputs} \rightarrow \text{Processes} \rightarrow \text{Outputs} \rightarrow \text{Outcomes}$$

That is, inputs are converted through management processes (which comprise staffing and assets and all information and control systems) into outputs, which in turn contribute to achieving the desired outcomes of the expenditure. A systemic performance audit evaluates the management processes and systems. A substantive efficiency audit evaluates whether a program or activity is being efficiently operated and a substantive effectiveness audit evaluates whether the outputs of a program or activity are achieving their intended outcomes. Auditing of performance indicators is a thread which potentially runs through all other aspects of performance audit. Performance indicators (or lack of them) are part of the management control systems evaluated in a systemic audit. Output indicators are also relevant to measuring performance under a substantive efficiency audit and outcome indicators assist in measuring performance under a substantive effectiveness audit.

Some relationship can be seen with the traditional financial and compliance (or regularity, as termed by INTOSAI) audit undertaken by national audit institutions which review compliance with applicable financial laws, regulations, and controls as well as providing a formal audit opinion on the reliability or fairness of presentation of the annual financial statements. For example, financial and compliance audits through their review of the internal control system may identify weaknesses in controls which have a material impact on performance. This is likely to reflect operational efficiency issues—for example, the adequacy of asset management, in particular inventory or plant assets, as discussed below in the section on the development of performance auditing. As Barzelay (1996b) notes, "efficiency has been one of the core values in all but the most legalistic of audit bodies."

Performance auditing is almost invariably ex post, although there are at least two examples of an ex-ante approach. The US Government Accountability Office (GAO) may review programs in advance of their implementation and also reviews or scores the agency performance plans developed by the executive branch. The German Federal Court of Audit has a specific role to provide independent advice to assist the appropriations committee of parliament in its review of the proposed government budget.[3] As part of this role the findings of its ex-post performance audits are used and special ex-ante performance studies may also be undertaken.

Development of performance auditing

In most OECD countries it appears that early developments in performance auditing have been separate from the development of other aspects of performance management in the public sector. However, Barzelay (1996a) notes that performance auditing is more developed in those countries which have more vigorously pursued what is described as the "new public management" or (NPM)[4]—with the exception of France and Germany, which have a long-established performance audit function but which have been relatively slow in adopting NPM concepts.

Performance issues as a legitimate audit concern first emerged in the 1950s.[5] The development of program evaluation in the US included its development in the GAO as effectiveness auditing in the late 1960 and 1970s, reflecting the view of the then head of the GAO that Congress needed such information to exercise appropriate oversight of the executive branch. However, performance auditing appears to have been stimulated in some countries from the early 1970s through the introduction of Planning, Programming, and Budgeting Systems (PPBSs) in their various forms.

From the 1960s new legislation formally expanded the mandate of national audit institutions in a range of countries including Australia (1979) and the UK (1983). These moves appear to reflect a number of factors including the wishes of parliaments and government concerns to improve public sector performance, and in some cases formalized moves already undertaken by audit institutions into examining economy and efficiency issues, arising out of their existing financial and compliance audits. For example, it is a relatively small step from the role of a traditional financial and compliance audit review of the adequacy of inventory management systems to produce reliable information about the level of inventory held (which is reported in the financial statements) and to ensure adequate controls over inventory, to a performance audit using this information to evaluate whether the right inventory is held at optimal levels. In essence some external audit institutions actively sought to expand their work into performance auditing and successfully sought political support for this, these performance auditing developments thus being, at least in part, supply driven. Some of the political support for these developments may also have reflected the view that given the application of market type mechanisms in some parts of the public sector, which provided a surrogate for performance measurement, the need for performance measurement and review in the remainder of the public sector becomes of greater importance.

The partly supply-driven nature of some country's moves to performance auditing is also suggested by the fact that in general, formal public sector management reform programs adopted by OECD governments and reflecting the NPM approach[6] made little or no explicit reference to the role of external audit in the overall performance management system.

The moves by many OECD governments from the late 1980s and early 1990s to develop more formal systems of performance measurement and thus to better measure and report on performance, to a large extent associated with NPM, also facilitated the moves to performance auditing. As discussed in Chapter 1, NPM has aimed to achieve a greater focus on performance through providing greater managerial flexibility, in return for which managers are required to achieve agreed results. This development has seen a greater focus on measuring performance through performance indicators and more in depth program evaluation, with performance measurement becoming part of ongoing management systems. Changes in country budgeting systems have reflected this approach—particularly through less-detailed appropriation controls and the publication of performance information in the budget documents.[7]

However, performance auditing has not necessarily been perceived as an important or integral part of this development. Perhaps reflecting this, a 2005 OECD questionnaire on the use of performance information in the budget process, prepared for the annual meeting of its senior budget officials (SBO) network, did not raise the issue of the role of performance audits (either substantive or systemic), although an earlier OECD (2002) review noted that in over half of OECD countries, performance information in budget documents was subject to some form of audit.

The more recent focus on developing (and using) performance information has seen the development of an external audit focus on performance information (New

Zealand, Brazil, Australia, the UK, Sweden, and France), although not necessarily extending as far as formal audit attestation of performance indicators, based on the view that claims about performance should be subject to some independent external review, particularly in view of the fact that most performance information is produced by the supplier of the services. In general, however, the development of performance auditing appears to have proceeded along a separate path from performance budgeting, although one exception is Sweden, as will be discussed later.

Substantive performance audits

Substantive performance audits are generally at organizational, program, or activity level, rather than whole of government. They examine performance (and usually by implication the performance of management) on an ex-post basis by reference to some type of results or process standards. They include:

- review of program effectiveness, that is, the extent to which programs are achieving their objectives
- review of government policy (but the audit mandate extends this broadly in only a few jurisdictions, which have a clear separation of powers between the parliament and the executive branch. Thus in Australia and the UK, which have traditions of strong executive government and where parliament is less at arm's length from the executive, the performance audit mandate specifically excludes any review of government policies. By contrast, the broader performance audit mandate of the US GAO reflects the role of Congress as an equal partner in government with and independent of the executive branch)
- review of operational efficiency, that is, whether outputs are being produced a lowest cost, consistent with quality requirements.

It can be noted that the auditor is not normally providing an overall opinion on the achievement of economy, efficiency, and effectiveness of the audited entity (INTOSAI Field Auditing Standard 4.0.23).

Studies of program effectiveness raise the issue of the boundaries between performance (effectiveness) audits and program evaluations. This also raises the question of whether effectiveness audits are an appropriate role for auditors, even recognizing that audit institutions have changed their personnel practices to acquire knowledge and skills for such auditing which go beyond those of a financial auditor. Pollitt and Summa (1997a) note the similarities between substantive performance auditing and external program evaluation as being a similar "toolkit" or methodology but note differences in terms of authority and processes, which are often reflected in different topic selection, relationship with the auditee, and "tone" and form of reporting.

A number of countries reviewed have a clear and significant effectiveness auditing role (Australia, Brazil, Netherlands, the UK, and the US) which exists in parallel with program evaluation carried out within the government. There are equally examples of countries where program evaluation is well developed but with no corresponding performance auditing role.[8]

Interestingly, INTOSAI has established separate working parties on performance auditing and program evaluation, but the basis of this distinction is not clear. As discussed later it seems clear that the methodologies of effectiveness auditing and program evaluation are similar, with the difference being mainly in concept of independent external review and the public reporting of evaluation results inherent in the audit function. However even these differences may not be a distinguishing feature of effectiveness audits. For example, all program evaluations in Chile are required to be carried out by independent "experts" and all evaluations must be published.

Reviews of performance indicators

The INTOSAI standards refer specifically to national audit institutions working toward "improving techniques for auditing the validity of performance measures" (Basic Principles 1.0.6(j) and 1.0.45) and comment that "the expanding audit role of auditors will require them to improve and develop techniques and methodologies to assess whether reasonable and valid performance measures are used by the audited entity" (Basic Principle 1.0.46).

External auditors appear to perceive the design and operation of information systems as an area in which they may have particular expertise, drawing from the evaluation of financial management systems as part of their financial audit work.

The scope of this type of systems review may vary—it may include review of the accuracy and validity of performance measures. This review may go so far as formal attestation as to whether the information is relevant and reliable, or be by exception—that is, reports on cases where the measures are perceived as inaccurate or invalid/misleading. In principle this role may also include reviewing the targets against which performance is assessed, although this is not common.[9]

In principle this may also extend to reviewing whether the performance indicators are appropriately used in decision-making—so as to actually improve performance. This has been a component of some substantive performance audits, as has also been the question of whether there is adequate performance focus in program implementation.[10] If this addresses the use of performance information by elected officials, it may be pushing the boundaries of performance auditing into the political arena (and potentially compromise the auditor's perceived political impartiality) in that it may question the appropriateness of elected officials making decisions on the basis of "political rationality," rather than using supposedly "objective" performance information. It also raises the issue of how, given the inherent limitations of many performance indicators, it may be possible to determine whether information has been used "appropriately."

The same issue arises in respect to the use of the other major types of performance information (in particular, program evaluation information and substantive performance audits) by decision-makers, including elected officials. However, this appears to have received less attention than the use of performance indicators.

The national audit institutions of New Zealand, the Netherlands, Brazil, and France have a formal role in reviewing of the validity and reliability of reported performance indicators, although the nature of the audit report may vary. For example, in the Netherlands and New Zealand there is a formal audit opinion on the performance information. Other audit institutions have a less formal review role (Sweden and the UK) but nevertheless an objective to see that reported performance information is at best not misleading.

There is also considerable work by external audit institutions in promoting good practice in performance measurement in the public sector (Australia, the Netherlands, New Zealand, Sweden, and the UK), in some cases through the audit institution itself developing guidance on good performance measurement or reviewing the level of adherence to other guidance issued on performance measurement.

Systemic performance audits

Pollitt and Summa (1997b) note that in five national audit institutions surveyed by them as part of a comparative study of performance auditing in Europe, the focus is on the adequacy of management systems—staffing, organizational structures, information systems, and other components of internal control, to enable the organization to operate effectively and efficiently, rather than on substantive performance measurement.

These systems are judged against generally accepted good practices, as developed by the management consultancy and other related professions. Individual organizations' performance is increasingly benchmarked against that of other relevant organizations using a range of business excellence models. Such work may make use of the balanced score card approach under which the adequacy of measures to maintain the capacity and responsiveness of the organization are also reviewed, along with the perceived service delivery performance of the organization.

Value added of performance auditing

Based on presentations to the 1995 OECD symposium and on their own publications describing their work, external auditors appear to perceive two main objectives for their performance auditing work:

1. enhancing the accountability of executive government to parliament and the public
2. improving the performance of the public sector.

These goals of performance improvement and performance accountability are not mutually exclusive. They are related but not identical. Barzelay (1996a) suggests they may not even be synergistic and notes that, if they were, the distinction would not be important. However, it seems from the experiences of a number of countries that there may be some difference in emphasis between these two objectives, reflecting different "cultures" in different audit institutions ranging from a collaborative relationship between the auditor and the auditee (reflecting a focus on performance improvement) to a more adversarial one (reflecting a focus on accountability), where critical audit reports may evoke a defensive or contested response. This may also reflect in part the two main different traditions of institutional arrangements for external audit—the Court of Accounts tradition where the external auditor is legally a court, passing judgments on the actions and accounts of officials (represented by France and Brazil) and the Auditor-General tradition where the external auditor has no such status, but also has a special reporting relationship with the legislature (represented by Australia, Canada, New Zealand, Sweden, and the UK). There may be of necessity be a more "judgmental" approach where the audit institution has the status of a court.

On the objective of performance improvement it can be noted that in a number of cases the identification of budget savings is specifically identified as an objective of this work. For example, the UK National Audit Office has its own performance objective of identifying potential savings nine times the overall cost of its operations. The US GAO has a similar approach in identifying potential savings or value added from its reports. The Brazilian Court of Accounts (TCU) reports annually on the percentage of its performance auditing recommendations adopted by the executive and the likely budget savings. And the UK Audit Commission (which audits local government entities) has stated that its prime objective is to assist local governments in achieving greater value for money. However, such an approach may lead to difficult debates about the level of such savings and whether they are attributable to audit work or were known anyway, which has led some countries (Australia) to eschew such an approach. Determining potential savings also requires detailed costing of all audit recommendations, which may be difficult.

The value added by external auditors is perceived by them to be independence and the professional audit standards which are required to be applied to the work—competence, due care, standards of planning, supervision and review, evidence and reporting, including consultation. The external public sector auditor also operates under a Code of Ethics and professional auditing standards promulgated by INTOSAI.[11] These codify such issues as required integrity, independence, objectivity, impartiality, professional secrecy, and competence. Arguably, such standards could also be developed by an "evaluation profession," which is emerging in some countries, assisted by the work of national and regional evaluation organizations which seek to promote high-quality, professional evaluation. The Canadian, American, European, and Australasian evaluation societies are major players in this area, and some have active involvement of their external audit institutions. The need for independent review may also be reinforced by the self-evaluation concept which is part of NPM, and as mentioned above by the fact that most performance information is prepared by the government organization which is managing the programs or activities.

Given the scope of the audit and the lack of a single criterion for arriving at conclusions, the performance audit report necessarily differs from the "short form" audit report on the financial statements. As INTOSAI standards state, "performance audit is wide ranging in nature and is more open to judgment and interpretation. As a consequence performance audit reports are varied and contain more discussion and reasoned argument" (Reporting Standard 4.0.21). This gives rise to two other issues which may impact on the auditor's independence—the making of recommendations for improvement and the impact on the relationship with auditees.

On the first issue, the performance improvement focus may include directly advising the auditee on how to improve performance measurement and management, as well as detailed audit recommendations on how performance might be improved. A traditional view of audit might perceive this as compromising the auditor's independence, in that the auditor is subsequently auditing systems which he/she has been involved in establishing. However, this does not accord with a more modern view of auditing. INTOSAI reporting standards state, inter alia:

- "Performance audits should not concentrate solely on criticism of the past but should be constructive. The auditors' conclusions and recommendations are an important aspect of the audit and, where appropriate, are written as a guide for action" (Reporting Standard 4.0.25).
- "Fairness implies the presentation of weaknesses or critical findings in such a way as to encourage correction, and to improve systems and guidance within the audited entity" (Reporting Standard 4.0.24).

Thus INTOSAI auditing standards now implicitly accept the importance of the external auditor adding value by contributing to performance improvement, and the making of recommendations for improvements is not perceived as compromising audit independence.[12]

In terms of relationships with auditees, both the Lima Declaration and INTOSAI standards refer to giving "due consideration to the points of view of the audited organizations in the audit findings and agreeing the facts with the audited entity to ensure they are complete, accurate and fairly presented in the audit report."[13] Thus there is a willingness by auditors to engage in a dialogue with the auditee on performance audit findings, which does not involve negotiating the conclusions of the audit. This is generally seen as enhancing the quality and likely impact of the audit, rather than compromising audit independence. Indeed it is the practice of many auditors to include auditee responses or comments in the audit report.

There is some debate, particularly among auditees, about the adequacy of audit skills to undertake substantive efficiency and, more particularly, effectiveness audits. However, it can be noted that to ensure a high-quality audit, performance audit staffing now routinely includes persons of varying professional backgrounds (for example, economics, management, engineering, social sciences), not just those with financial and compliance audit training and skills.[14] Even if such diverse professional skills are not part of the audit institution's staffing, they may be added to performance audit teams through consultancy arrangements. There is less debate on the adequacy of audit skills to undertake systemic performance audits, given traditional audit expertise in management and information systems.

Linking performance audits with the budget

A key issue is the link between performance audit activity and the budgetary process. To what extent do substantive and systemic performance audits feed into the budget dialogue, including any audit of performance indicators? In most countries there has been no direct study of the extent to which *substantive* performance audit studies have influenced budgetary decisions. In Australia an internal study by the Australian National Audit Office (ANAO) notes the difficulty of determining a causal relationship between performance audits and budget decisions. Nevertheless it documents a number of cases where performance audit reports have featured prominently in budget decisions, which appear to reflect performance audits focused on significant and topical issues with costed and specific recommendations for performance improvement. (See Box 6.1.)

Box 6.1 ANAO review

In 2005, the ANAO reviewed the impact of its performance audits and identified seven significant examples over the period 1999–2005 that demonstrated a direct link to budgetary initiatives. These included additional funding provided to the Taxation Office to realize efficiency gains and additional funding to strengthen quarantine operations, both following a detailed performance audit report. Other examples included changes in procedures for managing detention center contracts and the management of drought assistance programs.

The substantive performance audits of the UK Audit Commission, with their focus on identifying budgetary savings also appear to have a close link with the budgetary process.

It is clear that the link between performance indicators and budgetary allocations is necessarily an indirect one[15] in which performance information informs the budget process but does not control it through some mechanistic or rational link. The original New Zealand budget model of output-based appropriations suggested a direct linkage with outputs, but neither funding during the year nor the dialogue on the following year's budget appear to have been significantly influenced by the actual outputs produced.[16]

A key issue therefore is under what conditions public performance audit reports will feed into budget decision-making. The act of publication will in itself increase public and political pressure to implement performance audit recommendations. In addition, there are a number of other institutional factors which may increase the likelihood of recommendations being implemented, including:

- the extent to which there are formal requirements for a follow-up or response by the executive to the performance audit report. For example, Westminster-system countries (Australia, Canada, New Zealand, and the UK) typically have a system of Treasury minutes under which the Ministry of Finance (MoF) or equivalent is required to make a formal response to all audit reports, with this response being tabled in the parliament. In any case there is a well established parliamentary committee structure charged with following up audit reports. Even in the Court of Accounts tradition of auditing, although there is no direct constitutional relationship between the Court and the parliament, parliament is able to pursue matters raised in audit reports

- the extent to which cost savings or value gains are quantified in the audit report, and particularly whether they have been discussed and agreed with the organization being audited
- the extent to which parliament has committee structures in place to facilitate a linkage into budget decision-making. In many countries the parliamentary committee responsible for the review and follow-up of audit reports is the public accounts committee (or its equivalent), with no direct role in reviewing the government's proposed budget. In others countries (such as Germany), the roles of audit follow-up and budget scrutiny are combined
- the extent to which parliaments, which have budget-making powers independent of the executive branch, are interested in issues of performance when reviewing budget proposals. It appears that neither the Brazilian nor the US Congresses evince much interest in performance information, including performance audit reports.

The work of audit institutions in seeking to improve the quality of reported performance indicators which feed into the budget process, as discussed above, is another dimension of the linkage between performance auditing and performance budgeting. This appears particularly strong in Sweden, where the development of performance auditing focused upon the review of performance information which feeds into the budget process played an important role in developing and implementing the new results-based budgeting system developed from 1993 (see Sandberg and Larsson, 1996). This may also reflect the former status of the Swedish National Audit Office as an autonomous part of the MoF, with explicit responsibilities to assist in improving financial management. In any case it is one example of an audit institution playing an important role in the development of performance budgeting. It is also strong in the Netherlands and Australia, whose national audit institutions have played a significant role in reviewing the quality of performance information included in budget documents, in the former case involving a formal audit opinion on the performance information.

The Brazilian Court of Accounts has a special role in monitoring the physical and financial execution of public works projects and reporting to Congress to assist in decisions on budget allocations. This has a performance (efficiency) dimension through comparing physical progress to expenditures and budget.

A number of external audit institutions have carried out broad reviews of the operation of performance management initiatives, including performance budgeting. For example, the Canada Auditor-General's Office has had a long tradition of reviewing management reforms initiatives and seeking to support reforms to achieve a well functioning performance management system (see appendix). The US GAO has carried out reviews of such major performance management initiatives as the Government Performance and Results Act (GPRA) which is intended to bring about greater linkage between performance information and Congressional budget allocations, and of the Program Assessment and Review Tool (PART) used by the executive branch in formulating its budget proposals.

Conclusion

Performance auditing exhibits substantial differences between countries in terms of its origins, objectives, scope, and processes. While there has been significant discussion of performance auditing in professional and academic literature, there has been little discussion or analysis of its relationship with performance budgeting. However, in general it appears that performance auditing and performance budgeting have developed along separate paths, but recently have been brought more closely together through increasing emphasis on published performance indicators.

Clearly, rigorous and professional performance audits, on topical issues, whether substantive or systemic, can inform and improve a performance budgeting system. This appears to be the case in Sweden and also in Australia and the Netherlands. The linkage does not appear as strong in New Zealand, with its narrower focus on output measures in the formal budget system. In France it is too early to tell, given the very recent development of a performance budgeting approach (see Chapters 11 and 20). In Canada and the UK we do not as yet have enough evidence on the operation of performance budgeting and the impact of performance audit. In the US the position is complicated by the failure of Congress to embrace the performance budgeting concepts set out in its own legislation (the GPRA) which have been largely adopted by the executive branch. A similar position applies in Brazil, where the Congress has independent budget powers but has yet to embrace performance budgeting concepts, even though they are quite well developed in the executive branch.

Appendix: country summaries

Australia

The Australian National Audit Office has had a statutory mandate to carry out performance auditing since 1979, although at the earlier stages there was an emphasis on efficiency issues. It may review the economy, efficiency, and effectiveness of any public sector organization, program, or function—although, as in the case of the UK National Audit Office discussed below, it may not comment on the merits of government policy. Its performance audits will invariably include an assessment of the performance management system governing the organization, program, or function.

Reforms in the Australian budgetary process over the past 20 years have emphasized the importance of a performance culture supported by increased budgetary devolution and accountability. Performance information is presented in two main accountability documents: the portfolio budget statement (PBS) prepared by each department, and the annual reports of each department and agency. There is no formal requirement for this information to be audited. However, for both documents the ANAO has issued better practice guidance[17] to assist in improving performance measurement, in the former case jointly with the Department of Finance and Administration (ANAO, 2002; ANAO and Department of Finance and Administration, 2004). Portfolio budget statements reflect internal management and at the same time provide parliament with information to explain the proposed funding in terms of outcomes (including whole of government outcomes) and output classes and outputs. This information has also been used in the past for market testing of government activities, to determine whether they might be better contracted out to the private sector. Recent moves have seen greater emphasis placed on formalizing outcome measures as part of the budgetary process.

The requirements for annual reports are issued by the Department of Prime Minister and Cabinet and generally reflect information contained in the PBS. The ANAO has also in the past prepared reports reviewing the quality of performance information (ANAO, 2001, 2004) which have focused on the organization's performance framework, measurement and data quality, and quality of reporting.

Given the high profile of performance audit reports and the requirement for a formal response to them by the government, performance audits appear to have a significant impact on budget decisions. In an internal study the ANAO has identified a direct link between a number of its reports and budget decisions, including cases where it has identified the need for additional expenditures to improve performance.

It can be noted that in the State of Western Australia the Auditor-General has been required to provide a formal audit opinion on departmental and agency performance indicators in their annual reports since 1985 as well as to opine whether the organization has operated in an efficient manner. However, this mandate initially proved difficult to fulfill, given the evolving state of performance management and the perceived low value added of issuing large numbers of qualified audit reports. However, as performance management has developed to focus on a smaller number of key performance indicators (KPIs) and a closer linkage with the budget, moving from an output to an outcomes focus, the audit role has similarly developed. The Auditor-General reviews the appropriateness and quality of the performance indicators used in the budgetary process and the links between the indicators and budget decisions. In terms of the formal audit opinion, there has been a substantial reduction in the number of qualified audit reports on performance indicators in the past ten years.

Brazil

The Brazilian federal Court of Accounts (TCU) has a significant performance auditing role. First, it reviews the (four-volume) annual report of the President to Congress, which includes non-financial information as well as financial statements. Detailed performance indicators for each government program under the four-year National Plan (PPA) are primarily reviewed by the internal audit institution reporting to the MoF, the Federal Secretariat of Control (SFC), although the TCU may also review and comment on this work. The SFC operates its own database to monitor program objectives, expenditures, and results.

Second, the TCU carries out an extensive range of substantive effectiveness audits, in which it also makes detailed recommendations for improving performance. These focus on the priority social programs contained in the National Plan. The

TCU's annual report reviews the percentage of its recommendations adopted by the government and the estimated savings.

Finally, the TCU has a special role to oversee the implementation of major public works projects. The TCU reports on the physical and financial execution of these projects to Congress, to assist in decisions on the allocation of funds to these projects.

Canada

The Auditor-General Act of 1977 requires the Auditor-General to report to parliament on cases where it is observed that "money has been spent without due regard to economy or efficiency, or satisfactory measures have not been established to measure and report on the effectiveness of programs, where such procedure could appropriately and reasonable be implemented." This reflects the Canadian Comprehensive Auditing Foundation approach discussed earlier; there is substantive reporting on economy and efficiency, but not effectiveness, where the focus is on audit review of performance management systems. This performance auditing mandate followed the 1975 recommendations of an independent review committee.

Departments and agencies are required to monitor key aspects of the performance of their programs and operations as set out in key results commitments covering a three-year period, and to carry out appropriate evaluation and review. Central agencies have also regularly carried out major program and expenditure reviews. Performance management is the policy responsibility of the Treasury Board Secretariat, which prepares an annual report to parliament on the performance of departments and agencies, which also report performance in their annual reports to parliament. However, it does not appear that this reporting is against specific targets. Every department presents a Report on Plans and Priorities once the budget is passed, indicating how it intends to achieve the outcome results which have been set for it.

The Office of the Auditor-General (OAG) does not systematically audit the performance information presented to parliament, but may do so as part of a substantive performance audit and the review of a department or agency's performance management systems. Auditor-General's annual and special reports have commented generally on areas where performance management systems need improvement and cross-cutting issues and the OAG has a long history of proactive involvement in promoting improved performance management, as part of overall public sector management improvement. Examples are its 2000 report "Reporting Performance to Parliament: Progress too Slow" and its 2001 report on "Public Service Management Reform." Earlier studies in the late 1980s and 1990s included "Constraints on Productive Management in the Public Sector" and "Attributes of Well-Performing Organizations."

France

With the passing of the Loi Organique relative aux Lois des Finances (LOLF) in 2001, France has moved to restructure its budgetary system to one focusing on outcomes, with the first program budget being presented in 2004, and the system to be fully operational in the 2006 budget exercise (see Chapters by 11 and 20). The budget is broken down into some 47 missions and below that into around 150 programs and 500 sub-programs or activities. In return for increased budget and management flexibility program managers are required to produce agreed results, as set out in an annual performance plan (PAP) attached to the budget law, which contains main goals, performance indicators, expected results or targets, and expected costs. At year end actual results are reported in an annual performance report (RAP) attached to the budget review law. Overall some 1,500 performance indicators have been produced based on guidance produced by the Ministry of Finance, the parliament and the Cour des Comptes (Court of Accounts) for those who will produce, use, and verify the performance information. The indicators are required to be documented in such a way that they can be verified.

The Cour des Comptes has a broad performance auditing role, which includes substantive reviews of performance. Studies of the "good use of funds" have long been combined with studies of the "proper and legal use of funds." Although these reports were not generally made public, a 1991 decision of the Conseil d'Etat empowered the Court to undertake and publish specific audit reports. With the new performance budgeting approach, its work in this area is expanding to include examination of the "coherence and reliability" of the information in the budget documents, both ex ante and ex post. It may also comment on significant variances between targets and results. Its work in this area is complemented with an interdepartmental program audit committee (CIAP), comprising Inspectors-General of Finance from ministries, which reviews the quality of the information and the analysis contained in the annual performance plans and annual performance reports.

The Netherlands

The Ministry of Finance is responsible for coordinating performance measurement and reporting, with individual ministries responsible for measuring the performance of their policies and management. From 2001 a system of outcomes-based budgeting has been introduced and performance information covering both efficiency and effectiveness is required by the Government Accounts Act to be included in the budget documents. In addition the annual report of each ministry and a consolidated annual report of the government focus on the question of the achievement of goals as set out in the budget and their costs. There is thus a focus on increasing the informational value of the two major accountability documents—the budget documents and the annual reports. The Government Accounts Act allows performance indicators to be developed from in-depth expenditure evaluations, as set out in a separate regulation on performance data and evaluation.

Ministers are required to present a statement on management control, which includes the adequacy of internal systems to convert the budget inputs to appropriate outputs and outcomes, and this is included in each ministry's annual report.

The Court of Audit has a statutory mandate to review and report on efficiency and effectiveness, including reviews of performance measurement systems, administrative systems and program effectiveness, (but not questioning government policies) dating from 1976. It carried out program effectiveness audits and may also review those undertaken by ministries and agencies themselves. Under the Government Accounts Act it must express an opinion on the quality of non-financial information included in the government's annual report, including information on outcomes and outputs, covering both their reliability and appropriateness/relevance. In doing this it would prefer to rely on the work of the internal audit directorate of each ministry as it does for the audit of financial information, but this internal role has not yet been developed. Overall the Court considers further work is needed within government on developing good performance information, particularly outcomes, and has indicated that it will actively participate in this work. It can be noted that the Court expressed reservations in a 1997 report about the decision-making relevance of performance indicators developed earlier under Ministry of Finance guidance.

New Zealand

The Office of the Auditor-General has a broad performance-auditing mandate which enables it to examine the extent to which a public entity is carrying out its activities effectively and efficiently and complying with its statutory obligations, whether any waste may have resulted and whether there may have been lack of probity. Fifteen performance audits were completed in 2004/05—a relatively small portion of the OAG work at less than 10 percent, but the OAG's five-year strategy calls for an increase in this percentage and additional staff are being recruited to carry out performance audits.

As part of the financial audit, the OAG also expresses an audit opinion on the service performance (outputs) reports required from most public entities, which report actual performance covering quantity, quality, timing, and location for each class of output compared with targets, and form part of the financial statements of each public entity. The OAG's work here is governed by its Auditing Standard 4, the Audit of Service Performance Reports and by the Institute of Chartered Accountants of New Zealand standards for reporting performance information. The OAG's standard requires the auditor to form a judgment about the appropriateness of the performance measures, meaning that they must be relevant, complete, and understandable. The standard provides guidance on what tests might be applied to determine this. Reliability of the information is also to be tested through evaluating the systems and processes which produce the information. Where the auditor considers that the performance measures are "fundamentally misleading or senseless," and where those performance measures are "significant" (guidance on determining significance is also provided) these concerns must be discussed with management. "Special circumstances" which are also set out in the standard must be taken into account in any decision to issue a qualified audit report on a performance report.

The OAG standard also requires the auditor to review draft performance targets and measures and the processes for establishing those measures in consultation with management before public consultation and formal approval of the measures, thus providing for "upstream" audit involvement.

The OAG has also been proactive in promoting improved reporting of public sector performance, and its January 2002 report on Reporting Public Sector Performance (second edition) aimed to stimulate discussion about how public entities set direction and measure and report performance, and thereby improve the level of accountability—going well beyond the statement of service performance into issues of outcomes. This guidance supplements other guidance provided by both the Treasury and the State Services Commission on statements of service performance and annual reports.

Sweden

Performance management in Sweden reflects its governmental system in which most public services are provided by autonomous agencies, subject to some general policy supervision by umbrella ministries. In return for their significant autonomy agencies are required to achieve results. The Ministry of Finance, together with the National Financial Management Authority (ESV) has overall responsibility for the development of performance measurement systems, with parliament and the government determining what is to be achieved or objectives within the 47 expenditure policy areas, ministries specifying what is to be measured and agencies determining the relevant performance measures. Performance measurement tends to focus on its use in performance improvement and resource allocation through the budget, as well an accountability mechanism. Performance monitoring and evaluation are closely linked with the budgetary process (ESV, 2003).

Agencies prepare an annual report which includes financial, performance, and other information—including how they have met the objectives set by government for their operations, which forms the basis of a performance dialogue between ministries and agencies. The government also prepares a consolidated annual report for the central government sector setting out objectives aimed at and results achieved, and agencies thereafter present their budget request which sets out their objectives and results achieved, which together with the annual reports form the basis of detailed budget reviews by the relevant parliamentary committee. Performance information is further integrated into the budgetary process through special performance reports to parliament on various expenditure areas during the year.

Performance auditing dates from the early 1990s and was the main task of the National Audit Office (RRV), after financial auditing was largely devolved to agencies themselves. Audit is seen as having a moral responsibility to ensure that action is taken on its reports and has had an important role in bedding down results-based management and budgeting through promoting the development of the related performance indicators for the results-based budgeting system introduced from 1993.

The RRV was reconstituted in 2003 as a body headed by three separate and equal Auditors-General reporting to parliament as well as the government, and has a major performance auditing role which reflects the responsibilities of agency management for efficient operations, reliable reporting, and compliance with regulations (RRV, 2000). The RRV may comment on material cases where efficiency has not been achieved and identify possible efficiency gains. It reviews (but does not formally attest) the performance information in terms of whether the information published is true and fair. It will indicate cases where it considers that the information is not truly and fairly presented, is not free from significant errors, or is incomplete in meeting decision-makers' needs. That is, the reporting is on an exceptions basis. However, such adverse audit reports have been rare. This information is available to parliament when considering budget requests, so that there is considerable emphasis in ensuring that reliable and relevant information is available to decision-makers.

Finally, the RRV also plays a consultative role in assisting agencies to improve their performance measurement.

Although there has been no systematic study of the use of performance auditing findings in budget formulation, it can be noted that apart from the close integration of performance issues into the budget, the government is required to report to parliament annually on actions taken on RRV reports, and this may feed into parliament's review of the budget.

The United Kingdom

The National Audit Office has since 1983 had a formal mandate to examine and report on the economy, efficiency, and effectiveness of government organizations, programs, activities, and systems, although it may not go so far as to question "the merit of [Government] policy objectives." The 1983 mandate to some extent formalized a role which had already been developed. The formal extension of the NAO's mandate was strongly supported by the then Prime Minister, Margaret Thatcher, with her focus on efficiency and budget savings. About 50 percent of NAO resources are devoted to performance auditing through studies of "value for money."

The NAO has a Directorate of Performance Measurement to coordinate its work on performance measurement in financial audits, reviews of governance arrangements of central governance bodies, and value for money studies. As part of this role the NAO has provided guidance to public sector organizations on developing performance measurement systems as well as evaluations of these systems, as reflected in two major reports (NAO, 2000, 2001). It also collaborates with executive government in promoting good practices, through jointly issued guidance (HM Treasury et al., 2001, 2003) and through participation in the Performance Information Panel, a multi-stakeholder advisory group which has reviewed the robustness of draft performance measurement arrangements for departmental Public Service Agreement (PSA) targets (see Chapter 12). The Directorate also provides advice on the quality of performance data, covering both performance measures and the information systems which collect them, when requested by central government agencies.

For departments and ministries performance measurement now focuses on targets as set out in PSAs, begun in 1998 and negotiated with the Treasury, which cover a period of three years ahead or until the next envisaged expenditure review, which focus on desired outcomes, with related outputs set out in service delivery plans. The NAO may also validate these performance measurement systems.

The NAO plays a role in the external validation of performance measures. External validation to provide reasonable assurance of the quality of performance information for agencies and non-departmental public bodies is required where the achievement of targets affects the pay of staff. In all other cases it is left to the discretion of the responsible minister as to whether external validation should be required, but it is expected that validation will be undertaken where performance information is used to inform key strategic decisions such as allocation of resources or reporting to parliament. External validation can be provided by the NAO, by other external experts, or by the organization's own internal audit unit.

Although there has been no systematic review of the use of value for money audits in budget decisions, it can be noted that the NAO measures its own performance partly on achieving the objective of identifying budgetary savings from its performance audits of nine times its annual operating costs. And departments agree their PSA targets as part of the spending review process, so that in principle, resource allocation decisions have a link with performance.

For local government the Audit Commission specifies the standard performance indicators that local authorities are required to produce and publish each year, and also publishes a comparative set of these indicators, covering all local government units, to enable the performance of different local authorities to be compared. Auditors appointed by the Commission check that the systems used are robust enough to produce reliable information. In addition "best value performance indicators" reflecting the national interest in the delivery of local services are required, with an emphasis on targets that reflect continuous improvement. Auditors review whether the systems are producing reliable information and whether the required "best value performance plans" have been prepared according to the legislation.

The Audit Commission also carries out major value for money studies of public sector services which identify areas where performance can be improved and savings made in the delivery of local government services.

The United States

The Government Accountability Office assists Congress in its oversight of the executive branch, and about 70 percent of its work is in response to specific requests by Congress. Its performance auditing role covers economy, efficiency, and effectiveness, and much of its work is in-depth program evaluation. The scope of this work is defined in its auditing standards, commonly known as "the yellow book," which was updated in 1994. While there is no formal audit of the extensive performance information produced by agencies which cover effectiveness, efficiency, and service quality, the GAO's performance audits may review performance management systems and the quality of performance information in individual organizations.

The GAO also reviews cross-cutting performance management issues; for example, it has carried out a major review of the implementation of the Government Performance and Results Act, 1993, under which agencies are required to develop five-year strategic plans, set annual program goals, and develop output measures through annual performance plans and reports and link them with budget submissions. It has also reviewed the Program Assessment and Review Tool initiated in 2002 by the executive branch to better link performance with the budget.

Its reporting to Congress, mainly on issues identified by Congress as requiring review, suggests that its performance audits should closely inform Congressional decisions on the budget. However, no detailed study has been made of the use of its performance audits by Congress in the budget process.

The GAO's own performance measurement stresses the identification of savings and value for money improvements identified in its reports, which it endeavors to quantify in its own annual report to Congress.

Notes

1. This chapter focuses on external auditing. However, some reference is made to internal audit arrangements, and it can be seen that similar issues arise in internal audit.
2. Definitions of these three elements, commonly referred to as the "three E's," are not provided in the INTOSAI standards. However, there is extensive public sector management literature to assist in defining these concepts, some of it based on drawing a distinction between outputs (physical measures of goods or services delivered), which reflect efficiency and outcomes (which measure the achievement or otherwise of program objectives through those outputs), which reflect effectiveness. A new classification of service delivery quality, which may encompass elements of both efficiency and effectiveness, is also sometimes added. In all cases inputs, reflected in costs, are the other side of the performance coin.
3. See Zavelberg (1996, p. 201) for a description of this role. It can be noted that the President of the Federal Court of Audit is also designated as the Federal Commissioner for Efficiency.
4. NPM can be distinguished from earlier moves to results-based management concepts by its comprehensive approach, involving both management devolution and performance accountability. See OECD (1996b, 2005) for a fuller description of NPM developments in OECD member countries.
5. See Shand and Anand (1996) for a more detailed discussion of the origins of performance auditing. It can also be noted that INTOSAI does not appear to perceive performance auditing as a necessary part of the external audit function. Its discussion of the basic nature of audit in the Lima Declaration of Guidelines on Auditing Precepts adopted by INTOSAI in 1977 refers to legality, regularity, economy, efficiency of *financial management* (italics added), although this latter term is not defined. However, it also states that "the full scope of government audit includes regularity and performance audit."
6. For example, the Australian Financial Management Improvement Program which commenced in 1983, the UK Next Steps initiative of 1990, the Canada Public Service 2000 initiative of 1990 and the US National Performance Review of 1994.
7. See OECD-PUMA (1997) for a more detailed description of some of these changes to budget systems.
8. Chile, which has a well developed formal system of program evaluation led by the central budget office of the Ministry of Finance, is a good example.
9. The Finnish National Audit Office and the New Zealand Office of the Auditor-General are two institutions which have such a role.
10. For example, a 1990 Australian Auditor-General report criticized the administration of a grant program for having no clear criteria for the allocation of grants beyond apparent political rationality.
11. INTOSAI, Code of Ethics and Auditing Standards, available at <www.intosai.org>. However, there is no mechanism available to INTOSAI to enforce these standards, unlike auditing standards promulgated by the international accountancy profession through the International Federation of Accountants (IFAC). Public sector external auditors may also operate under their own local auditing standards and the international standards on auditing promulgated by IFAC.
12. However, it can be noted that some audit organizations believe that such recommendations should be general rather than specific, that is, the recommendations should indicate

the improvements needed but not necessarily the details of how to achieve or implement them.

13. Lima Declaration (see note 5 above) Section 20.2 and INTOSAI Reporting Standard 4.0.24 respectively.
14. Also, the Lima Declaration states that if special skills are not available among the audit staff, the national audit institution may call on external experts as necessary.
15. This issue is discussed in Moynihan (2003).
16. See Shand and Norman (2005) for a more detailed discussion of the New Zealand approach.
17. ANAO practice has been to develop better practice guides across a wide range of issues, so as to assist in improving public sector performance.

References

ANAO, 2001, "Performance Information in Portfolio Budget Statements," *ANAO Audit Report* 18 (Canberra: ANAO), November.

——, 2002, *Better Practice Guide. Performance Information in Portfolio Budget Statements* (Canberra: ANAO), May.

——, 2004, "Performance Management in the Australian Public Service," *ANAO Audit Report* 6 (Canberra: ANAO), August.

ANAO and Department of Finance and Administration, 2004, *Better Practice Guide. Better Practice in Annual Performance Reporting* (Canberra: ANAO and Department of Finance and Administration), April.

Barzelay, M., 1996a, "Performance Auditing and the New Public Management: Changing Roles and Strategies of Central Audit Institutions," in OECD, *Performance Auditing and the Modernization of Government* (Paris: OECD).

——, 1996b, "Central Audit Institutions and Performance Auditing: A Comparative Analysis of Organizational Strategies in the OECD." Unpublished paper, October.

ESV, 2003, *Performance Management in Swedish Central Government* (Stockholm: ESV).

HM Treasury, Cabinet Office, and National Audit Office, 2003, *Setting Key Targets for Executive Agencies: A Guide* (London: HM Treasury), November.

HM Treasury, Cabinet Office, National Audit Office, Audit Commission, and Office for National Statistics, 2001, *Choosing the Right Fabric: A Framework for Performance Information* (London: HM Treasury), March.

INTOSAI, 1992, Auditing Standards (issued by the Auditing Standards Committee at the XIVth Congress of INTOSAI, 1992, Washington DC, amended by the XVth Congress of INTOSAI, 1995, Cairo).

Moynihan, D., 2003, *Performance-Based Budgeting: Beyond Rhetoric*, World Bank PREM Public Sector Note No. 78, February (Washington: World Bank).

NAO, 2000, *Good Practice in Performance Reporting in Executive Agencies and Non-Departmental Public Bodies* (London: NAO), March.

——, 2001, *Measuring the Performance of Government Departments* (London: NAO), March.

OECD, 1996a, *Performance Auditing and the Modernization of Government* (Paris: OECD).

——, 1996b, *Governance in Transition: Public Management Reforms in OECD Countries* (Paris: OECD).

——, 2002, *Overview of Results Focused Management and Budgeting in OECD Member Countries* (Paris: OECD).

——, 2005, *Modernizing Government—The Way Forward* (Paris: OECD).

OECD-PUMA, 1997, *In Search of Results: Performance Management Practices* (Paris: OECD).

Pollitt, C., and H. Summa, 1997a, "Performance Audit: Travelers Tales," in *Evaluation for the 21st Century: A Handbook*, ed. E. Chelimsky and W. Shadish (Thousand Oaks, Calif., and London: Sage).

——, 1997b, "Performance Audits and Their Neighbours: Concepts and Practices in Five SAIs." Paper presented to the Conference of the European Evaluation Society, Stockholm.
RRV, 2000, *Audit Guide* (Stockholm: RRV).
Sandberg, B., and K. Larsson, 1996, "Role of Auditing in Performance Improvement in Sweden," in OECD, *Performance Auditing and the Modernization of Government* (Paris: OECD).
Shand, D., and P. Anand, 1996, "Performance Auditing in the Public Sector: Approaches and Issues in OECD Member Countries," in OECD, *Performance Auditing and the Modernization of Government* (Paris: OECD).
Shand, D., and R. Norman, 2005, "Performance Budgeting in New Zealand." Paper prepared for the IMF Conference on Performance Budgeting, December.
Zavelberg, H.G., 1996, "Legislatures and Performance Auditing: The German Experience," in OECD, *Performance Auditing and the Modernization of Government* (Paris: OECD).

Part Two

Linking Budgets to Performance

7
Making Performance Budgeting Work

Marc Robinson

Performance budgeting practice is not monolithic. There are different forms of performance budgeting which seek to link results and funding in different ways. Performance budgeting systems also vary in respect to their objectives—in particular, some place more emphasis upon allocative efficiency than upon technical efficiency, or vice versa. They also have, as discussed in Part One, differing information requirements. In Part Two, we turn our attention from information requirements to the type of link between results and funding which performance budgeting systems strive to build. The primary objective here is to identify and assess the mechanisms by which each form of performance budgeting aims to achieve its intended impact upon allocative and/or technical efficiency, with the aim of deepening our understanding of what approaches to performance budgeting work and in what context.

In surveying the key issues for Part Two, it is convenient to start by considering those forms of performance budgeting which aim primarily to improve allocative efficiency, particularly through better expenditure prioritization in the central budget. This is followed by a discussion of the key issues which arise in respect to newer forms of performance budgeting which seek to develop rather tighter links between funding and results, often with the primary objective of inducing better agency-level performance.

Ensuring performance information is used for expenditure prioritization

As discussed in Chapter 1, expenditure classification is a basic tool of all forms of performance budgeting which aim to improve expenditure prioritization. Good expenditure prioritization requires the classification of public expenditure in the budget process into categories which facilitate allocative decision-making. The most fundamental and enduring instrument for this purpose has been the program classification of expenditure, the methodology of which is discussed in Chapter 5. Some forms of performance budgeting, with less enduring influence, have sought to take the principle of expenditure classification to facilitate allocative decision-making purposes even further. Zero-base budgeting, for example, breaks down expenditure into a larger number of "decision packages"—usually within programs—in order to systematically assess options for increasing or reducing expenditure directed to particular objectives. The intention is, in either case, the same—that information about the costs and benefits of programs or decision packages will be used by decision-makers, together with information about alternative expenditure options, to make better decisions about where limited public funds can be used to best effect. To do this, information about program costs must, of course, be accompanied by information on program results (see Chapter 4).

Producing the *information* to permit better expenditure prioritization does not, however, ensure that this information will be used. There are many cases even in recent years of countries where considerable effort has been made to introduce program classification, and to develop measures of program performance, without any significant use having apparently been made of that information by budget decision-makers. It is for this reason that, as Schick (2002, p. 23) notes, "there is consensus these days that changing budget classifications does not itself change budget allocations." Even within OECD countries, as Teresa Curristine reports in Chapter 8, a large increase in the availability of performance information has not been matched by a corresponding increase in its use in the budget process.

There are, of course, a number of possible explanations for such a state of affairs. The problem may lie in part with the nature or adequacy of the performance information itself. It may reflect inflexibilities built into public expenditure—such as revenue earmarking and rigid civil service employment practices which make it hard to reallocate public employment from low priority to higher-priority purposes. It may be, more fundamentally, that political systems are so dysfunctional that there is negligible interest in efficiency and effectiveness as criteria for expenditure prioritization decisions. But even if none of these types of problems exist, and the ground is ripe for information on the costs and benefits of programs to have a substantial impact on the expenditure allocation, this will not happen unless the budget process facilitates the use of this information. Expressed differently, to the extent that "traditional" budget processes tend to have an inbuilt bias towards allocative inertia and so-called "incrementalism,"[1] performance budgeting is unlikely to succeed in improving expenditure prioritization unless the budget process is reformed by the inclusion of mechanisms and procedures which aim to facilitate allocative flexibility and which, more specifically, facilitate the effective use of performance information in allocative decisions.

What form should such expenditure prioritization mechanisms and procedures take if they are to work well? It cannot be expected that there should be a single answer to this question. Different mechanisms and procedures may be appropriate for different political and administrative systems and cultures. Nevertheless, international experience can shed significant light on what can work and what is unlikely to work. It is for this reason that a number of the chapters in this part of the volume—both case studies and thematic pieces—focus upon expenditure prioritization processes and their relation to performance budgeting. By way of background to these studies, a number of overarching points may be identified. Many of the issues are considered in greater depth by Jim Brumby in Chapter 9 on performance budgeting and allocative efficency.

The first point is that *expenditure prioritization needs to be conducted as a systematic routine integrated with the budget process*. Thus, for example, the British spending review process (see Chapter 12 by Peter Smith) involves a routine of biennial reviews which lead directly to the setting of three-year ministry spending envelopes. Another successful prioritization mechanism has been the Australian Expenditure Review Committee (ERC), a cabinet committee supported by the finance ministry which was established at the national government level in the early 1980s with the express task of reviewing both existing programs and new spending proposals in such a way as to feed into annual budget decisions (Xavier, 1998; Campos and Pradhan, 1999). The case study in this part of the volume by John Pierce and Michael Di Francesco (Chapter 14) outlines how a version of this system works in Australia's largest and most economically important State, New South Wales.

As both of these examples illustrate, expenditure prioritization tends to work best when the budget is put on a multi-annual basis, through either multi-year allocations or a system of rolling forward expenditure estimates. Expenditure prioritization is about choices between alternative policies, and the fiscal impact of specific policy choices can often not be measured by their cost in the prospective budget year. This point has long been recognized by performance budgeting advocates, well before the recent resurgence of interest in medium-term budgeting. The original US program budgeting system (PPBS), for example, aimed to plan expenditure over at least a five-year time horizon (Anshen, 1967, p. 356).

Expenditure prioritization-setting is most likely to be successful in terms of changing the actual allocation of resources if it is managed by the Ministry of Finance. Past experience with ad hoc reviews carried out by individuals appointed from outside government[2] was generally disappointing. So also has been experience with the model, common in many Latin American and African countries, where separate planning/development ministries develop medium/long-term development plans which set strategic priorities which are supposed to guide annual budget formulation. Because such planning is conducted away from the budget process and by people who are not budget decision-makers, it all too easily becomes a paper exercise with little real impact on the allocation of resources. This problem was also experienced in the implementation of Medium-Term Expenditure Frameworks (MTEFs) in countries where the sectoral expenditure prioritization component of the MTEF process was carried out in isolation from the budget process, either by consultants or by ministries other than the MoF (Le Houerou and Taliercio, 2002).

As the British and Australian examples make clear, the expenditure prioritization process must include *systematic routines for the review of existing programs*—that is, of ongoing "base" public expenditure. All too often, it is only *new* spending initiatives which receive any analytic attention in the budget preparation process. Many countries have established processes for the appraisal of new expenditure proposals, while requiring nothing from line agencies by way of justification of expenditure on established programs. Even in countries where there is an explicit strategic phase in the budget process—for example, a cabinet meeting early in the budget process to set overall spending priorities (see Chapter 9) or a development planning process of the type described above—"priority-setting" is all too often more about identifying new priorities for expenditure than about identifying low-priority areas which can be cut to make room for these new priorities. The absence of systematic processes for the review of base expenditure virtually guarantees that hopes about the impact of performance budgeting will be disappointed, since it is precisely in the review of existing programs that performance information can be expected to make its greatest contribution.

It is crucial that expenditure review should not be confined to so-called "discretionary" expenditure, but should encompass the full gamut of public expenditure. All too often, expenditure on items such as civil service salaries and "mandatory" items such as social security benefits is treated as untouchable and exempt from review. Where this happens, expectations of what performance budgeting can deliver are bound to be disappointed, as the Spanish case study (Chapter 17) indicates. Successful expenditure prioritization processes set up in the UK, Australia, and elsewhere make no distinction between discretionary and non-discretionary expenditure, and do not exclude standing appropriations from the expenditure review spotlight.[3] They recognize that all expenditure is flexible in the medium to long term, and that reducing the inflexibilities which inhibit the reallocation of funds is an important prerequisite of successful performance budgeting.

Important lessons about how to organize expenditure prioritization were learned from experience with the earliest form of program budgeting (especially US PPBS—see Chapter 1) and, subsequently, zero-base budgeting (ZBB). These systems strove to establish a central expenditure prioritization mechanism which was comprehensive—in the sense of encompassing the whole of the general government sector each year—and quite detailed. They were highly *centralist*, assuming "control in detail from the centre, as opposed to delegated authority, incentive structures and local initiative" (Spackman, 2002, p. 8), and viewed expenditure prioritization as essentially an exercise in central *planning*.[4]

Experience with these systems demonstrated that such comprehensive and detailed central expenditure prioritization mechanisms are too much for the budget process to handle. "Bounded rationality"—practical limits to how much information can be absorbed and how much complex rational calculation can be performed (see Chapter 2)—limits the scope for central planning of expenditure allocation in government just as it limits the scope for central planning of the economy as a whole. As a recent review of the history of performance budgeting by the Florida government put it:

> One important lesson to be learned from past experience is that ambitions of budget reforms have often outstripped the analytic and information management capacity of government agencies. The labor-intensive nature of these systems led to a recognition that they were not feasible. (Office of Program Policy Analysis and Government Accountability, 1997)

The failure of detailed comprehensive planning was particularly striking in the case of ZBB. The attempt to review every program *from bottom up* every fiscal year—that is, to systematically consider all options ranging from cutting out programs to expanding them—proved to be impossibly ambitious. Even a scaled-down version of ZBB known as "alternative budgeting" proved so cumbersome that it was abandoned quickly in all jurisdictions which tried it out.[5]

Central expenditure prioritization mechanisms therefore need to be designed in such a way that they facilitate the use of relevant information for good allocative decision-making while recognizing the limits on the capacity of central decision-makers to analyze and plan. A number of alternative approaches have been taken to this problem. One is to conduct periodic rather than annual reviews of priorities. The British Spending Review process is a good example—not only are the Spending Reviews biennial rather than annual, but the more in-depth "Comprehensive" Spending Reviews are conducted only infrequently (see Chapter 12). Another alternative is to aim for comprehensive review of expenditure priorities on a staggered timetable over a number of years. Thus the US Program Assessment Rating Tool (PART), discussed by Denise Fantone in Chapter 10, has been applied in a cycle in which 20 percent of government programs are reviewed, so that all programs are reviewed over a five-year cycle. Some other countries (for example, Chile, Australia) have taken a less deliberately structured approach, reviewing selected areas of public expenditure each year on the basis, not of a predetermined review plan, but of top-level judgments about which programs are most ripe for review.

There is widespread contemporary recognition that, in part because of the limits of central planning, central budget decision-makers should in general focus their attention on broad expenditure allocations—particularly at the sectoral level—and that it is both necessary and desirable that there should be substantial decentralized allocative decision-making at the line agency level (World Bank, 1998). This raises many important questions about the interface between central and decentralized expenditure allocation processes. A particularly important issue here is that of how the central budget process may be designed to create incentives for, and pressures on, line agencies to keep their own expenditure priorities under active review, and to make maximum use of performance information for this purpose. The more expenditure prioritization is carried out at the decentralized level, the more well-designed performance budgeting systems need to concern themselves with how to improve resource allocation within line agencies as well as in the central budget process. The starting point of encouraging agencies themselves to take good expenditure prioritization seriously is, however, to create good, performance-informed expenditure prioritization at the center. If line agencies know that central decision-makers will look hard at the performance of their programs when determining their budget funding, they will be motivated not only to prioritize their own budgets much more effectively, but also to improve program design and management. This, as Fantone makes clear, has been one of the aims of the US Office of Management and Budget in its implementation of the PART system.

The effectiveness of expenditure prioritization processes depends in part on the overall quality of the budget preparation process. It is particularly important that the initial macro-fiscal steps of the budget process be well-managed. Aggregate fiscal discipline and good expenditure prioritization have a mutually reinforcing effect. It is only in the context of a hard budget constraint that priority-setting can be effective—otherwise the temptation is to respond to new expenditure priorities by continually increasing aggregate expenditure, rather than reallocating expenditure from lower-priority or less effective programs. As Brumby points out in Chapter 9, there are strong grounds to believe that the converse is also true: namely, that good expenditure prioritization facilitates the enforcement of fiscal discipline. Better expenditure prioritization processes might be expected to deliver the capacity to achieve better-quality fiscal consolidation when and if necessary—because, if aggregate expenditure needs to be cut, an improved capacity to target cuts at lower-priority areas should in principle both make fiscal consolidation less difficult than it might otherwise be, and also make it more enduring. Moreover, a capacity to allocate expenditure more effectively should contribute to restraint in the longer-run rate of growth of public expenditure.

It is therefore not surprising that fiscal stress has not infrequently provided the impetus for the introduction of performance budgeting systems aimed at improving expenditure prioritization. A good recent example of this is Brazil, where severe fiscal crisis in 1995–96 (subsequently compounded by broader macroeconomic crisis) led directly to the introduction of a new priority-setting process—initially in the form of the *Brasil em Ação* mechanism (1996–98) aimed at prioritizing 42 major programs, and subsequently the development of improved systems of multi-annual performance budgeting. These budgeting reforms were closely integrated with reforms of aggregate fiscal policy-making (IMF, 2001). In other countries, less acute—but nevertheless very real—aggregate fiscal stress has played a similarly important role in promoting performance budgeting developments. Thus the case study of Spain (Chapter 17) makes it clear that the fiscal pressure associated with the Maastricht fiscal rules has been a crucial driving force behind performance budgeting reforms in that country.

Turning from the nature of the expenditure prioritization process to the actors in that process, the case studies in this part of the volume highlight the crucial role of the Ministry of Finance. If there is to be good expenditure prioritization, MoF officials must be able to advise political leaders on reallocation options—and, in particular, on where cuts may be made to fund new priorities and imperatives. It is therefore essential that the MoF concern itself closely with the type of performance information with which it is provided by line agencies, in order to assure itself that this information is what it and the political leadership require. The type of involvement which this requires is well-illustrated in the guiding role which, as Brice Lannaud makes clear in Chapter 11, the French finance ministry has played in the development of both the program classification and performance measurement system which underpins the new French performance budgeting system. Similarly, in Chile (see Chapter 13 by Marcela Guzmán) the budget directorate of the MOF not only specifies the key performance indicators to be provided by line agencies in the budget process, but also manages the system of program evaluation which is the distinctive feature of Chilean performance budgeting. In the US, it is Office of Management and Budget examiners—not outside evaluators, or other civil servants—who use PART to systematically gather from line agencies the information and assign summary performance ratings to programs for use in the budget process. As this example makes clear, it is critical that MoF officials carry out their own assessments of program performance, using the information available to them. They must, in short, become program analysts as well as financial analysts. This point is all too often overlooked by countries introducing performance budgeting, as is illustrated in the Spanish case study (Chapter 17), in which Ruiz-Herta et al. identify as a key problem the "imbalance" which exists between the volume of performance information which the MoF requests of line ministries, and its capacity to process and analyze that information.

The central role of the MoF makes the bureaucratic "muscle" of the MoF an important determinant of the success of performance budgeting in improving expenditure prioritization. This is a point which is well-illustrated by the examples of Chile and the UK, in both of which the finance ministry and finance minister have great authority vis-à-vis line agencies and ministers.

As crucial as the role of the MoF is, expenditure prioritization cannot be regarded as a purely technical task carried out by civil servants based solely upon technical criteria. As Curristine emphasizes in her overview of performance budgeting in OECD countries (Chapter 8), expenditure prioritization is necessarily political, and electoral calculus is inevitably important in the budgetary decisions taken by political leaders. To set up an expenditure prioritization mechanism which explicitly or implicitly excludes political input is almost certainly to doom it to irrelevance. In general, therefore, expenditure prioritization procedures need to be designed so as to feed useful information on the costs and results of existing programs, and expenditure alternatives, to the top political budget decision-makers, who can then weigh this information together with other relevant considerations including electoral pressures. This information, as Pierce and Di Francesco emphasize in Chapter 14, must be provided in a usable summary form which recognizes the severe time constraints facing political leaders.

The corollary of this, as Curristine again emphasizes, is that expenditure prioritization mechanisms will not work without strong commitment from the political executive. Not even the best-designed performance budgeting system can be expected to have any positive impact on expenditure prioritization if the political leadership of the executive branch is indifferent to the efficiency and effectiveness of public expenditure. One of the best examples of the positive impact of strong political commitment is the UK, where the Chancellor of the Exchequer (finance minister) actively leads the Spending Reviews and both the reviews and the associated Public Service Agreements have the strong support of the Prime Minister.[6] The best way of organizing political leadership of the expenditure prioritization process will vary from country to country, depending in part on the political system. In countries with a strong executive presidency—Chile being a case in point—the involvement of the President is of paramount importance. On the other hand, the more powerful the cabinet (council of ministers), the more important it is that expenditure prioritization be a systematically-organized cabinet process. Thus, an important feature of the Australian ERC mechanism referred to above is the way in which it secures cabinet consensus on key spending priorities, and strengthens the hand of the finance minister vis-à-vis spending ministers.[7] This is also one of the objectives which has been pursued in Spain through the establishment of the cabinet-level Spending Policy Commission which, as Ruiz-Huerta et al. make clear in Chapter 17, has been intended as an instrument to transform the spending prioritization into a multilateral negotiation process rather than a purely bilateral one between the finance ministry and each spending minister.

It is often asserted that it is crucial to the success of performance budgeting that legislators learn to make extensive use of performance information when voting on the expenditure priorities established in the annual budget. However, such hopes have in practice usually been disappointed. Thus Curristine reports survey results indicating that only 19 percent of OECD legislatures, and only 8 percent of members of legislative budget committees, make use of performance information in decision-making. Even in the UK, where the government has nailed its colors to the mast through explicit commitment to performance targets for public services, Smith (Chapter 12) reports that parliamentary scrutiny of performance against these targets has been rather limited. Perhaps a little more realism may be required in respect to parliamentary use of performance information. The time constraints, limited support services, and political incentives facing legislators are such that it may not be appropriate to expect too much from them by way of review of program performance. Moreover, in many political systems the actual power of the legislature over expenditure prioritization is quite limited. This is true, to a greater or lesser degree, in most parliamentary systems, where the fact that the political executive is drawn from the party or parties which control the parliament usually leaves real (as opposed to formal) power over expenditure prioritization in the hands of executive government. It is also true in a number of presidential systems where the budgetary power of the legislature is constitutionally constrained, often as a consequence of historical experience with legislative fiscal irresponsibility. Chile falls into this category, as also did France prior to the new budgeting reforms. Prior to the passage of the Loi Organique relative aux Lois de Finances (LOLF), the French parliament was unable to change in any way the allocation of resources in the budget proposed by the government. As Lannaud describes, a key breakthrough embodied in the LOLF is that the parliament has acquired the power to shift funds between "programs" within the same "mission" (although not between missions). France is unusual in that the prime impetus for the introduction of performance budgeting came from the legislature rather than executive government, and it will therefore be particularly interesting to see what use parliament makes use of its new powers, and of the extensive performance information with which it will be henceforth provided.

Linking results and funding more tightly to promote better agency performance

Improved expenditure prioritization is not the only objective of performance budgeting. Although it is the primary objective of program budgeting, there are other forms of performance budgeting which differ in the way in which they seek to link funding and results, and in the objectives which they aim to achieve by building that linkage. Chapter 1 identified three other performance budgeting mechanisms which have been an important part of recent performance budgeting developments, namely:

- funding-linked performance targets
- agency-level budgetary performance incentives
- formula funding.

None of these mechanisms are concerned with improving expenditure prioritization in the central budget. Rather, their aim is to put pressure on agencies to improve the effectiveness and/or efficiency with which they spend public money. To achieve this, each seeks to tighten further the link between funding and results. Program budgeting aims to deliver a significant, but nonetheless very loose, funding/results linkage—by ensuring that information on the effectiveness and efficiency of programs is systematically taken into account in making expenditure prioritization decisions. By contrast, the more contemporary performance budgeting mechanisms seek to build either or both tighter ex-ante and ex-post linkages between funding and results.

Tightening the ex-ante links between funding and results means relating the level of funding provided to each agency more closely to the results which that agency is *expected* to deliver with that funding. The tightest form of such linkage is formula funding, in which funding is a mathematical function of expected results. The idea of funding-linked performance targets, on the other hand, aims to ensure that targets are appropriate to the level of funding, so as to increase their credibility and motivational impact.

Performance-based financial incentives to agencies aim, by contrast, to tighten the ex-post linkage of funding to results. The linkage, in other words, flows from *actual* (rather than expected) performance to funding levels, and the expectation is that performance-contingent financial rewards or sanction will motivate agencies to perform better. The strongest form of performance-based financial incentive is that which is created by "purchaser-provider" models. As outlined in Chapter 1, in purchaser-provider systems funding is linked by formula to actual results ("payment-for-results") and, as a consequence, government agencies make profits or losses depending on their performance. "Performance bonuses" are a weaker version of the performance-based financial incentives mechanism, in which agencies receive top-up funding based on selected performance measures, as a supplement to core funding which is unrelated to actual performance.

One of the aims of the material in this part of the volume is to shed light on how well these mechanisms work, and under what circumstances. In this respect, certain key points emerge. The first is that the effort to build stronger links between funding and results has been most successful in *sectoral* performance budgeting systems. As Smith outlines in Chapter 12, the formula funding principle has been widely applied in the public sector in areas such as education and social services.

Perhaps the most striking example of the success of sectoral performance budgeting systems, however, is the "diagnosis related group" purchaser-provider system of hospital funding. There is strong evidence that this system has delivered significant improvements in technical efficiency and that fears that it would induce erosion of the quality and other perverse effects were largely unjustified.

It has not, on the other hand, proven possible to create such tight linkages at the level of the government budget as a whole. The "accrual output budgeting" experiment in New Zealand and Australia represented the most ambitious attempt ever to link funding and results tightly right across the budget sector, inspired by the purchaser-provider principle. As discussed in Chapter 16, it was not a success. A key reason for this is that the relationship between output and cost is, for many government services, too uncertain to permit a tight linkage of funding to the quantity of outputs delivered. The lesson to be learnt is that both the purchaser-provider mechanism, and the formula funding mechanism more generally, are impractical in the case of many public services.

At the level of the government budget as a whole, budget-linked performance targets seem to have worked better. The British Public Service Agreement (PSA) system, which Smith discusses in Chapter 12, appears to have been very successful in boosting public sector performance, although there is debate about perverse effects (see below). Two factors seem to have been particularly crucial to the success of the PSA system. The first is that the pressure on agencies to meet the targets is considerable, reflecting strong commitment from the political leadership. The second is that the targets are set as part of the budget process, under the leadership of the finance ministry and finance minister.

This contrasts markedly with experience elsewhere. Although the setting of agency-level performance targets has become quite common internationally—under the influence of the broader current of "managing-for-results" thinking—such target-setting is often beset by the problems that, first, the pressure on agencies to meet the targets is weak, and, second, that target-setting is carried out quite separately from, and often with no regard to, funding decisions. Underlying this, as Pollitt (1999, p. 5) notes, is the fact that "financial management and performance management systems tend to develop separately as parallel systems that may or may not (or only to varying degrees) be harmonious or even compatible." In many countries, government-wide performance management systems—including the processes for setting performance targets—are managed by institutions separate from the finance ministry (President's offices, Prime Minister's departments, or civil service commissions), without any links to the budget process.

By contrast, experience in countries like the UK or Chile suggests that assigning institutional responsibility for target-setting to a powerful finance ministry and finance minister underlines the political commitment to the targets and helps to ensure that they will be taken seriously by agencies. It does this partly by strengthening the perceived ex-post linkage between results and funding. In other words, if the finance minister and finance ministry are at the center of the target-setting process, agencies are far more likely to believe that their performance against those targets will be considered in determining future budget allocations.

A striking feature of the PSA system is that it is primarily outcome-focused; that is, the great majority of PSA targets focus on outcomes such as student knowledge, and reductions in rates of cancer and heart disease. This outcome-orientation is representative of a broader international trend in performance budgeting at the level of the government budget as a whole. The international vogue in the 1990s for output-focused performance budgeting—influenced by the New Zealand experiment—has now faded. The dominant contemporary view is now that, at the level of the government budget, the focus should be on outcomes. Outcomes are, after all, the true goals of public policy, whereas outputs are a means to that end.

The outcome focus puts a spotlight on the key question of how tightly one can link funding to results. As discussed in Chapter 4, the relationship between outcomes and funding is often particularly uncertain, because of the impact of "external factors" on both the magnitude and the timing of outcomes. For example, the results which can be achieved by public programs designed to reduce cancer are highly uncertain for a range of reasons, including the partially uncontrollable nature of the risk factors (dietary and smoking habits, environmental deterioration, and so on) which impact on the incidence of the disease. So if targets are to be set for the outcomes expected over, say, a three-year time horizon, and the level of funding provided is to be linked to these targets, how does one deal with this uncertainty? Exactly what type of results/funding linkage can be built under such circumstances?

The answer, as Smith makes clear, is that there can indeed be no tight calibration between outcome targets and the level of budget funding. Often, the linkage will be no tighter than an expectation that if funding is increased, tougher targets will be set. Even such a loose linkage is, however, arguably important and beneficial, particularly by contrast with a system in which targets are set completely independently of the budget process, and without regard to the funding levels provided.

This implies that the ex-post linkage between outcomes and funding must also be a loose one. As a number of studies in this part of the volume make clear, it is unrealistic to expect any mechanical linkage between past performance and future funding. Thus Fantone stresses that there is no automatic relationship between a program's PART performance rating and the level of funding proposed for that program in the President's budget. Curristine reports that survey results suggest the same to be true of OECD countries as a whole. This is hardly surprising. It is common sense that if a program is performing badly, there can be no assumption that a funding cut is the appropriate response. It may be that program redesign or management change is what is required, or even that additional funding is needed.

This suggests that it is not useful to think of the performance incentives which performance budgeting can create at the level of the government-wide budget as "rewards" and "sanctions" analogous to those which operate in market transactions and which are mimicked by sectoral purchaser-provider systems. It is notable in this context that the one attempt to create a government-wide system of explicit agency-level rewards for good performance—in the Canadian state of Ontario—endured only a couple of years. Nevertheless, even if agencies are well aware that there is no automatic connection between performance and future funding, the knowledge that past program performance will be an important consideration in expenditure prioritization decisions can be expected to help motivate them to perform better. So rather than treating the government-wide budget process as a means of creating financial rewards and sanctions for agency performance, it is probably better to focus on creating good, performance-informed expenditure prioritization in the knowledge that one of its by-products will be to encourage agencies to improve program design and management so as to reduce the risk of having their budgets cut in the prioritisation process.

Changing behavior through performance budgeting and management

There is a further set of important issues concerning the *behavioral* impact of those forms of contemporary forms of performance budgeting—and "managing-for-results" (MFR) more generally—which aim to encourage and pressure agencies to perform better through the specification of expected levels of performance, whether through performance targets or other means. One concerns the potential for *behavioral distortion*. It is well-established in both theory and practice that performance measures and targets which are incomplete or capable of manipulation can induce behavioral distortions (see, for example, Ridgway, 1956; Smith, 1990, 1995). Given that the "existence of such perverse effects is uncontroversial" (Pidd, 2005, p. 483), the real question at stake is whether their *magnitude* is such as to throw into doubt the very efficacy of MFR and MFR-related performance budgeting systems. This question has been the subject of vigorous public controversy in some countries. As Smith outlines, in the UK, critics of the Public Service Agreements regime have complained about the alleged perverse affects of PSA performance targets in a range of areas. Although there is considerable *general* literature relevant to the issue of perverse effects—such as literature in the field of organizational economics—there is relatively little analytic literature on the question in the *specific* context of the public sector. To the extent that the public sector has different characteristics to the for-profit sector, this presents difficulties. It has been important, therefore, to provide some treatment of this issue in this part—both through discussions in a number of the case studies (in particular, that of the UK), and also in a thematic chapter which examines questions of behavioral impact more generally.

The question of behavioral impacts is important not only because of the issue of behavioral distortions, but also because of the issue of the source of motivation to perform more generally. Although many contemporary forms of performance budgeting and MFR aim to induce agencies to perform better, it is not always completely clear how it is intended that this impact be achieved. In the case of those forms of performance budgeting which seek to create financial rewards for agencies with good performance, the mechanism is in a sense explicit. However, whether agency-level financial rewards are part of the performance budgeting mechanism or not, a more fundamental issue arises—how can the individuals who staff the agency be induced to perform better? Through stronger incentives—financial and other explicit rewards and sanctions such as performance pay—linked to the achievement of organizational goals and targets? If so, this reinforces the importance of considering the question of behavioral distortions, because it is once again a familiar theme in the literature that the more "high-powered" (stronger and more direct) performance incentives are, the greater the potential for behavioral distortions if the measures upon which those incentives are based are imperfect. Another concern raised by critics of MFR is that sharper extrinsic incentives may undermine more "altruistic" or public spirited motivation to perform, which it is argued is particularly important in many areas of the public sector. How serious are these concerns and what are their implications for performance budgeting? To the extent that public employees are primarily motivated by altruistic commitment to the public good, is giving them the *freedom to perform*—by reducing controls which limit their freedom of action—perhaps more important than giving them incentives to perform and monitoring their performance?

Despite the importance of these behavioral issues, they have not been well-researched. To deal with them thoroughly would require deep foundations in the theory and empirical literature of industrial motivation and behavior, which is something well beyond the scope of this volume. However, in recognition of their importance, Chapter 18 reviews relevant literature, attempting to suggest links between performance budgeting and sources of individual motivation, and to draw out implications for the design of incentive systems.

In conclusion, the objective of the thematic and case studies in this part is to shed light on what types of performance budgeting system can potentially work, and whether they are potentially effective at the central budget level and/or at the decentralized level. Knowing what can *potentially* work is clearly of great importance to those designing performance budgeting systems in deciding, from the menu of choices available, what type of system they should be attempting to build. It does not, however, provide all that is required to make such decisions. The other crucial consideration is whether relevant *preconditions* have been met for the successful adoption of certain forms of performance budgeting. Preconditions, as well as sequencing and implementation strategy, are considered in Part Three.

Notes

1. Incrementalism has been defined as "inattentiveness to the (budgetary) base"—in other words, that budgetary decision-makers take the budgetary base more or less for granted as the starting point in budget formulation, and focus their attention on the size of the increment (or, occasionally, decrement) in agency or program budgets (Berry, 1990).
2. Such as the Grace Commission appointed by President Reagan in the US or the Rayner scrutiny reports commissioned by the then Prime Minister, Margaret Thatcher, in the UK.
3. The need for expenditure prioritization to focus on the totality of government expenditure is closely related to the widely-accepted case for budget comprehensiveness (including by limiting the use of extrabudgetary funds) (see, for example, Allen and Tomasi, 2001, p. 49).
4. In the 1960s and 1970s, advocacy of the early program budgeting models was often linked with sympathy for so-called "indicative" planning of the economy as a whole.
5. Alternative budgeting, as noted in Chapter 1, involved requiring line ministries each year to present in their budget submissions options for, and analyses of the impact of, marginal

changes of predefined magnitudes in each program (for example, 10 percent cut, 5 percent cut, 5 percent increase).

6. Experience in the UK and a number of other countries makes clear that it is far too superficial to regard politics and budgetary rationality as mutually exclusive, in the way that many US academic commentators, in the tradition of Aaron Wildavsky, continue to do (see, for example, the assertion of Lu (1998, p. 167) that "[the] politics of public budgeting makes it almost impossible for decision-makers to use rational data to allocate resources"). Insofar as either (1) the effectiveness and efficiency of programs has electoral significance or (2) the political leadership is committed as a matter of principle to improved public sector performance, performance information may have a significant impact in the allocation of resources notwithstanding the fundamental importance of political considerations. The tendency of US analysts to treat politics and budgetary rationality as antitheses may owe much to the specific context of the US political system, with its fragmentation of budgetary power between Congress and the executive, and the incentives which individual Congressmen have to use their powers over the allocation of expenditure to win local and interest group support.
7. Particularly important is the involvement of the Prime Minister and inclusion of two or three powerful ministers with big spending portfolios. By assigning these spending ministers a key role in the enforcement of overall government spending priorities, one reduces the danger that they will use their power in the cabinet to defend the interests of spending ministries against the finance ministry.

References

Allen, R., and D. Tomasi (eds.), 2001, *Managing Public Expenditure: A Handbook for Transition Countries* (Paris: OECD).

Anshen, M., 1967, "The Program Budget in Operation," in *Program Budgeting: Program Analysis and the Federal Budget*, ed. D. Novick (Cambridge, Mass.: Harvard University Press).

Berry, W.D., 1990, "The Confusing Case of Budgetary Incrementalism: Too Many Meanings for a Single Concept," *Journal of Politics*, Vol. 52(1), pp. 167–96.

Campos, E.J., and S. Pradhan, 1999, "Budgetary Institutions and the Levels of Expenditure Outcomes in Australia and New Zealand," in *Fiscal Institutions and Fiscal Performance*, ed. James M. Poterba and Jürgen von Hagen (Chicago: University of Chicago Press).

IMF, 2001, *Brazil: Report on Observance of Standards and Codes (ROSC)—Fiscal Transparency Module* (Washington, DC: IMF).

Le Houerou, P., and R. Taliercio, 2002, *Medium Term Expenditure Frameworks: From Concept to Practice: Preliminary Lessons from Africa*, Africa Region Working Paper Series No. 28 (Washington, DC: World Bank).

Lu, H., 1998, "Performance Budgeting Resuscitated: Why is it Still Inviable?," *Journal of Public Budgeting, Accounting and Financial Management,* Vol. 10(2), pp. 151–72.

Office of Program Policy Analysis and Government Accountability, 1997, *Performance-Based Program Budgeting in Context: History and Comparison*, Report 96–77A. Florida Legislature.

Osborne, D., and T. Gaebler, 1993, *Reinventing Government: How the Entrepreneurial Spirit is Transforming the Public Sector* (New York: Plume).

Pidd, M., 2005, "Perversity in Public Service Performance Measurement," *International Journal of Productivity and Performance Management*, Vol. 54(5/6), pp. 482–93.

Pollitt, C., 1999, *Performance Management and Financial Management—How to Integrate Them?* (Paris: OECD).

Ridgway, V.F., 1956, "Dysfunctional Consequences of Performance Measurement," *Administrative Sciences Quarterly*, Vol. 1(2), pp. 240–7.

Schick, A., 2002, "Does Budgeting Have a Future?" *OECD Journal on Budgeting*, Vol. 2(2), pp. 7–48.

Smith, P.C., 1990, "The Use of Performance Indicators in the Public Sector," *Journal of the Royal Statistical Society, A*, Vol. 153 (1), pp. 53–72.

——, 1995, "On the Unintended Consequences of Publishing Performance Data in the Public Sector," *International Journal of Public Administration*, Vol. 18(2/3), pp. 277–310.

Spackman, M., 2002, "Multi-Year Perspective in Budgeting and Public Investment Planning," Draft background paper for discussion at session III.1 of the OECD Global Forum on Sustainable Development: Conference on Financing Environmental Dimension of Sustainable Development, OECD, Paris.

World Bank, 1998, *Public Expenditure Management Handbook* (Washington, DC: World Bank).

Xavier, J.A., 1998, "Budget Reform in Australia and Malaysia Compared," *Public Budgeting & Finance*, Vol. 18(1), pp. 99–118.

8
Experience of OECD Countries with Performance Budgeting

Teresa Curristine[1]

Over the past two decades, the majority of OECD governments have sought to shift the emphasis of budgeting from inputs towards results. Across OECD countries, this introduction of a performance focus to budgeting has proven to be a powerful idea with applications to different levels and sectors of government. There is no single model of performance budgeting. OECD governments have adopted different models and approaches depending on their particular national capacities and priorities.

Trends[2]

The introduction of performance information (PI) into budgeting by OECD governments is widespread and well established (nearly 75 percent of all OECD countries include non-finance performance data in their budget documents) albeit varied in the approaches taken to it. Seventy-seven percent of countries introduced their first government-wide initiative on outputs measures at least five to ten years ago, with over 40 percent working on outputs measures for more than ten years. Countries' approaches to performance budgeting are not static, but rather evolving, with 75 percent of countries having introduced new initiatives within the last five years (Curristine, 2005a, pp. 92–3).

Countries use a variety of different methods to assess non-financial performance, including performance measures, evaluations, and benchmarking. In the 2005 OECD Survey on PI, approximately 90 percent of countries reported developing both performance measures and evaluations to assess performance. Of those countries that have developed performance measures, over 50 percent produce a combination of outputs and outcomes for most of their programs (Curristine, 2005a, p. 90).

Issues

Despite the length of time OECD countries have been engaged in performance budgeting, two of the major issues they face are, first, the quality and relevance of the data used as the basis for performance budgeting, and, second, ensuring such PI is used in the budget process.

As regards the first issue, not only does the quality of PI vary widely across OECD countries but it also varies widely within countries themselves, from ministry to ministry and from sector to sector. On a positive note, in the 2005 OECD Survey on PI, countries reported that over the past five years the quality of performance data available to them has improved. However, despite this improvement, more progress is needed. For example 50 percent of Ministries of Finance (MoFs) who responded to the 2005 OECD Survey reported that the cost-effectiveness and value for money reviews provided by their spending ministries were insufficient, incomplete and, in many cases, inaccurate.

As regards the second issue, the extensive increase in the volume of PI available to OECD governments has not been matched by a corresponding increase in use. For performance budgeting to succeed, it is important that PI be used in budgetary decision-making. One of the first issues for countries to address is ensuring that there is a process in place for such information to be integrated into the budget process. While many countries have adopted such a process, how it has been instituted varies from country to country. Furthermore, countries' experiences show that even having a procedure in place to integrate performance information into the budget process does not guarantee its use in budgetary decision-making. Other factors influencing the use of PI include the quality, relevance, and credibility of the data, the institutional capacity of the relevant MoF and spending ministries, and the political and economic context.

For OECD countries, performance budgeting has proven a challenging task given the technical complexity of implementing it, as described above, and also given the behavioral changes it requires of decision-makers. Civil servants and politicians must learn to change their behavior and use PI in the decision-making process. In order to achieve this change, countries need to introduce reforms to create incentives to encourage civil servants and politicians to use this information in a manner whereby governments may reap positive benefits and avoid perverse incentives.

This chapter concentrates on performance budgeting (PB) at the central government level, and does not address the efforts of state or local governments in this area. Furthermore, it focuses on attempts to introduce a government-wide approach to PB. Throughout this chapter the term "performance information" is used to refer to both evaluations and performance measures.

This chapter is divided into three parts. The first examines attempts to integrate PI into the annual budget process. The second discusses the use of PI expenditure prioritization exercises, concentrating on spending reviews. The third examines other factors that influence the use of PI and the challenges OECD countries continue to encounter to improve its use in budgetary decision-making.

1. Integrating PI into the annual budget process

PI can be used at different stages and levels of the budget process. This section concentrates on the use of PI at the budget formulation stage in budget negotiations between the MoF and spending ministries and briefly addresses its use in negotiations between spending ministries and agencies.

PI in budget negotiations between the MoF and spending ministries

OECD countries have taken a variety of approaches to including PI in budget negotiations. These can be split broadly into formal and non-formal approaches to including PI in budget negotiations. Even within such categories, countries have adopted a wide variety of methods, some of which are described below.

Some countries have followed a formal *comprehensive* approach, in which the MoF requires *all* ministries to present performance plans and/or performance results along with their spending proposals. Other countries have a formal but non-comprehensive approach that requires performance plans or results either (1) from some ministries and sectors only, or (2) only when ministries present proposals bidding for *additional* funding (for either new or existing programs).

As regards non-formal approaches, some countries leave to individual ministries the decision as to whether to present PI to the MoF in the budget context. Certain other countries make systematic use of PI in negotiations between ministries and their subordinate agencies over performance contracts or agreements, while excluding PI from any significant role in budget between the MoF and ministries.

Even having formal requirements to present PI to the MoF does not mean it will be used in budget negotiations in all cases. As can be seen in Figure 8.1, in over three-quarters of countries that responded to the OECD 2005 Survey, performance measures are part of the budget discussions between the MoF and either *all* spending ministries (29 percent) or *some* spending ministries (50 percent). There is less use of evaluations: 51 percent of countries use them in budget negotiations, and less than 10 percent use them for budget negotiations in respect to *all* spending ministries.

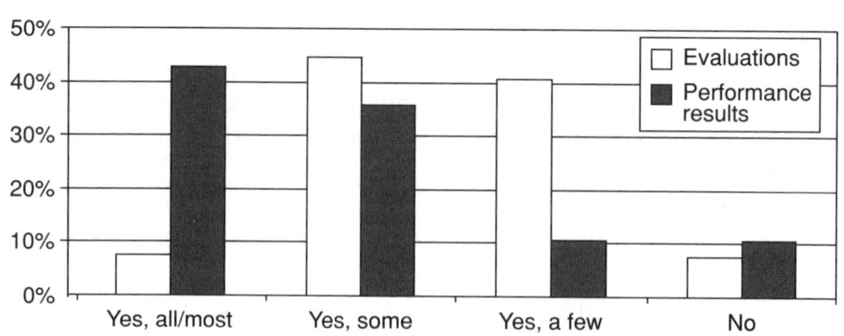

Figure 8.1 Is PI used as part of budget discussion between the MoF and spending ministries?

Source: OECD 2005 Survey on PI in the Budget Process.

When PI is part of the budget negotiation process, a key question is *how* it is used. One may distinguish between the use of PI by the MoF for planning purposes and for accountability purposes. In both these cases there is an issue about how PI should be linked to funding. In the first case, the question is the degree of linkage between funding and *expected* results. In the second case, the question is how far funding is affected by actual results achieved in the past.

Planning purposes

Most budget negotiations have traditionally included some element of discussion on planning—that is, about expected performance—as budgetary estimates often provide some indication of what a ministry aims to achieve with funding (for example, to build a certain number of roads or hospitals). The introduction of performance budgeting has formalized this process and placed a greater emphasis on setting explicit expectations or targets for the results to be delivered with the funding provided.

The majority of OECD countries do not have a systematic government-wide approach to linking expenditure to targets. As can be seen in Figure 8.2, over a third of OECD countries reported that expenditure is linked to some output or outcome targets, while over 46 percent of countries only link expenditure to a few or no outputs or outcome targets.

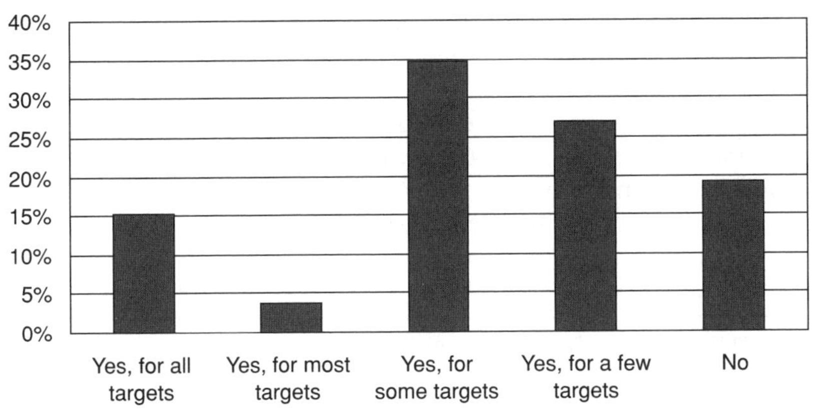

Figure 8.2 Are expenditures specifically linked to each output or outcome target?

Source: OECD/World Bank Survey on Budget Practices and Procedures 2003.

Of course, performance plans and targets are not necessarily discussed or approved during the budget process, but may take place outside of the budget process either with the MoF or with other central agencies. Indeed, the development of these plans can be part of an unconnected reform initiative. In some countries, planning is completely separated from budgeting, and strategic and performance plans are primarily presented and approved by the Prime Minister's/President's office, the Ministry of Planning, or the legislature.

Accountability purposes

The MoF can use PI to hold ministries and agencies accountable for their performance, including by taking the past performance record into account when deciding on budget allocations. A key issue in performance budgeting is how tightly funding can be linked to performance results. In practice in most OECD countries, there is, at the level of the budget as a whole, at best only a loose or indirect link between funding and performance results. The majority of MoFs engage in what might be referred to as "performance informed" budgeting—that is, performance data is used along with other information on fiscal policy, policy priorities, and political factors, to *inform but not to determine* budget allocations. According to the 2005 OECD Survey, 76 percent of MoFs frequently use performance measures, and 66 percent frequently use evaluations, to inform budget decisions (Curristine, 2005a). In these cases, there is no automatic or mechanical link between performance results and funding. PI is only one consideration in the decision-making process on the level of funding to be provided, and how much weight is given to it will be influenced by the wider economic and political context and specific characteristics of the relevant policy area.

The exception to this is performance budgeting based on formula budgeting. This approach is not used in OECD countries at the level of the budget as a whole but, rather, when it is used it is applied in specific sectors. Two-thirds of respondents to the 2005 OECD Survey on PI stated that they do not directly link performance results to appropriations. Formula funding is mainly applied to sectors such as health and education.

In the majority of cases, the MoF does not often use performance results to financially reward or punish agencies. Table 8.1 shows the percentage of MoFs in OECD countries that often use evaluations or performance measures to eliminate programs, to cut expenditure, or to determine pay.

Table 8.1 Percentage of OECD MoFs that often use PI for the listed courses of action

Performance measures		*Evaluations*	
To eliminate programs:	4%	To eliminate programs:	11%
To cut expenditure:	10%	To cut expenditure:	15%
To determine pay:	11%	To determine pay:	5%

As can been seen from these numbers, it is rare that PI is used by the MoF when deciding on these courses of action. The difficulty in linking funding to results reflects the fact that the issues and context surrounding budget decisions are complex. The capacity of the MoF to eliminate or even cut back programs may be restricted by lack of institutional capacity and power or lack of political support.

In addition, the actual decision-making power can rest with the Prime Minister or be the result of political negotiations within the cabinet. Budgetary decision-making takes place in a political context and proposals to cut back or eliminate programs can encounter political resistance, especially if these programs bring benefits to important political groups or are high political priorities.

It is questionable whether financially rewarding good performance and penalizing bad performance on a government-wide level is likely to lead to improved agency performance. To automatically cut funding without understanding the causes of poor performance could make the situation worse and condemn badly performing agencies to continue to underperform. Performance measures do not explain the underlying causes of poor performance. Performance in any given year can be influenced by a variety of factors both internal and external, which may or may not be within the control of an agency. In addition, in some OECD countries, it is uncertain if the PI is of high enough quality to be used in budgetary decision-making in this manner.

In addition, such an approach can generate perverse incentives and encourage agencies to manipulate data. Incentives to provide accurate information are influenced by the expectations of how it will be used in decision-making. If funding is tightly and automatically linked to results, there can be incentives to engage in gaming and to manipulate data in order to receive more money or to avoid receiving less. As Wildavsky (1974) pointed out over 30 years ago, it is politically irrational to expect agencies to provide objective information if it will be used to cut back their programs.

Automatically linking performance to results on a systematic government-wide scale is not the best approach to promoting the production of credible information and encouraging agencies to focus on maximizing their use of PI. No OECD country has done this, perhaps realizing the difficulties of adopting such a systematic approach.

While MoFs do not financially penalize or reward agencies for their performance, they do, however, still use PI to hold ministries to account. PI acts as a potentially useful signal of problems within programs and agencies and serves as a trigger for the MoF to more closely monitor or review agencies and programs. The most common course of action taken by MoFs against poorly performing agencies is that resources are not increased and the program is reviewed during the course of the year. Other actions include making the continuation of programs conditional on future performance.

PI in budget negotiations between spending ministries and their agencies

OECD research indicates that PI is more often used by spending ministries than by the MoF (OECD, 2005b). PI can be used at the budget formulation stage in negotiations between spending ministries and their agencies. In this context, a common approach to integrating PI into the budget process is through discussions on agencies' performance agreements and contracts. This is an approach widely used in countries with executive agencies, such as New Zealand, the UK, the Netherlands, and the Nordic countries.[3] These discussions may concentrate either on future targets or on past performance, or may involve a combination of both. With the exception of the purchaser-provider model used in New Zealand, in many cases there is only a loose link between funding and targets.

Another common use of PI by spending ministries is to redistribute resources (see Figure 8.3). The capacity of spending ministries to reallocate resources is influenced by the wider budgetary framework and rules. In most countries, ministries at the budget formulation stage have the capacity to propose changes in the distribution of resources between subordinate agencies and programs. Existing rules and procedures can sometimes force spending ministries to reallocate. The MoF in some countries—for example, New Zealand and Sweden—seeks to control expenditure and limit proposals for increased spending through the use of fixed spending caps. This requires ministries to remain within the set expenditure limits and forces them to cover any increase in spending through internal reallocations.

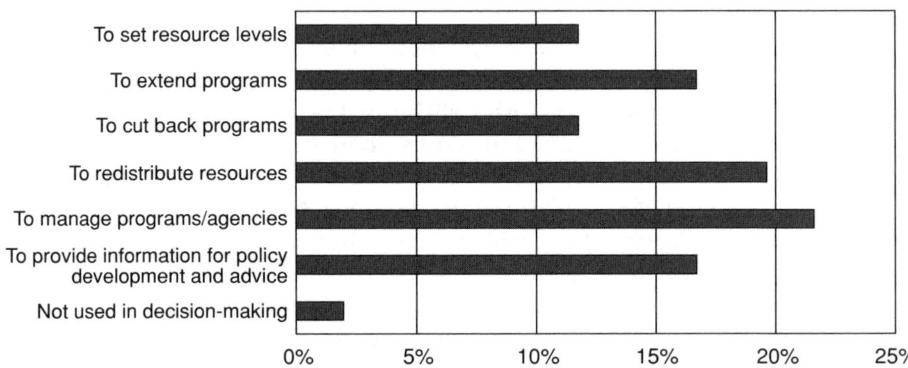

Figure 8.3 How are the results of performance measures generally used by spending ministries/departments? (Multiple responses possible)

Source: OECD 2005 Survey on PI in the Budget Process.

Across OECD countries there is a wide variation in the quality and use of PI by spending ministries in the budget process. Even within the same country, there can be wide variations among different ministries in terms of the quality, the extent of use, and the weight given to PI in budget discussions. For example, in Norway, PI is requested by the different ministries in their letter of instruction to agencies. Despite formal requirements and processes, many agencies have made only limited progress in developing meaningful performance measures. The character of PI changes from agency to agency. Some have defined objectives and developed a few performance measures; others do not develop any performance measures. These problems make it difficult for spending ministries to use this information in budget negotiations with agencies. Like many other OECD countries, Norway struggles with the problem of developing good-quality performance measures and data (OECD, 2006, p. 21).

As already indicated in this volume, PI is not just used for budgeting purposes; it also aims through the "managing-for-results" approach to improve the management of programs. As Figure 8.3 indicates, the most common use of performance measures by ministries is to manage programs.

PI has the potential, if it is of good quality, relevant, and timely, to be used in such a way as to improve programs. It can indicate the degree to which programs are achieving their objectives and help to identify which policies and processes work and why. These factors can help to improve program management and thereby boost efficiency and effectiveness. There are no comparative cross-country studies showing the extent to which the use of PI in this manner has in practice improved performance. These types of studies are difficult to conduct due to comparability issues and also to the difficulty of distinguishing the impact of the use of PI from that of other relevant initiatives and factors. However, in a national country context there are many anecdotal examples of how PI has improved operational efficiency, some of which are discussed elsewhere in this volume.

2. PI and expenditure prioritization

Expenditure prioritization is concerned with clarifying governments' key objectives and priorities and funneling funds towards high-priority areas and away from lower-level priorities. Expenditure prioritization seeks to improve allocative efficiency and to reallocate resources. The motives for governments to engage in central expenditure reallocations across government are diverse and include new political priorities, fiscal stress or abundance, program overspending, and substitutions of inputs such as changes in technology (OECD, 2005a, pp. 10–11). OECD countries have used a variety of methods and budget institutions to approach reallocation, which include medium-term frameworks, different rules for budgetary discipline, and spending reviews.

This section focuses on the approaches that potentially make use of PI in expenditure prioritization decisions, and therefore concentrates on spending reviews.

Expenditure prioritization and spending reviews

Here we examine the use of spending reviews as an approach to increasing allocation efficiency. Spending reviews can be ad hoc or systematic and part of the annual budget cycle or separate from it.

Program evaluation is a particularly useful input for spending reviews. As Figure 8.4 highlights, the majority of program evaluations are conducted by spending ministries. OECD MoFs have, however, found the quality of the evaluations produced by spending ministries to be poor, particularly in respect to evaluations of cost-effectiveness and "value for money." MoFs therefore in many cases conduct their own evaluations to provide them with information to be used in the budget process.

Spending reviews differ from ordinary program or policy evaluations in that they are centrally driven exercises and they concentrate on issues of allocative efficiency across government and examine the consequences of alterative funding levels.[4] These reviews may be conducted either on an ad hoc basis or as a systematic part of the budget process. The motives for engaging in spending reviews vary, although they are influenced by the underlying economic context and are more likely to occur under conditions of either fiscal stress or fiscal abundance.

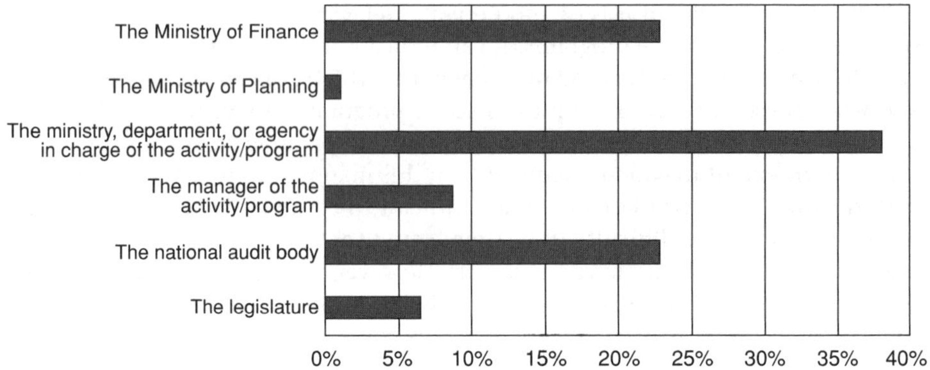

Figure 8.4 Who is responsible for conducting evaluations in your country?

Source: OECD 2005 Survey on PI in the Budget Process.

Ad hoc spending reviews

An example of expenditure prioritization and reallocation that took place under conditions of fiscal stress is the 1994 Canadian Program Review. This was a one-time exercise driven by a combination of factors, including high annual deficits, pressure from the financial markets, and the election of a new government. The review was driven from the center, which established the guidelines, set departmental spending, cut targets, and specified how departments were to go about reviewing their programs (including assessment of program objectives and purposes, the impact on society, whether the program should be provided by government, and means of improving program efficiency). Using these centrally established qualitative criteria, all departments provided action plans setting out their strategic priorities and alternative packages of programs and activities. Final plans were submitted to a special committee of ministers set up by the Prime Minister. The committee made specific recommendations on departmental programs to the MoF which incorporated them into the budget. The results were substantial cuts (averaging 21.5 percent) to departments' budgets (OECD, 2005a, pp. 14–15).

Given that this exercise took place under conditions of fiscal stress, while performance criteria on program effectiveness and efficiency were included it is not clear how much weight was given to this information during the decision-making process, especially since the decisions took place in a highly charged political context and involved discussions and negotiations between ministers.

Systematic spending reviews

Other countries have sought to design systematic cross-government expenditure reallocation mechanisms. These include the UK with its Spending Reviews (starting in 1998), the Netherlands interdepartmental policy reviews (1981), and value for money reviews in New Zealand (2001). All these reallocation initiatives were designed during times of fiscal abundance, and the primary objective in many cases was to improve the performance of the public sector and allocative efficiency (OECD, 2005a).

The UK process is discussed in greater detail in Chapter 12 by Peter Smith. The system was initiated with a Comprehensive Spending Review in 1998, followed by Spending Reviews in 2000, 2002, and 2004. A further Comprehensive Spending Review was underway at the time of writing, and was scheduled for completion in 2007. This biannual approach aims to reallocate money to key priorities and to improve the efficiency and delivery of public services. After a review of existing departmental spending, each department develops three-year spending plans and Public Service Agreements (PSAs). The Treasury negotiates with ministries their key performance targets for the next three-year period, which are included in their PSAs.

The Dutch approach differs from the UK approach in that it is an annual exercise which is not designed to be comprehensive. The Dutch policy reviews focus on a limited number of priority areas every year (approximately ten) and were originally conducted with the idea of developing alternative funding scenarios for these policies and recommendations on how to improve efficiency. The reviews are carried out by small working parties, which are often chaired by an external member and include participants from the relevant spending ministry, the MoF and the Ministry for General Affairs. The results of these reviews are published and submitted to parliament. These reviews have been used by both the spending ministries and the MoF during the budget process, and have also been used by cabinet and opposition parties (OECD, 2005a, p. 43).

Challenges with spending reviews and reallocation

The experiences of the UK and the Netherlands are seen as successful examples of spending reviews. By contrast, the New Zealand experience with value for money reviews underlines the difficulties in conducting these exercises. For the 2002 budget year, the New Zealand cabinet agreed to 17 reviews, but, despite the recommendations in these reviews, only two significant reallocations occurred. These instances were in ministries that had participated in the exercise voluntarily. The New Zealand reviews highlighted the need for obtaining the cooperation of spending ministries and political support in the recommendations if reviews are to be implemented (OECD, 2005a, p.19).

While spending reviews can highlight the need for cross-departmental reallocations, in order to actually implement change, high-level political support from the cabinet and/or the Prime Minister may be required and, depending on the nature of the political system, the legislature. This depends in part on the nature of the political and administrative systems and relevant power of the MoF. In only a few countries is the MoF powerful enough to carry out an exercise in cross-departmental reallocation without high-level political support. In the US system, the support of the legislature is also needed for most reallocations across departments.

Notwithstanding the examples discussed in this section, significant central reallocation across government is not common. In OECD governments' budgets, except in conditions of fiscal abundance, the funds available for reallocations are generally marginal because of the extent of mandatory spending, entitlement programs, and prior commitments. Politicians are often reluctant to place certain spending, such as entitlement programs, in the spotlight. In this sense, in many OECD countries much of the annual budget process remains incremental, and inputs still play a significant role. Even in circumstances when reallocation occurs, the reallocation is not necessarily the result of systematic spending reviews. This is just one of many possible reallocation institutions and mechanisms.

Although program performance can be a valuable input in spending reviews, one should not expect a mechanical linkage between performance and spending cuts or increases; particularly because budget decision-making takes place in a political context, so poorly performing programs and those with high-priority objectives may receive funding increases.

PI must compete for attention with other sources of information, priorities, and tools in the budget process. While the MoF and the budget office have the objective of improving allocative efficiency, their primary role is to maintain aggregate fiscal disciple. Although this volume argues that over the long term PB can help achieve this, other more traditional and perhaps more blunt tools such as centrally imposed spending cuts for ministries can help to achieve this in the short term, although there may be an issue with long-term sustainability. Even if PI is integrated into the process, timing issues can work against the use of PI. With the tight deadlines in the budget process, there is a danger that serious discussions of performance or even of targets are left out in favor of discussions on inputs.

3. General factors influencing the use of PI in the budget process

Sections 1 and 2 highlighted that, while having procedures to integrate PI into the budget process is important, it does not necessarily mean that PI will be used in decision-making. Key actors in the process must have the incentive to change their behavior and break from the traditional approach to budgeting.

Other general conditions and factors which influence the use of PI in the budget process include the quality of PI, the institutional capacity of MoFs and spending ministries, and the wider political and institutional context. This section concentrates on the latter two factors. OECD countries continue to face challenges regarding many of the technical aspects of these reforms and with providing incentives for key actors to use this information in budgetary decision-making.

Institutional capacity of the MoFs and spending ministries

The institutional capacity of the MoF influences the role it is able to play in promoting the use of PI in the budget process at all levels. The capacity to steer reform initiatives and expenditure prioritization exercises is influenced by its position in the wider institutional framework and its power vis-à-vis other central agencies and spending ministries. This affects the extent to which the MoF can impose its views, as opposed to being forced to rely on persuasion.

Across OECD countries, the role played by MoFs in developing PB initiatives, and their subsequent implementation, varies widely. It ranges from developing performance measures and setting and/or negotiating performance targets, to a completely decentralized approach in which the MoF has no involvement. In some countries, such as the UK and Chile, the MoF has a high degree of involvement and plays a strong and active role in developing and implementing these reforms. This more centralized approach contrasts with the much more decentralized one in, for example, Iceland, where the MoF has a low level of involvement and it is solely the responsibility of individual ministries to develop and implement these reforms.

The degree of involvement of the MoF is a function not only of the PB approach and the level of interest in these initiatives, but also of the relative position and power of the MoF in the wider institutional and political system. For example, in the UK, the Treasury has taken a PB approach, which involves expenditure prioritization through two-year Spending Reviews. The strong formal role for the MoF in this initiative has been promoted by a high level of political interest and the centralized administrative and institutional structure in which the Treasury has a powerful position.

There are risks with having too much or too little central involvement from the MoF or other central ministries in these reforms. Previous incarnations, such as the Planning, Programming, and Budgeting System (PPBS) and zero-base budgeting (ZBB) have been accused of being overcentralized. Too centralized an approach can result in those responsible for delivering the target lacking the flexibility and managerial freedom to get the job done and the motivation to deliver results. Furthermore, centrally set and driven performance targets can distort behavior at lower levels, creating incentives to cheat and twist information in order to meet requirements at the center. If PI is not used in the manner intended, given the extensive costs in generating it, it risks becoming an expensive paper exercise.

On the other hand, too little central involvement can result in no pressure to change. The risk is that reforms are announced and not implemented at lower levels. If there is too much decentralization, the center can lack the information necessary to make decisions. There can also be a lack of uniformity in the development and presentation of PI. This makes it difficult to compare performance across government and hinders expenditure prioritization. In addition, central coordination can promote the development of joint goals and initiatives which cut across ministries.

For each country, the relative risk of having too much or too little central involvement is influenced by the existing institutional structure. Those countries that operate in a decentralized system of public administration, in which the MoF has relative weak formal power, face a different set of challenges to those that operate in a more centralized system.

Resources in terms of staff and expertise also influence institutional capacity. PI is different from financial information. In order to make judgments and compare performance, the MoF needs the relevant expertise to be able to analyze and evaluate the information received from different spending ministries.

Since spending ministries are dependent on agencies for information, they, like the MoF, need the capacity to understand and evaluate the information they receive. This is necessary if they are to make judgments about the appropriateness and quality of performance measures, and about the realism of proposed targets. It is mostly the agencies that decide on detailed goals, priorities, performance measures, and targets. Even if the interest is there, ministries may not have the expertise or knowledge to develop performance measures or even to effectively monitor performance. The danger is that this can lead to the passive provision of data without it having any real weight in the decision-making process.

While this section has concentrated on the role of the MoF, it is not always the MoF that plays the central role in initiating or monitoring PB reforms. For example, in Brazil the Ministry of Planning is responsible for developing and monitoring PB reforms. In some countries the responsibilities are split across departments. For example, in Korea, the Ministry of Planning and Budgeting is responsible for performance budgeting and operates a system similar to the US Program Assessment Rating Tool (PART) system. The performance management side is divided between the Ministry of Government Administration and Home Affairs, which is in charge of general management, and the Civil Service Commission, which is responsible for personnel policy. The office of the Prime Minister coordinates the overall reform effort and other ministries work in this area.

Importance of politicians and the wider political and institutional context

Politicians have an important role to play in promoting the development and use of PI in the budget process. Their role potentially involves applying pressure on other actors to implement PB, playing an active role in setting objectives, and using PI in budgetary decision-making. The role of politicians in the legislature and executive will vary depending on the nature of the legislative-executive relationships in the budget process, which in turn is influenced by the type of political system—presidential, semi-presidential, or parliamentary.

Most models of PB and "managing-for-results" more generally assign to politicians the role of setting clear objectives for agencies and monitoring performance against those goals. Most OECD governments now present their objectives and performance results to the public either in government-wide annual performance plans and reports (as, for example, in the UK), or in ministerial-level plans and reports (as, for example, in Canada and the US) (OECD 2005b). This approach, if successfully implemented, can help to clarify what the government is trying to achieve and how programs contribute to governments' wider policy objectives or outcomes, and it can also help to improve transparency.

However, politicians have not always availed themselves of this opportunity. Setting clear objectives is one of the challenges that OECD countries continue to encounter. In any system with multiple principals, or lack of agreement on the role of an agency, there can be competing and even conflicting goals and demands for agencies. This problem is more pronounced in separation-of-powers systems in which control of the bureaucracy is divided between the legislative and executive arms of government, as in the US.

It has proven particularly difficult to get politicians in their capacity as legislators to pay attention to and to use PI.[5] Only 19 percent of OECD legislatures use PI in decision-making, and the figure is only 8 percent for members of legislative budget committees (OECD, 2005b, p. 72). This is despite the fact that in some cases these reforms were the initiatives of the legislature and not the executive; for example, the Government Performance and Results Act (GPRA) in the US.

A key challenge is to create good-quality and relevant information that takes account of the constraints of timing and the capacity under which political decision-makers operate. There has been a large increase in the volume of PI provided to the legislatures in OECD countries. This information has improved transparency, and it enables politicians in the legislature, should they wish to do so, to use this information to hold the government to account. There are examples of this both in the UK and Holland, where the government opposition has used the government's performance results to highlight problems.

In many cases, however, politicians complain about receiving too much information of variable quality and relevance. Not only is there a problem of information overload, but it is also often the case that performance information is not presented in a clear or comprehensible manner. Politicians in the legislature and the executive have different informational needs. To be useful, information needs to be tailored in such a way as to recognize these differing requirements. It should also be provided at the right time for the relevant decision.

In most countries these reforms have not resulted in any changes to procedures in the parliamentary budget process. The process has not been altered to integrate PI into budgetary decision-making. The exception to this is France, where the Loi Organique relative aux Lois de Finances (LOLF) reform has given a greater role to the legislature.

The support of politicians in the cabinet or that of the Prime Minister is often needed to implement the recommendations of spending review and expenditure prioritization exercises. However, their willingness to do so can be influenced by many factors in the wider political and economic environment. For example, coming close to an election, or during times of fiscal abundance, it can be difficult to obtain political support for recommendations to reduce spending even for programs that are inefficient. Furthermore, politicians want to be responsive to their constituents and special interests. In some political contexts, programs and agencies are continued even though their existence is questionable on efficiency and effectiveness grounds. Meeting these political needs is not necessarily conducive to using PI in budgeting decision-making.

This approach can be more of a challenge in systems where the legislature is powerful and influential in the budget process. For the reform to succeed it requires not only that the politicians in legislature and the executive change their behavior and support this approach, but also close cooperation between them. Whether the political system is consensual or adversarial will impact on their ability to cooperate and the use politicians make of PI.

It needs to be recognized that politicians are slow at changing approaches and methods, and they are faced with a different set of incentives and structures than civil servants. Many OECD countries continue to struggle with providing the right incentives to motivate politicians, especially those in the legislature, to use PI.[6]

Conclusion

There is no one model of PB, and OECD countries have adopted a variety of methods and approaches to it. OECD countries now have a mechanism which enables politicians and managers to set and clarify objectives and to monitor progress toward achieving these goals. PB has encouraged OECD countries to put greater emphasis on planning and to move towards an outcomes focus in policy design and delivery, and has also improved transparency by increasing the amount of information provided to the legislature and the public on the performance and results of the public sectors.

Despite these benefits, OECD countries continue to struggle with a number of challenges and issues. It has proven easier to increase the quantity of PI produced than to ensure that this information is actually used in budgetary decision-making. OECD countries have adopted a variety of processes to integrate PI into the budget. PI is part of budget negotiations in most OECD countries and in some cases it has been part of expenditure prioritization through spending reviews. Nevertheless, making sure that these processes work remains a challenge. Integrating PI into the budget process is a necessary but not sufficient condition to assure its use in decision-making. Most importantly, it is not just a matter of process, but also of having the right incentives to motivate decision-makers to use this information in the budget process.

OECD countries continue to face the question of how tightly to link funding to performance. The current practice on a government-wide scale in OECD countries is not automatically or mechanically to link funding to results. It is seriously questionable whether such an approach on a government-wide scale is even desirable given the quality, technical, behavioral, and incentive issues involved. PI is used in budget negotiations along with other information on fiscal factors and political priorities. It is used to inform but not to determine budget allocations. PI plays a greater role at the decentralized level. Spending ministries and agencies make the most use of PI, and do so principally to manage programs.

In most OECD governments' budgets there is little room to maneuver, and reallocation decisions are based on marginal funds. In making decisions on marginal funding, performance is only one of many factors that can be taken into consideration. The amount of weight given to this information depends on the information itself, the relevant sector or policy area, and the wider political and economic factors. PI must compete with other sources of information and budgetary tools to gain the attention of decision-makers.

Other factors influencing its use include the quality of the PI itself, the capacity of the MoF and spending ministries, and the wider institutional and political context. Although there are some exceptions, most OECD countries continue to struggle with providing good-quality and relevant information to decision-makers in a timely manner. They also continue to face the challenge of changing the behavior and culture of civil servants and especially politicians. What incentives to provide and the capacity to provide them are decisions influenced by the wider political and institutional structures.

As PB is intuitively appealing, it is easy to oversell and exaggerate its potential. In some OECD countries, reformers have failed to learn from earlier incarnations of PB, have initially been overambitious, and have oversold the reform potential to administrative and political leaders. This has resulted in unrealistic expectations about the capacity of PB to transform budgeting. It is important to bear in mind that the central budget process remains a political process, that inputs in most countries still play a central role and that, with the possible exception of times of fiscal constraints or abundance, budgeting remains in many cases largely incremental, with PI impacting on the margins.

There is no one approach to PB that can succeed in all countries. Rather, each model of PB needs to be adapted to the relevant context and be seen as part of a learning process. OECD countries' approaches are continuously evolving as they learn from their experiences and take account of PB's potential and its limitations.

Notes

1. The views expressed in this chapter are those of the author and do not represent the opinions of the OECD.
2. The data presented in this chapter are from two sources. First is the OECD 2005 Survey on the Development and Use of Performance Information in the Budget Process. This questionnaire was sent to the Ministries of Finance in all OECD countries and two observer countries—Chile and Israel. There was a high response rate: 26 out of 30 OECD countries and the two observers completed the questionnaire. All answers are self-reported. The second source is the 2003 OECD/World Bank Survey on Budget Practices and Procedures, for which 27 out of the 30 OECD countries completed this survey.
3. For more details on the definition and principles of executive agencies see Schick (2002).
4. In some of the literature the term "program review" is used refer to spending review.
5. The UK is an exception to this with its Special Cabinet Committee on public services and expenditure chaired by the Chancellor.
6. For a more detailed description of the possible incentives motivating politicians to change behavior see Curristine (2005b).

References

Curristine, T., 2005a, "Performance Information in the Budget Process: Results of the OECD 2005 Questionnaire," *OECD Journal on Budgeting*, Vol. 5, No. 2.

——, 2005b, "Government Performance: Lessons and Challenges," *OECD Journal on Budgeting*, Vol. 5, No. 1.

OECD, 2005a, *Reallocation: The Role of Budget Institutions* (Paris: OECD).

——, 2005b, *Modernizing Government: The Way Forward* (Paris: OECD).

——, 2006, "Budgeting in Norway," GOV/PGC/SBO(2006)7 (Paris: OECD).

Schick, A., 2002, "Agencies in Search of Principles," *OECD Journal on Budgeting*, Vol. 2, No. 1, OECD, Paris.

Wildavsky, A.B., 1974, *The Politics of the Budget Process* (New York: Little Brown and Company).

9

Improving Allocative Efficiency

Jim Brumby[1]

The traditional view of public finance attributes three major goals to the management of public finance: stabilization, reallocation, and redistribution.[2] It is the interrelationships between these that give rise to the major issues in public finance. For instance, provision of public educational services through the levying of taxation affects real income distribution, while distributional activities inevitably affect relative prices and consumer demands, and therefore the allocation of resources to the production of various goods. Of these interrelationships, there is perhaps no more crucial question for public finance than the following: How can society collectively determine the optimal amount of public goods, and how shall the costs of these goods be apportioned among individuals (Due and Friedlaender, 1973, p. 48)? The scope of this chapter is, first, to acknowledge the contribution that the answering of this question can have for the goal of stabilization through management of the aggregate fiscal position, but mainly to examine the specific mechanisms that can assist improving allocative efficiency through public budgeting.

The chapter begins by looking at the notion of allocative efficiency and reviewing the root causes of changes in allocative efficiency. It then sets up a tentative framework of modern budgeting mechanisms, prior to describing each of these mechanisms, focusing in particular on mechanisms to give effect to changes in government priorities and in relative prices of government intervention.

Defining allocative efficiency

A reasonable definition of allocative efficiency is the production of the best or optimal combination of outputs by means of the most efficient combination of inputs. Allocative efficiency involves the output combination which would be chosen by individual consumers responding in perfect markets to prices which reflect the true costs of production. Pareto optimal output involves the point at which the marginal social value equates with marginal social cost; accordingly, it involves efficiency in the product mix and efficiency in consumption.

Adapting the concept of allocative efficiency to the public sector is far from straightforward: resource allocations are not made by individuals; often, neither tastes nor outputs are well-articulated; the relationship between the output and some measure of welfare, such as outcome, may be difficult to gauge; input prices are often distorted and not transparent; and data on true costs of production are often not available. In addition, there is the problem of the aggregation of preferences—individuals with different preferences have different marginal rates of substitution at the efficient scale of output for publicly supplied goods. It is well appreciated that there is no market mechanism that will determine the efficient scale of output of publicly provided goods or allocate the costs of this production among the members of society. Political and bureaucratic institutions, in all their flawed glory, are left to do this.

Over the past decade, an accepted way of looking at budgetary institutions has been to see three levels of efficiency-related objectives associated with budgeting. At the highest level (Level 1), there is a concern about the aggregate expenditure control and the burden placed by the state on the productive sector of the economy. Nicholas Barr would call this macro efficiency, but many budget writers may just refer to this as being concerned with aggregate control (see Barr, 1998, p. 9; World Bank, 1998, p. 2).[3] At the second level (Level 2), the objective is to pursue interventions which are consistent with the priorities of society, as represented by decision makers. On occasion, this level is referred to as being concerned with allocative efficiency. The third level (Level 3) is concerned with the government's role as a supplier of services, seeking production of such services in a technically efficient way. Improving allocative efficiency would see reallocation from lower to higher priorities of government and from less effective to more effective programs.

Allocative efficiency and fiscal stabilization

It is axiomatic to the tasks of public budgeting that there are tensions between the aggregate and its parts. The three levels of efficiency-related objectives are interrelated. Perhaps it is trivial to make the point that without some form of constraint at the aggregate, there would be no scarcity, and there would be no public budgeting problem as such. But, alas, this would lead headlong into a dispute with what, from a stabilization point of view, the economy could sustain as an achievable aggregate fiscal position. The reality of budgeting is that the sum of the parts will hold as a constraint only if portfolio pressures are constrained. The realization of the need to manage this common pool problem has led to many reforms to strengthen this role of fiscal institutions, especially the central budget office, over the past 20 years or so.[4] Evidence of this is seen in the increased use of budget limits being placed on budget formulation by central budget offices, rather than allowing an aggregation of bids.[5]

The potential contribution of achieving productive efficiency (Level 3) objectives to assist with the achievement of (aggregate control) Level 1 objectives appears straightforward. Improved productive efficiency provides a choice for resource allocates (that is, those with decision rights over resource allocation), along the following lines:

- the efficiency gain can be reapplied to the same productive process to yield higher output;
- it can be reapplied to another output;
- it can flow through to the bottom line and result in fiscal consolidation (lowering the estimated cost of taxes through time); or
- it can be returned to taxpayers via a tax cut now, or in the future through lower debt.

Similarly, there is a potential contribution from improved expenditure prioritization (allocative efficiency) to Level 1 control objectives, along the following lines:

- a reduction in production of one output (or the level of resources to one intervention) may yield a fiscal dividend which can be reapplied; or, alternatively,
- an increase in an output (or resources devoted to an intervention) will need to be funded from some source (either through a transfer from another output, taxation, or debt).

The better the ability of government to identify its priorities, and as important, its non-priorities, the easier the task of managing the aggregate constraint and the more credible that constraint. Further, provided there is limited dissonance between government priorities and those of the people, there may be less pain associated with fiscal consolidation, even that involving fiscal retrenchment.

Linking allocative efficiency and performance budgeting

A public finance construct that sought to describe government, well-informed and non-distorted, as a central point for making decisions on the marginal welfare gains of alternative spending options or an additional dollar of spending versus a reduced dollar of taxation, could be considered somewhat fanciful. With apologies to Alchian and Demsetz (1972), if the firm is a nexus of contracts, then government organization is a labyrinth of (hard-to-measure) formal and informal contracts, executed in space protected from the self-correcting powers of the market.[6]

There are a number of factors associated with the state which introduce complexity on the design and oversight of resource allocation procedures (Gorringe, 2001, p. 126). These factors include:

- the power of the state (associated with tyranny, commitment, and capture);
- centralization (associated with making decisions and coordinating action, limited competition);
- organization (agency and other contracting issues); and
- collective choice (free-riders, rational ignorance of voters, limitations of voting systems, and so on).

Modern budget management attempts to address these factors. For instance, the twin initiatives of applying increased managerial flexibility alongside more accountability is a clear case where political decision-makers have assigned some of their rights to others. In this one area, there is a specialization of role and function, which deals with centralization; there is a control placed on government power, which deals with problems associated with credible commitment; and there are also issues associated with organizational management. If increased managerial flexibility is provided as a way of delivering on a harder and more credible budget constraint, consistent with the political objectives, then it would also be reasonable to expect such flexibility to be positively related to improved fiscal outturns.[7] Notwithstanding these sorts of initiatives, the characteristics of many of the services being supplied by government (such as policy advice and diplomatic representation) suggest that they rely at least to some degree on the organizational form of a bureaucracy, in which the costs of making decisions and implementing them are high (Ouchi, 1980).

As Schelling has pointed out (in a different context), a budget manager can take lessons from traffic signals—although planning is often associated with control, the crucial element is often coordination (Schelling, 1978, p. 121).

In this context, the role played by the provision of performance-based information can be considered. Such information moderates the problems associated with information asymmetry, allowing at least some informed consideration as to whether government interventions are working.

Changes in allocative efficiency

There are likely to be three main factors driving a reallocation of government resources reflecting changed priorities to increase allocative efficiency: preference changes; relative cost changes; and affordability changes caused by movements in national income.

Preference changes

There are several sources of change associated with preferences. By its nature, government is concerned with collective action and collective will. Those charged with power to allocate resources do so based on some concept of the will of the governed. Therefore, if either the will of the governed was seen to change or the way that that will was relayed politically, then that would amount to a preference change. At times, events may lead to rapid changes in preferences, such as an increased preference for domestic protection in the US following the terrorist attacks of September 11, 2001. Politicians are, of course, active players in the creation of, and interpretation of, public preferences.

In the language of performance budgeting, preferences are generally concerned with outcomes, with the concern being, for example, to improve the health of the population, its education achievement, or, perhaps, perceived safety. Although empirically, we can observe that at times the public or a political party may express their preferences in terms of an output (such as improved taxation inquiry services) or even inputs (such as having a preference for the public sector making some services, such as higher education), for the most part, it is reasonable to argue that changes in political preferences are concerned with desired outcomes. In this way, it is possible to see a corollary between changing preferences based on outcomes, and consumer theory, which is concerned with maximizing an individual's utility.

There are two important asides here. First, just with an individual, a lack of observed outcome success does not necessarily translate into more (or less) funding. It may lead to the redesign of the intervention. For instance, lack of success in drug enforcement programs may or may not yield an increase or a reduction in funding. Second, political agency problems and poor budgeting procedures can combine to make a mess of expenditure prioritization. Quite simply, governments have often allocated resources to poor uses. In poor budgeting systems, preferences are generally not well articulated—the clearest statement of preferences may come through analyzing actual budget allocations.

Relative cost changes

There are numerous ways in which the cost of an achieved public intervention may change. First, and most simply, changes in input prices may feed through to changes in output costs, ceteris paribus.[8] Second, while the output characteristics may not change, the input technologies may change, involving a different configuration of inputs, yielding a different output cost. Third, the nature of the output may change through a redesign of the intervention itself, such as by choosing a different policy instrument. (For instance, measures to reduce demand through preemptive interventions have been used in the judicial systems (pre-trial conferences), and have been recently adapted in some health systems, where telephone consultations between health providers and patients are used to sort patients into those who should access outpatient services and those who should not.) The task of the budgeter is to manage these potential sources of change in such a way as to achieve the agreed fiscal and budgetary objectives.

In some cases, there may appear to be a mixture of the two effects. For instance, the overwhelming evidence of an emerging aging problem—involving a smaller share of the population engaged in the workforce—produced a change in the perceived costs associated with universal pension schemes, and a relatively abrupt change in the tastes of some countries for universal, tax-supported pension and health systems. Arguably, the preference for financially sound older people did not change, but the realization of the non-affordability of achieving that through traditional policy means has led to a substitution of new forms of intervention, replacing the old forms.

Income changes

As the aggregate budget constraint may become relatively more relaxed as income increases, there are likely to be different mixes of consumption that will satisfy allocative efficiency. Decreasing marginal demand for certain goods or services is often associated with necessities, while increasing demand is associated with luxuries. In government, the (intended and revealed) consumption patterns of poor countries are discernibly different from those in advanced countries.

The particular budget management issues associated with sudden changes in affordability have given rise to a subset of budget management literature. In particular, additional strains can be placed on the quality of budget allocation in economies which are exposed to wide income variations perhaps related to high dependence on trade, especially commodities.[9]

From sources of change into plans of action

These sources of change to resource allocation are not always self-evident and frequently require considerable finesse to see them converted into reallocations. As Schick has commented, to achieve positive public expenditure outcomes, it is necessary that information, incentives, and other institutional arrangements be properly aligned (Schick, 1999, p. 2). Contributing to these institutions and mechanisms of budgeting is a skilled and informed Ministry of Finance (MoF) focused on these matters. The limited capacity of Ministries of Finance in developing countries is one factor constraining the efficiency of resource allocation in such countries—Caiden and Wildavsky refer to this as a lack of redundancy (1974).

The transformation of traditional command-and-control MoFs into today's modern MoFs is a necessary aspect of seizing and converting allocative change through preference, price, and affordability changes. This transformation has been commented on elsewhere (Schick, 1997, and more recently, Wanna et al., 2003). Modern MoFs are responsible for designing systems of coordination which bring together information at appropriate times, in digestible forms, to be acted upon by decision-makers who have their incentives aligned to the allocative efficiency goal. Their task is to design a budget allocation system which, through the behaviors of the participants, augment rather than detract from the goal of allocative efficiency. This requires information about the production and cost of government-funded outputs, and the degree to which these outputs contribute to the achievement of government outcomes.

Reallocative mechanisms

The desire to reallocate often stems from factors outside the budgeting system. For example, political preferences may abruptly change due to a change in government, or as a result of a natural or economic disaster. However, even in such circumstances, the use of performance information in the budget process assists as an instrument for translating preferences (including those of a new government) more effectively into expenditure allocations—that is, as an instrument for better prioritizing expenditure.

Practices across countries in the past two decades or so indicate that there have been changes associated basic mechanisms to assist improving allocative efficiency, in particular:[10]

- the medium-term orientation to the budget has been strengthened to identify current and future costs of policies;

- efforts have been made to align better budget resources with the policy priorities of government, and to reduce fragmentation across government.

In support of this, a high proportion of advanced countries and a growing proportion of emerging and developing economies introduced government-wide initiatives to improve output information at least five to ten years ago. And ongoing adaptation is continuing, with Organization for Economic Cooperation and Development (OECD) countries recording major ongoing initiatives in the past five years as well (Curristine, 2005, p. 6). Nowadays, fully three-quarters of OECD countries include performance information with their budgets (Joumard et al., 2003, p. 129).

Mechanisms to deal with changes in fiscal fortunes

An increase in available resources gives the government an opportunity to allocate these resources to their best use. The choice basically comes down to deciding whether to strengthen the financial position of government or not (to be more precise, whether to use money to increase net financial worth, or whether to spend it on increased services or lower taxes). In the first category are decisions that would hold the increased resources as financial assets (whether in a stabilization reserve or other), or use the windfall to pay down debt; in the second category may be decisions to lower the tax rates, or to increase spending in a particular way. The opposite occurs during a downturn, with the particular way that such a downturn will flow through to the fiscal position being influenced by whether the overarching control is a deficit limit control—thereby forcing either an increase in taxation or a reduction in spending—or an appropriation control, in turn forcing an increase in taxation or an increase in debt in order to meet appropriation requirements.[11]

When countries face high fiscal stress, then prioritization may be most important and crucial. A failure to prioritize may see an unaffordable increase in aggregate spending, with ensuing flow-ons to the tax rate, and associated deadweight costs. If the fiscal scoring system relies on cash rather than accrual accounting, then capital spending is particularly at risk. This was the case in Europe during the 1990s (Brumby, 2000, p. 3). But history suggests that governments have often stumbled in allocative efficiency in good times as well. When the marginal value of each tax dollar seems lower, then the decision-maker may be prone to allocating it particularly poorly.

In the same way that the free cashflow problem has been documented as a *bête noire* for firms seeking high-returning investments (Jensen and Meckling, 1976), fiscal abundance can induce growing allocative inefficiency. In both cases, there is a lack of credible constraints on the power of the decision-makers. Bigger, more diversified government does not necessarily satisfy voters, just as bigger, more diversified firms do not necessarily satisfy shareholders. Indeed, one recent empirical study showed that governments interested in maximizing the life satisfaction of their voters should, regardless of their ideology, limit their direct interventions in the economy to allow voters a high degree of personal freedom (Bjornskov et al., 2005, p. 23). To the end of constraining the available discretion, there have been two major initiatives in recent years: the development of fiscal rules, and the creation of fiscal boards.[12]

Mechanisms to reflect political preferences through strategy management

Allocative efficiency can be enhanced if, assuming a robust political process, resources flow to where they are most valued by the ruling government, as agents of the people. An important source of articulation of these preferences may be through the strategic phase of the budget process. The strategic phase involves agreeing to the following:

- an aggregate constraint to apply to all spending, in the context of the outlook for the economy over the medium term;
- an indicative scope for the pursuit of major new initiatives;
- identification of sectors/policies and programs for special treatment, either for cuts or additional spending; and
- identification of the general rule to apply in transmitting limits to government departments.

Box 9.1 Budget formulation in developing countries

The benefits from the strategic phase of the budget may be more tenuous in countries where the annual budget is not implemented as presented and fiscal blight occurs regularly. In such circumstances, many of the decisions which actually allocate resources are not made during formulation at all but are, in reality, made during execution, often via cash rationing. In such circumstances, the immediate need is to put in place a budget which could be considered realistic and which has some hope of implementation. Sadly, the chronic disconnect between budgeting and planning in many poor countries was identified by Caiden and Wildavsky in *Planning and Budgeting in Poor Countries* (1974) some 30 years ago. At the very least, a credible strategic phase of the budget will require effective budget implementation.

In addition to the problems of perpetual fiscal blight, some developing countries may have suffered from resource misallocation associated with corruption. One mechanism designed to exert pressure on improving the quality of the internal control systems in order to ensure that resources go to where they are meant to go is the Public Expenditure Tracking Survey (PETS). The initial set of PETSs carried out in countries such as Uganda and Mozambique showed there to be a high proportion of leakage from the intended purpose stated in the budget.

One explanation for the lack of credibility associated with the development of robust budgeting systems in such countries is that they are ineffective in constraining or dealing with the types of uncertainties that such countries face. In particular, high levels of uncertainty may induce short-sighted behavior and a preference for systems which can be manipulated to meet short-term needs. An extreme form of this dynamic incentive (and misallocative equilibrium) could be associated with high adult mortality rates. In such circumstances, adults are unlikely to invest in actions that generate long-term benefits and short-term costs, preferring instead to take actions generating short-term benefits at long-term costs.[a]

[a] See a recent study by Lorentzen et al. (2005).

Aggregate constraint

The advice to government on the aggregate expenditure limit is generally the core work of the minister of finance. This is where Musgrave's concern for stabilization and efficient allocation between the public and private sectors come to the fore (Musgrave and Musgrave, 1959). The minister needs to convince his colleagues of the desirability of a limited spending envelope. To do this, he would be expected to enlist the leader's assistance. The argument for the aggregate limit may need to focus on the advisable tax take, the appropriate debt setting, and the pressures from the community to spend—the sorts of issues that Schick has raised in terms of sustainability. By focusing on the limit and the collective aspirations of the government as a whole, it may be possible for the leaders to gain collective agreement.

Managing the baseline

Decision-making behaviors suggest that unless there is real growth in the expenditure aggregate to allow new allocations, decision-makers will be faced in an unsolvable dispute where no one spender will be prepared to give up resources to fund the initiatives of another spender.[13] The Minister of Finance can try to break this impasse, without adding to real spending, by imposing an across-the-board rebasing of all agencies. The determination of the amount of and the reasoning behind this device may differ through time and between jurisdictions, but its purpose is clear: to meet the need to constrain the aggregate and provide some funds for new initiatives or higher priority spending (or reductions in taxation). In some cases, this may be subject to a very simple rule—that ministries' budgets will not increase in nominal terms—while on other occasions, there may be a set of quite specific deflators (or adjustors) attached to different input or output types. Though it could be argued from an allocative efficiency point of view that such across-the-board cuts are likely to induce misallocations, this can be disputed if the cuts are kept reasonably modest, in the 1–2 percentage point range of administrative spending. Notwithstanding the very large productivity increases witnessed in knowledge-intensive industries in advanced economies over the past 15 years or so, there appears to be reluctance for government to impose a standard efficiency dividend of more than 1.5 percent of administrative costs.[14]

The degree of flexibility on the spending side can also be assisted by the specific identification of spending programs that will be disbanded. But in many cases, there are no incentives for ministers to bring forward such plans unless they believe that they will receive a comparable level of resources returned to them. There are several ways that this can be dealt with—one is to seek indicative proposals for, say, 2–5 percent cuts from each ministry, with the Ministry of Finance reviewing the veracity of the claims, and the ministers determining collectively which they would like to pursue. There are two important ingredients to ensuring a contribution from this sort of exercise: (1), to ensure that incentives are working to have agencies' reveal the right information; and (2), to ensure that the MoF's officials are sufficiently knowledgeable in the areas of the agencies' businesses that they can interrogate the agency staff. Another way is to use some fomalized program review, either collectively or bilaterally—this is discussed later.

Identification of specific initiatives

During the strategic phase, individual ministers or spending agencies can be expected to make arguments that their initiatives which may require additional funding are supportive of the government's key priorities. In so doing, they would be expected to align their requests with perceived shifts in public opinion and the policies of the government. For a government already in office, the underlying argument is that the particular initiatives will yield better results than those lost from reductions in spending in other areas. For a newly elected government, the argument is that some of the results that have been achieved are not those that are valued by the new government—which has a set of different preferred results—which have been endorsed by the people, and are thus legitimate. In both cases—newly elected and continuing government—choices concerning policy priorities will draw on some form of citizen legitimization.

This is the core strategic management task. Strategic decision-making requires acceptance of a framework for considering trade-offs. In the 1960s, this was seen as part of the initiative to use Planning, Programming, and Budgeting Systems (PPBSs), which focused mainly on the planning task aimed at more systematic strategic decision-making, but failed to achieve this for a range of reasons including the excess bureaucratic paperwork and failed to deal adequately with the incentive problems faced by operational management. There is a general consensus that the PPBS exercises bore little fruit for a variety of reasons (Boston et al., 1996, p. 384) including their creation of an excess of bureaucratic paperwork.

Determination of the bounds of strategic versus operational management lies at the heart of the decentralization dilemma (see the appendix to this chapter). Clearly, cabinet could not run a process which considered all manner of operational decisions, as it would become overburdened, and the information needs would grind effective decision-making to a halt. Accordingly, central government agencies need to frame the agenda and the preparation of materials for the strategic phase. Different approaches to this task have been adopted; with a majority of OECD countries saying that they have in recent years introduced mechanisms to increase the focus on overall priorities (Joumard et al., 2003, p. 121).

The budget process can usefully differentiate the management of the resource base to meet the costs of pre-existing policies, and the management of new initiatives. Depending on the size and complexity of agencies, it may also prove useful to allow some discretion for reallocation to new priorities at the level of portfolio ministers. In such circumstances, not all funding requests for new initiatives would be referred to the minister of finance or the cabinet. Instead, a rule would be created to determine the characteristics of new priorities that would need to be considered by central decision-makers, versus those that could be treated at agency level. Generally, the more detailed the appropriation law, the less discretion can be provided at the agency level. Arguably, all new proposals involving substantial additional funding should be considered at the center; and presumably all initiatives which may invoke public debate should be referred to the center, whether they involve additional funds from the center, or can be funded from reallocation at the agency. Different jurisdictions, and different ruling parties within the same jurisdictions, may take a range of approaches to this issue of determining the degree of discretion over new initiatives at the agency level.

One important safeguard to ensuring that the center is not overrun by work is to assign a gatekeeper role. In this role, perhaps through an officials' committee, all new expenditure initiatives are first assessed to ensure that they are bona fide, and that the cost implications are correctly estimated. This ensures that only validated initiatives are considered by central decision-makers, and that all baselines remain firm. Simply put, it is likely that the top-level central decision-makers (in a parliamentary system, the cabinet) will find things more manageable if such a committee is set up.

In the case of a newly formed government, the strategic phase may run somewhat differently. There may have already been a government formation process—to which officials may or may not have been a part—which has specified the most important policies and objectives for the government. These may be identified in a coalition agreement or similar other. As such, an agreement or existence of a government policy platform would be taken as the starting position for the strategic phase.

Planning period

An extended planning period—beyond the annual focus of the budget—provides a means to assess sustainability of policy settings, but is complicated with issues associated with uncertainty. Most governments have sought to use the outyear estimates to assess current settings rather than formalize this information as formal budgets. Such updated information, through, say, a forward estimates system, can assist in interpreting the dynamic position of the budget and the key drivers of change.

Alignment and fragmentation

Much of the literature about medium-term expenditure frameworks suggests that there is a role for the representation of government preferences in terms of sectoral or functional spending limits (see World Bank, 1998; Le Houerou and Taliercio, 2002, p. 10). However, there can be difficulties with converting such spending limits onto the business plans and organizational allocations that agencies require for their operations. If there is no specific responsibility aligned to the functional or sectoral area, as is often the case, then the allocation of resources within that functional area may be a fraught process involving conflicting priorities and political power, with perceptions of winners and losers. In such cases, the estimates provided are little more than numbers on a page. In an assessment of public expenditure management systems carried out by the World Bank and the IMF, this lack of integration between planning and medium-term budgeting was found to be common, with 18 of the 25 countries being assessed as having medium-term projections poorly integrated into their annual budget cycle (IDA and IMF, 2005, p. 26).

There are two main responses to address this issue: either reorganize to better align accountabilities and functional classification, or change the definitions of sectors and functions to move them away from their pre-existing definitions to better approximate the distribution of accountabilities (this is the case, for example,

Box 9.2 Managing the fragmentation threat to allocative efficiency

Government administrations have introduced many devices which have the potential to fragment the budget and protect particular interests. These can counteract the goal of allocative efficiency by lessening the degree of scrutiny on these arrangements and by introducing multiple sets of priorities, serving different interests.

Form of fragmentation	*Cause of potential misallocation*	*Remedial action to improve allocative efficiency*
External loans and grants	Imposition of donors' priorities; draining of matching resources	General budget support
Dual budgeting	Failure to link capital and operating may lead to new non-productive assets	Integration between capital planning and operations planning; business plans
Extrabudgetary funds, autonomous agencies	Own priorities dominate those of government	Clearing house for consideration of all expenditures (virtual funds); contractual mechanisms
Tax earmarking/ user charges	Over-resourcing to one area at the expense of others	Clearing house for consideration of all expenditures; contractual mechanisms
Tax expenditures	Benefits mistargeted and poorly measured	Estimation and reporting of the cost; consideration with all expenditures
Uncontrolled virement between programs	Substitution of different purpose expenditure	Specifying clear rules about purpose and virement
Quasi-fiscal activities (QFAs)	Subsidies being captured by special interests	Transparency or allocation of community service obligations and other QFAs
Single-year consideration	Lack of awareness on emerging fiscal trends leading to abrupt changes in allocations	Multi-year budget frameworks

in Sweden, with the use of expenditure area limits). As the distribution of decision rights within government addresses many issues, many of which may be directly political, then the second approach may prove more expedient.[15]

Alignment between sectoral limits and ministerial or bureaucratic authority may be not sufficient to deal with some forms of fragmentation, a number of which are described in Box 9.2. Many of the institutional arrangements described are designed to remove resource allocation discretion from the center, in some cases, hard-wiring it through specific devices and in others, subjecting it to other forces, with the effect of biasing the allocation of resources.

Treatment of capital

A standout feature of much of the traditional public budget in many countries has been the homogeneous treatment of capital and operating expenditures. Given the different economic characteristics of capital and operating expenditures, the failure to measure and treat them differently would likely lead to misallocation.[16]

At the agency level, capital budgeting needs to mirror the strategic planning processes of governments as a whole; in particular, business cases need to be made in relation to the following: expanding operations; reducing costs through substitution of labor or other inputs by capital; and replacement or refurbishment of old capital stock. A capital budgeting system needs to be able to cope with all these different demands for capital funds. Consideration of the different characteristics of capital spending does not in itself increase fragmentation—indeed, examination of the linkage between asset creation and operating activities is a crucial component to strategic planning. An aspect worthy of consideration is whether there may be opportunities to make use of private sector involvement in public investment. A key long-term allocative consideration to be taken into account is the nature of and exposure to financial risks—this is a large topic to be dealt with elsewhere.

Mechanisms to consider changes in the form of intervention

The substitution of one form of intervention over another to achieve the same outcome is a means of improving allocative efficiency. In such cases, the redistribution of resources to the new intervention will be carried out if the new intervention dominates the old intervention in terms of effectiveness and, most probably, value for money.[17] There have been a number of ways that budget systems have been reformed to attempt to bring consideration of the type of intervention to the fore in considering resource allocation. Some of these measures have been particularly high profile, such as the redirection of resources to consumers through vouchers, rather than the consumption of resources as suppliers of government services. To varying degrees, all these mechanisms seek to deal with the issue of informing the central decision makers, so that they can compare the effectiveness of spending programs across functional and organizational areas. A critical issue remains concerning the quantum of information to be sent to the center and the span of the center's decision control, versus the nature of decisions left in spending agencies. Accordingly, some mechanisms which tend to focus more on routine or operational management issues tend to transmit information to the local level only, whereas more strategic information (or more material) information needs to find its way to the central decision-makers.

The following mechanisms have been used by administrations in recent years:

- formal program review processes—also known as fundamental reviews—zero-base reviews, and output price reviews, sometimes resulting in change of policy instrument or type of intervention;
- ongoing policy advice and review, sometimes associated with a decoupling of policy, funder, and provider; and
- requirements to produce performance information, which in turn may be considered by auditors either in attest auditing, or via performance audits.[18]

Box 9.3 Integrating government resource allocation practices: Victoria's Integrated Management Cycle

The State of Victoria, Australia, is one of many jurisdictions that implemented formally integrated planning cycles to government. The Integrated Management Cycle (IMC), which was introduced more than ten years ago, seeks to improve government sector performance by:

- enhancing responsiveness to government's desired outcomes and priorities;
- strengthening resource allocation and management processes;
- improving the quality of service provision; and
- facilitating corporate and individual performance assessment.

The components include:

- whole-of-government budget sector planning;
- departmental and agency planning;
- annual budget and resource allocation;
- legislative planning;
- internal government evaluation, review, and reporting; and
- external information, reporting, and accountability requirements.

The first stage—known as Setting the Budget Strategy—is the process by which the Expenditure Review Committee of cabinet (ERC) reviews the government's short- to medium-term overall policy and financial strategy, and sets the government's strategic direction and framework for the upcoming budget, including: aggregate budget strategy, targets and objectives; strategic output and asset investment priorities; and department-specific initiatives that may be considered for funding at ERC Stage 2.

In setting the budget strategic output and asset investment priorities, the cabinet committee's decisions are based on a range of information, including:

- the government's broad long-term social, economic, and environmental goals and measures;
- a presentation by the Treasurer containing information on the fiscal and economic outlook including actual and projected performance against budget targets and objectives;
- presentations from portfolio ministers on departmental strategic priorities, including proposed cross-portfolio initiatives; and
- information and/or advice from other stakeholders.

Subject to capacity constraints, specific initiatives that are consistent with the agreed budget priorities are approved by ERC for consideration for funding at ERC Stage 2. Decisions made in ERC Stage 1 provide direction to ministers and departments in developing detailed new initiatives in the annual budget process by indicating the short- to medium-term strategic priorities of government and those initiatives that ERC may consider for funding in ERC Stage 2, in which detailed proposals from ministers for new output and asset initiatives that were agreed upon in ERC Stage 1 are considered for funding.

Source: Department of Treasury and Finance (Australia) (2005).

Program review processes

These processes can be distinguished by the fact that they are managed by the center of government—most usually, the cabinet office or budget office (Kraan, 2005, p. 39). Typically, such processes involve the targeted review of certain programs, with respect to certain fundamental questions:

- whether the program is justified for government intervention at all;
- whether the program should be administered by a different level of government;
- whether the program uses the appropriate policy instrument for its purposes; and
- whether the program is sufficiently targeted to ensure that its benefits flow to the intended recipients.

Not surprisingly, program review represents a struggle between the center and line agencies. Portfolio ministers can attempt to bypass such review mechanisms. The UK and the Netherlands currently have formal program review mechanisms, while a particularly celebrated case in terms of reallocation was carried out as part of the fiscal consolidation efforts in Canada during the 1990s. In the Canadian case, the central focus was provided for this task by the cabinet office (known there as the Privy Council Office).[19] In coalition governments, it is important to have broad representation on the program review's overseeing body so that program review does not turn into a witch hunt of one party or another. It is fundamental that support occurs at the highest level, and, if necessary, the Minister of Finance's own programs and those of the premier should be included early in the round.

Arguably, institutionalized program review is nothing more than what a modern, analytically informed budget office should be doing routinely and should have been doing for some time. Through its assessment of policy and the use of intervention analysis, the budget office acts as the agent of the center, making recommendations to government decision-makers on improving the allocation of resources. This role as a contester of agency programs and priorities is fundamental to the modern role of the budget office, seeing it move away from command and control; instead, it would restructure institutional arrangements to alter the incentives on key players, in particular ensuring that the traditional problems of information asymmetry associated with government activity are mitigated to some extent. The need to perform program review means that the budget office is forever moving closer to the role of an office of strategic management, with capability in many of the major policy lines of government (such as education) and a need for more deeply developed analytical skills, rather than the clerical skills of yesteryear. Quite simply, budget offices no longer do the degree of transaction-oriented work they used to do.

The logical frame of reference for program review can be adjusted as needs be. For instance, the affordability concerns with aspects of the welfare state in the context of changing demographics appear to have triggered very high-profile individual cases of program review on such issues as the affect of the aging population, or universal access to some welfare benefits, on the budget. These cases may directly spin out of the concern for strategic management at the center and the need to position the fiscal aggregates into a long-term sustainable position. By far the majority of OECD countries have carried out reviews in the past decade or so concerning the affects of aging.

Program review may result in the determination that the service should not be funded through general taxation, but instead should rely on user charges. A number of goals can be addressed through the appropriate use of user charging, with many having an allocative aspect. For example, the choice of who to charge may give rise to the question of whether those being charged (or their representatives) can effectively monitor standards, exert countervailing pressure on costs, and find alternatives to public provision. The additional inflow of income to the government and the possible reduction in production volume can provide some flexibility for the line agency or the government decision-makers to consider alternative uses for the funds. Guides exist as to the economic circumstances when user charging is beneficial, and the appropriate design associated with effective implementation.[20]

Ongoing policy evaluation and review

Program review may be supported by an ongoing cycle of program evaluation. Some jurisdictions have set goals of reviewing all government spending programs over a period of time and, consistent with that goal, have introduced mechanisms such as agency-based evaluations to ensure that critical information is flowing continually within agencies and—whenever possible—to the center about the effect of government interventions. However, this form of review is chiefly distinguished from program review by its requirement for a lower level of involvement from the center. Notwithstanding, the center sets the rules for this form of review and draws selectively on the information uncovered. A problem remains with information congestion, as the amount of data created by an evaluation each year of, say, 20 percent of all government programs can be overwhelming. Leverage can be gathered by the judicious allocation of budget office staff, or other independent analysts with similar orientations, to the evaluation teams involved in such work. Further advantage can be gained by requiring the transmission, and perhaps even publication, of all such reports to the center.

While different nomenclature may be used in different jurisdictions, the basic forms of evaluation can be about improvements in program design, improvements in process, or whether the program has contributed in a valid way to outcomes.

Role of performance information

The assessment as to whether policy and administration are addressing the priorities of government requires information about the performance of the policies. This is a topic worthy of separate consideration; suffice to say that information about the use of inputs, the production of outputs and the affects on outcomes is central to assessing whether interventions are achieving the desired goals in a cost-effective manner. This issue is extensively covered in Part Three of this book.

Summing-up: ten rules of thumb to assist with allocating resources in accordance with priorities

The foregoing discussion leads to the view that the way in which the budget is managed can lead to resource allocation which more closely reflects priorities. In other words, the design of budgetary mechanisms matters. Budgeting in accordance with priorities is not purely a matter of political will or some exogenous factor applied to decision-making. The preparedness to make decisions and the quality of those decisions can be influenced by the mechanisms at hand. In drawing the chapter to a conclusion, ten rules of thumb are recommended; of these, five relate to institutional design, and five relate to information requirements.

Institutional design factors

Item 1: A committee of the cabinet should be established to represent the collective interest in overseeing the budget. This committee should in turn be supported by a technical committee, which acts to ensure that only justifiable claims can be made on the agenda of the cabinet committee.

Item 2: The budget entity should be defined broadly to ensure that all public programs and public financial exposures are appropriately captured. There should be an absence of unconstrained fragmentation mechanisms.

Item 3: The performance and accountability system should be integrated with budget management concerns; agency performance in its use of resources is an important aspect of the assessment of the performance of government chief executives.

Item 4: An efficiency or productivity factor should be applied to the baselines of all agencies. In the absence of any empirical evidence to the contrary, the factor should be applied at the rate of 1.5 percent per year.

Item 5: A system of fundamental program reviews should be instituted, with the reports being communicated through the officers' technical committee through to the cabinet committee. The trigger for such reviews should be agreed at a political level, and while can include criteria such as when a department seeks additional resources to produce the same level of outputs, they should also be cast wider to ensure that low-profile programs are also subjected to such reviews.

Information factors

Item 1: Intended outcomes are required during budget formulation and are also reported to the legislature, alongside the budget proposal. Proposals to change budgetary allocations are informed by consideration of the changes in intended outcomes. Ex-post reporting on these is required.

Item 2: The outputs to be produced in support of achieving the outcomes are also reported to the decision-makers at the agency, in the executive, and the legislature.

Item 3: Forward estimates (for at least three years) of the cost of unchanged policy are provided to the legislature on a classification basis which is well aligned to the political and bureaucratic distribution of authority.

Item 4: Performance reporting, in terms of the outputs produced, is subject to ex-post attestation through audit.

Item 5: All cost information should be full (accrual-based) cost.

Appendix: public budgeting and decentralization

Public budgeting involves the distribution of decision rights via the institutions available to government. As such, it presents as a case of the decentralized dilemma.

The knowledge of decision-makers is limited by both current scientific progress and also by their capacity to absorb, comprehend, and process the available knowledge (Zoghi, 2002, p. 6). This introduces trade-offs in the optimal point of allocation for decisions. Jensen and Meckling (1990, p. 4) point out that when knowledge is valuable in decision-making, there are benefits to collocating decision authority with the knowledge that is valuable to those decisions. There are few approaches to achieving this: moving knowledge to the individual with the decision rights; alternatively to shift the decision rights to the individual who possesses the knowledge; or a combination of the two.

The first approach leaves the organization faced with the costs of transporting knowledge. Radner (1992, p. 1393), drawing from the literature of computer science, defines four aspects of the processing of information that involve costs: observation of the data about the environment, capabilities and resources of the processors, the communication network that stores and moves the data, and the delay between the observation of the environment and the implementation of the decision. The magnitude of these costs will be influenced by the type of knowledge being transferred, current technology, and the organizational structure. As a result, the nature of these costs will be uniquely determined for any given organization, or sets of organizations, such as a government. By example, the movement of too many decisions to the center will overload it, as decision-makers are human with only a finite amount of time available to allocate to each decision—for instance, under the then Czechoslovakian state planning system, planners were reputed to have had only six minutes available to spend on planning each industry (Gorringe, 2001, p. 142). The second approach of shifting decisions to those with knowledge leaves the organization faced with agency costs that result from transferring decision rights—a problem of coordinating the decentralized decisions. These costs include the costs of developing and enforcing a set of contracts among agents with conflicting interests.

In making the determination of the best location for decision rights, and hence seeking to achieve allocative efficiency through these decision-makers, an organization is faced with trading off between agency costs and knowledge transfer costs. Figure 9.1 shows the intuition behind this.[21] On the left-hand side, there is complete centralization—one single planner makes all decisions and all relevant knowledge is transferred to him or her. This results in zero agency costs—the principal and the agent are one. A movement toward the right side of the figure indicates decentralization, which increases agency costs and decreases the cost of transmitting information. When all decision rights have been transferred to the individuals in possession of specific knowledge, the organization is completely decentralized, as indicated by the vertical line on the far right of Figure 9.1. At this point, agency costs are at their highest, and information costs at their lowest. Optimally, a location of decision rights that minimizes the sum of these two costs would be chosen.

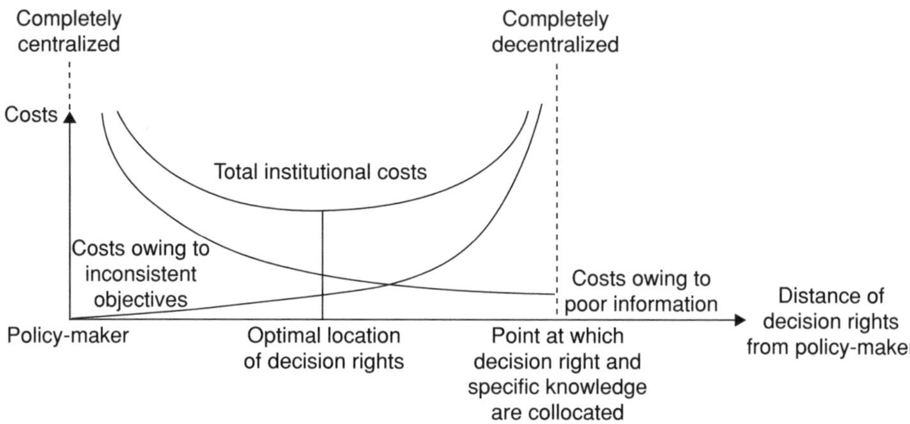

Figure 9.1 Trade-offs between inconsistent objectives and poor information

Source: Adapted from Jensen and Meckling (1990).

The relevance for reallocation of resources between competing priorities is clear. The more a resourcing decision relates to the choice over the type and purpose of intervention, and thus influenced by the political preferences, the higher the costs of moving critical information to the decision-makers will be. Conversely, the more a decision relates to dealing with local conditions, the better placed the local agent is to respond to this information, but the more there is a need to make government policy clear so that the action can be consistent with that policy. As Schick has suggested, the center requires strategic capacity, and the organizations of government require operational information (Schick, 1997, p. 17).

Different administrative structures deal differently with this trade-off in the allocation of discretion. Some countries, such as Sweden, New Zealand, the Netherlands, and the UK, are characterized by strong devolution, whereas some others such as Italy, France, and Germany are characterized both by more legalistic traditions and more central control (Kraan, 2005, p. 25). The introduction of the Next Step agencies in the UK could be considered a case where the value accorded to local operating information was given precedence over the value given to closeness to political control. While there may be differences between jurisdictions in terms of the relative value put on decentralization, it is also clear that there are differences within jurisdictions as well. For instance, the relatively new budget control or appropriation taxonomies in New Zealand and the UK, which have different controls for administrative costs, transfers, and capital expenditures, demonstrate differentiated discretion according to the underlying economic nature of the expenditures.

Notes

1. The author would like to acknowledge comments on this chapter from colleagues including Holger van Eden, Marc Robinson, and Theo Thomas, and from Professor Philip Joyce. Any errors remain the author's.
2. Developed by Musgrave in the classic work *The Theory of Public Finance* (Musgrave and Musgrave, 1959).
3. Literature exists which assesses governments that are too small and thus unable to deliver the merit and public goods necessary for efficient operation of the economy. On the other hand, burgeoning government relies on increasing rates of taxation, which encompass increasing marginal rates of deadweight loss. A consequence of this is that not only must the positive welfare consequences of public intervention increase to offset the growing deadweight costs of taxation, but also that variability in tax rates will, ceteris paribus, lead to higher deadweight cost than raising the same revenue through a constant rate of taxation over the same period. This, accordingly, relates aggregate management of expenditure very directly to broader allocative efficiency.
4. This is the focus of writing associated with Von Hagen, among others. The idea that a common pool problem is intrinsically rooted in the typical public budget process can be traced back to Weingast et al. (1981).
5. Whereas 60 percent of US states used no ceilings in 1970, this number had fallen to 3 percent by 2000 (Burns and Lee, 2004, p. 3).
6. Political agency problems can induce distortions in resource allocation; accordingly, the degree of the political agency problems is likely related to the observed rate of distortion. For instance, as Alesina and Tabellini recently argued, the pro-cyclical nature of fiscal policy in developing countries is evidence of voters—poorly informed and victims of an agency problem which will not allow rents to be pushed to zero—seeking a second-best solution to constraining politicians through pro-cyclical fiscal policy. This has the effect of starving the Leviathan, but with associated welfare losses (Alesina and Tabellini, 2005, p. 3).
7. The argument is that the more responsive movement of resources at the line management level is, the less pressure is placed on spending caps, the more likely fiscal consolidation exercises that rely on reductions in spending are to be successful. There has been a lack of empirical research on this question.
8. Some jurisdictions will refer to this as an output price, as there is an arm's-length contract between the funder and the supplier, even where the supplier is a government agency.
9. For instance, see Davis et al. (2003).
10. One could also argue that fiscal rules that have variously set limits on expenditures, deficit levels, taxes, or debt, have also contributed substantially to the incentives for reallocation. Without such constraints, the desire to meet new priorities can be added on to an expenditure base, rather than involve a reallocation from lower-priority areas to higher-priority areas. But fiscal rules are the subject of other analyses.
11. In some cases, even where the overarching control is an appropriation control, the executive retains the right to vary downward spending from these appropriation limits. In other cases, the appropriation control may be seen as a floor and a ceiling.
12. Fiscal rules should be anchored in a medium-term perspective, be defined over the cycle, and be unambiguous in their coverage. Fiscal rules should distinguish the balance sheet effects of different forms of expenditure, so as to counteract the bias to cut capital spending first. Independent fiscal boards are a relatively new innovation, which has

been touted as an aggregate control protector in certain circumstances (see Bonato et al., 2005, p. 4).

While neither of these conditions may look profound, it is worth noting that Fund staff recently argued that the fiscal framework rule applying in Sweden had been interpreted as a yearly structural balance and as an average balance—nominal or structural—over the cycle (Bonato et al., 2005, p. 12).

The Fund has identified two types of fiscal agencies: Independent Fiscal Agencies (IFAs), which mimic independent central banks on the fiscal side, and which could be mandated to enforce fiscal balance targets; and fiscal councils, which would not receive any authority over policy, but rather would provide independent analysis and assessment of fiscal developments (IMF, 2007, p. 2). The rationale for the agencies depends on the extent to which they could be expected to diminish the risks of an injudicious use of discretion. The Fund points out that to date, there is no IFA in operation in any country.

13. This behavior is called loss aversion, in which the marginal utility from a gain is strictly less than the marginal utility from an equivalent loss. Reallocations will not naturally occur as decision makers (spenders) will fight extremely hard to protect themselves from the loss associated with reductions in resources (Kahnemann and Tversky, 1979).
14. Introduced first into Sweden and Australia, the idea of the efficiency dividend was to take from baselines that amount of spending which otherwise would have been converted into increased outputs or higher-than-necessary input prices.
15. In this context, it is perhaps worth recalling that the internationally-accepted functional definitions of government are primarily to assist the comparative analysis of government. Accordingly, the functional depiction has clear analytical uses, but perhaps less clear decision-making use. Rather than being an instrument for allocation, such functional data represent the allocations made.
16. A case in point would be a fiscal scoring system that focused solely on a measure such as the Public Sector Borrowing Requirement.
17. In many cases, this may involve substituting one output with another, but on some occasions it may principally involve substituting regulation or law for an output.
18. The use of performance information in attest auditing requires there to have been an accounting standard issued by the jurisdiction's accounting standards setter.
19. The Privy Council Office, the Ministry of Finance and the Treasury Board operated together to pursue this change agenda; however, the Privy Council Office, which reports directly to the Prime Minister, was the lead.
20. See, for example, New Zealand Treasury (2002) and OECD (1998).
21. The figure is used with the permission of Professor Jensen.

References

Alchian, A., and H. Demsetz, 1972, "Production, Information Costs and Economic Organization," *American Economic Review*, Vol. 62(5), pp. 777–95.

Alesina, A., and G. Tabellini, 2005, *Why Do Politicians Delegate?* NBER Working Paper, WP11531 (Cambridge, Mass.: NBER).

Barr, N., 1998, *The Economics of the Welfare State* (Oxford: Oxford University Press).

Bjornskov, C., A. Dreher, and J. Fischer, 2005, "The Bigger the Better? Evidence on the effect of Government Size on Life Satisfaction Around the World," *Institute of Economic Research Economic Working Paper Series* (Zurich: Swiss Federal Institute of Technology).

Bonato, L., E. Tsounta, and F. Balassone, 2005, *Sweden: Article IV Selected Issues* (Washington: International Monetary Fund).

Boston, J., J. Martin, J. Pallot, and P. Walsh, 1996, *Public Management. The New Zealand Model* (Oxford: Oxford University Press).

Brumby, J., 2000, *Budgetary Devices That Deliver*, Oxford Policy Institute Policy Brief No. 3 (Oxford: Oxford Policy Institute).

Burns, J.C., and R.D. Lee, 2004, "The Ups and Downs of State Budget Process Reform: Experience of Three Decades," *Public Budgeting and Finance*, Fall, pp. 1–19.
Caiden, N., and A. Wildavsky, 1974, *Planning and Budgeting in Poor Countries* (New York: Wiley).
Curristine, T., 2005, *Performance Information in the Budget Process: Results of OECD 2005 Questionnaire*, GOV/PGC/SBO(2005)6 (Paris: OECD).
Davis, J., R. Ossowski, and A. Fedelino, 2003, *Fiscal Policy Formulation and Implementation in Oil Producing Countries* (Washington: International Monetary Fund).
Department of Treasury and Finance (Australia), 2005, *The Integrated Management Cycle* (Melbourne: Treasury of Victoria).
Due, J.F., and A.F. Friedlaender, 1973, *Government Finance. Economics of the Public Sector* (Irwin: Homewood).
Gorringe, P., 2001, *Economics for Policy* (Wellington: Institute of Policy Studies).
IDA and IMF, 2005, *Update on the Assessments and Implementation of Action Plans to Strengthen Capacity of HIPCs to Track Poverty Reducing Public Spending* (Washington: International Monetary Fund).
IMF, 2007, *Promoting Fiscal Discipline—Is There a Role for Fiscal Agencies?* forthcoming (Washington: International Monetary Fund).
Jensen, M.C., and W.H. Meckling, 1976, *Theory of the Firm: Managerial Behavior, Agency Costs and Ownership Structure* (Cambridge, Mass.: Harvard University Press).
——, 1990, "Specific and General Knowledge and Organizational Structure," in *Contract Economics*, ed. L. Werin and H. Wijkander (Oxford: Blackwell), pp. 251–74. Available at SSRN: <http://ssrn.com/abstract=6658 <http://ssrn.com/abstract=6658>.
Joumard, I., P. M. Kongsrud, Y.S. Nam, and R. Price, 2003/2, "Enhancing the Cost Effectiveness of Public Spending: Experience in OECD Countries," *OECD Economic Studies*, Issue 2, No. 37, pp. 109–61 (Paris: OECD).
Kahneman, D., and A. Tversky, 1979, "Prospect Theory: An Analysis of Decision under Risk," *Econometrica*, pp. 263–91.
Kraan, D-J., 2005, *Reallocation: The Role of Budgetary Institutions* (Paris: OECD).
Le Houerou, P., and R. Taliercio, 2002, *Medium Term Expenditure Frameworks: From Concept to Practice. Preliminary Lessons from Africa*, Africa Region Working Paper 28 (Washington: World Bank).
Lorentzen, P., J. McMillan, and R. Wacziarg, 2005, *Death and Development*, CDDRL Working Paper No. 48 (Stanford: Stanford University Press).
Musgrave, R.A. and P.B. Musgrave, 1959, *The Theory of Public Finance* (New York: McGraw-Hill).
New Zealand Treasury, 2002, *Guidelines for Setting Charges in the Public Sector* (Wellington: New Zealand Treasury). Available at: <www.treasury.govt.nz/publicsector/charges/>.
OECD, 1998, *Best Practice Guidelines for User Charging for Government Services* (Paris: OECD). Available at: <www.oecd.org/dataoecd/19/38/1901769.pdf>.
Ouchi, W., 1980, "Bureaucracy, Markets and Clans," *Administrative Science Quarterly*, Vol. 25, pp. 129–45.
Radner, R., 1992, "Hierarchy: The Economics of Managing," *Journal of Economic Literature*, Vol. 30, pp. 1382–415.
Schelling, T., 1978, *Micromotives and Macrobehavior* (New York: Norton).
Schick, A., 1997, *The Changing Role of the Central Budget Office*, OCDE/GD/(97)109 (Paris: OECD).
——, 1999, *A Contemporary Approach to Public Expenditure Management* (Washington: World Bank Institute).
Wanna, J., L. Jensen, and J. de Vries, 2003, *Controlling Public Expenditure* (Northampton: Edward Elgar).
Wanna, J., J. Kelly, and J. Forster, 2000, *Managing Public Expenditure in Australia* (Crows Nest: Allen & Unwin).

Weingast, B., K. Shepsle, and C. Johnsen, 1981, "The Political Economy of Benefits and Costs: A Neoclassical Approach to Distributive Politics," *Journal of Political Economy*, Vol. 89(4), pp. 642–64.
World Bank, 1998, *Public Expenditure Management Handbook* (Washington: World Bank).
Zoghi, C., 2002, *The Distribution of Decision Rights within the Workplace: Evidence from Canadian, Australian and UK Establishments*, BLS Working Paper No. 363 (Washington: Bureau of Labor Statistics).

10
US Program Assessment Rating Tool

Denise M. Fantone[1]

For over 50 years the US federal government has attempted to better align resource decisions and expected performance. Although several government-wide reforms contributed to the evolving concept of performance budgeting in the United States, all fell short of linking performance to budget decision-making. Building on the strategic planning, reporting, and measurement processes of the Government Performance and Results Act (GPRA), the current administration believes its Program Assessment Rating Tool (PART) succeeds where other reforms failed. At the time of writing, the Office of Management and Budget (OMB) was in its final year of a five-year effort to use PART to rate the program design, strategic planning, management, and results of all US federal programs as a part of its executive branch budget formulation process. This chapter draws on General Accounting Office (GAO) reviews[2] that described PART's development and use, and assessed its strengths and weaknesses as a budget and evaluation tool.

Introduction

The US federal government is built on a system of checks and balances that makes shared power and responsibility necessary. In practice, both the legislative branch (the Congress) and the President oversee and manage agencies and their missions. At times, this leads to significant differences in policy direction and complicates how, for what, and to whom agencies are held accountable. In allocating resources, the Congress plays a pivotal role stemming from the Constitution, which states: "No Money shall be drawn from the Treasury, but in Consequence of Appropriations made by Law…"[3] Although the Congress exercises power through a many-layered system of committees, the Appropriations Committees are at the heart of the Congressional budget process. They control the budget structure and make annual funding decisions for most of the activities—other than entitlements[4]—that are carried out by the US government or third parties acting in the federal government's behalf. Since the President does not have the final say on funding or its purpose, it may appear that he is disadvantaged. However, the President has an opportunity to propose overall fiscal policy targets and specific funding levels for programs and activities through his budget to Congress, which serves as the starting point for Congressional deliberations. Moreover, even though Congressional committees in their various roles continue to oversee agencies throughout the year, presidential influence increases once spending bills are enacted and executive branch agencies implement their programs (Fantone and Posner, 2003).

The Office of Management and Budget, located in the Executive Office of the President, is responsible primarily for the annual preparation of the President's budget request. To the extent that it is possible with a staff of just over 500, OMB also oversees the management of executive branch agencies. As the President's budget office, OMB provides guidance on the content and presentation of agency budget requests; develops policy options and funding recommendations; approves agency spending plans, and drafts legislation in support of presidential initiatives. In addition to monitoring the efficacy of agencies' operations, OMB promulgates government-wide guidance and regulations for federal organizations primarily in the areas of financial management, information technology, performance planning, regulatory program activities, and federal acquisitions.

OMB periodically is criticized for not paying sufficient attention to management issues because of its preoccupation with budgetary matters. But those familiar with OMB claim that agency management and program performance have always been examined along with budget requests. In contrast, OMB's efforts have been inconsistent, and some believe neglectful, in encouraging implementation of government-wide management reforms and oversight of day-to-day agency operations. This has been attributed to limited staff resources, few tools (beyond the budget) to motivate performance improvements, and the changing management priorities of each administration (Tanaka et al., 2003).

Past performance budgeting initiatives

Recent efforts in the US to improve the linkage of performance information and budgeting in the federal government are part of a continuum over the past 50 years.[5] Since World War II and prior to the current Government Performance and Results Act of 1993, there have been four government-wide initiatives aimed at linking performance with the federal budget process.

The Hoover Commission of 1949 was established, in part, to identify ways to reduce war debt and downsize the post-war government. At a time when the federal government primarily provided goods and services directly, it was not surprising that the Commission recommended a shift in the focus of budget decision-making from inputs to measuring workload and efficiency of government functions and activities. Although it did not mention performance budgeting directly, Congress enacted the Budget and Accounting Procedures Act of 1950 (BAPA), which required the President to present performance information, primarily on "workload" (output or activity in modern terminology) and unit cost.

The next government-wide reform came in the mid-1960s when the Department of Defense's Planning, Programming, and Budgeting System (PPBS) was extended to civilian agencies. PPBS introduced a framework for budget formulation that allowed comparisons to be made among policy choices and encouraged multiple strategies for achieving objectives. Multi-year planning based on an agency's program structure offered the possibility of linking outputs to long-term objectives. Systems analysis and measurement were seen as essential elements for understanding the costs and benefits of government services. Confident that management techniques could modernize the federal government, President Johnson predicted that PPBS

> will help us find new ways to do jobs faster, to do jobs better, and to do jobs less expensively. It will insure a much sounder judgment through more accurate information, pinpointing those things that we ought to do more, spotlighting those things that we ought to do less. It will make our decision-making process as up-to-date, I think, as our space-exploring program.

The third and fourth reforms borrowed ideas from the private sector and state government. President Nixon introduced Management by Objectives (MBO) in 1973 as an approach that added the element of holding agency managers responsible for agreed-upon outputs and sought to define performance in terms that today we would call "outcomes." The intent of this initiative was to centralize goal-setting decisions while at the same time allowing managers to choose how to achieve the goals. MBO continued only one year after President Nixon resigned and was followed in 1977 by the Carter administration's zero-base budgeting (ZBB), a process transplanted from the state of Georgia to the federal government. ZBB sought to optimize accomplishments by setting priorities based on program results that could be achieved at alternative spending levels. In developing budgets, these alternatives were to be ranked sequentially from the lowest level organization up through the department in an attempt to move away from traditional incremental budgeting and towards an annual reconsideration of how all resources would be used.

Although there is general agreement that all four of these efforts fell short of their stated goals, each has contributed to some aspect of the evolution of performance budgeting in the United States and their influences still can be seen today (GAO, 1998a).

Government Performance and Results Act

The most recent statutory reform, the Government Performance and Results Act of 1993,[6] was designed to avoid a number of weaknesses identified in earlier reforms. First, the authors of the legislation hoped to strengthen the credibility and use of GPRA plans and reports by requiring consultation between the executive and legislative branches on overall agency goals and missions. Second, by linking planning and goal-setting to the program activity structures in agency budget requests, they wanted to increase the possibility that this information could be used directly in budget deliberations. Third, the backers of this legislation recognized that it would take time for the federal government to build capacity and create a receptive environment. In response, they phased the development of the GPRA strategic planning and reporting process, did not prescribe how plans would be organized as long as they were comprehensive, and, while they preferred outcome measures, accepted a range of measures initially.

GPRA was intended to address several broad purposes, including strengthening the confidence of the American people in their government; improving federal program effectiveness, accountability, and service delivery; and enhancing Congressional decision-making by providing more objective information on program performance. These objectives were to be achieved through three key elements:

1. A multi-year strategic plan for every executive agency—covering five years and updated every three, the plan must include an agency mission statement and long-term general goals and objectives, describe strategies for achieving these goals, and explain the key external factors that could affect the achievement of goals.
2. An annual performance plan—covering each program activity presented in agency budget requests,[7] the plan aligns annual goals with long-term strategic goals. Agencies are required to have performance measures to gauge progress towards goals and to explain how the resulting performance data will be verified.
3. An annual performance report—an agency review and discussion of its performance for the prior year compared with the performance goals established in its annual performance plan. Agencies are expected to explain any differences and to provide baseline and trend data to help ensure that their performance is reviewed in context (GAO, 1997).

Ten years after enactment, GPRA's achievement record is mixed. Although the committee report accompanying the Act suggested that developing the capacity to relate the level of program activity with program costs, such as costs per unit of result, cost per unit of service, or cost per unit of output, should be a high priority, it was not a requirement of GPRA. In a 2004 survey of federal managers, GAO found that only 31 percent of those surveyed reported having such measures to a great or very great extent (GAO, 2004a). Among the issues that managers identified were difficulties in distinguishing between the results produced by the federal program and results caused by external factors or non-federal actors, such as with grants programs. Timely and useful performance information was not always available to federal agencies, making it more difficult to assess and report on progress achieved. Those who expected that GPRA would be used to determine which programs should or should not be funded, or who viewed performance budgeting as a contractual arrangement, that is, a certain level of funding for an agreed-upon level of performance, were bound to be disappointed with the progress made under GPRA.

A factor in the development of the Program Assessment Rating Tool was the current administration's frustration with the inability to use GPRA information meaningfully in the budget process. Former OMB Director Mitch Daniels testified that "agencies spend an inordinate amount of time preparing reports to comply with it [GPRA] producing volumes of information of questionable value" (Daniels, 2002). Still, the current administration owes much to GPRA for providing the planning and performance reporting framework, and metrics on which to base and build its management initiatives.[8]

Program Assessment Rating Tool[9]

In outlining his management priorities shortly after taking office, President Bush put federal agencies on notice that

> [u]nderperforming agencies are sometimes given incentives to improve, but rarely face consequences for persistent failure. This all-carrot-no-stick approach is unlikely to elicit improvement from troubled organizations. Instead, we should identify mismanaged, wasteful or duplicative government programs, with an eye to cutting their funding, redesigning them, or eliminating them altogether. (OMB, 2001)

To make good on this strategy, OMB developed PART, a 25-item questionnaire to help assess a program's strengths and weaknesses. Designed to be evidence-based, PART does not create new information, but instead is expected to draw on a variety of sources, including authorizing legislation; strategic plans, annual plans, and performance reports required by the Government Performance and Results Act (GPRA); financial statements; independent program evaluations; and inspector general and GAO reports. Once a PART assessment is completed, the program receives one of four overall ratings: effective, moderately effective, adequate, or ineffective. A fifth rating, results not demonstrated, may be given—independent of a program's numerical score—if OMB decides that performance information, performance measures, or both are insufficient or inadequate. This last category was added to make a distinction between unknown effectiveness and evidence that a program was performing poorly.

Divided into four sections each with its own weight,[10] the PART questions address: (1) program purpose and design (20 percent), (2) strategic planning (10 percent), (3) program management (20 percent), and (4) program results (50 percent). Several additional questions are asked depending on which of seven program types best describes how services are delivered.[11] For federal programs that do not fit easily into any one category, OMB allows a "mixed" PART questionnaire, provided that the agency and OMB agree on which additional questions are relevant. Table 10.1 provides examples of the types of questions asked in each of the four sections.

The first three sections use a yes/no format and the last uses a four-point scale—yes/large extent/small extent/no—that allows examiners to give agencies credit for progress in achieving goals. The results of the assessment, including explanations for each response, supporting evidence, and recommended follow-on actions, are publicly available on OMB's website.[12] Figure 10.1 provides an example from the

Table 10.1 Selected PART questions

Section	*Questions*
Program Purpose and Design	Is the program design effectively targeted, so that resources will reach intended beneficiaries and/or otherwise address the program's purpose directly?
Strategic Planning	Does the program have a limited number of specific long-term performance measures that focus on outcomes and meaningfully reflect the program purpose?
Program Management	Are federal managers and program partners (including grantees, sub-grantees, contractors, cost-sharing partners, and government partners) held accountable for cost, schedule, and performance results?
Program Results/ Accountability	Do independent evaluations of sufficient scope and quality indicate that the program is effective and achieving results?

Source: US Office of Management and Budget.

worksheet for the US Department of Labor's Job Corps program for questions 4.3 and 4.4 (Section 4: Program Results, questions 3 and 4). This program provides education and training services to disadvantaged youth.

Although this detail is available online, the PART results are primarily communicated through summary sheets in the budget.[13] A PART summary sheet displays the program's key performance measures, three years of budget information, significant findings, and follow-on actions in addition to the overall ratings and the individual numerical section scores. For those approximately 20 percent of programs that have been reassessed, the summary sheet also shows the year the program was last assessed and the status of follow-on actions. (Status markers include "no action taken," "action taken but not completed," and "completed.") Figure 10.2 illustrates the PART summary for the Job Corps program, which was assessed for the first time in 2004.

The release of the President's fiscal year 2007 budget in February marked the fourth year of a five-year effort by the US to formally assess all federal programs at least once in its executive branch budget formulation process. OMB's plan to review approximately 20 percent of programs—or an equivalent percentage of the budget— annually has resulted in assessments of nearly 800 federal programs to date. With the exception of some support functions for programs assessed separately in earlier years and—according to OMB—some defense programs, OMB is on schedule to meet its goal.

Developing the Program Assessment Rating Tool

The President's fiscal year 2004 budget request was the first time that the PART questionnaire was used, but it was the second year that OMB had assessed programs and presented the results in the President's budget proposal. In its initial effort, OMB rated selected programs either as effective or ineffective and provided a brief

PART Performance Measurements

Program: Job Corps
Agency: Department of Labor
Bureau: ETA
Type(s): Direct Federal

Section Scores				Rating
1	2	3	4	Moderately
100%	81%	87%	49%	Effective

4.3 **Does the program demonstrate improved efficiencies or cost effectiveness in achieving program goals each year?** Answer: NO Question Weight:19%

Explanation: Although the program tracks cost-per-participant, the program provides no evidence of overall improved efficiencies or cost effectiveness from year to year (e.g, in the form of cost per outcome or output). The program provides some smaller examples of savings it achieved in PY 2002.

Evidence: OJC reports that from PY 2001 to PY 2002, it reduced its workers' compensation costs by 1.3% ($53,000); communications costs by 29.2% ($2.5 million); student post-termination settlements by 15.8% ($1.2 million). DOL also notes that in PY 2003, with a 4% increase in its operations budget, it achieved a 17% increase in its high school diploma attainment rate (which it argues is a sign of efficiency, although the placement and retention rates declined in PY 2001).

4.4 **Does the performance of this program compare favorably to other programs, including government, private, etc., with similar purpose and goals?** Answer: YES Question Weight:19%

Explanation: According to comparisons conducted by Mathematica Policy Research, Inc., during the National Job Corps Study, Job Corps' results compare favorably to other federal youth training programs and demonstration initiatives. Mathematica concluded that 'Job Corps remains the only large-scale program to produce sustained and significant earnings gains for its participants.' As measured by placement rate (87% in PY 2002), Job Corps is more successful than the Youth Activities program (which had PY 2002 results of 69.5% for older youth), although it is significantly more expensive on a per-participant and per-placement basis. While no national youth training programs have matched Job Corps' effectiveness, some less costly local models (San Jose's Center for Employment and Training (CET) and its replication sites) have shown positive results.

Evidence: Mathematica Policy Research, "Summary of the National Job Corps Study" (June 2001), and related documents. Based on PY02 data, Job Corps costs more than $22,000 per participant versus less than $3,000 under Youth Activities, and almost $30,000 per placement, versus under $6,000. CET was among 13 projects funded under Jobstart, a demonstration designed to replicate Job Corps' success in serving disadvantaged high school dropouts using a less costly approach. An early 1990's study showed sustained annual earnings gains in CET--participants earned 40% more than control group counterparts at costs per enrollee of $4,200 (DOL Office of the Chief Economist, "What's Working (and what's not)," 1/95). At 30 months, MDRC found positive effects at certain replication sites for young women, but employment-related impacts for men were negative or negligible (MDRC, "Working With Disadvantaged Youth, 30-Month Findings from the Evaluation of the CET Replication Sites," 6/03). Final results will be available in 2005.

Figure 10.1 Example of a worksheet for the Job Corps program

Source: US Office of Management and Budget.

Program: *Job Corps*

Agency: *Department of Labor*
Bureau: *ETA*

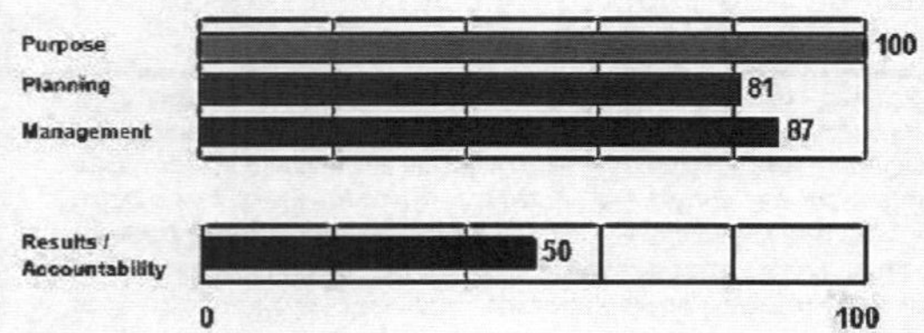

Key Performance Measures from Latest PART

Key Performance Measures from Latest PART	Year	Target	Actual
Annual Measure: Percentage of participants entering employment or enrolling in post-secondary education, the military or advanced training/occupational skills training	2002	80%	87%
	2003	90%	90%
	2004	85%	
	2005	85%	
Annual Measure: Percentage of participants who achieve literacy or numeracy gains of one or more educational functioning levels.	2004	45%	
	2005	46%	
	2006	47%	
	2007	48%	
Annual Measure: Percentage of participants that earn a high school diploma, GED, or certificate.	2004	64%	
	2005	64%	
	2006	65%	
	2007	65%	

Rating: *Moderately Effective*

Program Type: *Direct Federal*

Program Summary:

Through a national network of 122 primarily residential centers, the Job Corps program provides intensive education and training services to disadvantaged youth ages 16-24.

The PART found:

- Job Corps' results are positive, and compare favorably to other federal youth training programs. While the program is expensive on a per-participant basis (almost $23,000) owing to its primarily residential design, its benefits exceed costs.
- The four-year findings of an experimental evaluation of Job Corps were that program participants fared better than their control-group counterparts in terms of employment and earnings increases, literacy and numeracy gains, and reduction in involvement with crime. However, Hispanic youths and 18 and 19-year olds did not have employment or earnings gains; and those who failed to complete vocational training or earn a GED derived no benefit from Job Corps.
- Job Corps has historically not provided capital asset planning information in support of its budget request, does not have a formal capital asset plan, and does not involve the Chief Financial Officer or Procurement Executive in its capital planning process.
- Although the program tracks cost per participant, Job Corps cannot provide evidence of overall year-to-year efficiency or cost effectiveness improvements.
- Job Corps' budget justification displays output and outcome measures alongside the request, but does not present resource needs in a transparent way.

In response to these findings, the Department of Labor will:

1. Improve the employment and earnings outcomes of Hispanic and 18 and 19-year-old enrollees and reduce the share of enrollees (currently half) who fail to complete the program.
2. Provide capital asset information during budget formulation and involve the CFO and Procurement Executive in its capital planning process.
3. Improve program efficiency by, for example, using non-residential centers for a larger portion of the population and increasing employer and provider cost sharing.
4. Revise its budget presentation to show clearly the components of the program' s $1.5 billion budget.
5. Proceed with common measures implementation, which has been delayed.

(Note: 2002 and 2003 placement rate reflects the previous measure, which tracks only program graduates versus all individuals who leave the program. Including non-completers will make this goal more challenging, so the levels have been reduced.)

Program Funding Level (in millions of dollars)

2004 Actual	2005 Estimate	2006 Estimate
1,566	1,576	1,547

Figure 10.2 Summary assessment for the Job Corps program

Source: US Office of Management and Budget.

narrative explanation for the rating. However, because there was no explanation for either the methodology or sources used to reach conclusions, reactions generally were negative.

Responding to this criticism, OMB created PART the following year and tested the instrument on 67 programs using a couple of approaches to train its program examiners (OMB, 2002a). First, OMB developed guidance that explained the purpose of each question and described the evidence required to support a yes or no answer. Although not expected to cover every situation, the instructions established general standards for PART assessments. Second, OMB tasked its Performance Evaluation Team (PET)—the group of examiners who developed the PART—to continue as advisors during the first round of PART reviews.[14] This had the two-fold benefit of providing a source for examiners to ask questions and giving PET members an understanding of where the questionnaire or process needed to be clarified or revised.

In addition, OMB sought input from external groups (including GAO) during the pilot phase and assistance from outside budget and management experts who helped guide PART's first year of implementation as members of the Performance Measurement Advisory Council (PMAC) (OMB, 2002b). As a result of these steps, some important changes were made. OMB agreed to publish individual section scores because it was suggested that these better represented OMB's views of a program's strengths and weaknesses than the overall rating alone. To recognize program differences, OMB created sub-sets of questions for each of the seven program types and, in section 1, purpose questions were dropped or de-emphasized (reviewers thought they were too political) so that only questions about program design remained. In section 4 on program results, responses were changed from the yes/no format to a four-point scale, and performance targets and at least one efficiency measure were now required for all programs (OMB, 2002b). OMB concluded that these PART revisions lessened subjectivity and reduced the likelihood that the tool would be applied inconsistently (OMB, 2002c).

At the end of the first rating cycle, OMB organized a group of OMB staff and agency officials to check for consistency. The Interagency Review Panel (IRP) examined 10 percent of the PART assessments using a sub-set of the PART questions that OMB staff identified as being the most subjective or difficult to interpret. The IRP also reviewed the results of formal agency appeals to see if similar situations were treated equitably. The IRP was not reconstituted for the fiscal year 2005 budget process, but OMB requested a similar review by the National Academy of Public Administration (NAPA), the results of which were not made public. Since then, OMB has done consistency checks using its own staff (OMB, 2003a).

Although some changes were made to the PART questions between the first and second year, subsequent changes to the tool have mainly been refinements. However, OMB continues to make process improvements and to further clarify terms and concepts each cycle. Notably, OMB has shifted the timing of PART reviews so that they occur in the summer in advance of OMB's fall review of agency budget requests. OMB has also worked with the evaluation community to identify evaluation approaches considered best suited for different types of programs (OMB, 2003b, 2004). The fiscal year 2006 PART process has a new option for an abbreviated reassessment. Abbreviated reassessments allow updating of selected questions instead of the entire PART, which is intended to give programs the opportunity to begin using and reporting on new performance measures more quickly than if they were to complete a full reassessment (OMB, 2006).

Using PART to rate programs

The need for a credible evidence-based rating tool for programs was a major impetus in developing PART. However, there is no single bottom-line for most federal programs. Given that programs almost always have multiple purposes and goals, OMB staff had to decide how to apply general principles to specific cases. Inevitably, bottom-line ratings force choices as to which of multiple goals best exemplify a program's mission. It is not surprising that GAO's first PART review found inconsistencies in application or that OMB's internal reviews point to continuing issues (GAO, 2004b). The pressure on agencies (and OMB) to show improvement encourages a determination of program effectiveness even when performance data are unavailable, the quality of those data is uneven, or they convey a mixed message on performance. To create an instrument that is comprehensive without being overwhelming and broad enough to capture information across dissimilar programs, yet meaningful for a specific program, is a tall order. Consequently, PART reflects trade-offs.

OMB's effort to standardize by using a yes/no format has at times resulted in oversimplified answers and confusion about what was being rated. Agency officials commented that the yes/no format is a crude reflection of reality in which progress in planning, management, or results is more likely to resemble a continuum than an on/off switch. This was particularly troublesome for questions containing multiple criteria for a "yes" answer, which contributed to a number of inconsistencies across program reviews in the first year. OMB responded by either splitting questions or making clear that each element of a multi-part criteria must be answered yes to answer the question affirmatively (GAO, 2004b).

Other discrepancies occurred when the responses to related questions were contradictory or when it was left to OMB examiners to decide whether a measure was long-term or an intermediate target. Again, OMB highlighted the relationship between linked questions to reduce this problem. Although OMB has tried to clarify terms, many PART questions still contain subjective language that is open to interpretation. Examples include terms such as "ambitious" describing sought-after performance measures. Because the appropriateness of a performance measure depends on the program's purpose, and because program purposes can vary immensely, an ambitious goal for one program might be unrealistic for a similar but more narrowly defined program (GAO, 2004b).

Inconsistencies continue to surface in examiners' responses to agency progress—some examiners give credit for improvements while others do not. The limited availability of credible evidence on program results is a longstanding condition that continues to constrain OMB's ability to use PART to rate programs' effectiveness. The PART confirmed findings by GAO and others on agency data and evaluation capacity generally—that federal agencies do not have sufficient data and studies to evaluate the impact of federal programs (GAO, 1998b; Blalock and Barnow, 2002). Table 10.2 shows that except for 2005, "results not demonstrated" is the rating given most frequently to programs.

Table 10.2 The cumulative PART program results by rating category, 2002–05

Ratings	*2002*	*2003*	*2004*	*2005*
Effective	6%	11%	15%	15%
Moderately effective	24%	26%	26%	29%
Adequate	15%	20%	26%	28%
Ineffective	5%	5%	4%	4%
Results not demonstrated	50%	38%	29%	24%
Total programs	234	407	607	794

Source: US Office of Management and Budget.

"Results not demonstrated" or RND ratings have implications beyond PART because they can negatively affect how an agency is rated by another high-visibility indicator, the President's Management Agenda (PMA) scorecard. Using a simple "stoplight" grading system, agencies are assessed each quarter on meeting standards for five government-wide initiatives: (1) Human Capital, (2) Competitive Sourcing, (3) Financial Performance, (4) E-Government, and (5) Budget and Performance Integration. To get to "yellow" status on the Budget and Performance Integration initiative, agencies must not have more than 50 percent of their programs rated RND. For an agency to achieve "green" on the scorecard, fewer than 10 percent of its programs could have received a RND PART rating for more than two years in a row. This rating is given not only when OMB determines that there are insufficient data to assess a program, but also when it and the agency cannot reach agreement on which goals or measures to use. As one agency official remarked to GAO, "they really understand incentives at OMB" (GAO, 2005b).

This increased focus on performance is often reflected in improved ratings when programs originally rated RND are reassessed. OMB gives priority to these programs, and agencies are motivated to make changes. GAO found that when reassessed, 86 percent of these programs were rated "adequate," "moderately effective," or "effective." Better results might be expected because programs are only reassessed when OMB determines that significant changes had been made to address deficiencies. However, what is less obvious is that the critical determinant of whether a program moves out of RND when reassessed is how high the program scored initially in the program results section (section 4). In other words, positive changes in program purpose and design, strategic planning, and program management were inconsequential if the program had scored low on program results (Government Accountablility Office, 2005a).

Then there is the question of the unit of analysis used to assess program performance. Since there is no standard definition for a program,[15] what to rate and how useful the results will be often depends on who will use the information and for what purpose.[16] In some instances, what was rated aligned with an "account"—for example, the visa and consular services of the Department of State—which is the level at which congressional appropriators make funding decisions. In other cases—such as Medicare[17]—the unit of analysis for the PART assessment is commonly recognized as a federal program. More often, however, OMB created units of analysis tied to discrete funding levels by both disaggregating and aggregating certain activities that make up a PART-defined program. In some cases, disaggregating for PART reviews ignored interdependencies by artificially isolating related activities from the larger contexts in which they operate. Conversely, in other cases in which OMB aggregated multiple activities with diverse missions and outcomes, it became difficult to settle on a single measure (or set of measures) that accurately captured the multiple missions of these diverse components. Although OMB acknowledges that there is a need for flexibility in defining a program when the budget structure does not reflect the way a program is managed, both of these "unit of analysis" issues exacerbated the problems caused by the lack of available planning and performance information (GAO, 2004b).

PART and the Government Performance and Results Act

OMB should be given credit for creating a tool that reflects the administration's management principles and the priority given to using performance information in OMB's decision-making process, but its focus primarily on program-level assessments contrasts with the emphasis of GPRA on an agency's goal structure and the contributions of multiple programs in achieving results. Although the two processes can be complementary, the intent of the legislative framework was to bring all interested stakeholders into the process to build broad support and give credibility to the results. So while GPRA and OMB's PART initiative share similar goals—including identifying what is working well and what is not—PART clearly is designed first and foremost to meet OMB's needs in the federal budget process.

OMB has tried to clarify the relationship between GPRA and PART, but has mainly relied on agencies to decide how they should integrate the two requirements. According to OMB, PART reinforces performance measurement under GPRA by encouraging development of performance measures according to the outcome-oriented standards of the law and by requiring that agency goals be appropriately ambitious.

> The PART process should also help agencies develop and identify meaningful performance measures to support their GPRA reporting....When annual plans and reports include programs that have been assessed in the PART, the measures used for GPRA should be the same as those included in the PART. In all cases, performance measures included in GPRA plans and reports should meet the standards of the PART—they must be outcome oriented, relate to the overall purpose of the program, and have ambitious targets. (OMB, 2006)

To provide decision-makers with program-specific, outcome-based performance data useful for executive budget formulation, OMB had stated its intention to modify and at times replace GPRA goals and measures with those developed under PART. As a result, the goals and measures used in strategic planning are expected to conform to those judged by OMB to be most useful, even if the result eliminated or conflicted with the goals and measures of other GPRA stakeholders. The federal budget process, which is closed until decisions are made, does not provide an opportunity to vet changes with other stakeholders until after the fact. Moreover, while PART does not eliminate the departmental strategic plans created under GPRA, many OMB and agency officials told GAO that PART is being used to shape strategic plans. The emphasis is shifting so that eventually the performance measures developed for PART will drive agencies' strategic planning processes (GAO, 2004b).

This also was made clear when OMB guidance called for agencies to substitute a performance budget structure starting in fiscal year 2005 for the annual GPRA performance plan[18] (OMB, 2003c). Although related primarily to the President's Management Agenda budget and performance integration initiative and not directly to PART, OMB expects that agencies will analyze programs that contribute to a goal, "including their relative roles and effectiveness, using Program Assessment Rating Tool (PART) assessments when available" (OMB, 2003d). These performance budget presentations generally have not been well received by appropriators. There are a number of reasons for this, not least of which is that it is not the structure used to appropriate funds. In its most recent guidance OMB has suggested that agencies "should consult with relevant congressional appropriations committees to ensure their support for modifications to the format, including the use of the results of PART assessments, of your agency budget documents" (OMB, 2005a).

Integrating PART into executive branch budget formulation

OMB has taken the fruits of the GPRA planning process—goal-setting and performance measurement—and strategically applied them to budget formulation using PART. Not only is OMB invested in using PART for its reviews, but as the timing of PART assessments has moved earlier in the budget formulation process, OMB has made clear that it hopes to influence internal agency budget deliberations as well.

Over the four years of its existence, PART has evolved into a more interactive process between agencies and the OMB staff who rate their programs. Agency self-assessments are no longer optional as they were the first year. Instead, they have become the first step in the assessment process with agencies providing support that they hope will lead to positive ratings by OMB. Agencies increasingly are involved in negotiating which programs will be assessed during the year, setting performance targets, and recommending follow-on actions. OMB holds regular meetings with agency leads responsible for fostering budget and performance integration in their organizations. In turn, PART appears to be a catalyst for bringing agency budget, planning, and program staffs together to respond to PART assessments.

OMB believes that PART provides a systematic way of asking performance-related questions that have always been important in OMB's reviews of agencies' budget requests. Both OMB and agency officials said that this has helped to ensure that OMB staff with varying levels of experience are asking the same types of questions and that it has also fostered a more disciplined approach to discussing program performance and agency management.

Agency officials told GAO that, by encouraging more communication between departments and OMB, PART helped illuminate both how OMB makes budget decisions and the way examiners think about program management. OMB managers and staff reported that it led to richer discussions during internal deliberations on what a program should be achieving, whether the program was performing effectively, and, if not, how program performance could be improve. In addition, both agency and OMB officials said that the attention given to programs that were not routinely reviewed was a benefit, although some agency officials complained that this was a burden for small programs that did not have as many resources to devote to the reviews (GAO, 2004b).

By 2003—the second year of PART—OMB had developed tools to help collect and transmit data, but agencies still reported that it was a strain on resources to comply with the PART process. They also provided anecdotal evidence of OMB examiners who had not had sufficient time to review PART reassessments (Government Accountability Office, 2005b). OMB acknowledged that resource constraints were partially responsible because reassessments are taking almost as long as the original reviews.

With PART now in the middle of its fifth year, there continues to be concern that assessments are time-consuming for both agencies and OMB. According to some agency officials, OMB has tried to reduce program examiners' workload by defining programs in larger units or limiting the number of programs reassessed annually. Whether these managers' perceptions are the exception or not, capacity issues remain even after OMB limited reassessments to those programs where there was significant evidence of change. OMB for the first time in the current cycle has given agencies under certain conditions the option of seeking an abbreviated program reassessment instead of a full reassessment (OMB, 2006). Whether done, as stated, to speed update of performance information, it also suggests that the PART process continues to be labor-intensive.

Table 10.3 provides a timeline for the executive branch budget formulation process with milestones for the PART assessment denoted in bold.

OMB claims that PART has proven its value in helping the President formulate budget priorities. No doubt PART has played some role, but it is not always clear how much weight a PART assessment carries in resource decisions (although there have been any number of regression analyses done to try to glean this information, including by GAO in the 2004 PART report). A better measure may be found in the list of programs that the administration proposed for termination, reduction, or major reform in its fiscal year 2006 budget proposal (OMB, 2005d).[19] Of the approximately 150 discretionary programs proposed for termination or reduction, no more than a third had gone through a PART assessment.

Similarly, OMB identified 35 programs in 11 agencies that contributed to some aspect of community and economic development. The President's proposal consolidated 18 of the 35 programs, which OMB claimed accounted for 89 percent of

Table 10.3 Major steps in the executive branch budget formulation process

What happens?	*When?*
Agencies and OMB agree on programs to be assessed or reassessed	**Early March**
The Performance and Evaluation Team (PET) provides revised PART guidance and workbook, training for agencies and for examiners on PART and PARTWeb	**March**
OMB issues planning and policy guidance for the next President's budget	Spring
Agencies' draft responses/evidence for PART program reviews due to Resource Management Offices (RMOs)[a]	**April**
OMB and executive branch agencies discuss budget issues, presidential priorities, and options that will be developed for OMB's upcoming fall budget reviews.	Spring/ Summer
Discussions about PART program assessments between agencies and OMB	**May/early June**
OMB issues instructions for submitting budget data and materials	July
RMOs submit PART assessments to PET for consistency check and feedback	**June/July**
RMOs give revised PART assessments and related draft summaries to agencies	**July**
Agency PART appeals and comments due to OMB	**Early August**
Appeals board provides decisions	**Mid-August**
PARTs updated to reflect appeals board decisions	**Late August**
Executive branch agencies provide budget requests with supporting materials including how they will address OMB follow-on actions for new and reassessed PARTs	September
RMOs draft summaries and agree to improvement plans	**September**
Conduct PART Director's Review	**Mid-October**
OMB conducts Fall budget reviews. OMB staff review agency budget proposals in light of presidential priorities, program performance, and budget constraints. They raise issues and present options to the Director and other OMB policy officials	October–November
Agencies submit year-end performance data for all measures for all PART assessments (old and new). Update follow-up actions for previously assessed PART programs. New actions may be added if earlier actions completed	**Mid-November**
OMB briefs the President and advisors on proposed budget policies. The OMB Director makes funding recommendations for the President's budget request	Late November
Decisions on budget requests are passed back to executive branch agencies	Late November
President's budget request to Congress	Early February
PART assessments released with the President's budget request and supporting information posed to ExpectMore.gov	

[a] OMB is organized into Resource Management Offices (RMOs), three statutory management offices that oversee government-wide federal financial management, federal procurement, and information technology and regulations, plus a number of OMB-wide staff and support offices. Program examiners are employed in the RMOs, which are organized by broad areas of government, such as National Security and International Affairs, and Natural Resources, Energy and Science. Examiners review agency budget submissions and make recommendations on funding, policy, and management issues. Currently this process includes assessing selected programs with PART.

Source: GAO adaptation of OMB information.

the $16.2 billion spent annually for this area. Many assumed that the consolidation proposal was backed by PART assessments when in fact only 8 out of the 18 programs had gone through such an assessment. Ultimately the proposal was not enacted, but it did promote closer examination of these programs, led to Congressional hearings, and gained considerable media coverage. Moreover, agency officials whose programs would have been affected described benefits from the cross-cutting PART review. In the short term, it helped them reach agreement with OMB on goals and objectives for similar programs and several expected that better coordination among program managers would continue as well.

Although OMB generally proposed to increase funding for programs that received ratings of "effective" or "moderately effective" and proposed to cut funding for those programs that were rated "ineffective," GAO's reviews confirmed OMB's statements that funding decisions were not applied mechanically and the relationship between performance levels and budget decisions is not one-dimensional (GAO, 2004b). OMB has consistently said that a good rating does not guarantee a specific level of funding and, that if the obstacle to program improvement was budgetary, a program that had received a low score might get an increase to correct deficiencies. Different choices might be made in other situations. For example, if the program's problems are prohibitively difficult or costly to fix, shifting funds to a related program with better results might be the best solution. If anything, OMB guidance suggests that most programs should expect to operate with flat budgets. Agencies are asked to set targets that are achievable with their current program characteristics and to assume current budget levels (OMB, 2005b). The President's budget for fiscal year 2006 made clear, however, that programs that cannot demonstrate their value over several years are likely to see their resources moved to higher-performing programs (OMB, 2005c).

There are several messages to be taken from this. First, no one should be surprised that presidential proposals reflect policy positions made with or without performance analysis. Second, in gaining relevance to the resource allocation process, PART illustrates the trade-offs and risks associated with this more active approach to performance management and budgeting. Far from removing politics from budgeting, the linkage of performance to budgeting raises the stakes associated with performance goals and measures. As such, the performance analysis marshaled to support budget decisions is potentially more vulnerable to political debate and conflict. Third, the "success" of performance budgeting initiatives should not be judged simply by budget changes or program terminations. Previous reforms have been doomed by inflated and unrealistic expectations that performance data could resolve thorny political problems and dilemmas. However, performance information can certainly be helpful to policy-makers in demonstrating whether programs are contributing to their stated goals, are well coordinated with related initiatives, and are targeted to the intended beneficiaries.

PART and program improvement

OMB has stated that PART's purpose is much broader than assessment and its use in budget decision-making; OMB's goal is to create a results-oriented federal government in which programs continue to improve. To understand better what this means in practice, GAO analyzed the 1,700 follow-on actions OMB expected agencies to take as the result of PART assessments for 2002–04, all the information available at the time of GAO's 2005 review.[20] As Figure 10.3 shows, these actions have been distributed fairly consistently each year among those expected to improve program management, assessment, or design. The percentage of recommendations explicitly linked to funding proposals has steadily declined from 20 percent in 2002 to 12 percent in 2004.

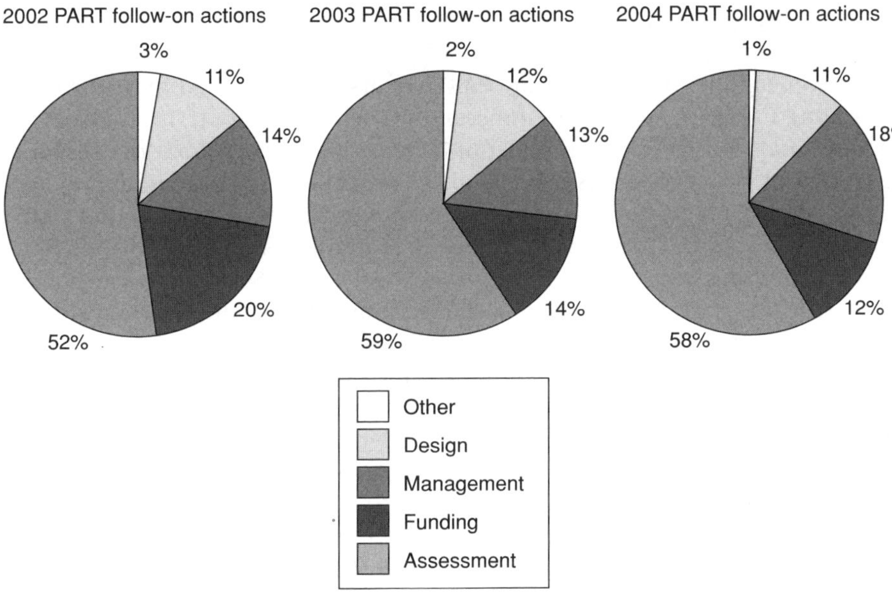

Figure 10.3 PART recommendations by program type

Source: GAO analysis of OMB data.

GAO found that problems identified by the PART assessments and the recommendations intended to address them were not always clear. Regardless of what types of deficiencies were identified in a PART assessment, more than half of all PART recommendations were aimed at improving the process of program assessment through developing outcome measures and/or goals, creating efficiency measures, or improving data collection. This was especially true for programs rated "results not demonstrated," but was also a common follow-on action for programs rated "effective" and "moderately effective." Moreover, programs assessed for the first time in 2004—the most recent year for which data were available—were just as likely to get a recommendation to improve performance assessment information as during the first PART cycle. Of the 797 follow-on actions recommended in the first two years, OMB reported that 30 percent were considered fully implemented, and nearly half of these were for improvements in performance measures or data.

In many ways these findings could have been anticipated because of the number of programs that OMB determined had insufficient or inadequate information to rate their performance. It is also consistent to assert that improving managers' ability to assess program outcomes and identifying information gaps are necessary steps before expecting observable program improvements. OMB has set an ambitious agenda and it may be that eventually PART will be credited with the program improvements that the administration and others claim (Government Accountability Office, 2005a).

Congressional response to PART

Despite some effort to communicate PART results, OMB has had limited success in engaging Congress in the PART process. In GAO's 2005 report, interviews with Congressional staff revealed a number of issues and concerns about the design of the PART tool, results of assessments, and the way OMB has communicated PART results.[21] Many Congressional staff of both parties expressed skepticism that OMB's assessments could be impartial and devoid of political influence or that PART could be anything other than an executive branch tool. Some thought that the assessments were targeted for a general audience and did not allow a sophisticated analysis that they or their members would find useful. Some were frustrated with the lack of detail provided in PART summary sheets as to why a program was rated a certain way. Congressional staffs were unlikely to accept conclusions about a program's performance without seeing the evidence used in support, particularly when the rating was contrary to what they believed to be true about a program. Several said that finding information on OMB's website was too time-consuming and difficult to use. Others felt that posting information to a website was not a meaningful communication tool if OMB wanted to signal the importance of PART results to Congress.

As with reconciling PART with GPRA requirements, agencies have been at the front line in explaining PART and the result of program assessments to their Congressional committees of jurisdiction. In the view of some Congressional staff, agencies are not in a position to explain the decisions made in OMB's assessments or to promote the value of PART, particularly if they have received poor assessments. Without consultation by OMB staff on how PART might serve Congressional needs and agreement on what to assess and how to measure performance, Congressional staff almost universally remained unconvinced of the value of PART assessments and ratings to Congressional committees (Government Accountability Office, 2005a). Congressional committees have expressed their support and displeasure with PART in committee reports, but if the House version of the fiscal 2007 appropriations bill for Labor, Health and Human Services and Education becomes law, it will include a general provision that would increase the role of the Congress in the administration's PART studies. Specifically, the provision states that,

> Unless specifically exempted, no funds are provided in the Act to conduct or participate in the conduct of a PART analysis or study unless the Committees on

Appropriations of the House and Senate have approved of the study, inclusive of the data on which the analysis will be based, the methodology to be employed and the relative weight of each of the four factors that will be assigned to the study in determining a final score.[22]

Future of PART

The introduction of PART marks another milestone for performance management and the federal government's 50-year quest to have performance budgeting take root. Underlying PART and previous efforts is the belief that performance information will only be taken seriously once it becomes institutionalized and serves as a primary driver behind management, including funding decisions. GPRA created a structure for formulating strategic goals and measures, and standardized reporting of this information. Given that strategic plans were the exception and not the rule in federal civilian agencies, this was no small achievement. However, unlike GPRA which is based in statute, PART may end as it began with this administration. Whether or not an assessment process continues, agency officials GAO interviewed credited the PART with increasing attention to the use of performance measurement in day-to-day program management. According to many of these officials, PART has lent support to internal agency initiatives and—despite the limitations of scorecards and bottom-line ratings—has highlighted the need for improvements, motivated agencies to seek more ambitious measures, and underscored the need for quality evaluations (Government Accountability Office, 2005a).

After five years of considerable effort OMB has an infrastructure in place for what could be argued is a missing piece of GPRA, an assessment component that brings planning and performance full circle. Since its inception, the creators of PART have tried to build discipline and standardization through guidance, training, consultation, and formalized assessment consistency checks. And they have developed the PARTweb to help ease the exchange of information between agencies and OMB. With the release of the President's fiscal year 2007 budget request, OMB launched ExpectMore.gov, a website "aimed specifically at making performance information transparent and readily available to the American people (that is, the first purpose)" (OMB, 2006). This latest effort is aimed at creating demand and expectation by the public that assessments of federal program performance will continue. Figure 10.4 displays information on the US Department of Labor's Job Corps program, used in previous examples, and what OMB has done to make the results more accessible on its new website.

The challenge in continuing PART or another systematic approach to assessment is how to use such a tool for cross-cutting reviews of spending programs and tax expenditures that contribute to a goal or policy. Some initial efforts at developing common measures have had mixed reviews from the agencies involved and more will need to be done to ensure that the measures are meaningful and provide fair assessments across similar activities. OMB made the decision that it was important to have 100 percent coverage of federal programs, but by doing so it placed less emphasis on examining the relationship between and among programs, which limits

PROGRAM ASSESSMENT	
PROGRAM View Similar Programs	**Job Corps** • This program provides intensive education and training services to disadvantaged youth ages 16–24. These services are intended to help these youth obtain jobs, seek further education, or enter the military. The program serves 60,000 youth nationwide through 122 centers, most of which are also the youths' residences.
RATING What This Rating Means	**PERFORMING** **Moderately Effective** • **The program's performance results are positive, and the program compares favorably to other Federal training programs for youth.** A four-year experimental evaluation found that most participants fared better than comparable non-participants in terms of employment and earnings increases, improvements in literacy and numeracy, and reduced involvement in crime. • **The program's benefits exceed its costs.** The cost per participant is expensive (about $24,000) because most participants reside in the center that serves them. However, society benefits from the program because graduates gain important vocational skills and attain educational levels higher than those who do not attend the program. • **The program's planning for construction and capital assets is insufficient.** The program did not have a formal capital asset plan until 2005, and it did not include the Department of Labor's or the Employment and Training Administration's Chief Financial Officer or Procurement Executive in the planning process.
IMPROVEMENT PLAN About Improvement Plans	**We are taking the following actions to improve the performance of the program:** • Reducing the proportion of program participants who fail to complete the program. Currently, 40 percent of all youth who enroll in the program do not complete it. • Developing an annual, formal capital asset plan and planning process. • Collecting data to allow comparison with other youth training programs on performance relating to key outcomes like entry into a job or post-secondary education, literacy, and earning a diploma.

Figure 10.4 PART assessment for the Job Corps program on ExpectMore.gov[a]

[a] ExpectMore.gov includes more detailed information about the PART assessment rating process, supporting documents for the specific assessment, and program-related information from the agency's website.

Source: US Office of Management and Budget.

PART's usefulness in re-examining or restructuring federal missions. The administration may have recognized this when it sent a legislative proposal to Congress last year that, if enacted as proposed, would create two kinds of commissions that would continue to rely on PART-like assessments.

The Government Reorganization and Program Performance Improvement Act of 2005 will shift responsibility for program assessment away from OMB to commissions established by Congress that report to the President. The President will decide what agencies or programs the result commissions will study, but target overlap in program, policy areas, or jurisdictions with the goal of "consider[ing] and revis[ing] Administrative proposals to restructure or consolidate programs or agencies to improve their performance." The second type of commission—a Sunset Commission—will "consider Presidential proposals to retain, restructure, or terminate programs" following a schedule of regular review—at least every ten years— and reauthorization. Programs will be terminated automatically if they are not reauthorized by Congress two years after the review or after four years if Congress chooses to extend the deadline for reauthorization (OMB, 2005e).

Conclusions

OMB, through its development and use of the PART, has more explicitly infused performance information into the budget formulation process, increased the attention paid to performance measurement and program evaluation, and challenged Congressional decision-makers and others to act on the PART assessments. The commitment of senior OMB officials and staff clearly signals the importance of this strategy in meeting the priorities outlined in the President's Management Agenda, and PART provides agencies with powerful incentives for improving data quality and availability. If these measures and supporting data meet the needs of other stakeholders as well, then eventual acceptance of performance metrics in budgeting may come as the result of a "culture change" brought about by generation of valid information (Joyce, 1993). At the very least, OMB should be credited with opening up for scrutiny—and potential criticism—its review of program performance and then making these assessments available to a potentially wider audience.

Performance budgeting initiatives, such as PART, should not be expected to provide the answers to resource allocation questions in some automatic or formula-driven process. Despite its bottom-line conclusions, PART is diagnostic not definitive, and while it can add an important perspective, it is, as OMB has acknowledged, only one among many factors in making resource decisions. In fact, long after PART ratings have been forgotten, this OMB's influence over measures and data collection may be the true legacy of the PART process. Moreover, if PART ratings continue to highlight the need for evaluation research and data, and if, in turn, this leads to better program design, greater effectiveness, or increased efficiency, then the enormous time and effort put into the PART process by OMB and agencies may pay off. What is harder to predict is whether assessments will continue—and in what form—after OMB reaches its milestone next year of assessing all federal programs at least once.

As noted above, performance questions and problems do not have a single budgetary answer—performance problems may at times warrant greater investments to improve operations while high-performing programs may suffer cuts if they prove to be lower in priority than other competing claims. As the agenda formation literature suggests, reframing the kinds of questions raised in policy debates constitutes an important political event with potentially major consequences for decisions (Kingdon, 2002). Thus, we might reasonably expect performance budgeting reforms like PART to force issues associated with outcomes and efficiency of programs onto decision-makers' radar screens. At the same time, we should recognize that technical or analytic exercises do not do a good job of addressing equity considerations, unmet societal needs, and the competing values of policy choices for different communities and individuals. Other factors such as the overall budget situation, the state of the economy, and the appropriate role of the federal government are also important considerations (Government Accountability Office, 2005a). This we leave to elected officials and the political process, where as citizens we can provide our own assessments of how well the federal government is doing at election time.

Notes

1. The author would like to acknowledge Paul Posner, Jackie Nowicki, and others who contributed to the 2004 and 2005 GAO PART reviews.
2. In addition to OMB documents related to the President's Management Agenda and its Budget and Performance Integration initiative, the other main sources for this chapter are GAO (2004b, 2005b).

   We examined the first year of PART's implementation (2002) and use in the fiscal year 2004 budget process in our first report. Our objectives were to determine if PART was being applied consistently and whether it complemented the existing statutory framework established by the Government Performance and Results Act (GPRA) (Pub. L. No. 103–62 (1993)). We were also asked to identify the strengths and weaknesses of PART as a budget and evaluation tool. For that report, GAO reviewed OMB materials on the development and implementation of the PART as well as PART assessment results. To assess whether PART was applied consistently, GAO performed analyses of data from the PART program summary and assessment worksheets for each of the 234 programs rated. GAO also reviewed 28 programs in nine clusters covering food safety, water supply, military equipment, procurement, provision of health care, statistical agencies, block grants to assist vulnerable populations, energy research programs, wildlife management, and disability compensation to determine if comparable or disparate criteria were applied in producing the PART results for these program clusters.

   As part of GAO's examination of the usefulness of the PART as an evaluation tool and to obtain agency perspectives on the relationship between PART and GPRA, GAO interviewed department and agency officials including senior managers, and program, planning, and budget staffs at the Departments of Health and Human Services (HHS), Energy (DOE), and Interior (DOI). Concurrently, OMB officials at each level of the organization were interviewed regarding their experiences. We selected these three departments because they had a variety of program types (for example, block/formula grants, competitive grants, direct federal, and research and development) that were subject to the PART and could provide a broad-based perspective on how PART was applied to different programs. Although not generalizable, the consistency and frequency with which similar issues were raised by OMB and agency officials suggested that our review reliably captures significant aspects of PART as a budget and evaluation tool. Finally, GAO did a series of regression analyses to show the relationship between PART scores and funding levels in the President's fiscal year 2004 budget. Overall PART scores had a positive and statistically significant effect on discretionary program funding. The programs evaluated by OMB include both mandatory and discretionary programs. Since funding for mandatory programs (mainly entitlements) are in almost all cases not the result of annual budget decisions, regression results for mandatory programs showed—as expected—no relationship between PART scores and the level of funding in the President's budget proposal. PART scores explained at most about 15 percent of the proposed funding changes in fiscal year 2004, leaving a large portion of the variability in proposed funding changes unexplained. This suggests that most of the variance is due to institutional factors, program specifics, and other unquantifiable factors.

Our October report revisited some of the findings raised in our earlier report—the relationship of PART and GPRA, unit of analysis and measurement concerns, and workload issues. However, the focus of our recent work was on the effect PART recommended follow-on actions were having on program operations and results, and congressional perspectives on OMB's efforts to involve Congress in the PART process. Once again we interviewed OMB officials and agency managers at HHS and DOE. In addition we spoke with officials at the Department of Labor (DOL) and an independent agency, the Small Business Administration (SBA). We compiled a database of PART assessments and recommendations for the three years available, 2002 through 2004. Our purpose was to discern possible changes or patterns in recommended follow-on actions and the relationships between the type of recommendation made, overall ratings, PART section scores, and answers to selected PART questions. For our final objective, to gauge the effectiveness of OMB's outreach to Congress, we interviewed House and Senate staff (majority and minority) of the Authorization and Appropriations Committees with oversight jurisdiction for our selected departments and agency. We also reviewed Congressional hearing records and reports for any mention of the PART or PART results for specific programs. Our findings are not generalizable to the PART process for all years or all programs.

These and other GAO reports are available at GAO's website: <www.gao.gov>. The General Accounting Office was later renamed the Government Accountability Office.

3. Article I, section 9, clause 7 (the so-called Appropriations Clause) refers to the power of Congress not only to appropriate funds, but also to prescribe the conditions governing the use of those funds. This clause has been described as the most important single curb on Presidential power in the US Constitution.
4. Entitlements currently account for over two-thirds of federal expenditures annually and are growing at a much faster rate than funding for what are referred to as discretionary programs. Entitlements are most often formula based or determined by eligibility criteria that changes infrequently, unlike funding for discretionary programs, which is controlled by the Appropriations Committees and subject to shifting priorities of the political process.
5. For an in-depth discussion of earlier reforms, implementation approaches, and contributions to performance budgeting in the US federal government, see GAO (1998a).
6. The Government Performance and Results Act (Pub. L. No. 103–62 (1993)) requires federal agencies to develop strategic plans, annual performance plans, and annual program performance reports. GAO has published a large body of work on GPRA that can be found at it website, but two reports in particular are worth noting. (1) *The Government Performance and Results Act: 1997 Governmentwide Implementation Will Be Uneven*, (GAO, 1997). Under the GPRA Act, GAO was required to report to Congress on agencies' progress in implementing GPRA and the prospects for compliance by executive agencies beyond those participating in the pilot phase. The last of the reports to meet this mandate included the results of a survey of federal civilian managers and senior executives to get their perspectives on the Act and implementation challenges. (2) *Results-Oriented Government: GPRA Has Established a Solid Foundation for Achieving Greater Results* (GAO, 2004a). This ten-year GPRA retrospective found that the Act had succeeded in establishing strategic planning and a more results-oriented focus in the federal government, but that many challenges remained, including difficulties in setting outcome-oriented goals, collecting useful data on results, linking institutional, program, unit, and individual performance measurement and reward systems, as well as inconsistent leadership commitment in agencies.
7. By requiring that an agency's annual performance plan cover each program activity in the President's budget request for that agency, GPRA established a basic foundation for linking resource allocation decisions and results. However, recognizing that agencies' program structure is not consistent across appropriations accounts (the level that ties to funding decisions), the Act allows agencies to consolidate, aggregate or disaggregate program activities so long as no major function or operation of the agency is omitted

or minimized. For a recent in-depth discussion of restructuring efforts related to OMB's performance and budget integration initiative, see GAO (2005a).

8. The President's Management Agenda includes five government-wide initiatives: (1) Strategic Management of Human Capital, (2) Competitive Sourcing, (3) Improved Financial Performance, (4) Expanded Electronic Government, and (5) Budget and Performance Integration, of which the Program Assessment Rating Tool (PART) is a key element.
9. In February 2006, OMB released the most recent set of PART assessments along with the President's fiscal year 2007 budget request. Although GAO has not reviewed this latest PART cycle, information from OMB on the results of these assessments has been included in tables and narrative as appropriate to provide the latest information available.
10. The weight given to questions can be altered to emphasize key factors for a specific program and a "not applicable" response is sometimes used when a question is not relevant. However, the overall weight given to a section is the same for all PART assessments.
11. The seven program types are: (1) competitive grants, (2) block/formula grants, (3) capital assets and service acquisition programs, (4) credit programs, (5) regulatory-based programs, (6) direct, federally-delivered programs, and (7) research and development programs.
12. <www.whitehouse.gov/omb/part/index.html>. This website also includes guidance and further information on the Budget and Performance Initiative of the President's Management Agenda.
13. Summary sheets were published the first year in a separate volume of the President's fiscal year 2004 budget and in subsequent years on a CD-ROM included in the *Analytical Perspectives of the President's Budget* volume and at OMB's website. A comprehensive list of programs, with their ratings and funding, is updated annually in the *Analytical Perspectives*.
14. The PET model has continued to be used with members rotating in and out at the beginning of a new cycle of assessments. In the last two cycles, the PET has also conducted consistency checks after PARTs are completed, but before the final PART is passed back to the agency and agencies have the opportunity to appeal.
15. There is no standard definition for the term "program" in the US federal budget. For purposes of PART, OMB describes a program (or unit of analysis) as (1) an activity or set of activities clearly recognized as a program by the public, OMB, and/or Congress; (2) having a discrete level of funding clearly associated with it; and (3) corresponding to the level at which budget decisions are made. Although these criteria may be reasonable, not having a recognized definition for a program complicates the PART assessment process because it adds another potential point of disagreement between OMB, the agency, and Congress on what should be included or excluded in an assessment. Consider the possible advantages or disadvantages if a PART-defined program is (a) an entire agency, including administrative functions; (b) a "name-brand" program that is recognized as such by the agency, Congress, and the public, for example, Job Corps; (c) one piece of a larger program, for example, the enforcement component of the customs service; or (d) a group of related activities that are not managed together because they are in different agencies and, in some instances, different departments, for example, rural water supply projects, grants, and loans.
16. A companion effort to the PART under the Budget and Performance Initiative of the PMA was to have agencies submit a "performance budget" as a way of rationalizing what is currently an appropriations account structure that was not created as a single integrated framework, but rather developed incrementally to address specific needs. Beginning with the fiscal year 2005 President's budget request, agencies were instructed to, where possible, restructure their appropriations accounts in a way that would align accounts and program activities with "programs or the components of the programs that contribute to a single strategic goal or objective" (OMB, 2003c, pp. 51–3). The response generally from appropriators and their staff was that the restructured budgets did not meet their needs, did not align with how agencies operate, were not supported by agency accounting systems, and did not provide information that was useful (OMB, 2005b).

17. The US federal health insurance program for people 65 years or older, certain younger people with disabilities, and people with end-stage renal disease.
18. OMB defines a performance budget as a presentation that clearly explains the relationship between performance goals and the costs for achieving targeted levels of performance. The requirements for the performance budget include an overview of what an agency expects to accomplish by strategic goal; what it has accomplished; strategies used to influence outcomes; an analysis of programs that contribute to a strategic goal, their relative roles, effectiveness as identified by PART and other evaluations; performance targets for current and budget years, how they will be achieved, and how they relate in a "pyramid" of outcomes; what resources are requested; and, to the extent possible, the full cost of the program. This should be cross-walked to the budget structure used by appropriations committees.
19. Since entitlement programs and other types of direct spending are not subject to the annual budget process, this information applies only to those budget proposals that would affect funding for discretionary programs. Discretionary programs are defined in the US federal budget process as funding for programs that are provided in and controlled by appropriations acts, other than those that fund mandatory programs.
20. A GAO study of PART follow on actions related to evaluation can be found at the GAO website. See GAO (2005c).
21. GAO interviewed House and Senate committee staff (majority and minority) for the Authorizing and Appropriations Subcommittees with jurisdiction over the four agencies selected for our case study. Additional views of legislative staff can be found in the GAO 2005 report entitled: *Performance Budgeting: PART Focuses Attention on Program Performance, but More Can Be Done to Engage Congress* (GAO, 2005b).
22. H.R. 5647, Department of Labor, Health and Human Services, Education and Related Agencies Appropriations Act, 2007, Title V—General Provisions, Sec. 521.

References

Blalock, A.B., and B.S. Barnow, 2002, "Is the New Obsession with Performance Management Masking the Truth About Social Programs?" in *Quicker, Better, Cheaper?: Managing Performance in American Government*, ed. Dale Forsythe (Albany, NY: Rockefeller Institute).

Daniels, M.E., 2002, "Linking Program Funding to Performance Results." Testimony before the Subcommittee on Government Efficiency, Financial Management and Intergovernmental Relations of the House Committee on Government Reform, 107th Cong., 2nd Session (Washington: US Government Printing Office).

Fantone, D.M., and P.L. Posner, 2003, "United States Case Study on Accountability and Control in Modernization Reforms," paper presented at the OECD Expert Meeting on Accountability and Control, Madrid, October 29–30, 2003.

General Accounting Office (GAO), 1997, *The Government Performance and Results Act: 1997 Government-wide Implementation Will Be Uneven*, GAO/GGD-97–109, June 2, 1997 (Washington: GAO), pp. 3, 15, 26–9.

——, 1998a, *Performance Budgeting: Past Initiatives Offer Insights for GPRA Implementation*, GAO/AIMD-97–46, March 27 (Washington: GAO), pp. 4–6, 35, 42.

——, 1998b, *Program Evaluation: Agencies Challenged by New Demand for Information on Program Results*, GAO/GGD-98–53, April 24 (Washington: GAO), pp. 23–4.

——, 2004a, *Results-Oriented Government: GPRA Has Established a Solid Foundation for Achieving Greater Results*, GAO-04–38, March 10 (Washington: GAO), p. 64.

——, 2004b, *Performance Budgeting: Observations on the Use of OMB's Program Assessment Rating Tool for the Fiscal Year 2004 Budget*, GAO-04-174, January 30 (Washington: GAO).

Government Accountability Office, 2005a, *Performance Budgeting: Efforts to Restructure Budgets to Better Align Resources with Performance*, GAO-05–117SP, February (Washington: GAO).

——, 2005b, *Performance Budgeting: PART Focuses Attention on Program Performance, But More Can Be Done to Engage Congress,* GAO-06–28, October 28 (Washington: GAO).

——, 2005c, *Program Evaluation: OMB's PART Reviews Increased Agencies' Attention to Improving Evidence of Program Results*, GAO-06–67, October 28 (Washington: GAO).

Joyce, P.G., 1993, "Using Performance Measures for Federal Budgeting: Proposals and Prospects," *Public Budgeting and Finance,* Vol. 13(4), pp. 3–17.

Kingdon, J., 2002, *Agendas, Alternatives, and Public Policies* (New York: Longman Press).

Office of Management and Budget (OMB), 2001, *The President's Management Agenda—FY2002,* August 2001 (Washington: OMB), p. 9.

——, 2002a, OMB Budget Procedures Memorandum No. 852, Addendum 1, Attachment A , *Spring Review Program Effectiveness Ratings, Guidance for Selecting Programs* and Attachment B, *Instructions for the Program Assessment Ratings Tool, General Guidance*, May 10, 2002 (Washington: OMB).

——, 2002b, National Advisory Council, Performance Measurement Advisory Council (PMAC), *Summary of Meeting,* June 27, 2002 (Washington: OMB).

——, 2002c, OMB Memoranda to the Heads of Departments and Agencies, M-02–10, *Program Performance Assessments for the FY 2004 Budget*, July 26, 2002 (Washington: OMB).

——, 2003a, Executive Office of the President. *Analytical Perspectives, Budget of the United States Government, Fiscal Year 2004* (Washington: US Government Printing Office), pp. 4–5.

——, 2003b, OMB Budget Procedures Memorandum No. 861, *Completing the Program Assessment Rating Tool (PART) for the FY2005 Review Process*, May 5, 2003 (Washington: OMB).

——, 2003c, Executive Office of the President, OMB Circular A-1l, *Preparation, Submission, and Execution of the Budget, Fiscal Year 2003*, Part 6, Sec. 220 (Washington: US Government Printing Office).

——, 2003d, OMB Memoranda to the Heads of Departments and Agencies, M-03–17, *Program Assessment Rating Tool (PART) Update*, July 16, 2003 (Washington: OMB).

——, 2004, OMB Budget Data Request No. 04–31, *Completing the Program Assessment Rating Tool (PART) for the FY2006 Review Process*, March 22, 2004 (Washington: OMB).

——, 2005a, Executive Office of the President, OMB Circular A-11, *Preparation, Submission, and Execution of the Budget*, Sec. 51, November 2, 2005 (Washington: US Government Printing Office).

——, 2005b, Budget Procedures Memorandum No. 879, Addendum 2, *Additional Guidance to Improve Consistency in PART Assessments and Updated 2005 PART Process Schedule*, September 30, 2005 (Washington: OMB).

——, 2005c, Executive Office of the President, *Analytical Perspectives, Budget of the United States Government, Fiscal Year 2006* (Washington: US Government Printing Office), pp. 10–12.

——, 2005d, Executive Office of the President, *Major Savings and Reforms in the President's 2006 Budget*, February 11 (Washington: US Government Printing Office).

——, 2005e, Executive Office of the President, *The Government Reorganization and Program Performance Improvement Act of 2005*, June 30 (Washington: US Government Printing Office).

——, 2006, OMB Program Assessment Rating Tool Guidance No. 2006–02, *Guidance for Completing 2006 PARTs*, March 10, 2006 (Washington: OMB), pp. 65, 68.

Tanaka, S., J. O'Neill, and A. Holen, 2003, "Above the Fray: The Role of the US Office of Management and Budget," in *Controlling Public Expenditure: The Changing Roles of Central Budget Agencies—Better Guardians?* ed. J. Wanna et al. (Cheltenham: Edward Edgar), pp. 57, 80.

11

Performance in the New French Budget System

Brice Lannaud

On August 1, 2001, when parliament passed a new organic budget law—the Loi Organique relative aux Lois des Finances (LOLF)—France acquired a new system of expenditure planning and execution. The LOLF has been progressively implemented and came fully into effect on January 1, 2006.

This new system replaces the traditional budgeting system, in force since 1959, which had become unsatisfactory. In a context of high debt levels and burdensome levels of taxation and social security contributions, France had to devise a more efficient way of managing public resources. This was not possible under the traditional budgeting system.

Under the new system, parliament has acquired increased power over the budget. Line ministries and agencies (henceforth "line agencies") have acquired increased managerial autonomy in exchange for committing themselves to improving the effectiveness and efficiency of their expenditures. The essential aim of the new system is to improve the results delivered by public expenditure and the government agencies that manage that expenditure, for any given level of resources.

Reasons for reform

The previous budgeting system instituted in 1959 was weak

The budgeting system which LOLF has replaced was established by an organic budget law dating from 1959. This law was not conducive to efficient public expenditure management and severely restricted parliament's control over the budget. For example, the process of parliamentary approval of the annual budget under the 1959 law promoted incrementalism by requiring a two-stage budget approval process. The first stage involved making general appropriations for maintaining the expenditure necessary to ensure continuity in public services and for meeting government commitments (the "current services appropriations"—*services votés*).

These accounted for 95 percent of the total budget. The second phase, which was more detailed, concerned measures for achieving savings or increases in appropriations for "new expenditure authorizations" (*mesures nouvelles*). This covered less than 5 percent of the budget.

In addition, the annual budget law was a traditional "line-item" budget which appropriated expenditure by ministry and by economic classification (remuneration, operating, capital, and so on). Appropriations were not linked to public expenditure objectives, and the appropriation process was therefore not conducive to optimal resource allocation.

In the execution of the budget, the 1959 system did not encourage the proactive management of appropriations. Indeed, approved budgets were extremely fragmented, broken down into 850 capped appropriation "envelopes" for central government managers (the "budget chapters") and 2,000 capped appropriation envelopes for decentralized government units (that is, service delivery units of the state located in the regional) and regional or *département*-level directorates (the "estimates articles"—*articles de prévision*). As each of these appropriation envelopes was further broken down by economic classification, whenever managers wished to redeploy appropriations from, say, operating expenditure to capital expenditure—for example, to implement public policy—they had to seek approval at a higher administrative level (central government in the case of decentralized units, and the Ministry of Finance and the Prime Minister in the case of central government units). This hampered the reallocation of appropriations.

There was, as a consequence of the appropriations regime, very limited discussion or debate at the end of the fiscal year about budget performance. In particular, the focus of discussions between the Ministry of Finance and line agencies was upon the extent to which appropriated amounts were spent, and not on the efficiency of expenditure or on the extent to which expenditure objectives had been achieved.

The 1959 system severely restricted parliament's power to amend the budget to the extent that parliament was virtually powerless to change the appropriations proposed in the budget law proposed by the government. Article 40 of the 1958 Constitution provided that "bills and amendments introduced by Members of Parliament shall not be admissible where their adoption would have as a consequence either a diminution of public resources or the creation or increase of an item of public expenditure." Article 42 of the 1959 organic budget law made these provisions much tougher by confining parliamentary budget amendments to those "eliminating or effectively reducing an expenditure, creating or increasing an item of revenue." This barred parliament not only from increasing *aggregate* expenditure or reducing *aggregate* revenue relative to the levels envisaged in the government's draft budget, but also from increasing any *individual* item of expenditure or reducing any *individual* revenue item. The result was a diminution of parliament's power to authorize and debate the budget within the framework of "rational parliamentarism" (one law, one vote, with the assumption of responsibility for an overall legislative package), markedly modifying prior practices that were more favorable to parliament but which had led to substantial budget instability.

The time was ripe for reform

There were, over the years, 35 attempts in parliament to reform the 1959 organic budget law, all of which failed. Only in 2001, with the passage of the LOLF, was reform achieved. This was because, finally, the external context made it possible to effect reforms which had become pressing as a result of the traditional budgeting system's inherent flaws. The key factors which came together to produce this change were:

- *A more demanding society, in a more difficult fiscal context.* Mounting government deficits and debt from the 1980s onward led to spirited debates on public expenditure. In a context of ever scarcer resources and increasingly burdensome levels of taxation and social security contributions, the debate naturally focused on the proper use of the taxes paid by citizens and, therefore, on the effectiveness and efficiency of expenditure. This led naturally to discussion of the improvement of government management, the introduction of new management methods, more decentralized management, the decentralization process itself, and even the outsourcing of certain government activities. In a more general way, citizens—who are both users of public services and taxpayers—began to seek a better understanding of public expenditure and to demand more transparency as well as greater efficiency and quality. With public debt exceeding 60 percent of GDP and public expenditure alone representing 54.7 percent of GDP (2003 figures), the issue of governance reform could not be ignored.
- *A supportive international environment.* Financial governance issues were underscored by various international organizations, and some countries set up systems to improve governance. The OECD and the IMF had both developed codes of good practice on financial governance. Relevant elements of these codes include, in particular, strengthening parliamentary control over finances, greater accountability of line ministries to the Ministry of Finance, transparency of budget information, and establishment of accrual accounting similar to corporate accounting. Also, many other countries had initiated or developed governance improvement processes, including Canada (through its program review exercises), the United Kingdom (multi-year budgets, performance budgeting, accounting, and so on), and the Netherlands (performance budgeting). France closely studied these various experiments in other countries, particularly through the mission headed by the Inspector-General of Finance, Henri Guillaume, on performance management. Finally, with the Stability and Growth Pact, the Economic and Monetary Union established the requirement of multi-year fiscal programming for all the governments of the European Union.
- *Parliamentary initiative.* The origin of the LOLF reform can be traced directly to a parliamentary initiative. As early as 1998, a working group on the effectiveness of public expenditure and parliamentary control had been formed in the National Assembly by its President, Laurent Fabius. A specialized parliamentary committee was then established alongside the assessment and audit mission (the MEC). A further impetus arose from a political debate

begun in late 1999 on the credibility of big tax revenue surpluses claimed by the government (the "tax jackpot" debate), which led a strong push in the Senate for greater transparency in financial reporting. The political response was an announcement on March 16, 2000, by Prime Minister Lionel Jospin that the 1959 organic budget law would be reformed.

With the way cleared by parliament, the National Assembly's general rapporteur on the budget, Didier Migaud, tabled an initial draft of the LOLF in the National Assembly on July 11, 2000. He was supported by Alain Lambert, President of the Senate Finance Committee, who agreed to work on the drafting of the new law. Cooperation between the National Assembly, the Senate, and the government gave rise to an agreement to reform the budgetary system without touching the Constitution itself. Both the government and the Audit Office (Cours des Comptes) contributed to the drafting. The result was that when the new law was presented to the parliament, there were no amendments from the government (Laurent Fabius, formerly President of the National Assembly, was by then Minister of Finance) and the vote was nearly unanimous (with only the communists in the Senate abstaining).

The new budgeting system is aimed at moving from input-based to performance-based fiscal management in France, essentially by strengthening the managerial autonomy of government units and increasing parliamentary control of the budget.

Strengthening governmental autonomy and parliamentary control

Strengthening managerial autonomy of government units

Based on the notion that financial managers in the field are in the best position to facilitate the optimal use of available resources, the French budget reform seeks primarily to increase the autonomy of these managers. Accordingly, the appropriations structure of the budget has been reformed. The number of capped appropriation envelopes allocated to ministries and approved by Parliament was reduced from 850 to 133.[1] This multiplied by a factor of six the average size of the appropriation envelopes available to each minister. On the other hand, restrictions on the movement of appropriations within the fiscal year are tighter under the LOLF than they were under the organic law of 1959 (see Box 11.1).

Crucially, these capped appropriation envelopes are now based on "programs" which are defined by purpose—in other words, by public policy objective rather than by input type.[2] Within each program, appropriations can therefore in large measure be used freely for capital, operating, and personnel expenditure, as long as they contribute to the public policy involved. There is only one restriction on the free use of appropriations: within the appropriations for a program, a ceiling on personnel expenditure must be observed. Although it is possible to redeploy appropriations from personnel to operating or capital expenditure, the reverse is not allowed. This is what is known as "asymmetrical fungibility." This control of personnel expenditure is reinforced by a separate ceiling on the numbers of civil servants (expressed in full-time equivalents) each ministry is permitted to employ. The special treatment

Box 11.1 Changing budget allocations during the fiscal year

Under the LOLF, a distinction is made between the *transfer* of appropriations, and the *virement* of appropriations.

The *transfer* of appropriations refers to changes in the ministry responsible for executing the expenditure, which nevertheless leave unchanged the programmatic purpose of the expenditure. That is, the transferred appropriations must still be used to finance an action that could be funded by the program for which that expenditure was originally appropriated (for example, co-financing a joint commitment or research concerning individual ministries). Such transfers are now authorized by decree of the Prime Minister, whereas under the system established by the 1959 law they only required ministerial authorization.

The *virement* of appropriations refers to "changing the distribution of appropriations among the programs of a given ministry." Virement modifies parliamentary expenditure authorizations more significantly than do transfers, inasmuch as they change the *purpose* of the expenditure. The LOLF provides that "the total amount, during a single year, of appropriations that have been vired may not exceed 2 percent of appropriations allocated by the annual budget law to each of the programs concerned." Technically, the purpose of this procedure is to correct budgeting errors or cover specific management contingencies. However, in practice they will have the broader consequence of facilitating programmatic reallocations within the 2 percent limit. Under LOLF, virement modifies the purposes for which money is being spent, whereas under the 1959 system, it changed the type of input upon which money was spent (albeit within a single ministry and within the limit of 10 percent of the initial appropriation for each of the chapters concerned). Overall, the margin for shifting appropriations remains approximately the same, although slightly greater by virtue of moving from a redeployment limit divided by five (that is, 2 percent of the appropriation instead of 10 percent) to a basis divided by six, with the change from 850 chapters to 133 programs under the general budget.

of personnel expenditure is a reflection of the long-term rigidity that characterizes such expenditure within the framework of the employment guarantee that comes with civil servant status in France.

A "program manager" is appointed for each program, more often than not selected from among central government directors. These program managers are empowered to allocate and reallocate appropriations *within* programs, and to set performance objectives for the services covered by the program. Figure 11.1, as an example, illustrates the new budget structure of appropriations for the Ministry of Justice.

The government has been careful not to simply base programs on existing organizational units ("directorates"). Thus, of 124 non-grant programs, 56 do not correspond to a particular central government directorate. The government's aim has, rather, been to define centers of responsibility. With respect to the relationship of programs and organizational structure, three cases may be distinguished:

- A program corresponds to a specific organizational unit, usually a central government directorate. Such a one-to-one correspondence is to be expected insofar as there are directorates with mandates focused on specific public policy objectives which are naturally designated as programs under the new system (police, gendarmerie, judicial system, correctional system, and so on).

- A central government directorate handles several programs because the breadth of the role of the directorate made it logical to recognize it as pursuing several distinct programmatic objectives. One consequence of this has been that there are a number of cases where the same individual serves as program manager for more than one program.[3]
- A single program involves several central government directorates. Examples of this include the "heritage" program of the Ministry of Culture, which brings together six directorates, or the "central and local government tax and financial management" program of the Ministry of Finance, which brings together the two major directorates with networks (General Tax Directorate and General Directorate of Government Accounting), as well as part of Customs.[4]

As discussed in Chapter 20, the reform of organizational structures was not considered to be an element of the LOLF reforms at the time of their introduction. Nevertheless, this new budget structure should gradually encourage agencies to adapt their organizational structures to the new budgeting and management framework, usually through the regrouping of central government directorates.

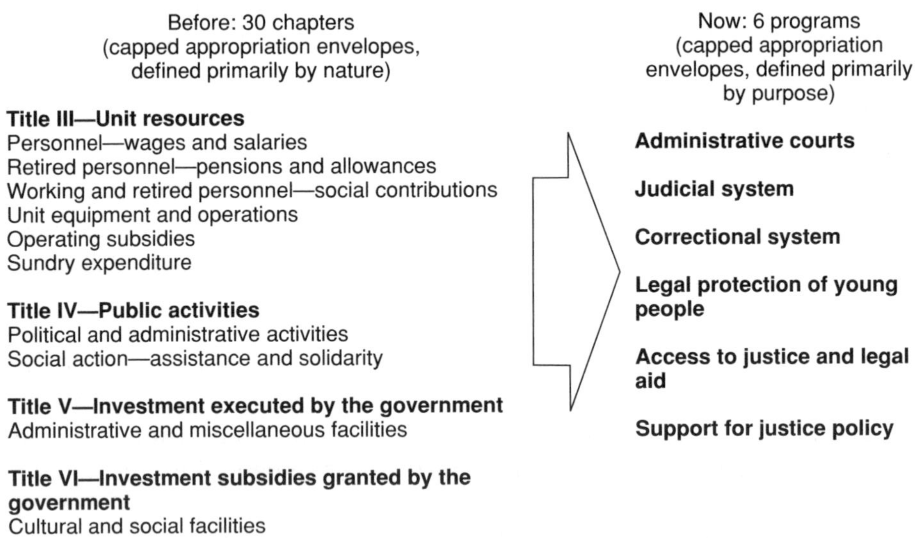

Figure 11.1 New budget structure of appropriations for the Ministry of Justice

In those cases where organizational and program structures differ, each program has been asked to develop a "management charter" specifying the manner in which the program's budget allocation will be shared between the directorates concerned, as well as the responsibilities of each directorate in contributing to the overall performance of the program. In most cases where a number of directorates contribute to a single program, the program manager will be the head of one of the directorates concerned. He or she will, as a consequence, have no hierarchical authority over his or her colleagues. The management charter is intended as a means of specifying the rules of the game under these types of circumstances. However, this objective has not yet been fully achieved, because there are a number of cases where the management charters that have been developed for specific programs do not as yet accord to the program manager the full extent of authority that they ought to have.

Apart from affecting central government managers, the budget reform is intended to increase the managerial autonomy of the decentralized government units that manage a large proportion of government appropriations and actually deliver the services through which many public policy objectives are realized. With this in mind, each ministry has been asked to accord to its own decentralized units the flexibility afforded to the ministry as a whole under the new budget framework. To understand what this means, it needs to be borne in mind that each budgetary program is broken down within ministries into a number of "operational program budgets," more often than not at the regional level (which would mean that one program could be broken into 22 operational program budgets, in line with the number of regions in metropolitan France). The new system has created considerably greater flexibility at the local level, by contrast with the 1959 system under which there were a far larger number of capped appropriation envelopes which local level managers were obliged to observe. In fact, the amount of resources that the manager of an "operational program budget" can freely use has thus multiplied about twelve-fold relative to the 1959 system. Unfortunately, some central government units have prevented local managers from benefiting fully from such expenditure flexibility by imposing additional disaggregated controls on how the operational program budgets may be spent. Furthermore, although the size of the appropriations allocated to the decentralized level was increased, parallel practices of "earmarking" appropriations persist through various instructions that may limit the options of the decentralized units.

As noted above, this enhanced managerial autonomy is combined with increased parliamentary control of the budget.

Increased parliamentary control of the budget

Parliament now has the power to redeploy appropriations across programs, subject to certain conditions described below. In the budget law, the 133 programs are grouped into 34 missions that are linked to major areas of public policy, of which the programs constitute subdivisions. Some missions may be interministerial and encompass programs falling under the authority of various ministers.

Within a single mission, parliament can change the distribution of appropriations among the various programs, thus departing from the initial breakdown proposed by the government. Interpreting the Constitution, Article 47 of the LOLF opens up the possibility of parliamentary amendments to expenditure: "within the meaning of Articles 34 and 40 of the Constitution, the responsibility is understood, in respect of amendments applicable to appropriations, to be that of the mission." Therefore, *amendments proposing increased appropriations for a program offset by an offsetting reduction in appropriations for another program within the same mission are now admissible*. This interpretation of the Constitution has been approved by the Conseil Constitutionnel, France's constitutional court. Parliament's capacity to amend the budget still remains limited by a bar on changes in the aggregate level expenditure proposed in the government's budget, even if financed by equivalent changes in taxations so as to leave the fiscal balance unchanged. Changes by parliament to the distribution of appropriations among missions are also prohibited.

Since missions are established by government initiative, members of parliament may not create new missions. They may, however, create or abolish programs within missions. It is for this reason that the government began consultations with the finance committees of the National Assembly and the Senate on the new budget architecture, two years before the organic law came into force. Parliament wanted to ensure that the number of programs would be large enough for it to exercise real power of amendment. It therefore became necessary to strike a balance between parliament's wishes and the objective of making appropriations fungible in order to allow for more efficient management. The government developed a prototype program/mission classification and submitted it to parliament in January 2004. In response to the views expressed by the parliament, the government modified this classification by adopting most of the suggestions made jointly by both the National Assembly and the Senate, including the establishment of new interministerial missions such as "Security" and "Territorial Policy," and increasing the total number of programs.

The corollary of this increased power of parliament to amend the appropriations proposed in the government's draft budget has been the disappearance of the distinction between "current services appropriations" (*services votés*) and "new expenditure authorizations" (*mesures nouvelles*), which—as noted at the outset of this chapter—tended to promote incremental adjustments to expenditure from one year to the next. Under the new system, parliament may now question any program expenditure. This puts pressure on government units to justify the total amount allocated to each program, rather than simply any incremental changes relative to the previous year. This idea has been captured under the system by reference to the principle of *justification au premier euro*. This "justification from the first euro" is intended to lead to better information on the output and activity content of programs, and not only their expenditure content. Specifically, the intention is that agencies will be required to clarify the drivers behind the program appropriations requested of parliament. This will include physical drivers (number of users, volume of activity, number of staff, building floor space, and so on), financial drivers (determinants of a wage bill, unit costs of intervention mechanisms, and so on), or a combination of the two. Such information is to be included in annexes to the draft budget law, and should enable members of parliament to gain a more in-depth understanding of what each program involves. The overarching consideration here is that the fungibility of appropriations within broad programs should not result, especially for parliament, in a loss of information concerning the purpose and nature of expenditure relative to the current situation. It is also intended that the principle of "justification from the first euro" will also be applied to end-of-the-financial-year reporting on program performance, in such a way as to strengthen the link between expenditure planning and execution.

These new arrangements are likely to lead to less inertia in the process of allocating budget resources.

Formal commitments by government units to enhance expenditure effectiveness

In exchange for increased managerial autonomy, agencies are now required to commit formally to the achievement of objectives for improved efficiency and effectiveness. These objectives, specified in terms of performance indicators and associated performance targets, must now (according to Articles 7 and 51 of the LOLF) be specified in "annual performance plans" (*projets annuels de performances*) presented as annexes to the draft budget law. At the end of the fiscal year, the results achieved must be reported and commented upon in "annual performance reports" (*rapports annuels de performances*) presented as annexes to budget closure law[5] (Article 54 of the LOLF). Performance targets may be set, on an annual or multi-year basis, for periods of up to five years.

This procedure is based on the application of a number of key principles which were agreed to by parliament, the Audit Office, and the government, and which are embodied in a methodological guide entitled *The Performance-Based Approach* (June 2004). Prior to the LOLF coming into full force, these principles were tested by all ministries through the publication of pilot annual performance plans in the fall of 2004. The further refinement of these principles has been facilitated by the review of these pilot plans by the finance committees of the National Assembly and the Senate, as well as by the Audit Office and the Interministerial Program Audit Committee. In addition, several pilots carried out at the decentralized level by certain ministries during 2003, 2004, and 2005 have also provided an opportunity to investigate the practical effects of applying these principles.

Objectives aimed at enhancing expenditure effectiveness: "spending better"

The objective of the performance-based approach is to "spend better." This approach encourages those who design and manage public policies and the personnel who implement them to improve the results achieved by public services and the quality of those services, at least cost and within the framework of the resources allocated to programs.

Accordingly, agencies are expected to articulate three types of objective in their annual performance plans:

- *Outcome objectives, reflecting citizen expectations*. These outcome objectives should spell out the expected benefits for citizens or society which each program will deliver, in terms of changes brought about to economic, social, ecological, health, or cultural conditions. They are intended to indicate the socioeconomic impact which the government's actions are intended to have, rather than the services (outputs) delivered. For example, the socioeconomic effectiveness objective of the "public elementary education" program is "to result in all pupils mastering essential basic skills by the time they complete primary education."

- *Service quality objectives, reflecting expectations of the users of public services.* These objectives define the expected quality of services delivered to users, that is, the suitability of the service to meet the needs of the recipient, whether the recipient is a willing customer of the service or an unwilling subject (prison inmate, for example). The user may be an external user (user of a public service) or, in the case of programs based on internal support services (such as senior management and resource management), an internal user (that is, staff of the supported programs). For example, a service quality objective in the "development, urban planning, and public engineering" program is "to provide users and local governments with quality service in the delivery of urban planning permits."
- *Management efficiency objectives, reflecting taxpayer expectations.* These objectives relate to technical efficiency—that is, the maximization of the outputs or activities delivered given the level of resources. For example, the efficiency objective of the "central government and local public sector tax and financial management" program is "to reduce the cost of tax management."

Objectives related to the reallocation of inputs or activities within programs to achieve new priorities are also recognized as management efficiency objectives.

It is expected that each of these three types of objectives will, to the extent possible, be specified for each program. The improvement of public expenditure should be pursued in each of these three dimensions simultaneously, all the more because the expectations of citizens, users, and taxpayers do not always coincide. Experience has shown that citizen expectations for socioeconomic outcomes often tend to receive more consideration than user expectations in terms of service quality, which in turn tend to receive more attention than taxpayer expectations with respect to efficiency. Accordingly, of all the objectives contained in the pilot annual performance plans published in 2005, 39 percent related to outcomes, 18 percent to service quality, and 25 percent to efficiency (with 18 percent not falling into any of these categories). Parliament therefore requested that the objectives related to quality and especially to efficiency be strengthened, and that the management efficiency objectives be specified in respect to the bulk of program appropriations. In the annual performance plans published with the draft 2006 budget law, outcome objectives account for 54 percent of the total, service quality objectives 18 percent, and management efficiency objectives 28 percent.

Activity, input, and output quantity objectives are not covered in the performance-based approach, as they are attained mainly as a result of increases in the volume of resources and therefore are not evidence of improvements in spending effectiveness and efficiency. The specification of such objectives would tend to undermine the objective of providing increased managerial autonomy because it would in many cases, in effect, reduce the flexibility provided by the new budget framework with respect to managerial choices in the use of allocated inputs. Although 13 percent of the objectives in the 2004 pilot annual performance plans related to inputs or activities, such objectives had virtually disappeared from the 2006 annual performance plans.

It has been deemed essential that these objectives be assigned to a specific program manager, and that the program manager and his/her minister should be accountable to parliament for the achievement of their assigned objectives. An objective can be assigned to a program if:

1. its achievement depends on the activities, appropriations, tax expenditure, or personnel of that specific program
2. it is feasible for the program manager and his/her minister to commit to a target for performance within a timeframe not exceeding five years.

In the pilot annual performance plans of 2004, approximately 5 percent of objectives could not be assigned to programs because they did not meet these criteria.

In some cases, programs have wide-ranging objectives which go beyond the field of competence of a single program manager. In these cases, responsibility for performance in respect to that objective has been assigned to a minister appointed to take the leading role in respect to the cross-cutting policy objective concerned. This is the case, for instance, with certain interministerial public policy objectives of considerable budgetary significance, identified by the Prime Minister, which related to several programs falling under the authority of various ministries and not necessarily belonging to the same *mission*. The lead minister appointed by the Prime Minister is responsible for coordinating the activities of the various programs involved, with a view to achieving the common socioeconomic results shared by those programs. Because of the coordination powers vested in the lead minister, the program can have cross-sectoral objectives reflecting the combined impacts of the activities being carried out under several programs.

As regards the cross-sectoral policy on road safety, for example, the road safety program, as one covered by the lead minister, has a cross-sectoral objective—namely reducing the number of deaths on the roads—that is clearly beyond the scope of this program alone. Other programs which support the achievement of this objective have more specific objectives which fall within their specific fields of competence but which contribute to the higher-level common objective. Thus the national police and national gendarmerie programs will seek to increase the effectiveness of traffic-related controls in their respective areas of competence, while the national road network program will seek to reduce the dangerous aspects of the road infrastructure.

In addition to its annual performance plans, the lead ministry is also responsible for producing a cross-cutting policy document (*document de politique transversale*—DPT), annexed to the draft budget law, which spells out its coordination role. The DPT describes the overall strategy of the cross-sectoral policy and contains a structured presentation of the strategic objectives included in the various programs covering aspects of that policy. An objective presented in the DPT must also be shown in an annual performance plan, as only the latter document is required by the LOLF. The purpose of the DPT is to facilitate coordination of the objectives of various programs, rather than to institute a parallel, competing management mechanism. (See Table 11.1.)

Table 11.1 lists cross-cutting policies covered by a DPT and the respective lead ministers.

Table 11.1 Cross-cutting policies covered by a DPT

Cross-sectoral policies	*Lead minister*
Civil security	Interior
Overseas territories	Overseas Territories
Road safety	Community Facilities
Action outside the country	Foreign Affairs
Official development assistance	Foreign Affairs
Urban affairs	Urban Affairs
Higher education	National Education
Combating exclusion	Social Affairs

A limited number of objectives reflecting priorities and based on a decisive approach

It has been decided that the number of objectives specified for programs should be limited, to ensure the overall readability of the budget law and prevent a dispersal of efforts that would lead to the pursuit of too many objectives at once. Ideally, there should be no more than about six objectives per program. This means that the objectives specified for each program are not necessarily comprehensive, but rather reflect the most important program objectives.

In the annual performance plans for 2006, each program contains five objectives on average,[6] with an average of two performance indicators for each of these objectives.[7] Each objective relies, moreover, on the implementation of specific courses of action (*lévier d'action*) or action plans. These courses of action may be defined as any change in the way in which inputs are used, or in the activities used to deliver services, which can assist in maximizing outcomes, quality, and efficiency. Thus performance with respect to program objectives, within given resource constraints, may be enhanced through:

- redesign of the policy; and/or
- changes in the way in which services are delivered. For example, to improve service quality with given resources, the following intervention strategies might be used: adoption of a service quality approach, training of staff, retooling of processes, a change in opening hours, and so on.

Operational objectives

The performance objectives set out in the annual performance plans give agencies considerable autonomy in deciding how those objectives should be achieved, as they do not specify in detail which activities should be carried out, the appropriations to be used, or the intervention strategies to be employed. It is up to agencies to make the best possible use of the new flexibility provided by the LOLF, through the fungibility of appropriations, to decide on the most appropriate course of action to achieve their objectives.

Agencies are therefore asked to put in place a performance-based steering mechanism to focus the overall action of their staff on the attainment of objectives. To this end, the strategic objectives presented to parliament are translated by agencies into operational objectives related to each of the "operational program budgets" (see above) of which the program is comprised. Indicators and targets are then specified for these operational objectives.

Objectives defined within the framework of the budget process

One of the key phases of the annual budget discussion is the discussion and joint determination of objectives, indicators, and targets.

At the beginning of the year, the ministries first discuss with the Ministry of Finance, under the authority of the Prime Minister, the amount of each ministry's appropriation envelope for the following year and the structural reforms likely to generate savings. Program managers then discuss, in the context of the envelopes allocated by their minister, the results obtained during the previous fiscal year, and the targets appropriate for the future. New objectives are defined as needed. The same Ministry of Finance staff are involved throughout this dialogue.

Results achieved and objectives for the coming year are not used to determine the allocation of expenditure between programs, because this has been determined prior to the definition of objectives. Around June, after these discussions are over, a provisional list of objectives and indicators under consideration for the next draft budget law, without targets, is submitted to parliament. Although parliament has no power of amendment of these objectives and indicators, it can make its views known. In doing so, it can make use of the annual performance reports published with the budget closure law. The government can decide to change certain objectives or indicators in response to the views expressed by the Parliament.

Performance targets in respect of the chosen indicators may be adjusted further during the summer months, in the event that program appropriation envelopes change as a result of new trade-off discussions. The finalized annual performance plans, including objectives, indicators and targets, are placed before parliament on the first Tuesday of October.

Audited indicators

The inspection unit of each ministry, the Interministerial Program Audit Committee, the Audit Office, and parliament audit the accuracy of the results reported by ministries.

The Interministerial Program Audit Committee

The Interministerial Program Audit Committee (CIAP) is a body composed of representatives of the various audit and inspection units. It is accorded by the government with responsibility for auditing the quality of the data presented in annual performance plans and reports. It assesses the consistency of objectives and related indicators, the reliability of the information systems that produce the indicators, the pertinence of the action plans adopted to achieve the objectives, the quality of the system for managing the networks of decentralized units in the management control system, the accuracy of reported results, and the objectivity and completeness of the analysis of variances between targets and actual results.

The Audit Office

The Audit Office functions independently of the government and is specifically responsible for auditing the proper use of public funds. In its annual work auditing the execution of the budget, the Audit Office analyzes the consistency and reliability of the data presented in the budget documents, especially with regard to performance, as well as any major variances between targeted and actual performance. In addition, more in-depth audits, which may be undertaken at the request of parliament, are conducted to ensure that government actions recorded in the budget laws are performed in accordance with established rules.

Parliament

The special rapporteurs,[8] who are members of the parliamentary Finance Committees, may use their powers to conduct off-site and on-site audits, particularly with a view to testing the reliability of the results announced. The Finance Committees are authorized, on the occasion of assessment and audit missions, to verify—if necessary with the support of specialized bodies or the Audit Office—the methods used in compiling and reporting performance data. The work of the members of parliament involved also consists of determining, in the field, the reliability, quality, continuity, and use made of the performance indicators associated with each program.

Improving results within the framework of the allocated inputs

The link between budgeting and performance

In France's performance budgeting system, the link between appropriations and performance is not automatic. On the contrary, an improvement in outcomes or service quality is sought with given inputs, based, for example, on program redesign or changes in the input mix.

In addition, performance commitments are made for given levels of appropriated resources, after the allocation of expenditure to programs has already been determined based on the political priority given to certain areas. The challenge is to assure parliament that government units will seek the best possible use of the funds granted to them, for a given policy.

Nor do the results achieved automatically affect the amount of appropriations for the following year. The review of results achieved should, first of all, raise questions about the courses of action used—that is, the design of policies and the nature of the activities and input mix used—prior to any discussion of the level of program funding. Nevertheless, the performance-based approach may lead indirectly to decisions concerning the level of resources provided. Indeed, the availability of information about the results achieved by programs provides members of parliament with a valuable tool for analyzing both the quality of program management and the pertinence of the underlying objectives. This information may, when necessary and along with other factors, lead members of parliament to propose amendments aimed at reallocating appropriations between programs grouped under the same mission.

Use of performance information in the budgeting and management process

The Ministry of Finance, parliament, the ministry head offices, and the decentralized units all use performance information at various stages of the budget process. As a result, the performance-based approach changes the budget dialogue, by encouraging reviews or reforms of ineffective interventions and by setting objectives when program appropriations increase in order to ensure that additional funding is used optimally. During and at the end of the fiscal year, performance is used to guide the agency management toward the achievement of priority objectives, to define corrective measures, and to identify and share best practices.

In practice, when the budget is being compiled:

- the Ministry of Finance looks for objectives that reflect reforms deemed necessary, making it possible to reduce appropriations or improve their use in real terms; it also looks for objectives that will impose performance pressure on the program
- when a decision has been made to increase the appropriations for a program, the Ministry of Finance looks for objectives that will allow for future verification that the appropriations were used in the best way possible, especially in cases where it may have preferred another, less costly approach to achieving the objectives concerned
- once the objectives have been formulated, the Ministry of Finance tries to ensure that performance targets are set which are consistent with the best possible use of the appropriations in question
- program managers individually seek to define objectives that will enable them to energize and mobilize decentralized units, by assigning them a number of clear priorities to achieve during the fiscal year.

During the fiscal year:

- program managers monitor performance measurements, so as to take corrective steps when necessary: speeding up a reform, reallocating resources, and so on
- program managers can immediately redeploy, within a program, any savings generated by performance improvements.

At the end of the fiscal year:

- program managers compare the results achieved by the various decentralized units contributing to the program. From this comparison, they determine which are the best practices or the most effective actions for achieving the best results with similar resources. They then disseminate these good practices, the adoption of which they recommend to all decentralized units. Over time, this exercise leads to overall improvements in program performance

- when the desired program results have not been achieved, the program manager analyzes the reasons for this and defines the remedial measures needed to improve future results
- where applicable, the results achieved and the analysis of the reasons for them can, along with other factors, lead to a decision to change the amount of program appropriations, in the event that there is a concomitant major revision of the procedures for implementing the policy in question.

Future paths

Experience to date has led to the development of a more substantial link, within programs, between appropriations and performance and between compensation and performance. These arrangements are aimed at rewarding the most successful units or staff members within programs, rather than providing rewards to programs which perform better than other programs. For example:

- within a number of government units, such as the General Directorate of Taxes, the achievement of targeted results by decentralized units results in their being allocated additional funding for specific purposes such as improving working conditions for staff
- the national police directorate has introduced a performance-based compensation system under which staff in better-performing units receive individual bonuses.

In each of these cases, the fact that performance measures have been used by management for some years has put the agencies in a good position to identify appropriate indicators on which to base their systems of rewards. Most other government units have not yet reached this stage of maturity in performance measurement. At the same time, experiments carried out in other decentralized units suggest that the autonomy granted through the fungibility of appropriations, together with the setting of explicit performance objectives, are capable of significantly increasing the motivation to perform of both management and staff.

Finally, the Ministry of Finance has entered into discussions with certain volunteer ministries with a view to concluding multi-year performance contracts.[9] These contracts will provide the ministries in question with a multi-year perspective on the appropriations they receive, in exchange for the attainment of ambitious performance objectives based on major reforms. The multi-year framework is intended to promote the accomplishment of major reforms, as such reforms often require considerable time for formulation and implementation, and their effects can only be felt in the medium term. The multi-year perspective on the amount of appropriations allotted helps to create a stable framework conducive to the success of the reforms. The contract also allows for determining, in advance, the portion of potential savings that can be reallocated to the program in exchange for the efforts made.

* * *

In conclusion, the new French budget reform seeks to make the allocation of resources more transparent and more flexible, based on the new budget architecture which is defined by purpose and on increased parliamentary control of the budget. It also seeks to make the use of allotted resources more effective by giving greater managerial autonomy to central and decentralized government units, in exchange for commitments on the results to be achieved.

Notes

1. In the 2006 budget law.
2. There is an exception to this principle: certain resource management functions (human resources, property management, and so on), senior management functions (ministerial office, inspections), and certain joint expenses (investment in a joint information system for the ministry as a whole) are still classified under support programs because they cannot be distributed among public policy programs, or could only be so distributed to the detriment of their effectiveness. To compensate for this exception, the documents annexed to the draft budget law contain, for information purposes, an analysis of the costs of public policies, which consists in breaking down the support appropriations, using allocative keys, across the public policy programs, in order to reconstruct the full cost.
3. There are, in fact, nine senior servants—including the Deputy Director of Employment, the General Director of the Treasury and the General Director of Local Government—who are program managers for three or more programs.
4. This example is discussed further in Chapter 20.
5. The law which, after the closure of the accounts for the financial year, serves as the means for parliament to note and discuss the financial results for the year.
6. Among programs with objectives, programs without performance objectives.
7. A total of 629 objectives for the general budget, consisting of 133 programs, 118 of which have objectives; 1,284 indicators for the general budget.
8. The general rapporteur on the budget, appointed by the finance committee of each assembly, is the person chiefly responsible for reviewing the budget law. Special rapporteurs are appointed to analyze the budget of each mission. In early 2005, in preparation for the LOLF, the two assemblies adapted the committees' organization and work methods by appointing rapporteurs, no longer by ministerial budget document, but by mission. Within each finance committee in the National Assembly and in the Senate, the general rapporteur analyzes the draft budget laws and proposes amendments. He lays out his findings before the committee and submits his proposals for amendments, which are then debated. The commission votes on each amendment and each article of the draft law. At the end of the debates, the general rapporteur drafts a report setting forth the opinion of the committee and submits the amendments agreed upon by the majority of the committee. The other committees to which the draft budget law was submitted for comment appoint a special rapporteur to analyze and submit a report for comment on the relevant missions. In addition to the amendments selected by the finance committee, members of parliament may enter other amendments on which the finance committee has expressed an opinion. Once the draft reports of the special rapporteurs of the other

committees have been collected and the report of the general finance committee has been adopted, the draft budget law is discussed in open session.

9. Multi-year performance contracts covering the period 2006–08 have been concluded with the General Directorates of Taxes and Public Accounting (tax and financial management program of the central government and the local public sector); the General Directorates of Competition, Consumption, Suppression of Fraud, and Customs and Indirect Duties (program to regulate and protect trade in goods and services); and the Ministry of Foreign Affairs.

12

Performance Budgeting in England: Public Service Agreements

Peter C. Smith[1]

When it came to power in 1997, the Blair government sought to revolutionize the way in which UK public services are planned and delivered. In particular, it put in place mechanisms that sought:

- to improve the way in which priorities are set between public services
- to focus the actions of specific public services on explicit objectives and targets
- to transmit national objectives clearly to local service providers
- to improve coordination and performance of public services.

To this end, the principal initiatives that have been introduced are:

- a system of explicit objectives and measurable national targets for government ministries, in the form of what are known as Public Service Agreements (PSAs)
- a high-profile "delivery unit" charged with monitoring progress against PSA targets and where necessary demanding corrective action
- a range of instruments designed by individual ministries to encourage local service providers to meet the national PSA targets.

The PSA system is a major departure for UK public services, seeking to introduce a level of coherence and transparency to policy-making that had never been attempted hitherto. It is a major test-bed for the principles of performance budgeting, and has without question delivered many benefits in the planning and delivery of public services. However, it has also led to serious tensions within some of those services, and exposed some major difficulties that arise in the implementation of performance budgeting. This chapter first summarizes the history of PSAs, and illustrates with an example from the health ministry. It then discusses some of the major issues that have arisen in seeking to implement the PSA regime, and assesses its effectiveness. The chapter ends with some comments on the relationship between PSAs and performance budgeting.

Background

The United Kingdom has traditionally been a highly centralized state, with a strong central government and circumscribed local autonomy. Since 1999 there has been some devolution of powers to national governments in Scotland and Wales, leading to increased divergence in policies. However, strong central control has remained a feature of English government, where weak regional and local government offer little counterbalance to national powers. Throughout this chapter, the discussion relates to performance budgeting systems put in place in England, which accounts for 84 percent of the population of the United Kingdom.

Responsibility for financial management of public expenditure rests with the finance ministry (known as Her Majesty's Treasury), led within the government by the Chancellor of the Exchequer (who throughout the period under discussion was Gordon Brown). Traditionally, other government departments negotiated annual budgets with the Treasury. With the exception of some "demand led" spending (such as welfare payments) there has been a strong culture of adherence to such budgets within English government.

The Blair government came to power in 1997 with a commitment to evidence-based policy, to systematic priority-setting, and to explicit performance targets throughout the public services. This led Gordon Brown to undertake in 1998 a Comprehensive Spending Review (CSR) that set three-year budgets in advance for government departments. The break with annual budgets was a new departure, and was intended to offer departments more medium-term certainty within which to plan reforms. After the budgetary agreements were concluded, a set of Public Service Agreements with each department was announced, intended to signal priorities across the entire range of government activity. These were expressed in the form of about 600 specific objectives, many of which were expressed as a target in measurable form, and expected to be achieved within designated timeframes. (Access to these and all subsequent Treasury documents can be secured through <www.hm-treasury.gov.uk/spending_review/spend_index.cfm>.)

A distinctive feature of PSAs was the intention to focus on the outcomes of the public services, rather than operational activities of public service delivery. Although this principle was pursued as an ambition, for many departments the initial targets related more to processes, procedures or outputs. For example, a target for the Ministry of Defence was to "create new Joint Rapid Reaction Forces, which will be fully operational by October 2001." A second feature of the PSAs was the incorporation within each of a productivity target, intended to signal the high priority given to value for money across all government activity. For example, an efficiency target of 2 percent per year was set for police services, and a system of annual efficiency plans introduced.

The PSA process signaled the Blair government's determination to make the management of public services more transparent, and to give departments clear statements of priorities. However, in this first round, the detail, specificity and measurability of the PSA targets were highly variable. For example, the Home Office had a very specific target by 2001 to halve the time from arrest to sentence for persistent young offenders, alongside a much vaguer target to "improve victims' and witnesses' satisfaction with their treatment by the criminal justice system," for which there was no baseline or measurement instrument specified. It was, moreover, also clear that the number of targets was excessive, seriously diminishing their impact.

The intention was to review PSAs biennially, so the first set of PSAs was reviewed two years later in the government's first Spending Review (SR2000). Several principles were applied in the review, including a commitment to focusing on only the government's key priorities, to moving towards a more widespread emphasis on outcomes rather than processes or outputs, and to adopting a longer time horizon. This resulted in a marked reduction in targets (from 600 to about 160), covering a reduced number of departments, and the introduction of four "cross-cutting" PSAs that introduced joint targets across departments.

Moreover, the published documentation associated with the 2000 PSAs became more systematic and uniform. The new format included for each ministry: an overarching aim; a set of broad objectives; specific, measurable targets associated with each target; a value for money (efficiency) target; and a statement of who was responsible for delivery (usually the relevant minister). The PSAs were supported by a series of Technical Notes giving detailed technical specifications of each target, including its formal definition and the measurement instrument to be used to judge success. In addition, a more operational Service Delivery Agreement was developed for each department, giving details of how the PSAs would be delivered.

The apparent reduction in the number of targets was to some extent illusory. The Service Delivery Agreements included many lower-level operational targets, intended to support planning and implementation associated with the departmental PSA. Moreover, although the Spending Review covered the usual three-year planning horizon, some of the targets now covered much longer periods. For example, the Ministry of Agriculture, Fisheries and Food, was asked to "reverse the long term decline in the number of farmland birds by 2020, as measured annually against underlying trends." This highlights an important emerging feature of PSAs: that they may relate to time periods well beyond the budgetary time horizon. Progress towards such targets nevertheless continued to be monitored, to determine whether the department remained on track.

The next Spending Review occurred in 2002 (SR2002). The stated number of targets was further reduced from 160 to 130, and there was much improved continuity in their scope and definition. An important new development was the increased direct interest of the Prime Minister in the PSA process, reflecting the high profile given to the delivery of public services in his successful 2001 election campaign. This was manifest in the creation of the Prime Minister's Delivery Unit (PMDU), with the objective of assuring progress towards key PSA targets, especially in health, education, crime, and transport. The PMDU seeks to "improve public services by working with departments to help them meet their PSA targets consistent with fiscal rules" (<www.cabinetoffice.gov.uk/pmdu/>). In doing so, it offers challenge and practical guidance to the relevant departments and provides regular performance updates directly to the Prime Minister.

The SR2004 offered further consolidation and refinement of the principles developed for the PSA regime. A key development was the abandonment of the value for money (VFM) targets. These had sometimes given rise to difficulties, such as contradicting a department's other PSA targets (an issue discussed further below). Abolition of VFM targets was made possible by an Independent Review of Public Sector Efficiency, led by Sir Peter Gershon, which calculated (in £millions) concrete "efficiency" savings to be delivered by each department (Gershon, 2004). The review made many detailed recommendations on the scope for efficiency improvements, and the Office for Government Commerce became responsible for ensuring the efficiency programme is implemented. Another review (led by Sir Tony Atkinson) advocated new approaches towards measuring the productivity of government services in the national accounts, which are now being implemented by the Office for National Statistics (Atkinson, 2005).

The number of stated targets was further reduced to 126. Again, to some extent this reduction was illusory. Some previous targets were replaced by PSA "standards." These indicated a continued level of performance that was required once a previous PSA target had been achieved. For example, the Department of Trade and Industry was given a standard to "maintain the UK's standing as one of the best places in the world for online business." Performance against standards continued to be monitored, but there was no requirement for further improvement. The PMDU rendered the detailed service delivery agreements largely redundant, and they were abandoned in SR2004.

At the time of writing, a second Comprehensive Spending Review is under way, which will report in 2007.

Case study: PSAs for the Department of Health

In order to illustrate the issues that emerge in setting departmental PSA targets, this section examines experience with the Department of Health. In common with other government ministries, the department has been set strategic targets as part of the PSA system since 1998. Its 2004 PSA targets are set out in Box 12.1. They are based on four broad objectives, as follows:

1. improve the health of the population. By 2010 increase life expectancy at birth in England to 78.6 years for men and to 82.5 years for women
2. improve health outcomes for people with long-term conditions
3. improve access to services, in particular waiting times
4. improve the patient and user experience

Detailed targets associated with the objectives are given in Box 12.1. At the bottom of the box, there are in addition four standards to be maintained, reflecting targets

Box 12.1 Department of Health Public Service Agreement targets, 2004

Objective I: Improve the health of the population. By 2010 increase life expectancy at birth in England to 78.6 years for men and to 82.5 years for women.

1. Substantially reduce mortality rates by 2010:
   - from heart disease and stroke and related diseases by at least 40% in people under 75,with at least a 40% reduction in the inequalities gap between the fifth of areas with the worst health and deprivation indicators and the population as a whole;
   - from cancer by at least 20% in people under 75,with a reduction in the inequalities gap of at least 6% between the fifth of areas with the worst health and deprivation indicators and the population as a whole; and
   - from suicide and undetermined injury by at least 20%.
2. Reduce health inequalities by 10% by 2010 as measured by infant mortality and life expectancy at birth.
3. Tackle the underlying determinants of ill health and health inequalities by:
   - reducing adult smoking rates to 21% or less by 2010, with a reduction in prevalence among routine and manual groups to 26% or less;
   - halting the year-on-year rise in obesity among children under 11 by 2010 in the context of a broader strategy to tackle obesity in the population as a whole; and
   - reducing the under-18 conception rate by 50% by 2010 as part of a broader strategy to improve sexual health.

Objective II: Improve health outcomes for people with long-term conditions.

4. To improve health outcomes for people with long-term conditions by offering a personalised care plan for vulnerable people most at risk; and to reduce emergency bed days by 5% by 2008, through improved care in primary care and community settings for people with long-term conditions.

Objective III: Improve access to services.

5. To ensure that by 2008 no one waits more than 18 weeks from GP referral to hospital treatment.
6. Increase the participation of problem drug users in drug treatment programmes by 100% by 2008 and increase year on year the proportion of users successfully sustaining or completing treatment programmes.

Objective IV: Improve the patient and user experience.

7. Secure sustained national improvements in NHS patient experience by 2008, as measured by independently validated surveys, ensuring that individuals are fully involved in decisions about their healthcare, including choice of provider.
8. Improve the quality of life and independence of vulnerable older people by supporting them to live in their own homes where possible by:
   - increasing the proportion of older people being supported to live in their own home by 1% annually in 2007 and 2008; and
   - increasing by 2008, the proportion of those supported intensively to live at home to 34% of the total of those being supported at home or in residential care.

Standards

- A four hour maximum wait in Accident and Emergency from arrival to admission, transfer or discharge.
- Guaranteed access to a primary care professional within 24 hours and to a primary care doctor within 48 hours.
- Every hospital appointment booked for the convenience of the patient, making it easier for patients and their GPs to choose the hospital and consultant that best meets their needs.
- Improve life outcomes of adults and children with mental health problems, by ensuring that all patients who need them have access to crisis services and a comprehensive Child and Adolescent Mental Health Service.

Source: HM Treasury (2004a).

secured through previous PSAs that must continue to be achieved. A set of even more detailed Technical Notes accompanies the targets, giving the context, data sources, and measurement instruments. An example showing the Technical Note for the obesity target is given in Box 12.2.

Box 12.2 Example of a PSA Technical Note (SR 2002 joint Obesity Target for Department of Health and Department for Education and Skills)

PSA Target: Halting the year-on-year rise in obesity among children under 11 by 2010, in the context of a broader strategy to tackle obesity in the population as a whole

Scope: Children aged between 2 and 10 years (inclusive) in England.

Obesity: Prevalence of obesity as defined by the National BMI percentile classification (from the 1990 reference population from T J Cole et al) and measured through the Health Survey for England. Children above the 95th percentile of the 1990 reference curve are defined as obese.

Halt the year on year increase: Obesity in 2–10 year olds rose, on average, by 0.8% per year between 1995 and 2002. Halting the increase would mean no significant change in prevalence between the two three year periods 2005/06/07 and 2008/09/10.

Data source: Health Survey for England. We are also exploring with colleagues in DH and DfES the cost and feasibility of options for other sources of data in order to obtain more local level information.

Baseline year: Due to the small sample size, the baseline will be the weighted average for the three-year period 2002/03/04.

Target Year: By 31 December 2010, in practice this will mean 2010–11 financial year.

Reporting: Annually (aggregate trend data will be available every three years). The lag between the end of the collecting period and data being published is around 12–15 months.

OGD contributions to PSA: The delivery of this joint PSA target will be supported by a range of programmes including:

a) the joint DfES and DCMS PE, School Sport and Club Links project which seeks to increase the percentage of school children who spend a minimum of two hours each week on high quality PE and school sport within and beyond the curriculum;

b) the joint DfES and DH National Healthy Schools Programme which seeks to promote a whole school approach to healthy living;

c) the joint DfES and DH "Food in Schools" Programme which seeks to promote a whole school approach to a range of food issues.

Throughout the PSA regime, a central role of the Department of Health has been to devise operational instruments that transmit the national PSA targets to the local level. To this end, the most important initiative was the development of a system of "performance ratings" for individual National Health Service (NHS) organizations. Since 2001, every organization (including local health authorities and NHS providers of care) has been ranked annually on a four-point scale (zero to three stars) according to a series of about 40 performance indicators. The indicators are intended directly to reflect the objectives of the NHS, as embodied in the national PSA targets (Department of Health, 2001).

For each NHS organization, the indicators are combined according to a complex algorithm to produce the star rating. The most important determinant of an organization's rating was its performance against a set of about ten "key indicators," which hitherto have been dominated by measures of various aspects of patient waiting times. This was augmented by a composite measure of performance based on the 30 or so subsidiary indicators, combined in the form of a "balanced scorecard" view of the organization. Clinical quality comprised only a small element of the calculation. Since 2004, a new health care regulator, the Healthcare Commission, took over responsibility for preparing the star ratings from the health ministry. The performance indicators used to determine its ratings of acute hospitals in 2004 are shown in Box 12.3 (Healthcare Commission, 2004).

The most striking innovation associated with performance ratings was the introduction of very strong managerial incentives dependent on the level of attainment, which some commentators characterize as a regime of "terror" (Bevan and Hood, 2006a). The jobs of senior executives of poorly performing organizations came under severe threat, and the performance indicators (especially the key targets) became a prime focus of managerial attention. Rewards for performing well included some element of increased organizational autonomy. For example, the best performers in the acute hospital sector became eligible to apply for Foundation status, implying considerably greater autonomy from direct NHS control.

The response to performance ratings among NHS managers has been mixed. Many have criticized the system because of some of the apparently arbitrary way in which the ratings are calculated, and their sensitivity to small data fluctuations (Barker et al., 2004). However, there are some who acknowledge that the system does give managers better focus, and a real lever with which to affect organizational behaviour and clinical practice. Reaction among health care professionals has been less ambiguous, with a widespread view that they distort clinical priorities and undermine professional autonomy (Mannion et al., 2005). This is hardly surprising, as one of the aims of the national and local targets was precisely to challenge traditional clinical behavior, and to direct more attention to issues such as waiting times that had not always been a high priority.

There is, however, no doubt that performance ratings have delivered major improvements in the aspects of NHS care that they targeted (Bevan and Hood, 2006b), and have secured marked progress towards some of the PSA targets. For example, very long waits for non-urgent inpatient treatment, a prime focus of the PSA regime, have been rapidly eliminated. Moreover, compared to Wales and Scotland, which have not been subject to the PSA regime and have not implemented performance ratings, targeted aspects of English health care have improved markedly, even though funding levels are less than in the other two countries (Hauck and Street, forthcoming).

Less satisfactorily, the high-level PSAs shown in Box 12.1 include important public health targets under objective 1, such as reduced mortality rates from heart

Box 12.3 Indicators for constructing acute hospitals' performance ratings, 2003–04

Key targets
12 hour wait standard for emergency inpatient admission
two week wait for first appointment for suspected cancer
achieving financial balance
satisfactory hospital cleanliness
improving working lives of staff
achieving targets for booking outpatient and elective appointments
outpatient waiting standards (21 weeks reducing to 17 weeks over course of the year)
non-emergency inpatient waiting standards (12 months reducing to 9 months over course of the year)
accident and emergency wait of 4 hours or less

Balanced scorecard indicators

Clinical focus

child protection
clinical governance composite indicator
clinical negligence
composite of participation in clinical audits
deaths following a heart bypass operation
deaths following selected non-elective surgical procedures
emergency readmission following discharge (adults)
emergency readmission following discharge for a fractured hip
indicator on stroke care
infection control
thrombolysis—30 minute door to needle time
infection control

Patient focus

A&E emergency admission waits (4 hours)
adult inpatient and young patient surveys: access and waiting
adult inpatient and young patient surveys: better information, more choice
adult inpatient and young patient surveys: building closer relationships
adult inpatient and young patient surveys: clean, comfortable, friendly place to be
adult inpatient and young patient surveys: safe, high-quality, coordinated care
better hospital food
breast cancer: 1 month diagnosis to treatment
breast cancer: 2 month GP urgent referral to treatment
cancelled operations
day case patient booking
delayed transfers of care
patient complaints
patients waiting longer than standard for revascularisation
six month inpatient waits
thirteen week outpatient waits

Capacity and capability

implementing specialist appraisal
data quality on patient ethnic groups
information governance
junior doctors' hours
staff opinion survey: health, safety and incidents
staff opinion survey: human resource management
staff opinion survey: staff attitudes

Source: Healthcare Commission, <http://ratings2004.healthcarecommission.org.uk/home.asp> (accessed April 26, 2005).

disease and cancer, reductions of health inequalities, and reduced rates of smoking, childhood obesity, and teenage pregnancy. Converting these high-level public health objectives into meaningful local targets through the medium of the performance ratings system has proved far less straightforward than in the waiting time domain. Public health has therefore not received anything like the sustained managerial attention enjoyed by the health service delivery targets (Marks and Hunter, 2005). There is therefore concern that local managers are concentrating on targeted and readily managed aspects of health care (most notably objective 3, waiting times) at the expense of less controllable and less immediate concerns, such as public health (objective 1).

While retaining the principle of rating performance on a simple composite measure, it is noteworthy that the Healthcare Commission in 2006 implemented a major change to the assessment regime that pays more attention to a broader spectrum of performance, most notably clinical quality (Healthcare Commission, 2005). It places increased emphasis on self-reporting, and reports clinical performance and financial performance separately.

Discussion

PSAs, and in particular the associated targets, have become a central element of political discourse in England. They have without question succeeded in shaping the priorities and delivery of public services, although whether that influence is for the good remains a matter of fierce debate. On the one side are those who claim that, by focusing on outcomes and stating firm measurable targets, they have helped to "modernize" public services. On the other side are those who claim that, through their simplistic view of priorities, they are undermining the traditional public service ethos and rendering those services dysfunctional.

PSA targets have certainly delivered noteworthy successes, such as the reduction in NHS waiting times, improvements in measured police performance, and focusing attention on numeracy and literacy in schools. However, alongside the manifest intended improvements in many of the measured PSA targets there are widespread reports of adverse side-effects in other, often unmeasured, aspects of public services (Bevan and Hood, 2006a). Many of these reports are anecdotal and may be apocryphal, but some have been credibly documented by the House of Commons Public Administration Select Committee (2003) and Bevan and Hood (2006b). Examples from health care include neglect of unmeasured aspects of performance (for example, clinical priorities being sacrificed in the pursuit of reduced waiting times), distorted behavior (such as refusing to admit patients to accident departments until a four-hour waiting time target was achievable), and fraud (manipulation of waiting lists).

Unintended and adverse responses such as these were readily predictable from the Soviet literature (Nove, 1980). They offer a powerful caution against a sole reliance on a targets regime for securing improvement, and the need to put in countervailing instruments where necessary (Smith, 1995). These might include: a strong national data audit and surveillance capacity; a system of professional inspection that monitors and reports on unintended consequences; careful scrutiny of performance beyond targets by organizational boards of governors; some sort of democratic "voice" in the control of local public service organizations; and empowerment of service users through improved information and systems of redress.

The Social Market Foundation (2005) summarized the criticisms of the targets regime under five headings:

1. there are too many targets
2. they are too rigid and undermine the morale of staff
3. they have perverse and unintended consequences
4. it is not always clear who is responsible for meeting the target
5. the data are often not credible.

The history summarized above demonstrates the learning that has been necessary over its lifetime, and the need to change key elements of the PSA infrastructure in order to resolve such difficulties. This section summarizes some of the most important questions that have arisen in the development of the PSA system under eight headings: Who should choose the targets? What targets should be chosen? When should outcomes be used as a basis for targets? How should targets be measured and set? How should cross-departmental targets be handled? How should attainment be scrutinized? How should departmental objectives be transmitted to local organizations? How should efficiency be incorporated into the PSA regime?

Who should choose the targets?

In principle, it seems perfectly reasonable and indeed honorable for a legitimately elected government to set out its objectives and targets in the explicit fashion of the PSAs. The PSAs serve many purposes, but one is to enhance political accountability. Through the PSAs, the government can be held to account by parliament and the electorate, both for its choice of priorities, and for its performance against the targets. Indeed it is a sign of the success of the PSA process that much of the public debate surrounding targets now refers less to the principle of setting targets and more to the details of what those targets should be.

However, there remains disagreement about the processes by which priorities are chosen and targets are set. For example, many argue that the government's excessive emphasis on waiting times in its targets for the National Health Service ignores the prime objective of health care, which is to improve health, and therefore poses a threat to clinical quality. Because of such outcomes, some have argued that the professionals delivering the public services should have a greater say in influencing the nature of the targets. There is an element of good sense in this principle, because the outcomes of many public services rely very heavily on the engagement and commitment of front-line professionals. And yet it is also the case that the priorities and working practices of those professionals can impede progress towards better performance. To some extent, the PSA process seeks to challenge traditional ways of delivering public services, and it will therefore at times come into conflict with the professions.

There are also those who argue that parliament should have a greater say in target setting. In this respect, a crucial role of parliament is to scrutinize the choice of priorities and the attainment of targets. However, it is difficult to see how the involvement of the legislature in choosing targets would enhance the PSA process. No government will pursue objectives with total commitment when it does not fully control their nature. (This principle also applies, of course, to the devolved organizations charged with delivering public services, and gives rise to some of the problems of morale and alienation discussed further below.)

It is also frequently suggested that service users should have more say in setting PSA targets. There is of course much to commend wide consultation with user groups in identifying priorities for improvement. However, setting objectives involves considerations beyond immediate users of a particular service, such as the taxpayer perspective, the interests of future users, and the interests of users of other services. The user perspective is therefore important, but cannot be the sole influence on priority setting, which in any case involves judgments about the relative importance of different user groups.

Thus, any prudent government seeking to implement a PSA-type process would be well-advised to consult many relevant stakeholders about the choice of objectives and the nature of the targets. However, uncritical accommodation of every interest group would render the PSA process meaningless, for example, leading to an unwieldy proliferation of priorities. A prime role of government is to balance conflicting claims on public resources, and PSAs should in the end be an explicit and succinct statement of the government's choice in that respect.

What targets should be chosen?

Multiple objectives are a characteristic of public services—indeed it can be argued that the existence of multiple objectives is one of the defining characteristics of public services, and is one of the reasons why they cannot (at least in their entirety) be delivered by competitive markets.

However, one of the intentions of the PSA system is to focus on a limited number of objectives. This requires tough political choices to be taken. The 1998 suite of PSAs failed to recognize this, and therefore in many domains failed to have a detectable impact. Subsequent Spending Reviews addressed this issue by focusing on a greatly reduced number of targets. It is nevertheless important to note that some of the numerical reduction was deceptive—the health example above indicates how some targets became multidimensional, for example, seeking to address both overall health improvement and reductions in inequalities in health. Furthermore, as noted above, a number of previous targets have now been converted into standards, indicating a level of attainment secured in previous periods. To many, these retained the appearance of targets, albeit in a different guise.

It is noteworthy that, having identified a priority, the government has sought to include an associated objective into a department's PSA, even when attainment is hard to measure. Indeed in recent Spending Reviews an attempt has been made to quantify attainment of even the most elusive objective, such as measuring improvements in "children's communication, social and emotional development" through use of a new national survey instrument by the education ministry. Quantification is without question a good principle to pursue, as it will in general allow the government to set departments concrete targets. However, it does run the risk of distracting managerial attention from important qualitative aspects of performance, and suggests that reports of progress towards quantified targets should be accompanied by a narrative describing success and failure in more qualitative terms.

The move towards standards indicates that, as the Social Market Foundation suggests, targets should focus on domains where manifest change is required. If a domain is not included in the targets regime, this is not necessarily an indication that it is unimportant. Rather, it may suggest that it is not a priority for urgent change. The key focus of PSA targets should be where change is required, and maintenance of standards in other domains should be secured through other instruments, such as routine regulation, inspection, or market mechanisms.

More generally, it is noteworthy that successful ministries manage to maintain a balance between the pursuit of PSA targets and the maintenance of standards in other domains (Cabinet Office, 2006a). In contrast, the Home Office pursued its PSA targets with great vigor and some success, but was judged very adversely in a "capability review" that assessed its general fitness for purpose (Cabinet Office, 2006b).

When should outcomes be used as a basis for targets?

From the outset, the architects of the PSA system recognized that it is usually the outcomes of public services that matter to most service users and the broader public. In principle, the outcomes focus enables public service organizations to look beyond traditional ways of delivering their services and traditional organizational boundaries. It has had some marked successes in the English PSA system, such as a reorientation in police services from the traditional perspective of solving crime to a concern with crime prevention and reducing the fear of crime.

However, the focus on outcomes can give rise to difficulties. For example, some outcomes (such as wars averted by the Foreign Office) are intrinsically unmeasurable. Even if they can be measured, some outcomes (such as reduced mortality from smoking) can take years to materialize, beyond the lifetime of most governments. Furthermore, some outcomes (such as the alleviation of world poverty) are particularly vulnerable to influences beyond the control of the government department under scrutiny. Each of these difficulties offers the department an excuse for apparent failure, and can undermine the PSA process.

On the other hand, it is clear that the use of output measures can distort behaviour, and lead to unintended outcomes. For example, the Department for Education and Skills was asked in 2004 to "increase the stock of...registered childcare by 10%" by 2008. The real desired outcomes, as stated in SR2004 were, "supporting child development, removing barriers to parental employment and alleviating child poverty." However, it is not at all clear that the chosen output target will necessarily address these issues. The target is readily subverted—for example, attainment might be secured merely by registering existing unregistered capacity. Or it might lead to perverse outcomes—the new places may be taken up predominantly by wealthy parents. Therefore, if the chosen output target is pursued without regard to the eventual outcomes, it may be ineffective. Additional assurance will be needed that the desired outcomes have indeed been secured. Yet if outcome data are available to provide that assurance, they should have formed the basis for the original target.

In short, outcome measures address what matters to the service user and the citizen, and are less vulnerable to distortion. It therefore seems unanswerable that outcomes should inform all PSA objectives. However, there will be occasions when a carefully chosen output or process measure—which evidence shows is clearly linked to the eventual outcome—may form a more effective basis for a target.

How should targets be measured and set?

A central feature of the PSA debate has been how—once objectives have been identified—the associated targets should be set, in terms of the measurement instrument to be used and the level of attainment to be required. A number of governmental agencies and regulators collaborated to advise departments on how they might set targets for their front-line delivery organizations (HM Treasury et al., 2001). Their report advocated the use of specific, measurable, achievable, relevant, and timed (SMART) targets, and the Treasury has sought to pursue these principles in the setting of PSA targets.

The Royal Statistical Society (Bird et al., 2005) put forward a more comprehensive set of desirable general principles for setting targets, as follows:

- Indicators should be directly relevant to the primary objective, or be an obviously adequate proxy measure.
- Definitions need to be precise but practicable.
- Survey-based indicators, such as of user satisfaction, should use a shared methodology and common questions between institutions.
- Indicators and definitions should be consistent over time.
- Indicators and definitions should obviate, rather than create, perverse behaviors.
- Indicators should be straightforward to interpret, avoiding ambiguity about whether the performance being monitored has improved or deteriorated.
- Indicators that are not collected for the whole population should have sufficient coverage to ensure against misleading results; that is, potential bias compared to measuring the target population should be small.
- Technical properties of the indicator should be adequate.
- Indicators should have the statistical potential to exhibit or identify change within the intended timescale.
- Indicators should be produced with appropriate frequency, disaggregation, and adjustment for context.
- Indicators should conform to international standards if these exist.
- Indicators should not impose an undue burden—in terms of cost, personnel, or intrusion—on those providing the information.
- Measurement costs should be commensurate with the likely information gain.

The National Audit Office (2005, 2006a) scrutinized the data systems used to monitor and report progress against all PSA targets from SR2002, and found varying levels of success:

- 30 percent were fit for purpose
- 29 percent were broadly appropriate, but systems needed strengthening, such as improving controls over data collection and documentation, and improving checks on data obtained from external bodies
- 18 percent were broadly appropriate, but disclosure needed strengthening to explain data limitations to the public
- 12 percent were not fit for purpose, most commonly because of design problems, where the systems established did not measure adequately the aspects of performance included in the target
- 6 percent were not yet established
- for 5 percent it was too early to judge.

The Statistics Commission (2006) scrutinized all SR2004 targets in detail to assess whether the statistical evidence to support PSA targets was adequate for the purpose of achieving government policy objectives. Among its findings, it noted that:

- there are some cases in which important technical aspects of targets are not explained in the Technical Notes
- the complexity of some targets can become a serious obstacle to understanding and accountability
- not all the data used to monitor targets were collected, managed, and published in line with the National Statistics Code of Practice
- the transparency and independence of the qualitative assessments of performance were variable
- long time-lags between the end of the target period and the data becoming available can be a serious weakness.

A number of approaches exist to overcome some of these weaknesses. For example, the Royal Statistical Society advocates adoption of a multi-stage measurement "protocol" for each target, that would explicitly explain all stages of the measurement process, from choice of indicator to publication of results. It also recommends publication of levels of uncertainty alongside all attainment measures. In the same vein, the Statistics Commission advocates publication of interim attainment measures for longer-term targets.

A particular feature of PSA targets is the specification of explicit levels of attainment to be achieved. This is an important element of the process, but it has been applied with inconsistent rigor. Some targets have been little more than unattainable aspirations, while others can be secured with little effort on the part of ministries. Furthermore, there are conflicting pressures within the targets regime. To be effective managerial instruments, targets should be stretching but attainable, suggesting (say) a one-in-three risk of failure. However, few governments would want to face parliament or the electorate with such a high proportion of failures. From an accountability perspective, a government would wish to feel there was a good chance of attaining all targets. It is difficult to see how this tension can be satisfactorily resolved, unless the political process becomes mature enough to recognize that some failure is inevitable and not necessarily adverse if progress is nevertheless being secured.

How should cross-departmental targets be handled?

A focus on outcomes sometimes gives rise to objectives that are not obviously attached to a particular ministry, leading to the need to specify "joint" targets that transcend departmental boundaries. These have given rise to particular difficulties in the PSA process. In a joint report, the National Audit Office and the Audit Commission (2006) have examined three particular joint targets requiring especially complex cross-departmental "delivery chains": supplying affordable housing, promoting bus use, and halting the rise in child obesity. They find no ready solutions, but advocate much stronger collaboration between national and local government, and stronger engagement with non-governmental organizations. In short, such targets give rise to problems of coordination, persuasion and engagement that must be addressed if they are to be successful.

The Social Market Foundation recognized that some targets cannot be broken down into individual components, and therefore required a joint effort by two or more departments. However, it recommended that all targets should be unambiguously attributed to a single department, and that targets that must be delivered by more than one department should always have a "lead" department that takes responsibility for the meeting of the target. It is noteworthy that in launching the 2007 CSR, Gordon Brown announced that he would review areas that require cross-departmental collaboration, with a view to seeking innovative solutions for the challenges they pose.

How should attainment be scrutinized?

For a mechanism that has played such a central part in the recent development of English public services, there has been surprisingly little attention paid to the public reporting and scrutiny of attainment against targets. An exception was the report by the House of Commons Public Administration Select Committee (2003), which sought to identify attainment of 249 measurable targets from CSR1998. They found that 67.1 percent had been met; 7.6 percent had been partially met; 10.0 percent had been not met; and for 14.9 percent there was inadequate data on achievement.

These results were not readily available, and the Committee had to undertake research to secure them. In their original form, performance reports were found in a variety of formats, with varying levels of clarity, in the annual reports of individual ministries. The Treasury website merely offered links to these reports. The Committee recommended that progress towards targets and eventual attainment should be reported consistently and regularly on a single, authoritative website.

Within the UK parliamentary system, parliament appoints scrutiny committees for most ministries, and these would be the natural focus of holding the government accountable through routine reporting of progress towards PSA targets. However, systematic parliamentary scrutiny has not yet become routine, and instead scrutiny has been piecemeal, in the form, for example, of occasional reports from pressure groups, the media, and public service regulators.

A particularly important issue within the PSA regime has been the need for independent audit of the reliability of the data used to assess attainment. Hood (2006) reports a range of evidence to suggest that officials implementing the PSA system have given little explicit consideration to potential gaming responses and the associated data audit and regulatory requirements. Indeed, few within government have an interest in challenging information that reports apparent performance improvements and attainment of targets. Considerable popular scepticism has therefore developed about the veracity of information provided by the government on its own performance. The National Audit Office examines the processes for data collection, but is not in a position to assure the accuracy of all data (see Chapter 6 on performance auditing). In this respect, it is noteworthy that the government has announced its intention to make the Office for National Statistics more independent of government than hitherto. An important objective of this initiative is to dispel the perception that reports of government performance may be unreliable.

Far greater attention has been given within government to scrutiny of progress towards targets. The initial instrument for assuring implementation of PSAs was the set of service delivery agreements with departments. However, these proved unwieldy and ineffective, and they have been replaced by the Prime Minister's Delivery Unit (PMDU). The PMDU has been a very important element of the more mature PSA system, indicating a perception within government that continuous monitoring, strong, and timely intervention powers, and continued political attention at the highest level has made an essential contribution to the longevity and sustained high profile of the system.

How should departmental objectives be transmitted to local organizations?

In most cases, attainment of national ministerial targets relies on securing satisfactory improvement in local organizations charged with delivering services. Therefore much depends on how the ministerial priorities are transmitted to local services. In the early rounds of the PSA process, such transmission mechanisms were often crude and ineffective. For example, the national objective to "increase the percentage of children who achieve level 4 in each of the Key Stage 2 English and maths tests ...to 80% in English and 75% in maths" was initially translated by the education ministry into a simple-minded requirement that each school should secure that outcome, regardless of its existing level of attainment and the difficulty of the local circumstances.

Such approaches lead to manifest problems. Organizations already performing well have no incentive to improve, while those with disadvantaged populations may stand no chance of success, and become alienated. Indeed, if such regimes were sustained, it may become difficult to recruit public service workers in disadvantaged areas, exacerbating existing problems. As a result, many national departments have introduced more subtle target regimes for local organizations, seeking to encourage all to improve in the chosen measures, from whatever baseline they start.

However, the tension between national objectives and local discretion has become an important unresolved issue within the PSA regime, especially in the local government sector, where there should be some legitimate flexibility to set local priorities. The prevailing lack of flexibility was highlighted in a report by the Audit Commission (2003) that criticized the neglect of local government discretion in earlier PSAs.

In response, the Treasury set up a review of devolved decision-making to examine how national priorities and local flexibility can be accommodated within the PSA system. It has signaled an intention to move in the medium term towards the publication of local performance data as an alternative to national targets (HM Treasury, 2004b), with a view to allowing local people, rather than the national government, to hold local services to account for their chosen priorities and performance. However, while a policy of devolution clearly has relevance to services that are the responsibility of local governments, such as schools and personal social services, it has not yet been made clear how it local accountability will work in services (such as health care) that do not have a local democratic decision-making mechanism.

How should efficiency be incorporated into the PSA regime?

Most PSA targets address issues of effectiveness, as measured in the outcome targets. However, governments are also profoundly concerned with issues of cost-effectiveness, and so the Treasury has naturally sought to incorporate value for money considerations into the PSA system. From a theoretical perspective this may appear misguided—most departments are given a fixed budget, and the assumption must be that (if they spend the budget wisely) they will strive to secure their PSA objectives within that budget, and inefficiencies will naturally be driven out of the system. In short, issues of cost-effectiveness could be addressed naturally by ensuring that departments seek out maximum effectiveness within their budget constraints.

However, probably sensibly, the Treasury never believed that an emphasis on outcomes alone would ensure VFM, and they have therefore been seeking other ways of improving VFM. At first, this was attempted through the specification of an explicit VFM target within the PSA system. However, this gave rise to manifest anomalies. For example, the Department of Health VFM target was based on year-on-year improvements in the outputs of the NHS (such as hospital admissions, weighted for severity) divided by its expenditure. This target was weak for a number of reasons. First, it focused on outputs rather than outcomes, thereby breaching a guiding principle of PSAs and giving rise to obvious potential for distortion. And second, it was very selective in its coverage of outputs, and therefore offered only a partial glimpse of the department's overall VFM. Implicitly it emphasized the department's health care objectives, at the expense of health improvement.

The Treasury has therefore sought to implement other instruments alongside PSAs to ensure pursuit of VFM. For example, the implementation of Sir Peter Gershon's detailed review of government efficiency included operational efficiency initiatives for specific ministries, such as improved procurement of IT services and relocation of civil servants to low-cost parts of the country.

More recently, it has become clear that VFM will become a central feature of the 2007 CSR, and the Treasury has published a paper discussing how VFM can be embedded into the PSA system (HM Treasury, 2006). The discussion paper raises a number of obvious approaches to promoting VFM, such as seeking out further operational efficiencies, in line with the Gershon agenda, and strengthening the capacity for financial management within government departments. However, it also discusses more radical approaches to securing VFM, such as empowering users (giving them more say in the shaping of their services and more choice of providers) and enhancing local democratic accountability.

Implicit in proposals such as these is a desire to focus the PSA targets on national priority outcomes only, and to move away from rigid central targets in other domains (perhaps relying on minimum local standards). This approach may address some of the criticisms of inflexibility inherent in the PSA system hitherto, and reduce the reported alienation of professionals charged with service delivery. However, to be successful it will require the provision of better-quality data, of relevance to service users and taxpayers, on the performance of local services. It will also require major enhancements to the weak systems of local democratic accountability currently in place for many public services.

Assessment

In introducing the PSA system in 1998, the government had a number of objectives (House of Commons Public Administration Select Committee, 2003):

- offering a clear statement of what it is trying to achieve
- giving a clear sense of direction and ambition
- introducing a focus on delivering results
- forming a basis for deciding what is and what is not working
- improving accountability.

In broad terms, it is difficult to argue with the claim that it has been successful in these respects. However, the PSA regime remains a work in progress. It has introduced numerous challenges and anomalies, the most important of which are documented above. As experience unfolds, it is becoming clear that to be successful the PSA regime must be augmented by a number of other mechanisms. A series of departmental Capability Reviews by the Cabinet Office (2006a, 2006b) has noted that "while progress against PSAs and other top targets is necessary and welcome, it is not sufficient for delivering high-quality performance across the whole system."

Some of the more important institutional requirements for the implementation of regimes such as the English PSA system include:

- sustained political commitment to the PSA system, at the very highest level
- a nimble central government organization (the PMDU) responsible for timely monitoring, reporting, and (where necessary) intervention

- continued monitoring and regulation in domains not directly covered by PSA targets
- high-quality performance management skills within the ministries
- carefully crafted mechanisms for transmitting national targets to the local level
- strong collaborative arrangements where necessary for domains that cross traditional ministerial boundaries
- careful integration of central and local government priorities
- mechanisms for ensuring VFM that are consistent with the PSA outcome targets
- engagement, as appropriate, with relevant stakeholders, including user groups, professional organizations, and the voluntary sector.

A number of commentators have offered suggestions on the architecture of the targets regime. For example, the Social Market Foundation (2005) raises the following issues:

- Targets should be set only when change is required or for aspects of public services which are exceptionally important.
- There should be a fairly small number of targets in place at any one time.
- While an outcome orientation is desirable, "process" and "input" targets may sometimes be appropriate, especially if the organization in question has limited influence over the outcome.
- Targets add most value where other mechanisms, such as user choice and the threat of exit, or the contestability of providers, are not in place.
- Proportionate sanctions and incentives are important. An organization missing a stretching target by a narrow margin should not be sanctioned for failure, but rather rewarded for its progress.
- Public service targets should be fully integrated into departmental performance management, audit, and inspection regimes.
- Joint targets that need to be delivered by more than one department should always have a "lead" department which takes responsibility for the meeting of the target.
- Greater use could be made of targets relating to public satisfaction for a number of public service areas.

In addition, the Royal Statistical Society and Statistics Commission have given detailed guidance on technical aspects of performance measurement. The work of the National Audit Office emphasizes the need for improved quality of data, and there is clear evidence that genuinely independent scrutiny and audit of the data have become a central requirement of the PSA regime.

Performance budgeting seeks to strengthen the linkage between the funding and results of public services. On the face of it, the English PSA system offers immense potential in this respect. It applies a consistent approach to setting priorities across all government activity, focuses on the outcomes of government endeavor, and creates a comprehensive framework for measuring attainment. Moreover, it has been developed within the framework of the Treasury's expenditure negotiations with ministries.

However, it remains the case that—notwithstanding rhetoric to the contrary—the link between the PSA system and the funding mechanism remains weak. In examining why this is the case, it is useful to think of three broad roles for the PSA system: setting priorities, measuring attainment, and offering incentives to ministries (James, 2004).

Without question, the PSA system offers a useful framework within which to set governmental priorities. It offers the finance ministry an opportunity to survey the whole domain of public services, to assess the relative merit of alternative claims on resources, and to choose objectives. In this respect, it contributes to the budgetary process, by requiring that departments expose their plans to critical scrutiny and receive funding conditional on acceptance of explicit targets.

However, there is no direct link between the PSA objectives set for a department and the funding it receives. In principle, the Treasury could make the allocation of a department's budget conditional on acceptance of an ambitious PSA target. As noted above, PSA targets are probably strongest when signaling a change of priorities or a new policy direction. In these circumstances, additional money for a ministry can be made conditional. For example, the health ministry's allocation of extra funding since 2000 was to some extent conditional on acceptance of targets embodied in its PSAs, and the more detailed NHS Plan (Department of Health, 2000). More usually, however, the detailed targets emerge from a process of negotiation after budgets have been set.

Another priority-setting area where PSAs can in principle make a major contribution is in cross-departmental domains, which historically have received low levels of attention from individual ministries. Although England is still struggling to find an entirely satisfactory mechanism for addressing cross-cutting objectives, the PSA system offers some promise for this especially difficult aspect of government. One possible future development may be to "carve out" budgets specifically for cross-departmental domains.

The retrospective measurement of attainment inherent in the PSA system can also furnish important evidence for expenditure reviews. First, it might identify "delinquent" ministries that are not making good use of their budgets. And second it might signal domains where government spending is highly effective (or ineffective), irrespective of the ministry's competence. However, interpreting measures of attainment will always be problematic. The Soviet experience offers numerous examples of the perverse incentives that arise when budgets are based on attainment of central targets, and the associated distortionary consequences. Therefore, there is a strong case for viewing measures of attainment with caution, and maintaining a very loose linkage between performance against targets and departmental budgets.

In contrast to many previous "target" initiatives, a noteworthy feature of the PSA regime has been its success in securing sustained attention at the highest ministerial level. The responsibility for attainment of targets lies with ministers, and there is one instance of a minister resigning in response to poor performance against targets (the Education Minister, Estelle Morris). However, as noted above, there is in general rather weak public and parliamentary scrutiny of performance, and it is unusual for a minister to feel fatally exposed by poor performance. Furthermore, James (2004) found extensive use of stratagems to shift the blame for poor performance away from ministers. Nevertheless, the main (quite powerful) incentive operating on ministers will be to attain targets in order to maintain a reputation for competence. Senior civil servants will similarly have a concern for reputation.

James found limited evidence of any material incentives operating on departments more generally. Perhaps the most direct incentive operating is the threat of receiving a "hard time" from the Treasury or the Delivery Unit. Serious underperformance will lead to escalating levels of intervention from the PMDU, with loss of autonomy and potential damage to reputation for those directly involved. The more recent "capability reviews" also have important incentive effects, although their remit extends well beyond the PSA system. However, there is little scope for using funding allocations as a major component of the incentive regime.

The National Audit Office (2006b) found that the majority of departments are increasingly using outcome-based performance information for reporting, accountability, and planning purposes. However, they found less use of PSA outcomes being made to inform financial management decisions or to maximise efficiency and effectiveness. This is perhaps where the major scope lies for strengthening the link between the PSA system and funding. In principle, the chosen PSA targets should inform the internal decisions of departments in evaluating existing activity, and assessing the virtues of new initiatives. A major challenge is therefore to embed the PSA principles within departmental decision-making in this way.

In conclusion, the English PSA system is an important new development with strong links to the principles of performance budgeting. It offers an immensely rich source of experience in seeking to apply consistent outcome-based performance criteria to the management of public services, and has without question delivered some major successes within the English public services. However, it has also exposed important implementation difficulties. It therefore merits careful examination by all those involved in the development of performance budgeting systems.

Note

1. I am indebted to Alex Hill (HM Treasury) for informal discussions and an invaluable paper on the history and mechanics of UK experience presented at the IMF performance budgeting seminar. I also benefited from membership of the Treasury's Performance Information Panel, which scrutinized technical aspects of the PSA target-setting process, and participation in the Royal Statistical Society and Social Market Foundation commentaries on the PSA targets regime. I thank my fellow committee members and co-authors for their many perceptive insights, which may, I fear, not always be fully acknowledged in the text. I should also like to thank Marc Robinson for constructive comments and guidance. All errors and opinions remain my own responsibility.

References

Atkinson, T., 2005, *Measurement of Government Output and Productivity for National Accounts*, Basingstoke: Palgrave Macmillan, <www.statistics.gov.uk/about/data/methodology/specific/PublicSector/atkinson/downloads/Atkinson_Report_Full.pdf>.

Audit Commission, 2003, *Targets in the Public Sector*, London: The Stationery Office, <www.audit-commission.gov.uk/reports/NATIONAL-REPORT.asp?CategoryID=&ProdID=B02E376A-01D5–485b-A866–3C7117DC435A>.

Barker, R., M. Pearce, and M. Irving, 2004, "Star Wars, NHS Style," *British Medical Journal*, Vol. 329, pp. 107–9.

Bevan, G., and C. Hood, 2006a, "What's Measured is What Matters: Targets and Gaming in the English Public Health Care System," *Public Administration*, Vol. 84(3), pp. 517–38.

——, 2006b, "Have Targets Improved Performance in the English NHS?" *British Medical Journal*, Vol. 332, pp. 419–22.

Bird, S.M., D. Cox, V.T. Farewell, H. Goldstein, T. Holt, and P. Smith, 2005, "Performance Indicators: Good, Bad and Ugly," *Journal of the Royal Statistical Society, Series A*, Vol. 168(1), pp. 1–25, <www.rss.org.uk/PDF/PerformanceMonitoring.pdf>.

Cabinet Office, 2006a, *Capability Review of the Home Office* (London: Cabinet Office), <www.civilservice.gov.uk/reform/capability_reviews/reports.asp>.

——, 2006b, *Capability Reviews: The Findings of the First Four Reviews* (London: Cabinet Office), <www.civilservice.gov.uk/reform/capability_reviews/reports.asp>.

Department of Health, 2000, *The NHS Plan: A Plan for Investment, a Plan for Reform* (London: The Stationery Office).

——, 2001, *NHS Performance Ratings Acute Trusts 2000/01*, <www.doh.gov.uk/performanceratings/>.

Gershon, P., 2004, *Releasing Resources for the Frontline: Independent Review of Public Sector Efficiency* (London: HMSO), <www.hm-treasury.gov.uk/media/B2C/11/efficiency_review120704.pdf>.

Hauck, K. and A. Street, forthcoming, "Do Targets Matter? A Comparison of English and Welsh National Health Priorities," *Health Economics*, forthcoming.

Healthcare Commission, 2004, *Performance Ratings 2003/2004* (London: Healthcare Commission).

——, 2005, *Assessment for Improvement. The Annual Health Check. Measuring What Matters* (London: Healthcare Commission), <http://annualhealthcheckratings.healthcarecommission.org.uk/annualhealthcheckratings.cfm>.

HM Treasury, 2004a, *Stability, Security and Opportunity for All: Investing for Britain's Long-term Future. New Public Spending Plans 2005–2008* (London: The Stationery Office), <www.hm-treasury.gov.uk/spending_review/spend_sr04/spend_sr04_index.cfm>.

——, 2004b, *Devolving Decision Making: 1—Delivering Better Public Services: Refining Targets and Performance Management* (London: The Stationery Office), <www.hm-treasury.gov.uk/media//53886/devolving_decision1_409.pdf>.

——, 2006, *Releasing the Resources to Meet the Challenges Ahead: Value for Money in the 2007 Comprehensive Spending Review* (London: The Stationery Office), <www.hm-treasury.gov.uk/spending_review/spend_csr07/spend_crs07_resources.cfm>.

HM Treasury, Cabinet Office, National Audit Office, Audit Commission, and Office for National Statistics, 2001, *Choosing the Right Fabric: A Framework for Performance Information* (London: HM Treasury), <www.hm-treasury.gov.uk/media/EDE/5E/229.pdf>.

Hood, C., 2006, "Gaming in Targetworld: The Targets Approach to Managing British Public Services," *Public Administration Review*, pp. 515–21.

House of Commons Public Administration Select Committee, 2003, *On Target? Government By Measurement. Fifth Report of Session 2002–03* (London: House of Commons), <www.publications.parliament.uk/pa/cm200203/cmselect/cmpubadm/62/6202.htm>.

James, O., 2004, "The UK Core Executive's Use of Public Service Agreements as a Tool of Governance," *Public Administration*, Vol. 82(2), pp. 397–419.

Mannion, R., H. Davies, and M. Marshall, 2005, "Impact of Star Performance Ratings in English Acute Hospital Trusts," *Journal of Health Services Research and Policy*, Vol. 10(1), pp. 18–24.

Marks, L., and D. Hunter, 2005, "Moving Upstream or Muddying the Waters? Incentives for Managing for Health," *Public Health*, Vol. 119, pp. 974–80.

National Audit Office, 2005, *Public Service Agreements: Managing Data Quality—Compendium Report* (London: The Stationery Office), <www.nao.org.uk/pn/04–05/0405476.htm>.

——, 2006a, *Second Validation Compendium Report. 2003–06 PSA data systems* (London: The Stationery Office), <www.nao.org.uk/pn/05–06/0506985.htm>.

——, 2006b, *PSA Targets: Performance Information* (London: The Stationery Office), <www.nao.org.uk/publications/nao_reports/05–06/Acting_on_Information.pdf>.

National Audit Office and Audit Commission, 2006, *Delivering Efficiently: Strengthening the Links in Public Service Delivery Chains* (London: The Stationery Office), <www.nao.org.uk/pn/05–06/0506940.htm>.

Nove, A., 1980, *The Soviet Economic System*, second edition (London: Allen and Unwin).

Smith, P., 1995, "On the Unintended Consequences of Publishing Performance Data in the Public Sector," *International Journal of Public Administration*, Vol. 18(2/3), pp. 277–310.

Social Market Foundation, 2005, *To the Point: A Blueprint for Good Targets*, Report of the Commission on Targets in the Public Services (London: Social Market Foundation).

Statistics Commission, 2006, *PSA Targets: The Devil in the Detail* (London: Statistics Commission), <www.statscom.org.uk/media_pdfs/reports/Final%20PSA%20Targets%20Report.pdf>.

13
The Chilean Experience

Marcela Guzmán

In Chile, the Budget Directorate of the Ministry of Finance has over recent years sought systematically to improve the formulation, execution, and transparency of the government budget by increasingly focusing budget management—and public management more generally—on the results delivered by public expenditure. These management and budgeting reforms, referred to collectively as the Management Control System, comprise initiatives in the following areas: performance indicators; program and agency performance evaluations; the introduction of a new standard format for submission of results-oriented funding requests for public programs; agency management improvement programs linked to performance-based pay for staff; and agency performance reports.[1]

The Chilean system of performance management and budgeting has evolved under a presidential regime that grants the President of the Republic exclusive initiative with respect to bills concerning the financial and budgetary management of the central government. In particular, legislation having a financial impact may only be initiated by the executive branch. In the process of discussing and approving the budget, the National Congress may neither increase nor decrease the revenue estimate, and may only reduce expenditure. Consequently, parliament's capacity to modify the budget is limited. This makes the executive branch responsible for administration and management of public finances. It has also led to the development of a system in which the budget has become the central instrument not only for funding decisions, but for public management reform.

The executive branch's budgetary responsibilities are borne primarily by the Ministry of Finance,[2] and within the MoF by the Budget Directorate. The Budget Directorate's main function is to prepare the budget and apply budgetary policy in the framework of national plans and objectives. It manages budgeting formulation and execution. In the budget formulation the Budget Directorate works closely with spending ministries in meetings of technical groups and senior officials.

There are a number of other distinctive aspects of the Chilean experience, particularly:

- *The indirect method of using performance information in budget decisions.*[3] The link between performance information and decisions on resource allocation is in general neither mechanical (formularized) nor direct. In particular, poor performance does not necessarily lead to funding cuts. Formula funding is, however, used on a selective basis for certain services.[4]
- *The existence of various performance evaluation and monitoring instruments.* The system currently in operation includes various performance management and evaluation instruments, which are being developed and used in a complementary and synergistic manner. The instruments are based on methodologies and formats of varying degrees of complexity and cost, with a view to meeting information needs efficiently and effectively.
- *Gradual development.* The various instruments in use were introduced gradually, commencing with the introduction of performance indicators in 1994. They were introduced as part of the budgetary process, without the need for new legislation.
- *Information on both past performance and expected future performance is used*—the former in the case of existing programs and activities, and the latter in the case of new investment projects and programs.
- *The identification of the objectives of expenditure.* The structure of the budget classification classifies most (although not yet all) expenditure by function and objective.[5]
- *The degree of flexibility given to spending agencies.* The rules governing agency operations, including the financial management regulations, provide a considerable degree of managerial freedom.[6]

Description of instruments, uses, and results[7]

Performance indicators

The introduction of performance indicators into the budgetary process in 1994 had the aim of making information on agency performance available in order to enhance the analysis used in budget formulation and in budget debates in the National Congress.

In the Chilean system, performance indicators are categorized according to the various performance dimensions (effectiveness, efficiency, economy, and quality) and also according to the steps in the results chain (processes, outputs, intermediate and high-level outcomes). Selected key performance indicators are submitted to the National Congress as part of the supplementary budget documentation which accompanies the budget bill. The performance targets are defined considering the budget funding provided for each of these key indicators.

The process whereby these key performance indicators and targets are identified, formulated, and monitored is detailed in Box 13.1.

The process of developing good indicators and targets took time. Particular progress was made during the period 2001–06, especially in the selection of better and more exacting targets. There was in this period an increase from 275 indicators covering 72 agencies in the 2001 budget to 1,552 indicators covering 136 agencies

Box 13.1 The use of performance indicators in the budget process

The use of performance indicators in the budget process involves three main steps, as follows:

1. Selection of the key indicators that will be used in the budget process.
   - The Budget Directorate makes an initial selection of indicators from different available sources of information, including indicators used in the previous year's budget process and indicators used in program evaluations or in the Comprehensive Management Report (*Balance de Gestión Integral*—BGI).
   - These key indicators are sent to the agencies in the forms that are used to prepare the budget bill. The agencies can modify, refine, and/or expand the initial selection and put forward their own proposals, including in respect to targets. The indicators and targets must be submitted together with agency budget proposals to the Budget Directorate during the budget formulation phase.
   - Once agencies have submitted the proposed indicators and targets to the Budget Directorate, the Directorate carries out a review and, together with the agency, selects the final indicators and targets that will be incorporated in the budget documentation accompanying the budget bill. This stage includes a technical analysis and a check to ensure the relevance and consistency between the established target and the allocated budget.
2. Submission of performance indicators and targets to the National Congress, as part of the budget bill documentation.
3. Monitoring. This final stage involves the evaluation of actual performance against the targets specified in the budget documentation. Information about performance against targets is sent, together with supporting information, to the Congress.

in the 2006 draft budget (that is, an average of 11.4 indicators per agency)[8] (see Table 13.1). Of the total number of indicators formulated, 19 percent are process-based indicators, 63.1 percent are output-based, and 17.7 percent are outcome-based (either intermediate or high-level outcomes).

Table 13.1 Growth of performance indicators, 2001–05

Year	*No. of indicators*	*No. of agencies*	*Average per institution*
2001	275	72	3.8
2002	537	109	4.9
2003	1,039	111	9.4
2004	1,684	132	12.8
2005	1,588	133	11.9
2006	1,552	136	11.4

Source: Budget Directorate.

Target-setting has focused primarily on the most important outputs (goods and services) produced by agencies. The process of identifying targets aims to takes all available previously existing information into consideration to set exacting targets for the budget allocations established for each budget cycle. It recognizes that, particularly in the case of targets for effectiveness and quality, there is no precise mathematical relationship between expected results and resources. In respect to efficiency targets, the target-setting process makes use of information on past resource use ratios together with best-case scenarios for the future.

Performance against targets has been assessed each year, and the percentage of targets achieved increased in the period 2001–04 from 69 percent to 86 percent (see Table 13.2).[9]

Table 13.2 Achievement of indicator targets, 2001–04

Achievement ranges	*2001*	*2002*	*2003*	*2004*
95–100	80%	69%	76%	86%
90–94	6%	9%	5%	3%
80–89	4%	8%	7%	4%
< 80	10%	15%	12%	7%
Total no. assessed	163	394	958	1,579
Assessed/formulated	79%	73%	92%	94%

Source: Budget Directorate.

Information on performance against targets is reported to Congress. It is also used in the budgetary process—specifically, in the assessment of budget execution, which is part of the work schedule of the Budget Directorate, where the information is analyzed together with other available financial and performance information.

The work on the use of performance indicators in the budget has been complemented and reinforced by the increased use of indicators in other aspects of performance management discussed below, including the agency Management Information System (SIG) (which is part of the broader Management Improvement Program), in the development of the logical frameworks used in program evaluations, and in the standard format for program presentation in budget formulation.

Program and agency evaluation

Since 1997 the government has sought by a variety of means to make greater use of evaluation in order to make information available to support management, analysis, and decision-making in the allocation of public resources. This commenced with the introduction of Government Program Evaluation (*Evaluación de Programas Gubernamentales*—EPG), which was followed by Impact Evaluation (*Evaluación de Impacto*—EI) and, subsequently, by the agency-focused instrument known as Comprehensive Expenditure Evaluation (*Evaluación Comprehensiva del Gasto*—ECG). These evaluation instruments were originally outlined in a number of memoranda signed with Congress, the aims of which were to improve the allocation and use of public resources. Since 2003, these memoranda have been supported by regulations.

The EPG approach was based on the logical framework methodology used by multilateral development agencies. That methodology identifies the program objectives and then determines the consistency of their design and results with those objectives. In this manner the main aspects of program performance can be assessed, on the basis of past and current information, at reasonable cost and within an appropriate timeframe.

In view of the fact that, generally speaking, the logical framework methodology used in the EPG approach makes use of program information that becomes available within a relatively short time, it can be difficult to assess high-level outcomes using this methodology. This difficulty led in 2001 to the introduction of the EI approach, which uses more comprehensive instruments and methodologies for data collection and analysis.

ECGs, which were introduced in 2002, are evaluations of agencies as a whole, and as such aim to assess the most important policies, programs, and procedures of each agency which is evaluated. They include the assessment of consistency of the agency's objectives, its organizational structure and internal allocation of functions, as well as the evaluation of its effectiveness, efficiency, and economy in the use of resources.

The design of each of these three evaluation instruments reflects common principles and requirements—namely independence, reliability, public disclosure, relevance, efficiency, and timeliness.[10] The process by which they are implemented is outlined in Box 13.2.

During its nine years of existence, the evaluation program has encompassed a total of 188 evaluations of public programs and 19 evaluations of agencies (see Table 13.3).

Table 13.3 Number of evaluations, 1997–2005

	1997–99	*2000*	*2001*	*2002*	*2003*	*2004*	*2005*	*Total*
Government Program Evaluations (EPG)	80	20	18	14	13	13	14	172
Impact Evaluations (EI)			2	4	4	4	2[a]	16
Comprehensive Expenditure Evaluations (ECG)								
– No. of evaluations				1	2	2	1[a]	6
– No. of agencies				8	2	4	5	19

[a] Evaluations in progress.

To date, expenditure subject to *program* evaluation covers 61 percent of the total budget that can feasibly be assessed with the methodologies used, and represents annual expenditure of some $3.75 billion. Agency evaluations based on the ECG methodology have so far (that is, during the period 2002–05) covered agencies with expenditure of $685 million, equivalent to 4 percent of the total budget.

Regarding the quality and pertinence of the evaluations, it should be noted that the items covered by the evaluations and the methodologies used in the various approaches are considered appropriate by the various parties involved (principally agencies and evaluators).[11] These aspects have also been assessed by outside experts.[12]

Box 13.2 Evaluation of programs and agencies

The evaluation process comprises eight stages, as follows:

1. *Selection of programs or agencies.* The evaluation process begins with the selection of the programs to be evaluated. The selection is made in consultation with the National Congress, based on a proposal submitted by the Ministry of Finance.[a]
2. *Selection of consultants.* Once the programs and agencies have been selected, consultants are selected via public tender to undertake the evaluation.
3. *Preparation of background information.* In tandem with the selection of the evaluators, the agencies concerned are informed that the evaluation process is about to begin, and are asked to prepare the background information required to conduct the evaluation and to identify the key program issues. The same request is made to the person in the Budget Directorate responsible for the specific sector.
4. *Training and preparation of logical frameworks.* The basic methodological aspects used in the evaluations are explained to the staff of the agency. In the case of an EPG, prior to the beginning of an evaluation, evaluators and professionals of units responsible for the programs receive training in the methodology of logical frameworks. Initial preparation of these frameworks for each relevant program is undertaken by the program professionals.
5. *Conduction of the evaluation.* This involves the preparation of both preliminary and final evaluation reports. Both the agency being evaluated and the Budget Directorate comment on these reports. The final evaluation report must include recommendations to improve the program or agency on the basis of the evaluation findings. The result of each evaluation is revised and analyzed by the Budget Directorate and appropriate decisions are taken.
6. *Submission to Congress.* The final evaluation report is submitted to the National Congress, together with an executive summary prepared by the Budget Directorate and comments by the agency concerned.
7. *Formalization of commitments.* Based on the recommendations made by the evaluators, specific formal commitments are defined between the agency and the Budget Directorate with the aim of improving the performance of the program or agency.
8. *Monitoring.* The follow-up on the commitments made on the basis of the recommendations is carried out by the Budget Directorate on December 31 and June 30 of each year.

[a] The selection of programs to be assessed each year is based on the following:

1. performance background on the programs available in the Budget Directorate of the Ministry of Finance, based on its budgetary and management control functions
2. whether or not a program has already been assessed in the framework of the evaluation program of the Budget Directorate of the Ministry of Finance, or as part of other evaluation mechanisms, and the year in which that took place
3. program execution schedule and priority
4. suggestions from the General Secretariat of the Presidency (Ministerio Secretaría General de la Presidencia—SESPRES) and the Ministry of Planning (Ministerio de Planificación—MIDEPLAN), both of which are members of the program's Interministerial Committee
5. suggestions made at meetings of the Special Joint Committee on the Budget and the budget subcommittees during the review of the draft budget law in Congress.

The Budget Directorate of the Ministry of Finance considers these factors and drafts a proposal for programs to be assessed. This proposal is then examined with the members of the Special Joint Committee on the Budget of the National Congress, and a memorandum of understanding (MOU) is drafted. The MOU accompanies the approved draft budget law and contains a final list of programs.

The improvement of the technical quality of evaluations in recent years has resulted in more relevant recommendations, which better reflect the issues identified and the changes required to address those issues. The improved quality of the evaluations has made them more useful in the resource allocation process as well as in the process of agency management improvement. This is illustrated by the fact that from 2000 to 2005, out of a total of 118 programs assessed,[13] 24 percent were substantially redesigned, 38 percent underwent major changes in the design of internal management components and/or processes, and 24 percent were the subject of minor adjustments to their information systems, monitoring systems, or other administrative processes. In 5 percent of the programs, some reassignment of program responsibilities between agencies was recommended; 9 percent of the programs were terminated because the results and/or objectives no longer fully met the new needs and/or the better solution was that some components or activities of the program were absorbed by other programs (see Table 13.4).

Table 13.4 Actions arising from Government Program Evaluations and Impact Evaluations undertaken in 2000–05

Categories of effects	*Percentage of programs*
1. Minor adjustments Includes programs that primarily require minor adjustments, such as optimization of their information, monitoring, and oversight systems, clarification of some design aspects, and/or adjustments to internal administrative or management processes.	24
2. Important changes to the design of internal management components and/or processes Includes programs that require major changes in the design of some of their components and/or activities or in their internal management procedures. The most important of these are: revision of methodological instruments; design and implementation of information systems to enhance oversight and monitoring of results; changes to internal and/or external agency coordination in program delivery; and improvement of administrative processes relating to transfers of financial resources.	38
3. Substantial program redesign Includes programs that require extensive and in-depth reformulations or restructuring of the program design internal management processes, or organizational structure, or where substantial aspects of the design must be further developed for the program to meet its objectives.	24
4. Reassignment of agency responsibility for the program Includes programs that, based on their objectives, require a change of reporting authority.	5
5. Program termination Includes programs that, based on their results, cannot justify their budget appropriations; or are reaching the end of their commitment period and for which the extension of further funding is not warranted; or that require such substantial changes that it would be tantamount to the wholesale replacement of the program or its absorption into the institutional function.	9
Total programs (118)	100

In the case of the ECG, from 2002 to 2004, out of a total of 14 agencies, 72 percent made major changes to their design or internal management, while 21 percent underwent minor adjustments, mainly in strategic definitions and information and monitoring systems (see Table 13.5).

Table 13.5 Actions arising from Comprehensive Expenditure Evaluations undertaken in 2002–04

Categories of effects	*Percentage of programs*
1. Minor adjustments Includes agencies that are identified as requiring minor adjustments, such as the fine-tuning of their strategic definitions, information, monitoring, and oversight systems, or the results measurement systems.	21
2. Important changes to design or internal management Includes agencies that require changes, whether to the design of aspects of their organizational structure, to their strategic goals, and/or to their internal management.	72
3. Substantial redesign of agency management or design Includes agencies that require extensive and in-depth reformulation or restructuring, whether in the design of a large part of their organizational structure, their strategic definitions, or their internal management.	7
Total agencies (14)	100

Since 2000, the effects and implications of each program and agency evaluation have been reviewed jointly by the professional staff of the programs concerned and those of the Budget Directorate of the Ministry of Finance. This review process results in the agency commitment to incorporate changes in the program, with specific indications of how the problems or inadequacies identified in the evaluation are to be addressed and in what timeframe.

These agency commitments have been the subject of a rigorous and regular monitoring process to determine the extent to which the necessary changes are made in the areas assessed. Since 2001, the information from this monitoring progress has been used, in conjunction with other performance information, in the budget process. This monitoring indicates that, in the period up to June 2005, in respect to the commitments made by agencies following 98 program evaluations and 12 agency evaluations, 80 percent had been fully met, and 16 percent partially met during the established timeframe. Only 4 percent of commitments had not been met at all. Monitoring results also indicate that there has, over the years, been an increase in the rate of fulfillment of commitments.

The use of program evaluations has thus resulted in managerial changes incorporated to improve performance. But it has also had a substantial impact on the allocation of resources in recent years, contributing to the goal of efficient resource allocation. The resource allocation effect is shown in Table 13.6, which indicates that programs in which substantial design changes were made as a result of evaluation tended also to experience more substantial budget funding reductions than did those that were the subject of minor adjustments or smaller design changes.

Table 13.6 Budgetary effects of program evaluations, 2002–05 (millions of 2006 pesos)

	Categories of effects					
	1. Minor adjustments, changes to the design of some internal management components and/or processes, and/or institutional relocation		*2. Substantial program redesign*		*3. Termination*[a]	
Evaluation process	*Base budget*[b]	*Rate of change of budget*[c]	*Base budget*	*Rate of change of budget*	*Base budget*	*Rate of change of budget*
2002	92,770	2.2%	34,731	–1.8%	4,717	–46.5%
2003	75,026	–0.8%	15,938	–30.4%	5,890	–65.3%
2004	49,751	16.7%	167,798	10.1%	1,672	–19.0%
2005	93,514	15.7%	30,190	–11.9%	1,886	–66.3%

[a] Programs in the "termination" category receive funding to cover commitments already made, which explains why the budget is not immediately reduced to zero.

[b] For EPGs, the figure is based on expenditure of the program in the year in which the evaluation was conducted. In the case of EIs, it is expenditure in the year immediately preceding the year in which the evaluation results were taken into consideration in the formulation of the budget.

[c] Corresponds to the percentage change in the budgets of the programs assessed in the year ($t + 1$) (that is, the year in which the evaluation results were taken into consideration in the budget) relative to their budgets in the base year (t).

Submission of programs for financing, standard format, and resources for innovation

Beginning with the 2001 budget formulation process, a standard format for submitting new expenditure proposals to the Budget Directorate was introduced,[14] with the aim of making higher-quality information available in a format more appropriate for review and analysis during budget formulation. From 2001 to 2003, this format was used as a methodology for prioritizing "discretionary" expenditure, allowing such expenditure to be allocated on the basis of the best new initiatives and extensions of the best existing programs. This was done on the basis of better technical explanations, better identification of anticipated results, and better past performance information in the case of existing programs.

This new format was subsequently extended to serve as the basis for consideration in the budget process of the level of funding which would be allocated to programs that had been evaluated; to grants from one ministry to public agencies for specific purposes; and also programs which serve as the basis of budget appropriations.[15] The use of the submission format covers only a portion of the budget, thus allowing for reasonable management of the procedure and use of the information by the Budget Directorate and by the agencies themselves.

Management Improvement Programs

Management Improvement Programs (*Programas de Mejoramiento de Gestión*—PMGs) are another important tool in the Chilean system of performance-based budgeting and management. PMGs provide for staff monetary incentives linked to the achievement of management objectives.[16]

Since 2001, PMGs have been structured around a number of managerial systems of public sector agencies—namely human resources, user services, management planning and control, internal audit, decentralization, accounting/financial management, and gender issues. Under what is known as the Framework Program, a number of stages of development are defined in respect to each of these managerial system. Each stage is defined specifying its content and requirements, so that with completion of the final stage, the system is implemented in accordance with pre-established characteristics and requisites. In 2005, the PMG system was further refined with the development of the so-called Advanced Framework Program, which applies the international quality standard ISO 9001:2000 to the preparation and certification stages for each of the managerial systems of PMGs.

The 2006 budget process represented the sixth consecutive year in which the PMG has been applied. During these six years, the system has evolved to a stage which has made it possible to use it as the basis for monetary incentives to staff.

PMGs cover a total of 179 agencies[17] and more than 62,000 staff members. The 2004 evaluation of PMGs showed that 74.9 percent of the agencies achieved between 90 percent and 100 percent of their PMG managerial improvement objectives and that, as a result, more than 56,000 staff members received bonuses equal on average to 5 percent of their pay (see Table 13.7). Of the total agencies, 48 percent fulfilled 100 percent of their commitments.

Table 13.7 Degree of compliance, PMGs, 2001–04

Percentage of compliance	*Agencies 2001* No.	*Agencies 2001* Participation rate	*Agencies 2002* No.	*Agencies 2002* Participation rate	*Agencies 2003* No.	*Agencies 2003* Participation rate	*Agencies 2004* No.	*Agencies 2004* Participation rate
90–100	116	66.3%	139	79.4%	132	75.0%	134	74.9%
75–89	29	16.6%	28	16.0%	36	20.5%	35	19.6%
< 75	30	17.1%	8	4.6%	8	4.5%	10	5.5%
	175	100%	175	100%	176	100%	179	100%

Source: Budget Directorate.

PMGs have made the following contributions to performance-based management and budgeting: (1) as of 2002, information on the achievement of management objectives has been used in the budgetary process, alongside other performance information; (2) developments in the financial/accounting system of the Framework Program have improved the quality of financial information, leading to better quality of financial management; (3) developments in the Management Planning and Control System have generated better indicators for presentation with the budget bill, as well as for use in evaluations.

Other important changes intended to link incentives to staff with agency performance have been coordinated with the PMG. This is the case of the performance pay mechanism established by Law 19,882,[18] which requires that indicators and targets related to work unit performance must be linked to the mission, strategic objectives, and relevant outputs of their agencies (as specified in the Management Planning and Control component of the PMG). This system will also serve as a basis for performance agreements, which the same law requires, between the ministries and the heads of the agencies as part of the Public Senior Management System. In addition, the PMG results were used as selection criteria for the award of the Annual Prize for Agency Excellence. Lastly, arrangements were introduced in 2004 to accord additional flexibility in budget execution[19] to agencies that have complied with a set of conditions relating to the development of their PMG and financial discipline. Fifteen agencies benefited from such additional budget flexibility in 2005.

Comprehensive Management Report

Since the end of the 1990s, the Budget Law has required that central government agencies provide information concerning their objectives, management targets, and results. To give effect to this requirement, Decree-Law 47 (1999) of the Ministry of Finance imposed upon agencies the obligation to produce a Comprehensive Management Report (*Balance de Gestión Integral*—BGI), which would be provided to the National Congress as a public report.

BGIs have been prepared since 1998. In 2000, significant improvements were made to their required content and format, based on the experience of the first few years. In 2006, a total of 113 agencies submitted BGIs. As well as being provided to Congress and the public, the information they contain is also used in the budget process[20] and in the program and agency evaluations (where they serve as baseline information).

Factors explaining the development of the Chilean experience

A series of factors has fostered the development of performance-based management and budgeting in Chile, namely:

1. a politically stable framework since 1990, when the country resumed its path towards democracy
2. the development of each of the instruments as part of a broader process of financial modernization and government reform[21] underpinned, particularly in recent years, by strong political support
3. strong financial management, in terms of aggregate fiscal discipline, transparency, and productive efficiency,[22] that has facilitated the development of performance-based management instruments and budgeting, and created conditions for the use of performance information in budgeting and management
4. the credibility and prestige of the Budget Directorate of the Ministry of Finance, which, combined with the strong role that the Directorate plays in programmatic and financial decision-making, has facilitated the changes in practices that the new performance-oriented management and budgeting techniques have required
5. a basic consensus among the political players, as reflected in memoranda of understanding with Congress on transparency and efficiency in the management

of public resources, as well as in new financial management guidelines.[23] Particularly since 2003, these have been an important part of the regular work of the Congressional Budget Committee
6. gradualism in the development and introduction of new management and budgeting techniques, and complementarity between them. This has allowed the agencies to gradually move up the learning curve in respect to both the technical and operational aspects and the use of the information in decision-making processes
7. a strong institutional framework to support the introduction of these reforms, including interministerial committees, a unit overseeing the system in the Budget Directorate, and formal work networks in the agencies
8. the existence of the necessary levels of professional capacity within both government agencies and private consultancies in respect to public management reform and evaluation—capacity that has been progressively strengthened as consequence of the experience gathered during the reform process.

Conclusions and future challenges

Progress in the development and consolidation of each of the performance management and budgeting instruments described above has resulted in the increased use of performance information by the Ministry of Finance and other central government agencies.[24] This has fostered and promoted management improvements in public programs and agencies, as demonstrated, for example, by the formulation of agency performance-improvement commitments and their fulfillment, the sustained increase in the number and quality of performance indicators, the achievement of performance targets, and progress in the development of management systems through the PMG. Increasingly, this has meant that more and better information is available during the budget cycle, which is then used in analytical and decision-making processes in respect to both current and capital expenditure, thus also contributing to transparency in budget management. In summary, there has been considerable progress in the establishment of a viable performance-based budget model, the objectives and components of which are increasingly widely understood and supported by the various agents upon whom it depends and to whom it is linked.

Notwithstanding what has been achieved to date, there is a need to continue to improve the availability of performance information in the spending agencies and to further develop procedures and practices relating to the use of that information in agency decision-making processes. This would not only help to improve agency management, but would also permit further increases in budgetary flexibility.

Notes

1. In addition to these instruments, there is the ex-ante evaluation system for public investment under the aegis of the Ministry of Planning.
2. In Chile, unlike many other countries, the Ministry of Planning has no responsibility in fiscal administration.

3. For the classification of direct and indirect links, see OECD (2003).
4. Some examples are: the school subsidy system, per-beneficiary funding of primary care, flexible adult care programs, public defender services in criminal cases, and support for forestry development.
5. In particular, the expenditure for each public investment project is fully identified in budget appropriations. Furthermore, a large number of public programs are organized financially under budget programs that include their total expenditure.
6. Public services have authority in a number of areas, the most important being the hiring of personnel, purchases and acquisitions, cash management, prioritization of recommended technical investment projects, and reallocations under the budget subheading "Goods, Services, and Personnel."
7. For more information, see Budget Directorate (2005).
8. Over the past three years, the number of indicators per agencies has been in the range identified for the medium term, so that users can have access to a manageable set of relevant indicators.
9. Achievement is defined as a performance in the range of 95–100 percent of the target level.
10. To meet the independence criterion, it was decided that the evaluation would be conducted by entities outside the public sector, through panels of experts, universities, or consulting firms, selected on a competitive basis. The public nature of the information is established through the formal transmittal of the final reports on each evaluation to the National Congress and to the public agencies responsible for making decisions affecting the respective program, such reports being available to anyone who requests them. In addition, summary reports on the evaluations are included in the information attached to the draft budget bill. The relevance of the evaluations is addressed in the definition of the scope of the evaluation included in the methodological design, and in the requirement for recommendations to improve performance on the basis of such evaluations. The efficiency criterion is related to the need for evaluations to be made at a manageable cost; along with the preceding criteria, it aims to ensure that evaluation opinions that meet the principal needs for performance information on programs and agencies are obtained within reasonable timeframes and at reasonable cost. Lastly, the timeliness criterion is related to the need for the evaluation results to be available for the budget preparation process.
11. Budget Directorate, Surveys of Evaluation Procedures: EPG, EI, and ECG, 2000–05.
12. See World Bank (2005).
13. The number of programs assessed does not correspond to the number of evaluations shown in Table 13.3, as an evaluation may include more than one program.
14. The key aspects of the format are: (1) strategic objectives and outputs of the agency to which the initiative or program is linked; (2) justification; (3) targeting and beneficiary population; (4) background information on budget, expenditure, and budget proposals; (5) goal and purpose of the initiative or program; (6) description of components; and (7) indicators and means of verification.
15. Budgetary classification that incorporate different appropriations covering the total cost of the program.
16. Law 19,553 of February 1998 and Decree-Law 475 of May 1998, amended by Laws 19,618 and 19,882. The monetary incentive provides that achievement of the management objectives established in an annual PMG shall entitle the staff of the respective agency to a 5 percent pay increase during the following year, provided that the agency has recorded an achievement rate for the annual objectives it has pledged to meet that is equal to or greater than 90 percent. The staff shall be entitled to a 2.5 percent increase if the achievement rate is equal to or greater than 75 percent and less than 90 percent.
17. Since 2001, agencies governed by different pre-existing laws regarding the establishment of management objectives linked to staff incentives have voluntarily adhered to this system. The 2006 formulation includes eight agencies in that category.

18. The law was published in June 2003.
19. This refers to the following procedures: (a) carryover: inclusion of an opening cash balance that exceeds the approved budget estimate as a result of higher revenue or permanent savings; (b) reallocating resources between investment projects: flexibility in reallocating resources under items 61–74 of subheading 31 (Real Investment) up to the amount authorized in the Budget Law, so long as the favorable economic and technical recommendation (RS) of the Ministry of Planning and Cooperation (MIDEPLAN) is maintained.
20. Specifically, in the Internal Evaluation of Budget Execution (*Evaluación Interna de la Ejecución Presupuestaria*), which is conducted in the Budget Directorate as one of the stages in the budget cycle.
21. The most important reforms include: definition and observance of a fiscal policy rule; growing dissemination of information and adaptation of fiscal statistics to international standards; improvements in the budget management legal framework; development of a financial management and information system; reforms in human resource management; establishment of a Public Senior Management system; and growing emergence of e-government. See *Informes de Finanzas Públicas* (Public Finance Report) 2000–05; *Evaluación de la Gestión Financiera* (Financial Management Evaluation) 2003–05; *Estudios de Finanzas Públicas: Balance Estructural del Gobierno Central* (Public Finance Studies: Structural Balance of the Central Government) 2001; and *Sostenibilidad y Regla Fiscal* (Sustainability and Fiscal Rules) 2003, at <www.dipres.cl>.
22. See World Bank and Inter-American Development Bank (2004) and OECD (2004).
23. Regulation of the reserved spending lines (*gastos reservados*); disclosure of the budgetary data of the national defense agencies; inclusion of annual budgetary norms in permanent legislation (for example, the obligation for the Ministry of Finance to conduct public program evaluations); and strengthening of the powers of the Congress, among other legal matters.
24. Surveys sent to institutional agents in 2004, particularly to those in charge of assessed programs and to the directors of the financial departments of public agencies, show that over 50 percent of them report making use of the information in the analyses of institutional resource allocation ("Efectos y Usos de las Evaluaciones de Programas en los Servicios Públicos" (Effects and Uses of Program Evaluations in Public Institutions), Budget Directorate, July 2004). The assessment conducted by the World Bank in 2004 shows similar experiences.

References

Budget Directorate, 2005, *Sistema de Control de Gestión y Presupuestos por Resultados. La Experienca Chilena* (Management and Control System and Performance-based Budgeting. The Chilean Experience) (Chile: Budget Directorate, Ministry of Finance).

OECD, 2003, *Public Sector Modernization: Governing for Performance* (Paris: OECD), November.

——, 2004, *Budgeting in Chile* (Paris: OECD).

World Bank, 2005, *Chile—Evaluation of the Program Evaluation System* (Washington: World Bank), April.

World Bank and Inter-American Development Bank, 2004, *Chile—Country Financial Accountability Assessment* (Washington: World Bank).

14
Results and Services Plans and Budget Reform in New South Wales

John Pierce and Michael Di Francesco

Getting the incentive structures "right" in public sector institutions is, to borrow a metaphor, a race with an ever-receding finish line. Performance budgeting, which can be defined as funding processes that use performance information to strengthen the link between resources and achievement, is one set of techniques to design these incentives, although the strategies vary significantly.

There is a large and growing menu of performance budgeting practices, and this volume aims to assess the options by asking three key questions: How effective are different types of performance budgeting as incentive structures? What implementation strategies were employed to effect behavioral change? If successful, to what extent are the critical success factors transferable?

This case study will describe the development and implementation of a distinctive form of performance budgeting adopted in the Australian State of New South Wales—a "funding plan" model that uses performance narrative as the basis for understanding the relationship between funding and results, and for discussing the continuing relevance of "baseline" funding. The chapter covers policy and organizational developments up to September 2005.

Using the performance budgeting taxonomy developed for this volume, the New South Wales model—known as the Results and Services Plan Budget process—corresponds with those categories of performance budgeting that aim for "looser" links between funding and results, one example of which is "program budgeting." Its core objectives are to better align ministerial and bureaucratic priorities, and to deliver performance information about cost, service accomplishment, and results achievement that can *inform* allocation decisions.

The case study will profile some of the defining features of the New South Wales model and its implementation, including its focus on:

- an annual budget process framed around a service funding plan—the Results and Services Plan—so that strategic discussion about incremental funding and policy issues occurs in the context of a "whole plan"
- the use of "performance stories"—the results logic—to contextualize high-level discussion about the relative priority of funding issues and to clarify financial and non-financial performance expectations
- a commitment to building agency capacity for both strategic planning and resource management through the results and services planning approach
- the use of regular consultative review processes to test process modifications and work towards closer meshing between ministerial and bureaucratic priority setting and resource allocation decision-making.

Against the grain? Performance budgeting in New South Wales

Why is New South Wales of interest? During the late 1980s and early 1990s the Australian State of New South Wales was seen by many observers as a pioneer in public sector financial management reform. It was one of the first jurisdictions in the world to introduce full accrual accounting in the sub-national public sector, including consolidated financial statements, and in the commercial sector New South Wales implemented a systematic reform program that corporatized government businesses (mainly energy and transport utilities) to replicate commercial sector corporate governance and incentive structures (see Steering Committee on Government Trading Enterprises, 1988, for an overview of how the policy framework developed).

Since the mid to late 1990s, however, budget sector reform orthodoxy in Australia has revolved around accrual output budgeting, defined broadly as the purchase and monitoring of contractually specified outputs from service delivery agencies on a full accrual cost basis (see, for example, Robinson, 1999, 2002; Carlin and Guthrie, 2001). While in New South Wales the preparation of departmental budget estimates has been on a "program" basis since 1986, and rolling three-year expenditure limits (forward estimates) in place since 1989, these developments represented the farthest distance traveled on the performance budgeting road.[1] As a consequence, according to some commentators, New South Wales has earned a reputation among the Australian states for being "somewhat recalcitrant" (see Carlin and Guthrie, 2003, p. 150). The criticism is undeserved, for three important reasons.

First, it disregards historical legacy. Sub-national (or State) government administration in Australia is fundamentally about the efficient delivery of essential services, and as such the priorities for organizational reform are often driven by the practicalities of ensuring that service provision meets the demands of local constituencies. Prominent students of Australian State political systems have observed that, by comparison with its State siblings, New South Wales's political and bureaucratic culture has little inclination for radical reform and has more often than not been marked by a "climate of skepticism" about managerial change (see, for example, Painter, 1987; Halligan and Power, 1992; Alaba, 1994).

Second, it discounts intention. New South Wales Treasury has employed a deliberate strategy of "watching and learning," as much to avoid costly errors as to learn lessons about which elements of systematic reform programs could be applied in this jurisdiction. New South Wales has questioned the practicability of implementing accrual output budgeting, chiefly on the basis that output purchase models adopted in other jurisdictions have yet to demonstrate clearly that they improve the way government works in practice.[2]

Third, it overlooks context. Between 1995 and 2005 the Council on the Cost and Quality of Government (CoCQoG) operated as a key advisory body to the New South Wales Government on the review and reporting of service delivery performance in the public sector. A key output of the Council were whole-of-government Service Efforts and Accomplishments (SEAs) reviews that summarized the activities and performance of budget dependent agencies on a policy sector basis (for example, the law, order, and public safety sector) (see CoCQoG, 2003, 2004). While the reviews were largely a consolidation of historical data—each year's review reported sectoral performance on a rolling basis for the previous five years—the SEAs initiative did give the development of performance indicator standards a higher profile across the public sector.

Against this background then, the service funding model of performance budgeting that has emerged in New South Wales reflects a distinctly "pragmatic" response to national and international budget reform trends, and is a product—sometimes based on careful "trial and error"—of a strategy of lesson-drawing.

Expenditure budget process in New South Wales: key institutions

To aid understanding of the performance budgeting reform process, this section will introduce the State of New South Wales and provide an overview of the key institutions of government and their role in the current expenditure budget process.

Situated on the eastern seaboard of the Australian continent, New South Wales is the oldest, largest, and wealthiest of the six States (and two Territories) that comprise the Commonwealth of Australia.[3] Its population of 6.7 million is highly urbanized and dominated by the mid-coastal conurbation centered on Sydney, Australia's largest city, and bounded by the old industrial cities of Newcastle in the north and Wollongong in the south.

The New South Wales economy accounts for over one-third of national output and, while highly diversified, like other advanced economies is increasingly services-based. Sydney is a center for financial, insurance, and information and communications technology services in the Asia Pacific region, while the State economy retains significant strengths in agricultural production, mining and minerals processing, and manufacturing.

New South Wales has a Westminster form of responsible parliamentary government where traditionally the executive government has significant influence over taxation measures and the details of expenditure (see, for example, Parker, 1978; Smith, 2003). It does, however, also operate within the system of intergovernmental financial arrangements that mark Australian federalism. While sub-national government in Australia delivers many "everyday" functions like hospital, school, urban transport, policing, infrastructure, and recreational services, revenue-raising capacity lies principally with the federal government.[4] The federal government's use of specific purpose (or "tied") funding mechanisms mean that State discretion over the nature of some key services is increasingly constrained, while the distribution of general purpose (or "untied") grants is governed by a complex system that seeks to equalize States' capacity to provide services, resulting in significant per capita transfers from larger to smaller States.[5]

As in other Westminster systems the annual expenditure budget process is an executive government responsibility. Budget preparation involves four key institutions: cabinet, the central agencies (including New South Wales Treasury—hereafter "the Treasury"—and the Cabinet Office), portfolio ministers, and service delivery agencies. The following discussion will profile the role of Cabinet and the central agencies.

Cabinet, which in New South Wales comprises the ministry,[6] is the peak decision-making forum for executive government. Two of its standing committees have responsibility for resource allocation.

- The *Standing Committee on the Budget* or *Budget Committee* (made up of the Premier and Treasurer, Deputy Premier and Minister for Transport, the Minister for Finance, and the Assistant Treasurer) sets the budget strategy (including major budget targets); approves updated forward estimates; reviews recommendations from the Treasury on portfolio funding proposals and options for portfolio savings; and determines final budget allocations and savings requirements for ministers and portfolio agencies.
- The *Standing Committee on Infrastructure and Planning* (which is also chaired by the Premier) sets strategic direction for urban and regional infrastructure development—for example, the Metropolitan Strategy for managing urban development in and around Sydney. It also reviews infrastructure proposals, and makes recommendations to Budget Committee for infrastructure financing decisions.

The executive government's key public service advisor in the budget process is the Treasury.[7] The Treasury supports the Budget Committee by maintaining the three-year forward estimates system, advising on budget aggregates (or "the budget result"), advising on the merits of individual portfolio funding proposals, and advising on infrastructure proposals and individual agency capital programs. The Cabinet Office, which is the Premier's principal source of advice on whole-of-government priorities, works with the Treasury to review the consistency of current and proposed funding with government priorities.

In the early 1990s the New South Wales Budget system was described as "multi-year target budgeting with discretionary (global) estimates in a program framework" (Nicholls, 1991, pp. 182, 190) and, by and large, this is still the case. In other words, estimates are prepared for the budget and three forward years on a "no policy change" basis; there are elements of "target budgeting" in that the forward estimates act as a baseline (or target) for agency expenditure; there are elements of conventional "bid and review" budgeting in which ministers and agencies are invited to submit program-based funding proposals;[8] and ministers, to whom allocations are made, have limited discretion to transfer recurrent funds between programs within their portfolio.

Budget authorization requires approval by parliament. In May each year the executive government presents its budget to parliament, setting out the estimates of expenditure for the financial year commencing in July.[9] In New South Wales while estimates of agency expenses are prepared and reported on an accrual basis, parliament appropriates from the Consolidated Fund the *cash* funding required to fund total expenses in the year.[10] This is referred to as a "net appropriation" since service delivery agencies are able to retain revenue from their own sources (such as user charges) such that the cash appropriation approximates the "net cost of services"; that is, the difference between total expenses, retained revenue and the gain/loss on disposal of non-current assets.[11]

The final institutional setting informing the expenditure budget process is legislative "fiscal rules." Between 1995 and 2005, governments in New South Wales were required to consider the fiscal policy framework set out in the General Government Debt Elimination Act 1995.[12] The principal objective of the legislation was to "maintain fiscal results that are fiscally sustainable in the medium and long term."[13] The Act set out specific fiscal strategy "targets"—for example, in the medium term, "to reduce general government net debt to sustainable levels by 30 June 2005"—as well as fiscal principles to guide budget management—for example, that "the budget should be framed to achieve a fiscal result for the general government sector consistent with the fiscal targets." The budget targets set by Budget Committee in the early stages of each year's expenditure budget process were determined with reference to these targets and principles. Following the achievement of the Act's short- and medium-term targets in 2005, the key fiscal targets and principles have been updated to focus on controlling the level of general government liabilities and constraining long run average growth in expenditure.[14]

Having profiled the key institutions in the expenditure budget process, the three sections that follow will describe the development and implementation of the service funding model of performance budgeting that has emerged in New South Wales.

Starting point: service and resource allocation agreements (stage 1 reform)

The starting point for recent budget reform in New South Wales was the issue of the Financial Management Framework in December 2000 (NSW Treasury, 2000a). A distinctly pragmatic approach to improving financial management and budgeting, the Framework is a "consolidation" of the periodic modifications made over the previous 15 years (and discussed briefly in this chapter). It is aimed squarely at delivering "value for money" by building incentives for government agencies to assist "resource allocation" and improve "resource management" (which equate broadly to allocative and productive efficiency, the key concepts used in this volume).[15] While these objectives are consistent with reform agendas in comparable jurisdictions, the means of achieving them have been different.

The Framework noted the widespread adoption in Australia of "output budgeting" (the system of "accrual output budgeting" referred to earlier) and expressed concerns about its "complexity" and "practicability of implementation" (NSW Treasury, 2000a, p. 13). Output budgeting hinges on the capacity of central decision-makers in executive government to specify desired outputs in detail (and hence surmount its "relative lack of knowledge about program and service delivery options") as well as a preparedness to involve itself in the detail of service delivery. Often, despite the best intentions, the reality of government administration does not allow for this. In addition, experience in comparable jurisdictions suggested that contractual purchase and monitoring of "output" potentially can create perverse incentives, including incentives to focus on what is *done* rather than what is *achieved*.

As a consequence, New South Wales set a different course towards performance budgeting based on *funding a service delivery plan*. Under this approach, the executive government sets high-level desired outcomes and associated performance targets, with program and service delivery design and implementation devolved to agencies. Each service delivery agency is then accountable to the executive government for the efficient implementation of the plan as well as for demonstrating progress towards achieving the desired outcomes.

The platform for this performance budgeting approach was the Service and Resource Allocation Agreement (SRAA). The SRAA was a service delivery agreement negotiated with the Treasury where agencies "describe the way in which the funding allocated to them is used, accompanied by efficiency and effectiveness data" (NSW Treasury, 2000a, p. 9). It aimed to integrate characteristics of a funding agreement (linking an agency's budget funding to its service delivery), a performance agreement (linking the service delivery to financial and non-financial performance targets), and a strategic plan (linking agency planning to emerging community need and changing executive government priorities).

SRAA implementation applied an "output and outcomes" methodology. The agreements were framed around detailed "outcome statements" prepared for each of the desired outcomes that an agency sought to achieve. However, the pilot format for the SRAA, introduced in 1999–2000, focused implementation on full coverage of agency outputs, and encouraged agencies to develop performance targets for output delivery as a preliminary basis for monitoring financial performance against quarterly budgets.[16] While the SRAA was intended to link funding to measurable outcomes, the pilot experience quickly found that the agreements were framed around outputs and output-related performance information (and specifically a preponderance of quantity measures, for example, the number of tasks performed). This indicated that agency (and Treasury) understanding of the relationship between outputs and outcomes was at a rudimentary level.

A key development, introduced for the 2001–02 budget cycle, was to supplement the output and financial compliance focus with broader organizational performance measures and indicators. The "balanced scorecard" method for mapping and measuring non-financial (customer, business, and capability) perspectives on organizational performance was the preferred framework (NSW Treasury, 2000b, pp. 9–13; for more information about the "balanced scorecard" see Kaplan and Norton, 1992).

The 2001–02 budget process also clarified the key objectives of the SRAA process as supporting strategic discussion between the Treasurer and portfolio ministers (and between the Treasury and agencies) about issues that could be addressed in the budget process, and providing a common framework for assessing agency performance. To meet these objectives, early in the budget cycle agencies were asked to submit draft SRAA outcome statements prepared on a "no policy change" basis along with agency funding proposals. In other words, it was intended that the draft SRAA and SRAA budget proposals comprise an agency's budget proposal documentation.[17] At the end of budget preparation, the final SRAA would be updated to reflect decisions of Budget Committee and signed off by both the Treasurer and the portfolio minister as an agreement.

For the pilot agencies, the SRAA budget process was used during the 2001–02, 2002–03, and 2003–04 budget cycles. Each year's experience was subject to a comprehensive review, and a number of implementation issues appeared regularly.[18] While there was a general recognition that the SRAA sharpened the focus on "what the Government wants," and signaled a consistent approach to understanding agency issues, the agreement process suffered from a number of flaws. The SRAA's aspirations to "comprehensiveness" meant that each agency's agreement was lengthy and unwieldy—agencies were encouraged to list *all* relevant indicators rather than concentrating on those actually *used* by agencies to manage program delivery. This was compounded by an agency perception that the Treasury did not use the SRAA for either agency discussions or budget monitoring, and that the SRAA—as a planning exercise associated strongly with the Treasury—had marginal relevance for ministers. Evidence for this came from its absence in bilateral discussions between the Treasurer and portfolio ministers about funding proposals.

This perception was mirrored in internal Treasury feedback. To Treasury analysts (that is, budget officers) the SRAA seemed to be an "add-on" to the budget process and its credibility was undermined when stakeholders did not see it referred to directly by ministers or executives. As a consequence there was a tendency for Treasury analysts to see negotiation of the agreement with their agencies as a task that added negligible value to their relationship management role. In short, the SRAA was seen as a "separate exercise" and hence disconnected from the budget process.

The links between resource allocation and resource management also remained at a delicate stage for agencies. The SRAA was (generally) prepared at some distance from more established internal agency planning processes. At the same time, suspicions were raised about the Treasury's intentions for the SRAA budget process. For example, some agencies expressed concerns about the prospect of Treasury analysts linking short-term fluctuations in performance targets with specific discussion about current and future funding levels. These agencies wanted the Treasury to give more emphasis in the SRAA process to understanding what influences the relationship between an agency's activities and the government's long-term outcomes, and how this should be gauged.

Against this background the 2003–04 budget process proved to be a transition stage in the development of a service funding model. In a pre-election period[19] the government established the ad hoc Major Issues and Strategies Committee (MISC) of Cabinet to steer priority-setting. Operation of the MISC confirmed that the SRAA had a low profile in high-level officer consideration of funding and service delivery priorities. In effect, the 2003–04 budget process crystalized Treasury thinking about how to integrate the agreements with cabinet processes. In particular, the weight of both ministerial and agency feedback hastened the adoption of a more intuitive approach to understanding and measuring agency performance—this took the form of "performance stories" that could explain the contribution that agency activities made to desired outcomes and help guide the selection of performance indicators.

Linking planning and budgeting: results and services plans (stage 2 reform)

After the March 2003 State election the government announced a renewed commitment to improving public service delivery within existing allocations and reprioritizing current programs and activities to fund new initiatives.[20] There was a growing realization in government that a combination of temporary stresses and structural dynamics were emerging as a risk to achievement of the fiscal strategy. The former included an expected decline in the rate of growth in New South Wales's most important own source revenue stream—transfer duties on property sales—while the latter principally comprised a smaller proportion for New South Wales of federal (Goods and Services Tax) revenue (discussed briefly in this chapter). Better management of these risks required both aggregate expenditure restraint and reinforcement of budgeting tools for identifying and implementing priorities.

The configuration of cabinet structures—and the signals these send throughout the public sector—is one of the first tools available to any executive government. Service delivery improvement and expenditure restraint were embedded through the creation by cabinet of a new standing committee, the Service Provision and Financial Management (SP&FM) Committee. It is important to note that this committee's *resource monitoring* function was intended to complement the Budget Committee's *resource allocation* role. The SP&FM Committee was to maintain the spotlight on high-profile service delivery portfolios and monitor both budget compliance and, particularly for funded initiatives commencing in the budget year, service delivery performance against agreed indicators and targets.

The Treasury also recognized that the service delivery focus required an overhaul of the budget process to integrate it with new cabinet structures—hence the 2004–05 budget process was a significant departure from the traditional budget cycle. The pre-election MISC experience confirmed that the conventional "bid and review" process could be made both more efficient and more strategic (acknowledging the potential for improved *collective* priority-setting mechanisms early in the process).[21] In effect, the existing process asked, "What additional budget allocation do you want?" rather than "How well are you using your existing budget allocation?" and "How can you improve service delivery?"

The response was a two-stage budget process. The first "scene-setting" stage was framed by dedicated meetings of the Budget Committee (and an advisory group of high-level officers) to discuss emerging policy issues and to determine broad priority-spending areas.[22] These meetings were informed by a series of chief executive-level meetings designed to discuss funding and service delivery issues that might need to be addressed in the budget process.

While all ministers and agencies were invited to submit maintenance of effort funding proposals, the outcomes of the scene-setting meetings formed the basis for a second "invitation" stage where ministers and agencies were selected to submit enhancement of effort funding proposals. The process would be anchored by a common information base for assessing services and their cost, the Results and Services Plan (RSP).

The RSP replaced the SRAA at the beginning of the 2004–05 budget process and extended service delivery and funding plans to *all* budget dependent agencies.[23] The RSP developed initially as a "summary" of the SRAA (and pilot SRAA agencies were grandfathered into the new arrangements by preparing their RSP as an overview to their current year agreement). While the RSP reflects the intent of the SRAA, it addresses some of the performance budgeting issues raised in the SRAA pilot in different ways.

The RSP is a high-level business plan that sets out the services that can be delivered and the results that can be achieved with an agency's current budget allocation. Learning from the SRAA experience, the foundation of an RSP is a clearer description of the relationship between an agency's activities and the outcomes it expects to achieve in the community, economy, or environment. Learning from the experience of comparable jurisdictions, the RSP uses "intervention logic" (or what is referred to in New South Wales as "results logic") to develop and convey performance narrative information (NSW Treasury, 2004a; for more information about intervention logic, see Schacter, 2002; Baehler, 2003).[24]

The structure and content of an RSP are set out in Figure 14.1. An RSP is a short, plain-English planning document—a maximum of only ten pages, compared with the 30-plus pages of an SRAA—that captures the salient information being generated by an agency's more detailed internal planning processes. As this suggests, it is important that the RSP be a "by-product" of agencies' strategic and operational planning; it also indicates that the plan's brevity is designed to give ministers and high-level officers a "snapshot" of priorities and resource deployment.[25]

As Figure 14.1 explains, an RSP consists of eight parts that capture performance narrative, and funding issues relating to, for instance, strategic scanning, efficiency improvement, organizational capability planning, and risk assessment and management. The foundation, however, is the results logic—or "performance story"—diagram that appears in Part 1 of an RSP. Results logic is a form of business strategy mapping that is both a *method* for guiding selection of a core set of performance indicators and a *context* for explaining the impact of funding and

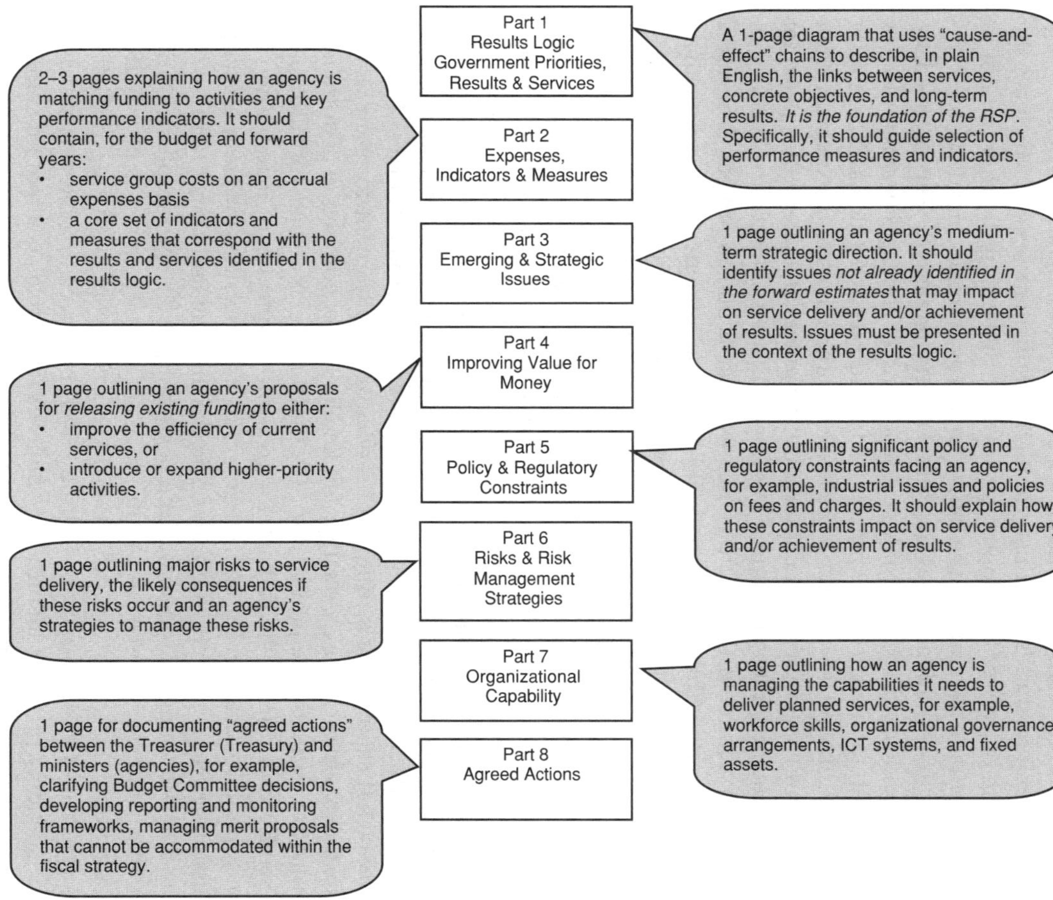

Figure 14.1 Structure and content of the Results and Services Plan

other issues on each part of the plan; that is, how planned service delivery can be managed with variations to the plan.

There is then merit in describing results logic methodology in more detail. Figure 14.2 is extracted from Treasury guidance material and shows the one-page results logic for a fictional law enforcement agency, Southland Department of Law Enforcement (see NSW Treasury, 2004b). This results logic is used by Southland to explain its *capacity to influence results* and to justify its *selection of performance measures*.

The level of influence is explained through intermediate results, which are the more concrete objectives that Southland needs to achieve in the shorter term in order to contribute to results in the longer term. For example, one desirable long-term result is "fewer violent crimes and crimes against property."[26] The intermediate results should demonstrate plausible "cause and effect" linkages between services and this result; for instance, if community education services (such as community awareness campaigns about crime prevention) are delivered as expected, then Southland can expect increased community awareness of strategies for personal safety and property protection, and if this impact is achieved, then the agency can be reasonably confident that more people will take action to protect themselves and their property. While Southland will have some influence over intermediate results, it should have full control over how efficiently it delivers services.

In this way the results logic can be used by Southland as a high-level context for explaining its capacity to influence long-term results and hence clarifying with the Treasury the performance expectations against which it can be held accountable. Stepping down through the results logic shows how accountability for "performance" will match the capacity to influence. This is also illustrated in Figures 14.3 and 14.4, which are also extracted from Treasury guidance material. Figure 14.3 shows a small selection of agreed result indicators that correspond with the intermediate results identified in the results logic; Figure 14.4 sets out a manageable number of service measures that capture key attributes of service accomplishment for each service group, for example, efficiency, quality, and timeliness. For both sets of performance information estimates are provided for the budget year and three forward years. The service measures provide a basis for Treasury monitoring of planned service delivery performance over the short term; result indicators can inform ministerial discussion of relative funding priorities over the medium and longer term.

The 2004–05 budget process was the beginning of a staged implementation of a more strategic resource allocation process. Certainly, in terms of workflow management, the invitation process worked efficiently, with the number of enhancement of effort proposals declining from hundreds to a few dozen, based on the spending priorities identified by Budget Committee. As a tool for strategic discussion the RSP had mixed success. Agencies were given a tight timeframe to prepare the plans, and the average quality reflected this. The intended role of the chief executive meetings—as the main conduit for agencies to raise emerging funding risks—was blunted by inconsistent implementation by central agencies. As some agencies later explained, the purpose of the meetings was heavily dependent on an agency's relationship with its Treasury analyst.

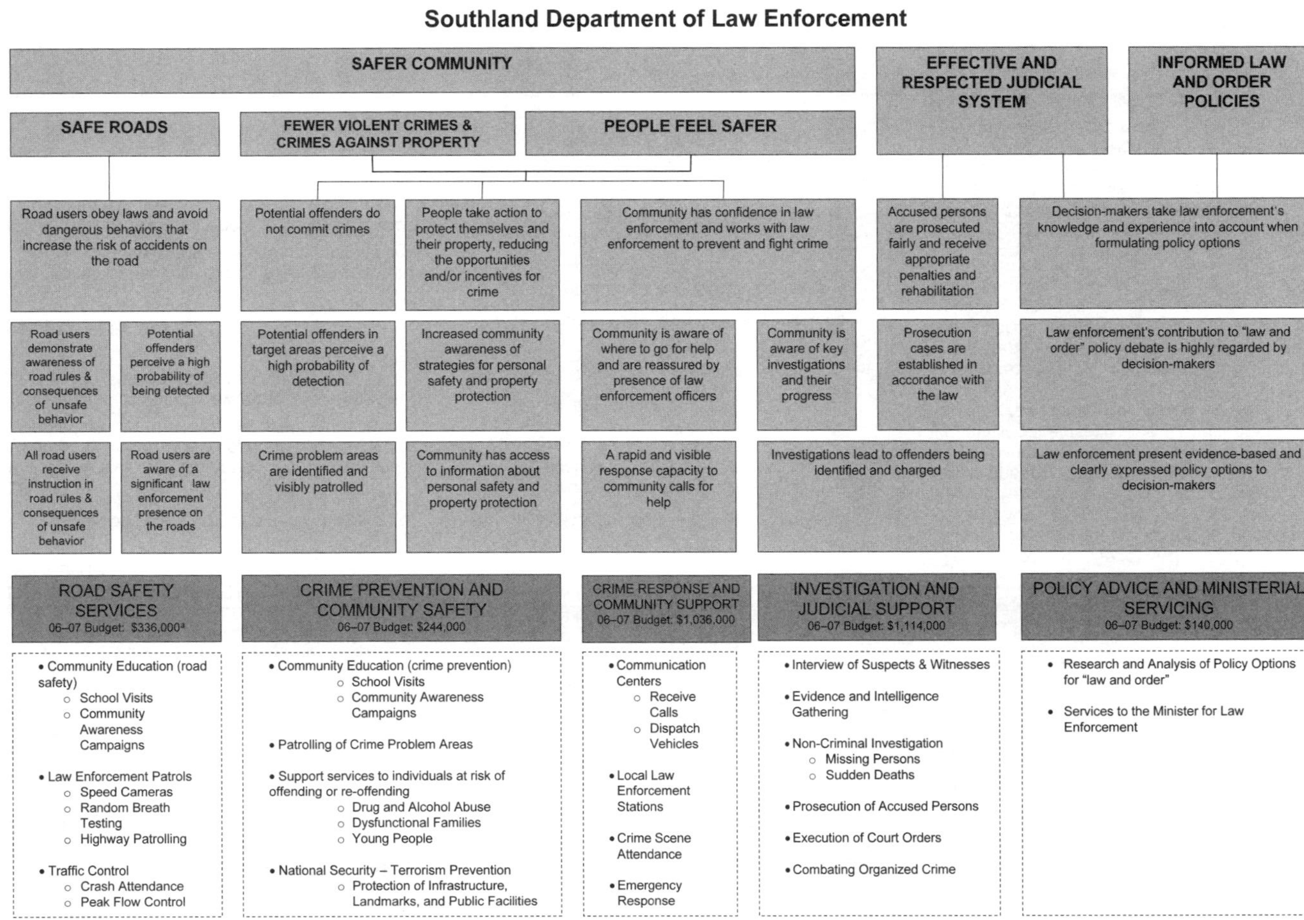

[a] 06–07 budget figures are in $ 000s.

Figure 14.2 2006–07 Results logic (results hierarchy)

Result indicators

	RESULTS & INTERMEDIATE RESULTS	RESULT INDICATORS	04–05	05–06	06–07 est.	07–08 est.	08–09 est.	09–10 est.
KEY RESULT 1: SAFER COMMUNITY	**SAFE ROADS**	• Road deaths per 100,000 people	100	100	95	90	90	90
	• Road users obey laws and avoid dangerous behavior • Road users demonstrate an increased awareness of road rules and consequences of unsafe behavior	• Traffic infringement notices issued per 100,000 people						
		• % of people who indicate that in the last 12 months, they have regularly:						
		- exceeded the speed limit by 10km/h or more						
		- driven with a Blood Alcohol Level exceeding 0.05	30%	29%	29%	28%	28%	25%
	FEWER VIOLENT CRIMES & CRIMES AGAINST PROPERTY							
	• Potential offenders do not commit crimes	• Recorded victims of violent crimes						
	• People take action to protect themselves and their property, reducing the opportunities and/or incentives for crime	• Recorded victims of crimes against property						
	• Increased community awareness of strategies for personal safety and property protection	• Reporting rates for violent crime • Reporting rates for burglary						
	PEOPLE FEEL SAFE							
	• Community has confidence in law enforcement and works with law enforcement to prevent and fight crime	• Calls to "Stop Crime" Police Info Line • % of suburbs with a Neighborhood Watch coordinator						
	• Community aware of where to go for help and are reassured by the presence of law enforcement officers	• Proportion of people who feel safe at home after dark • Proportion of people who feel safe walking locally after dark						

The Safe Roads result group is an example of a shared result. It is listed by both the DLE and the Southland Traffic Management Agency.

Data for these indicators are collected in an annual survey conducted by an independent research body. They were chosen for the RSP because they indicate the extent to which road users are actually changing their behavior—a key intermediate result.

The number of **"Recorded Victims"** is based only on crimes actually reported to the DLE.

The **"Reporting Rate"** is based on an independent national survey, conducted every four years. It is the proportion of people identifying themselves as "victims of crime" who actually reported the incident to the DLE.

When assessing whether results are being delivered, these indicators should be read in conjunction with one another. They will indicate whether fewer crimes are occurring and also the community's level of confidence in reporting crimes to the DLE.

"Proportion of people who feel safe"
These result indicators can also be used as Risk Indicators for one of the Risks outlined in Part 6: *"that a decrease in actual crime rates does not lead to people feeling safer."*

Figure 14.3 Result indicators

In March 2004 the Treasury conducted a comprehensive post-implementation review where three issues loomed large:

- the need for the Treasury to provide more detailed guidance and support to agencies on RSP preparation
- the potential for better collaboration and information sharing between agencies on RSP development (including the incorporation of "cross-agency" issues)
- tighter integration with agency corporate planning processes and the need for agency senior executive engagement with the process as a priority-setting exercise.

The process for the 2005–06 budget was modified to reflect these concerns. The initial step was consolidating the development of the RSP as an "agency" business plan. The Treasury's communications strategy reinforced the underlying rationale for the new process—the RSP was about better planning, and the key to better planning was the results logic method. A clear message from the better-practice agencies was that significant benefits for performance and financial management could be realized by integrating the RSP with existing agency planning processes (for example, strategic, corporate, business, resource, and risk management planning).[27] Hence a secondary focus for Treasury implementation was "selling" the message that the RSP should be a by-product of internal agency planning processes and not a stand-alone exercise. This would take time—the introduction of the RSP for the 2004–05 budget process had not been timed to feed into these annual planning processes.

These RSP development initiatives accompanied further modification of the new budget process. The two-stage invitation process was retained and the "scene-setting" phase was enhanced to enable an early exchange of information about service delivery issues and/or risks that could be addressed in the budget and forward years. For the first time, however, the scene-setting meetings would "roundtable" with portfolio ministers on a "cluster" basis.[28] Meeting on a cluster basis was intended to promote broad discussion about the quantum and relative priority of ministers' spending intentions in the context of "sectoral" spending areas. It was also designed to examine how funding pressures and opportunities for joint service delivery initiatives—for example, integrated client management in human services—could be addressed on a cross-agency or cross-portfolio basis. The outcomes of the cluster-based scene-setting phase would assist the Budget Committee in determining maintenance of effort funding and invitations for enhancement of effort proposals.

The cluster-based ministerial scene-setting meetings were informed by trilateral chief executive level meetings between agencies, the Treasury, and the Cabinet Office. Both sets of meetings were tasked with answering key questions about strategic and emerging issues and key organizational capability issues in the context of an agency's RSP. These issues were designed to expose funding and service delivery issues not currently captured in the forward estimates, and medium-term risks to the sustainability of service delivery, including how the agency proposed to manage these risks. In this way the RSP was "built in" to the scene-setting phase.

Service Groups are those listed in the Results Logic diagram—see Figure 14.2

SERVICE GROUP	SERVICE MEASURES	04–05	05–06	06–07 est.	07–08 est.	08–09 est.	09–10 est.
ROAD SAFETY SERVICES • Community Education (Road Safety) • Law Enforcement Patrols • Traffic Control	• % of primary students attending road safety education classes	50%	55%	60%	62%	64%	66%
	• Expenditure per capita on road safety and patrols[a]	$26	$26.90	$27.70	$28.50	$29.40	$30.30
	• Average number of traffic infringement notices issued per patrol vehicle						
CRIME PREVENTION AND COMMUNITY SAFETY • Community Education (Crime Prevention) • Patrolling of Crime Problem Areas • Support Services to At-Risk Individuals	• % of community aware of information campaigns on crime prevention and safety						
	• Expenditure per capita on Community Safety and Crime Prevention Education[a]	$5.40	$5.60	$6.20	$6.30	$6.50	$6.70
	• % of identified crime problem areas patrolled	75%	85%	90%	92%	93%	94%
INVESTIGATION AND JUDICIAL SUPPORT • Interview of Suspects and Witnesses • Evidence and Intelligence Gathering • Non-Criminal Investigations • Prosecution of Accused Persons • Combating Organized Crime	• % of violent crime and property crime investigations resolved within 30 days of offense being reported to Law Enforcement[b]	45%	48%	51%	53%	55%	55%
	• % of serious offenders DNA Tested						2%
	• % of "cold hits" from DNA						2%
	• % of failed prosecutions						2%

"Expenditure per capita"
These are measures of the *efficiency* of service delivery and should be read in conjunction with other indicators that show effectiveness.
A decrease in per capita expenditure might indicate progress if services are effective.

Where annual data are not available for a measure, or if a time lag exists in reporting data, agencies should provide a brief explanation to assist readers. For example:
"This measure is reported with a one-year time lag since it requires actual comparative data from several jurisdictions. This means that results reported for 03–04 will be actual figures from 02–03."

CRIME RESPONSE AND COMMUNITY SUPPORT • Communication Centers • Emergency Response • Local Law Enforcement Stations • Crime Scene Attendance	• % of emergency calls attended within 10 minutes	75%	80%	85%	85%	90%	90%
	• % of reported non-urgent matters reported to the Community Assistance Line	20%					
	• average time taken to respond to non-urgent matters	24 hours	24 hours	24 hours	12 hours	12 hours	12 hours
POLICY ADVICE AND MINISTERIAL SERVICING • Research and Analysis of Policy Options for Law and Order • Services to the Minister for Law Enforcement	• % of policy papers that the Minister for Law Enforcement is satisfied meet prescribed standards for policy advice	85%	87%	95%	95%	95%	95%
	• % of draft replies to correspondence provided within 20 days	95%	88%	95%	98%	98%	98%

> A strategy to improve value for money (see Part 4) is to encourage reporting of non-urgent matters to the Community Assistance Line rather than in person at a Law Enforcement Station.
>
> An increase in this % will indicate that this strategy is being successfully implemented.

[a] Adapted from Steering Committee for the Review of Government Service Provision (2004).
[b] Adapted from CoCQoG (2004).

Figure 14.4 Service measures

The relationship between resource allocation (the budget process) and resource monitoring (a function of the SP&FM Committee of Cabinet, discussed earlier) also become more established around the RSP. The service delivery and budget compliance focus initiated after the March 2003 election continued through the 2005–06 budget process, and was transformed into a more searching "expenditure review" process designed to determine the continuing relevance of current activities. For those ministers and agencies appearing before the committee, the RSP was the first port of call for explaining the current services profile and allocation of resources. The RSP provided a "window" on the *quality* of agency planning and the activities that could be *targeted* for more detailed examination.

Finally, in conjunction with modifications to both the RSP and the budget process, the Treasury began to address its own organizational capability issues. In July 2004 an internal initiative to better define the role of the Treasury analyst (or budget officer) began; its key objective was to align expanding expectations about performance budgeting with the wherewithal to deliver advice on agency financial and non-financial performance. Taking the new RSP budget process as its centerpiece, the initiative examined how "performance analysis" capacity could be strengthened, for example, using team construction to get the "skill set" right, re-emphasizing the "relationship management" aspect of the analyst's role, and, within the contours of often pressing work flows, encouraging a more strategic approach to assessing and managing funding issues.

A more strategic budget process: using the results and services plan as a funding plan (stage 3 reform)

The current 2006–07 budget process, which commenced in September 2005, is the next stage of reform. The first two iterations of the Results and Services Plan budget process acknowledged that the quality of the RSP was important to generating "demand" for performance information, and so the focus has been on raising awareness and building planning capability among agencies and Treasury analysts alike.[29] The current stage aims to consolidate the use of the RSP as a tool for strategic discussion about funding and performance, but also commences use of the RSP as a "funding plan" within a proposed "performance management and budgeting" framework (set out in Figure 14.5).

The previous section of this chapter discussed progress in establishing more effective planning structures and a supporting information base. The next steps involve using the RSP to build stronger links between each further element of the performance management cycle—funding, monitoring, and reporting. In broad terms the framework could develop along the following lines.

As an agreement between the Budget Committee and portfolio ministers, the RSP sets a small number of key performance indicators that ministers and agencies will report on and manage towards. These indicators will align chief executive performance agreements with agency strategic plans and business unit service delivery plans. Planned performance based on the results, services, estimates of expenses, and key performance indicators agreed in the RSP will be reported in

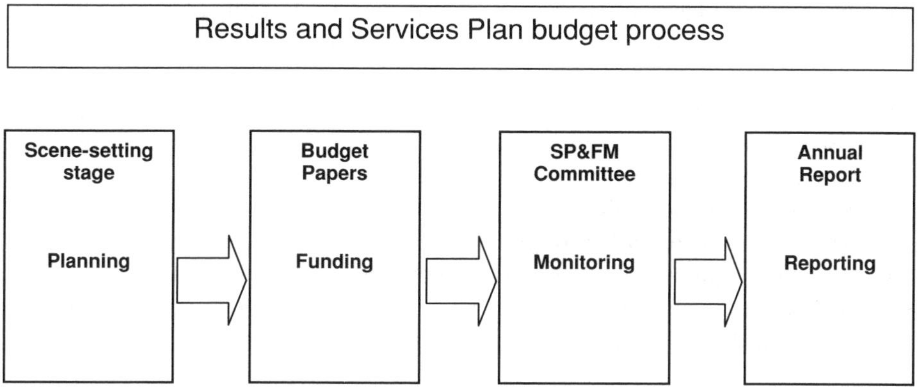

Figure 14.5 A proposed "performance management and budgeting" framework

the annual Budget Papers presented to parliament. Performance indicators are currently being negotiated as part of the budget process, and Budget Paper reporting is transitioning to a results and services format.

Over time the SP&FM Committee could hold portfolio ministers and agencies accountable for the delivery of the agreed level of service delivery performance in the Results and Services Plan. This will be achieved by regular monitoring of actual performance against that planned in the RSP. At the same time the SP&FM Committee will also monitor any efficiency targets required of agencies (including the impact on achievement as set out in the RSP). Initially this may concentrate effort to ensure that large portfolio ministers and agencies deliver services within budget.

Closing the performance management cycle is the reporting of actual performance. The performance information developed for the RSP could provide a core set of data to meet external reporting requirements. One option is to report actual financial and non-financial performance for the previous year in departmental Annual Reports.

Learning from the New South Wales experience

This chapter traces the development of the New South Wales Results and Services Plan Budget process over the last five years and describes the key features of the model. It introduced the New South Wales model as one of those performance budgeting systems that sought to establish "looser" links between funding and results. "Looser" linkages means an intention to build among decision-makers both a commitment to a small set of priority actions (and associated indicators of progress) as well as an awareness that selecting between competing priorities will always carry an opportunity cost. The descriptive case study has confirmed this: reform has focused on process modification that aims to embed high-level planning and performance information in the budget process.

The Results and Services Plan budget process remains in the early stages of implementation. However, four key features of the model stand out:

- an annual budget process framed around a service funding plan—the RSP—so that strategic discussion about incremental funding and policy issues occurs in the context of a "whole plan"
- the use of "performance stories"—the results logic—to contextualize high-level discussion about the relative priority of funding issues and to clarify financial and non-financial performance expectations
- a commitment to building agency capacity for both strategic planning and resource management through the results and services planning approach
- the use of regular consultative review processes to test process modifications and work towards closer meshing between ministerial and bureaucratic priority setting and resource allocation decision-making.

While the budget reform process is far from complete, there are some key lessons that can be drawn from the New South Wales experience in terms of both the *approach* to reform and the *preliminary outcomes* for performance budgeting.

The first lesson relates to the value of the "performance story" approach as a foundation for strategic discussion. The Results and Services Plan budget process is about creating a climate in which performance information forms unobtrusive background for discussion about funding and policy issues. Results logic uses simplified "cause and effect" narratives to help decision-makers understand the assumptions underlying service delivery strategies and to review how resources are currently allocated to these activities. While the RSP is also developing as a basis for matching funding to a small set of performance information, it is fundamentally directed at raising the level of central-line agency discussion in (and around) the budget process.

There is a growing list of examples of how the RSP is supporting better communication between the Treasury and agencies. Feedback from agency chief executives has confirmed that the RSP has been particularly useful in structuring high-level officer discussions, including debate about the continuing relevance of functions and activities. In a small number of cases the RSP process has helped restructured agencies identify functions (and associated resources) that do not fit within results logic and hence provided options for shifting activities from one agency to another. The RSP has also been employed as a platform for agreeing how longer-term issues and "merit" funding proposals (those which are assessed to be of worth but unable to be funded within existing constraints) can be managed without recourse to budget support.

This type of utilization is, however, not easy to achieve. It is clear that *procedural* integration (that is, mandating plans, changing templates, issuing timetables) is only ever the starting point. *Substantive* integration (that is, modified behaviors and attitudinal change) is dependent on making the procedural changes visible in the most basic, everyday ways. As in any organizational setting the urgent has a way of displacing the strategic, and senior management has recognized the importance of demonstrating a clear commitment to talking "performance" and signaling "ownership."

A second, related lesson revolves around the capture and use of performance information; that is, information on the results achieved and the costs of achieving those results. As this volume notes, accessing and deploying this information does not come cheaply. So how did New South Wales try to reduce the costs of performance information?

Initially, the Results and Services Plan budget process aims to manage the "costs" of performance by dealing with the *information asymmetry* that characterizes the relationship between central and line agencies. By framing the planning process as an information-sharing exercise, the RSP was as much about increasing an agency's understanding of its own business as providing a tool for expanding the Treasury analyst's knowledge.

Again, learning from the SRAA trial, a second focus is addressing *bounded rationality*. Acknowledging the potential for decision-makers to experience information overload, a key concern in designing the RSP was to make performance information resonate with the intended users. Performance stories—presented in the form of a one-page "results logic" diagram—use plain English narrative and visual displays to give users a snapshot of an agency's current service delivery priorities and the extent to which these are aligned with government priorities. The performance story, however, is only half the story. To build commitment, ministers and chief executives must own a small number of key performance indicators that make sense in the context of the performance story.

The RSP process sought also to manage problems associated with *outcomes measurement*. The RSP is as much a methodology for thinking about how and why services are delivered, as it is a discrete strategic planning exercise. The results logic sets out key strategies (how services are delivered) and identifies priorities that can be used to drive performance management within an organization. Further, it helps to "frame" central-line discussion about performance expectations because "cause and effect" chains mark out an agency's capacity to influence results (and hence its "accountability" for results achievement).

A third lesson relates to the importance of managing expectations about budget reform and the pace at which it can progress. The Treasury considers that a hallmark of the Results and Services Plan budget process has been an implementation strategy based on "trial and error"—there has been a preparedness to test different approaches to planning and priority-setting and an acceptance that some of these initiatives would need to be modified. The development of budget reform has also reinforced the significance of ongoing review of agencies' implementation and the need to work closely with those officers who are actually preparing the plans. Finally, a central budget agency should not underestimate the value of candor in the reform strategy and acknowledge up front that change processes will be long and grinding.

Conclusion

Performance budgeting in New South Wales is a product of both a distinctly pragmatic approach to public sector reform and an intentional strategy to "watch and learn" the experience of more radical reform in comparable jurisdictions. The Results and Services Plan budget process can be categorized as a "loose" performance budgeting system; that is, the process is designed primarily to give strategic context to discussion about relative funding priorities. While the change initiative is in the early stages of implementation, New South Wales Treasury remains committed to gradual, long-term budget reform and believes that significant progress has been made in linking planning and performance information with the way that resource allocation choices are considered.

Notes

1. The definition of a "program" in the New South Wales context remained at a high level and was applied inconsistently across service delivery agencies. In general, a program comprised a group of activities that contributed to a specific objective, for example, road maintenance tasks contribute to the development of road network infrastructure. Agency financial estimates are still presented on a "program" basis for the Budget year, but are reported at an aggregate level for the three forward years. For an example see *2005–06 Budget Paper 3* (NSW Treasury, 2005).
2. This type of studied neutrality has been applied by New South Wales in matters of public sector reform more generally. For example, in the late 1990s the Premier's Department, which has responsibility for public sector performance improvement, noted similar concerns in its study of international experience with structural reforms separating policy and operational functions (NSW Premier's Department, 1998).
3. Australia has a federal system of government. The national government in Canberra is variously described as the "Australian," "Commonwealth," or "federal" government.
4. In the 2005–06 budget 41 per cent of total budgeted revenues were sourced from the federal government (see NSW Treasury, 2005: Chapter 3 of 2005–06 Budget Paper 2).
5. The chief component of general purpose grants is revenue from the Goods and Services Tax (GST), a federal value added tax. The grants are distributed among the States on the basis of per capita relativities calculated by the independent Commonwealth Grants Commission. The key elements of the funding system, and donor states' concerns about the way per capita relativities are calculated, are set out in Review of Commonwealth-State Funding (2002).
6. That is, all Ministers of the Crown, as distinct from a smaller grouping of senior ministers.
7. Established in 1824, New South Wales Treasury consists of two separate agencies: the Office of Financial Management (which advises on financial management policy and economic conditions) and the Office of State Revenue (which administers state taxation, collects revenue, and develops taxation policy and legislation). In this chapter, a reference to the Treasury means the Office of Financial Management.
8. Portfolio ministers and their agencies prepare two types of funding proposals—a *maintenance of effort* proposal (which seeks funding outside the forward estimates to maintain current service delivery levels) and an *enhancement of effort* proposal (which seeks funding outside the forward estimates to expand current services or introduce new services).
9. The financial (or budget) year runs from July 1 to June 30. The Appropriation Bill sets out estimates of payments for both recurrent services and capital works and services from the Consolidated Fund. An Appropriation Act must pass both Houses of Parliament—the Legislative Assembly (the lower house) and the Legislative Council (the upper house). However, where there is a disagreement between the Houses, the *Constitution Act 1902* provides that the upper house has no power to prevent passage of appropria-

tions for "ordinary annual services." For more detailed discussion see Twomey (2004, pp. 530–82).

10. Cash allocations from the Consolidated Fund are appropriated to ministers and lapse at financial year's end.
11. The "net cost of services" is the key administrative control Treasury uses to manage the impact of service delivery agency expenses on the budget aggregates in the budget and forward years.
12. The Act required that governments "aim to pursue" policy in accordance with the Act's fiscal principles and targets (s10), but did not create enforceable obligations (s27). The Treasurer was, however, required to include in the annual budget papers a statement explaining the reasons for any departure from the principles (s10). In any event, the government has provided regular progress reports in Paper 2 of the Budget Papers (see, for example, NSW Treasury, 2005).
13. The Act defines "fiscal sustainability" as requiring "that the Government be able to manage financial shocks in future periods without having to introduce significant and economically or socially destabilising expenditure or revenue adjustments in those future periods."
14. See Fiscal Responsibility Act 2005. For discussion about fiscal target achievement see Chapter 1 of 2005–06 Budget Paper 2 (NSW Treasury, 2005).
15. *Value for money* is defined as the requirement "that the limited resources available to Government be applied in such a way that community needs and expectations are satisfied to the greatest extent possible both now and in the future"; *resource allocation* is the "best mix of programs and services within the funding and expenditure constraints set by the State's fiscal strategy"; and *resource management* is "selecting and managing the mix of labour, capital assets and other resources available in such a way that they deliver the greatest quantity and quality of programs and services possible" (NSW Treasury, 2000a, p. 6).
16. The trial agencies were the Attorney-General's Department, the Office of State Revenue and the Departments of Agriculture and Urban Affairs and Planning. Later pilots would cover almost three-quarters of the General Government sector budget, including (in addition to the four trial agencies) the Departments of Health, Education and Training, Corrective Services and Land and Water Conservation, as well as the Roads and Traffic Authority.
17. Although the "request" to submit an SRAA was issued to agencies as part of the allocation letter (the formal advice from the Treasury about Budget and forward year estimates), the process was not mandated, for example in a Treasury Circular. Instead, the implementation strategy sought to create "incentives" for better planning by demonstrating the value of stronger linkages between strategic planning and the budget process. This approach continues with the Results and Services Plan budget process.
18. In each year the Treasury conducted a post-implementation review using a consistent data collection format, that is, participant interviews with agency chief executive officers, senior agency officers involved in the budget process, Treasury executive officers and Treasury analysts (budget officers).
19. The Constitution Act 1902 provides for a fixed four-year term for the parliament of New South Wales, that is, a general election is held every four years.
20. The initiative was framed as "better services for New South Wales" and reflected the priorities of a third-term government aware of the need to consolidate and deliver on its election commitments.
21. Internal Treasury analysis indicated that, on average, agencies submitted enhancement proposals valued at about 3 percent of the total budget and that only about 10 percent of these proposals were finally approved. In effect, in a typical budget cycle, the efforts of agencies and government are directed at funding that is worth less than 1 percent of total budget expenditure.

22. These priority review processes drew on similar arrangements operating in other jurisdictions, for example, the Senior Ministers Review process run by the Commonwealth Department of Finance and Administration.
23. At the start of the 2004–05 budget process SRAA implementation remained in pilot stage with 11 service delivery agencies.
24. There were a number of sources inspiring the development of results logic. In the early 1990s the NSW Premier's Department pioneered the use of "outcomes hierarchy" methodology to support better program evaluation (NSW Office of Public Management, 1990). More recent models include the use of "logic chains" by the Oregon Progress Board in the United States, the application of "intervention logic" in the preparation of Statements of Intent in New Zealand, and the promotion of "performance stories" by the Office of the Auditor General of Canada.
25. The RSP also emphasizes the use of everyday language to make technical information more accessible to non-specialist audiences, both ministerial and bureaucratic (the most obvious example being the replacement of "outcomes and outputs" with "results and services"). The use of everyday language was extended to the key questions that helped agencies prepare an RSP: "What do you do?" "Why do you do it?" "How do you know you are doing a good job?"
26. Agencies are encouraged to describe results (and intermediate results) as "end-points to be aimed for." The result or intermediate result should then be used to select an indicator that can capture whether a situation is changing or improving.
27. An illustrative better practice agency was the Department of Community Services (DoCS) which has responsibility for child protection services, parenting supports, and early intervention programs. During this period the DoCS Executive used the RSP approach to drive organizational reform and clarify service delivery priorities. This is illustrated in the integration of results logic methodology with the DoCS corporate plan (see DoCS 2004).
28. A "cluster" refers to a grouping of ministers (and their agencies) around shared functions or closely related policy objectives. For example, the "human services" cluster might comprise the Ministers for Health, Community Services, Aging Disability and Home Care, Education and Training, Aboriginal Affairs and Housing. While there were existing cabinet-level forums for some ministerial clusters, these arrangements were not aligned closely with the annual budget process.
29. In March 2005 the Treasury used "stages of development" criteria to assess agency RSPs submitted as part of the 2004–05 and 2005–06 budget processes. The findings indicate that there has been a steady improvement in the average quality of result logic development and performance information.

References

Alaba, R., 1994, *Inside Bureaucratic Power: The Wilenski Review of NSW Government* (Sydney: Hale & Iremonger).

Baehler, K., 2003, "Managing for Outcomes: Accountability and Thrust," *Australian Journal of Public Administration*, Vol. 62(4), pp. 23–34.

Carlin, T.M., and J. Guthrie, 2001, "Lessons From Australian and New Zealand Experiences with Accrual Based Output Budgeting Systems," in *Learning From International Public Management Reform*, Vol. II, ed. L. Jones, J. Guthrie, and P. Steane (New York: JAI), pp. 89–100.

——, 2003, "Accrual Output Based Budgeting Systems in Australia: The Rhetoric-Reality Gap," *Public Management Review*, Vol. 5(2), pp. 145–62.

CoCQoG (Council on the Cost and Quality of Government), 2003, *Overview of New South Wales Government Services, 1996–2001,* November, <www.ccqg.nsw.gov.au/Site07Jul2004/performance_reports/index.html>.

——, 2004, *Overview of New South Wales Government Services, 1997–2002*, March, <www.ccqg.nsw.gov.au/Site07Jul2004/performance_reports/index.html>.

DoCS (Department of Community Services), 2004, *Corporate Plan 2004/05—2008/09*, <www.community.nsw.gov.au/documents/corp_plan05.pdf>.

Halligan, J., and J. Power, 1992, *Political Management in the 1990s* (Oxford: Oxford University Press).

Kaplan, R.S., and D.P. Norton, 1992, "The Balanced Scorecard: Measures that Drive Performance," *Harvard Business Review*, January–February, pp. 71–9.

NSW Premier's Department, 1998, *Directions for Public Sector Reform in New South Wales: Discussion Paper* (Sydney: NSW Premier's Department).

NSW Office of Public Management, 1990, "Clarifying Program Objectives for Program Evaluation," *Program Evaluation Bulletin*, 1/90 January (Sydney: NSW Premier's Department).

NSW Treasury, 2000a, *Financial Management Framework: The Financial Management Framework for the General Government Sector*, TPP00–4, December, <www.treasury.nsw.gov.au/pubs/tpp00_4/tpp00–4.pdf>.

——, 2000b, "Budget Outcomes and Outputs: A Guide to Performance Management," TRP00–2, October. Internal NSW Treasury document.

——, 2004a, *What You Do and Why: An Agency Guide to Defining Results and Services*, TPP04–4, October, <www.treasury.nsw.gov.au/pubs/tpp2004/tpp04–4.pdf>.

——, 2004b, "Example Results and Services Plan: Southland Department of Law Enforcement." Internal NSW Treasury document.

——, 2004c, *Office of Financial Management Corporate Plan, 2004–07*, July, <www.treasury.nsw.gov.au/pubs/2004–07plan/2004–07-corp-plan.pdf>.

——, 2005, *Budget Papers, 2005–2006*, <www.treasury.nsw.gov.au/bp05–06/bpapers.htm>.

Nicholls, D., 1991, *Managing State Finance: The New South Wales Experience* (Sydney: NSW Treasury).

Painter, M., 1987, *Steering the Modern State: Changes in Central Coordination in Three Australian State Governments* (Sydney: Sydney University Press).

Parker, R.S., 1978, *The Government of New South Wales* (St Lucia: University of Queensland Press).

Review of Commonwealth-State Funding, 2002, *Final Report: A Review of the Allocation of Commonwealth Grants to the States and Territories* (Melbourne: Committee for the Review of Commonwealth-State Funding), August.

Robinson, M., 1999, "Contract Budgeting," *Public Administration*, Vol. 78(1), pp. 75–95.

——, 2002, "Output-Purchase Funding and Budgeting Systems in the Public Sector," *Public Budgeting and Finance*, Vol. 22(4), pp. 17–33.

Schacter, M., 2002, *Not a "Tool Kit": Practitioner's Guide to Measuring the Performance of Public Programs*, Institute on Governance, <www.iog.ca/publications/guide.pdf>.

Smith, R., 2003, "New South Wales" in *Australian Politics and Government: The Commonwealth, the States and the Territories*, ed. C. Sharman and J. Moon (Cambridge: Cambridge University Press), pp. 41–73.

Steering Committee on Government Trading Enterprises, 1988, *Policy Framework: Government Trading Enterprises*, September, <www.treasury.nsw.gov.au/comframe/gte_perf.pdf>.

Steering Committee for the Review of Government Service Provision, 2004, *Report on Government Services 2004* (Canberra: Steering Committee for the Review of Government Service Provision, Productivity Commission).

Twomey, A., 2004, *The Constitution of New South Wales* (Sydney: The Federation Press).

15
Formula Funding and Performance Budgeting

Peter C. Smith[1]

Numerous instruments are needed to make operational the principles of performance budgeting. Among the most important is the mechanism whereby individual local agencies are financed. This chapter focuses on one particular type of financing mechanism: the use of mathematical formulas to determine the magnitude of funds directed towards a local public service organization. The use of such formulas has become increasingly widespread in many public services. When properly designed, it can be strongly aligned to the principle of program budgeting, as a means of systematically transmitting central policies to specific local organizations. However, formula funding also embraces a number of perils that must be addressed if it is to contribute successfully to the performance budgeting process.

This chapter summarizes the "state of the art" of formula funding as it relates to performance budgeting. It begins with a brief overview of the funding flows that are addressed by formula funding, and then explains what formula funding is. It next examines the rationale for adopting formula funding within a performance budgeting framework. The following section then describes in some detail the two main types of formula funding—case payments and capitation methods. The chapter concludes with a discussion of the incentives under formula funding, and the circumstances in which it can be aligned successfully with the performance budgeting process.

Flow of funds in public services

Most public expenditure is undertaken locally. However, the methods put in place by the national government for funding local public services have crucial implications for their nature, effectiveness, and efficiency. Figure 15.1 offers a conceptual framework for the flow of funds implicit in the financing of most public services. The prime source of central government funds is usually taxation, paid in a variety of forms by citizens and businesses. This creates a pool of revenue (A) available to the government, which must decide how it will allocate the funds to support locally delivered public service programs, either wholly or in part, consistent with its performance objectives.

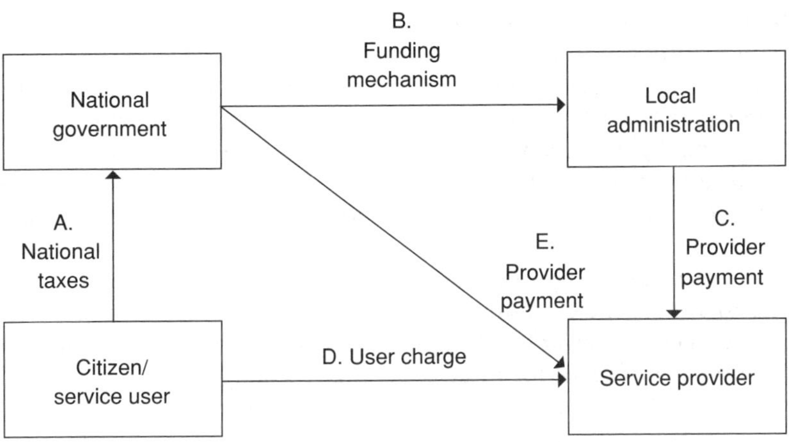

Figure 15.1 Flow of funds in public services

The central government might pay local providers directly (E), as in many national systems of university education. In contrast, it might devolve purchasing powers to lower tiers of administration. In this chapter I emphasize the case where the local purchaser is an agency of the national government. The case where the agency is a local government, with some degree of local accountability, independent revenue sources, and an element of autonomy from the national government is not treated explicitly in this chapter, although many of the principles remain valid when services are devolved to local governments. My book gives an extended treatment of this topic (Smith, 2006).

Where they are used, the national government must give local purchasers the means to carry out their purchasing functions (flow B). Local service providers then receive payments either directly from the national government (flow E) or from its local administration (flow C). In some circumstances, the distinction between local purchaser and provider may be unclear (for example, schools are often directly provided for by local administrations). However, even where there is no explicit payment mechanism, local administrations must in principle purchase their services from vertically integrated providers. Finally, the service user might pay a charge to the service provider (D).

This chapter is centrally concerned with two of the funding flows represented in Figure 15.1: the mechanisms for funding local administrations from national revenues (B); and the mechanisms used for paying providers (E and C). Throughout, I shall refer to the national disburser of funds as the payer, whether the payment is made to a local administration or to a provider. From a performance budgeting perspective, a central challenge for the payer is to design a payment mechanism that secures its policy objectives.

Determining satisfactory mechanisms for making financial allocations to local agencies can give rise to serious challenges for the payer. First, it is a difficult technical exercise to determine where public money is best spent in line with performance objectives. Second, any funding mechanism introduces powerful incentives for local organizations, and it is important to ensure they are in line with the payer's intentions. Third, the political ramifications of any funding choice can be acute, particularly when parliamentary representatives are elected on a geographical basis. And finally, a national government requires reassurance that public expenditure is being spent locally in line with intentions, yet monitoring the effectiveness and efficiency of local spending is often a difficult undertaking. This is of course a fundamental concern of program budgeting.

There are numerous ways in which a national payer could determine the allocation of public funds to local agencies. At its crudest, the distribution could be based on political patronage, perhaps rewarding localities according to their political support in the past, or their importance for future elections. Although few payers would admit openly to engaging in such patronage, there is ample evidence to suggest that to some extent it informs many allocation systems that are supposedly non-partisan (Gibson, 1998; John and Ward, 2001).

Financial allocations could instead be made according to how much localities actually spend. This approach will usually contradict principles of good public finance, as it is likely to encourage spending in excess of optimal levels and offers few incentives for efficient local management. However, it has historically formed the basis for many rudimentary funding mechanisms as it has minimal monitoring requirements, and it can be used to encourage spending when local agencies would otherwise spend below optimal levels.

Another approach in widespread use is to distribute public funds according to historical precedent. Politically, it has the great attraction that it minimizes disruption to existing public services, and avoids potentially large swings from year to year inherent in other allocation mechanisms. Its popularity is manifest in the way that more systematic approaches to distribution are frequently abated by "damping" mechanisms that seek to reduce the magnitude of year-on-year financial losses and gains to local agencies. However, sole reliance on such methods would leave a payer hostage to history, and offers few incentives for service reform or improved performance.

A fourth possibility is to allocate funds according to bids submitted by local agencies, or to make allocations contingent on some measure of local performance. In principle, this approach has much to commend it from a performance budgeting perspective. If undertaken properly, it could ensure that public funds are spent in line with national policy intentions, in a cost-effective manner. Its major weakness is that it usually entails large transaction costs, in the form of central scrutiny and policing, and the preparation of bids by local agencies. It also makes local budgets dependent on the quality of local management, and so may lead to large inequalities. Moreover, unsuccessful agencies may perceive that the allocations have been made according to patronage rather than the quality of bids, leading to further potential for perceived unfairness.

In practice, most systems of financing local public service institutions use a mix of all four types of mechanism to allocate funds. However, a fifth approach—allocation by mathematical formula—is increasingly becoming the favored approach towards determining local financial allocations. It can be defined in broad terms as the use of mechanical rules to determine the level of public funds a devolved organization should receive for delivering a specified public service. The next section examines formula funding in more detail.

What is formula funding?

Under formula funding the payer specifies in advance mathematical rules that determine the magnitude of the funding received by a local organization. Those rules might be very simple (for example, a fixed amount of funding for each user) or very complex. However, the overarching objectives of formula funding are (a) to create a budget for the local entity with which it is expected to provide local public services, and (b) to offer appropriate incentives to provide those services in line with the payer's objectives.

With many systems of formula funding, the payer's objective is merely to enable all local agencies to deliver some "standard" package of services. As stated, this criterion usually ducks the issue of what that standard might be. In practice, the standard is often interpreted as the national average level of services, given a locality's social, economic, and geographical circumstances. The standard package might be defined in terms of expenditure (for example, a certain level of spending on each citizen in need of services), service levels (a stated service entitlement for citizens with specified needs), or outcome (a stated level of outcome to be secured for all users). However the standard is defined, when applied to a locality it implies a certain level of expected expenditure, which is the local agency's "spending need." It is this spending need that the funding formula seeks to estimate.

This traditional "needs based" funding formula makes little direct reference to performance, other than an implicit expectation that the local agency will perform at the national average level. As stated, the needs based approach offers only the *opportunity* to deliver the standard, and on its own offers no direct incentive to secure any performance standard whatsoever. Performance budgeting signals a desire to move away from this traditional approach of "funding needs," toward a principle of "funding results."

There are two broad approaches to the use of formula funding. The first reimburses the local agency on the basis of some measure of output, typically a count of the number of service users. Such *case payment* mechanisms are widespread in education (counts of pupils) and health care (counts of patients), and they are especially relevant when an unambiguous indicator of a service user's need for the service can be established. Case payment methods give rise to a variable budget for the local agency, based on recorded output. They therefore incentivize increased output, but can give rise to perverse incentives to create unwarranted or inappropriate service utilization.

The other approach to formula funding is to reimburse according to the *expected* level of local activity. Typically, this takes a measure of the size and characteristics of a local population, and infers the expected level of local service expenditure without reference to actual local output. Because these methods are based on population counts, they have become known as *capitation* funding methods. They circumvent some of the perverse incentives inherent in case payment, because they do not rely on a count of service users. However, they introduce their own difficulties—most notably the failure to incenticize any sort of output, whether warranted or not. The incentives inherent in formula funding methods are discussed in more detail in the sections below.

Whatever the chosen mechanism, four institutional aspects must be in place for formula funding to be effective. First, there must exist at least some local autonomy regarding how the local public service is delivered. The recipient of funds could be very large (such as a regional government) or very small (even extending to an individual citizen in receipt of a voucher to spend on specified services). However, unless this local agency enjoys at least some autonomy as to how it can use the funds, the funding mechanism becomes one of merely reimbursing specific activities, and offers few incentives for efficiency.

Second, there must be adequate data, available on a consistent basis across all local organizations, to which can be applied a mechanical formula that determines the level of funding to be allocated to those organizations. The data should of course be verifiable and timely. Also, the formulaic rules should be specified ex ante, so that there are no immediate provisions for altering the consequent level of funding. The possibility of ex-post adjustments to the rules suggests that formula funding budgets are being moderated by considerations of actual spending or political patronage.

Third, there should be some explicit performance criteria against which the performance of the local agency is to be judged. It is meaningless to devolve funds without some statement as to their use. However, the chosen performance criteria might range from a very rudimentary check that services are delivered with some basic adherence to quality standards, to the very complex quality assurance regimes now emerging in some education and health systems (Smith and York, 2004). It is noteworthy that many existing formula funding mechanisms pay little regard to such performance issues.

Finally, there must exist some incentive to adhere to the financial allocation implied by the formula. Formula funding is a mere ritual if the recipients of public finances can with impunity ignore the resulting budgetary limits. Sanctions and rewards may take many forms. And they might apply to an organization, to a team, or to an individual manager. For example, a head teacher might face dismissal if a school's financial allocation is persistently exceeded. Or a for-profit provider might be threatened with bankruptcy if it fails to secure enough business. There is no requirement that the sanctions should be as "hard" as these examples, but there must be some incentive for recipients of formula finance to take notice of their allocations.

Formula funding is becoming the dominant mechanism for devolving public finances. For example, Smith (2003) estimates that annually at least £150 billion of UK public expenditure is devolved in this way, and Louis et al. (2003) suggest an equivalent figure of $250 billion for federal spending in the United States. It is nevertheless important to note that many existing mechanisms have been designed primarily to address issues of fairness between local areas, and have not been explicitly aligned with the payer's performance requirements. The extent to which they can address performance budgeting requirements is discussed in the next section.

Rationale for formula funding

There are three broad reasons why a government might introduce formula funding, relating to efficiency, equity, and political arguments. Performance budgeting "refers to public sector funding mechanisms designed to strengthen the linkage between funding and results" (Chapter 1). The interest in this chapter is the extent to which formula funding can promote performance budgeting, and efficiency concerns are therefore likely to be paramount. This section therefore examines those efficiency arguments in some detail. However, it is important to bear in mind that payers may also turn to formula funding to address equity and political objectives, so the section concludes with a brief summary of arguments in those domains.

Economic efficiency has a number of connotations. The two most fundamental are allocative efficiency (the extent to which allocations of resources are in line with society's preferences) and managerial efficiency (the extent to which agencies perform specified functions at least resource costs). Formula funding is intended to address both aspects of efficiency. First, it seeks to align resource allocations and incentives with the payer's intentions; second, it seeks to promote efficient management among local organizations.

No coherent system of financial transfers can be developed without first establishing clear objectives for the financial regime. Once objectives have been set, the fundamental efficiency argument for implementing formula funding is that—if properly designed—it allows the payer to implement an optimal allocation of finance in line with those objectives. Any deviation from such a formula implies a reduction in the effectiveness with which funds are used, and therefore a loss of efficiency. For example, if objectives are set in terms of service outcomes—such as maximizing school examination results—the formula should be designed to secure that objective at a national level, subject to an aggregate budget constraint. This implies designing allocations such that the expected marginal benefit (marginal improvement in exam results) for an extra unit of expenditure is equal for all local agencies. Any departure from this criterion leads to a loss in total examination success. Of course the key empirical challenge then becomes one of successfully designing a formula in line with that objective.

It could be argued that an efficient allocation could be secured through means other than formula funding. For example, one could envisage an iterative mechanism under which the national government makes incremental changes to local budgets each year in the light of where it feels the funds are best spent (increasing budgets where the marginal benefit appears high, and reducing them where it seems low). Apart from requiring an indefinite time horizon over which to converge to an optimal allocation, such methods are vulnerable to gaming on the part of the local agencies. For example, they may have an incentive to underperform in order to imply that they would benefit from increased funding. In contrast, well-designed formulas can secure an instantaneous solution, and can be designed so that they are not susceptible to such gaming.

A central concern of many payers is the extent to which the mechanism for financing local organizations relies on data provided those same agencies. This can give rise to two difficulties: data manipulation and fraud, and the creation of perverse behavioral incentives. An example from the nineteenth century illustrates both issues. The government rejected a proposal to reimburse English local authorities according to the number of "indoor paupers"—or workhouse residents—(a) because the count of "indoor" paupers was vulnerable to fraud and (b) it may have encouraged unnecessary use of the workhouse (in order to raise numbers of indoor paupers, the proposed basis for payment). Even in systems in which such responses are rare, a suspicion that they exist may undermine the credibility of the funding mechanism.

Many of the most creative systems of formula funding therefore seek deliberately to minimize the use of data emanating from local agencies, or to rely only on independently verified and audited data, so reducing the danger of moral hazard in the actions and reporting of local agencies. Such approaches allow the center to develop funding mechanisms that rely more on objective indicators of service needs and outcomes, and that are therefore independent of special pleading or gaming on the part of the local organization. Formula funding therefore offers a practical means of accommodating the information asymmetry between the payer and the local agency.

Implicit in these arguments is the belief that the use of formulas economizes on the analysis, audit, and oversight required at the center. With careful design, the payer can reduce the need for detailed scrutiny of the case for funding local agencies. In turn, the local agency does not need to make a case to the center, and must instead concentrate on delivering local services. Furthermore, and perhaps most importantly, it has less incentive or opportunity to distort behavior in order to suggest a need for more funding. Compared with most other funding mechanisms, formula funding can therefore economize on agency costs, both at the center and locality. Of course, in practice, even under a formula funding system, local agencies are likely to make representations to the center about the accuracy or fairness of the formula. However, special pleading is likely to be less profitable and more easily rebutted if a well-designed formula is in place.

Formula funding can have important implications for managerial efficiency, as it leads to the creation of clearly defined incentives and rules for the creation of budgets in the local agency. A clearly defined and predictable system of reimbursement enables the local agency to put in place proper financial management and business planning arrangements. When implemented alongside decentralization of power, the setting of a clear budgetary regime offers local organizations freedom to respond to local circumstances, to innovate, and to seek out economies, in line with the prescriptions of the new public management (Osborne and Gaebler, 1992). Properly designed, the use of mathematical formulas is an important means of enabling the center to set a credible and robust budgetary regime that can be used to promote its performance objectives.

Rather than these efficiency concerns, which are central to the principles of performance budgeting, many systems of formula funding have traditionally been concerned more with promoting some concept of equity, in seeking to reimburse "needs" rather than "results." So far as a payer is concerned, the pursuit of equity might be valued for its own sake, or it might be valued because it secures acceptance for the redistribution implicit in the assignment of government revenues to pay for local public services. Central governments raise much of their revenue through national taxes, levied at some standard rate across the country. In order to secure support for such taxation, they may wish to redistribute revenues in a fashion that appears fair and in line with concepts of natural justice (Rice and Smith, 2001b).

Indeed, there is a rich "political economy" of formula funding (Glennerster et al., 2000; McLean, 2005). It may appear that, by delegating the rules for setting budgets to the technical domain, formula funding circumvents the political problem. Such a view assumes the existence of an enlightened payer able to articulate an explicit set of objectives in respect of public services. However, enlightenment may not be the only principle informing the payer's motivations, and a more self-interested payer may wish to use a funding formula to further its own interests.

Moreover, there are numerous actors associated with the funding of public services beyond the immediate payer who may seek to influence the deployment of funding formulas, including politicians, central and local bureaucrats, local governments, providers, interest groups, and the general public. Depending on the institutional arrangements in place, such actors may play an important role in influencing, constraining, or enabling the design and implementation of funding formulas. Indeed, the payer may use the formula funding mechanism to reconcile these various interests. In short, it is important to note the complex political economy underlying the design of public service funding mechanisms.

In reading the literature on funding formulas, therefore, it should be kept in mind that many existing systems have been used not to promote performance objectives, but rather to resolve the competing claims of various agencies. Hence the frequent emphasis on needs-based funding. This is an important and legitimate role of formula funding. However, it is not considered further here. Instead, the following sections focus on the role of formulas in systems of results-based funding.

Elements of formula funding

This section describes the two broad approaches to designing funding formulas in common use. In the case payment approach, local services are reimbursed according to some measure of the *actual* level of output. In the capitation approach, an estimate is made of the *expected* costs the local agency will experience if it were to deliver some standard level of service to its local population. The section concludes with a discussion of the information needs of formula funding.

Case payments: reimbursing according to outputs

It is often perfectly feasible to quantify the outputs of a local agency, for example, in the form of the number of users who receive a specified service. Such counts form the basis of most systems of case payment. An example is schooling, where the number of pupils completing some specified program can usually be readily counted. Other services where outputs can be readily counted and audited, and therefore case payments are likely to be feasible, include much of health care, long-term social care, prisons, and housing.

The fundamental objectives of case payment methods are (a) to encourage local agencies to increase the number of service users and (b) to implement efficiency improvements so as to reduce unit costs. Case payment methods are therefore often strongly aligned with performance budgeting when the payer's objectives are to stimulate the volume of outputs and to increase technical efficiency.

The usual approach to case payment is to reimburse according to some measure of the expected expenditure on a service user. For example, the case payment might be based on an estimate of the national average cost per case, perhaps with some reduction for assumed efficiency gains. Or it might be based on (say) the lower 25 percentile of costs, assuming these represent a challenging but feasible cost target for the majority of service providers. Any surplus of the case payment over the local cost is usually retained by the agency.

When users are reasonably homogeneous, such as university students, it may be feasible to use a single case payment for all users. However, for most services, a fundamental challenge with case payment methods is that service users are often not homogeneous. For example, in health care, it is clearly the case that the expected expenditure on a patient requiring an appendectomy is much in excess of that on a patient requiring treatment for minor abrasions. If such variations in spending needs exist and a case payment system does not reimburse providers fairly for the costs of more intensive users, providers may seek to "cream-skim" only low-cost users. More intensive users may then find it difficult to secure access to services because their expected costs exceed reimbursement levels. For example, if reimbursed at a flat rate per pupil, schools might seek to recruit only pupils who have a high probability of completing their studies without undue difficulty, and to deter pupils with higher perceived probabilities of failure or other complications.

The potential for cream-skimming has led to the development of the methods of "risk adjustment," which seek to vary payments according to the dependency of users. The most celebrated of such schemes is the system of "diagnosis related groups" (DRGs) used in many health systems, under which the case payment varies according to the diagnosis of the patient (Fetter et al., 1980; Fetter, 1991) (see Box 15.1). DRG payment systems are now used in most mature health systems (Langenbrunner et al., 2005). They are demanding to design, and introduce potentially costly data recording and audit requirements to ensure that providers

Box 15.1 Diagnosis related groups in health care

The longest-standing and most celebrated of case payment mechanisms in health care is the system of diagnosis related groups (DRGs) introduced in 1983 as the basis for reimbursing providers under the US Medicare system. It led to manifest cost savings and efficiency improvements compared to the previous "fee-for-service" reimbursement system (Fetter, 1991). Medicare's DRG system was the starting point for other DRG systems inside the US. It also secured great international interest, and health systems throughout the developed world have adopted their own versions of the DRG payment mechanism (Busse et al., 2006).

The first purpose of DRGs is to offer an accurate assessment of the costs of treating a given patient, in the light of observable and measurable patient characteristics, especially the diagnosis—but, to a varying degree, also the interventions chosen. Indeed, the antecedents of today's DRG systems were developed as a method of adjusting the performance of providers for the different mixes of patients they treat rather than a mechanism for reimbursing providers (Fetter et al., 1980).

In this role, the main challenge is a technical one of ensuring that the risk adjustment process is unbiased and accurate. This requires careful decisions on the design of the DRG system, such as the hierarchy and algorithms used to classify patients into a limited number of groups. In principle, patients within one group should have homogeneous costs. Moreover, cases allocated to one group should form a clinically distinguishable entity based on main diagnosis, severity, co-morbidity, and/or treatment performed. But what exactly is homogeneous? When are costs and/or clinical diagnoses so different that a group should be split? In practice, most DRG-type systems use several hundred different categories of patient, based on criteria such as clinical diagnosis, procedures undertaken, length of hospital stay, and age.

However, the role of DRGs as a payment mechanism is not only to reimburse providers fairly for the work they undertake, but also to encourage efficient delivery and discourage the provision of unnecessary services. This requires carefully balanced incentives as well as a methodologically sound system. The sorts of incentives a DRG-type system introduces include:

- encouraging treatment of patients whose expected costs are lower than the associated reimbursement. This might be beneficial (if those patients will benefit from treatment) or adverse (if the benefits are questionable)
- discouraging treatment of patients whose expected costs are higher than the associated reimbursement (so-called "dumping" of high-dependency patients)
- encouraging more coding of complications ("upcoding") if this leads to an upgrading in the severity of DRG, and therefore increased reimbursement
- encouraging more intensive treatment of patients if such treatment leads to an upgrading in the severity of DRG, and therefore increased reimbursement (but only if the increase in reimbursement exceeds the increased costs of treatment)
- within a treatment group, the payment mechanism gives a strong incentive to minimize costs, or to shift the costs of treatment onto other parties (such as the user or a social care agency)
- on their own, pure case payments offer no incentive to maintain quality of care (indeed there may be strong incentives for "quality skimping").

Therefore, in addition to quantifying the associated efficiency improvements, any evaluation of a DRG-type system should examine the extent to which low-risk patients are favored at the expense of high-risk patients ("cream-skimming"), unnecessary treatment is provided (for example, supplier-induced demand), data manipulation or fraud occurs, or the quality of care is compromised. Many of the continuing design challenges reflect attempts to address these concerns (Schreyögg et al., 2006).

record the diagnosis accurately. However, they are needed in order to reimburse providers fairly and avoid widespread cream-skimming. Analogous systems are needed in schooling when the abilities of pupils (and therefore their expenditure needs) show marked variations.

There may be considerable variation in patient costs even within a DRG, so there may still be an incentive to cream-skim within the group. Generally, the local provider always has a clearer picture of the likely costs of a specific user than the central payer. This information asymmetry between payer and provider leads to pressures to define a finer gradation of user types, for example, by increasing the number of DRGs. However (even if this is technically feasible), as the gradation becomes finer, so the payment becomes closer to reimbursing providers according to actual costs. The incentive to reduce costs becomes diluted. There is therefore a fine balance to be struck between the coarseness of the case payment categories, the incentives for cost-reduction, and the incentives for cream-skimming.

Under case payments, local organizations usually have an incentive to reduce unit costs, subject to satisfying the payer's quality requirements. Yet they also have an incentive to ensure that they secure the maximum possible case payment for each service user. Where risk adjustment is used, it is often the case that the level of case payment depends to some extent on the type of service delivered. This may encourage providers to "gold-plate" services in order to secure a higher case payment (where the extra case payment outweighs the additional costs of service delivery).

For example, under many DRG systems, a patient's case payment category may increase if there are "complications" associated with the treatment, in some cases offering physicians an incentive to over-treat patients in order to secure a higher DRG payment. The phenomenon of "DRG creep" has been a source of widespread concern in health care. Even if provider treatment patterns do not change, the DRG system offers incentives to ensure that all possible indicators of case severity are properly recorded, and software packages have been developed to help medical coders maximize DRG revenue, giving rise to the phenomenon known as "upcoding."

Case payment systems are especially prevalent where users have the freedom to choose their provider. They effectively enable the payer to offer the user a voucher for the service in question, which the user is free to spend on approved providers (Steuerle et al., 2000). The voucher will usually be for a fixed payment for a specified service. Therefore, use of vouchers requires a clear assessment of the needs of the user and the services to which the user is entitled. This might be quite straightforward in (say) education, where there pupils are reasonably homogeneous. However, it becomes much more problematic in (say) health care, where the professional assessing patient needs may be the same professional delivering the service. A particularly interesting example of user needs assessment is found in English social care, where some local governments are experimenting with offering individualized vouchers to adults requiring long-term care on the basis of a periodic independent "needs assessment" (Commission for Social Care Inspection, 2004).

Case payment methods rely fundamentally on the local quantification of the volume of outputs, in the form of the number of service users and (where appropriate) their risk characteristics. Payers should always be alert to the dangers of reliance on counts of service users as the basis for reimbursement for a number of reasons, such as:

- the counts often rely on the local organization's own information sources and so may be vulnerable to fraud and difficult to verify
- using the actual number of service users as a basis for reimbursement may encourage the local organization to stimulate demand for services rather than invest in preventative measures or otherwise manage local demand
- the payer does not know in advance the total number of service users, and so may not be able to control aggregate expenditure satisfactorily.

The use of case payments therefore generates fundamental requirements to check on the validity of the local data, and the appropriateness of the services being delivered. Such audit requirements will in some circumstances be costly and administratively demanding.

Furthermore, although encouraging increases in outputs, case payment methods rarely consider the ultimate outcomes to service users, and local agencies therefore often have an incentive to stint on quality if the payer places no quality constraints on them. For example, further education colleges in England were for a while reimbursed according to numbers of students enrolled in courses. Without countervailing quality controls, this created an incentive to enroll students in courses without regard to their suitability or probability of success, and led to high student dropout rates and a clearly inefficient outcome. Subsequent reforms therefore based case payments on the numbers of students completing their courses of study (Learning and Skills Council, 2004).

Thus, although in many respects consistent with the principles of performance budgeting, case payment methods can give rise to important unintended consequences. The issue of incentives under formula funding, and how they might be aligned with performance budgeting, are discussed further below.

Capitation funding: reimbursement according to expected activity

Case payment methods reimburse local agencies according to actual output. In contrast, capitation methods seek to estimate an agency's expected level of output, and to reimburse accordingly. In contrast to case payments, which are attached only to service users, a capitation payment is attached to every member of the population "at risk." So, for example, an annual case payment of $400 might be attached to each user of a day center for older people. The service provider's revenue is then the number of users multiplied by $400. However, if the probability of a member of the "at risk" older population requiring the service is only 0.15, then the equivalent capitation payment would be $\$400 \times 0.15 = \$60$. The service provider's revenue would then be the size of the entire "at risk" older population multiplied by $60. The revenue would of course be the same under both payment mechanisms if 15 percent of the local older population did in fact use the service. This highlights the key difference between case payment and capitation methods: under the latter, the local agency almost always has an incentive to reduce demand for its services, as it receives the same revenue regardless of output, while under the former the incentive will often be to stimulate demand.

The reduction in output associated with capitation may in some circumstances be desired. For example, if the output of the fire service is measured in numbers of fires attended, it would clearly be perverse to use case payment methods, and thereby stimulate demand for fire-fighting. Properly designed fixed budgets, in the form of capitation payments, are more likely to stimulate preventative measures, and a desired reduction in demand for fire-fighting. Similar arguments are likely to be relevant to other public protection services, such as public health and policing.

However, the objective of capitation systems is usually to reimburse local agencies for variations in needs, and not to encourage efficiency among local agencies. For the reasons set out above, addressing equity issues has often been a higher priority among national payers than funding results. Capitation methods are well aligned with such needs equalization. However, although, properly designed, they may give a local agency the means to deliver the payer's desired levels of output, on their own they offer no incentive to reach that level. They are therefore often in conflict with the objectives of performance budgeting when results are measured in terms of volume of services, and so should be deployed with caution.

Under capitation, the most rudimentary formula for paying the locality is to reimburse an equal amount per head of population, without regard to variations in the personal characteristics of that population. This approach can be justified when differences in expected service use between citizens in different social circumstances are not substantial, or when the local agencies in receipt of funds have only small differences in socio-demographic profile. It may also be justified if there is no further information with which to refine payments. However, simple capitation methods are manifestly crude, and will not satisfy the payer's efficiency objectives when there are substantial differences between the expected service use of different types of citizen.

A modest refinement to the crude capitation payment may be to confine the population "at risk" to any obvious demographic stratum from which service users will be drawn. For example, school financing is clearly better distributed according to the estimated number of children than the total population. An example of such simple stratified capitation funding is the formula for social services for older people in England (Office of the Deputy Prime Minister, 2003). In 2003, this formula implied an expected expenditure requirement of £337.77 for each person over 65.

However, capitation payments are often further adjusted to account for more subtle variations in expected spending needs, using the principles of risk adjustment discussed under case payments. For example, the expected expenditure requirement of a person for personal social services is known to increase with age, so the estimates of expected expenditure needs should therefore be disaggregated by age. The above social services example was refined using an age adjustment that implies a capitation payment of £158.62 for people aged 65–74, £482.97 for people aged 75–84, and £1,252.54 for people aged over 84. This sort of risk adjustment amends the capitation payment attached to an individual according to certain measured characteristics of the population.

In principle, numerous approaches to risk adjustment can be envisaged, ranging from such rudimentary age adjustments, to the extraordinarily ambitious schemes found in some health care systems (Rice and Smith, 2001a). As new risk adjusters are added, so the capitation payments can be presented in the form of a contingency table. A particularly comprehensive example is a matrix of capitation payments developed for Stockholm health care. This took advantage of a comprehensive register of Swedish citizens that records both personal characteristics and health care utilization in some detail.

In such circumstances, the number of potential capitation payments to be estimated could in principle be very large—for example, with age (two groups), sex (two), social class (five), employment status (three), housing tenure (two), and marital status (two), the number of distinct capitation payments to be estimated might in principle be $8 \times 2 \times 5 \times 3 \times 2 \times 2 = 2{,}160$. Under these circumstances, an important challenge is to reduce the potentially massive matrix of capitation payments to manageable proportions, by minimizing the number of risk adjusters used and amalgamating cells of the matrix wherever possible (Andersson et al., 2000). The abridged matrix of capitation payments recommended for Stockholm acute care, giving estimates of the expected monthly expenditure on health care, is summarized in Table 15.1.

Table 15.1 The abridged Stockholm capitation matrix for medical and surgical health care, 1994 (Swedish krona per month)

Age	*Owner occupier*		*Rented*
<1		7,200[a]	
1–24	1,900		2,100
Higher non-manual	3,100		3,600
Other non-manual	3,700		4,300
Manual	4,000		4,400
Not employed	5,300		6,400
Higher non-manual	3,600		3,900
Other non-manual	3,600		4,200
Manual	3,900		4,600
Not employed	5,100		5,400
Cohabiting	13,500		16,500
Living alone	15,400		18,200
Cohabiting	27,600		29,800
Living alone	24,200		29,400

[a] Same level of payment irrespective of owner/rented status.

Source: Diderichsen et al. (1997).

Capitation methods promote aggregate cost control and address equity concerns. However, they offer no incentive to increase outputs, and share many of the weaknesses of case payment methods, such as a lack of attention to the quality of outcomes. The principal reason they might prove attractive to payers from a performance budgeting perspective are (a) they may encourage appropriate preventative measures for services where this is an important objective of the payer, (b) they remove the incentive for supplier induced demand, where this is a problem under case payment, and (c) they reduce reliance on output data provided by local providers, and therefore avoid the incentives for manipulation and fraud discussed above. The issue of data under both types of funding mechanism is now briefly discussed further.

Data considerations

Fundamental to any type of formula funding is the information to be used as the basis for reimbursing local organizations. It is very rare to have available independent "engineering" evidence of what levels of reimbursement each devolved entity should receive. Instead, in order to infer optimal reimbursement levels, payers are highly dependent on historical expenditure patterns among the intended recipients of funds. The reliance on past spending as a basis for current funding can give rise to profound philosophical and practical difficulties for the payer.

These difficulties can be illustrated in their most extreme form when the payer bases reimbursement to each organization solely on the historical spending of that organization—for example, by basing the organization's current budget on expenditure last year. Such budget-setting rules are endemic within many bureaucracies, and were also a central feature of the Soviet planning system, which tended to set production levels and budgets "from the achieved level" (Nove, 1980). They lead to many adverse consequences, and contain few incentives for efficiency or effectiveness.

As a result, payers have sought out funding mechanisms that reduce the reliance on an organization's own past expenditure in setting its future budgets, and instead rely on some form of statistical analysis of general patterns of expenditure among all (or at least a substantial proportion) of the public service organizations that will be in receipt of the payer's funds. This section summarizes the main considerations that arise when relying on such empirical data as the basis for formula funding.

In the first instance, case payment methods require a reliable count of the number of service users. This can be straightforward, as in school education, or highly contested, as, for example, in a count of people in "need" of sheltered housing accommodation. A prerequisite for satisfactory case payment methods is a clear statement by the payer of the national criteria that entitle a user to secure access to the service, in order to yield the required measure of output. In contrast, capitation methods can allow an element of local discretion on entitlement. The difficulty and reliability of specifying entitlement and counting the numbers of service users will often be an important determinant of whether case payment or capitation methods are preferred.

Capitation methods require a verifiable count of population, disaggregated where necessary into demographic groups. Although the population count used in a capitation system is often uncontentious, it can give rise to difficulties when it relies on local reporting, as there are obvious incentives for local organizations to maximize the population on which their revenues are based. For example, for many years UK general medical practitioners received a large part of their income on the basis of unreliable estimates of the size of the population registered with the practice. There was widespread acknowledgment that the registered population sizes were inflated to very different extents in different practices, arising from factors such as delay in removing patients from the register when they died or changed provider, transient populations, and fraud (Ashworth et al., 2005).

Although counts of the number of service users or the "at risk" population can be problematic, it is usually the risk adjustment process that leads to most technical debate, and where the analysis of past expenditure patterns comes into play. Key issues are the choice of characteristics to include as "risk adjusters," and the relative weight to attach to each factor. Different technical choices can lead to major changes in payment rates, and there is often little methodological guidance for those seeking to design risk adjustment schemes.

It is important to note that in many circumstances the range of satisfactory data available for risk adjustment purposes may be highly circumscribed. The first criterion in the design of risk adjustment will therefore always be feasibility. For example, some obvious risk adjusters in health care would be measures of chronic health status. However, these can rarely be reliably collected at reasonable cost, although some imaginative schemes have been tested, such as the use of routine prescribing data as a proxy for some chronic health condition (Fishman and Shay, 1999).

Even where potentially useful data do exist, there is frequently tension in the design of formulas between a desire to model expected expenditure accurately, and a desire to avoid perverse incentives. For example, in health care the best predictor of an individual's current health care expenditure is his/her previous history of expenditure and utilization, and such variables are often used in systems of competitive health insurance in order to model individual expenditure accurately (and so reduce the incentive for insurers to cream-skim only healthy patients) (Van de Ven and Ellis, 2000). However, policy-makers in other countries have sought to avoid the use of such data in the design of health service formulae, on the grounds that they may offer a perverse incentive for providers to increase provision in order to secure an increased capitation payment for the individual in the future.

Any proposed risk adjuster must be reliably and consistently recorded across all recipients of funds. There will often be a need for a strong audit function to reassure all localities that payments are fair. A suggestion that some localities are manipulating information may be seriously corrosive. For this reason, a payer may often feel unable to use some otherwise suitable metrics as risk adjusters because they cannot be satisfactorily verified. This is an important reason for the use in many funding mechanisms of area-wide data, such as those collected from periodic censuses of population, which obviates reliance on data provided by local agencies. Fraud is an ever-present danger when funding systems are based on data provided by the recipients of funds and has been a persistent concern in the US Medicare scheme (Becker et al., 2005). A fundamental constraint hampering many analytic endeavors is the extent to which the scope for misrepresentation may rule out the use of certain types of risk adjustment.

Risk adjusters should be plausible, in the sense of being manifest drivers of expenditure. But the payer will wish to use only factors that are *legitimate* drivers of expenditure, and will seek to avoid use of illegitimate factors (Rice and Smith, 2001a). Loosely speaking, legitimate drivers of expenditure are influences on the costs of delivering the required service that lie entirely outside the control of local organizations, and so can be used as risk adjusters. Examples might be local input prices and some (but not necessarily all) user characteristics. Illegitimate drivers of expenditure are influences on costs function that arise from the organizations' own policy choices, and so should not be used as risk adjusters.

A persistent theme in the literature is the tension between parsimony in the use of data and the need to model spending needs sensitively. Generally speaking, many payers prefer simple funding mechanisms as they can be more readily understood and therefore promote accountability. However, there will often be an element of rough justice in a simple funding formula, so those local organizations that feel they are adversely affected by the choice of a simple mechanism will press for "refinement," in the form of an increased number of risk adjusters and added complexity. Balancing simplicity and sensitivity of the funding mechanism is a key role for the payer.

One final issue of great importance relates to the variation in expenditure that is not captured by the chosen funding model. Even on those rare occasions when the statistical methodology explains a high proportion of individual variation in expenditure, a considerable element of unexplained variation often remains. The unexplained variation can be ascribed to two broad sources: omitted explanatory variables and random fluctuation. Clearly, given the paucity of data available, there is an ever-present danger of variable omission, especially as some important but illegitimate determinants of expenditure (such as variations in teacher effectiveness in education) may have to be omitted from the funding model.

However, it is also important to recognize that there is a large element of unpredictable variation in the use of many public services (most notably health care) that will always defy systematic modeling. This is particularly true under capitation, when both the probability of using a service and the expected costs of that use are subject to large random variation. For example, although an average health care capitation payment of (say) £550 per annum may be assigned to a male aged 40–44, it would be absurd to expect every such individual to require that level of expenditure *per annum*. Rather, the capitation payment offers an *expected* level of expenditure, around which there might exist substantial variation.

In summary, numerous criteria for selecting risk adjustment characteristics have been indicated. For example, they should:

- be feasible, with low administrative cost
- be consistently, reliably, verifiably, and universally recorded
- not be vulnerable to manipulation or fraud
- be legitimate predictors of expected public service expenditure
- encourage efficient delivery of public services, and be free from perverse incentives

- respect confidentiality requirements
- be parsimonious and plausible, thereby promoting transparency and accountability.

In practice, this often severely limits the choice of variables, as in many contexts only very restricted information on the characteristics of individuals or areas exists that conforms to such criteria.

Incentives under formula funding

It is important to note that funding formulas are more than reimbursement mechanisms. The previous sections imply the existence of some very strong incentives for the recipient of funds that are inherent in pure formula funding systems. Under case payments these include:

- increasing activity
- cream-skimming
- cost containment and increasing technical efficiency
- skimping on service quality
- upcoding
- manipulating data.

Under capitation they include:

- reducing outputs
- preventative measures and reducing demand for services
- encouraging low effort and technical inefficiency
- skimping on service quality.

Some of these are intended and virtuous, and serve to promote the payer's performance objectives. Others are unintended and adverse, and may thwart such objectives. The payer will therefore wish to reinforce the intended incentives and abate the adverse responses.

To some extent this can be achieved by adjusting the payment mechanism. Possibilities include refining the risk adjustment mechanism (to reduce the gains from cream-skimming) and using mixed payment systems (to moderate the stark activity incentives inherent in the pure systems). For example, if a capitation system of fixed budgets is inducing local agencies to underprovide certain services, this might be addressed by augmenting the fixed budgets with a certain element of case payment. If a pure case payment system is inhibiting access for some high-needs service users, then it might be augmented by a degree of cost sharing between payer and locality if the expenditure on a particular user exceeds some threshold. Such blended mechanisms are far more likely to be effective if specified explicitly ex ante, by means of a formula, than if addressed arbitrarily on a case-by-case basis.

However, the payer will usually also have to augment any payment mechanism with other regulatory instruments in order to ensure that desired outcomes are secured. In short, although a well-designed payment mechanism is a necessary condition for securing the payer's objectives, it is not on its own sufficient. In the context of this chapter, formula funding must be viewed not in isolation, but within the context of the entire system of performance budgeting. This section summarizes some of the more important tools for ensuring the payment mechanism works as intended.

Under either funding method, but especially capitation, there is no direct incentive for local organizations to deliver services to any standard. There is therefore a fundamental need for the payer to put in place mechanisms to ensure that services are delivered at the required level and quality. These mechanisms might take a number of forms. For example, a frequently used but costly regulatory instrument is to undertake periodic inspection of local services. This is especially important for provider organizations, and is routinely found in schooling and health care, where it is often the case that only accredited organizations are permitted to provide public services.

Performance measurement is another widely used instrument for ensuring service standards. By collecting and disseminating data on issues such as unit costs, access to services, activities, and outcomes, payers can compare organizations, identify those where performance is anomalous, and put in place corrective action. Such data can often form the basis for managerial incentives and concerted organizational improvement efforts.

Many payers are experimenting specifically with *public* reporting of local performance data. Here the intention is to help citizens (as taxpayers) to hold their local services to account, often via the media. Performance reporting is therefore likely to be especially effective where strong local democratic procedures are in place. However, its effectiveness depends heavily on the precise mode of dissemination. For example, researchers in health care have found low impact of public dissemination of performance data where little attention is paid to how the data are presented to the public or their representatives (Mannion and Goddard, 2001). In contrast, aggregating a local organization's performance data into a "star rating," with extensive media coverage, has been highly influential in attracting public attention to NHS performance in England (Smith, 2002). The appropriate means of disseminating performance data to managers, the media, the public, and local governing boards is a promising area for future research.

Another mechanism for stimulating performance improvement is to offer public service users a choice of services within a local market of providers. The success of this approach depends heavily on ensuring real competition between providers, and giving users the means to make an informed choice. Performance data should therefore also play a central role in the implementation of formula funding. Citizens as service users are likely to require more detailed information than citizens as taxpayers, the nature and effectiveness of which is also an important research issue (Hibbard et al., 2003). It is noteworthy that such market systems must usually rely, at least in part, on some sort of case payment mechanism for reimbursing providers.

The ultimate logic of the principle of provider choice is to offer users a voucher for the service to which they are entitled that can be used with any accredited provider. Systems such as DRG payments in health care and pupil case payments in schooling effectively become voucher systems when the user has a degree of choice over the provider. Important policy choices for the payer are then the range of providers from which a user may choose, and the extent to which users are able to "top up" the case payment with their own private payment if the provider charges a fee in excess of the case payment. Formula funding has a fundamental role to play in voucher systems in setting the level of reimbursement for the provider.

User choice can also be applied to local purchasers as well as providers. For example, a number of health care systems, such as Belgium, Germany, Israel, the Netherlands, and Switzerland, offer citizens a choice of social health insurers (Saltman et al., 2004). In the UK, the system of general practitioner fundholding offered patients some choice of GP purchasers (Glennerster et al., 1994). In these systems, the use of a capitation payment (as a pseudo insurance premium) becomes the main funding mechanism, and securing an adequate funding formula to set the level of this "premium" becomes a key determinant of the success of the policy.

Implementing managerial incentives alongside formula funding is one of the most effective approaches to correcting some of the adverse organizational incentives inherent in payment mechanisms. Managerial incentives can take many forms other than direct financial rewards, such as increased autonomy and personal advancement. For example, the systems of organizational ratings used in much of the English public sector (such as the NHS performance ratings and local government comprehensive performance assessments) are directed mainly at the prestige and career prospects of senior management (Smith, 2002). They have undoubtedly been successful in focusing the attention of managers on the national government's performance priorities, although of course poorly designed managerial incentives can in turn produce their own unintended consequences (Smith, 1995).

Moreover, it is possible to incorporate quality standards directly into the payment mechanism (Smith and York, 2004). Carefully designed, this is likely to be fruitful when paying providers, especially when a local provider market is operating. However, to make financial allocations to local purchasers conditional on performance risks exposing citizens to a double jeopardy—in one period they could experience poor-quality services, and as a consequence their local administration would secure lower budgets in a future period. This is likely to be inefficient, and to offend most concepts of natural justice. Rather, it is likely that the most promising innovations would be to direct rewards (and sanctions) for organizational performance at the managers of such organizations.

Finally, a central theme of this chapter has been the key role that information plays in all funding mechanisms, both to serve as a basis for calculating funding levels and as a means of checking on performance standards. More generally it is a crucial input into activities as diverse as inspection, user decisions and setting managerial rewards. Much of the information on which the public services rely emanates from the services themselves, and there is a clear danger that data will become corrupted as the stakes attached to them increase. Any threat to the perceived probity of the public services risks undermining confidence in those services, and popular support for them. Therefore, a key role for the payer is to decide on the nature and scope of independent data audit needed to counter any incentives for manipulation.

This section has sketched in only the briefest outline some of the additional mechanisms a payer may need to implement alongside formula funding in order to reinforce desired behavior and address perverse incentives. A full treatment is beyond the scope of this chapter. Rather, the intention has been to alert the policy-maker of the need to consider how formula funding fits into the whole system of performance budgeting. Most of the initiatives, such as inspection, performance reporting, user choice, provider markets, and managerial incentives, are means of correcting the natural tendency of funding mechanisms to reduce service standards or (in the case of capitation) to ignore technical efficiency considerations. The payer has a formidable challenge in ensuring they fit together into a coherent design for the whole public service system.

Conclusions

The central objective of performance budgeting is to align the funding of public agencies with the results they achieve. Formula funding is a key instrument within many public sectors, and this chapter has examined the extent to which it can promote or hinder the implementation of performance budgeting.

Any funding mechanism must give local agencies both the means and the incentives to deliver the payer's objectives if it is to promote the objectives of performance budgeting. Hitherto, most formula funding systems have emphasized the first role, often seeking to give local agencies the resources needed to deliver some standard level of service. In contrast, relatively few payers have paid much attention to whether the incentives for local agencies implicit in formula funding are aligned with their performance objectives.

The chapter has identified two broad types of formula funding mechanism: case payments and capitation payments. Case payment systems generally give local agencies the incentive to increase output and efficiency, which in many circumstances will be a central objective of the payer. Therefore, they will in important respects often be strongly aligned with the principles of performance budgeting. However, I have also drawn attention to some of the potential weaknesses of case payment methods, most notably the risks of cream-skimming, and the challenges in addressing those weaknesses.

Capitation methods generally emphasize the "fair funding" principle of giving the local agency the means to deliver some standard of service, with few if any direct incentives to secure the desired results. They are in general therefore less well aligned with performance budgeting. However, they may be appropriate when the services in question are mainly preventative in nature (crime, public health, fire). They are also often less demanding of administrative data and audit requirements than case payment methods. Because of the stark incentives inherent in pure case payment and capitation systems, it may be the case that some blend of the two mechanisms may be appropriate for many systems of performance budgeting.

Moreover, neither approach addresses the issue of service quality at all securely, mirroring the preoccupation in many performance budgeting systems with outputs rather than outcomes. The ultimate objective of performance budgeting should be to move towards an outcomes-based concept of performance, so the logic should be that formula funding systems should focus on outcomes, in the form of the quality of outputs. In this respect, there are some interesting developments in health care, where the "payment for results" movement has assumed increasing importance, particularly in the United States (Casalino et al., 2003). The notion of making case payments wholly or partially contingent on outcomes has also made some headway in education services (Ross and Levacic, 1999).

The chapter indicates that formula funding has an important role to play in making operational the principles of performance budgeting. It has nevertheless concluded that funding mechanisms cannot on their own secure all the objectives of performance budgeting. There will always be a need to align other performance budgeting instruments with formula funding mechanisms if they are to be effective. Examples include policies on regulation, provider markets, performance reporting, and good-practice guidelines. However, if these instruments are deployed carefully, and are made to articulate with each other, they offer the potential for enormous gains in the performance of public services.

Note

1. The author would like to thank the participants at the IMF seminar, and especially Marc Robinson, for perceptive and constructive comments on earlier drafts. This chapter draws on my forthcoming book *Formula Funding of Public Services* to be published by Routledge. Preparation of the book was funded by UK Economic and Social Research Council fellowship R000271253.

References

Andersson, P., E. Varde, and F. Diderichsen, 2000, "Modelling of Resource Allocation to Health Care Authorities in Stockholm County," *Health Care Management Science*, Vol. 3(2), pp. 141–50.

Ashworth, M., M. Jenkins, K. Burgess, H. Keynes, M. Wallace, D. Roberts, and A. Majeed, 2005, "Which General Practices have Higher List Inflation? An Exploratory Study," *Family Practice*, Vol. 22(5), pp. 529–31.

Becker, D., D. Kessler, and M. McClellan, 2005, "Detecting Medicare Abuse," *Journal of Health Economics*, Vol. 24(1), pp. 189–210.

Busse, R., J. Schreyögg, and P. Smith, 2006, "Special Issue on Hospital Case Payment Systems in Europe," *Health Care Management Science*, Vol. 9(3).

Casalino, L., R. Gillies, S. Shortell, J. Schmittdiel, T. Bodenheimer, J. Robinson, T. Rundall, N. Oswald, H. Schauffler, and M. Wang, 2003, "External Incentives, Information Technology, and Organized Processes to Improve Health Care Quality for Patients with Chronic Diseases," *Journal of the American Medical Association*, Vol. 289(4), pp. 434–41.

Commission for Social Care Inspection, 2004, *Direct Payments: What are the Barriers?* (London: Commission for Social Care Inspection).

Diderichsen, F., E. Varde, and M. Whitehead, 1997, "Resource Allocation to Health Authorities: The Quest for an Equitable Formula in Britain and Sweden," *British Medical Journal*, Vol. 315, pp. 875–8.

Fetter, R., 1991, "Diagnosis Related Groups: Understanding Hospital Performance," *Interfaces*, Vol. 21(1), pp. 6–26.

Fetter, R., Y. Shin, J. Freeman, R. Averill, and J. Thompson, 1980, "Case Mix Definition by Diagnosis-Related Groups," *Medical Care*, Vol. 18(2), pp. 1–53.

Fishman, P.A., and D.K. Shay, 1999, "Development and Estimation of a Pediatric Chronic Disease Score Using Automated Pharmacy Data," *Medical Care*, Vol. 37, pp. 874–83.

Gibson, J., 1998, "Political Manipulation or Feedback in English Local Authorities' Standard Spending Assessments? The Case of the Abolition of the Inner London Education Authority," *Public Administration*, Vol. 76(4), pp. 629–47.

Glennerster, H., J. Hills, and T. Travers, 2000, *Paying for Health, Education, and Housing: How Does the Centre Pull the Purse Strings?* (Oxford: Oxford University Press).

Glennerster, H., M. Matsaganis, and P. Owens, 1994, *Implementing GP Fundholding: Wild Card or Winning Hand?* (Buckingham: Open University Press).

Hibbard, J., J. Stockard, and M. Tusler, 2003, "Does Publicizing Hospital Performance Stimulate Quality Improvement Efforts?" *Health Affairs*, Vol. 22(3), pp. 84–94.

John, P., and H. Ward, 2001, "Political Manipulation in a Majoritarian Democracy: Central Government Target of Public Funds to English Subnational Government, in Space and Across Time," *British Journal of Politics and International Relations*, Vol. 3(3), pp. 308–39.

Langenbrunner, J., E. Orosz, J. Kutzin, and M. Wiley, 2005, "Purchasing and Paying Providers," in *Purchasing to Improve Health Systems Performance*, ed. J. Figueras, R. Robinson, and E. Jakubowski (Maidenhead: Open University Press).

Learning and Skills Council, 2004, *Funding Guidance for Further Education in 2004–05* (Coventry: Learning and Skills Council).

Louis, T., T. Jabine, and M. Gerstein (eds.), 2003, *Statistical Issues in Allocating Funds by Formula: Panel on Formula Allocations* (Washington: National Academies Press).

Mannion, R., and M. Goddard, 2001, "Impact of Published Clinical Outcomes Data: Case Study in NHS Hospital Trusts," *British Medical Journal*, Vol. 323, pp. 260–3.

McLean, I., 2005, *The Fiscal Crisis of the United Kingdom* (Basingstoke: Palgrave Macmillan).

Nove, A., 1980, *The Soviet Economic System*, second edition (London: Allen and Unwin).

Office of the Deputy Prime Minister, 2003, *Local Government Finance Report 2003/04* (London: Office of the Deputy Prime Minister).

Osborne, D., and T. Gaebler, 1992, *Reinventing Government: How the Entrepreneurial Spirit is Transforming the Public Sector* (New York: Penguin Books).

Rice, N., and P. Smith, 2001a, "Capitation and Risk Adjustment in Health Care Financing: An International Progress Report," *Milbank Quarterly*, Vol. 79(1), pp. 81–113.

——, 2001b, "Ethics and Geographical Equity in Health Care," *Journal of Medical Ethics*, Vol. 27(4), pp. 256–61.

Ross, K., and R. Levacic (eds.), 1999, *Needs-based Resource Allocation in Education: Via Formula Funding of Schools* (Paris: UNESCO).

Saltman, R., R. Busse, and J. Figueras (eds.), 2004, *Social Health Insurance Systems in Western Europe* (Maidenhead: Open University Press).

Schreyögg, J., T. Stargardt, O. Tiemann, and R. Busse, 2006, "Methods to Determine Reimbursement Rates for Diagnosis Related Groups (DRG): A Comparison of Nine European Countries," *Health Care Management Science*, Vol. 9(3).

Smith, P., 1995, "On the Unintended Consequences of Publishing Performance Data in the Public Sector," *International Journal of Public Administration*, Vol. 18(2/3), pp. 277–310.

——, 2002, "Performance Management in British Health Care: Will it Deliver?" *Health Affairs*, Vol. 21(3), pp. 103–15.

——, 2003, "Formula Funding of Public Services: An Economic Analysis," *Oxford Review of Economic Policy*, Vol. 19(2), pp. 301–22.

Smith, P., 2006, *Formula Funding of Public Services* (London: Routledge).

Smith, P., and N. York, 2004, "Quality Incentives: The Case of UK General Practitioners," *Health Affairs*, Vol. 23, p. 112.

Steuerle, C., V. Ooms, G. Peterson, and R. Reischauer (eds.), 2000, *Vouchers and the Provision of Public Services* (Washington: Brookings Institution).

Van de Ven, W.P.M.M., and R. Ellis, 2000, "Risk Adjustment in Competitive Health Plan Markets," in *Handbook of Health Economics*, ed. J.P. Newhouse and A.J. Culyer (Amsterdam: Elsevier).

16
Purchaser-Provider Systems

Marc Robinson

This chapter considers the scope for applying the purchaser-provider (henceforth "PP") principle as a performance budgeting technique. It builds upon the previous chapter on formula funding systems, of which PP is one specific type. The chapter commences with a discussion of the properties of PP systems. It then identifies certain criteria which determine to which types of services the PP mechanism may be successfully applied. Following this is a discussion of the experiment with government-wide budgeting on a PP basis in Australia, which commenced in the late 1990s. The fourth section considers the ways in which agencies might be motivated to focus on their financial result under a PP arrangement. Conclusions then follow.

PP systems aim to simulate market transactions between arm's-length purchasers and providers (suppliers) for the supply of products at pre-specified prices. They seek to create, by these means, a particularly tight link between results and funding in order to put strong pressure on the provider agency to maximize its technical efficiency. The PP mechanism was introduced in Chapter 1 by way of a short-hand definition based on two properties:

- government pays the public sector service delivery ("provider") agency a per unit "price" for its outputs, with the agency making a profit or a loss reflecting any difference between what it is paid and the cost of producing those outputs
- the agency only receives payment for the outputs it actually delivers to the community (the principle of "payment-for-results").

This can be regarded as a good working definition, upon which most of the analysis in this chapter will be based. It should, however, be emphasized that the definition should not be construed as suggesting that the unit price need be constant irrespective of the quantity of output "purchased."[1] It requires, rather, that funding be by formula. The definition is also a little too narrow in suggesting that PP arrangements may only be used to "purchase" *outputs*, and not *outcomes*, and also in implicitly focusing only on output quantity. It is true that, for reasons which are discussed further below, it tends to be difficult to apply the PP mechanism to the funding of outcomes or output quality. There are, nevertheless, some cases where this is possible. It is convenient in the analysis below to focus on the use of PP arrangements for funding output quantity, and to then consider separately (and more briefly) the scope for paying for outcomes or output quality.

The PP mechanism is capable of substantially boosting technical efficiency when applied to at least some public services (such as the hospitals via the DRG-based case payments system outlined in the last chapter[2]). The success of the PP principle in certain sectors has generated considerable international interest in extending its application more broadly within the public sector.

The broader application of the PP principle would be a particularly useful way of realizing the performance budgeting goal of linking funding and results in order to boost public sector performance. It is therefore highly desirable to identify the types of public service in relation to which this tool may be used to positive effect. With this in mind, the main objective of this chapter is to identify key characteristics of public services which determine whether or not they are suitable candidates for the application of the PP funding mechanism. A subsidiary objective is to clarify further the nature and modus operandi of PP systems.

The essence of the PP principle is the introduction of the distinction between the price received by the provider for its output and the cost incurred in producing that output, so that the agency will make a loss if its costs of production exceed the price paid. To achieve this, the price must be set at a level which will put pressure on the agency concerned to improve its technical efficiency, the *degree* of pressure imposed being a matter of policy choice.[3]

The PP principle therefore requires that the financial result become an important management and operational objective for the provider agency.[4] A prerequisite of this is that the agency is able to measure its financial bottom line. To do this, it must adopt business accounting in the place of traditional government accounting, which treats government agencies as cost centers with no financial bottom line. Business accounting requires, first, accrual accounting, because accrual accounting is designed to produce an accounting measure of the costs of producing outputs. Second, it requires that the government's "payments" to the agency for outputs be recognized in agency accounts as *revenue*, so that the operating statement measures the difference between the payments the provider receives for delivery of outputs and its cost of production. Such an accounting treatment contrasts with usual government accounting practice, in which funding from the budget is not accounted for as agency revenue because it is more in the nature of a spending allowance than market revenue.[5]

The question arises as to how, and indeed whether, the introduction of such a "quasi-market" arrangement changes the behavior of the provider agency and motivates it to improve technical efficiency. This issue is discussed in the final section of this chapter. In the meantime, it will be assumed for analytic purposes that the provider agency does have an incentive to worry about its bottom line. More precisely, the assumption is made that the introduction of a PP arrangement transforms the agency into a *loss avoider*, although not necessarily into a profit maximizer.

When does the purchaser-provider mechanism work?

Purchaser-provider arrangements are appropriate for some types of services, but not for others. This can be clarified by considering a number of concrete examples.

The first is *veterinary services for emergency response to animal disease outbreaks*. Such a service requires the maintenance on a continuing basis of an animal control disease center, with appropriate specialist veterinary expertise capable of determining the appropriate strategy to fight an outbreak. There needs to be an associated veterinary diagnostic laboratory armed with the specialist staff and equipment to enable it to identify a wide range of unusual and unexpected diseases. Contingency and support plans need to be prepared and periodically updated, and simulation exercises and training undertaken. Research capacity capable of diagnosing hitherto unknown diseases should, at least in wealthier countries, also be maintained (Geering et al., 1999).

Although it is possible to make some peripheral day-to-day use of certain of these facilities (for example, the diagnostic laboratory), the key characteristic of such a service is that it is not maintained in order to produce outputs on a day-to-day basis. It may, in fact, remain ready to respond to emergencies for years at a time without being called into action. A PP arrangement would therefore fail to provide such a service with the funding it requires.

This is an example of a *contingent capacity service*. As defined in Chapter 4, these are services the demand for which is unpredictably variable, and for which there is an *essentiality* and *immediacy* to supply—in other words, it is considered important that when a demand for the service arises, the service be supplied promptly. As pointed out in that chapter, there are many such services maintained by government, including the armed forces and a range of emergency services. For contingent capacity services, budget funding is not about paying for outputs, but rather about paying for the maintenance of the capacity to deliver essential outputs when and if they are needed.

The second example is *investment facilitation services*, that is, the service which many governments provide to potential large-scale foreign investors in order to encourage investment and boost growth. Such a service typically covers a range of assistance such as:

- advice on and facilitation of development approvals (environmental, urban planning, health and safety, and so on)
- identification, and assistance in the assurance, of necessary infrastructure and utility services
- advice on industrial relations issues
- (in many countries) the provision of financial incentives.

The extent of assistance provided to any given potential investor will tend to be highly variable, depending on factors such as the size of the potential investment, the complexity of the regulatory issues involved, and the political importance of the specific project. The cost per potential investor assisted (that is, per unit of output) could therefore be expected to be quite variable and unpredictable, not only within each financial year, but over time.

It would clearly make no sense to finance a service such as this on a purchaser-provider basis, paying the same "price" to the government agency concerned for each project for which it provided assistance. If such an approach were adopted, an obvious response by the agency would be to reduce significantly the degree of assistance offered to the most complex and important potential projects, so as to avoid making unsustainable losses.

Investment facilitation services are an example of an output type which is highly *heterogeneous* (non-standardized). As discussed in Chapter 3, a service is heterogeneous when there is a *deliberate* variation in the amount and/or types of activities received by each client/case of the "same" service, particularly in response to differences in client or case characteristics. The consequence of heterogeneity is that the unit cost of delivering the service will vary from one client/case to another, for reasons which reflect variations in case complexity and have nothing whatsoever to do with inefficiency (see Chapter 4).

This is not an isolated example. Heterogeneity is very common among services delivered by government (and, indeed, increasingly common in the economy as a whole). Consider just one other example—*child protection services*, which refers to the protection of children who are abused or at risk of abuse. The degree and type of assistance provided to each child can and should vary enormously, depending on a range of factors such as the degree of investigation required to ascertain whether abuse is occurring, the severity of the abuse, whether it is feasible to leave the child with the parent, whether psychological treatment is necessary, and the child's geographical location. Again, paying a uniform amount per child assisted might well lead to a marked reduction in services to the children most in need of assistance.

The tendency of a PP system to result in the underservicing of more complex clients/cases is a familiar phenomenon which economists have labeled "skimping" (Allen and Gertler, 1991; Ellis, 1998). It is not, however, the only type of perverse behavior which can result from the inappropriate use of PP financing of a highly heterogeneous service. The other great danger is "cream-skimming," which refers to the deliberate avoidance by providers of complex, and therefore high-cost, clients/cases.[6]

The heterogeneity problem is, of course, in no sense specific to the public sector—consider, for example, most types of legal services. It is for precisely this reason that many private sector services are not supplied by way of contracts with pre-specified output prices, but by a range of other forms of contracting many of which involve a substantial degree of risk sharing (see, for example, Williamson, 1985). The emergence of the "service society" has seen a major shift away from the dominance of standardized mass manufacturing towards a focus on heterogeneous services and goods produced in a working environment "more artisanal than industrial" (Cohen, 2006, p. 14).

It should not, however, be assumed that *any* degree of heterogeneity rules out the use of the PP mechanism. A PP arrangement may well work if, notwithstanding complexity-related variations in cost, the *average* cost per unit of output is reasonably stable—in other words, if the additional cost of the more complex cases is offset by the lower cost of less complex cases. If this is the case, the provider agency could finance the losses on more complex cases by the profits made on less complex cases. If the provider were a loss avoider (rather than a profit maximizer) it would then be under no pressure to engage in skimping or cream-skimming. Such a "swings and roundabouts" approach to higher-cost patients on the part of hospitals is an important reason for the success of the DRG hospital payments systems, notwithstanding the degree of complexity-related variability which exists even within the DRG output categories upon which the system is based. The DRG example highlights another important point—that average cost is, other things being equal, more likely to be stable if the quantities of output for the service concerned are large,[7] as is the case for many hospital services.[8]

It follows from this that heterogeneity makes services unsuitable for the use of the PP mechanism when it is not possible to define output groups for which average cost is reasonable, stable, and predictable. This would not be true of investment facilitation services, nor probably for child protection services. A little reflection would suggest that a great many government-provided services are like this.

The other important criteria governing the scope for applying the PP mechanism is information costs. As highlighted in Chapter 4, more complex performance budgeting mechanisms such as PP are considerably more demanding of performance information. To implement a PP system, one has to develop reasonably reliable unit cost measures. Price-setting also requires relevant cost information (such as comparative cost information obtained through cost benchmarking) which can inform the purchaser's decision about just how much price pressure to impose. Such information does not come cheaply, and will only be worth obtaining if the potential savings from increased technical efficiency for the services concerned are substantial. This will tend to rule out the use of PP arrangements except in the case of services which absorb quite a large amount of government expenditure.

In summary, the PP mechanism is most suitable for relatively standardized services produced in large volumes.

Against this background, we can return to the question of PP arrangements based on outcomes and output quality. As mentioned at the outset of the chapter, PP arrangements are normally applied to outputs rather than outcomes. There are some enthusiasts who have called for the widespread application across government of outcome-based PP contracts, on the familiar grounds that it is outcomes and not outputs which are the true objective of public policy (Osborne and Gaebler, 1993, p. 139). However, this is in general impracticable because of the two key problems identified in Chapter 3:

- the uncertainty which often characterizes the relationship between funding and outcomes, due to the impact of "external factors": if the provider agency has only limited control over the outcome, an arrangement in which its core funding is outcome-based may expose it to unsustainably large random volatility in revenue
- the difficulty of measuring many outcomes, leading often to reliance on quite imperfect proxies.

Consider, for example, the practical implications of attempting to fund an investment facilitation service by the number of projects it succeeded in attracting, or of funding a hospital emergency service by the number of lives it succeeded in saving.

The impracticability of funding on the basis of outcomes is greater the higher-level the outcomes concerned, because both the attribution and measurement problems tend to be more severe. Conversely, the limited opportunities which exist to apply the PP principle to outcomes arise in respect to certain proximate outcomes which have a higher degree of controllability.[9]

By contrast, the incorporation of an explicit quality component in the payment mechanism in PP systems is an idea which is attracting growing interest in sectors such as health (Berwick et al., 2003; Salber and Bradley, 2002). The practical challenge of this is, of course, that of quality measurement. Notwithstanding the complexities of quality measurement, this is an area where, as Smith indicated in Chapter 15, progress may be expected in future.

Accrual output budgeting in Australia: a government-wide PP experiment

As outlined in Chapter 1, there were experiments in New Zealand[10] (starting in the mid-1990s) and Australia (late 1990s) which sought to apply the purchaser-provider principle to the budget system as a whole. These experiments yielded important lessons about the limitations of the PP model. What follows focuses particularly on the Australian experience. This section is based partly on extensive interviews conducted by the author with officials of both the national and certain State governments.[11]

In Australia both the national government and all but one[12] of its eight State and territorial governments attempted to implement what came to be known generically as "accrual output budgeting" (AOB). AOB was intended to transform the budget into a mechanism whereby the government would "purchase" outputs from its own agencies "at specified levels of quantity, quality and price" (VDTF, 1997, p. 11). As the then head of the Australian Finance Department put it, "the Government will know what [outputs] it is being offered and at what prices…[and] can then actively decide what it wants to buy and how much it wants to pay" (Boxall, 1998).[13] Budget funding was reconceptualized as a "price" paid to agencies for delivery of outputs, as in a simple market transaction between arm's-length purchasers and providers. It was intended that this system would place government-owned agencies and potential private suppliers of publicly financed services on an equal competitive footing, thus facilitating contestability and creating a "new competitive world" (Boxall, 1998).

Under AOB, the parliamentary budget appropriations mechanism was transformed to make the principal line of funding a "payment for outputs" appropriation based on the prices to be paid for outputs.[14] As in New Zealand,[15] there was an explicit intention to introduce into the general government sector the business distinction between the cost of production and the price at which products were sold, so that if output "costs exceed funding, agencies incur an operating deficit" (QT, 1998, p. 12). Accordingly, not only was accrual accounting introduced, but the payments for outputs received by ministries from the government were recognized as revenue in their accounts, giving government ministries for the first time a bottom-line profit/loss measure.

As in any purchaser-provider system, it was intended that the price paid for outputs would be set so as to impose pressure on agencies to improve their technical efficiency. The explicitly stated intention in all jurisdictions[16] was that, after an initial period where for practical reasons the "price" would be based upon cost, there would be a rapid transition to a position where output prices would be set on the basis of what might be called the *efficient* cost of production, which would be measured by cost benchmarking or by market price references. As the Australian finance department put it, "departmental output appropriations will progressively be based on market (or benchmark) prices, rather than accrual based input costs" (DOFA, 1999, p. 27). This would mean that if an agency's actual cost of production exceeded the "efficient" cost, it would run an operating deficit the magnitude of which would be indicative of the extent of its technical inefficiency. This was intended, in the parlance widely used in New Zealand, to transform "budget pressure" into "purchase pressure" (New Zealand Treasury, 1996); that is, to engineer a situation where agencies would be pressured to respond to reduced funding by improving technical efficiency rather than by cutting services.

The Australian finance ministry and a number of its State counterparts explicitly stated, at the time of the introduction of AOB, their intention of implementing the principle of payment-for-results. To be more precise, what they intended to do was to apply this principle in an accounting sense so that "recognition of Departmental output appropriations" would "reflect agencies [sic] delivery of their outputs" (DOFA, 1999, p. 43).[17] What this meant was that agency accounts would record as revenue earned, not the actual budget appropriation, but that part of the budget appropriation which the agency was deemed to have actually earned by delivering outputs.[18] Simplifying a little, if an agency were provided with $1 million in the budget in the expectation that it would deliver 1,000 units of output, but due to inefficiency spent its full appropriation and only delivered 600 units, it would be recorded as having only earned $600,000 and as therefore having made a loss of $400,000. The formal mechanism for such a system of payment-for-results was actually established in the State of Victoria. Each department in that State was for some years required to present quarterly "invoices" stating the outputs it had delivered. The idea was that the finance ministry would scrutinize the invoice and determine what payment was due and could be recognized as income in the relevant department's accounts (VDTF, 1998, pp. 302–3).

A number of key difficulties arose during the implementation stage of the AOB reforms. The first was that the demanding performance information requirements of the system were not met. AOB required the clear specification of the outputs to be delivered, and good measurement of the quantity, quality, and cost of what was actually delivered. In practice, however, there was a "lack of rigour in the definition and measurement of outputs" (Carlin and Guthrie, 2001, p. 97; 2003, p. 154). Given the large number of types of service delivered by governments, this was hardly surprising. Even in a country which had moved some years before to develop performance measurement systems, the performance measurement requirements of the new AOB system were a formidable challenge. Output costing systems also tended to be quite inadequately developed, echoing earlier experience in New Zealand, where a 1995 review determined that cost allocation to specific products was so "inappropriate" that the resultant information "fell well short of playing a useful role for management decision-making" (Coopers & Lybrand, 1995).

A second key difficulty arose from a certain imprecision about exactly what it meant when AOB proponents said that budget funding would be based on "prices." The logic of AOB required the specification of *per-unit* prices for each output (or, more generally, a funding formula). Without a formula to indicate how much revenue was payable for any given quantity of output delivered, there would be no way that the finance ministry could implement the principle of payment-for-results. It would be unable to determine, in the event of the failure of an agency to deliver the full quantity of output which was expected of it, what portion of its "payment-for-outputs" appropriation it would be permitted to recognize as revenue in its operating statement.

The official documentation at the time of inception of the system made it clear that, reflecting the market analogy upon which AOB was based, many of the system's proponents did indeed have in mind a model based on unit prices of outputs. Thus, for example, the Victorian finance ministry stated that "[budget] funding will be based on a single quantity and unit cost measure for each output. Major quantity measures should allow a *quantity x unit cost = expenditure* equation to be derived where possible" (VDTF, 1997, p. 18).

Very little consideration had, however, been given to the practicability of the principle of unit pricing, and it quickly became clear that there were many services for which formularized funding based upon unit prices was difficult to implement. There was great puzzlement as officials sought to apply the principles of AOB to heterogeneous and contingent capacity services such as defense, international representation, and environmental regulation. In the upshot, there was very little success across the country during the implementation phase in developing funding formulas to underpin the "prices" set in budget appropriations. The greatest efforts made in this respect were at the national government level, where the finance ministry attempted to give effect to the New Zealand idea of "purchase agreements" (New Zealand Treasury, 1995, 1996) with individual ministries (see Box 16.1). This had limited success, and led to only a small sub-set of the services delivered by that government being placed on a formula funding footing.

Box 16.1 Setting output prices for immigration services

The experience of the Australian immigration department—an agency which produces more relatively standardized services which are suited to formularized output funding than most other national government agencies—exemplifies the difficulties which arose with formula funding as the basis of PP arrangements. At the time of introduction of AOB, the finance ministry and immigration department entered into a formal "purchasing agreement"[a] which set unit prices for many of the department's outputs. There were, for example, unit prices for each of 14 different categories of visa application. Prices were also specified for each of three different categories of "removals" of illegal immigrants—that is, the management of forced repatriations. Even though the purchasing agreement only covered those immigration services which appeared more suited to the purchaser-provider treatment, the problem of heterogeneity still manifested itself. For example, one of the visa output categories used for funding purposes covered a number of complex types of visa application including spouse visa applications—that is, applications for entry status by persons on the grounds of marriage to a citizen. (Immigration's mandate in respect to such applications is to prevent abuse of spousal entry through contrived marriages contracted solely for immigration purposes.) It became clear, however, that there is such great variability in the extent of investigative activity which spouse visa applications require as to make this particular type of visa application entirely unsuited to funding via a fixed per-case amount. Immigration might, for example, be faced in a given year with a set of spouse visa applications of more than usual average complexity, in which case it would find itself under considerable financial pressure to investigate cases with less than adequate thoroughness.

[a] An interim purchasing agreement with the immigration ministry was formulated in 1999–2000, and by 2001 this had developed into a three-year agreement covering 2001–04 (DIMA/DOFA, 2001).

Closely related to this was the third problem—the difficulty of implementing the principle of payment-for-results. Victoria was the only jurisdiction which made an across-the-board attempt to do so. Its quarterly invoicing system did not achieve its intended purpose. During the time the invoicing procedures remained in place, there was no instance where an agency was not permitted to recognize its full payment-for-outputs appropriation as revenue. The Victorian finance ministry made a couple of initial attempts to so penalize departments which it saw as underperforming, but these were blocked at the political level: no minister was prepared to accept what would in effect be a public censure of his or her department's performance. The fundamental technical problem with the system was the inevitable subjectivity of any assessment of departmental delivery performance in a context where there was no unit price for outputs and, in many cases, not even good measures of output quantity.

At the national government level, the initial enthusiasm of the finance ministry to apply the principle of payment-for-results led to robust interaction with the Auditor-General. The latter was concerned that revenue recognition based upon highly subjective assessments of output delivery performance would create wide scope for the manipulation of agency accounts. In this debate, the Auditor-General was in a strong position because of his power to qualify agency accounts, and Finance was obliged to largely give way. The upshot was agreement that budgetary payment-for-outputs appropriations would be recognized as revenue at the time the appropriations legislation became law, unless there was a purchasing agreement or something similar which would clearly state how output delivery performance would be measured (DOFA, 2002, p. 20; ANAO, 2002, pp. 24–5). Because purchasing agreements made so little headway, the second option remained a dead letter.

The fourth key problem was the difficulty of giving effect to the stated intention to pay prices based on the efficient cost of production. AOB required finance ministries to determine the efficient cost of production of each of the myriad of outputs produced by budget sector agencies. This would have required a monumental effort even if the necessary analytic techniques had been available. However, the AOB enthusiasm for the use of market price comparisons and benchmarking overlooked the considerable practical limitations upon the use of those techniques. Benchmarking can be a most valuable management tool for services where good benchmarking partners are available. However, there are many areas of government where it is very difficult or even impossible to find other organizations sufficiently similar to permit cost-effective benchmarking. Moreover, even where benchmarking is feasible, it remains a costly and demanding process. As for market price comparators, these tend to be available only for a minority of government outputs (indeed, where they are available, the question arises as to why the government is producing the service concerned rather than buying it from the private sector or leaving it to market provision).

The difficulty of determining the "efficient" price was experienced most intensely in the course of an "output pricing review" process which was initiated at the national government level at the outset of the AOB experiment. The intention of the finance ministry was to conduct an intensive review of every ministry budget over a period of a couple of years in order to determine the appropriate prices which the government should be paying for departmental outputs. This process turned out to be not only exhausting, but also ultimately unsatisfactory, to both Finance and the line agencies concerned. Output pricing reviews which were intended to be accomplished in one year extended to two and sometimes three years. Even then, it turned out to be frustratingly difficult to draw strong conclusions about either the scope for efficiency gains or priority-setting issues. Benchmarking to determine efficient cost proved to be very difficult.[19]

The consequence of this series of implementation difficulties was that in no jurisdiction did it prove possible to realize the original vision of AOB—that is, of a system in which agencies would experience intense "purchase" pressure to improve efficiency as a result of being forced to earn revenue for outputs actually delivered at prices reflecting efficient operation. This mirrored earlier experience in New Zealand.[20] At root, this failure reflected both the inappropriateness of the PP model for many government services, and the formidable informational challenges of implementing such a system.

By 2003, there was a widespread view within the bureaucracy in Australia that AOB had not been a success. There was also, according to senior officials, considerable ministerial dissatisfaction with the system.[21] The result was the dismantlement of many of the purchaser-provider elements of the system. At the Commonwealth level, for example, the output pricing review process was a formally dropped as the result of a Budget Estimates and Framework Review recommendation that as of July 1, 2003, these reviews be "rolled into a broader input-based cost analysis model involving a detailed analysis of agency expenditure." Benchmarking essentially disappeared as an element of the central budget process. The "purchasing agreements" and most other formularized output funding arrangements between Finance and ministries—including that with Immigration—also disappeared. The AOB appropriations framework, with its "payment-for-outputs" appropriations, remained, but essentially as a matter of form.

The PP experiment was a bold attempt to revolutionize public budgeting so as to apply strong pressure for improved efficiency. It was, in the words of one senior official, a "brave experiment...that didn't quite come off" (quoted in Kelly and Wanna, 2004, p. 106).

Profits, losses, and the motivation to perform

It is via the financial bottom line that PP aims to motivate government agencies to perform better. But why should the agency be concerned about its financial result? Manifestly, it cannot be because its owners' incentives have changed: if government is both owner and purchaser, the financial consequences for it of any given level of agency inefficiency are the same whether there is a PP contract or not. Clearly, the objective of the PP mechanism must be to improve the motivation of agency management and staff ("agents") to perform, just as in the case of internal purchaser-provider arrangements within private enterprises. What are therefore crucial are the *consequences* of the agency's financial performance and how these impact on agents.

A crucial question here is whether the "revenue earned" by the provider agency for the delivery of outputs actually determines the funding made available to it by government. In sectoral PP arrangements with, say, hospitals and universities, this is the case. By contrast, as outlined above, AOB envisaged that revenue earned would be an accounting entry distinct from the amount of budget funding.

If revenue earned determines funding, an agency which is making losses will receive a level of government funding insufficient to cover its operating costs. This would place it under strong pressure to reduce its costs, and might ultimately put it at risk of closure. The unpleasant consequences for agents could be expected to motivate loss-avoiding behavior. Such motivation may also be reinforced by the non-self-interested commitment of staff to the objectives of their organization, which would further strengthen their desire to see their organization survive (see Chapter 18). The result would be to transform the agency into a loss avoider. The impact may, however, be asymmetrical, generating little motivation to make profits. This would be consistent with evidence that the DRG payments system works principally by motivating hospitals to seek to avoid losses—the "pressure matters" thesis (see Chapter 18).

Such an approach requires that the provider agency be accorded key operational freedoms normally accorded to public enterprises and private businesses. In order to be able to cut expenses when required, the agencies would require considerable flexibility in areas such as hiring and firing staff and setting salaries. Crucially, it would also require the power to borrow in order to be able to remain afloat in the face of losses, because it could not be expected that any and all losses could be offset immediately by cutting wages and other expenses.[22] Such a degree of operational freedom is not usually enjoyed by government ministries—even when accorded the enhanced autonomy advocated by "management-for-results"—and creates certain risks which need to be carefully weighed prior to any decision to adopt this version of the PP mechanism.

A further important consideration in deciding whether to take such an approach is the credibility of the threat (implicit or explicit) of closure of chronically loss-making agencies. This threat will be most credible if there are alternative service providers (for example, other hospitals) or if the service concerned is one which the government could readily cease providing. Conversely, if the supplier agency is the sole supplier of a crucial public service, no threat of closure is likely to be credible.

It was perhaps because such an approach seemed unsuited to the funding of many core government ministries that AOB exponents envisaged the alternative of treating revenue earned as purely an accounting entry.[23] The implication of such an approach is, of course, that any loss made as a result of the cost of production exceeding the output price will also be a purely accounting loss, with no direct impact on the resources available to the agency. To make the agency focus on its financial performance, it would be necessary for the government as owner to establish specific sanctions and rewards for management based on the financial result. The efficacy of such an approach would, however, depend critically on the credibility of financial result as a measure of agency performance, which would in turn depend on factors including the appropriateness of the output prices set. If the PP mechanism was applied to the wrong type of service, with the consequence that the price was an arbitrary one, it could not be expected that the financial result would have credibility as a performance measure for either the agency or the government.

Conclusion

The analysis in this chapter suggests that the purchaser-provider form of performance budgeting can serve as a powerful instrument with which to pressure government agencies to improve technical efficiency. It is a mechanism that can be effectively used as the basis for sectoral funding systems for services which are relatively standardized and produced in large volumes. There are, however, many government services which are unsuited to the application of the purchaser-provider principle, including services which are characterized by high levels of heterogeneity or which are "contingent capacity" in nature. Because the purchaser-provider model is only suitable for selective application, it is an inappropriate model upon which to base a government-wide budgeting system.

Notes

1. One related additional point on definition: PP systems do not necessarily require that *all* funding provided is a function of results delivered. Some PP systems are hybrids in which, in addition to the payment-for-results, agencies receive some element of funding which is not based upon results delivered.
2. See Robinson and Brumby (2005) for a review of the empirical evidence on the success of this system.
3. Imposing pressure for improved technical efficiency requires, in a static context, that the price set is below the costs of production prevailing prior to the introduction of the PP system. The greatest pressure would be imposed by setting prices to reflect cost which would prevail if there were 100 percent technical efficiency. In a context where there are multiple providers of the service, one less stringent possibility is to set prices equal to the average costs of all providers so as to put pressure on those with below-average levels of efficiency (an approach mentioned in Chapter 4 in relation to hospital funding). In a dynamic context, pressure would be imposed over time by setting an initial price equal to the costs of production, but then increasing it more slowly than the pre-PP trend rate of cost increase for the service concerned. This was, approximately speaking, the objective when the first version of the DRG system—the Prospective Payment System—was introduced in the United States with the objective of restraining the rate of growth of hospital costs.
4. This does not, however, necessarily mean that these entities are expected to operate as profit maximizers. What it does certainly require is that there is a strong expectation that they should operate with the aim of avoiding losses.
5. Accrual accounting and the treatment of budget funding as revenue are quite separate matters. The introduction of accrual accounting in a government context does not in itself require that budget funding be treated as revenue. If there is no purchaser-provider arrangment, there is no logical reason for treating budget funding as revenue, nor any case for producing an agency-level profit/loss figure. To put the matter in business terminology, it is because PP seeks to turn government agencies into *profit centers* (rather than cost centers) that both elements of business accounting are required.
6. The avoidance of high-cost cases is known as "dumping." Cream-skimming can involve either or both dumping and "creaming," which is the deliberate selection of low-cost clients/cases (and, in the extreme, the delivery of services to clients/cases who don't need them).
7. This is related to what statisticians call the "law of large numbers."
8. Another key point highlighted by the DRG example is that the severity of the output heterogeneity problem can sometimes be reduced by defining output types more narrowly so as to reduce the cost variability (to make them more "iso-cost," in DRG terminology). Take, for example, the treatment of hip fracture patients, where it transpired that there was such variability in case complexity that it was problematic to pay the same amount for the treatment of every patient. The response, as the DRG system evolved, was to split hip fracture patients into a number of groups—such as elderly hip fracture patients and hip fracture patients with secondary medical problems—attracting different prices. This is an example of what Smith refers to in the previous chapter as finer "risk adjustment." There are, however, limits to how far heterogeneity may be resolved by adopting finer output classification. DRG systems also make use of special payment arrangements for high-cost "outlier" cases to further reduce the heterogeneity problem. This, however, raises the further problem of how to prevent the inappropriate classification of cases as outliers.
9. Such as the Ethiopian university funding system described in Chapter 24, which pays universities for successful course completions (a proximate outcome measure) rather than simply for courses undertaken (an output measure). What is crucial here is that

the proximate outcome upon which payment is based is sufficiently controllable by the provider agency to make the revenue risk manageable.

10. For the New Zealand experience, see, for example, Schick (1996) and Robinson (2000).
11. Including, but not confined to, intensive interviews conducted in Canberra in 2003. State government officials were also interviewed in Victoria, Queensland, and Western Australia.
12. The exception being Australia's largest State, New South Wales. The very different approach to performance budgeting taken in that State is the subject of Chapter 14.
13. It was curious given these clear statements of the output-purchase philosophy of the system that the national finance ministry subsequently rejected the "purchaser-provider" label for its new budgeting system (DOFA, 2001), and claimed that it was different from the New Zealand system in that it supposedly put equal emphasis on outcomes as on outputs.
14. The new appropriation regime—which included "capital injection" appropriations and a distinction between departmental and "administered" expenses—is discussed in detail in Robinson (2002a).
15. Where Ian Ball, the principal finance ministry architect of the system, described it in the following terms: "it means revenue and cost flows are split. 'Surplus' then has a real meaning and can be used as a key ownership performance measure" (Ball, 1992, p. 21).
16. See Robinson (2002b, p. 19, n6) for references to statements of this position in the official documentation of State governments.
17. As the Western Australian Treasury put it, that the "recognition of appropriation revenues" were to "be tied to output acquittal performance" (WAT, 2001a, p. 13).
18. As the West Australian Treasury (2001b, p. 5) put it: "Agencies will only be entitled to recognise appropriation drawdowns as revenue 'earned,' when the associated output delivery has been successfully acquitted. Appropriations drawn prior to the acquittal process, will be recognised as revenue in advance (a liability). If an agency's outputs are not acquitted (in full or in part), an operating loss will be reported for the period.)"
19. Some agency personnel interviewed suggested that an additional reason for the lack of success of benchmarking in certain areas where intra-government benchmarking was attempted (for example, policy advice) was an uncooperative stance taken by many government departments to sharing cost data.
20. Where Coopers & Lybrand (1995, p. 40) found in a review commissioned by the finance ministry that there was "little evidence of significant purchase pressure (as opposed to budget pressure)."
21. The author was told this by a number of senior officials during interviews in 2003. It is also confirmed in Kelly and Wanna (2004).
22. In a private sector context, if losses are made, it is rarely the case that employees bear the full consequences of any losses, particularly in the short term. A key ownership function is risk taking, and economists analyse the appropriate allocation of risk between owners and their agents by reference to "optimal risk sharing." It is one of the virtues of market mechanisms that external capital—whether in the form of equity or loans—breaks the short-run nexus between a firm's earnings and its operating costs.
23. The New Zealand Treasury (1996, p. 38) at one stage floated the idea that "in the future departments may possibly be required to show their outputs have been produced before the Government pays the 'price' and hands over the appropriated output funding." The idea was not implemented.

References

Allen, R., and P. Gertler, 1991, "Regulation and the Provision of Quality to Heterogeneous consumers: The Case of Prospective Pricing of Medical Services," *Journal of Regulatory Economics*, Vol. 3, December, pp. 361–75.

ANAO (Australian National Audit Office), 2002, *A Model Agency: Illustrative Financial Statements for the Year 30 June 2003* (Canberra: ANAO).

Ball, I., 1992, "The New Approach: Financial Management Reform," *Accountants' Journal*, June, p. 21.

Berwick, D.M., et al., 2003, "Paying for Performance: Medicare Should Lead," *Health Affairs*, Vol. 22(6), pp. 8–9.

Boxall, P., 1998, "The Revolution in Government Accounting," *Australian CPA*, Vol. 6(3), pp. 18–20.

Carlin, T.M., and J. Guthrie, 2001, "Lessons form Australian and New Zealand Experiences with Output-Based Budgeting," in *Learning from International Public Management Reform*, ed. L.R. Jones, J. Guthrie, and P. Steane (Amsterdam: Elsevier).

——, 2003, "Accrual Output Based Budgeting Systems in Australia: The Rhetoric-Reality Gap," *Public Management Review*, Vol. 5(2), pp. 146–62.

Cohen, D., 2006, *Trois Leçons sur la Société Post-Industrielle* (Paris: Seuil).

Coopers & Lybrand, 1995, *Review of Costing Systems and User Charges, Commissioned by the Treasury* (Wellington: Treasury of New Zealand).

DIMA/DOFA (Department of Immigration and Multicultural Affairs and Department of Finance and Administration), 2001, "Purchasing Agreement, 1 July 2001–30 June 2004." Unpublished.

DOFA, 1999, *Commonwealth Accrual Budgeting Guidelines* (Canberra: DOFA).

——, 2001, *Finance Brief No. 1: Accrual Accounting in Respect to "Department Revenue from Government," 2000–01* (Canberra: DOFA).

——, 2002, *Requirements and Guidance for the Preparation of Financial Statements of Commonwealth Agencies and Authorities, 2002–03* (Canberra: DOFA).

Ellis, R.P., 1998, "Creaming, Skimping and Dumping: Provider Competition on the Intensive and Extensive Margins," *Journal of Health Economics*, Vol. 17(5), pp. 537–56.

Geering, W.L., P.L. Roeder, and T.U. Obi, 1999, *Manual on the Preparation of National Animal Disease Emergency Preparedness Plans* (Rome: Food and Agriculture Organization), <www.fao.org/docrep/004/x2096e/X2096E00.HTM.>, accessed November 2006.

Kelly, J., and J. Wanna, 2004, "Crashing Through with Accrual-Output Price Budgeting in Australia," *American Review of Public Administration*, Vol. 34(1), pp. 94–111.

New Zealand Treasury, 1995, *Purchase Agreements Guidelines, with Best Practice for Output Performance Measures* (Wellington: Treasury of New Zealand).

——, 1996, *Putting It Together: An Explanatory Guide to the New Zealand Financial Management System* (Wellington: Treasury of New Zealand).

Osborne, D., and T. Gaebler, 1993, *Reinventing Government: How the Entrepreneurial Spirit Is Transforming the Public Sector* (New York: Plume).

QT (Queensland Treasury), 1998, *Managing for Outcomes: Output Costing Guidelines* (Brisbane: Queensland Treasury).

Robinson, M., 2000, "Contract Budgeting," *Public Administration*, Vol. 78(1), pp. 75–90.

——, 2002a, "Financial Control in Australian Government Budgeting," *Public Budgeting and Finance*, Vol. 22(1), pp. 80–93.

——, 2002b, "Output-Purchase Funding and Budgeting Systems in the Public Sector," *Public Budgeting and Finance*, Vol. 22(4), pp. 17–33.

Robinson, M., and J. Brumby, 2005, *Does Performance Budgeting Work? An Analytical Review of the Empirical Literature*, IMF Working Paper 05/210 (Washington: IMF).

Salber, P.R., and B.E. Bradley, 2002, "Adding Quality to the Health Care Purchasing Equation," *Health Affairs*, November.

Schick, A., 1996, *The Spirit of Reform: Managing the New Zealand State Sector in a Time of Change* (Wellington: State Services Commission).

VDTF (Department of Treasury and Finance, Victoria), 1997, *Reform of the Budget Sector: Elements of Financial Management* (Melbourne: Victorian Treasury).

——, 1998, *Accrual Accounting Manual* (Melbourne: Victorian Treasury).

WAT (West Australian Treasury), 2001a, *Accrual Appropriations and Capital User Charge: A User Manual* (Perth: Treasury).
——, 2001b, *Questions and Answers on the New Appropriation Regime and Capital User Charge* (Perth: Treasury).
Williamson, O., 1985, *The Economic Institutions of Capitalism: Firms, Markets, Relational Contracting* (New York: The Free Press).

17
Three Decades of Reforms in Spain

Jesús Ruiz-Huerta, Eduardo Zapico, Javier Loscos, and Tamón Takahashi[1]

As in other continental European countries, public administration in Spain has a legalistic tradition focused heavily on the detailed regulation of procedures and the application of strict control mechanisms. The budgeting system has traditionally been focused on compliance—that is, on the control of the level and objects of spending rather than on the results of spending. Civil servants responsible for budget preparation and execution therefore have concentrated their efforts on complying with the budget legislation and instructions established in regulations, without much concern with the efficiency and effectiveness of their initiatives.

Since the mid-1970s various forms of budgeting by objectives or results (hereinafter performance budgeting—PB) have been prepared for introduction in Spain.[2] Since that time continuous efforts have been made to move from administrative line-item budgeting to budgeting for results. As explained later, some relevant improvements have taken place. However, change proposals and tools have been focused on formulating new legislation and incorporating the main formal or technical elements of PB. After three decades of efforts to implement a PB-like model (for example, Planning, Programming, and Budgeting System—PPBS, zero-base budgeting—ZBB) there seems to be a new momentum for a new budget reform effort. At this stage it is important to review previous experience in order to get a better understanding of how best to move ahead and to avoid committing the same errors made in previous budget reform exercises. So far, insufficient attention has been paid to the behavioral effects and conditions imposed by this type of budget reform on those responsible for the reform and its stakeholders.

The aims of this chapter are to: (a) present an overview of Spanish experience with PB; (b) outline the current status and ongoing reforms; (c) discuss certain new challenges and opportunities for the further development of PB; and (d) present some thoughts on main lessons learned on the design and implementation of PB reform.

Historical background

The traditional approach to budgeting prevailed until the approval of the democratic Constitution of 1978. There were, however, a number of initial steps toward reform in the early 1970s, of which the most important, from a performance budgeting perspective, was the establishment of Development Plans (*Planes de Desarrollo*), which for the first time introduced provisions aimed at measuring programs and objectives. Associated with this, interdepartmental commissions were created to develop methodologies (such as ex-ante assessments and cost-benefit analysis) for evaluating public investment projects.

However, the initiative had numerous limitations. The analysis was applied to investment projects only, and these were analyzed in isolation from their current expenditure implications. Consequently, the global effects of the programs evaluated were not known. Moreover, the difficulties that arose when endeavoring to measure the non-financial benefits and costs of projects led to an analytic focus on programs or departments with a clearly economic/financial focus (public works, agriculture, and so on) (see Lozano Irueste, 1982). Another problem was the limited connection between the cost estimates obtained in the project evaluation process and the budget allocations to the project. A key reason for this was that budget allocations did not include the civil service wage costs of projects, because wage costs were treated as a ministry overhead cost assigned to the ministry central office (see Carreño Rodriguez-Maribona and González Finat, 1979). Civil servants' lack of motivation and capacity for program-based management was a further obstacle (see Barea and Carreño, 1971).

Strong growth of the economy and public spending in the 1970s and 1980s was not accompanied by commensurate advances in financial and budgetary management capacities. During those years, public spending in Spain nearly doubled, rising to the level of the most developed countries. However, at the end of the 1970s the budget process remained in a very traditional mode. In effect, it was a process of incremental allocation of resources, in which:

- the main interest of budget implementers was in spending, by the end of the fiscal year, all the resources allocated to them, in order to be regarded as "effective" and avoid budget cuts in the following year
- financial control focused on formal compliance with budgetary and accounting regulations, with spending limits and fraud prevention constituting the primary objectives, and with control mechanisms based on an extremely rigid and detailed ex-ante control of every expenditure item
- parliamentary control of budget execution was based on the role of the Court of Auditors, also legalistic by nature, and the approval of the General Ledger of the State (that is, the formal approval of the report on the execution of the budget) tended not to attract great interest on the part of members of parliament (se Argüello and Palacios, 1979).

It is clear that, at the end of the 1970s, the main priority of the Ministry of Economy and Finance (*Ministerio de Economía y Hacienda*—MEH) was focused on control of aggregate spending levels and compliance with budget and accounting regulations. Budget preparation was largely an exercise in administrative calculations (projections of spending increases stemming from administrative decisions, new laws, inflation, and so on) (see Gunther, 1980) and budgetary and financial control focused on the legality of procedures. Evaluation and planning played no significant role.

Since that time, however, the Spanish government has been reforming budgeting, in parallel with broader reforms in economic policy and management. It began, first, to pay greater attention to the economy, efficiency, and effectiveness of public spending, while at the same time focusing on aggregate fiscal discipline and sound macroeconomic policy.

In 1977, a new organic budget law (*Ley General Presupuestaria*—LGP) was adopted which included a number of important provisions for budget reform oriented toward achieving greater spending efficiency and effectiveness. The new democratic Constitution (*Constitución Española*—CE) adopted in 1978 also set out a basic framework for the modernization of government finance management, stipulating that the programming and execution of public expenditure should meet the criteria of efficiency and economy (Article 31.2 CE), and that public administration should comply with the principle of efficiency (Article 103.1 CE).

In the late 1970s, the MEH started to require some departments to formulate their budgets by programs. This was extended to the government as a whole in the mid-1980s, with the development of a functional budget structure in which all expenditure was classified by programs. In the late 1980s, the focus of budget reform moved away from budget classification to the budget process: among other things, it focused on performance budgeting and the development of new multilateral budget negotiation mechanisms.

In more detail, the first step toward the introduction of program budgeting in Spain was taken in the 1979 budget preparation guidelines. It was quite partial (not involving a genuine change in traditional budgeting approaches) and limited to only two departments (see Sánchez Revenga, 2005, pp. 29–30). The extension of this across the whole Spanish administration in the 1984 budget was more formal than substantive: there was no requirement that program objectives be specified or that program performance indicators be identified. The sole requirement was for a program classification of expenditure, which in many cases ended up being a simple transposition of the organizational structure (cf. Ministerial Order of June 17, 1983, and Sánchez Revenga, 2005, pp. 30–1).

The need to improve on this was recognized in the Ministerial Order of April 23, 1984, requiring a more complete classification by programs identifying objectives to be pursued. The Ministerial Order also gave spending units authority to shift funding *within* programs (Sánchez Revenga, 2005, p. 31). It also mandated program performance indicators, by means of so-called *program indicator sheets* which were to include "in concise and clear form…the objectives, indicators, and measures proposed to reduce spending or spending increases as needed in order to carry out the program anticipated at its level [as well as] the regulations in force affecting the program, with reference to the conditions derived from same as to the rigidity of and changes in spending."[3]

Alongside these advances, the government was placing much greater emphasis on fiscal discipline. In 1988, it approved the first Macroeconomic and Budgetary Scenarios (four-year projections signaling spending ceilings for the first year and updated annually). The Maastricht Treaty (1992) and the creation of the European Monetary Union (1999) increased the pressure for fiscal discipline. In 2001, parliament approved two Budget Stability Laws (one for the national and one for the regional governments),[4] which were amended in 2006 to re-specify the budget balance requirement in cyclically adjusted terms.

In this context, there has been an increasing recognition of the need to reinforce aggregate spending discipline with greater effectiveness and efficiency of public managers. Several other innovations have been introduced to improve the budget process with a new system for the monitoring of objectives (see Sánchez Revenga, 2005, pp. 31–3) and the new multilateral budget negotiation arrangements based on the creation of the Spending Policy Commissions and Program Analysis Commissions (PAC) (see below). Negotiation at the PAC is the stage which features the most intensive debates between the Directorate-General of the Budget and the departments responsible for spending policies. At the beginning, the PACs were intended to introduce multilateral debates into the budget process, rather than to rely only on bilateral discussions between each ministry and the MEH. The multilateral negotiations would have encouraged departments and spending units to negotiate and compete among themselves for resources in a zero-sum game context, thus increasing the effectiveness of aggregate expenditure discipline. However, traditional bilateral meetings persisted.[5] There was no political will to implement this approach to budget negotiations.

In the last two decades, the General Audit Office (*Intervención General de la Administración del Estado*—IGAE) has made important efforts to follow up and report on the results of a selected group of budget programs. However, the performance information produced by the IGAE has not been considered as very relevant for budgeting.[6] Furthermore, a Law on the Organization and Functioning of the General Administration of the State was approved in 1997,[7] and the first steps were taken toward preparing a new organic budget law to be approved in 2003.

Current situation of performance budgeting

Performance budgeting developments are currently progressing along two different paths: the improvement of budgetary techniques and processes (particularly in the context of the new General Budgetary Law of 2003), and the refinement of the evaluation and control systems and their linkage with the budget process. But before analyzing these improvements it is necessary to present a brief description of the budget procedure and main actors.

Overview of the budget process

The budget preparation process starts each January when the MEH prepares a three-year budget outline and draft expenditure ceilings for the next year, and submits these to the Council of Ministers. The MEH then draws up the Multi-year Budgetary

Scenario.[8] To this end, the Directorate-General of Budget (DGP) in collaboration with the budget offices of spending departments prepares projections for a long-term scenario and submits them to the DGP. The DGP adds the revenue projections and sends them to the MEH who presents the Scenario to the Council of Ministers (CoM). The MEH then prepares recommendations for the Council of Ministers on budget stability objectives for both the national and regional governments ("Autonomous Communities"). The CoM decides on the budget policy—including a multi-year macroeconomic framework contained in the Stability Program drawn up in accordance with the EU Stability and Growth Pact—and submits it to the parliament, which reviews and either approves or rejects the proposed budget framework.[9]

Key institutional players in the budget preparation process include the following:

1. The *Spending Policy Commission,* chaired by the Minister of Economy and Finance with the assistance of the Secretary of State for Finance and Budget and with the participation of spending ministers or other top officials representing them. The role of this Commission is to reach agreement on an initial allocation of budgetary resources which is consistent with government priorities and aggregate fiscal policy. The Commission sets ceilings within which each spending department prepares its budget proposal.
2. The *Revenue Commission*, chaired by the Secretary of State for Finance and Budget, which is responsible for coordinating the preparation of the revenue forecasts.
3. The *Departmental Budget Commissions* composed of the representatives from within the relevant departments, and chaired by its Deputy Secretary. The task of these commissions is to make proposals for the preliminary draft budget, formulate priority criteria, review existing programs, and monitor their execution.[10]
4. The *Program Analysis Commissions* (at least one per department, chaired by the Secretary of State for Finance and Budget), whose functions include the analysis of the adequacy and validity of spending programs consistent with priorities defined by the Spending Policy Commission (see below for further details on these Commissions).[11]

The Preliminary Draft Budget is discussed and approved by the CoM in September, and is then submitted to the Congress by October 1. In considering the budget, Congress first sets an aggregate expenditure ceiling and then debates the allocation of spending within that ceiling. Normally, the debate at the parliament does not pay attention to program performance.

Budget execution is a highly regulated process with a particular concern on legal compliance. The functions of auditing and control are vested in various institutions: the internal audit done by the IGAE and the external audit done by the Court of Auditors (*Tribunal de Cuentas*).

A solid framework and clear rules of the budgetary game

As noted above, one of the key forces behind the budgetary reform process was the macroeconomic pressure to restrict public spending and comply with budgetary stability objectives. This demands not only the control of aggregate spending, but also improved *quality* of spending (Pollit and Bouckaert, 2004, p. 67). Budget stability and performance budgeting therefore need to be addressed in a coherent and complementary manner. The synergy between these issues is well captured in the four basic principles articulated in the Budget Stability Laws, namely: budgetary stability, multi-year projections (scenarios with first-year spending limits), transparency, and efficiency in the allocation and use of public funds.[12]

The MEH formulated a new organic budget law—the General Budgetary Law (LGP) of 2003—in order to give effect to these principles, and in particular to the one referring to efficiency in financial management. As observed by Sánchez Revenga (2005), "the substance of the new LGP 2003 shows a keen interest in establishing an appropriate normative framework, making it possible to apply efficiency approaches into budgeting and to develop a management by results culture in respect to expenditure."

The law requires a multi-year programming and the definition of objectives on regular basis. It seeks to establish a systematic linkage between budget allocations and the objectives for departments and spending management units,[13] by the following means:

1. *Development of a system of spending management by objectives*. Public managers are required to be effective in attaining their objectives, and to focus on results in programming and implementation expenditure initiatives. For each program, spending management units are required to specify a relevant set of objectives appropriate to their organization. These objectives must be included in their annual multi-year program.[14]
2. *Development of information and performance monitoring systems*. The management and control systems of public spending must be oriented towards results as well as financial compliance. Spending management units should prepare an annual report on the achievement of their objectives, which shall be included in their annual reports and in the multi-year programming.[15]
3. *Continuous evaluation of spending policies*. The MEH, in collaboration with the various spending management units, leads and coordinates the evaluation of budget programs with the purpose of ensuring that spending policies achieve their strategic and socioeconomic objectives.

Strengthening the budget process

At the end of 2004, in response to the opportunity offered by new legislation for developing performance budgeting, the Secretary of State for Budgeting created several working groups to study possible measures for improving the budget process and documentation. Two of these groups focused respectively on the role of the Program Analysis Commissions and on the quality of information presented in budget programs.

Improving the Commissions for Program Analysis (PACs)

The main official functions of the PACs are: analyzing the adequacy and validity of spending programs in relation to their objectives; allocating resources within the budget ceilings for each department or program; and ensuring that proposed allocations are consistent with priorities set at the political level. It is also intended that PACs should review and take into consideration program results in the preceding year.[16]

Although from an instrumental point of view the PACs have not been very successful, from other points of view they add value to the budget process. The symbolic and relational role played by the PACs in the process of preparing the budget should be underlined. As Zapico Goñi points out (2005):

> They embody expenditure review and oversight...They significantly facilitate direct relationships among senior officials and shape expectations and standards of behavior or decision-making style facilitating progress towards reaching budget agreements. The PACs make it possible for technical specialists to obtain direct information on agreements or disagreements at the policy levels...

The capacity of the PACs to facilitate information sharing and useful debate on performance in the budget process remains at this stage quite limited. This is due to both technical and political factors. The major weaknesses identified by the working group in the preparation and functioning of the PACs are:

- shortcomings in the instructions received at the Program Analysis from Commissions from the Spending Policy Commissions. These instructions are neither concrete nor effectively communicated
- inadequate communication and collaboration between spending management departments and the Directorate-General of Budget
- insufficient use of the analytical capacities of the DGP and other actors in the budget process. Better preparation of the starting positions for negotiation in both parts would facilitate more efficiency in the debates
- limited scope of the debate in the PACs. Discussions are mainly focused on the projections of spending line-items according to expected variations in inflation, or according to new legislation (see Zapico Goñi, 2005, pp. 40–2; Dirección General de Presupuestos, 2005).

Many other specific weaknesses may be mentioned. There is a tendency to avoid conflict rather than deal with it in a transparent manner. At a more technical level, there is sometimes a major imbalance between the volume of information requested by the DGP and that received from the spending management units. This information often arrives at the very last minute. The capacity to process and analyze this information is limited. Most of the information is financial in nature, and the amount of relevant performance information remains very limited. Analysis lacks sufficient depth, with most budget commitments being considered unavoidable (for example, personnel) and the scope for discretionary decision-making for budget corrections being therefore perceived as very limited. While this might be right in the short term, it is not necessarily the case over the medium- or long-term horizon.

Spending management departments often don't have sufficient accurate information about the budget implications of departmental plans, reform programs, or legislative proposals, complicating oversight over the adaptation of annual plans to the medium-term budget scenarios.

There is not enough time for debate in the PAC meetings. In general, the focus of PAC discussions is incremental and, frequently, focused on the maximum percentage increases authorized for budget chapters. There is scarcely any systematic debate about spending policies or ministerial priorities and past or expected performance. There is also no debate on interdepartmental programs. So far, budget scenarios seem to have been considered as a mere formal exercise complementary to the annual budget. Instead it should be the other way around. Annual budgeting should be an extension of the budget scenarios.

> The efficient allocation of resources in the framework of budgetary scenarios prepared with transparency (better knowledge on sector programs and information on performance) and with the active participation of spending managers, would be much more effective and relevant than the current annual program budget negotiations focus on chapters or line items expenditures. (Zapico Goñi, 2005, p. 43)

The suggestions made by the working group to improve the functioning of the PACs in the short or medium term involve: incorporating a more strategic and selective approach into the negotiations, introducing a multi-year perspective in the debate, and taking into account information sensitive to the institutional and political context. In particular, it is deemed necessary to strengthen the political leadership and supporting role that must be played by the Minister of Economy and Finance with a view to improving the functioning of the PACs.

Specific lines proposed for improving the PACs model are as follows (see Zapico Goñi, 2005, pp. 40–2; Dirección General de Presupuestos, 2005):

1. *Modification of the role and competencies of the DGP in the budget process.* When preparing PAC meetings, the DGP must reorient its efforts and resources toward the analysis of selective strategic spending. Debates at the PACs should focus on long-term effects or impacts.
2. *Applying resource allocation criteria in order to encourage the application of spending management by objectives.* One of the main focuses of debates at the PACs should be on ensuring the consistency of budget programs with sector plans of spending ministries and/or with government priorities. Also, other types of analysis (for example, assessment of socioeconomic and environmental impact of policies, or cost-effective analysis) could be prepared in collaboration with external experts (see Zapico Goñi, 2005; CECAEE, 2004).
3. *Introduction of new types of PAC meetings, and revision of their composition and size.* Four types of meetings are suggested: (a) preparatory meetings, with experts from the budget offices and representatives of the IGAE in spending ministries; (b) main interface meeting between the DGP and spending ministry officials; (c)

meetings to follow up compliance with agreements and solving controversies in a transparent manner; and (d) final meetings, at top level, after which no changes would be accepted unless accompanied by offsetting proposals from the same department (see Zapico Goñi, 2005; Dirección General de Presupuestos, 2005). The composition and size of the PACs should be adjusted depending on the different types of meetings in order to ensure flexible and efficient functioning.

4. *Improvement of the information used in PAC decision-making.* To bring about this improvement it has been suggested, first, that the DGP develop a more proactive behavior during the preparation of new sector plans and programs in spending ministries. Officials of the DGP should be searching for information at early stages of sector policy-making on the potential budget impact of the main future initiatives. This would allow them to anticipate possible risks of excessive spending, and to ensure sound programming (that is, relating resources to objectives and actions; choosing relevant indicators, and so on), so that subsequent monitoring and evaluation are feasible.
5. *Introducing incentives for coordination and collaboration between the DGP, budget offices, and management operational services.* The study also recommends the use of incentives that have been applied in other countries to enhance collaboration among budget and management officials, such as: (a) sharing the "profits" derived from performance budgeting between the Ministry of Economy and Finance and the spending management units, rewarding savings resulting from cutbacks or from efficiency gains, or granting flexibility to allocate a portion of the profits in accordance with predetermined criteria; (b) creating a Reserve Fund for innovation and productivity, to be distributed on a competitive basis; (c) signing budget agreements specifying the information on resources, objectives, and activities which must be submitted to the Ministry of Economy and Finance by the spending management units for purposes of monitoring special budget programs; (d) using indicators of outcomes or impacts that require the cooperation of several services; (e) focusing evaluation efforts more on recognizing and promoting desirable management styles than on the identification of spending misbehavior or non-compliance; and (f) making the provision of funds contingent on meeting the information requirements of the Ministry of Economy and Finance so as to penalize resistance or delays in the provision of data on the budgetary impact of plans, or poor quality information on budgetary programs (see OECD, 2001; UK Cabinet Office, 1999; Chile National Budget Office, 2003).

Improving performance information presented in budget programs

The working party on performance information included representatives from the DGP (Budget), the IGAE (Financial Controller), and the budget offices of specific spending management departments. Its aim was to examine and suggest ways of improving the quality of program information presented in the budget documents (see Ministerio de Economía y Hacienda, 2004, pp. 3–5). Six "pilot programs" were analyzed with a view to assessing and proposing improvements in their structure, the consistency of their main elements (that is, objectives, activities, and indicators), and their level of "evaluability."[17]

The main weaknesses identified were:

- overly broad nature of many programs. The design of the program classification tends to be somewhat artificial. Normally it is a translation of the organic (organizational) classification of spending
- lack of a useful definition of needs or problems being addressed
- absence of a clear identification of the program target groups and their main characteristics
- ill-defined objectives. Use of excessively general definitions, insufficiently focused on problem-solving, or not well supported with operational objectives and performance measures
- lack, or inadequacy, of logical or conceptual framework of programs
- failure to adequately link main components of the programs: for example, objectives not always related to activities and resources
- performance indicators based on available data and statistics, rather than using goal-driven data and information
- predominance of indicators based on resources, activities, or immediate output; almost no information on outcomes or external impacts on society.

In general, prior to 2005, public programs presented in the budget document were not sufficiently well specified to allow proper performance follow-up and evaluation. A key reason for the poor quality of budget programs in this respect was the lack of participation and ownership of managers. The incentive for public managers to actively participate in the budget reform has been a missing factor in the efforts made so far done to introduce PB in Spain.

The main future steps decided upon were (Espadas, 2005a, 2005b; Dirección General de Presupuestos, 2006): correcting inconsistencies found for the pilot programs studied, extending the effort to other programs, improving program monitoring and information systems, identifying units dealing with program evaluation in spending departments, promoting greater involvement of managers, and conducting full quality appraisals (including options and management risks of programs, the adequacy of organizational structures, human resources, performance incentives, and information collection systems). Furthermore, the program classification will be better linked to a functional classification adapted to international standards.

The working party prepared guidelines for spending management centers covering the basic requirements that must be met during the preparation of budget programs in order to achieve the proposed aims, provide adequate systems for the follow-up and evaluation of program achievements, and provide the information necessary for the adoption of performance-based decisions during the process of resource allocation (Ministerio de Economía y Hacienda, 2004, pp. 3–5; 2005, p. 3). Regarding the functional classification of expenditures, the guidelines provide a better and clear link between programs and spending policies, and also continue to move forward with the alignment with international classifications (see Ministerio de Economía y Hacienda, 2005, p. 6).

In particular, strong emphasis is placed on identifying the so-called "Areas of Activity" and their corresponding objectives and performance indicators. The areas of activity may be defined as a set of activities aimed at achieving one or more common objectives. These areas of activity make it possible to identify the policy function and main internal components, the type of activities to be carried out and the ends pursued by them. Once the area of activity is identified, it can be associated with the strategic and operational objectives. For instance, the program "To promote labour insertion and stability" has as one of the areas of activity "Vocational training" with the strategic objective of developing working skills and enhancing business competitiveness. This strategic goal is to be operationalized through two specific objectives: (a) to promote access to a job through vocational training, and (b) to promote continued participation in the labor market through updating professional qualifications (Ministerio de Economía y Hacienda, 2005, p. 7).

The strategic objectives must consider the context of the program and the interaction with other programs sharing the same aim, thereby taking into account the consistency of all the initiatives associated with it. The number of strategic objectives of a program should not be excessive. They are complemented by operational objectives and at least one of them must address the issues related to performance-based expenditure management: efficiency and effectiveness. In addition, they should refer to key aspects of the program, that is, to activities that consume a sizable amount of resources. Some strategic objectives refer to the program globally, while others refer to specific areas of activity of the program. The operational objectives constitute a further breakdown of the strategic objectives at a lower level, thereby facilitating the linkages with the activities of the program concerned (see Ministerio de Economía y Hacienda, 2005, pp. 10–15).

All these innovations may be regarded as technical steps toward the consolidation of performance budgeting, but they are not enough. While the formal structure required for PB is strengthened, it remains to be seen whether it will be used and whether there will be the political will and support at all levels needed to move beyond "incrementalist" spending behavior.

Strengthening evaluation and performance audit

Budget offices within each spending ministry could play an important role in the development of these functions, as they are responsible for estimating the budget needs of each department. However, in general, their capacity for analysis and evaluation is very limited. They are understaffed and/or overloaded with a long list of bureaucratic functions.

Program evaluation and performance audit are now emerging in diverse policy spheres owing to the influence of a number of factors including the European integration, the regional decentralization process, and growing demands for effectiveness in public services. Budget-cutting scenarios have also had an influence on the increasing demand for these management assessment tools. Traditionally, these kinds of evaluation and analysis efforts have been developed in Spain on the initiative of the central government, but the role played in recent years by the universities and regional and local governments has been essential and is increasing.

The IGAE has made substantial efforts to use performance auditing for the follow-up of budgetary programs. The Budget Stability Laws of 2001 and 2006 and the General Budget Law of 2003 strengthened the role of the IGAE as the main internal control body in government, highlighting not only its traditional functions of accounting and financial audit, but also its performance auditing on public expenditure management. Clearly there has been a shift from ex-ante compliance controls and financial audits towards the so-called integrated auditing, including the follow-up of budget programs through the performance monitoring of the achievements of objectives. A new National Agency for Evaluation (*Agencia Estatal de Evaluacion*) is being created in the Ministry of Public Administration.

Despite these developments, program evaluation and performance audit still have a long way to go.

Outlook: performance budgeting under decentralization

The outlook for the immediate future of PB in Spain needs to take into account the consequences of the current strong trend towards decentralization. Decentralization in Spain has two different dimensions. The first is an internal one aiming at administrative or management decentralization within central government. The second is an external one associated with the political decentralization or regionalization process that started with the new Constitution (1975).

Management decentralization within central government

The prospects in the immediate future for PB have been affected significantly by the recent approval, in 2006, of the Law of State Agencies (LSA) for the improvement of public services.[18] The aim of this law is to provide a general organizational model for central government based on a high degree of managerial autonomy for state agencies and simultaneously on strengthened mechanisms for accountability focused on results.[19]

State agencies' managers will have the authority to make decisions on their own resources and they will be held accountable for achieving their objectives. To this end, the law introduces a system of Transparent Management by Objectives based on the notion of multi-year management contracts (Article 13, LSA). These contracts must present, among other elements, (a) the objectives to be pursued, outcomes to be obtained, and, in general, the activity to be carried out; (b) the plans necessary for achieving the objectives, specifying the corresponding timeframes and the projects associated with each strategy and its time period, as well as the indicators for evaluating the results; (c) the staffing, material, and budgetary resources to be provided to achieving the objectives; (d) the effects associated with the degree of compliance with established objectives; (e) the procedure to be followed for covering whatever annual deficits may arise owing to a shortage in real revenue from the estimated levels, and the consequences in terms of accountability for management which may result from such deficits; and (f) the procedure for introducing annual changes or adaptations which may occur, as appropriate.

The management contract also determines the mechanisms of accountability for failing to achieve the objectives. Agencies are required to prepare an annual action plan, an activity report on the preceding fiscal year, and annual accounts, which will be available to the public (Article 15, LSA).

As regards their financial management regime, the law creates a new freedom for agencies to shift estimates between types of inputs (line-items), with the exception of personnel costs.[20] Agencies are subject to the accounting principles and system established for public entities and subject to external auditing by the Court of Auditors and oversight by the IGAE.

This reorganization of central government is complementary to the PB reform. Both are based on the same rational decision-making model. However, it remains unclear to what extent and how the two departments responsible for them, respectively the MEH and the Ministry of Public Administration, will share the credit of the reforms and will coordinate efforts. As in past experiences, collective action incentives will be needed.

Performance budgeting in a regionalized state

The development of the Constitution of 1975 has led to a shift from a highly centralized political regime, in which virtually all power was vested in central government, to a highly decentralized model in which the Autonomous Communities (regional governments) are now the level of government with the greatest public spending authority (accounting for 34.6 percent of public expenditure).[21]

Inevitably, this shift has had an impact on regional government budgeting and management. In the near future it is expected that there will be a considerable effort to develop these budgeting techniques. These efforts may yield significant improvements in the quality of their public services (see Rosen, 1999, p. 476 et seq.).

A good illustration on the advances made in this line is the reform process initiated by the Catalonian government with the preparation of the budget for 2006. A serious effort has been made to introduce PB with a view to ensuring that the budget fulfills its dual role as an instrument for fiscal discipline and for spending management. The reform emphasizes the strategic dimensions of this type of budgeting, associated with a long-term perspective, the development of participation, and management flexibility. Also noteworthy are the PB implications of the need for changing the administrative culture and the development of information and evaluation systems focused on outcomes, serving as elements for feeding the budget decision-making under a framework of transparency (in these respects, see Maluquer and Tarrach, 2006).

The preparation process for the 2006 Catalonian budget[22] required the broadening of the institutional scope of the budget (according to the European System of Accounts); the revision of the organizational, economic, and functional classifications of the budget; the implementation of a program budget, and the improvement of budgetary information and its accessibility.[23] The next stage calls for the reform of the Catalonian Finance Law, as well as the improvement of the design of programs and their main components, the development of cost accounting and a comprehensive system of indicators, as well as policy evaluation and reporting (Maluquer and Tarrach, 2006).

The development of these initiatives in this and other Autonomous Communities promises to be one of the most important initiatives in the near future of performance budgeting in the whole Spanish public sector. Improving public expenditure management in regional governments may also have relevant consequences for the programming and budgeting of intergovernmental initiatives that may need sound and comprehensive information on the total resources and overall effects and impact of public policies shared by different levels of governments. Encouraging rational collective behavior among different layers will be a critical factor for the success of any effort towards public-sector-wide PB.

Conclusions: main lessons

The traditional main concern of the MEH has been controlling financial compliance of spending procedures. There have been three decades of budget reform efforts focused on changing the budget document, the program structure, and the formal process of resource allocation. In addition, performance auditing efforts have been specially focused on the follow-up and evaluation of a selected group of budget programs. These reforms began to yield benefits in the mid-1990s (see Sánchez Revenga, 1989, p. 70). It is now generally accepted that the new budget structure offers improved classification and more information on PB technical components and program performance.

However, the budget system in Spain still needs further improvements to consolidate an effective and sound performance budgeting system. For example, accountability for results is still in a phase of development; and better integration among main stakeholders—interministerial or intergovernmental coordination—is needed for efficient and effective public policy results. Currently, additional efforts are being made to further develop performance monitoring, program evaluation, and financial management capacities within the MEH, in spending departments, and in regional governments. The capacity to carry out these functions is gradually being improved. Yet there are several issues and factors to be considered for a substantial qualitative improvement for performance budgeting.

Reflecting on past experience, the following points appear important for further development of PB in Spain:

1. Continuous political support is necessary. One explanation for the limited success of performance budgeting to date is the weakness or lack of continuity of political support. There has been strong commitment and political will in the MEH for supporting the use of efficiency and effectiveness criteria in public expenditure management. However, this interest has not been maintained over time.
2. The formal introduction of the technical components of performance budgeting is not enough. Attention also needs to be paid to cultural values and behavior

of budget main actors and stakeholders. Future advances in the quality of performance budgeting need to take into account, among others, the following conditions and considerations:

(a) *Budgeting cannot be assumed to be a neutral and technical exercise for economic and financial prediction, or a mere legislative process.* Some of the problems identified in this work relate to the attempts to impose reform processes from the center on the basis of a technically ideal solution. A non-participatory approach to budget reform might result in either a merely formal compliance, "creative budgeting," or even the rejection of performance budgeting. Conflicts and negotiations in the process should not be perceived as dysfunctions to be avoided or solved by "objective or neutral" analysis and the corresponding "automatic" decision-making. Uncertainty, conflict, and interdependence are part of the reality of the budget process and its reform. Specifying objectives, measuring performance, analyzing options, and structuring the budget by programs may facilitate stability and predictability in budgeting, but do not guarantee an efficient allocation of resources. Programming does not eliminate risk or the need for conflict management.

(b) *Respecting legal tradition should be complemented by the development of a management culture.* There is a general feeling that the legal perspective of public budgeting is incompatible with a management approach. There is a perception that there is a trade-off between both of them. On the contrary, it is necessary to complement the concern with legality of spending with a new emphasis on performance. However, it seems to be difficult to apply this new perspective to budget reform itself. The efforts of the MEH have been based primarily on introducing new legislation and guidelines for implementing changes in budgeting, auditing, and evaluation.[24] The follow-up and evaluation of the reform have been until recently neglected. A continuous effort is required to assess the impact of the reforms.

    Spending managers adapt their information systems and financial procedures to the requirements of the MEH, but do not regard them as genuinely valuable for their own management interests. The main values and elements of the reform model and implementation strategy are: hierarchical relationships, the assumption that the reform objectives are generally accepted, reliance on rules and norms, and "neutral" professionalism. Legal and hierarchical traditions are deeply rooted: new norms are proposed in the belief that success will be achieved once the "perfect" norm is established and strictly applied. Although the importance of formal procedures and accountability systems should not be underestimated, such systems are not sufficient by themselves to ensure the successful development of performance budgeting. It is necessary to apply the same model to the management of the reform (by results).

3. The collective rationality of the reforms should hold sway over the specific reform preferences of each department. The importance of cooperation and coordination has not been sufficiently considered. The promoters of financial management or performance budgeting initiatives do not have sole responsibility or credit for the results of the reform. There should be more emphasis on the importance of managing interdependence for change. Conditions such as political support, the right incentives to ensure active participation of public managers in the reform and effective integration of new PB, program follow-up and evaluation, government reorganization, and interdepartmental and intergovernmental initiatives, have so far constrained reform results.[25]
4. Learning capacity must be developed. Performance budgeting represents an ideal budgeting model which facilitates improvement in management performance and is perceived as the only solution possible—and the best one—for the public sector as a whole. The applicability of this model to different contexts or types of public organizations has not been questioned. Management and budgeting by results is regarded as a universally valid model. This may explain the difficulties identified when it comes to learning how to introduce the model or how to adapt it to a specific organizational contexts. The contingencies affecting its viability or validity need to be examined: inappropriate contexts, insufficient capacity to managing the reform, or a hierarchical or legalistic approach may affect the proper completion of the reform, even if the implementation strategy is correct.[26]

In short, the development of PB and management by results will depend on sustained political support for the reform, enhancing learning capacity, and introducing the right incentives (for example, accountability for results). Cross-cutting these three success factors, further emphasis should be placed on efforts to increase interaction and cooperation between reform stakeholders so as to overcome risk-averse behavior that may be blocking any collective efforts to move forward or to adapt the reforms to specific contexts.

Notes

1. The authors thank L. Espadas and J.L. Ruiz, of the Ministry of Economy and Finance of Spain, and M. Pazos, of the Institute for Fiscal Studies (Spain), for the information they provided. The opinions expressed in this chapter—and any possible errors—are solely the responsibility of the authors, and do not represent official positions of the Spanish government.
2. Effectiveness and efficiency are not the only valid criteria for measuring government performance: other key factors, such as participation, transparency, sustainability, might need to be considered (Schick, 2003).
3. Ministerial Order of April 23, 1984, of the Ministry of Economy and Finance.
4. Law 18/2001 of December 12, General Budget Stability Law (LGEP) and Organic Law 5/2001 of December 13, Supplementing the General Budget Stability Law (LOCGEP).
5. If full agreement cannot then be reached on a bilateral basis between a ministry and the Directorate-General of Budget, it will be taken to a higher level—ultimately to the Council of Ministers.

6. The IGAE is a body for the *internal audit* of the Administration, but is *external* to the spending units of the departments.
7. Law 6/1997 of April 14.
8. Article 12 of Law 18/2001, General Law on Budgetary Stability, and Article 28 of Law 47/2003, General Budgetary Law.
9. Article 8 of Law 18/2001, General Law on Budgetary Stability.
10. Article 2 of Royal Decree 2855/1979.
11. With regard to the functioning of the Program Analysis Commissions, see Zapico Goñi (2005).
12. See Articles 3–6 LGEP.
13. See Article 31 LGP.
14. Article 29.6 LGP.
15. Cf. Title V of the LGP ("State public sector accounting").
16. See Article 2.1 of Order EHA/1032/2006 of April 6, establishing the rules for preparing the Budgets for 2007.
17. The programs are "Highway Safety," "State Actions Abroad," "Creation of Road Infrastructure," "Coastal Activities," "Energy, Environmental, and Technological Research," and "Promotion of Labor Insertion and Stability." See Espadas (2005a, 2005b).
18. Ley 28/2006, de 18 de julio, de Agencias estatales para la mejora de los servicios públicos (BOE 19 de julio), <www.map.es/iniciativas/mejora_de_la_administracion_general_del_estado/servicios_publicos/ley_agencias_estatales/parrafo/00/document_es/ley_de_agencias.pdf>.
19. Articles 26–31 LSA indicate that budgets are "limitative in respect of their overall amount and estimative for the internal distribution , except personnel expenditure, with a…[changing power shared]…between the MEH— for…the overall budget and…personnel expenditure—and the Agency Director—for the remaining spending." Preamble LSA.
20. Preamble and Article 27 LSA.
21. The next largest spending is that of social security (30 percent). Both are well ahead of central government (17.8 percent) and local governments (15.2 percent). Data are for 2006.
22. *Diari Oficial de la Generalitat de Catalunya*, no. 4398 (June 3, 2005), p. 16172 et seq.
23. The budget preparation order for 2006 and the main annexed budget documents may be consulted on the internet, <www.gencat.net/economia/ambits/finances/pressupost/elaboracio/2006/index.html>.
24. This emphasis reflects both a lack of political support for change and a bias in favor of a "normative" approach to reforms.
25. Many of the changes promoted in the last three decades by the MEH and by the Ministry of Public Administration with a view to introduce performance budgeting and management by results were not sufficiently integrated.
26. This type of budget model is more adapted to a context of stability and increasing resources (see Metcalfe and Richards, 1989, p. 203) and might not be feasible or valid in conditions of uncertainty (that is, unstable policies, diversity of interests with regard to objectives, problems with measuring returns or with establishing cause-effect relationships between programs and outcomes, and so on).

References

Argüello, C., and J. Palacios, 1979, "El Presupuesto por Programas en España," *Hacienda Pública Española*, No. 50.

Barea, J., and A. Carreño, 1971, "Pasos para la Implantación en España de un Presupuesto por Programas," *Hacienda Pública Española*, No. 11.

Carreño Rodríguez-Maribona, A., and A. González Finat, 1979, "El Primer Presupuesto por Programas del Ministerio de Obras Públicas y Urbanismo," *Hacienda Pública Española*, No. 58.

CECAEE (Comisión de Estudio de Creación de la Agencia Estatal de Evaluación), 2004, *Informe para creación de la Agencia Estatal de Evaluación de la Calidad de las Políticas y Servicios Públicos* (Madrid: MAP).

Chile National Budget Office, 2003, *Systems of Management Control and Results-Based Budgeting: The Chilean Experience* (Santiago: Management Control Div. Santiago de Chile).

Dirección General de Presupuestos (Directorate-General of the Budget), 2005, "Propuestas para mejorar las Comisiones de Análisis de Programas: Notas para debate (Informe del Grupo de Trabajo No. 13)," unpublished, Madrid, February 20.

——, 2006, "Informe de progreso sobre fortalecimiento de programas," unpublished, Madrid, n.d.

Espadas, L., 2005a, "Elaboración de los P.G.E.: Mejora de procedimientos," in *Temas de actualidad en la Gestión del Gasto Público* (Sevilla: Universidad Internacional Menéndez Pelayo).

——, 2005b, "La Gestión Presupuestaria por Objetivos en la Ley General Presupuestaria," in *La Política Fiscal en España: Retos y Perspectivas* (Santander: Universidad Internacional Menéndez Pelayo).

Gunther, R., 1980, *Public Policy in a No-Party State: Spanish Planning and Budgeting in the Twilight of the Franquist Era* (Berkeley: University of California Press).

Lozano Irueste, J.M., 1982, *Apuntes de Cátedra de Hacienda Publica* (Madrid: Universidad Complutense).

Maluquer, S., and A. Tarrach, 2006, "La reforma pressupostària de la Generalitat de Catalunya," in *Jornades sobre pressupostació orientada a resultats* (Barcelona: Escola d'Administració Pública de Catalunya).

Metcalfe, L., and S. Richards, 1989, *Improving Public Management* (London: Sage).

Ministerio de Economía y Hacienda (Ministry of Economy and Finance), 2004, "Elementos Claves en el Fortalecimiento de la Presupuestación por Programas," *Notas Técnicas* de la Dirección General de Presupuestos (Subdirección General de Análisis y Evaluación de las Políticas del Gasto).

——, 2005, "Guía para la Elaboración de Programas Presupuestarios," Dirección General de Presupuestos, Subdirección General de Análisis y Evaluación de las Políticas del Gasto.

OECD, 2001, *Outcome Focused Management and Budgeting* (Paris: SBO).

Pollit, C., and G. Bouckaert, 2004, *Public Management Reform: A Comparative Analysis* (New York: Oxford University Press).

Rosen, H.S., 1999, *Hacienda Pública* (Madrid: McGraw-Hill),

Sánchez Revenga, J., 1989, *Presupuestos Generales del Estado y aspectos básicos del presupuesto general de las CEE* (Barcelona: Ariel).

——, 2005, "El Presupuesto por Programas en España," *Economistas*, Vol. 105, pp. 29–37.

Schick, A., 2003, "The Performing State: Reflection on an Idea Whose Time Has Come but Whose Implementation Has Not." Paper for the 24th Annual Meeting of Senior Budget Officials, Rome, June 3–4, 2003. Organization for Economic Cooperation and Development (GOV/PUMA/SBO(2003)17; May 2, 2003).

UK Cabinet Office, 1999, *Next Steps: Moving On* (Cm 2450) (London: HMSO).

Zapico Goñi, E., 2005, "Comisiones de análisis de programas y asignación eficiente del gasto público," *Economistas*, Vol. 105, pp. 39–50.

18
Performance Budgeting, Motivation, and Incentives

Elisabeth Paul and Marc Robinson

As noted in Chapter 1, many contemporary forms of performance budgeting are part of the broader "managing-for-results" (MFR) approach to public sector reform. Like MFR in general, the primary focus of these forms of performance budgeting is upon *motivating* agencies to perform better, and in this sense they differ from, for example, classic forms of performance budgeting the primary focus of which is better central expenditure prioritization. This is true of contemporary performance budgeting models which contain one or more of the following elements:

- agency-level performance targets which are intended to be linked to the level of resourcing provided
- funding formulas which implicitly set, through the funding formula, targets for the results expected to be achieved
- agency-level financial incentives, under which good performance by the agency results in higher levels of funding, and poor performance possibly leads to financial sanctions.

Motivating agencies to perform better is also important if the full benefits of input control relaxation are to be realized.

These contemporary approaches to performance budgeting all subscribe to the MFR view that the most fundamental tools for improving agency performance are the explicit specification of objectives, the measurement of performance against those objectives, and the setting of performance targets. This points, however, to a crucial question. Exactly how is it that the specification of objectives, measures, and targets impacts—to the extent it actually does—on agency performance? In asking this question, we need to bear in mind that agencies are comprised of individuals, and it is those individuals who need to perform better if the agency as a whole is to perform better. Therefore, to ask about the motivational impact on agencies is really to ask about the motivational impact *upon individuals* within the agency of objectives, measures, and targets specified for the agency as a whole.

There is a widespread contemporary view that the key to more effectively motivating individual public sector employees to perform is *individual performance incentives,*[1] and that, conversely, the biggest motivational problem in the "traditional" employment arrangements has been the weakness of such performance incentives. From this perspective, the "transmission mechanism" by which MFR in general—and performance budgeting in particular—can succeed in inducing better agency performance might be seen as comprising two critical elements. The first is the development of individual and work-group performance measures and targets which are clearly linked to organizational objectives—in order to create what the US General Accounting Office (GAO) (2005, p. 21; 2002, p. 11) refers to as "a line of sight that shows how individual performance can contribute to organizational goals" by "cascading organizational goals and objectives down to the individual performance level." The second element is the systematic linkage of these performance measures to individual incentives—both to traditional incentives (for example, promotion) and also increasingly to "higher-powered" incentives such as performance pay (also known as "merit" pay). Individual "contracts" are increasingly used for this purpose.

Consistent with this approach, there has been considerable expansion in recent years in the use of performance incentives in the public sector. Both the incidence of performance pay schemes for civil servants and the levels of incentives paid under those schemes have been increasing in a number of countries. In the US, for example, between 1998 and 2000 alone there was an increase from 14.3 percent to 64 percent in state governments using performance bonuses linked to measures of individual performance (Government Performance Project, 2003, p. 111).[2] The OECD (2005, p. 175) recently reported that countries with "extended, formalized performance-related pay policy for civil servants" include Denmark, Finland, Korea, New Zealand, Switzerland, and the UK.

Performance pay is also increasingly being used in areas of front-line service delivery such as health service (for example, nursing) and teaching. A prime example is teacher performance pay—what the recent US Teaching Commission report (2004, p. 22) calls "paying teachers more for high performance, as measured by fair evaluations and clear evidence of improved student learning." Many such schemes have been introduced into school jurisdictions in the US over the past decade, and a similar trend has been under way in some other countries. A national teacher performance pay scheme was, for example, introduced in the UK in 1999, taking effect in 2001. Other countries where such schemes have been tried include Kenya and Israel. Similar arrangements have been introduced for nursing pay in a number of countries including the UK.

Performance budgeting systems which incorporate agency-level funding "incentives" would seem to fit naturally with this approach to motivating individual performance—at least if there is a link between agency level funding rewards and individual incentives. Perhaps the most striking example of such a link is the Canadian province of Ontario, which recently experimented with a system in which the overall performance of all ministries was rated and the performance pay pool (that is, the amount of money made available to fund individual performance pay) made available to each ministry was linked to that rating (GAO, 2002, p. 20). An example of something similar at the sectoral level is a system announced in late 2005 in Texas (Perry, 2005) under which:

- schools that serve a large population of economically disadvantaged students that show marked improvement in student performance will be eligible for a grant of at least $100,000
- local school officials will have discretion to distribute the grant to the teachers they determine are having the greatest impact, with a requirement that a minimum of 75 percent of the grant must go directly to the "hardworking teachers who are improving the learning environment."

In most cases, however, the linkage between agency financial incentives and individual incentives has been less clear than in these instances. Moreover, as noted earlier, many versions of performance budgeting do not attempt to provide agencies with financial incentives for performance, but instead focus on strengthening the link between funding and expected future performance. In these systems, performance budgeting is more about strengthening the credibility of target-setting, rather than about linking individual performance incentives to the overall level of agency funding.

The proposition that the key to better public sector performance is stronger individual performance incentives linked to measured performance and performance targets may be very influential in contemporary thought and practice, but it is also controversial. There are many who oppose stronger individual performance incentives, arguing that they actually lead to a deterioration in public sector performance. Critics emphasize the perverse effects which can arise from linking high-powered incentives to inherently imperfect targets and measures. Many also suggest that the emphasis on incentives is based on a misunderstanding of the true nature of workplace motivation, and that high-powered incentives are more likely to demotivate than to motivate.

There has been vigorous public debate on these issues in recent years in a number of countries. In Britain, for example, critics have attacked the Public Service Agreements (PSAs) target-setting regime on the grounds that targets "are arbitrary...focus people on the wrong things...(and) demotivate" (Seddon, 2002). The British government has been criticized for its teacher performance pay initiative by those who see such schemes as "unfair and divisive, with a negative effect on team-working and co-operation" (Richardson, quoted in BBC, 1999). Similarly, in California, a November 2005 constitutional referendum proposition put forward by Governor Schwarzenegger to permit merit pay for teachers was attacked by the California Federation of Teachers (2005) on the grounds that

- it would "poison...the school atmosphere with unnecessary and unproductive competitive pressures"

- previous experience with merit pay scheme indicated that "to maximize pay, some teachers ignored their best and worst students, concentrating on the middle group, because they assumed the best would score well anyway, and the worst demanded too much time."

Critics often suggest that a regime of individual incentives based on measures and targets is particularly unsuitable in the public sector and, more generally, that the public sector has specific characteristics which mean that caution needs to be applied when importing management practices—whether in this or other areas—from the private sector. However, this debate is in no sense confined to the public sector. There are many management thinkers and practitioners who believe that high-powered individual performance incentives are damaging to organizational performance in a private sector context—and who believe that, although "we are often encouraged to believe that rewarding people for what they do will cause them to work harder and better," in fact "research and our long-term experiences... suggest exactly the opposite" (Kohn, 1998). The critics of performance incentives draw a sharp distinction between the level of pay and incentive pay. Their advice to managers is: "Pay people well. Pay people fairly. And then do everything in your power to take people's minds off of money" (Kohn, 1998).

It is relevant to this debate that although the current level of use of individual performance incentives in the public sector is certainly much higher than ever before, the use of these incentives are in no sense new. There was, in fact, a previous wave of enthusiasm in the 1970s and 1980s associated, for example, with the introduction of performance pay as part of the new "senior executive service" in the US, the influence of which then spread to many other countries. Critics assert that the preponderance of empirical research[3] on these earlier civil service schemes indicates that they were ineffective. The OECD's recent interpretation of this evidence is similar:

> The impact of performance pay on motivation is ambivalent: while it appears to motivate a minority of staff, it seems that a large majority often do not see performance-related pay as an incentive...Job content and career development have been found to be the strongest incentives for public employees. Performance-related pay is unlikely to motivate a substantial majority of staff, irrespective of the design. (OECD, 2005, pp. 176–7)

Similar claims about the weight of empirical evidence have been made in other public and private sector contexts. Thus the respected management academic Jeffrey Pfeffer recently claimed that "the last 100 years' worth of research shows that incentive pay does not produce better results in education, even though this is a lesson that seems to be continually relearned" (Pfeffer, 2005). He also argues that broader research in both public and private sector contexts suggests that the increased pay dispersion associated with performance pay schemes "can often reduce job satisfaction, disrupt social relationships in the workplace, decrease performance...decrease quality...and increase [staff] turnover" (Ferraro and Pfeffer, 2005, p. 20).

Against this background, the objective of this chapter is to consider the motivational "transmission mechanism" of performance budgeting. More precisely, it is to review, drawing upon the existing literature, what is known or what might be reasonably hypothesized about the efficacy of strategies for motivating public sector employees, and the implications of this for performance budgeting and for the "managing-for-results" mechanisms of which certain performance budgeting models are part.

The first and most fundamental question examined is therefore that of how far the correct approach to motivating better agency performance in the public sector is through stronger performance-based individual incentives, including not only performance pay but the more systematic linking of other incentives to measured performance. This question raises a number of more specific issues, including:

- How severe are the problems which arise for individual incentive schemes from imperfections in individual performance measurement?
- To what extent should one be concerned about stronger incentives undermining what is sometimes referred to as "intrinsic" or "public service" motivation?
- To the extent that motivations other than material self-interest are important, what should be the respective role of incentives and other strategies for motivating people?

To consider these questions, we start in the second section with a review of the literature of what might be called classic institutional economics, the most well-known element of which is agency theory. This is a literature which models workplace behavior on the assumption that individuals' motivation is essentially self-interested and materialistic. This literature explores formally the implications of this assumption for the role and design of performance incentives in the presence of both imperfect performance measurement and uncertainty (risk).

The third section turns to a body of literature which emphasizes the importance of non-materialistic motivations—social motivation, intrinsic motivation, and moral motivation. Most of this literature comes from the fields of psychology and management, although in recent years economists have also done important work based on richer motivational models. We also provide some additional views which do not necessarily emerge clearly from the literature.

The section following this considers—albeit in a rather speculative manner, given the limitations of the literature—the implications of these findings about the nature of individual motivation for the motivational transmission mechanism of performance budgeting.

In the final section, we consider briefly the implications of this analysis for the issues of motivating performance in the special circumstances which often characterize developing countries. We finally draw the main conclusions for motivating individuals in the context of performance management.

Mainstream economic literature

The mainstream economic literature on incentives uses various currents of the new institutional economics, including transaction costs economics, organization and property rights theories, and predominantly the principal-agent theory. It is a literature which assumes that individuals act rationally to pursue their self-interest. Crucially, self-interested motivation is not construed in the broad sense—to refer to the pursuit of anything from which individuals derive utility—but in the much narrower sense of the pursuit of material (monetary equivalent) well-being.[4] As Le Grand (2003, p. 25) puts it, the assumption is that rational *Homo economicus* is "a genus of individuals whose self-interest is defined solely in terms of their own consumption: that is, such individuals are motivated entirely by the desire to acquire material wealth that they consume themselves for their own benefit." In short, this literature assumes that individuals are, at least as an approximation, exclusively motivated by *materialistic self-interest.*

This literature assumes that people have a preference for leisure, so that work is wholly unpleasant. From this it follows that, to the extent they can succeed in doing so without being caught—or are not adequately motivated by incentives—agents will shirk in order to avoid the disutility of working. Because agents are assumed to be motivated solely by materialistic self-interest, "incentives" in this context refer exclusively to monetary incentives, on the one hand, and sanctions (including the threat of dismissal), assessed in terms of their monetary equivalent effect, on the other hand. The term "incentives" will, accordingly, be used in this manner throughout this chapter.

The assumption that individuals are motivated solely by materialistic self-interest distinguishes the mainstream economic literature from the psychological, management, and economic literatures discussed in the third section of this chapter, which focus upon a range of "non-self-interested" and "altruistic" motivations.[5] It is perhaps useful, however, to make clear at this point that we are not satisfied with this classification of motivation. We readily accept the existence of genuinely selfless motivation. However, as discussed in the third section, we regard the pursuit of *some* (not all) so-called "non-self-interested" objectives—such as the non-material psychological benefits associated with status and power—as fundamentally self-interested. Therefore, instead of adhering to the classification of self-interested versus non-self-interested motivations, we rather distinguish between "materialistic" self-interested motivations and "non-materialistic" motivations.

Although the materialistic self-interest postulate of the mainstream economic literature is quite reductionist, this literature has nevertheless yielded important results.[6] In particular, the conclusion of the bulk of this literature is that "high-powered" (performance-related) incentives are problematic in most employment relationships.

In this section, we overview key themes of this literature which are relevant for the question of individual motivation in a context of performance management. We start with the general literature, which generally assumes a private sector context, and after that consider the specifics of the public sector context.

Measurement, uncertainty, and the employment relationship

The mainstream economic literature treats the employment relationship as a principal-agent relationship in which a "principal" (for example, an employer) delegates work to one or several "agents" (for example, the workers). The agent's *effort* (activity) yields results for the principal. These results can be thought of, at least as a starting point, as the worker's "output."[7] The objective of the principal is to manage and motivate the agent to deliver the best results possible. Agent remuneration may, in principle, be based on effort, on output, or on some mix of the two. The principal needs, among other things, to decide the appropriate remuneration mix—in other words, how "high-powered" remuneration should be. Remuneration is more "high-powered" the more strongly and more directly it is linked to worker output—or more generally, worker results—and is more "low-powered" the weaker and more indirect that link. Piecework pay is, for example, extremely high-powered, while time-based pay is extremely low-powered.

To the extent that the principal can readily observe and measure the quantity and quality of the agent's effort, remuneration can be unproblematically based on effort with little or no consideration of worker output. However, in many employment relationships, the agent's effort is not perfectly or costlessly observable by the principal. If this is the case, the proxy measures of effort upon which remuneration is based—most obviously, hours worked—are flawed, and basing remuneration upon them allows considerable scope for shirking. The obvious response to this is the monitoring of agent effort by the principal (that is, work supervision). This is, however, not a fully satisfactory solution because for many types of jobs monitoring is imprecise and has a high cost. This is particularly true for managerial and other "knowledge worker" jobs where the precise activities which the agent should carry out in the interests of the principal cannot be fully specified in advance.

Where effort is not easy to measure, and supervision is costly and/or imprecise, it might be thought that the obvious alternative is to link pay more to output (for example, via piece rates or commissions), so that workers have a strong incentive to exert more effort and thereby to increase production. The use of high-powered incentives has the added advantage of screening workers on the basis of their ability (Lazear, 1986, 2000). In other words, because the most able workers have the prospect of earning more under such incentive schemes, these workers would be attracted to working for firms offering strong performance incentives.

The mainstream economic literature points, however, to major informational and uncertainty/risk problems which limit the scope for paying workers on the basis of their output. It explains by reference to these factors the limited use of high-powered incentives within firms—that is, in the context of the employment relationships—relative to their use in market transactions between firms.

In the first place, the measurement of worker "outputs" may be affected by a range of output measurement problems—for example, if the output concerned is a service rather than a physical good, quality may be particularly hard to measure. The self-interest postulate implies that, faced with high-powered incentives linked to imperfect output measures, agents will ruthlessly focus all effort on what is measured, neglecting what is not measured and which does not therefore enter into their compensation scheme. This will be a problem in any "multi-tasking" context—that is, when the work to be performed encompasses several dimensions (for example, quantity and quality, production and maintenance of the productive asset, and so on), some of which are less measurable than others. The result will be *dysfunctional (perverse) behavior*—that is, behavior which is to the detriment of the principal's interests (Holmström and Milgrom, 1991). The other consequence will be that agents may "game" the system, that is, manipulate information so as to be sure to get their output-based payments. Moreover, some degree of output measurement difficulty affects the bulk of jobs.

A further problem arises when, as is so often the case, outputs are produced by teams of workers and it may not be possible readily to distinguish the contribution of one worker from other workers in the team (Alchian and Demsetz, 1972). Under such circumstances, a measure of team output may be used as a proxy for individual output. However, group incentives entail the risk of the so-called free-rider problem, meaning that a member of the group could be tempted to reduce his own effort, while hoping to get the performance premium if the group as a whole meets the target.[8] But if most members act non-cooperatively and do not exert sufficient effort, performance will be low and the group will not receive any premium.

The further problem is that some agents—managers in particular—do not produce specific final or intermediate outputs, but are rather engaged in "overhead" tasks such as strategy formulation and the organization of production processes. In these circumstances, the ideal high-powered incentive would not be payment by output, but payment based on the agent's contribution to the principal's ultimate objective (which can be taken to be the maximization of the firm's total value). In reality, however, this generally is impossible to measure. Great difficulties arise in seeking to distinguish good performance from the impact of uncontrollable external factors. Disentangling one individual's contribution to the results achieved from that of others it exceedingly difficult, particularly given the substantial and variable time lag between managerial actions and their consequences (Feltham and Xie, 1994). Under these circumstances, if a high-powered incentive scheme based upon objective performance measures is to be used, there tends to be little choice but to use overall measures of firm performance (for example, accounting profit or changes in the firm's share price, or performance relative to competitors or to the market as a whole) which do not seek to distinguish the contribution of specific individuals and which, in general, do a poor job of netting out the impact of uncontrollable external factors. The inevitable imperfection of such performance measures leads to perverse effects (Baker, 1992; Gibbons, 1998). For example, they may lead to actions which boost short-term profitability (and thereby the short-term share price in an imperfectly informed equity market) at the expense of longer-term value maximization.

This points to a further related problem to which high-powered incentives are subject—the impact of uncertainty. To the extent that high-powered incentives for workers are based upon measures of outcomes or outputs which are subject to uncertainty due to uncontrollable external factors, the use of such incentives makes worker income uncertain, and transfers risks from the firm to its workers. The implication of this is that, if workers are more risk averse that the firm's principals, the appropriate role of high-powered incentives will be correspondingly lessened (Stiglitz, 1974).[9]

In summary, the conclusion of this literature is that *the less measurable are worker results (outputs or outcomes), and the greater the uncertainty about the relationship between worker effort and the results measures available, the less use should be made of high-powered incentives based upon objective performance measures*. The principal should, in general, *trade off the increase in incentives and the problems associated with them, that is, risk and distortions* (Baker, 2002). Insofar as high-powered incentives are used, the performance measures should be selected taking into account their degree of controllability by the agent and their alignment with the principal's objective (Feltham and Xie, 1994).

The role of medium-powered incentives

The mainstream economic literature also considers the merits of a number of other remuneration strategies which fall somewhere between the high-powered and low-powered ends of the spectrum.

One of these is the use of *subjective* performance "measures" as a way to mitigate incentive distortions arising from imperfect *objective* performance measures.[10] Subjective "measures" are performance ratings by supervisors which are intended to capture aspects of the workers' contribution to the firm which are hard to measure. However, subjective measures come with their own set of problems. As they cannot be costlessly verified by outsiders, subjective performance measures may possibly be manipulated or distorted (when, for example, supervisors compress ratings around the mean or when workers waste time currying favor) and entail the risk of opportunistic behavior by the principal (Prendergast, 1999). In particular, the risk of influence activities on the part of employees involves costs to the organization, both in degrading the quality of decision-making and in diverting attention and effort (Milgrom and Roberts, 1988). Subjective performance measures make sense only in ongoing relationships where the credibility of both players is important.

In practice, objective and subjective performance measures are often used in combination. Baker et al. (1994) show that in some circumstances, objective and subjective measures are complements, leading to better results than either explicit or implicit contracts alone. At the bottom line, the mix of objective and subjective measures should thus be based on a trade-off between the perverse effects and the distortions arising from the two kinds of measures.

Promotional incentives (referred to in some of the literature as "career concerns") have the advantage that they break the immediacy of the connection between assessed performance and the reward (Dewatripont et al., 1999a). This helps reduce the incidence of perverse effects and gaming with only a misleading short-term impact on measured performance. However, promotional incentives also raise another more general risk. This is that any incentives which are awarded on the basis of *relative performance*[11] (that is, the performance of one worker assessed in comparison with other workers' performance) entail the risk that agents will take actions that reduce the chances that other players "win the prize"—that is, employees may sabotage each other's work or output. This risk is, however, considerably greater for higher-powered incentives such as, at the extreme, the process which has been adopted by some companies wherein all employees are rated relative to one another and those at the top are rewarded richly while those at the bottom are fired. The literature warns strongly on the risk of using such "tournament" processes in contexts where cooperation and team work are critical to firm performance (Borjas, 2000, pp. 444–5; Lazear, 1986; Holmström and Milgrom, 1994).

The literature also suggests a number of other mechanisms which may be used to create more balanced incentives for materially self-interested workers in the presence of performance measurement difficulties, namely:

- *deferred compensation,* such as seniority pay (underpayment followed by overpayment) and pensions provide incentives to exert effort, and they reduce turnover
- *better working conditions,* which the hedonic theory of wages suggests can reduce the opportunity cost of worker effort
- *"efficiency" wages:* the idea here is that paying above-market wage rates will, by raising the opportunity cost of being fired, increase the desire of workers to perform in order to keep their jobs.[12]

Further theoretical results

Although this literature points to strong reasons for caution about high-powered incentives in many employment contexts, it clearly implies that the extent to which such incentives may be used varies enormously between different contexts. The literature points to a set of factors which determine the nature of the optimal employment and remuneration regime for particular types of work. These include the ease and cost of monitoring effort, the availability and quality of measures of work output or contribution to the firm's results, the importance of work-group cooperation, and the length of the employment relationship. In some contexts, it may be optimal from the principal's point of view to rely largely or wholly upon high-powered incentives—for example, if workers are responsible as individuals for producing an easily-measurable product (permitting, for example, piecework for outsourced clothing workers). However, the circumstances of most employment relationships are far removed from this, and more limited use of high-powered incentives is appropriate as a result.

With few early exceptions (for example, Alchian and Demsetz, 1972), the mainstream economic literature hardly mentions the information cost of performance information (that is, of information about outputs and outcomes achieved) as a factor in determining the appropriate role of high-powered incentives. In the main, it is only in respect to the monitoring of worker effort that information costs are taken into account as a determining factor for the choice between low-powered and high-powered incentives (for example, Garen, 1998). However, clearly the higher the costs of performance information, the smaller the appropriate role for high-powered incentives, other things being equal.

Generally speaking, in multi-task settings, it is often helpful to use multiple instruments to provide a balanced package of incentives (Gibbons, 1998).[13] In other words, optimal employment arrangements will often tend to be based upon a mix of low-powered and medium- or high-powered remuneration instruments of varying types, including use of objective and subjective measures. Among low-powered remuneration, time-based payment will often be important, supported by significant monitoring activity. In addition, rules constraining employees' behavior can play an important role in many contexts (Holmström and Milgrom, 1994).

Empirical results

The general empirical evidence with respect to the motivating power of money, which is notably surveyed in Gupta and Shaw (1998), Jenkins et al. (1998), and Prendergast (1999), is relatively consistent, and shows that financial incentives are associated with higher performance—or, more precisely, that they are associated with higher quantity of worker output.[14] However, this evidence relates almost exclusively to jobs with routine tasks (see, for example, Lazear, 2000) or to corporate managers' compensation (see, for example, Kole, 1997), and says little about other jobs where measurement is difficult. Thus, for example, the available literature on impacts on performance *quality* is inconclusive (Gupta and Shaw, 1998). In a managerial context, empirical evidence suggests that there is indeed a statistically significant relationship between managerial pay and firm performance, but only a weak one (Barkema et al., 1997). Moreover, there is little empirical endorsement of the principal-agent theory, in the sense that contracts are rarely designed as predicted by theoretical models (Prendergast, 1999).

The literature on dysfunctional responses—perverse effects and gaming—to compensation schemes in a private sector context is reviewed in Prendergast (1999, pp. 25–9), and provides some evidence that these effects are real. Baker et al. (1994) also offer a series of examples illustrating the dysfunctional behaviors due to a payment-for-results system based on "distortionary" performance measures. However, this empirical evidence is quite limited (it is inherently difficult to test, because of measurement difficulties), being based on only a handful of case studies.

Yet the real empirical question is not so much whether perverse effects exist, but rather what is their magnitude, and whether their costs (in conjunction with other problems) outweigh the benefits of incentives. A related question is how they can be mitigated, be it through additional constraints (supervision) to secure quality (Holmström and Milgrom, 1991) and/or other types of motivation (see below).

Application of these results to the public sector

Most of the mainstream economic literature assumes a private sector context. However, a number of economists, and some political scientists, have applied this framework to the public sector. Their general conclusion is that the special characteristics of the public sector mean that the problems affecting the use of high-powered incentives tend to be particularly severe, and that financial performance incentives may therefore *optimally* be absent or very low-powered in the public sector (Burgess and Ratto, 2003; Tirole, 1994; Dixit, 2002; Dewatripont et al., 1999b).

A key reason for this is that output measurement difficulties tend on average to be more severe in the public sector, because (as discussed in Chapter 3) the general government sector has a heavy concentration of services as opposed to physical goods, and many of these services are heterogeneous or contingent capacity in nature. Moreover, performance data is often only available at an aggregate level, hence the need to focus on team performance (Burgess and Ratto, 2003). At the level of outcomes, there is usually no measure of overall agency results equivalent to profit or market capitalization in the private sector. All of the other difficulties of measuring individual managers' contributions to results—the impact of external factors, uncertain and variable time lags, and the team nature of outcomes—also apply. By contrast to private firms which, at least approximately speaking, have a single clear ultimate objective (value maximization), government agencies pursue multiple social welfare objectives which frequently conflict (for example, efficiency versus equity) and which must therefore be traded off against one another. Moreover, as noted again in Chapter 3, there is often a measure of ex-ante ambiguity about objectives, one reason for which is unresolved competing views at the political level or within agencies. Relevant to this is the widespread presence of what the literature refers to as "multiple principals" in the public sector. In other words, rather than having only one boss to please, public organizations often face competing pressures from, for example, politicians and the public, or from political leaders in executive government versus those within the legislature. For all these reasons, it is often the case that results are harder to measure than actions (effort) (Dixit, 2002).

Moreover, the multiplicity of missions and measurement difficulties mean that the "multi-tasking" problem tends to be particularly severe in the public sector, the implication of which is that high-powered incentives may entail even more unforeseen and dysfunctional side-effects than in firms with clear goals. It has also been suggested that the importance of worker cooperation in some sectors is so great that excessive wage differential between workers of the same level would be very damaging to team cooperation (Lazear, 1986).

Prendergast (2002) argues that overseeing public officials' behavior is often carried out by investigating the details of the cases they handle, not on a random basis, but instead upon information received from consumers—that is, based on complaints. This system creates agency problems because those consumers who are given rents by mistake do not complain, while those who feel mistreated do complain.

A further difficulty for high-powered incentives in the public sector is the absence of the type of link between the level of performance of an agency and its funding which exists in the private sector where firms that perform well will tend to enjoy strong profits that can be used to provide performance incentives to employees.

This is a formidable list of difficulties, and the literature suggests that it is in significant measure as a consequence of these specificities that incentives are generally weaker in the public sector and that public agencies rather resort preponderantly on other types of lower-powered incentives such as promotion (see, for example, Dewatripont et al., 1999a, 1999b; Rose-Ackerman, 1986). The implication of this is that work supervision, as well as task assignment and work organization, are all even more important in the public than in the private sector in promoting better performance (Burgess and Ratto, 2003). Holmström and Milgrom's (1994) argument that the effectiveness of low-powered incentives may be enhanced by simultaneously placing constraints on the employee's freedom to act has also been used to explain the widespread use of bureaucratic rules regulating the behavior of public employees (Prendergast, 1999).

It must, however, be borne in mind that there is considerable variation within the public sector (as in the private sector) in the type of work being performed and therefore in relation to such factors as the costs of performance information and effort monitoring. What is more important to determine the power of incentives is not whether the tasks are performed in the public or private sector per se, but the nature of the tasks. For instance, a survey of the evidence on incentives in organizations by Burgess and Metcalfe (1999) shows that there is no difference between public and private organizations in the likelihood of an agency operating a performance pay scheme for manual workers; however, public service agencies are much less likely to operate a performance pay scheme for non-manual workers. They also find that merit pay based on subjective assessments is, as might be expected, more widely used than "objective" performance in the remuneration of non-manual workers (whose output is harder to measure), and that the reverse is true for manual workers. Generally speaking, incentive schemes for "operational" staff ought to adapt to the characteristics of the tasks, such as ease of monitoring, availability of good performance measure, and degree of cooperation needed between workers—just as in the private sector.

Non-materialistic motivation

The key deficiency of the mainstream economic literature is its strict adherence to the materialistic self-interest postulate. There is, however, considerable evidence indicating that people often act contrary to their material self-interest (Frey and Jegen, 2001; Fehr et al., 2002; Gintis et al., 2003; Fehr and Rockenbach, 2003). Moreover, the assumption that workers will shirk in the absence of sufficient incentives is one for which there is little empirical evidence (Minkler, 2004). The evidence points to the existence of informal norms and socio-psychological forces that may often motivate workers more powerfully than financial incentives do (Baron, 1988). Such non-monetary motivations have been studied for decades by social scientists (for example, Herzberg, 1968) and in particular social psychologists (for example, Deci, 1971; Deci and Ryan, 1985; Lepper and Greene, 1978).

With some honorable early exceptions (for example, Akerlof, 1982), economists for a long time ignored this literature. However, in recent years more and more economists have been using the findings of social sciences on the nature of work motivation, taking their analysis to a more sophisticated level than that offered by the strict material self-interest postulate (for example, Frey, 1993, 1997; Kreps, 1997;

Murdock, 2002; Bénabou and Tirole, 2003; Minkler, 2004; Le Grand, 2003). The importance of this is captured well by Gibbons (1998, p. 130), who observed that

> one simple possibility is that economic models that ignore social psychology may be incomplete (but perhaps still useful) descriptions of incentives in organizations. A more troubling possibility is that management practices based on economic models may dampen (or even destroy) non-economic realities such as intrinsic motivation and social relations.

No unified theory of non-materialistic motivation has emerged yet, and a range of different concepts of such motivation can be found in the literature. The lack of consensus in the literature makes it necessary to suggest a working classification of such motivation as a framework for the analysis in this chapter. To this end, we propose to distinguish between social motivation and internal motivation, and within the latter category between intrinsic motivation and moral motivation. In doing so, it is, however, important to stress the close interactions between these various sources of motivation. Moreover, the distinction between motivation and motivators is, as discussed below, an important one.

It is worth emphasizing that the recognition of these additional sources of motivation allows us to adapt—rather than completely reject—the rational choice approach preferred by economists. Indeed, adjusted to take into account non-pecuniary motivation, economic models may account for much of the pro-social or altruistic behavior now broadly evidenced in the literature (Baron, 1988; DiIulio, 1994; Bénabou and Tirole, 2003). Technically, of course, one can incorporate non-materialistic factors into the worker's utility maximization problem and still use (a modified version of) the rational choice approach (Minkler, 2004).

Social motivation

We define social motivation as referring to the pursuit by individuals of certain types of social relationships in the workplace—such as the acceptance and approval of others, adherence to norms, and search for status and power—for reasons which are separate from, or additional to, any material advantage which may arise from those social relationships.

The sources of social motivation identified by sociologists and psychologists include the human tendency to identify with groups, which translates into group loyalty and group utility (Gupta et al., 1997); the adherence to norms (general rules of voluntary behavior); and more generally, the desire to reciprocate, to avoid social disapproval and to get "social rewards." The importance of these sources of motivation has been clearly demonstrated in the psycho-sociological literature, even if their raison d'être is not as yet perfectly explained by social cognitive science (see, for example, Falk and Fehr, 2002; Fehr et al., 2002; Gintis et al., 2003; Fehr and Fischbacher, 2004; Janssen and Mendys-Kamphorst, 2004).

The sense of fairness is one crucial element of social motivation. Fairness is about how people feel they are treated (materially and also symbolically) relative to others in their reference group. Fairness often centers on reciprocity, and numerous experimental studies indicate that people tend to voluntarily cooperate, if treated fairly, and to punish unfair behavior (see, for example, Fehr et al., 1997; Fehr et al., 2002; Fehr and Schmidt, 2004). Fairness is very important to consider in the workplace, because workers who believe they are being fairly treated are more likely to put forth effort and commitment, even if it runs counter to their material self-interest; while workers who feel unfairly treated may quit, reduce their effort level, steal from the employer, or even sabotage output (Ehrenberg and Smith, 1997). Fairness and, more generally, social comparison would appear to be very important to human beings in general, but are perhaps even more important in some societies (for example, Japan—see Levine, 1993) than in others.

One of the few economists who recognized early the importance of social motivation is Akerlof (1982), whose partial gift exchange model involves the concepts of *norms, reciprocity*, and *fair treatment* (the latter being, for the most part, based on comparison of one's own situation with that of an appropriate reference group).

Internal motivations

We define internal motivations as those deriving from a desire of the individual to behave in a certain manner for reasons that are independent of any immediate external pressure or inducement. This contrasts with social motivations, which are activated by reference to the actual or anticipated reactions of others to one's own behavior.

Moral motivation is the first type of internal motivation we consider—and the most altruistic one. We define moral motivation as the desire to behave in accordance with one's moral beliefs and values, for reasons separate from any personal advantages (material or social) which may accrue from such behavior. Moral motivations encompass the desire to act altruistically in pursuit of a cause one believes to be just, or in the interests of external beneficiaries whom one believes one has a responsibility to assist (Minkler, 2004). They also encompass the work ethic, in the sense of an internalized commitment to work.

In a workplace context, belief in the "mission"—the social purpose—of the organization can be an important element in moral motivation. This is particularly true in public service and not-for-profit organizations. In a public sector context, the term "public service motivation" is, as discussed later, often used to describe this type of motivation.

Intrinsic motivation will be used in what follows to refer to motivation which derives from the enjoyment of work—that is, from the pleasure of undertaking activities one likes (input orientation) or from internal satisfaction derived from work achievements (and independent of any social or material rewards which those achievements might generate). Intrinsic motivation thus refers to working "for its own sake" (Deci and Ryan, 1985).

In the literature, the term "intrinsic" motivation is sometimes used in this narrow sense. But it is frequently used more broadly. For some authors, it encompasses some or all forms of what we call internal motivations.[15] For others, it includes even elements of social motivation.

The degree of intrinsic motivation clearly varies enormously between individuals and between types of jobs. Little intrinsic motivation may exist in some narrowly repetitive manual jobs, whereas the intrinsic motivation for, say, a musician may be extremely high.

The interrelationship between different kinds of motivation

Although the divergent use of terminology in the literature makes the presentation of the above taxonomy of sources of motivation necessary for purpose of clarity, it must be immediately acknowledged that social, intrinsic, and moral motivations are closely interconnected. For example, whereas an individual may initially be driven by social motivation to act in accordance with values held by others in his/her social milieu, over time such values are often internalized by the individual, thus becoming part of moral motivation. Intrinsic motivation and moral motivation arising from the work ethic can also be closely linked in practice.[16]

As noted earlier, the taxonomy presented here does not rely on the distinction between self-interested and non-self-interested motivation. In our typology, social motivations and intrinsic motivation are to an important degree self-interested in nature, although not in a material sense. This is obviously the case in respect to the desire for recognition or power, or the desire to avoid being socially "punished" by peers for unfair or non-cooperative behavior. It is for this reason that we reject the use of the term "self-interest" to refer to monetary and material objectives alone, and instead describe this as "materialistic" self-interest.

Some economists and game theorists argue that supposedly non-self-interested motivations are, at least in part, "rational." The most trite (but still erroneous[17]) form of this proposition uses the term "rational" not in the narrow sense of the search for material self-interest, but in the broader standard economic sense of the pursuit of utility (satisfaction). The proposition is then that individuals only do what gives them utility (satisfaction), and that therefore even supposedly altruistic acts must be selfish in the sense that they yield utility to the individual. A more credible proposition is that, as Kreps (1997) points out, it can be hard to distinguish between internal motivation and the worker's response to fuzzy extrinsic motivators, such as fear of discharge, censure by fellow employees, or even the desire of co-workers' esteem. Altruistic and cooperative behavior may also be in the self-interest—including the material self-interest—of individuals.[18] These points may readily be accepted insofar as they are not inconsistent with the basic propositions that (a) people are capable of behavior which is not only not self-interested, but which runs contrary to their self-interest, and (b) individual self-interest pertains to social as well as material objectives.

In our view, the essence of non-materialistic motivation is that it focuses on sources of motivation the mobilization of which requires different types of external motivators from financial ones, and/or which can operate without any external motivator.

Motivators and the mobilization of non-materialistic motivation

An important distinction which is not often made in the literature is that between motivation and motivators. Motivators are external actions or conditions which can impact upon the degree of motivation. Incentives—monetary and material rewards and sanctions—are thus a motivator which acts upon materialistic motivation. Crucially, however, they are not the only motivator, and the mobilization of non-materialistic motivations requires different types of motivators.

Social pressure—expressions of approbation, disapprobation, respect, and so on, from others—is a particularly important motivator which acts directly on social motivation. The literature focuses mainly on *peer pressure*, which may significantly constrain free-riding under group incentive schemes.[19] The importance of mutual monitoring and group norms in teams has been shown empirically (see, for example, Hamilton et al., 2003; Knez and Simester, 2001). Social pressure from respected superiors and/or subordinates may, however, also impact upon social motivation.

The example of social pressure indicates the important point that specific motivators can impact upon more than one source of motivation. For example, individuals may act to avoid the disapproval of others not only because they find this unpleasant, but also because they know that a bad reputation even among peers (and certainly on the part of superiors) may well damage their future material interests. The key point, however, is that the existence of social motivation means that social pressure can have a much more powerful impact than it would if people were motivated only by materialistic self-interest. The same point applies to some "incentives." The most obvious example is promotional incentives, which work not only because of monetary motivation, but also because of the way they mobilize certain forms of social motivation (desire for status). Perceptions of how fairly one is being treated similarly play on both monetary motivation and status concerns.

Social pressure may, up to a point, be mobilized by the principal in the employment relationship. For instance, Akerlof (1982) argues that firms can succeed in raising group work norms, which in turn raise average effort and performance, by paying workers a gift of wages in excess of the minimum required (efficiency wage).[20] As already mentioned, social motivation may also be enhanced by actions targeted at fairness and reciprocity.

Although moral motivation is not subject to immediate external influences, the extent of such motivation and its nature can under some circumstances be changed over time by a different type of motivator—what might be called management or leadership—as well as by social pressure. Managers may "sell" desired behaviors by linking them to values which workers already hold. They may also act to persuade workers to modify their values to some extent, so as to increase their commitment to the objectives of the firm. Such leadership complements the "screening" of employees by commitment to the mission in mission-oriented organizations (Leete, 2000; Besley and Ghatak, 2003a).

Other motivators identified in the literature include task enrichment, empowerment, and participation possibilities in the firm (for example, Herzberg, 1968; Frey, 1997). Motivators may also be positive and/or negative. In other words, some external actions and conditions—such as perceived unfair treatment and bad working conditions—may actually reduce worker motivation.[21] Leete (2000), for example, finds that wage equity is related to worker motivation. The concept of "strong reciprocity" developed by cognitive psychologists is highly relevant here.

This refers to the propensity of people to voluntarily cooperate, if treated fairly, and to punish non-cooperators (Fehr et al., 2002). Strong reciprocity is shown to be a powerful device for the enforcement of social norms, in particular for explaining altruistic behavior (Gintis et al., 2003).

Advantages and disadvantages of non-materialistic motivations

Non-materialistic motivations have a number of potential advantages. They can provide powerful motivations for behaviors which are very difficult to measure, such as creative tasks and the transfer of tacit knowledge (Osterloh and Frey, 2000). Most importantly, because these motivations generate a desire to perform per se, they are not prone to induce the types of behavioral distortions—perverse effects and gaming—associated with imperfect performance measurement under monetary incentive schemes. In technical terms, internal motivation can help in reducing the multi-tasking problems arising from purely materially self-interested behavior when the contract cannot completely specify all relevant aspects of employee behavior and its desired outcomes. For instance, the erosion of output quality which might be expected to occur in a system with incentives linked to output quantity, might be in some measure mediated by the presence of a moral commitment on the part of workers to the maintenance of service quality. Moreover, the more widespread the moral commitment at the workplace to certain objectives, the greater the social pressure there is likely to be on those who are less internally committed to those goals. Peer pressure has the added advantage of mobilizing information on effort and results which is more readily available to peers than to management. Hamilton et al. (2003) confirm the presence of mutual learning and group norms in teams.

The crucial implication of this is that, in workplace contexts where internal and social motivations are substantial, the conventional economic literature may somewhat overestimate the extent of the perverse effects and gaming which is likely to arise from the use of performance incentives in the context of imperfect performance measurement.

A further potential advantage of non-materialistic motivation, from the principal's point of view, is that the stronger such motivation, the less emphasis that needs to be placed upon incentives to elicit any given level of effort (Minkler, 2004). Potentially, therefore, leadership efforts by the principal to strengthen the sense of mission may be worthwhile. One should, however, be cautious on this point, because the marginal cost of increasing the sense of mission may in many work contexts be quite high. Expressed differently, one should safeguard against an exaggerated sense of the malleability of the workforce.

Internal motivations are not, however, without their risks and limitations. Intrinsic motivation, for example, can perhaps best be mobilized for creative tasks which need quality, but not for repetitive tasks. Internal motivation in general is fragile and difficult to manage (Frey, 1993). Moral motivations may be somewhat inconsistent with the objectives of the organization, so that it does not always work to the benefit of the employer (Osterloh and Frey, 2000). For instance, in the context of the US Job Training Partnership Act (JTPA) training program, training centers were shown to manifest preferences for serving the most disadvantaged. This had the benefit of acting as a counterweight to potential dysfunctional behavior induced by the funding formula, in the form of "cream-skimming." However, from the perspective of policy-makers, the extent of the case-worker bias towards the most disadvantaged is a problem, because it leads to too large a portion of resources going to clients who are, on average, least likely to succeed in re-entering the labor market even with substantial training assistance (Heckman et al., 1997). This example illustrates that sometimes, internal motivations may be myopic—for example, placing too much weight on equity issues, and too little weight on cost-effectiveness ones. We return to this important point below in the specific context of the public sector.

Impact of incentives on non-materialistic motivation

An important lesson from incentive theory is that, as new motivational instruments are added, the key is to evaluate them not in isolation, but as part of a coherent incentive system (Holmström and Milgrom, 1994, p. 990). This is particularly the case when the role of non-materialistic motivations is recognized. Behavior driven by either social or internal motivation is likely to be seen by people as "voluntary," and is preferred to action forced through either economic incentives or the threat of external sanctions. This means that material incentives are likely to be more effective when they are designed in a way that emphasizes the voluntary nature of the desired behavior (Kreps, 1997).

A crucial and controversial question is the impact of performance incentives—material rewards and sanctions for performance—upon the level of non-materialistic motivation. One possibility—the more attractive one—is that the mobilization of materialistic motivation by stronger incentives might not effect the degree of non-materialistic motivation. If this were the case, materialistic and non-materialistic motivation would be substitutes, so that the stronger the degree of non-materialistic motivation the less would be the need for financial incentives (Minkler, 2004). Another appealing possibility is that materialistic and non-materialistic motivations are mutually complementary, so that financial incentives and moral motivation might each be able to counterbalance the problems which could be expected to arise from relying exclusively on the other.

The other possibility, however, is that the increased activation of materialistic motivation by incentives might *reduce* the degree of an individual's non-materialistic motivation. Such interaction between materialistic and non-materialistic motivation is the subject of "crowding" theory. First studied by social psychologists (in particular, Deci, 1971; Deci and Ryan, 1985; Lepper and Greene, 1978), the possibility that the degree of non-materialistic motivation might be affected by material incentives has more recently been recognized by some economists (for example, Frey, 1993, 1997; Kreps, 1997; Murdock, 2002; Bénabou and Tirole, 2003; Minkler, 2004). Crowding effects have mostly been studied with respect to what we call internal motivation, but also, to a lesser degree, in respect to social motivation.[22] It has been persuasively argued that crowding theory helps to explain some of the empirical evidence which is inconsistent with principal-agent theory (Frey, 1997).

The greatest concern raised by this literature is that incentives may reduce ("crowd out") non-materialistic motivation. The extreme possibility is that the crowding-out effect reduces non-materialistic motivation by a greater amount than the increase in self-interested motivation which those incentives are aimed to induce, with the result that the total effect on motivation, and thus on workers' performance, may be negative (Frey, 1997). However, it has also been argued that—at least at low levels—incentives can "crowd in" (increase) the level of non-material motivation. The explanation for crowding out is to be found on socio-psychological grounds, as explained in Box 18.1.

It should however, be noted that there is forceful debate about the empirical evidence on the detrimental effects of rewards. On the one hand, a meta-analysis

Box 18.1 Explanations for motivational crowding effects

Cognitive evaluation theorists argue that an understanding of the effects of rewards and controls requires a consideration of the *interpretation* that the recipients are likely to give to them, in relation to their feelings of self-determination and competence. They suggest that the *perception* of external interventions affects individual motivations. People may perceive external interventions, such as monetary incentives, in two ways: either as *controlling* of their behavior, or as *informational* (for example, as an indicator of a worker's competence) (Deci and Ryan, 1980, 1985). The former perception tends to move away the perceived locus of control and to constrain self-regulation, and has a negative effect on intrinsic motivation; while the latter has a positive effect over it. If the controlling aspect dominates, the external intervention undermines intrinsic motivation (Deci, 1971; Deci et al., 1999). Thus, the "control costs" that workers associate with various systems of rewards and monitoring labor play a major role in affecting how workers respond to a given employment system.

Alternative explanations of crowding effects have been proposed, such as the so-called "hidden cost of reward" due to the "over-justification hypothesis" (Lepper et al., 1973; Lepper and Greene, 1978). The latter is based on the premise that, in the presence of external controls, people attribute their behavior to an external agent. If they are faced with too many external reasons (justifications) for performing the activity, the role of intrinsic reasons will be discounted, resulting in a decline in intrinsic motivation. If after some time the external control is removed, future internal motivation will have declined and so will performance.

The results obtained by Gneezy and Rustichini (2000) also suggest that behavior is influenced by agents' perception of the contract that is offered to them. They argue that when the contract offers money, the environment is perceived as monetary. In such cases, high financial premiums will be necessary to foster performance. However, when the environment is perceived as non-monetary, performance may be high without resorting to premiums. Agents thus respond in a qualitatively different way in monetary and non-monetary environments.

From these socio-psychological explanations and related evidence, some economists have developed models aiming at offering explanations of the crowding effect which bridge the gap with the rational choice approach. Frey (1997) uses the idea that external interventions have both a disciplining effect and a crowding-out effect. The total effect on work performance depends on the relative size of marginal effects. For their part, Bénabou and Tirole (2003) base their explanation on the informational impact of rewards, arguing that when the agent has imperfect knowledge of his ability, he can derive information from the incentive scheme through an inference process. If the agent reviews his perception of the task or of his own abilities, incentives may then have only a weak positive effect in the short run, and a negative one in the long run.

of the literature leads Deci et al. (1999) to conclude that "the evidence indicates clearly that strategies that focus primarily on the use of extrinsic rewards do, indeed, run a serious risk of diminishing rather than promoting intrinsic motivation." On the other hand, meta-analyses by Cameron and Pierce (1994) and Eisenberger and Cameron (1996) conclude that, apart from very limited situations, rewards do not negatively affect intrinsic motivation. Moreover, the literature concerned with the effects of rewards on intrinsic motivation draws almost exclusively from experimental investigations—and little from work settings. But there is also experimental and econometric work by economists suggesting that, in some cases, the provision of extrinsic incentives, and in particular monetary rewards, may adversely affect agents' internal motivation (for example, Frey, 1994; Frey and Oberholzer-Gee, 1997; Frey and Jegen, 2001).

What seems unquestioned is that extrinsic incentives and internal motivation do not always conflict, but do so rather under specific circumstances. The crowding-out effect can occur only if there are high levels of intrinsic motivation in the first place (Kreps, 1997; Frey, 1997; Osterloh and Frey, 2000).[23] Different complementary conditions are advanced in the literature. In particular, the crowding-out effects may take place when an external intervention is perceived to be controlling; by contrast, when the intervention is perceived as informative, intrinsic motivation is unaffected or may even rise. Contingent, tangible, and expected rewards entail the risk of reducing intrinsic motivation, while verbal rewards do not (Cameron and Pierce, 1994; Deci et al., 1999).[24]

This suggests that, according to the way they are designed and thus perceived, explicit contracts based on objective measures can either reinforce implicit contracts based on subjective measures and/or non-materialistic motivations, or crowd them out. Our view on that issue is that the possible demotivating effect of non-materialistic motivations deserves some attention. More precisely, the long-term effects of incentives on motivation are to be considered with care (Deci et al., 1999; Bénabou and Tirole, 2003). However, it is possible that the crowding-out effect may be largely avoided by avoiding the conditions which are recognized to prompt it (see, for example, Frey, 1997; Eisenberger and Cameron, 1996). So that, at the bottom line, using financial incentives as a complement to non-materialistic motivations and motivators, as part of a coherent system, may be fruitful.

Public sector

It has been suggested by many analysts that non-materialistic motivation, especially moral motivation, is particularly strong in the public sector, or at least in parts thereof (Perry and Wise, 1990; Le Grand, 2003). Indeed a specific term, "public service motivation" (PSM), has been widely used in this context. PSM may be defined as an altruistic motivation to serve the interests of the community, which leads public sector employees to commit effort because of the value they attach to a social service or other public goal (François, 2000). Expressed differently, the idea is that "mission-oriented" organizations—that is, organizations staffed by motivated agents who are committed to their basic goals—are more common in the public than in the private sector (Besley and Ghatak, 2003b). There is considerable evidence that

PSM exists within the public sector (for example, Perry, 1996, 1997; Brewer et al., 2000; Wright, 2001), and that public service organizations tend to attract people for whom the mission is important (Houston, 2000). There is also empirical evidence that the same type of moral motivation exists, to varying degrees, in the non-profit sector and even, in certain cases, the private sector (Wittmer, 1991).

It has been argued that PSM plays a crucial role precisely because the use of higher-powered performance incentives is more risky—more likely to induce perverse effects and gaming—in the public sector, because of factors such as particularly severe performance measurement problems and goal ambiguity (Baker, 1992, p. 599). The organizational goals of non-profit organizations are therefore often best achieved by intrinsically motivated employees and by employees who identify very closely with the goals of the organization (Leete, 2000). In this context, the lesser use of performance incentives, and lower remuneration in general, have been viewed as playing an important screening role. That is, by discouraging people with stronger materialistic motivation, it helps to match employee mission preferences to those of the agency in a way which increases organizational efficiency and economizes on the need for high-powered incentives (Besley and Ghatak, 2003a). Public organizations attracting staff with high levels of public service motivation are thus likely to be less dependent on material incentives to manage individual performance effectively (Perry and Wise, 1990).

The picture of public employees which such literature paints is one which differs greatly from the narrow *Homo economicus* of the mainstream economic literature. Thus DiIulio (1994) speaks of "principled agents" as workers who do not shirk, subvert, or steal on the job even when the pecuniary and other tangible incentives to refrain from these behaviors are weak or non-existent.

In this context, action to boost and shape non-materialistic motivation is viewed as generally even more important than it is in the private sector. The role of leaders is, for example, seen as crucial to shaping moral commitments (DiIulio, 1994).[25] Socialization and organizational culture are viewed as especially important. Thus Wilson (1989) underlines the importance of developing a "sense of mission" in bureaucracies, as well as the role of "professionals" and "narrow specialists" in creating such a sense of mission. The manner in which the organization is managed may also be important—thus Moynihan and Pandey (forthcoming) find that red tape and length of organizational membership are negatively related to public service motivation, while hierarchical authority and reform efforts are positively related to it. This suggests that is it important to create an environment that allows employees to feel that they are contributing to the public good.

Some analysts suggest that the prevalence of public spirit greatly entails the danger that high-powered incentives will induce crowding out (Frey and Oberholzer-Gee, 1997). Perry and Wise (1990) warn that the great risk in treating the public service like private enterprise is that it fails to acknowledge unique motives underlying public sector employment.[26]

The first implication of this literature is that performance incentives should work less well in the public sector than in the private sector and, in the extreme, might not work at all or actually be counterproductive. Recent empirical evidence on this seems to show, in the main, that performance related pay systems in the public sector can result in increased performance, but that the effects are not strong (Propper and Wilson, 2003). The literature surveyed in Burgess et al. (2001) suggests that performance-related pay in education in the US had only limited effects, while Atkinson et al. (2004) show that while the scheme for teachers in England did improve test scores and value added, the results were quite heterogeneous and sometimes nil. In the health sector, some anecdotal evidence finds that fee-for-service resulted in a higher quantity of primary care services provided compared with capitation (Gosden et al., 2001). However, Arrowsmith et al. (2001) conclude that performance-related pay in the British public health sector has had, at most, only a very modest beneficial impact. Overall, little reliable evidence is available on the impact and effect of incentive and reward strategies in health care (Buchan et al., 2000). However, by contrast, a study by Kahn et al. (2001) finds that the introduction of performance pay in the Brazilian tax collection authority had a dramatic effect. Empirical evidence questioning the efficacy of "first generation" pay for performance systems in the civil service was mentioned earlier.

The other implication of the public service motivation thesis is that the extent of perverse effects and gaming should be less than would be the case if actors were entirely materially self-interested. Counterfactual propositions of this type are not easy to test. There is some systematic (non-anecdotal) evidence—although not a great deal—on perverse effects and gaming in general in the public sector (Propper and Wilson, 2003). However, a key problem with this evidence is that in nearly all cases it examines the impact of organization-wide performance measures and targets without making it clear to what extent individual employees within those organizations received incentives linked to those organization-wide measures and targets.

Perhaps the most systematically studied area is the "diagnosis related group" based hospital funding system pioneered in the US and subsequently adopted in many public hospital systems around the world—an output-based funding system outlined in Chapter 1. The empirical literature on this (surveyed in Robinson and Brumby, 2005) overwhelmingly suggests that, despite quite strong financial incentives for hospitals linked to imperfect performance measures (in particular, output measures without a quality dimension), much-feared perverse effects largely failed to eventuate. On the other hand, researchers have reached mixed conclusions about the widely-studied training program managed under the US JTPA. Heckman et al. (2002) found that the degree of "cream-skimming" (selection of lower-cost clients and exclusion of higher-cost ones) is small, which suggests that training centers do not respond blindly to the dysfunctional doors opened by the system, and instead have some consideration for the disadvantaged. By contrast, Courty and Marschke (2004) reported that training agencies "game" the incentive system, which is consistent with the hypothesis that performance incentives in organizations lead to costly distortions in agent behavior. Prendergast (2002) shows how a new supervision system introduced in a police department led to dysfunctional behavior on the part of police officers, who changed their behavior to avoid the risk of being the subject of complaints from members of the public, with the result that crime rates increased.

It may be concluded that the jury is still out on the implications of the above considerations for the appropriate role of incentives in the public sector. This raises the question of the possible ways, other than through linkage to individual incentives, in which measures and targets may impact upon public sector employee motivation. We return to this in the next section.

Additional views on motivation under performance management

The above analysis makes it clear that when considering how best to motivate employees to perform, it is important not merely to think about the role of incentives, but to think about *motivators* more generally. "Motivators," as indicated above, refer to all external factors which impact upon worker motivation, and include, as well as materialistic incentives, factors such as the quality of leadership, the social recognition given for performance, peer review processes, the "fairness" with which people are treated, and other aspects of the quality of the working environment. The term "motivational system" can be used to refer to the set of such motivators in place at any given time. The use of the term "system" recognizes the interactions between various types of motivators, and the manner in which certain motivators can act upon multiple sources of motivation. As Holmström and Milgrom (1994) emphasize, it is crucial to assess proposed new motivational instruments not in isolation, but in relation to other incentives—and, in our language, in the context of the rest of the motivational system.

To decide what is the best way of improving performance, then, the starting point should be an assessment of the initial (baseline) situation. What are the deficiencies, if any, in the existing set of motivators? Depending upon the answer to this question, quite different responses may be required. If, for example, the biggest motivational problem is that the employees of an agency feel themselves to be inequitably treated in base pay relative to similar workers elsewhere, and as a consequence of a sense of injustice their level of non-materialistic motivation is lower than might be expected, adding performance pay may be much less appropriate and effective than increasing the basic wage. In making baseline assessments, it is probably important to recognize that the degree of sensitivity of workers with respect to the different types of motivations can be culture-specific.

It is also important to identify explicitly the areas in which agency performance is most in need of improvement, with respect to the ultimate objective of the motivational system to be put in place. For example, is the main performance improvement imperative to increase efficiency (that is, to reduce the unit costs of production)? Or is improving the quality of service to customers the more pressing concern? The appropriate type of change in the motivational scheme will depend critically on the answers to these questions. Thus if increasing efficiency is the priority, stronger incentives may be the answer. If, however, the priority is quality improvement, efforts to build upon the sense of mission (through better leadership, peer review, and other similar strategies) may be more appropriate.

The interaction of various motivators is, as discussed above, an important theme of the literature, particularly in respect to "crowding out" or "crowding in" impacts of performance incentives on the degree of internal motivation of public sector employees. Setting aside such interactions, it is also worth bearing in mind that the effectiveness of each type of motivator is almost certainly subject to diminishing returns.[27] Thus, if the level of public service motivation is already high, it may not be cost-effective to put much effort into raising it even higher. But conversely, if it is low, there may be great gains to be realized from efforts to build morale. If that is true, assessing the baseline situation in terms of existing motivation and motivators is crucial, because it can allow the identification of which motivations may already be quasi-saturated, and therefore which motivators are likely to best repay increased managerial attention.

In short, the choice of a motivation scheme should be based, as far as it is possible, on a cost-effectiveness analysis. It should, in other words, be based upon a comparison of the incremental benefits of options for changes to the motivational system, relative to the total additional cost of such changes. Of course, it will generally be impossible to quantify these costs and benefits, but bearing in mind the basic cost-benefit principle is nevertheless useful because one can often form a rough view of the likely orders of magnitude of such costs and benefits.

Finally, it is important always to bear in mind the real-world constraints on public sector motivational schemes. Thus the overall public sector budget constraint imposes important limits on the scope for performance incentives. Similarly, mechanisms designed to protect integrity and independence against nepotism and political corruption of the civil service may impose other constraints.

Implications for performance budgeting

The analysis of individual motivation above makes it clear that it is a mistake to think of material incentives as the only, or even principle, means of motivating individuals to perform well. Similarly, it is a mistake to think of performance budgeting—or "managing-for-results" more generally—as capable of improving agency performance only through a linkage with individual performance incentives. There are, rather, a number of channels through which they may impact also upon public service motivation and non-materialistic motivation more generally.

Consider first the role of performance measures. Principal-agent literature encourages one to think of performance measures mainly as a means by which principals can inform themselves on the extent to which agents are doing what is expected of them. This is clearly an important function. However, performance measures may also under some circumstances play the role of informing agents themselves of the degree of success they are having in achieving missions to which they have an internalized commitment—and may in this way assist in mobilizing public service motivation more effectively. It is possible that comparative indicators—for example, measures indicating the comparative performance of regional or local service delivery units in achieving important national objectives—are particularly useful for this purpose.[28] The important proviso about this role for performance measures is that it is *completely* dependent upon service providers regarding the measures concerned as valid—even if partial and imperfect—measures of internalized goals. This is a powerful argument to reinforce the importance of the consultative development, rather than mere imposition from on high, of performance measures.

The setting of *targets* in respect to goals in relation to which there is an existing internalized workforce commitment, as a means of harnessing public service motivation, raises the additional issues of credibility and realism. It is counter-productive for the center, or agency management, to set arbitrary targets to which the workforce feels no commitment and which it regards as unrealistic. As the Royal Statistical Society (2003, p. 11) puts it, "motivational targets which are not rational may demoralize." This makes collaborative development, rather than imposition, even more important for targets than it is for performance measures.[29] Insofar as performance budgeting succeeds in "calibrating" agency performance targets better to the level of funding provided, it should improve the credibility of targets and therefore their motivational force. Once again, however, this raises question marks about target-setting for high-level outcomes in respect to which there is limited controllability or, expressed differently, there is great uncertainty about timeframes and the relation between resources and possible outcomes. Further experience with some of the major target-focused managing-for-results regimes around the world will hopefully help to clarify the scope for useful performance target-setting.

MFR processes should also be viewed as potentially playing a valuable role in boosting, and in some measure reshaping, the sense of mission held by agency employees. Advocates of corporate planning processes view this, implicitly or explicitly, as a primary function of the process of articulating agency missions and objectives. Some skepticism about these processes is understandable, because there is a widespread sense that they deteriorate all too often into paper exercises which have negligible impact on the internalized values and motivation of staff. Notwithstanding this, the process of clarifying organizational goals can, if properly handled, potentially be a valuable one with a real impact on the level and direction of public service motivation.

It is important in this context to start with an explicit understanding of the way in which agency employees conceive their mission—and, more particularly, of any differences which exist between the employee sense of mission and the objectives held by the government. MFR processes may then be thought of as a potential tool for bridging any gaps which exist in the way principals and agents view agency goals. It was suggested earlier, for example, that it may not be uncommon for service delivery staff to be so focused on delivering good service to individual clients that they give insufficient weight to overall cost-effectiveness considerations, and that this may be in part the result of myopia—service deliverers can see what they are doing for individual clients, but have perhaps less sense of the opportunity cost of this in terms of services which could have been provided to others. Under such circumstances, it may be a key part of the leadership function to help employees understand that by paying more attention to cost-effectiveness, the overall mission of the organization may be able to be carried out more effectively.

What about the role of performance budgeting more specifically? As noted above, insofar as the credibility of targets can be improved by linking them better to the level of resourcing, this can assist in boosting performance. The other possible role of performance budgeting is through agency-level financial incentives. As emphasized throughout this volume, only some contemporary forms of performance budgeting aim to create a relationship between past performance and future funding in order to create "incentives" at the agency level. Such a linkage raises numerous difficulties, and can arguably work only in certain circumstances. The relevant point here, however, is that such agency-level incentives might impact upon individual motivation in ways other than, and in addition to, their impact on individual material self-interest.

It may be instructive in this context to consider again the experience of the diagnosis related group (DRG) payment system for hospital services. DRG systems were not generally characterized by any individual staff performance incentives linked to the overall financial success of the hospital under the DRG system. However, because under DRG funding hospitals are, approximately speaking, paid a fixed amount per service irrespective of their costs, the financial consequences of inefficiency are serious—leading to the need for major cutbacks or even, at the limit, to closure of the hospital concerned. American research on initial experience with DRG payment in that country provided strong evidence for a "pressure matters" thesis, to the effect that hospital performance was quite sensitive to the risk of losses, but not to the incentive to make profits.[30] It appears that the very considerable success of the DRG system—not only in the US, but elsewhere around the world (Robinson and Brumby, 2005)—arises from the fact that the financial pressure for efficiency placed on hospitals provided a powerful tool with which to convince physicians and other treating practitioners of the importance of efficiency, and to persuade them to take efficiency considerations systematically into account in clinical decision-making so as, in particular, to cut down on over-servicing. As Averill et al. (1996, p. 18) observe, "the DRG-based prospective payment rates created a natural language for communicating to the medical community the financial implications of clinical decisions." Analyzing the difference between hospitals which were "winners" under the DRG payment system and those which were "losers," Bray et al. (1994, p. 50) found that winners were hospitals where management "successfully engaged physicians in efforts to control costs (for example, physician-led task forces, routine financial information sharing with physicians, and appointments of senior physicians to management team positions)," whereas, by contrast, loser hospitals tended to be characterized by adversarial management/physician relationships (in the extreme, resulting in physician actions to push up costs as a means of undermining management). It seems plausible to hypothesize that what was at play here may have been more than just the self-interested motivation of physicians in seeing the hospitals where they work survive, and that it is a distinct possibility that much of the impact of the DRG system came from, and was dependent upon success in, mobilizing the "public service motivation" and professional commitment of physicians, as well as their sense of organizational loyalty.

Unfortunately, there is little empirical literature clarifying the way in which agency-level financial incentives impact within the public sector, and one can do no more than speculate on the issue. It seems clear, however, that it is inappropriate to think of non-profit public sector agencies as being impacted upon by financial incentives in entirely the same manner as for-profit corporations. Beyond this, it seems plausible to hypothesize that, in agencies characterized by strong public service motivation, agency-level financial incentives which are not linked to individual performance incentives may have an asymmetric effect: that is, the fear of losses which may put the existence of the agency at risk and thereby jeopardize its mission may have considerably more force in motivating improved performance than the prospect of agency-level financial rewards for good performance.

On a final point, MFR and performance budgeting emphasize the twin themes of greater *freedom* to perform and greater *pressure* to perform. Greater freedom usually refers to the decontrol of input choices, but in some cases also refers to greater managerial freedom in output choices (that is, in the choice of the means of meeting certain objectives). It is often suggested that greater freedom to perform can only work in the presence of stronger incentives to perform. However, it seems reasonable to suggest that the greater the degree of public service motivation in a given sector of public service delivery, the greater the impact which increased freedom to perform may have, irrespective of whether stronger performance incentives are offered. That is, the reduction of central controls may also be viewed as a means for providing scope for service providers to more effectively achieve public service goals to which they have a strong internalized commitment.

Special features of developing countries

As noted in the above analysis, the selection of motivators to boost public sector performance should take fully into account the institutional context, notably the existing incentives, organizational features, and history. It was also suggested in passing that individuals from different cultural backgrounds are probably likely to be more sensitive to certain specific kinds of motivations and motivators, especially with respect to non-materialistic motivations. Reference was made in this context to Levine's (1993) study showing that Japanese workers are more prone to social comparison than their American counterparts.

The cultural norms in many developing countries are undoubtedly very different from those of industrial countries, upon which almost all of the economic literature on incentives has been implicitly based. It is plausible to assume that workers in developing countries will tend to react somewhat differently to external interventions than Western workers. In addition to different social norms, developing countries also have a series of characteristics and constraints which may impede the use of some kinds of incentives, which would otherwise be recommended in industrial countries.

In the present section, we do not claim to be able to present a comprehensive analysis and recommendations on the issue of incentives in developing countries. We rather propose some reflections which build on the literature and the authors' experience (particularly in sub-Saharan Africa) and relate them to the lessons drawn in this chapter on motivation. Some features drawn below might of course not apply to the entire developing world, but reflect the situation in at least some regions—parts of Africa but also perhaps of the Pacific, Latin America and Asia. What follows, then, is a brief overview of some specific incentive problems encountered in developing countries, a series of potential causes, and finally some implications for the motivation of public employees in these countries.

Overview of problems

Public service in developing countries is often plagued with many deficiencies like ineffectiveness, inefficiency, and poor quality of services; endemic corruption; service provider absenteeism; and the high turnover of high-level staff which precludes the transfer of knowledge and the building of strong institutional cultures. These take place in a context of "informality," that is, where informal rules often dominate the formal rules of official institutions. In particular in sub-Saharan Africa, it appears that formal institutions are at odds with societal behavior, expectations, and incentive systems, and therefore face a crisis of legitimacy and enforcement (Dia, 1996). This makes the design of incentive schemes more difficult. Box 18.2 illustrates some of these problems.

Box 18.2 Excerpts from the *World Development Report* (*WDR*) *2004*, "Making Services Work for Poor People"

The World Bank's *World Development Report* (*WDR*) *2004* builds an analytical and practical framework centered on stakeholders' incentives to provide basic services, such as health and education, to poor people. It focuses on strengthening relationships of accountability between policy-makers, providers, and citizens. Some of the motivational problems faced by service providers in developing countries are highlighted in the following excerpts.

> They [teachers, doctors, nurses] are often mired in a system where the incentives for effective service delivery are weak, wages may not be paid, corruption is rife, and political patronage is a way of life. Highly trained doctors seldom wish to serve in rural areas. Since those who do serve there are rarely monitored, the penalties for not being at work are low. A survey of primary health care facilities in Bangladesh found the absentee rate among doctors to be 74 percent...When present, some service providers treat poor people badly. "They treat us like animals," says a patient in West Africa...By no means all frontline service providers behave this way. Many, often the majority, are driven by an intrinsic motivation to serve. Be it through professional pride or a genuine commitment to help poor people (or both), many teachers and health workers deliver timely, efficient, and courteous services, often in difficult circumstances—collapsing buildings, overflowing latrines—and with few resources—clinics without drugs, classes without textbooks...The challenge is to reinforce this experience—to replicate the professional ethics, intrinsic motivation, and other incentives of these providers in the rest of the service work force. (p. 4)
>
> Since the contract cannot be fully specified, policymakers look to others means of eliciting pro-poor services from providers. One way is to choose providers who have an intrinsic motivation to serve the poor. A study of faith-based health care providers in Uganda estimates that they work for 28 percent less than government and private for-profit staff, and yet provide a significantly higher quality of care than the public sector...Another way is to increase incentives to serve the poor or work in underserved areas. But one study of Indonesia shows that it would require multiples of current pay levels to get doctors to live in West Papua, for instance (where the vacancy rate is 60 percent)...A third way is to solicit bids for services and use the competition in the bidding process to monitor and discipline providers. (pp. 8–9)

Special constraints of the incentive systems

The incentive systems in many developing countries face a number of additional constraints relating to the various motivations and motivators we have presented in this chapter.

First, a number of characteristics worsen the agency problems. Performance information is, of course, in general much less available in developing countries than in industrial countries. Sometimes there is not even reliable information on inputs, let alone on outputs or outcomes (as for fiscal data see, for example, Lienert, 2003; Moussa, 2004). This results in acute measurement problems. At the same time, direct monitoring of work effort is made more difficult to the extent that at least some of these countries have a shortage of well-trained (and honest) supervisors. The scarcity of resources also increases the opportunity cost of such direct managerial control. A generalized lack of transparency makes it easier for some civil servant cliques to manipulate the information provided to others in their agencies and to the government as a whole—creating fertile conditions for collusion (Tirole, 1986).

Second, the predisposition of workers to various sources of non-materialistic motivations is probably different in developing countries than in Western societies. Some characteristics of workers may worsen the incentive problem, while others may offer opportunities. One problem lies in the low level of civil service pay—which has, for example, been shown to have a statistically and economically significant relationship with corruption (Van Rijckeghem and Weder, 2001). This relates to the issue of fairness: many civil servants in developing countries do not consider themselves as fairly treated, which decreases their loyalty to the organization and justifies "sabotage" behaviors. For example, a negotiation (or blackmail) tool regularly used by health staff unions in Senegal is to call for the retention of information on the part of health care providers, which considerably hampers the follow-up of patients (Paul, 2005). Together with low levels of *institutionalized* public service motivation, and implicit social acceptance of behaviors like absenteeism and corruption, civil servants may have quite low levels of social and moral motivation to perform.[31] As for the level of intrinsic motivation, it may be hampered by demotivating factors and external constraints such as a poor working environment. However, as the *WDR 2004* highlights, some service providers do possess a genuine dedication to serve, which should be carefully considered when thinking of designing an appropriate incentive scheme.

Finally, there are major constraints that hamper the increased use of material performance incentives in developing countries. These countries very often face particularly tight budget constraints, which can prevent them from setting the otherwise economically optimal incentive scheme (such as paying performance premiums, for instance). Inadequate judicial systems make it harder to enforce contracts and to punish deviant behavior.[32] This may reduce or even destroy the value of ex-post controls (Leruth and Paul, 2006). The use of peer pressure to increase work dedication is also hampered by the widespread lack of a long tradition of public service.

Implications for motivation

In the face of these additional pervasive problems in developing economies, the question of how to motivate agents to perform is even more difficult than elsewhere. This issue has been a (baffling) puzzle for consultants and technical assistants for decades, and it is impossible to provide here a magic bullet to the problem. However, we present a few ideas which build on the analysis developed in this chapter, which may at least contribute to the debate.

First, we believe the issue of fairness deserves great attention. As long as civil servants believe they are unfairly treated, one should expect to witness dysfunctional behaviors on their part, such as absenteeism and corruption. In terms of principal-agent theory, paying higher basic wages could help satisfy agents' "individual rationality constraint" and guarantee their participation in the contract.[33] When civil servants believe themselves to be the victims of serious pay injustice, attempts to introduce pay-for-performance are likely to be misunderstood. For example, the pilot introduction of performance premiums for health workers in a Senegalese region ended up as being considered as a (legitimate) increase in salary, with absolutely no connection to any consideration for performance. It even spread to other regions as a claim for a general increase in salaries (Paul, 2005).

More generally, although introducing payment-for-results in developing countries has the potential of increasing workers' effort, it should be considered with particular caution for others reasons as well. Practically speaking, the measurement problem may be such that it may be impossible (in the short run and at reasonable cost) to get the adequate information to sustain a system of performance measurement and control. Together with the cost of supervision (considering the risk of collusion) and that of performance premiums (cf. the example of Indonesia quoted in Box 18.2, where multiples of current pay levels would be required to get doctors to live in West Papua), using financial incentives may be prohibitively costly considering the government's cash constraint.[34] We have hypothesized earlier in this chapter that the potential dysfunctional behaviors theoretically associated with payment-for-results may be less important in practice than predicted by theory, because non-materialistic motivations may counterbalance these negative aspects. However, such counterbalancing effects may be weaker in some developing countries, where non-materialistic motivations might not be strong enough to sufficiently restrain dysfunctional responses to stronger financial performance incentives. If these hypotheses are valid, it may be the case that the danger of inducing increased dysfunctional behaviors (such as focusing on rewarded tasks, at the expense of others, or gaming the system) is so great as to eliminate the potential benefit of financial performance incentives. Finally, incentive schemes are generally ineffective in unstable situations (Pallez, 2003), which is often the case in developing countries.

It appears clear from the problems overviewed in this section that the civil service in many developing countries crucially lacks an adequate system of sanctions. The "culture of non-punishment" which is prevalent in some countries is due to various factors such as the absence of a functional and independent judicial system, the low work norms in place, the close-knit nature of society which precludes harming other members of one's social network, together with the risk of reciprocal punishment in case the worker you punish today becomes your boss the day after. The result is that the threats which exist in theory become meaningless in practice. It therefore seems essential that any motivational scheme is accompanied by a real (and fair) system of sanctions.

Mobilizing non-materialistic motivations is therefore probably particularly important in developing countries. Improving work norms, professional ethics, and public service motivation through human resource management initiatives appears to be essential. It is significant in this context that Rauch and Evans (2000) show that meritocratic recruitment is a statistically significant determinant of bureaucratic performance in less-developed countries. Other factors mentioned in the current chapter appear particularly adapted for increasing public service motivation (for example, reducing red tape, undertaking reform that clarifies goals and empowers employees, and so on; see Moynihan and Pandey, forthcoming) and intrinsic motivation (enriching tasks and improving working conditions) in developing countries.

Nevertheless, reliance on non-materialistic motivation rather than on explicit incentive contracts should not preclude the increased use of performance data for performance management more generally. For example, it may be fruitful to use performance indicators (for example, health center process indicators) to clarify goals, manage staff, and increase their awareness and ability.

Finally, the basic performance management problems may be of a different nature in developing countries. While performance-based funding systems in industrial countries often aim to reduce costs, the first problem to handle in developing countries is perhaps to increase output (and its quality). This probably calls for designing alternative incentive systems rather than importing those developed in industrial countries.

Conclusions

A major theme of contemporary performance budgeting is the building of tighter links between results and funding as a means of encouraging and pressuring agencies to improve their performance. This can only work insofar as individual public employees are motivated to perform better. This is particularly relevant when introducing new MFR systems, because reforms call for an extra amount of effort and cooperation, and a reform has little chance of being successfully sustained if those who manage it do not have appropriate incentives at crucial stages of implementation (Drazen, 2000).

This chapter has considered the manner in which performance budgeting—and managing-for-results more generally—can be linked to actions to boost individual performance motivation. The literature surveyed indicates that no definitive unified theory exists on the motivation of public personnel for performance. However, certain key points do emerge.

It is a mistake to focus exclusively or primarily upon material incentives as the means of strengthening individual motivation to perform. While materialistic self-interest is an important element of individual motivation, so also in many areas of government are non-materialistic motivations (social, moral, and intrinsic). MFR processes—defining objectives more clearly, and measuring performance and setting targets—have the potential, within limits and if managed appropriately, to boost individual performance by acting on these other sources of motivation as well as through links with individual incentives. Leadership and other mechanisms for strengthening and shaping the sense of mission in public sector agencies are enormously important. Agency-level financial performance "incentives," where appropriate, may also act in part through the mobilization of employee commitment to the mission of the agency as well as through the impact on individual material self-interest. Moreover, a first step before considering how to motivate workers to perform better may be to remove the factors which demotivate them—such as unfair pay or poor working conditions.

In determining the best means of boosting individual motivation to perform, account needs to be taken of many factors including the nature of the work and the existing areas of motivational deficit. If, for example, public service motivations (and moral motivation generally) are low in an area of service delivery where they could be expected to be high, action to boost such motivation may be considerably more important than, say, the introduction of performance pay mechanisms.

The jury is out on the extent to which the greater use of incentives such as performance pay can boost performance in the public sector. It is not true, as is sometimes claimed, that the empirical literature demonstrates that the contrary is the case—there are, in fact, a significant number of studies which suggest beneficial effects, although these are generally small in magnitude. As for the danger of behavioral distortions arising from the use of unavoidably imperfect performance measures and targets, the empirical (as opposed to anecdotal) evidence is quite limited. It is, in general, desirable that further experiments in the use of such incentives take place and that the results continue to be dispassionately assessed. But there are sufficiently strong theoretical grounds to suggest that caution should be exercised in respect to the degree of emphasis placed upon "high-powered" incentives, especially in those many areas of the public sector where performance measurement difficulties are greatest.

In the same vein, it also appears that the question of the possible demotivating effect of material incentives upon non-materialistic motivations deserves some attention, in particular in order to avoid situations which are recognized to demotivate people (see, for example, Frey, 1997).

There are, however, reasons to believe that the distorting effect of performance measures and targets can be expected to be less than sometimes warned against in the public sector, to the extent that either or both (a) non-materialistic motivations are strong and (b) the connection between measures and targets and individual incentives is attenuated in various ways (such as their combination with subjective assessments, and the use of longer-term promotional incentives). Therefore, contrary to the crowding-out hypothesis, it may be fruitful to use financial incentives to complement non-materialistic motivations and motivators, as part of a coherent system.

At the bottom line, one should keep in mind that the choice of an appropriate motivational system should be made using the logic of a cost-effectiveness analysis, that is, by comparing the *incremental* benefit prompted by the proposed instruments (increase in output and/or reduction in production unit costs) with all their costs. In particular, the extent to which contingent material rewards to individuals are cost-effective depends upon (a) the extent to which perverse effects arise as a result of the imperfection of individual performance assessment; (b) the risk (noise) in the performance measure; (c) the extent to which financial incentives may have demotivating or "crowding-out" effects; (d) the risks associated with the negative effect of individual incentives on cooperation; and (e) (if our assumption of diminishing marginal returns is valid) the initial degree to which material motivation is mobilized.

Moreover, agency-level performance measures and targets may potentially have significant motivational effects even when they are not strongly linked to individual incentives. They may, at least under certain circumstances, be important sources of information to public employees about the extent to which they are successful in achieving objectives to which they have strong internalized commitment. Experience with target-based systems such as the US GPRA model and the UK PSA model (see Chapters 10 and 12) will hopefully help to shed further light on the extent of such effects.

It is, finally, important to bear in mind that the bulk of the literature on incentives has been conceived in the context of industrial countries (especially the US), and that developing countries are characterized by special features and constraints and therefore deserve a special attention. Motivational strategies adapted to industrial countries cannot be blindly exported to these settings. Two crucial issues which appear to hamper the incentive systems in some of these countries, and which should be tackled in priority, are public employees' perceptions of unfair treatment (due to low wages, nepotism, lack of recognition) and the absence of proper systems of sanctions. The construction of a strong public service ethos, the enhancement of work norms, and the mobilization of intrinsic motivations are also extremely important tasks facing many developing countries.

Appendix: a stylized model and a roadmap for assessing incentive schemes

The literature generally studies the benefits of incentives, possibly some of their hidden costs (dysfunctional behavior, crowding-out effect), but hardly considers the full costs of incentive schemes. Yet we argue that the choice of an incentive scheme should, as far as possible, be grounded on a cost-effectiveness analysis. In this appendix, we design a simple model aimed at guiding the choice between alternative incentive schemes, depending on the characteristics of the initial context. We do not aim to solve for the theoretical optimal solution, but rather to outline the factors which should be taken into account when considering the introduction of new incentives in a given situation.

Consider a simple production function, where the output X is a concave function of the effort e exerted by the worker, that is, $X(e)$ with $X' > 0$ and $X'' < 0$. Consider also that the worker's utility is a function of his different sources of motivation, of the following form:

$$U_i = u_i\left(w\left(X\left(e\right)\right)\right) - \theta_i C\left(e,c\right) + \delta_i S\left(e,s\right) + \lambda_i I\left(e,i\right) + \gamma_i M\left(X\left(e\right),m\right)$$

where:

- u_i measures worker *i*'s utility, with $u' > 0$ and $u'' < 0$; w is the total wage received by the worker, which (at least partly) depends on his performance
- θ_i measures worker *i*'s laziness (effort aversion); C is a cost of effort function; c represents what Herzberg (1968) calls "hygiene" factors (like working conditions), that is, external factors which impact on the cost function; with $C_e > 0$, $C_{ee} > 0$, $C_c \leq 0$, and $C_{cc} \geq 0$
- δ_i measures worker *i*'s sensitivity to social pressure; S is a function capturing social pressure; s represents the social motivators in place (work norms, peer pressure, and so on); with $S_e \geq 0$, $S_{ee} \leq 0$, $S_s \geq 0$, and $S_{ss} \leq 0$
- λ_i measures worker *i*'s interest in the tasks performed; I is a function capturing intrinsic motivation; i represents the intrinsic motivators in place (empowerment, participation, and so on); with $I_e \geq 0$, $I_{ee} \leq 0$, $I_i \leq 0$ and $I_{ii} \leq 0$
- γ_i measures worker *i*'s moral (including public service) dedication; M is a function capturing moral (including public service) motivation (it depends on the output value); m represents the moral/public service motivators in place (for example, public service culture, acknowledgment of the service to the population); with $M_{X(e)} \geq 0$, $M_{XX} \leq 0$, $M_m \geq 0$, and $M_{mm} \leq 0$.

The worker will set his effort level by optimizing his utility level:

$$\partial U_i / \partial e = \left(\partial u_i / \partial w\right)\left(\partial w / \partial X\right)X'\left(e\right) - \theta_i C_e\left(e,c\right) + \delta_i S_e\left(e,s\right) + \lambda_i I_e\left(e,n\right) + \gamma_i\left(\partial M\left(X\left(e\right),m\right)/\partial X\right)X'\left(e\right) = 0$$
$$C_e\left(e,c\right) = \left(1/\theta_i\right)\left\{\left(\partial u_i / \partial w\right)\left(\partial w / \partial X\right)X'\left(e\right) + \delta_i S_e\left(e,s\right) + \lambda_i I_e\left(e,n\right) + \gamma_i\left(\partial M\left(X\left(e\right),m\right)/\partial X\right)X'\left(e\right)\right\}$$

This equation informs on the different ways that can be used to increase workers' effort:

- directly, through financial incentives (w) and/or the non-materialistic motivators (c, s, n and/or m)
- in a more indirect way, through selecting workers with high degrees of sensitivity to the different non-materialistic motivations (δ, λ, γ) and/or little effort aversion (θ).

This simple model captures the fact that acting on each source of motivation has diminishing returns to scale. However, because of its additive form, it implicitly assumes that the different sources of motivation are substitutes. It thus hides the potential cross-effects between the various sources of motivation and motivators, for instance, whether two types of motivations entail positive (crowd-in) or negative (crowd-out) externalities on each other. To take account of these considerations into the model, we need to introduce assumptions about motivators' cross-elasticity.

For example, if the crowding-out theory holds, increasing wage is supposed to have a positive direct effect on effort: $(\partial e/\partial w)|_{Dir.} \geq 0$; but might have a negative indirect effect on, for example, intrinsic motivation: $(\partial N/\partial w)|_{Ind.} \leq 0$. If the latter effect dominates, it could happen than the total effect on effort is negative $(\partial e/\partial w)|_{Total} \leq 0$. As another example, measures aimed at increasing moral motivation (for example, acknowledging the service to disadvantaged people) could also indirectly increase the social motivation (desire of co-workers' esteem): $(\partial S/\partial m)|_{Ind.} \geq 0$; so that the total effect on effort is superior to the direct effect on moral motivation: $(\partial e/\partial m)|_{Total} \geq (\partial e/\partial m)|_{Dir.}$.

The value of new incentive tools could be assessed, using the analytical tool presented above, according to the following "roadmap." (Note that the precise data will probably not be available; however, reasonable appraisals may be hypothesized.)

1. *Assess the baseline*

The additional effectiveness of new incentives will depend on the initial situation, which should be carefully assessed in order to identify possible motivational gaps. One should evaluate, as much as possible:

1.1 What is the "innate" sensitivity of workers to the different motivation sources, as well as their degree of effort aversion (according to personal characteristics and cultural norms, for instance)?

1.2 At what degree do the existing incentives mobilize each source of motivation? In particular:

- Is workers' "individual rationality constraint" met by the initial pay level?
- What are the "hygiene" factors which raise or decrease job hardness?
- How strong are the work norms, and how does peer (and social) pressure play in the workplace?
- How are internal motivations currently mobilized?

1.3 What are the actual motivations which are (quasi-)saturated, and what are those which could be incrementally raised?

2. *Consider the interaction of the new incentives on the existing system*

As emphasized by Holmström and Milgrom (1994, p. 990), one should evaluate new instruments not in isolation, but as part of a coherent incentive system. Both direct and indirect effects of motivators should thus be taken into consideration.

2.1 What is the potential *incremental* direct effect of the considered instrument on its "target" motivation (that is, for example, $(\partial e/\partial w)|_{Dir.}$, $(\partial e/\partial s)|_{Dir.}$, and so on)?

2.2 What is the potential *externality* effect of the considered instrument on the efficacy of existing incentives, and on other motivation sources (that is, for example, $(\partial S/\partial m)|_{Ind.}$)?

- In particular, the crowding out of internal motivation by financial rewards is shown to take place only (a) if the level of internal motivation is high at the outset; (b) if certain conditions hold (for example, the external intervention is perceived as controlling and not informing, rewards are highly contingent on performance). Depending on the initial situation, one could assess whether $(\partial N/\partial w)|_{Ind.} \leq 0$, $(\partial M/\partial w)|_{Ind.} \leq 0$, and at the bottom line whether $(\partial e/\partial w)|_{Total} \leq 0$.

3. *Run a cost-benefit analysis*
The introduction of a new (system of) instrument(s) should not be done unless its benefits outweigh its total costs. One should therefore assess:

3.1 What is the *total incremental cost* of the considered new instrument? Including:

- its monetary cost (rewards and/or motivational scheme and/or supervision, and so on)
- the monetary cost of the additional information required
- the potential bias, risk, and dysfunctional behavior due to imperfect indicators
- the potential crowding-out effect
- the possible ratchet or gaming effect (and thus impossibility to get the true information, for other (strategic) purposes).

3.2 Compare this cost with the *incremental* benefit in terms of increased effort and thus production (including its quality).

4. *Consider alternatives*
The "cost-effectiveness ratio" of the considered new instrument should be compared with that of possible alternative systems. For instance, financial schemes could be supplemented by, for example:

- mobilizing the intrinsic, moral, or social motivations
- using performance information to build a public sector ethos, decrease goal ambiguity, and increase civil servants' pride, rather than linking pay to it
- meeting the "individual rationality constraint" of workers and thus increasing their fairness perception, so as to win their loyalty to the organization
- offering efficiency wages, together with an appropriate system of sanctions.

Notes

1. By which term is meant, in what follows, all material rewards *and sanctions* applied to individuals including salary, remuneration in kind, promotional (career) rewards, and the threat of dismissal.

2. And also an increase from 20 percent to 38 percent in states using bonuses linked to measures of group performance.
3. See, for an outline of this research, Ingraham (1993) and Kellough and Lu (1993).
4. "Material" self-interest will be understood in what follows to also include things such as personal safety and quality of the physical environment, which are not part of social motivation as defined in the third section of this chapter. Thus, for example, the hedonic theory of wages—which argues that workers are interested in maximizing their *net* utility and therefore are willing to "exchange" that which produces utility to get reductions in something which yields disutility (for example, reducing the risks of injury associated to their job)—is firmly part of the mainstream "rational choice" tradition.
5. The mainstream economic approach does not necessarily reject so-called "intrinsic" motivation, but insofar as it does recognize it, it tends to regard it as irrelevant on the grounds that it allegedly only shifts the labor curve rightwards, without any impact on the marginal decisions with respect to work performance (Frey, 1997).
6. For a survey on that literature, see Prendergast (1999).
7. Which, in the language of Chapter 3, can mean either final or intermediate outputs.
8. The literature suggests several different ways to overcome the free-rider problem. In small groups, cheating may be easily detected, so that it is easy to enforce cooperation through the threat of group punishments (peer pressure). Teamwork associated with a group incentive may even allow the costs of supervision to be reduced, if individual effort is more difficult to observe for outsiders than for team members (FitzRoy and Kraft, 1985, 1987). In large groups, however, such mutual monitoring is not possible. The way out of the free-rider problem must then come from other sources, such as organizational loyalty (Ehrenberg and Smith, 1997). The implication of this is that, depending on the severity of the free-rider problem, team bonuses may or may not increase team productivity (McConnell and Brue, 1989).
9. The empirical evidence for this so-called risk insurance/efficiency trade-off is not strong (Prendergast, 1999; Foss and Laursen, 2005).
10. Technically, the literature often models the use of objective performance measures through static models, while subjective measures necessitate some repeated interaction for contracts to be enforceable.
11. Mechanisms based on relative performance ratings are referred to in the economic literature as "tournaments."
12. Paying efficiency wages consists in providing incentives through paying workers a wage above the market-clearing level: an efficiency wage is such that the marginal cost of increasing the wage exactly equals the marginal gain in productivity. This theory is based on the premise of a wage-productivity dependency. The presumed link between wages and productivity is explained by different reasons: a high wage is supposed to increase the cost of shirking, to influence the "sociology" of the organization, to reduce turnover costs, and to attract a "select" pool of workers (if their reservation utility depends on their ability). The theory thus assumes that wage rents and supervisors are substitutes. However, the efficiency wages theory suffers both from theoretical criticisms (bonding theory) and a lack of solid empirical foundations (nevertheless, Goldsmith et al. (2000) find that receiving an efficiency wage enhances effort). Moreover, it is less adapted to the public service where the fear of being fired is quasi-inexistent for many civil servants.
13. Feltham and Xie (1994) show that adding an additional measure to the performance assessment process will improve that process if (and only if) the additional measure adds additional information. However, this analysis does not consider the cost of information.
14. In one representative case study, Lazear (2000) shows that the switch to piece-rate pay in a glass corporation had a significant effect on average levels of output per worker. About half of this resulted from the average worker producing more because of incentive effects, and the rest arose from an ability to hire more productive workers, as well as, possibly, from a reduction in departures.

15. Thus Frey (1997) regards all moral motivations as forms of "intrinsic" motivation. Deci and Ryan (1985) regard the work ethic as a form of intrinsic motivation.
16. Although clearly if one does something one does not enjoy out of a sense of work ethic, one is being driven not by intrinsic but by moral motivation. François (2000) provides a criteria for differentiating between "intrinsic" and "public service" motivations: he argues that if agents get utility from some aspects of the task itself (intrinsic motivation), in terms of principal-agent theory, this affects both the participation and the incentive constraints; while if all that matters is the result from working (public service motivation), the nature of the actions performed is irrelevant, and the only constraint altered is the incentive compatibility one.
17. In that moral motivation sometimes leads people to make great sacrifices which can hardly be said—without abusing the language unacceptably—to yield them satisfaction.
18. Thus Rotemberg (1994) suggests that feelings of altruism can be individually rational in certain settings in which the variables controlled by the workers are strategically linked ("equilibrium altruism"), and Che and Yoo (2001) explain cooperation as a self-enforcing behavior, in a context where team members interact repeatedly.
19. Kandel and Lazear (1992) explore how peer pressure operates and how factors such as profit sharing, shame, guilt, norms, mutual monitoring, and empathy interact to create incentives in the firm.
20. As mentioned above, one of the explanations for the link between wage and productivity lies in influencing the "sociology" of the organization.
21. Herzberg (1968) notices the puzzling fact that the factors involved in producing job satisfaction (and motivation) appear to be separate and distinct from the factors that lead to job dissatisfaction. The author argues that motivator factors are *intrinsic* to the job (for example, achievement, recognition, the work itself, and responsibility), while dissatisfaction-avoidance (or hygiene) factors are *extrinsic* to the job (for example, supervision, interpersonal relationships, working conditions, and salary).
22. Including impacts on social rewards (for example, Janssen and Mendys-Kamphorst, 2004), reciprocity-driven voluntary cooperation (for example, Fehr and Gächter, 2000), and compliance with rules (for example, Falk and Fehr, 2002).
23. As argued in the appendix to this chapter, the introduction of new incentives should be preceded by an assessment of the baseline situation, including workers' initial degree of internal motivation. For instance, Lazear (2000) finds that the hypothesis that monetary incentives may actually reduce output is unambiguously refuted by his data on blue-collar work.
24. Bénabou and Tirole (2003) develop an interesting alternative explanation for crowding out, based on an informational inference process. They argue that when the agent has imperfect knowledge of his ability, he can derive information from the incentive scheme. In that view, the "crowding-out" case requires that the agent be less knowledgeable in some dimensions than the principal, and that a sorting condition holds (the principal is more inclined to offer rewards when the agent has limited ability or the task is unattractive). By offering low-powered incentives, the principal signals that he trusts the agent. Conversely, rewards have a limited impact on current performance, and reduce the agent's motivation to undertake similar tasks in the future.
25. Generally speaking, "management matters." For instance, a study of the largest US federal agencies finds that front-line supervisors play an important role in organizational performance and effectiveness, and supervisory management is an important determinant of high performance (Brewer, 2005).
26. More generally, critics argue that increasing "managerialism" in the public sector entails the risk that impartiality, equal treatment, and general interest (that is, the ethic component of common goods) disappear (Rawls, 1987).
27. The point we want to make here is about the efficacy of increasing the level of incentives, other motivators being constant—and notwithstanding the cross-effects of one type of motivator on motivations other than its "target" one. For instance, it would

seem to be a common-sense proposition that increasing monetary incentives might increase productivity up to a point, but raising pay to the infinite will not raise effort correspondingly.

28. Another example of comparative performance measures playing a valuable informational role for service deliverers is to be found in the development of measures of the comparative success rates of alternative procedures for treating given medical conditions, which is part of the broader movement over recent years to more "evidence-based" medical practice. In the absence of such information, it was quite possible for doctors to continue using procedures which had become outmoded and which were less effective that current best practice, in the sincere belief that they were giving their patients the most appropriate treatment. Such an approach becomes much more difficult when good information is developed and the use of such information is reinforced by peer review processes.
29. This is a lesson which has, for example, been learned in Britain where, particularly following the 2003 report of the House of Commons Public Administration Select Committee, *On Target: Government by Measurement*, the government has proclaimed its intention of improving consultation in the setting of national Public Service Agreement targets and permitting greater local autonomy in the translation of those targets to the "coal-face" level.
30. See the evidence surveyed in Coulam and Gaumer (1991, p. 51). It should be noted that most of the US hospitals concerned were private rather than public. However, at that stage, they were generally non-profit, and therefore possessed very similar characteristics to public hospitals.
31. Gatti et al. (2003) show that the social environment plays an important role in determining individual attitudes toward corruption. The presence of social effects implies that at the individual level, incentives to fight corruption can be low.
32. For examples of enforcement failures for regulatory contracts in Africa, see Laffont (2003). As for the lack of penalties in budgeting and financial management, see for example, Ramakrishnan (1998), and Sekwat (1997).
33. Van Rijckeghem and Weder (2001) suggest that higher relative salaries for public officials are associated with lower corruption. Dabla-Norris (2002) and Dabla-Norris and Paul (2006) argue that, as formal contracts fall short of their reservation utility, public agents in developing countries are offered "implicit contracts" which tolerate a certain degree of rent capture.
34. Van Rijckeghem and Weder (2001) also show that a rather large increase in wages is required to eradicate corruption.

References

Akerlof, G., 1982, "Labor Contracts as Partial Gift Exchanges," *Quarterly Journal of Economics*, Vol. 97(4), pp. 543–69.

Alchian, A., and H. Demsetz, 1972, "Production, Information Costs, and Economic Organization," *American Economic Review*, Vol. 62, pp. 777–95.

Arrowsmith, J., S. French, M. Gilman, and R. Richardson, 2001, "Performance-Related Pay in Health Care," *Journal of Health Services Research and Policy*, Vol. 6(2), pp. 114–19.

Atkinson, A., S. Burgess, B. Croxson, P. Gregg, C. Propper, H. Slater, and D. Wilson, 2004, "Evaluating the Impact of Performance-Related Pay for Teachers in England," *CMPO Working Paper* No. 04/113, University of Bristol.

Averill, R.F., M.J. Kalison, J.C. Vertrees, and N.I. Goldfield, 1996, "Achieving Short-Term Medicare Savings through the Expansion of the Prospective Payment System," *Health Care Management Review*, Vol. 21(4), pp. 18–25.

Baker, G., 1992, "Incentive Contracts and Performance Measurement," *Journal of Political Economy*, Vol. 100(3), pp. 598–614.

——, 2002, "Distortion and Risk in Optimal Incentive Contracts," *Journal of Human Resources,* Vol. 37(4), pp. 728–51.

Baker, G., R. Gibbons, and K. Murphy, 1994, "Subjective Performance Measures in Optimal Incentive Contracts," *Quarterly Journal of Economics,* Vol. 109, pp. 1125–56.

Barkema, H., P. Geroski, and J. Schwalbach, 1997, "Managerial Compensation, Strategy and Firm Performance: An Introduction," *International Journal of Industrial Organization,* Vol. 15(4), pp. 413–16.

Baron, J., 1988, "The Employment Relation as a Social Relation," *Journal of the Japanese and International Economies,* Vol. 2(4), pp. 492–525.

BBC, 1999, "Warning over Teacher's Performance Pay," 22 September, <http://news.bbc.co.uk/1/hi/education/specials/green_paper/453862.stm>.

Bénabou, R., and J. Tirole, 2003, "Intrinsic and Extrinsic Motivation," *Review of Economic Studies,* Vol. 70(3), pp. 489–520.

Besley, T., and M. Ghatak, 2003a, "Competition and Incentives with Motivated Agents." Unpublished, London School of Economics, September.

——, 2003b, "Incentives, Choice and Accountability in the Provision of Public Services," *Oxford Review of Economic Policy,* Vol. 19(2), pp. 235–49.

Borjas, G., 2000, *Labor Economics,* second edition (New York: McGraw-Hill).

Bray, N., C. Carter, A. Dobson, M.J. Watt and S. Shortell, 1994, "An Examination of Winners and Losers under Medicare's Prospective Payment System," *Health Care Management Review,* Vol. 19(1), p. 44 passim.

Brewer, G., 2005, "In the Eye of the Storm: Frontline Supervisors and Federal Agency Performance," *Journal of Public Administration Research and Theory,* Vol. 15(4), pp. 505–27.

Brewer, G., S. Coleman, and R.L. Facer, 2000, "Individual Conceptions of Public Service Motivation," *Public Administration Review,* Vol. 60(3), pp. 204–14.

Buchan, J., M. Thompson, and F. O'May, 2000, "Health Workforce Incentive and Remuneration—A Research Review," *Issues in Health Services Delivery. Discussion Paper No. 4* (Geneva: World Health Organization).

Burgess, S., B. Croxson, P. Gregg, and C. Pepper, 2001, "The Intricacies of the Relationship Between Pay and Performance for Teachers: Do Teachers Respond to Performance Related Pay Schemes?" *CMPO Working Paper* No. 01/35, University of Bristol.

Burgess, S., and P. Metcalfe, 1999, "The Use of Incentive Schemes in the Public and Private Sectors: Evidence from British Establishments," *CMPO Working Paper* No. 99/015, University of Bristol.

Burgess, S., and M. Ratto, 2003, "The Role of Incentives in the Public Sector: Issues and Evidence," *Oxford Review of Economic Policy,* Vol. 19(2), pp. 285–300.

California Federation of Teachers, 2005, "Responding to the Governor's Attacks: Oppose Merit Pay Schemes," <www.cft.org/resources/leg/news/talkptsmerit.html>, accessed November 7, 2005.

Cameron, J., and W.D. Pierce, 1994, "Reinforcement, Reward, and Intrinsic Motivation: A Meta-Analysis," *Review of Educational Research,* Vol. 64(3), pp. 363–423.

Che, Y.-K., and S.-W. Yoo, 2001, "Optimal Incentives for Teams," *American Economic Review,* Vol. 91(3), pp. 525–41.

Coulam, R., and G. Gaumer, 1991, "Medicare's Prospective Payment System: A Critical Appraisal," *Health Care Financing Review,* 1991 Annual Supplement, pp. 45–77.

Courty, P., and G. Marschke, 2004, "An Empirical Investigation of Gaming Responses to Explicit Performance Incentives," *Journal of Labor Economics,* Vol. 22(1), pp. 23–56.

Dabla-Norris, E., 2002, "A Game-Theoretic Analysis of Corruption in Bureaucracies," in *Governance, Macroeconomics, and the IMF,* ed. G. Abed and S. Gupta (Washington: International Monetary Fund).

Dabla-Norris, E., and E. Paul, 2006, "What Transparency Can Do When Incentives Fail. An Analysis of Rent Capture," *IMF Working Paper* 06/146 (Washington: International Monetary Fund).

Deci, E., 1971, "The Effects of Externally Mediated Rewards on Intrinsic Motivation," *Journal of Personality and Social Psychology*, Vol. 18(1), pp. 105–15.

Deci, E., R. Koestner, and R. Ryan, 1999, "A Meta-Analytic Review of Experiments Examining the Effects of Extrinsic Rewards on Intrinsic Motivation," *Psychological Bulletin*, Vol. 125(6), pp. 627–68.

Deci, E.L., and R.M. Ryan, 1980, "The Empirical Exploration of Intrinsic Motivational Processes," in *Advances in Experimental Social Psychology*, Vol. 13, ed. L. Berkowitz (New York: Academic Press), pp. 39–80.

——, 1985, *Intrinsic Motivation and Self-determination in Human Behavior* (New York: Plenum).

Dewatripont, M., I. Jewitt and J. Tirole, 1999a, "The Economics of Career Concerns, Part I: Comparing Information Structures," *Review of Economic Studies*, Vol. 66(1), pp. 183–98.

——, 1999b, "The Economics of Career Concerns, Part II: Application to Missions and Accountability of Government Agencies," *Review of Economic Studies*, Vol. 66, pp. 199–217.

Dia, M., 1996, *Africa's Management in the 1990s and Beyond: Reconciling Indigenous and Transplanted Institutions* (Washington: World Bank).

DiIulio, J., 1994, "Principled Agents: The Cultural Bases of Behavior in a Federal Government Bureaucracy," *Journal of Public Administration Research and Theory*, Vol. 4(3), pp. 277–318.

Dixit, A., 2002, "Incentives and Organizations in the Public Sector: An Interpretative Review," *Journal of Human Resources*, Vol. 37(4), pp. 696–727.

Drazen, A., 2000, *Political Economy in Macroeconomics* (Princeton: Princeton University Press).

Ehrenberg, R., and R. Smith, 1997, *Modern Labor Economics. Theory and Public Policy*, sixth edition (Reading, Mass.: Addison-Wesley).

Eisenberger, R., and J. Cameron, 1996, "Detrimental Effects of Reward: Reality or Myth?" *American Psychologist*, Vol. 51(11), pp. 1153–66.

Falk, A., and E. Fehr, 2002, "Psychological Foundations of Incentives," *CEPR Discussion Paper* No. 3185 (London: CEPR).

Fehr, E., and U. Fischbacher, 2004, "Social Norms and Human Cooperation," *Trends in Cognitive Sciences*, Vol. 8, pp. 185–90.

Fehr, E., U. Fischbacher, and S. Gächter, 2002, "Strong Reciprocity, Human Cooperation and the Enforcement of Social Norms," *Human Nature*, Vol. 13, pp. 1–25.

Fehr, E., and S. Gächter, 1999, "Collective Action as a Social Exchange," *Journal of Economic Behavior and Organization*, Vol. 39(4), pp. 341–69.

——, 2000, "Fairness and Retaliation: The Economics of Reciprocity," *Journal of Economic Perspectives*, Vol. 14(3): pp. 159–81.

Fehr, E., S. Gächter, and G. Kirchsteiger, 1997, "Reciprocity as a Contract Enforcement Device: Experimental Evidence," *Econometrica*, Vol. 65(4), pp. 833–60.

Fehr, E., and B. Rockenbach, 2003, "Detrimental Effects of Sanctions on Human Altruism," *Nature*, Vol. 422, pp. 137–40.

Fehr, E., and K. Schmidt, 2004, "Fairness and Incentives in a Multi-task Principal–Agent Model," *Scandinavian Journal of Economics*, Vol. 106(3), pp. 453–74.

Feltham, G., and J. Xie, 1994, "Performance Measure Congruity and Diversity in Multi-Task Principal/Agent Relations," *Accounting Review*, Vol. 69(3), pp. 429–53.

Ferraro, F., and J. Pfeffer, 2005, "Economics Language and Assumptions: How Theories Can Become Self-Fulfilling," *Academy of Management Review*, Vol. 30(1), pp. 8–24.

FitzRoy, F., and K. Kraft, 1985, "Unionization, Wages, and Efficiency: Theories and Evidence from the U.S. and West Germany," *Kyklos*, Vol. 38(4), pp. 537–54.

——, 1987, "Cooperation, Productivity, and Profit Sharing," *Quarterly Journal of Economics*, Vol. 102(1) (February), pp. 23–36.

——, 1995, "On the Choice of Incentives in Firms," *Journal of Economic Behavior and Organization*, Vol. 26(1), pp. 145–60.

Foss, N., and K. Laursen, 2005, "Performance Pay, Delegation and Multitasking under Uncertainty and Innovativeness: An Empirical Investigation," *Journal of Economic Behavior and Organization,* Vol. 58(2), pp. 246–76.

François, P., 2000, "'Public Service Motivation' as an Argument for Government Provision," *Journal of Public Economics,* Vol. 78, pp. 275–99.

Frey, B., 1993, "Motivation as a Limit to Pricing," *Journal of Economic Psychology,* Vol. 14(4) (December), pp. 635–64.

——, 1994, "How Intrinsic Motivation Is Crowded Out and In," *Rationality and Society,* Vol. 6, pp. 334–52.

——, 1997, "On the Relationship between Intrinsic and Extrinsic Work Motivation," *International Journal of Industrial Organization,* Vol. 15(4), pp. 427–39.

Frey, B., and R. Jegen, 2001, "Motivation Crowding Theory," *Journal of Economic Surveys,* Vol. 15(5), pp. 589–623.

Frey, B., and F. Oberholzer-Gee, 1997, "The Cost of Price Incentives: An Empirical Analysis of Motivation Crowding-Out," *American Economic Review,* Vol. 87(4), pp. 746–55.

Garen, J., 1998, "Self-Employment, Pay Systems, and the Theory of the Firm: An Empirical Analysis," *Journal of Economic Behavior and Organization,* Vol. 36(2), pp. 257–74.

Gatti, R., S. Paternostro, and J. Rigolini, 2003, "Individual Attitudes toward Corruption: Do Social Effects Matter?" *World Bank Policy Research Working Paper* No. 3122 (Washington: World Bank).

General Accounting Office (GAO), 2002, *Results-Oriented Cultures: Insights for U.S. Agencies from Other Countries' Performance Management Initiatives,* GAO-02–862 (Washington: GAO).

——, 2005, *Managing For Results: Enhancing Agency Use of Performance Information for Management Decision Making,* GAO-05–927 (Washington: GAO).

Gibbons, R., 1998, "Incentives in Organizations," *Journal of Economic Perspectives,* Vol. 12(4), pp. 115–32.

Gintis, H., S. Bowles, R. Boyd, and E. Fehr, 2003, "Explaining Altruistic Behavior in Humans," *Evolution and Human Behavior,* Vol. 24, pp. 153–72.

Gneezy, U., and A. Rustichini, 2000, "Pay Enough or Don't Pay at All," *Quarterly Journal of Economics,* Vol. 115(3), pp. 791–810.

Goldsmith, A., J. Veum, and W. Darity, Jr., 2000, "Working Hard for the Money? Efficiency Wages and Worker Effort," *Journal of Economic Psychology,* Vol. 21(4), pp. 351–85.

Gosden, T., F. Forland, I.S. Kristiansen, M. Sutton, B. Leese, A. Giuffrida, M. Sergison, and L. Pedersen, 2001, "Impact of Payment Method on Behaviour of Primary Care Physicians: A Systematic Review," *Journal of Health Services Research and Policy,* Vol. 6, pp. 44–55.

Government Performance Project, 2003, *Paths to Performance in State & Local Government: A Final Assessment from the Maxwell School of Citizenship and Public Affairs,* <www.maxwell.syr.edu/gpp/about/facts.asp>, accessed January 13, 2004.

Gupta, D., C.R. Hofstetter, and T. Buss, 1997, "Group Utility in the Micro Motivation of Collective Action: The Case of Membership in the AARP," *Journal of Economic Behavior and Organization,* Vol. 32(2), pp. 301–20.

Gupta, N., and J. Shaw, 1998, "Let the Evidence Speak: Financial Incentives Are Effective!!" *Compensation and Benefits Review,* Vol. 30(2), pp. 26, 28–32.

Hamilton, B., J. Nickerson, and H. Owan, 2003, "Team Incentives and Worker Heterogeneity: An Empirical Analysis of the Impact of Teams on Productivity and Participation," *Journal of Political Economy,* Vol. 111, pp. 465–97.

Heckman, J., C. Heinrich, and J. Smith, 1997, "Assessing the Performance of Performance Standards in Public Bureaucracies," *American Economic Review,* Vol. 87(2), pp. 389–95.

——, 2002, "The Performance of Performance Standards," *Journal of Human Resources,* Vol. 37(4) (Autumn), pp. 778–811.

Herzberg, F., 1968, "One More Time: How Do You Motivate Employees?" *Harvard Business Review* (January–February), pp. 53–62.

Holmström, B., and P. Milgrom, 1991, "Multi-Task Principal–Agent Analyses: Incentive Contracts, Asset Ownership and Job Design," *Journal of Law, Economics and Organization*, Vol. 7, pp. 24–52.

——, 1994, "The Firm as an Incentive System," *American Economic Review*, Vol. 84(4), pp. 972–91.

House of Commons Public Administration Select Committee, 2003, *On Target: Government by Measurement*, Fifth Report of Session 2002–2003, HC 62–1 (London: The Stationery Office).

Houston, D., 2000, "Public-Service Motivation: A Multivariate Test," *Journal of Public Administration Research and Theory*, Vol. 10(4), pp. 713–27.

Ingraham, P., 1993, "Pay for Performance in the States," *American Review of Public Administration*, Vol. 23(3), pp. 189–200.

Janssen, M., and E. Mendys-Kamphorst, 2004, "The Price of a Price: On the Crowding Out and In of Social Norms," *Journal of Economic Behavior and Organization*, Vol. 55(3), pp. 377–95.

Jenkins, G.D., A. Mitra, N. Gupta, and J. Shaw, 1998, "Are Financial Incentives Related to Performance? A Meta-Analytic Review of Empirical Research," *Journal of Applied Psychology*, Vol. 83(5), pp. 777–87.

Kahn, C., E. Silva, and J. Ziliak, 2001, "Performance-based Wages in Tax Collection: The Brazilian Tax Collection Reform and Its Effects," *Economic Journal*, Vol. 111(468), pp. 188–205.

Kandel, E., and E. Lazear, 1992, "Peer Pressure and Partnership," *Journal of Political Economy*, Vol. 100(4), pp. 801–17.

Kellough, J.E., and H. Lu, 1993, "The Paradox of Merit Pay in the Public Sector," *Review of Public Personnel Administration* (Spring), pp. 45–64.

Knez, M., and D. Simester, 2001, "Firm-Wide Incentives and Mutual Monitoring at Continental Airlines," *Journal of Labor Economics*, Vol. 19, pp. 743–72.

Kohn, A., 1998, "How Incentives Undermine Performance," *Journal for Quality and Participation*, Vol. 21(2), pp. 6–13.

Kole, S., 1997, "The Complexity of Compensation Contracts," *Journal of Financial Economics*, Vol. 43(1), pp. 79–104.

Kreps, D., 1997, "Intrinsic Motivation and Extrinsic Incentives," *American Economic Review*, Vol. 87(2), pp. 359–64.

Laffont, J.-J., 2003, "Enforcement, Regulation and Development," *Journal of African Economies*, Vol. 12, pp. 193–211.

Lazear, E., 1986, "Salaries and Piece Rates," *Journal of Business*, Vol. 59(3), pp. 405–31.

——, 2000, "Performance Pay and Productivity," *American Economic Review*, Vol. 90(5), pp. 1346–61.

Le Grand, J., 2003, *Motivation, Agency, and Public Policy. Of Knights and Knaves, Pawns and Queens* (Oxford: Oxford University Press).

Leete, L., 2000, "Wage Equity and Employee Motivation in Nonprofit and For-profit Organizations," *Journal of Economic Behavior and Organization*, Vol. 43(4), pp. 423–46.

Lepper, M., and D. Greene, 1978, "Overjustification Research and Beyond: Toward a Means-Ends Analysis of Intrinsic and Extrinsic Motivation," in *The Hidden Cost of Reward: New Perspectives on the Psychology of Human Motivation*, ed. M. Lepper and D. Greene (Hillsdale, NJ: Erlbaum).

Lepper, M., D. Greene, and R. Nisbett, 1973, "Undermining Children's Intrinsic Interest with Extrinsic Reward: A Test of the 'Overjustification' Hypothesis," *Journal of Personality and Social Psychology*, Vol. 28(1), pp. 129–37.

Leruth, L., and E. Paul, 2006, "The Design of Public Expenditure Management Systems in Developing Countries. Lessons from Principal–Agent Theory for Institutional Strengthening," *IMF Working Paper* 06/204 (Washington: International Monetary Fund).

Levine, D., 1993, "What Do Wages Buy?" *Administrative Science Quarterly*, Vol. 38(3), pp. 462–83.

Lienert, I., 2003, "A Comparison Between Two Public Expenditure Management Systems in Africa," *IMF Working Paper* 03/2 (Washington: International Monetary Fund).

McConnell, C., and S. Brue, 1989, *Contemporary Labor Economics*, third edition (New York: McGraw-Hill).

Milgrom, P., and J. Roberts, 1988, "An Economic Approach to Influence Activities in Organizations," *American Journal of Sociology*, Vol. 94, pp. S154–79.

Minkler, L., 2004, "Shirking and Motivations in Firms: Survey Evidence on Worker Attitudes," *International Journal of Industrial Organization,* Vol. 22(6), pp. 863–84.

Moussa, Y., 2004, "Public Expenditure Management in Francophone Africa: A Cross-Country Analysis," *IMF Working Paper* 04/42 (Washington: International Monetary Fund).

Moynihan, D., and S. Pandey, forthcoming, "The Role of Organizations in Fostering Public Service Motivation," *Public Administration Review.*

Murdock, K., 2002, "Intrinsic Motivation and Optimal Incentive Contract," *Rand Journal of Economics,* Vol. 33(4), pp. 650–71.

OECD, 2005, *Modernising Government: The Way Forward* (Paris: OECD).

Osterloh, M., and B. Frey, 2000, "Motivation, Knowledge Transfer, and Organizational Forms," *Organization Science*, Vol. 11(5), pp. 538–50.

Pallez, F., 2003, "Les instruments de la motivation du fonctionnaire, de l'intéressement à la considération," in *La motivation au travail dans les services publics*, ed. T. Duvillier, J.-L. Genard, and A. Piraux (Paris: L'Harmattan), pp. 141–56.

Paul, E., 2005, "L'approche sectorielle « Santé » au Sénégal: Analyse des incitants et des coûts de transaction," *Rapport de mission, Version finale du 17 octobre 2005,* Groupe de recherche sur les instruments de coopération en appui aux politiques sectorielles.

Perry, J., 1996, "Measuring Public Service Motivation: An Assessment of Construct Reliability and Validity," *Journal of Public Administration Research and Theory,* Vol. 6(1), pp. 5–22.

——, 1997, "Antecedents of Public Service Motivation," *Journal of Public Administration Research and Theory,* Vol. 7(2), pp. 181–97.

Perry, J., and L. Wise, 1990, "The Motivational Basis of Public Service," *Public Administration Review,* Vol. 50(3), pp. 367–73.

Perry, R., 2005, "Gov. Perry Orders Incentive Pay Program for Texas Teachers," Press Release, November 2, <www.governor.state.tx.us/divisions/press/pressreleases/PressRelease.2005-11-02.2856>.

Pfeffer, J., 2005, "Untested Assumptions May Have a Big Effect," Stanford Graduate School of Business News, June, <www.gsb.stanford.edu/news/research/lead_pfeffer_assumptions.shtml>.

Prendergast, C., 1999, "The Provision of Incentives in Firms," *Journal of Economic Literature,* Vol. 37, pp. 7–63.

——, 2002, "The Response of Los Angeles Police Department to Increased Oversight." Paper presented at the HM Treasury Conference on Public Services Productivity, June 13.

Propper, C., and D. Wilson, 2003, "The Use and Usefulness of Performance Measures in the Public Sector," *Oxford Review of Economic Policy,* Vol. 19(2), pp. 250–67.

Ramakrishnan, S., 1998, "Budgeting and Financial Management in Sub-Saharan Africa: Key Policy and Institutional Issues," *Development Discussion Paper* No. 622 (Cambridge, Mass.: Harvard Institute for International Development).

Rauch, J., and P. Evans, 2000, "Bureaucratic Structure and Bureaucratic Performance in Less Developed Countries," *Journal of Public Economics*, Vol. 75, pp. 49–71.

Rawls, J., 1987, *Théories de la justice* (Paris: Seuil).

Robinson, M., and J. Brumby, 2005, "Does Performance Budgeting Work? An Analytical Review of the Empirical Literature," *IMF Working Paper* 05/210 (Washington: International Monetary Fund).

Rose-Ackerman, S., 1986, "Reforming Public Bureaucracy through Economic Incentives?" *Journal of Law, Economics and Organization,* Vol. 2(1), pp. 131–61.

Rotemberg, J., 1994, "Human Relations in the Workplace," *Journal of Political Economy,* Vol. 102(4), pp. 684–717.

Royal Statistical Society, 2003, *Performance Indicators: Good, Bad and Ugly*, Report of the Royal Statistical Society Working Party on Performance Monitoring in the Public Services, <www.rss.org.uk>. accessed November 8, 2005.

Seddon, J., 2002, Memorandum by Mr. John Seddon, to House of Commons Select Committee on Public Administration, at <www.publications.parliament.uk>, accessed November 8, 2005.

Sekwat, A., 1997, "Public Budgeting Deficiencies in Sub-Saharan Africa: A Review," *Journal of Public Budgeting, Accounting and Financial Management,* Vol. 9(1), pp. 143–61.

Stiglitz, J., 1974, "Wage Determination and Unemployment in LDCs: The Labor Turnover Model," *Quarterly Journal of Economics*, Vol. 88, pp. 194–227.

Teaching Commission, 2004, *Teaching at Risk: A Call to Action*, <www.csl.usf.edu/teaching%20at%20risk.pdf>, accessed April 27, 2007.

Tirole, J., 1986, "Hierarchies and Bureaucracies: On the Role of Collusion in Organizations," *Journal of Law, Economics, and Organization*, Vol. 2(2), pp. 181–214.

——, 1994, "The Internal Organization of Government," *Oxford Economic Papers,* Vol. 46(1), pp. 1–29.

Van Rijckeghem, C., and B. Weder, 2001, "Bureaucratic Corruption and the Rate of Temptation: Do Wages in the Civil Service Affect Corruption, and by How Much?" *Journal of Development Economics*, Vol. 65, pp. 307–31.

Wilson, J.Q., 1989, *Bureaucracy: What Government Agencies Do and Why They Do It* (New York: Basic Books).

Wittmer, D., 1991, "Serving for People or Serving for Pay: Reward Preferences Among Government, Hybrid Sector, and Business Managers," *Public Productivity and Management Review*, Vol. 14, pp. 369–83.

World Bank, 2004, "Making Services Work for Poor People," *World Development Report 2004*, (Washington: World Bank).

Wright, B., 2001, "Public Sector Work Motivation: A Review of the Current Literature and a Revised Conceptual Model," *Journal of Public Administration Research and Theory*, Vol. 11(4), pp. 559–86.

Part Three

Implementation Strategy and Sequencing

19
Challenges to Implementation

Jack Diamond

Parts One and Two of this volume have distinguished among different types of performance budgeting (PB), and have assessed the various means employed to ensure that these efforts have improved the efficiency and effectiveness of government spending. Part Three focuses on the question of how countries have introduced PB, the typical challenges faced in implementation, how these have been overcome, and the lessons that can be learned by other countries who wish to introduce PB reforms.

Although interpreted differently by different countries, the challenge faced by countries in introducing PB arises from the common feature of this reform that it is usually interpreted as systemic. Although essentially it has to do with the way we budget—it is recognized as something more—it involves the entire budget process from the planning, budget preparation, and budget implementation to the ex-post evaluation phase. Following from its systemic nature, introducing PB involves a change in budget management, and, perhaps even more, represents something of a "cultural change" within the government sector. This is particularly pronounced in Chapters 20 and 21 that present case studies of France and Russia—both countries whose previous budgetary systems have influenced and formed models for many other countries. Both chapters argue that because the approach is comprehensive it needs to be reinforced by wider systemic changes, not only in government work practices, but in the institutional structure of government, its legal framework, and its human resource base. Ultimately it involves changes in motivation and the way performance is defined and enforced. In short, most contemporary forms of performance budgeting have close synergies with broader "managing-for-results" reforms (see Chapter 1).

These characteristics, its breadth and depth, point to a lengthy implementation process and one that must advance on a number of fronts, and not only within the budget process—features which are evident in the chapters presented in this part. In particular the Russian case study, documented by Elena Belyanova, Ole Hovland, and Alexey Lavrov in Chapter 21, perhaps most stresses the scope of the required reform effort, by a country with an ambitious reform program, and one undertaken on a massive scale. The recognition that introducing performance-based budgeting requires more than reforming budget processes but involves wider institutional and regulatory reforms is clearly brought out in this chapter. The candid discussion of the difficulties encountered and the tasks remaining, as well as the call for a more realistic timetable, are most instructive for other countries following a similar path. Similarly, Benoît Chevauchez's description of the French experience in Chapter 20 stresses the systemic view, arguing that introducing PB has implied modernizing the whole public administration. Accordingly, this has led policy-makers to pursue broader changes in three key areas: civil service reform, the organization of government, and the interaction between elected officials, ministers, and public servants—all challenges which the French currently face.

In this review of the implementation problems posed by this major reform, it is possible to identify some important lessons. First, *the introduction of PB requires suitable preconditions within the public expenditure management system.* It should be remembered that countries most successful in introducing these reforms started from a solid base in their budget system. Their systems were capable of controlling expenditure within budget appropriations, in adjusting fiscal aggregates to meet macroeconomic objectives, and only then were PB techniques introduced to enhance the efficiency and effectiveness of government spending. The need for a solid public financial management platform on which to base PB reforms should be emphasized.

Second, *successful implementation has required careful planning and organization,* both on the supply and the demand side. This reform should be considered not as a mere "add on" to other budget work, but as a dedicated activity, viewed as a major investment project requiring substantial human and financial resources. On the supply side it has usually involved a specialized reform team pushing for reform, and simultaneously the cultivation of the demand for these reforms by major stakeholders, both within and outside the budget system. Inevitably the costs involved are up-front, while the benefits tend to be longer-term and not as tangible.

As a consequence, the third lesson is *the importance of the sequencing and pace of the reforms.* While there is a danger in advancing too timidly there are obvious risks in advancing too fast. The chapters in this part give examples of both what might be termed the "big-bang" approach (for example, Russia) as opposed to a more phased, or sequential, approach (for example, France). Ultimately, the desirability of each approach is likely to be country specific and depend on the environment in which the reforms are launched. However, it will be evident that the big-bang approach appears the riskier of the two.

Last, but perhaps most problematic, since PB involves a wider systemic change in the way government does business, *its introduction typically requires parallel changes in the organizational and administrative structure of government and the legal framework in which it operates.* As a consequence budget reform needs to be paralleled by administrative and civil service reforms. If these are not in place, or do not advance fast enough, these wider conditioning factors may act as a brake on reform. Let us examine each of these issues in turn.

Preconditions should be established

There has been increasing recognition that PB reforms should be based on a solid financial management platform within government institutions. This "micro basis" of wider budget system reforms is easy to take for granted, but is problematic if neglected. In particular three areas have generally been found weak, especially in middle-income countries, but have not always been adequately emphasized: the internal control systems in budget institutions; mechanisms to meet the heavier demands for information, particularly of a performance nature; and the need for full costing of all government activities and programs. It is perhaps instructive to review the implementation problems caused by neglecting such prerequisites, which are touched on by several of the chapters in this part.

The essence of the PB approach is to let managers manage by devolving resource decision-making to the operational level. In moving away from the more traditional centralized controls, there it is often the need to strengthen institutions' internal control mechanisms to avoid any new financial freedoms, brought about by the dismantling of central controls, resulting in less effective use of funds. At the same time, this should be mirrored by a changing role for the central budget office, as discussed below.

Clearly PB is a heavy user of information. Detailed and robust financial information is demanded of managers to adequately track the costs of their operations, and at the same time additional performance information is required to relate these costs to their outputs and outcomes. In turn this implies PB management should be based on a firm IT platform. At its most general this will include software to assist in budget formulation, budget execution, and accounting operations. Specific demands of PB management will also require a progressive shift in the type of information used. This will be away from the traditional focus on annual cash requirements and uses, towards a more medium-term financial planning framework, with modification of existing information systems to capture additional performance data. In this move, as evidenced in some chapters in this volume, there are often difficult methodological problems faced in deriving indicators of performance, in setting and justifying target values for these indicators, and in deciding on how information will be combined and on how reporting systems will be designed. An important point stressed by Philip Joyce in Chapter 23, is not only that there is a need for appropriate information in order to make budgeting more results focused, but also that information needs to be properly used to make decisions. Again Joyce stresses the systemic nature of these reforms—there are multiple decisions to be made at every stage of the budget process, from its approval to final ex-post evaluation.

Kate Ashcroft, in Chapter 24, dealing with developing formulae for funding performance in higher education in low-income countries, gives an in-depth perspective on the importance of developing indicators flexible enough to allow incentives to managers but at the same time being practical enough to be applied.

While analyzing the principles underlying such formulae, much of the focus of the chapter is on the compromises required by poor or absent data and the lack of modern management systems in low-income countries. One of these compromises is the need for first developing indicators based on lower-level rather than high-level outcomes (for example, completed courses of study, rather than graduates employed in professional capacities). Another compromise is not to link funding too closely to performance in the short run, to allow institutions to adapt to different levels of funding and not be destabilized. Ashcroft offers many examples of funding formulas across the world based on inputs, outputs, or outcomes. Of course, not all higher education systems are funded by formulas, but the practice is growing and for good reasons: their transparency; their ability to fund complex systems; and their usefulness in focusing institutions on their core educational missions or goals, and so enforcing accountability. The essential point is that the design of the formula should allow it to be employed to promote better performance. Additionally, incentive funding can be set aside separately, so-called "top-slicing" available funds, to be targeted to different activities without disrupting the main formula. Of course, such targeting also demands more information.

At the same time there must be adequate mechanisms to fully cost programs and activities, so that they can be related to their outputs, and then to their ultimate benefits, in order to judge program performance. This approach involves public sector managers becoming more like private sector managers, required to capture the full costs of their operations. In turn, this has usually implied an accelerated move away from traditional cash accounting to at least partial accrual accounting. The case for moving to full accruals is less clear. For the few countries that have attempted it, the latter move has almost universally proved time consuming and costly, both financially and in terms of human resources. To adopt even partial accrual accounting has usually meant changes in budget classification and the adoption of new computerized accounting packages adapted from the private sector. Establishing these preconditions is highlighted in the Russian case study. In cases where full accruals has been introduced it has also meant the hiring of private sector accountants familiar with accrual concepts, typically in short supply, to supplement or even replace existing government accountants. Not surprisingly some countries have opted for the compromise position of only moving, at least initially, to a partial accrual accounting regime. It can be argued, therefore, that although performance budgeting does not require accruals, the approach will work better if over time accounting is moved, preferably in stages, onto an accrual basis.

Apart from the collection of performance data, managers must also ensure the timeliness of the data and its accessibility to allow various stakeholders, including civil society organizations and the general public, to monitor their performance. In turn this requires creating mechanisms to monitor program implementation, ex ante and within the fiscal year, as well as ex-post evaluation of the impact of programs. This should be complemented by procedures to ensure the integrity of all such functions. In turn this requires internal audit to be strengthened, to cover not only financial accounting and reporting but also correct measurement and reporting of non-financial indicators. In a similar way external audit should be performance-oriented. The case of Bogota clearly indicates the importance of the PB budget scrutiny by the legislative council, backed strongly by the external audit body (*Contraloria*), in highlighting budgetary issues and strengthening political oversight of the activities and outcomes achieved by the city administration. Joyce, in his chapter, argues that one of the ways that legislative bodies can impede performance is through the excessive use of budget controls. Rather it is essential that they engage in oversight designed to focus on performance. The elements are described: setting clear overall goals and direction for programs; focusing on appropriate performance and cost information; and exercising their oversight function on performance in a comprehensive way, so that it "allows legislatures to couple the grant of substantive policy-making with the capacity to discover what the executive branch has done with that power." Joyce admits, however, that such systematic oversight occurs less frequently than more episodic forms of legislative review.

Reform process needs to be mobilized

To ensure the adoption and the sustainability of PB reforms, it is important to fully appreciate that the workload of civil servants is likely to increase substantially. This is especially true in emerging market and developing countries. The requisite initial investment in systems could in the short run create resistance to reform. Civil servants can too easily view reform as a burden; especially in the initial phases when workload escalates without evident returns. There is also a longer-term problem—the cost of maintaining these systems is visible but gains are often less tangible.

In overcoming this resistance, the success in implementing PB reforms appears to rest critically on the change of management skills required to engineer the shift from one type of budget system to another. From this perspective some elements for successful implementation can be identified. First, there is the need to establish visible high-level commitment at the political level. Second, there is the need to form a consensus within the system that change is needed. Third, by building up and mobilizing this consensus, efforts must be made to ensure that it is strong enough to allow a common approach to be "sold" to the main stakeholders in the budget system and accepted as a central element of government policy. Fourth, and perhaps most important, a reform team has to be identified and empowered to carry out the reform led by a suitably powerful "champion" of the reforms. Fifth, there is also the need for a plan for sustaining the reform momentum, to institutionalize the changes so they become part of the management culture.

As indicated in the Bogota case study by Israel Fainboim Yaker in Chapter 22, the creation of a special unit in the Finance Secretariat to design and implement PB was of critical importance to the overall success of the reform. It should be underlined that this unit received political support from the highest level of the administration. In Russia, adopting a "big-bang" approach, Belyanova et al. report that while top-down pressure has been intense, a problem encountered has been that the implementation of reforms has been a shared responsibility between different institutions, sometimes difficult to coordinate. These case studies highlight the importance of a plan and the need for wider efforts to promote and institutionalize reforms.

To ensure that reforms were institutionalized it has usually been necessary to create the appropriate environment within the budget system and external to it. The latter has implied removing any institutional and legal constraints. Accordingly, most successful PB reform initiatives have led to changes in the way government is organized, and have been anchored on fundamental changes in budget system laws. We will return to this aspect later. Perhaps even more critical has been the creation of a suitable reform environment within the budget system.

The new PB budget model assumes that public officials will cease being administrators of public funds and assume a management role akin to that in the private sector. Unfortunately, this transformation is unlikely to occur without a substantial investment in human resources. The traditional compliance-oriented "command and control" management culture does not foster required PB managerial skills and while enforcing compliance does not encourage managerial responsibility. Management capacity needs to be identified and strengthened, but most important of all, mechanisms must be put in place to reward good performance while at the same time sanctioning poor performance. Put another way, at the same time as there is a need to upgrade basic management expertise there is the need to put into place a system of incentives for such expertise. This is not simple since performance becomes more difficult to judge. Where in the past managers were to be held accountable for the correct use of inputs, now they are to be held accountable for the results of using those inputs. This, as Chevauchez stresses in Chapter 20, has important wider ramifications for policy management, and in particular promotes the need for a clear definition of public policy objectives. Managers are unlikely to accept accountability for objectives that are unclear, inconsistent, and unachievable.

For reforms to be sustainable it may be necessary to strengthen the overall accountability framework. The focus has been on accountability within the executive branch and the need for the accountability of budget managers to be clearly defined and changed. However, this should be recognized as only one aspect of the overall accountability for the use of public funds. In addition there is the need for the executive to give an account to the legislature on how it is meeting its responsibilities as a whole, enforced by an independent external audit body, reporting at least annually, to the executive. However, as Chevauchez has pointed out, from the French experience improved accountability is likely to be wider than this, and may involve fundamentally redefining the roles of parliamentarians, ministers, and civil servants.

Often these latter dimensions of accountability also need to be strengthened. The accountability of the executive often needs to be enhanced by prescribing fuller reporting ex ante and ex post of fiscal policy strategies and intentions, as well as providing fuller reporting on the financial and non-financial outcomes. An effort designed to educate legislators on the use of these reports has also often proved beneficial. The external audit office also typically needs to be better resourced, made more clearly independent from the executive, and required to reorient its work to better serve the needs of the legislature (see Chapter 6 on the role of performance auditing). This, in the new PB model, has required the external audit institution to widen the scope of its audits away from narrow financial compliance with more emphasis on value-for-money audits.

A critical element in strengthening accountability and improving the effectiveness of the above approaches is to promote greater transparency within government. For low-income and emerging economies, this is also often an essential aspect of sustaining confidence in the government apparatus. This has become particularly acute with the exposure of fiscal policies to international financial markets arising from the increasing use of market financing of deficits. Such exposure has required many governments to modify past policies and so has assisted in achieving fiscal discipline and improved resource allocation. As argued below, it is also an essential ingredient in establishing the new budget management model.

Pace and sequencing of reforms is important

A realistic timeframe and the proper sequencing of reforms has been recognized as important. Experience from OECD countries warns of the dangers of being over-ambitious and underestimating the time required to complete budget system reforms. For countries with obvious administrative capacity constraints, a gradualist rather than a "big-bang" approach appears unavoidable. Moving from central controls where line ministries have little scope to manage their budgets, but rather administer them under central direction, implies new skills need to be developed or recruited. Accordingly management capacity needs to be strengthened as a prerequisite for devolving management decision-making. A "crawl before you walk and then run" approach inevitably takes time to implement. It also points to an implementation strategy that, rather than attempting blanket coverage, adopts a serial approach based on pilot agencies.

Unfortunately, a cautious step approach to reform could tend to make the reform process appear to lack coherence. All too easily, important legal and institutional initiatives and important programs and projects, while being identified as elements in the reform process, will not appear to fit together into an overall coordinated reform plan. With the incremental approach, it is difficult to specify a clear timetable for the reform process, nor to place emphasis on the sequencing of the individual components of the reform. It also allows more time for the opponents of change to organize themselves and increase resistance to the reform, and there is the ever-present danger of reform fatigue. It is not difficult to appreciate the lure of the "big-bang" approach to reform.

However, many of these drawbacks of a phased approach can be countered by a strong reform team with clearly designated and empowered agents of change. This raises questions about the role of the central budget office as a critical change agent where its work practices will need to undergo a fundamental change to "steer rather than row." Such a reorientation is often resisted. There are many reasons for this: fear of the unknown, reluctance to give up the power that goes with centralized controls, or simply the MoF having limited capacity for change management. Thus while the reform group may initially have to be located outside the central budget office (although ideally with its full participation), in the longer-run for PB reforms to be sustainable ideally the budget office should become the prime agent of change.

In implementing PB reforms, experience in some emerging market economies suggests the efficacy of a "scissors approach" to implementation: applying pressure from above to encourage managers to change, and increasing capacity from below to allow them to change. Top-down pressure on managers has come from a number of instruments: in-depth evaluations by the MoF of activities where managers are forced to justify the way they do business; institution of an "efficiency dividend," whereby managers are forced to find savings; improved accounting to ensure managers manage their assets better. However, this increased downward pressure must be matched by an improved ability of managers to adapt to it. Hence the second blade of the scissor: the need for a proactive role on the part of change managers at the center to develop good management in spending departments. This bottom-up approach can take several forms: promoting the idea of better management; developing standards for key management competencies and working with government institutions to apply them; reviewing outputs and performance indicators for each institution and providing specific expertise on demand when required so they can meet such requirements. For example, the Russian case study, while describing a top-down reform strategy, also highlights the importance of establishing a facilitating environment in budget institutions by offering them training and budgetary incentives to motivate them in supporting these reforms.

Providing an enabling environment is essential

The new PB reforms require continuous data-gathering, measurement, reporting, evaluation, and corrective action; that is, it makes "heavy" demands on managers. Consequently some offsetting incentives required. One obvious incentive is increased freedom for program managers, which is a key rationale of the PB approach. There must be some assurance that the information when manufactured can be used for better management decisions—that is, to assure a pay-off there must be flexibility in the budget. This assurance will not be provided if there is no scope for budget flexibility, if say, mandatory spending or "entitlements" consume nearly all the budget. Also the composition of spending is important—many budgets are transfer mechanisms rather than allocations for providing services. The latter are more susceptible to gains in using performance information well.

This also points to the importance of overall fiscal environment. While a sense of fiscal crisis can be a great spur to reform, if that crisis is too severe it will be difficult to invest heavily in longer-term reforms. Accordingly, it may prove easier to implement PB reforms in a resource-rich rather than a resource-poor budgetary environment, when there is some scope for visible pay-off rather than when expenditure cutbacks are required. Simply put, the timing has to be right. The Russian case study highlights that performance-based reforms were only undertaken when the macro-fiscal situation stabilized. The above considerations also point to the importance of introducing PB techniques selectively to those areas of expenditure, such as service provision where the pay-off is more visible to politicians and the public.

To sustain reforms an important challenge is to design comprehensive and effective incentive systems for program managers, typically with major structural constraints. Changes to civil service remuneration often imply fundamental administrative and civil service reforms. As the French case study stresses, this often can prove a most difficult element in reform.

The importance of increased labor flexibility to give public managers the freedom to deliver on their performance targets is a topic also taken up by Matt Davies, Marijn Verhoeven, and Victoria Gunnarsson in Chapter 25. To exercise this freedom the managers require a number of freedoms: the capacity to terminate employment, the capacity to shift people (either between agencies or between programs/activities), and the capacity to control remuneration structure and level. This chapter is important in relating these critical "micro" aspects of wage inflexibility to the aggregate wage bill inflexibility in the public sector as a whole and flexibility with respect to the labor market—recognized as important overall constraints in pursuing public sector management reforms. Their empirical analysis confirms that the wage bill is less flexible than other spending categories, with a consequent cost in terms of the quality of expenditure.

Chapter 25 also underlines that institutional processes—bureaucratic inertia, centralized pay scales and regulations, the rule of seniority, the importance of allowances and in-kind benefits, nationwide pay settlements, and all-powerful trade unions—contribute to this inflexibility, especially in lower-income countries. Given the generally hostile political environment, governance concerns, and the overriding need to ensure macroeconomic stability, the authors accordingly advocate a gradual approach to reforming public sector management. Davies et al. point to the tendency in OECD countries to reduce centralized controls over public sector employment and wage determination, and to cut powers to central civil service commissions, and so on, and to buttress the more general decentralization in public sector management. At the same time, they argue that some basic preconditions must be met so that such decentralization contributes to the quality of public management rather than simply increases the scope for corruption and nepotism. There should be no doubt that for performance budgeting to succeed, civil servant employment in low-efficiency or low-priority programs must be reduced—whether by redeployment, or by voluntary or involuntary redundancy. To ensure this, the transition to PB requires simultaneous coordinated reforms in traditionally rigid civil service employment regimes, usually with concurrent changes in the way budget institutions are organized and governed (see discussion below). Even if this is recognized it is often difficult to pursue such reforms simultaneously. This is made even more difficult when, as is typically the case, such reforms are designed and led by different teams so that coordination is problematic—a weakness identified in the present Russian reform efforts discussed by Belyanova et al.

Restructuring incentives by concentrating on the stakeholders within the budget system is unlikely to be enough—there is also the need for measures to activate the interests of clients to increase external demand for reform. One important external demand is that of the legislature in pursuing its oversight function. Joyce's chapter stresses the importance of the type of budget system substantially influences the way the legislature deals with the budget, and hence the scope to apply pressure for reform. While the focus of his chapter is on government systems where the legislature exercises independent control over the budget, there are important insights provided for systems with different degrees of legislative/executive separation in the move to performance budgeting. However, for him there are four critical actions contributing to better public sector performance with independent legislatures: establishing a clear schedule for authorizing or reviewing programs, investing in producing and reviewing performance data, increasing the transparency of legislative decision-making, and recognizing the performance implications of legislative constraints placed on executive branch agencies.

To bolster PB reform, and help to sustain it, clients also need to be empowered, and client feedback strengthened and made more transparent. One channel is through widely publicizing performance standards that should be expected from particular public agencies, and by spelling out the specific steps the public can take to force agencies to meet these standards. The UK Citizen's Charter attempted to do this at an aggregate level, but such initiatives are possible at a program level. A striking example of client involvement in improvements in public sector management is described in the Bogota case study. The *Bogota Como Vamos* project was promoted by the country's largest-circulation newspaper, a charitable foundation, and the Chamber of Commerce, to measure and report on quality of life and hence bring greater transparency to government operations.

The correct institutional underpinning of reform may also be an important factor in its success. In Chapter 20, Chevauchez highlights the importance of launching the new French budget process in 2006 by concentrating reform in the Ministry of the Budget and establishing a general directorate of government modernization to lead the reform process. But reform requires more than restructuring central institutions. Evidently, "managing-for-results" has certain well-defined characteristics: performance is defined in terms of outputs and outcomes and not just in controlling inputs; managers are given defined performance objectives and, often, quantitative targets and their results are measured against these; managers are given incentives and flexibility to achieve these results; and managers are held accountable for results achieved. Stemming from these characteristics it is important that operational authority be devolved from the center to accommodate this new accountability model which in turn has implied a more decentralized institutional structure for government. Often central institutions will need to be reorganized; for example, by removing the fragmentation in budget preparation (recurrent versus development budgets), and to operationalize the program approach as the basis of performance measurement. With a redefinition of programs, top-heavy large departments have often been reorganized around service delivery. In turn, this has often resulted in a decoupling of service providers from policy-makers and has given rise to the creation of "agencies" and other devolved government entities—a growing trend in most OECD countries.

Chevauchez, in the context of the French experience, highlights other common organizational problems faced in implementing these reforms; for example, the disconnect between the program structure and the institutional structure, and, in particular, the thorny question of multipurpose agencies. Another common problem encountered is that of "functional" directorates or support units, which ideally should be allocated to their respective program, but where often the soft option is taken, as in the French case, and a specific program is created for them. Unfortunately, as is rightly pointed out, this approach will delay and may even block the ultimate move to decentralizing such functions to the operating agencies, as is consistent with the PB model. Belyanova et al. emphasize that the Russian budget reforms are anchored on a fundamental restructuring of budget institutions, alongside a parallel reform of the civil service in the attempt to create the environment for greater performance and service orientation within the civil service. Fainboim Yaker also reports on the importance of parallel institutional changes, or what he terms "market-based governance" mechanisms, in supporting Bogota's performance budgeting reforms. These included the liquidation of a number of public agencies, restructuring entities through radical staff downsizing, the introduction of concessions, and outright privatization.

To create an enabling environment it is often necessary to remove any legal impediments to reform. The French case study points to the pivotal role of a new organic budget system law as the organizing framework in implementing reform. It also appears that a number of countries' budget system reforms were legislatively led, often in the form of fiscal responsibility laws, to force governments to commit credibly and assuage governance concerns. The basic idea of this approach is to create rules and procedures that impose costs on governments for deviating from fiscal responsibility. The pioneer in this field was New Zealand through the Fiscal Responsibility Act of 1994, which has often acted as a model for other countries. However, as a minimum, most countries will find it necessary either to supplement or replace existing legislation that supports a traditional budget process focused on financial compliance and the control of public monies.

It could be argued that the adoption of such legal frameworks is useful in facilitating budget reforms, but by themselves perhaps should not be considered a precondition for successful reform. While the French and Bogota case studies confirm that a suitable legislative framework underpinned the PB reforms, at the same time, to quote Fainboim Yaker,

> while it is important for PB to be incorporated into a law, since this would guarantee its permanency across changes of government, this is not a sufficient condition for success. It is the interest generated by the instrument among stakeholders (civil servants, legislature, citizens), and the use they give to it, that will determine its consolidation as a governance tool.

It should also be noted that in their candid assessment of the progress made and remaining tasks faced by the reform process, Belyanova et al. admit the need for further improvements in the legal and regulatory framework of budget management.

Concluding remarks

At first glance this brief survey of the challenges faced in introducing PB may appear quite daunting. However, in themselves each of these steps—establishing a strong public financial management base, organizing the reform process, investing in human resources, adopting a clear phased strategy, and putting in place an enabling legal and institutional environment—has individual merits and a pay-off in its own right. Moreover, it should always be remembered that these are steps that other countries have taken on the road to reforming their budget systems, so there is encouragement as well as lessons to be derived from their experience. The mere fact that PB reforms have been continued and extended in the countries that were first to adopt them should be a spur for those setting out on this reform path.

Nor should the prescription for reform described previously be considered unique or cast in stone. The fact is that all the more advanced countries have started from different initial conditions and have found their own solutions to these reform challenges, modifying and adapting these reforms to meet their own particular circumstances and specific political and economic environment. It is also worth remembering that the last word in budget system reform has not been written, and most likely never will. Even the most advanced PB systems continue to be subjected to new reform initiatives and experimentation. From this perspective, low- and middle-income countries who desire to advance PB reforms as fast as possible should recognize that there is no perfect system that can be taken "off the shelf" and applied without adaptation. What appears to work in one environment may not work in another. Rather, embarking on these reforms should be viewed as a learning process for all participants, and one that, once begun, should be expected to continue for many years into the future before its full results will be felt.

At the same time, while the pay-off may not be immediate, there should be no doubt about the advantages of pursuing these reforms, and the risks to countries in not pursuing them. Globalization in the international economy has had important repercussions for market-based economies, not only for their private sectors but also for their public sectors. The discipline of the global market has imposed constraints on private sector inefficiency and at the same time has also offered incentives for increased efficiency. Globalization has imposed similar discipline on governments. This has come not only directly through the channel of increased market financing of public sector deficits and public sector investments, but also indirectly but no less forcibly. An internationally competitive private sector requires an internationally competitive public sector providing its basic infrastructure of security, public health, an educated workforce, and basic utilities and transportation. PB is an attempt to ensure efficiency in the provision of public services and by so doing not only contributes to the sustainability of fiscal policies but removes constraints on private sector competitiveness.

Experience shows that the ultimate results can be profound. PB may have commenced narrowly by trying to promote improved service delivery, but has often ended up much more fundamentally reviewing what the role of government should be and changing the ground rules on how it should operate.

20
Public Management Reform in France

Benoît Chevauchez

Public sector reform (*la réforme de l'Etat*) is today a significant—although not dominant—theme of public debate in France. It is nonetheless an ambiguous term, denoting both change and modernization in public administration. The theme of public sector reform resurfaces periodically, with varying levels of intensity. Often, it is put forward as a slogan supposedly embodying a miracle solution for the ills besetting French society. The aspiration may be strong, but the specifics are usually lacking: there is little in the way of structured analysis, systematic vision, or comprehensive solutions. It is a theme of discussion only in the media and in intellectual and political circles. For the average citizen, public sector reform is of little genuine interest other than at the level of routine denunciations of "waste" and bureaucratic conservatism.

It is above all the French elite—government officials, graduates of the *grandes écoles*, and political insiders—which takes an interest in public sector reform. Over past decades, members of the elite have from time to time turned their attention to the subject in a deeper and more comprehensive manner than usual. Examples of this can be seen in the work of the "X-Crise" group in the 1930s, and also in that of the "club Jean Moulin" in the early 1960s. In the 1970s there was an attempt, spearheaded by economists from the Ministry of Finance and engineers from the Ministry of Infrastructure, to modernize budgeting under the banner of *Rationalisation des Choix Budgétaires* (RCB, Rationalization of Budgetary Choices), which was inspired by the US Planning, Programming, and Budgeting System. All of these efforts failed, however, because they were too exclusively technical and lacked political backing. More recently, an influential circle of government officials and academics have sought to disseminate within government analyses of the "sociology of organizations."[1]

During several periods over the decades, significant public sector reform has actually taken place: after the liberation of France, when the civil service was restructured and ENA (*Ecole Nationale d'Administration*) established; in 1959 with the return of General de Gaulle;[2] and, lastly, in 1983 when major decentralization reforms were implemented. Apart from these high points of reform, there has been a series of more incremental changes, arising, for example, from the redesign of organizational structures (with frequent splits and mergers of units), the work of numerous "axe committees,"[3] as well as with the far-reaching impact of new information technologies. Nevertheless, although the structure and operations of the government have not remained static throughout these decades, there was until recently no movement for public sector reform that was organized, systematic, and underpinned by an overall philosophy.

This situation began to change in the late 1980s–early 1990s with the *Renouveau du Service Public* (Public Service Renewal) movement under the Michel Rocard government. This focused on the development of a public service with greater managerial freedom and accountability for performance, on service delivery (with users of public services recast as "customers"), on contracts rather than rules, and similar themes. These ideas were embodied in the establishment of "accountability contracts"[4] between different levels of managerial responsibilities. Largely unnoticed by the wider public, this movement won the support of many senior civil servants, who still consider it a seminal milestone. However, it was not sustained and did not lead to genuine far-reaching changes.

Since that time, successive governments have maintained a small public sector reform unit (consisting of a few dozen people) associated with the Prime Minister's office and linked to the general directorate of the civil service.[5] Its work focused largely on issues such as organizational rationalization, service quality, and improving relations with "customers." However, lacking credibility among the greater mass of public servants and without any political backing, public sector reform languished. A handful of senior civil servants—heirs of the Jean Moulin clubs, the RCB, and *Renouveau du Service Public*—kept the torch burning. From contacts with their colleagues from other countries and in international organizations, they discovered the "new public management." However, even these reform enthusiasts were very pessimistic about the immediate prospects for genuine public sector reform in France.

The budget reform legislation of 2001—the Loi Organique relative aux Lois de Finances (Organic Law on Budget Laws, LOLF)—therefore came as something of a "bolt from the blue." This was particularly the case because it was an initiative that originated outside the bureaucracy. The impetus for the LOLF came from the parliament itself, reflecting the frustration of parliamentarians who no longer accepted that parliament's role should be confined to rubber-stamping faits accomplis. The aim of the reform was to restore parliament's budgetary powers and, more specifically, to broaden its powers to amend budget bills and to strengthen its right to budgetary information. The roots of this lay in major constitutional changes effected in 1958–59 with the establishment of the Fifth Republic under President de Gaulle. These constitutional changes brought about a major transfer of power from parliament to the executive branch, as a reaction to parliamentary excesses under the Fourth Republic. Particularly relevant here is the 1959 budget law, which many members of parliament never really accepted. Parliamentary criticism focused particularly on a provision (Article 40 of the Constitution) that prohibited any amendment of the budget bill by parliament that would lead to increased expenditures. When interpreted strictly, this provision prevented even expenditure reallocations that increased expenditure on some items without increasing aggregate expenditure. It was hardly surprising that parliament's limited role in the adoption of the budget came to be characterized as "Liturgy, Litany, Lethargy" (Edward Faure).

Prior to the LOLF of 2001, 35 proposals for budget law reform had been put forward by the members of parliament, most of them primarily to restore parliamentary powers in budgetary matters. Finally, and quite exceptionally in a country such as France, the right and the left alike agreed, in the period between 1998 and 2001, to unite and address the problem by adopting the LOLF.[6]

It is understandable that in these circumstances, the initial response of the Ministry of Economy, Finance, and Industry (MINEFI, with a staff of 175,000) to the draft LOLF was reticence. The proposal to restore parliament's powers raised some concern about a weakening of aggregate expenditure discipline. The bureaucracy did not, however, take the bill terribly seriously at first, seeing it as merely the 36th installment in a series of insignificant and ultimately unsuccessful attempts to change the budget law. However, the energy and commitment of the proponents of reform, the consensus of majority and opposition parties, and—decisively—the support of the Prime Minister all combined to ultimately overcome the Ministry of Finance's reluctance to revisit the 1959 organic law.

On the surface, the scope of the LOLF was apparently restricted to dry and technical matters of budgetary, accounting, and financial management (such as budget classification, more global budget appropriations, the expenditure process, accrual accounting, and the content of the budget documentation). Nowhere in the 68 Articles of the law was there any reference to the far-reaching changes in administrative structures, the civil service, or the broader system of governance that today appear as essential elements of the public sector reforms initiated by the LOLF. The 1959 organic law that the LOLF replaced was concerned only with budgeting, and the aims of the parliamentarians who worked during 2000–01 to secure the passage of the LOLF appeared also to be focused on budgeting rather than on broader public sector reform.[7]

It is therefore hardly surprising that few government officials at the time believed that passage of the LOLF would lead to broader public sector reform. However, during the four years of discussion and preparatory work from time of passage of the LOLF through parliament and its full entry into force on January 1, 2006, everyone gradually came to discover the true scope of a law that, if fully put into effect, would inevitably lead to substantial changes in the French public administration. It has thus become gradually apparent that in France performance budgeting reform will bring with it far-reaching changes that extend well beyond the technical realm in which it originated.

There are three key areas where this seemingly technical budgeting reform has led to much broader changes. These are the civil service, organization of government, and the government/policy relationship.

The civil service

By placing "the end before the means," performance budgeting lays the organizational groundwork in all areas of government operations for *a trade-off between efficiency and control*: there is a greater demand for government units to perform well, but in exchange for this demand, they are given greater freedom in their control of resources.

The most important of these freedoms is the "fungibility" of appropriations—that is, the removal (with certain exceptions[8]) of line-item controls by permitting spending agencies to transfer funds from one line-item category to another. For French managers, this was the main concrete innovation of the LOLF. The introduction of fungible appropriations led to a decision, taken after some hesitation, to do away almost entirely with what remained of the French system of ex-ante financial control.[9] Under this system, established in 1922, spending ministries required the prior approval of MoF financial controllers (posted within their organizations) before they could enter into expenditure commitments. This system had already been relaxed somewhat some years prior to the passage of the LOLF. However, appropriation fungibility eliminated the raison d'être for even this somewhat less strict form of ex-ante financial control.

However, although the LOLF deliberately increases managerial freedom, it does so only within the realm of the budget. Increasing budgetary freedom was not enough to meet all the requirements of government managers for greater managerial flexibility to meet new challenges and responsibilities. In France, as in many other countries, many of the strictures that constrain public management have their origins elsewhere than in budgetary rules. These strictures derive from rules and regulations covering such matters as public procurement, procedures for initiating and managing capital projects, the use of supplies and services, recruitment, personnel management, working hours, compensation scales, travel allowances, and so on. These standards, which are set not only by the Ministry of Finance, but also by other government units, and in particular by the Ministry of the Civil Service, are generally centralized and very rigid and therefore incompatible with "performance-based" management, which advocates instead the freedom to use resources to meet the demands of performance management. The relaxation of regulatory constraints on public management is consistent with the rationale of the LOLF. There has already been some movement in this direction in France since the passage of the LOLF (specifically, reform of the public procurement code, new rules for real estate management, and more flexible compensation arrangements, mainly for professionals). However, these developments still fall well short of meeting the aspirations of public managers, who are now generally supportive of the idea of reduced control to facilitate improved efficiency.

Before turning to the specific areas in which greater freedom is required, it should be stressed that increased flexibility does not mean ignoring the need to comply with some basic rules and fundamental laws. Resource use must continue to be regulated, and the fundamental principles of public service—neutrality, equity, continuity—must naturally be maintained. Furthermore, the quid pro quo for increased freedom must be increased transparency and accountability in respect to performance. Finally, the march toward increased managerial flexibility should be gradual and in tandem with progress in terms of results. The better an agency's performance, the more it can be freed of centralized regulatory constraints.

More flexibility in the civil service

In concrete terms, the area in which French managers run up against the greatest rigidities in the exercise of their daily responsibilities is human resource management. In service industries, whether in the public or private sector, human resources constitute the most important factor of production and their proper use is therefore the key determinant of success or failure. Managers, moreover, cannot be held responsible for results unless they are also given more freedom to manage the main resource used in the production process. French managers strongly demand greater freedom in the selection of their team members. At present, their authority in this area is very limited because personnel assignments are largely based on broad, centralized, and opaque mechanisms, notwithstanding that everyone knows that building competent and cohesive teams should be one of the major responsibilities of any manager. The other legitimate demand of managers in the French civil service concerns the way compensation is decided. Compensation decisions are currently centralized and rigid. Managers demand a role in compensation decisions in order to establish a link between each team member's *contribution* to the work unit's results and the *compensation* that team member receives.

Of course, this deregulation of management and the civil service is acceptable only if managers' accountability is reinforced by a system of incentives. The move from a traditional system based on *distrust* of managers (with a plethora of ex-ante controls of resources) to a new system based on *trust* (supported by ex-post accountability for results) can be envisaged only if performance leads to rewards or sanctions. Without incentives, ex-post accountability would be a purely academic exercise with no effect on actual managerial and professional behavior. While these principles are easy to articulate, implementing them is a more difficult matter. The system of incentives to be devised should be neither repressive nor demeaning, but should instead send the right signals to encourage effective and equitable management of government units by those in charge. The fundamental issue of accountability goes to the very heart of the culture and rules of the French civil service. The organizers of an important colloquium held in France in the summer of 2005 were not mistaken when they titled their conference "Accountability: The Other Reform," thus emphasizing that the success of the LOLF ultimately depends on setting up a completely new accountability/incentives system.

In reality, however, there have been over recent years been only a handful of limited changes in the French civil service, which remains characterized by the "career service" model (jobs for life, automatic advancement, rigid rules covering appointment and remuneration, compartmentalization of staff into narrow categories). Only very recently has the possibility of more far-reaching changes been raised. An important 2003 report of the Conseil d'Etat addressed the need for reduction of staffing levels, the simplification of rules, and increased use of contractual employment. However, for cultural and social reasons, such changes are difficult and no major changes have yet been implemented. The public stance of the authorities continues to be that the implementation of the LOLF does not imply any need to modify the civil service system, but if there is ultimately a move in the direction of civil service reform, the 2003 report should prove a valuable source of inspiration.

However, civil service reform does in fact seem an inevitable corollary to the LOLF. The traditional French civil service arrangements and the traditional budgeting systems embodied in the 1959 budget law were the two "pillars" of the post-war French of governance. Changes in the traditional budget system therefore call into question the traditional civil service system. If there is to be a performance-oriented budget, there must also be a performance-oriented civil service. More far-reaching reform of the civil service could thus emerge in coming years as the new frontier of public sector reform in France.

The LOLF has also had other consequences beyond the realm of budgeting—particularly in respect to the way ministries are organized and the relationship between the government and policy.

Organization of government

The introduction of performance budgeting must lead to sweeping changes in the distribution of powers and responsibilities in public administrations. As the French experience has shown, budget reform leads to at least two types of changes in the organization of government:

- the redesign of government agencies to make them customer-oriented rather than a producer-oriented
- the search for a new balance between the vertical and horizontal approaches to public policy management.

Organizational review

The implementation of performance budgeting has shaken up organizational structures, leading to changes in the distribution of powers and responsibilities between and within ministries. The pre-LOLF structures of directorates and ministries were not always built around clear and coherent public policy objectives, and often represented somewhat random configurations that could be explained only by historical evolution. Some organizational units contribute to several quite divergent government policy objectives. For example, the customs agency participates in tax collection *and* contributes to domestic security. Conversely, responsibility for some key policy objectives is in some cases split between several different agencies. Domestic security, for example, is the responsibility of several ministries: the Ministry of the Interior (which embraces the police), the Ministry of Defense (the gendarmerie), and the Ministry of Finance (the customs service). The new budget classification deliberately ignores these administrative divisions. Organized around comprehensive and coherent public policy objectives, it groups appropriations into *missions* and *programs* ("program" generically in what follows) which are focused on the services provided to users/citizens. By contrast, government organizational structures are often built around production processes and the constraints imposed by civil service regulations and processes. This disconnect between programs structures and organizational structures can in theory be addressed by two types of radical solution: programs can be made to fit the organizational structure or the organizational structure can be made to fit the programs. There are advantages and disadvantages to each of the two options: the first may quite simply prove incompatible with the performance budgeting approach, while the second can lead to sweeping changes in the administrative structure, with the attendant cultural, managerial, and social difficulties. The expectation in France has been that the structure of the organizational charts is logically expected to adapt to the contours of the programs.[10] However, in practice, after several months of fits and starts following the passage of the LOLF, compromise solutions lying between the two radical solutions have had to be found in France.

The managerial, political, and social ramifications of the consequences of budget classification for the organizational structure of public administration should not be underestimated. One recent French example illustrates the heavy impact that such apparently technical appearance matters can have on the political leadership of these administrative reforms.

For over two centuries, French financial administration—that is, the administration of public monies for both the central and local governments—has been divided into two services: one that assesses and audits taxes (the Directorate General of Taxes—DGI, with a staff of 75,000) and one that collects revenue and pays expenses (the Directorate General of Govenment Accounts—DGCP, with a staff of 56,000). This division of labor, based on historical considerations, has serious drawbacks, particularly in terms of cost. For the government, it resulted in a costly duplication of effort. For citizens, it leads to a need to deal with two agencies in a context where, in most other countries, there would be "one-stop shop" service. Recognition of this problem analysis led the government to attempt in 2000 (that is, prior to the LOLF) to resolve the problem. However, the magnitude of this attempted reform, tactical errors made in implementing it, and the traditional conservatism of French civil servants unions all combined to lead to failure after several weeks of strikes and the resignation of the Minister of Finance. This experience led to a deep trauma that fueled fears that this reform, although a good thing, was completely dead.

Rather surprisingly, the development of the new LOLF budget classification has led to progress in addressing the problem. After much hesitation prompted by the fear of revisiting a topic that had proved so volatile, it was decided to establish a program entitled "Public Finance Management," the purpose of which would be to collect taxes and manage public funds and which would pool the resources of both the DGI and the DGCP. Consistent with this, one program manager was appointed to oversee both directorates.[11] The two organizations remain separate. However, their budgetary resources, and their wage bill in particular, are being combined and managed by a single manager. The eventual merger of the DGI and the DGCP seems likely.

The thorny issue of "multipurpose agencies"

Another issue encountered in France warrants emphasis here because it is probably common to many countries—that of multipurpose agencies. As noted above, certain agencies contribute to very different public policy objectives. The example was mentioned of the dual roles of the customs agency in collecting taxes and contributing to domestic security. Other examples are the technical agencies of the Ministries of Agriculture and Industry, which contribute not only to enterprise and job creation, but also to environmental protection. There are several explanations for this situation, the most important of which is the strength of the production-oriented approach (based on competencies and skills) in the structuring of large organizations. Whenever, throughout the history of the formation of governments and public services, a new public policy need has emerged, it has often seemed wise to avoid establishing new agencies, and to see instead to what extent existing government units possess the resources and competencies needed. This may be a common-sense approach. However, a customer-oriented, program-based budget structure is not always consistent with such a producer-oriented way of organizing work. Of course, the solution to this problem does not necessarily consist in dividing the agency concerned into two entities. Such a solution, although sometimes appropriate, will often be too costly. A readier solution is to finance the multipurpose agency using two different budgetary appropriation lines. The issue becomes complicated, however, when a single staff member is contributing simultaneously to the achievement of two different policy objectives. For example, should the customs officer who stops and inspects freight trucks at the border receive his salary in two installments—one for his contribution to a revenue-collection objective, the other for his contribution to combating smuggling? Various pragmatic solutions consistent with the theoretical requirements of performance budgeting are of course possible, but therein lies a tangible difficulty which will often require much effort and imagination to develop appropriate practical solutions (cost accounting, charge back, outsourcing, and so on).

This issue of multipurpose units is not simply a technical question of how to allocate costs and financing. It also raises even more difficult managerial issues. Managing an organization that pursues several goals, some of which might even be contradictory, is no mean feat: what are the priorities? What objectives should teams focus on? To whom should conflicts between "programs" be referred?

Rethinking "functional" directorates

The funding of support functions raises issues similar to those raised by multipurpose units.[12] In France, the term "support function" refers to two rather different types of units: first, the top leadership of the ministry (the minister, his personal staff, the strategic bodies, and so on) and, second, the units such as property management, information technology, human resource management, and legal counsel that support the work of the various operational directorates. Maintaining single support units of this type, which serve all of the operational directorates of the ministry concerned, may seem desirable for technical, economic, and political reasons. The question then becomes one of finding out how to finance them and, in particular, to what line of a budget classification they should be allocated in a performance budgeting scenario. Since, for the most part, these units do not deal directly with the end user but instead work for the benefit of the operational directorates, the clearest theoretical solution would be for the operational directorates to fund such units through a charge-back system. This is how the headquarters or holding companies of large private groups are financed: their expenses are covered by contributions in various forms from the subsidiaries for whose benefit the headquarters is supposed to act. The French government did not go this far in its implementation of the LOLF. Under the new budget classification, it settled for creating specific appropriations lines for "support programs." This soft option has, however, been criticized and may only be provisional.

Under the LOLF, the functional units now have another more serious problem with which to contend. It is no longer just their financing arrangements that are posing a problem. Rather, their very existence is now an issue.

With the advent of performance budgeting, the role and place of functional services—and in particular "finances" and "personnel"—are changing. Today, these directorates, generally discreet but powerful, wield almost exclusive authority over the budgetary and human resources that they manage. However, in the years to come, the responsibility for managing these areas should be largely transferred to the "operational" directorates, those that implement public policies directly and assume responsibility for the "programs." The slogan for performance budgeting, "each minister must become his own finance minister," must be applied across the board: "each program director must become his own budget director." In France, the creation in most ministries of the position of "general secretary,"[13] while not a direct result of the LOLF, is particularly relevant given the profound structural changes brought about by budget reform. The appointment of general secretaries introduces a cross-cutting management approach in areas where the new programs structure sometimes encourages an excessively vertical management approach.

The dangers of verticalism

Verticalism—to coin a new term—is one of the great dangers for performance budgeting in France. French prefects[14] expressed great concern about verticalism at the very start of implementation of the reform. They reasoned that, with the advent of performance budgeting, each sectoral policy (agricultural development, transport, education, and so on) would be driven by overarching *national* objectives and the results achieved would be more closely monitored than in the past. The performance of officials working at the local level would be assessed and rewarded or penalized based on their success in achieving nationally defined goals and targets. The obvious danger was that these officials would focus their energy on achieving the national targets at the expense of local conditions. The responsibility of the prefects—coordination of ministries' local policies, adjustment of national priorities to specific territorial circumstances, and so on—therefore at first seemed inconsistent with the performance budgeting approach. A tense debate arose between the Ministry of the Interior and the Ministry of Finance in the years following passage of the LOLF. Ultimately, a compromise was reached, based on two concrete measures. First, the prefects would be recognized as partners in the preparation of the budgets of the ministries' local units. Second, they would have a [small] non-specific appropriations envelope that they would be permitted to use to address local priorities not sufficiently recognized in the national ministerial budgets.

In sum, the impact of performance budgeting on the organization of governments is a study in contrasts. The reorganization of services based on user needs and expectations is clearly the most positive aspect. However, everyone must bear in mind the risk of over-compartmentalization of public policies. Performance budgeting does not lead spontaneously to intersectoral consistency and to adjustment to specific local circumstances and constraints. Any structure and/or procedure intended to reinstate some horizontal view where verticalism is looming warrants attention.

The organization of ministries and central government units—over and above the merely financial aspect—will therefore be profoundly affected by the "public management" component of the LOLF.

The government/policy relationship

Performance budgeting affects not only public management but also public governance. In countries such as France, where politics and public administration are traditionally intertwined, the implementation of these new principles should bring about a profound change in the relationship between public servants and elected officials.

More emphasis on results first requires a clearer definition of public policy objectives, which should lead to the clarification of options, the setting of priorities, and the elimination of any ambiguities. The way public policy objectives are now set is often too general, unclear, ambiguous, and even contradictory. It contrasts with the performance-oriented approach, which dictates that objectives targeted through each of the public policies implemented by the central government must be clarified explicitly, in detail, and in quantitative terms. The LOLF therefore requires bold and responsible leadership.

Although politicians did not become spontaneously aware of this need, public servants, especially the program managers, can be counted on to raise awareness of this issue. If French government managers are to be prepared—as seems to be the case—to play the game of accountability, it will be on the condition that the objectives against which they are to be assessed and rewarded or sanctioned are clear, consistent, and achievable. A rigorous but fruitful dialogue should therefore take place between the politician who guides and monitors and the public servant who implements. The politician must demand results and the public servant must insist on the clarity of the objectives assigned to him.

More direct communication between public servants and parliamentarians

Significant change could also take place in the distribution of roles and responsibilities between parliamentarians, ministers, and public servants. Under the traditional arrangements that prevail in France today, things are simple: public servants are accountable to ministers, who issue them instructions and assess their performance; the minister in turn is accountable, along with the rest of government, to parliament. In this chain of accountability, typical of parliamentary democracy, public servants and parliamentarians, at least in theory, ignore each other. The LOLF, however, encourages unprecedented direct interaction between public servants and parliamentarians. From as early as 2001 there have been many indications that program managers would be questioned directly by parliamentarians on the objectives and results of the public policies entrusted to them, in line with practice abroad (especially in the United States). Granted, this development seems natural and consistent with the LOLF's spirit of accountability and transparency, and program managers will consider it flattering because of the visibility it will give their actions. This is not, however, without risk, as it is always possible that the minister and the public servant will not agree. In the relationship between the parliamentarian, the minister, and the public servant, the substitution of a new triangular construct for the classic linear relationship deserves to be closely monitored.

In any event, the LOLF is bringing to the fore a new category of super-high-ranking officials. Eighty "program managers"[15] pivotally positioned between the administration and politicians are to play an essential role in the reform. They can be expected to firmly assert their responsibility for implementing the strategy on which they will be judged. In this respect, the role and weight of the ministerial cabinets will have to be limited to prevent them from continuing to interfere in the management of staff, which is to be the purview of the program managers.[16]

The fact that the LOLF may remedy one of the recurring weaknesses of the French public governance is a clear sign that this is no mere technical reform.

Performance budgeting means permanent reform

The LOLF also leads to major changes in the annual budget decision-making process: the introduction of the "first euro budgeting" system,[17] inspired by zero-base budgeting, and the concomitant elimination of incremental budgeting. Coming at a time of budget stringency, these innovations introduced by the LOLF will complete the transformation of the budgetary procedure already underway since the Maastricht Treaty's Stability and Growth Pact. The purpose of the budgetary procedure is no longer to distribute supplementary appropriation margins generated by growth, but rather to achieve savings that can be used to finance government priorities. After years during which savings were achieved merely by cutting appropriations at the margin without substantially changing expenditure priorities, savings will in future need to be made mostly through structural reforms. The purpose of the new budgetary procedure established by the LOLF is to now to enable the government—and in particular the Prime Minister—to identify all conceivable reforms each year and decide which ones seem to be the most suitable for implementation: performance budgeting reform could itself become a "reform machine."

It would seem, therefore, that in France, public sector reform and budget reform are fast becoming synonymous.

What conclusions should be drawn?

One should not exaggerate the broader international relevance of the French case study discussed in this chapter. French government has very strong national features; long and deeply rooted traditions; a highly specific institutional, political, and cultural context; and its own way of conceiving change. These specific characteristics limit the scope of the broader lessons one might be tempted to draw. It is nevertheless impossible to resist the temptation of drawing a few lessons from this analysis of the French experience. One is that performance budgeting reform is not merely a technical reform. Performance budgeting is a systemic reform that affects all public management and public governance. It leads to a re-examination of the powers and responsibilities of all stakeholders, and goes to the very heart of the architecture of public organizations.

If, in a given country, a performance budgeting reform were to have no effect—in the medium term—on any of the three areas of public administration discussed in this chapter, one could conclude that the reform was no more than superficial. It is perfectly possibly to put a huge amount of effort into changing mechanisms and procedures, creating new documents, remodeling information technology systems and the like, without ultimately bringing about any real change. The sign of a successful budget performance reform is that it has led to wide-ranging and deep impacts on management and public governance—perhaps including in areas where they are least expected.

In principle, one should seek to consider all of the likely ramifications of performance budgeting reforms when embarking out on the path to reform. In practical terms, however, this can be difficult. A reform of this type is a dynamic process that develops over time. It would be wishful thinking to believe that it was possible to plan everything in detail in advance. It is certainly necessary to start with clear, simple, and solid principles, recognized by all, which will serve as a guide for the entire reform process. However, it is inevitable that many difficult challenges will become apparent only during the actual reform process, and solutions to these changes will have to be improvised over time, often on a case-by-case basis.

Finally, because budget reform is actually a form of broader public sector reform, consideration must be given to the role of the Ministry of Finance in leading the process. Admittedly, there are good arguments in favor of Ministries of Finance assuming the lead role in public sector reform. Fiscal restraint is often both the trigger and the expected result of the reforms. Finance ministries have a number of tools and levers to force reform; and their public servants tend to be highly competent and talented. Nevertheless, it must be recognized that the image of the financial agencies is not always the best suited to encourage others to change. Other government agencies will not necessarily recognize the legitimacy of the leadership role of a ministry that they may see as stubbornly bureaucratic, out of touch with users' real needs, and sensitive only to the accounting view of the government. This suggests that the involvement of the Ministry of Finance is necessary but not sufficient for the success of public sector reform.

In France, the formation of a new government in June 2005, headed by Dominique de Villepin, brought with it a clear and formal response to the issue at hand. Public sector reform and budget reform would be under the authority of a single minister, the Minister of the Budget, whereas previously public sector reform had been the responsibility of the Minister of the Civil Service. This decision was presented as "an absorption of the *budget* directorate by the ministry of *public sector reform*." A general directorate of government modernization was established, which brought together the Delegation for Public Sector Reform[18] with the Budgetary Reform Directorate, which had been set up in January 2003 to implement the LOLF. This rapprochement—a first in France—should give greater coherence to the reform program. It clearly demonstrated the conviction of government leaders that the LOLF would prove an instrument of broader public sector reform.

Notes

1. Largely inspired by the works of Michel Crozier.
2. The introduction of the role of regional prefect, town and country planning, and so on.
3. This generic term refers to the working groups or committees created from time to time—often at the suggestion of the Ministry of Finance—to identify and eliminate redundant administrative units or reduce their resource allocations. Experience indicates that the outcomes are generally disappointing.
4. Circular of February 23, 1989.
5. Known variously as the "Agency" [*Commissariat*] or "Delegation" [*Délégation*] for Public Sector Reform.
6. Law of August 1, 2001.
7. It bears noting, however, that A. Lambert, a senator and later Minister of the Budget and Budget Reform, considered budget reform a "prerequisite" to public sector reform.
8. In particular, the "asymmetric fungibility" provision governing wage expenditure, whereby agencies may not shift money from other input categories to wages, although the reverse in permitted. See Chapter 11 by Brice Lannaud.
9. Decree of January 27, 2005.
10. The restructuring of the central administration of the Ministry of National Education undertaken in France following implementation of the LOLF is one example of the impact of performance budgeting on administrative organization.
11. In the first instance, the General Secretary of the Ministry of Finance was appointed to this position—which clearly represents a temporary solution to the problem.
12. These issues are developed more broadly in Chapter 2.
13. General secretaries are senior officials who report directly to the minister and are responsible for managing the human and budgetary resources of all units. With rare exceptions, the general secretary has no say in the content of public policy.
14. In France, the prefect—a classic feature of the Napoleonic system of government—serves as the government's representative in the regions (22) and departments (98). Prefects have authority over the local representatives (external services) of each ministry and coordinate the latter's activities, while ensuring that the conditions are right for implementing national public policies at the local level.
15. A total of 80 managers for 132 programs, with some managers responsible for several programs.
16. The report by Alain Lambert and Didier Migaud on the implementation of the LOLF (*Rapport sur la mise en oeuvre de la LOLF*, September 2005) contains interesting proposals in this regard.
17. Which now draws inspiration from the zero-base budgeting method for its "justification of the first euro of expenditure" approach.
18. Delegation for the Modernization of Public Management and Government Agencies: Delegation for Users and Administrative Simplification; Agency for the Development of E-government.

21
Russia: A Case Study

Elena Belyanova, Ole Hovland, and Alexey Lavrov

Implementation of performance budgeting methods in Russia started in 2003. The system being built is essentially a program budgeting system with strategic goals and performance targets. The most important changes from January 2003–September 2005 have been achieved in the preparation of the federal budget. Limited progress has so far been reached in linking performance measures to budget execution, reporting, and evaluation procedures. This means that the performance budgeting concept is not fully implemented at this stage. Further important steps remain to be completed. The next years will be critical to ensure lasting positive effects of the reform.

This chapter will describe what steps have been taken so far, what is working well, what needs to be improved, and which additional measures need to be implemented.

History of the reform

The reform process started in spring 2003 when macroeconomic conditions were stabilized and the economic situation in Russia had improved. The budget showed surplus and macroeconomic indicators developed favorably, mainly due to higher oil prices, ruble devaluation, and some growth in the manufacturing sector.

When President Putin addressed the Federal Assembly in May 2003 he claimed that Russia's most severe problems were the ineffectiveness of the state and weak government. He advocated that the national goal of high competitiveness for the country should also include the activities of state bodies and local governments, and that the bureaucracy needed to be strengthened by modern and efficient managers. To achieve this it was necessary to carry out vital administrative reform programs.

Against this background the government launched a broad range of reforms in public governance:

- an administrative reform introducing a two-level government structure and aiming at optimization of government functions, reducing state interference in the economic activity of enterprises and in securing deregulation
- a civil service reform aiming at (1) creating a modern, merit-based, depoliticized, and professional civil service; (2) reducing corruption in the civil service; (3) increasing internal and external accountability and transparency; and (4) creating a performance and service orientation in the civil service (DFID/WB, 2005)
- a budget process reform.

The planning of the reform in the budget sector started in the Ministry of Finance (MoF) in early 2003. A Concept Paper for budget reform was developed through 2003 and approved by the government in May 2004, and one important element of the reform strategy proposed in the paper was the introduction of performance budgeting. The preparation of the 2004 budget in spring and summer 2003 was, however, based on an attempt to introduce performance-oriented budgeting in the budget preparation phase in parallel with traditional input budgeting. Input controls have remained in place, but at a less detailed level, mainly because of simplification and improvement of the economic classification.

The Concept Paper for reforming the budget sector included the following main elements:

1. improve budget classification and accounting
2. establish a distinction between "existing" and "proposed new" activities
3. improve medium-term financial planning
4. develop and extend the use of programs and performance budgeting methods
5. streamline procedures for budget formation and scrutiny.

The new budget classification was envisaged to be close to international best practices (*Government Finance Statistics Manual* (*GFSM*) *2001* modified to cash) and to take into account the new structure and functions of the government that followed the administrative reform. The new chart of accounts was to be integrated with budget classification and prepared for accrual accounting, and to allow for accounting of executed expenditures based on administrative, economic, functional, and program classifications.

The second and third areas of the budget reform were intended for securing increased reliability of medium-term budget planning by including in the framework a distinction between previous approved budget measures and new government policy priorities. Medium-term budget planning had in principle been in place for some time, but the plans were not integrated with the annual budgets or developed beyond the macro level and played a minor or non-existent role in the preparation of new budgets.

The fourth main reform area introduced performance budgeting as "*a procedure for evaluating the effectiveness of budget expenditures, a phased transition away from the principle of (input) line-item planning and financing of expenditures towards budgeting oriented to achievements of final socially important and measurable results (outcomes)."* The proposed procedure was intended to go beyond the use of performance information in budget preparation, so that when the system is fully developed expenditures should be linked to expected results. Reports on performance against the proposed targets were intended to be used in the budget preparation process for efficient allocation of future resources.

The fifth reform area highlighted improved administrative procedures to scrutinize annual and medium-term performance-oriented budgets, including more efficient budget procedures in the State Duma. The Concept Paper points out that the procedures for passing the budget through the State Duma and Federal Assembly are very time-consuming and need to be streamlined, and that the State Duma should focus more on evaluating priorities of budget policies. The Concept Paper further specifies that there is a need to clarify the differentiation of budget powers and responsibilities between the legislative and executive authorities. The differentiation of powers and responsibilities is vague and inconsistent under the present system.

The main reform events that have taken place in the period January 2003–September 2005 are presented in Table 21.1. The main accomplishments so far have been the following areas:

- Strategic goals, objectives, and performance indicators for budget administrators have been established.
- The government sector structure has been improved, and procedures have been started to avoid overlap of functions and to systematically go through what shall be government tasks in the future and what is better left to the markets and private sectors.
- The economic and functional classifications at the higher levels have been improved in line with international standards. A new chart of accounts has been developed prepared for accrual accounting.
- First steps have been taken to introduce medium-term budget planning as an integrated part of the budget process, and to present the results to the public in a user-friendly way.

Preconditions for introducing medium-term budgeting and performance budgeting

Many of the preconditions mentioned in the literature (see Diamond, 2003, 2004a, 2004b) for moving forward to introducing medium-term budget planning and performance-oriented methods were in place in Russia when the reform process started. As mentioned above, macroeconomic conditions were favorable, annual budgets were realistic, budgets were in surplus, most extrabudgetary funds had been integrated into the budget, and most of the revenues and expenditures from commercial activities were channeled through and recorded by a well-functioning Treasury. Budget execution in total was under the disciplined control of the Federal Treasury.

Table 21.1 Implementation of the budget reform: major events (February 2003–September 2005)

Date/period	*Regulations/processes*
Feb 18, 03	The first seminar on performance-oriented budgeting was initiated by the Budget Policy Department, MoF, with support of the EU-funded "State Budget Reform" project. The seminar addressed main managers of the federal budget funds (mostly ministries)
Jun–Jul 03	Main managers of budget funds developed Performance Reports for 2004–06 and submitted them to the MoF. The reports included strategic goals, objectives, and performance indicators for the two-year period
March 9, 04	Decree of the RF President No. 314, On the System and Structure of Federal Bodies of Executive Power. The government sector is restructured into ministries, federal services, and agencies. A total of 44 subjects of budget planning (usually ministries but also some federal services reporting directly to the President) will be responsible for all issues linked to budget preparation and execution, also for subordinate units
Apr 30, 04	RF Government Resolution No. 225 to establish the Government Commission to increase the effectiveness of budget expenditures, chaired by Deputy Prime Minister Alexander Zhukov
May 22, 04	RF Government Resolution No. 249 of May 22, 2004, On the Measures to Increase the Effectiveness of Budget Expenditures and the Concept of Reforming the Budget Process in the Russian Federation in the Years 2004–06. The concept contained an action plan for developing regulations to amend the budget process and specific requirements to produce Performance Reports
Jun–Jul 04	Subjects of budget planning (the name for ministries and a limited number of main managers of budget funds after the administrative reform) developed Performance Reports for 2005–07 and submitted them to the MoF and the Ministry for Economic Development and Trade
Aug 12, 04	Consolidated Report on the goals and indicators of the Russian Federation and subjects of budget planning for 2005–07 prepared by Deputy Prime Minister's Secretariat, presented to and approved by the government
Jun–Oct 04	Participants of the "Experiment" prepare the requested documentation. The "Experiment" is a two-year project where participating subjects of budget planning compete to be the best in using performance-oriented methods in the budget planning process. The winner(s) receive some additional funding to further improve procedures, to prioritize projects, and to upgrade staff qualifications
Nov 30, 04	RF Government Commission on the increase of budget expenditures' effectiveness approves the results (winners) of the "Experiment"
Dec 23, 04	The federal law, On the Introduction of Amendments to the Federal law "On the RF Budget Classification" and the RF Budget Code, No. 174-FZ was passed on December 23, 2004. The law gives the legal base for the improvements in the economic and functional classifications and to establish ministerial targeted programs
Mar 2, 05	RF Government Resolution No. 100, On the Government Commission on Budget Projections for the Current Year and for Medium-term Perspective, chaired by the Prime Minister, Michail Fradkov

Table 21.1 continued

Date/period	*Regulations/processes*
March 6, 05	RF Government Resolution No. 118, On Endorsing the Regulations on the Development of the Medium-term Financial Plan of the RF and the Draft Federal Budget Law for the next financial year
March 05	Methodical guidelines for preparation of 2006–08 Performance Reports by subject of budget planning is published on the MoF's website, <www.minfin.ru>
April–May 05	Subjects of budget planning submit their ministerial targeted programs claiming additional funding to the MoF
April 19, 05	RF Government Resolution No. 239 On Endorsing the Regulations on the Development, Endorsement and Implementation of Ministerial Targeted Programmes
April–July 05	Subjects of budget planning develop Performance Reports for 2006–08
July 05	Elaboration of a draft performance-oriented budget compliant Explanatory Note to be disseminated in the parliament alongside the traditional budget
July 16, 05	RF Government Resolution No. 440 On the Procedures for Keeping the Register of Spending Commitments of the Russian Federation
July 20, 05	Submission of the Performance Reports for 2006–08 to the MoF and the Ministry of Economic Development and Trade
July 05	Draft Consolidated Report on goals and indicators of the Russian Federation and subjects of budget planning for 2006–08 prepared by Deputy Prime Minister Secretariat and disseminated among experts for comments
Aug–Sept 05	Explanatory Note "Budget Policy 2006–08" approved and published on Ministry of Finance's website

It was also acknowledged that the reform process towards good governance should include a wide range of reforms, such as improving the structure of the government and the civil service in addition to the budget process. One particular area of the budget system that needed to be improved before the medium-term/performance budgeting reforms could be completed was the budget classification system and also the accounting system.

Input-based line-item controls were very detailed, allowing little flexibility for spending units to execute budgets in an efficient manner. Expenditures on heating were, for instance, split into several sub-categories (expenditures on heating, payment for natural gas consumption, payment for heating oil consumption, payment for electricity). This may be an advantage for internal control and information purposes, but when budget units are not allowed to shift funds between sub-categories, it reduces the possibilities for efficient and cost-effective use of resources. The economic classification did not follow international standards. The functional classification that had been used for parliamentary approval of the budget was also very detailed and contained a mixture of functional and economic elements (for example, it included investment as a "functional" category). The economic classification and the first and second levels of the functional classification have now been improved to follow international standards. The details of the functional classification still need to be improved. Earmarked expenditures and type of expenditures (the third and fourth levels of the functional classification) still contain a mixture of functional and economic elements that are not properly organized in a hierarchical structure.

It was also recognized that it was necessary to establish a well-functioning expenditure program structure as part of the reform process. Strategic goals and objectives of the federal ministries are to a large extent to be achieved by ministerial programs aimed at reaching specific measurable targets. The structure for establishing these ministerial targeted programs needed to be put in place. This issue was confused by the fact that the federal budget already included a number of federal targeted programs which were split between several ministries. These programs amounted in 2004 to some 7 percent of total expenditures. In principle these programs were linked to outcomes, but the formulation of the outcomes was in many cases so general that it was difficult to measure any kind of performance. The federal targeted programs need to be reorganized so program objectives can be linked to measurable indicators. Work in this area is still in progress.

The Concept Paper also pointed out weaknesses related to cash accounting. Cash accounting does not give the full cost of program execution, and makes it difficult to compare the costs of services provided by the state with the cost of obtaining the same services in the market. The Concept Paper further argued that accrual accounting will increase the transparency of the operations of the state and will give information showing the financial consequences of the decisions taken in the fiscal and budgetary sphere. A new chart of accounts developed to handle accrual accounting has been developed in Russia. Budget classification and budget accounting have been fully integrated.

The administrative reform approved in March 2004 was a radical reform aimed at strengthening top-down control and increasing the ability to implement structural and social reforms effectively. Effectiveness was to be increased through eliminating duplicating structures and by assigning a key role to ministers in order to strengthen internal accountability. Responsibilities were clarified. This was a precondition for setting strategic targets and specific performance indicators for each budget institution, and for avoiding overlap between institutions. The old system had six different kinds of government bodies: ministries, state committees, federal commissions, federal services, agencies, and federal inspections. The reformed system consisted of a two-level structure: ministries and their subordinate federal services and agencies.

The number of ministries was reduced from 23 to 16 and is now more in line with international recommendations. The size of the cabinet was reduced from 31 to 19. Ministries were reorganized; the number of departments within the ministries was reduced significantly. The old practice with a large number of deputy ministers in each ministry was also abolished. In the new system each minister has only one or two deputy ministers. The total number of government bodies increased, however, from 54 in the old system to 73 in the new system.

Federal services and agencies report normally to a ministry. The minister is responsible for approving annual budget plans, for performance indicators, and for submitting the performance report from all units within his or her responsibility. In this way the ministry determines the policies within its sector. The ministries are responsible for legislative drafting and for managing the performance of their services and agencies. This should include monitoring and evaluation of progress in government bodies within the ministry's jurisdiction.

The administrative reform was to be implemented from the middle of 2004. It is a huge reform. It was particularly challenging to change the government structure so dramatically in the middle of the budget year. The magnitude of the reform took some of the focus away from other budget preparation and execution reforms. The overall effects of the reform are far-reaching, but have not been properly evaluated at this stage. Some signs of reconsideration have emerged recently—for example, the agricultural agency is to be reintegrated in the ministry.

Performance information requirements

From the very start of the reform process, performance measurement was to be developed within a comprehensive framework. The reform process started actually more than a year before the government approved the Concept Paper. The MoF arranged a seminar in February 2003 on performance-oriented budget methods for budget administrators, supported by an EU-funded program, "State Budget Reform." This project was heavily supporting the reform process from January 2003 to September 2005 and is followed up now by the "Public Expenditure Management" project, also funded by the EU. This project lasted until the end of December 2006.

Budget administrators in Russia have normally sent a budget proposal to the MoF based on line-item budgeting in July each year. As part of the 2004 budget preparation, the MoF sent a letter to budget administrators requesting them to add performance information as part of the budget proposal. The request was far-reaching. Budget administrators were supposed to prepare performance reports describing strategic goals, objectives, functions, outputs and outcomes, performance indicators, and targets. The budget proposals were also to be linked to these goals and objectives. This request implied a lot of extra work. Many administrators were not prepared for this task, but most budget administrators included this information as part of the budget proposal.

The MoF had worked out a questionnaire to evaluate the reports. These evaluations were completed both by the budget institutions themselves and by the MoF with expert assistance. These evaluations were then used as information to develop the Concept Paper on budget reform.

According to the Concept Paper, ministries and agencies should identify both outputs and outcomes and identify the indicators to be used to measure progress. The annual performance reports should, according to the paper, include the following elements:

- identify main goals and objectives for activities within the responsibility of the ministries and their subordinate agencies and services, and show that these activities support government general policy priorities

- expenditures should be allocated to the relevant activity, including estimated revenues that are managed by the subject of budget planning
- measurable results in the reporting period and planned results for the medium term, should be linked with the budget programs aimed at achieving the targets
- expenditures should be allocated by goal targets and programs in the reporting and planning period
- the effectiveness of expenditures within the responsibility of the subject of budget planning should be assessed, and also what measures can be taken to increase effectiveness.

The performance reports have been prepared annually since mid-2003. Substantial progress has been made over these years in identifying strategic goals and indicators for output and outcome (see examples in Table 21.2).

Table 21.2 Output and outcome indicators from Performance Reports for 2006–08

Goal/objective of the ministry	*Output indicators*	*Outcome indicators*
Ministry of Agriculture		
Improving quality of products of agricultural, fishery, and food processing industries	Decrease in diseases common in humans and animals	Number of incidents of people infected through the use of food produced from bad quality raw materials of animal origin
Ministry of Industry and Energy		
Modernization of defense industry's production capacities	Rate of growth of investment in capital assets in the defense industry	Share of innovative products in the total output of the defense industry
Improving technical condition of heating and electric power plants and distribution systems	Number of investigated objects	Decrease in damage resulting from failures and accidents on such objects

Organization of the reform process

The MoF continued to push the reform process in 2004, and a number of seminars and training sessions were arranged with support from donors. As part of the 2005 budget preparation process, budget administrators were requested to prepare performance reports again.

Top levels of the government got heavily involved in the reform process after the presidential elections in March 2004. After the new government was formed, Deputy Prime Minister Zhukov was appointed to head the new Government Commission to increase the effectiveness of budget expenditures. The principal task of the Commission is to manage implementation of the public expenditure reforms in line with government decisions.

The Deputy Prime Minister and his secretariat developed a three-level goal tree with four main social and economic indicators at the top. Sub-goals and performance indicators were developed so progress could be measured within each level. The three-level goal tree was attached to the budget letter the MoF sent to budget administrators for preparing the 2005 budget. Each budget administrator was expected to show the relationship between their own goals and the goals at the national level (see Box 21.1). A number of working groups were set up by the Deputy Prime Minister and his secretariat to examine the 2005 budget proposals prepared by the budget administrators. The working groups were expected to ensure that goals were properly connected at all levels and that relevant indicators were formulated.

Box 21.1 Main social and economic goals and indicators at the national level

Goal 1. *"Increasing standards of living and improving the quality of life"*

Indicators:

- Share of citizens satisfied with their quality of life (by public surveys)
- Life expectancy at birth
- Fatalities per 1,000 people

Goal 2. *"Enhancing national security"*

Indicators:

- Share of military personnel serving on contract terms in the total number of privates and sergeants
- Number of deceased in natural and man-made catastrophes

Goal 3. *"Maintaining a high rate of sustainable economic growth"*

Indicators:

- GDP rate of growth
- Labor productivity
- Energy consumption per GDP unit (relative to 2003 level)

Goal 4. *"Creating potential for future development"*

Indicators: available for sub-goals only.

After the government approved the Concept Paper, the Ministry of Economic Development and Trade (MEDT) became part of the reform leadership. The MoF and the MEDT have been made jointly responsible for many legislative acts related to the performance budgeting reform. Both ministries are also responsible for consideration and approval of line ministry programs.

In addition, in March 2005, as the move to effective multi-year budget planning was under consideration, the Prime Minister was appointed to lead the Government Commission on budget projections for the current year and for the medium term. The Commission should revise both annual budget plans and medium-term budget plans before the plans are submitted to the government for approval.

Table 21.3 below illustrates some of the most important powers and responsibilities for the four key decision-makers in the reform process: the MoF, the MEDT, the Deputy Prime Minister's Commission, and the Prime Minister's Commission.

Having several main stakeholders in the reform process—MoF, the MEDT, the Deputy Prime Minister and his Commission and secretariat, the Prime Minister

Table 21.3 Main responsibilities for the major reform stakeholders

	MoF	*MEDT*	*Commission on budget projections (chaired by Prime Minister)*	*Commission to increase the effectiveness of budget expenditures (chaired by Deputy Prime Minister)*
Annual budget	Prepare draft annual budget, negotiate with budget administrators, fiscal policies and debt management	Forecasting of economic and social parameters Decide main economic and social parameters to be used in the budget preparation process Control of programs, investment, and other capital expenditures	Final revision of the draft budget before the draft is submitted to the government for approval	
Medium-term financial plan	Prepare draft medium-term financial plan, negotiate with budget administrators, fiscal policies and debt management for the medium term	Forecasts of economic and social parameters to be used in the medium-term budget plans Participate in preparing the medium-term plan	Preparation and final revision of the medium-term budget plan before the draft is submitted to the government for approval	
Ministerial targeted programs	Expertise (appraisal)		Settling disputes on the issues of resources required for programs	Settling disputes on goals and indicators
	Developing the list of ministerial targeted programs		Approving the list of ministerial targeted programs	Approves recommendations to increase the effectiveness of ministerial targeted programs
	Controlling implementation of ministerial targeted programs			
Reports on the results achieved (performance reports) and the main activities of a budget administrator	Developing methodical guidelines			Coordinating the preparation of reports

and his Commission and secretariat—has some advantages but probably more complications. It increases the pressure from above to make progress in reform implementation. On the other hand, the MoF and the MEDT often have conflicting views. Since both ministries have equal authority in settling many reform elements, this will complicate the decision-making process and delay reform progress. The

Prime Minister's involvement in budget preparation issues also raises difficulties: he will often have too many other responsibilities to be able to handle detailed budget preparation issues effectively.

All in all, the budget reform has enough top-down support. In addition to what has been mentioned above, the reform process has been fully supported by the President through his annual budget addresses, through speeches and government meetings broadcasted on TV. The problems lie in a reform leadership structure which is too top-heavy. This raises problems of coordination, decision-making, and conflicting signals sent to budget administrators, the overall effects of which could be reduced enthusiasm for the reform in line ministries and agencies and a slowing down of the reform process.

Human resources constraints

It is fair to say that budget administrators were relatively unprepared for the huge reforms that were introduced as part of the preparation of the 2004 budget. Line ministries and agencies are necessarily the most important stakeholders in the reform process. The MoF with donor project support arranged seminars presenting the new ideas, but most civil servants working on budget preparation and execution were firmly based in old budget traditions and procedures. The steps that have been taken so far have to a large degree been forced from above, and budget administrators have very much progressed in the way of "learning by doing." The MoF with support of donors has, however, provided substantial support through additional seminars, training in line ministries, and direct assistance to develop the necessary documents that were introduced as part of the reform process. When moving forward with a top-down approach, it is of course necessary and extremely important to get line ministries and agencies motivated for the reforms. Over time, it should be line ministries and agencies that perceive themselves as the "owners" of the reform.

An experiment conducted by the MoF towards the end of 2004 has been one important element in the emerging strategy to increase motivation. Candidate agencies were invited to improve their Performance Reports by supplementing them with medium-term budget projections, and information on the status and quality of the financial management and on their achievements in restructuring subordinate units. The participants of the "Experiment" were competing for relatively small amounts of funds. The most important motivating factor was probably not the funds but to show who was "the best" and in the lead in the reform process. The MoF was due to run a similar experiment in 2006, and can probably use this technique in future years to increase motivation.

In April–May 2005 the "State Budget Reform Project" conducted a survey among budget administrators to study how the participants in the budget process perceive the reform. A total of 73 participants from 34 federal executive bodies participated in the survey. Many respondents said that the reform had increased their workload without extra remuneration and that the work on the performance reform was complicated by the lack of a legal and methodical framework. However, many respondents recognized that the work on preparing the budget had become more interesting and saw possible future impacts in the effectiveness of public spending. All the interviewed officials thought that after ten years of reform implementation Russia would achieve either or both enhanced efficiency of public sector bodies and public spending, and improved quality of public services. Some main points emerging from the survey respondents were:

- the need for improved methodological support
- that the essence, goals, ideology, and instruments of the reform should have been explained better from the start. As a result of the failure to do this, when the formal reporting requirements are put in place, they will be seen as an additional burden
- the reform timetable should have been more realistic
- consensus should have been developed between reform leaders before implementation
- there is a need for clearer rules of the game—rules which are not changed every year
- increased responsibility and authority for program managers is needed
- reform leaders should listen to the opinions of ministries and subordinate units.

Phasing in of reform implementation

The Concept Paper identified the laws, regulations, and other documents that had to be drafted and approved to establish the necessary legal basis for the reform (see Table 21.4). These included a regulation for the layout and content of the performance reports that budget administrators should prepare. Such regulatory guidance is important, but is not sufficient to enable line ministries to grasp the total implications of the reform. Unfortunately, no detailed implementation plan or action plan was developed at this stage. The initial focus of the reform was also directed towards the budget preparation process with limited consequences for budget execution and reporting. Moreover, the anticipated timeframe for completing the reform was clearly too optimistic from the start.

The development of a medium-term budget plan lagged behind in the reform process. The first steps towards introducing multi-year budgeting on a rolling basis were taken as part of the 2006 budget preparation process. The reform process could have benefited from establishing fiscal policies and sector priorities for the medium term at an earlier stage in the process. More time could have been used to train line ministry staff in performance budgeting methods and in establishing administrative (ministerial programs) before this part of the reform was put in motion. The impact of the reform on the budget execution process and reporting should have been better developed at an earlier stage, including line ministries' responsibilities in shifting funds between programs to achieve more efficient allocation of resources.

Table 21.4 Concept Paper plan of measures for implementation of the concept of reforming the budget process in the Russian Federation in 2004–06

Task	*Form of document*	*Deadline for submission of draft to the RF government*	*Responsible ministry*
Making amendments to the budget classification	Draft federal law	Q3 2004	MoF
Amendments to the procedure for development, approval, and implementation of federal targeted programs	Draft resolution of the government	Q3 2004	MEDT MoF
Establishing the procedure for formation of the medium-term financial plan and the draft federal budget	Draft resolution of the government	Q4 2004	MoF MEDT
Establishing the procedure for keeping a register of spending commitments of the Russian Federation	Draft resolution of the government	Q1 2005	MoF
Establishing the procedure for the development, approval, and implementation of ministerial targeted programs	Draft resolution of the government	Q1 2005	MoF
Adoption of standards of accounting and financial reporting for bodies in the state management sector	Draft resolution of the government	Q1 2005	MoF
Introduction of amendments to the Budget Code of the Russian Federation concerning the regulation of the budget process	Draft federal law	Q2 2005	MoF
Establishing the procedure for the development, approval, and implementation of budget targeted programs financed from the federal budget	Draft resolution of the government	Q4 2005	MoF MEDT
Adoption of legal acts of the government of the Russian Federation, ensuing from the draft federal law "On Amendments to the Budget Code of the Russian Federation Concerning the Regulation of the Budget Process"	Drafts of acts of the government of the Russian Federation	Within three months after the adoption of the Draft Federal Law	MoF

Next steps

The reform process has been gaining momentum over the past three years, but success is not guaranteed. There is a lot of work that remains to be done. Some important next steps are discussed below. Unless substantial progress is made in these areas over the next two to three years, there is a clear danger that the reform will collapse, and that budget preparation and execution again will be based on traditional input budgeting, perhaps with some marginal use of performance indicators.

Complete the structure of administrative programs to finalize the overall framework of the reform. The overall structure and classification of federal targeted programs and ministerial programs needs to be finalized. The federal targeted programs need to be restructured (and if possible scaled down) to establish clear responsibilities and to avoid having sub-programs that span several functions and budget administrators. Programs should be "mono-functional" so that each program is linked to only one function.

The integration of both federal and ministerial programs with lower levels of the functional classification needs to be completed, and the lower levels of the functional classification need to be set up in a hierarchical structure. Each budget administrator (subjects of budget planning) needs to finalize the design of the ministerial programs that will govern the use of resources within his or her responsibilities. These programs must be linked to overall federal priorities, but be defined in a way that supports political decision-making and prioritization within the concerned sector. Programs should be hierarchically constructed. Each program can have a number of sub-programs; each sub-program can be decomposed into a number of activities and projects. Each sub-program must be linked to only one program and each activity or projects linked to only one sub-program. Program-based information must be included in the chart of accounts.

Plan and distribute budget expenditures in a multi-year framework. A regulatory framework for multi-year budgeting has been established, and more detailed procedures need to be further developed. Medium-term budget planning must be established on a rolling basis where the second year is the starting point for the next budget cycle. It is necessary to improve the integration of multi-year economic forecasts and the budget guidelines at the start of the budget cycle. The guidelines must be based on a clear fiscal policy for the medium term, with defined parameters of fiscal responsibilities. The capacity to develop such strategies needs to be strengthened within the MoF. It is probably necessary to start the budget preparation cycle earlier to allow time for improved annual and medium-term budget planning in the ministries and federal services.

Better integration of medium-term budgeting and performance-oriented budgeting. For the reform to be sustainable it is necessary to fully integrate performance budgeting with medium-term budget plans. This will give better predictability of budget expenditures and programs for specific budget sectors, and allow for more efficient allocation of resources within the sector and between the sectors. The quality of strategic budget policy decisions can be improved when moving from annual to multi-year budget plans, and budget plans can be developed within a sound overall fiscal policy for the medium term.

Improve the impact of performance measures on budget execution and later-year budgets. Performance measures must be designed so the results are useful in making decisions to allocate more or less resources to a specific program. Procedures to measure performance during the budget year on a regular basis need to be developed and be used together with information on program costing to improve the efficiency of resources during the year. This involves clear procedures for spending units' authority to reallocate resources between programs. End-of-year reporting, including information on program costing, must be structured to influence the allocation of resources for the medium-term planning period. It is necessary to provide more training and support to budget administrators on the use of performance measures to manage resources in a more effective way and to evaluate alternative courses of action.

Financial management. This must be fundamentally improved, with new, clear allocation of responsibilities for results and the activities and resources to achieve them. The Chart of Accounts and classification need further improvement to enable the information required for good financial management to be produced in a timely and user-friendly manner. The financial information system needs to be updated and coordinated with the development of the Federal Treasury system, to store and process the transactions that are needed to support and control the financial management.

Motivation. Budget negotiations between the hierarchies of institutions (ministry—agency/service—spending units) within the responsibility of one ministry or budget administrator should be based on performance targets and accountability mechanisms. This will strengthen the use of programs and performance indicators. It is important to further develop the framework to encourage and reward positive developments in resource management. The rewards and the criteria for the rewards must be transparent. Examples of spending agencies that succeed in attracting additional funding and managerial flexibility through high-quality planning and management should be published and used as positive examples.

The pace of the reform should be set to ensure a reasonable match between budget administrators' capacities and the innovations expected from them.

To reinforce budget administrators' commitment to the reform, effective incentive systems need to be developed and regularly updated. Some of the steps required (for example, changes in civil service remuneration) lag behind. The timing of budget administration and civil service reforms should be planned so each reform element can create positive synergy effects for other reforms.

The experiments that the MoF has been running in 2004 and 2006 to improve reporting, financial management capabilities, and the structure of subordinate units are one important measure to increase knowledge and motivation. The winners of the Experiments should receive a lot of positive publicity in media and government websites. Appreciation from high-level government officials could perhaps also encourage further efforts to improve the budget process among line ministries and agencies.

Reform leadership. It is necessary to establish a clearer allocation of powers and responsibilities among the key decision-makers—the MoF, the Ministry of Economic Development and Trade, the Prime Minister's Office, the Deputy Prime Minister's secretariat, and the Commission on Budget Projections. It is especially difficult to have two ministries involved in the reform with the same level of authority. The MoF should be given the overall ministerial responsibility for the reform process and the Ministry of Economic Development and Trade could play an advisory role.

Detailed plan of action. A detailed plan of action should be developed to cover the remaining parts of the performance budgeting reform including the introduction of a system of rolling forward medium-term budget plans. It is important that the plan has a clear distribution of responsibilities among the reform leaders. The outcome of each step of the process should be illustrated. The plan must also cover budget execution procedures and reporting, including line ministries' responsibilities and authorities in the reformed system.

Conclusions

In the last two years the performance budgeting reform in Russia has taken off from the government's blueprints and entered into the daily life of the Russian public sector. Most of the actual changes have so far been made to the budget preparation and planning phase at the federal level. The reform can be assessed as quite comprehensive and is based on international best practices, especially in the conceptual design. Compared to similar experiences in other countries, the Russian reform can be characterized by a combination of rapid pace and massive scale. Using the lessons available from international experiences, Russian reformers have adopted an implementation strategy that combines the benefits of uniform sequential implementation and implementation through selected in-depth pilot projects.

In this chapter, we have described what has been achieved in Russia since spring 2003 to introduce performance budgeting into the budget preparation phase at the federal level. The analysis also reveals that much remains to be done in the future. This is not surprising: for example, after almost six decades the US Comptroller General stated that "developing credible information on outcomes achieved through federal programs remains a work in progress" (GAO, 2002, p. 10).

In our view, the reform has now reached a critical stage. To advance further it is necessary to capitalize on the achieved gains and address the following main challenges:

- the design of a comprehensive and effective incentive systems for reform stakeholders
- the achievement of some tangible results visible to the reform participants and to the general public.

References

DFID/WB Donor Secretariat for Civil Service and Administrative Reform in Russia, 2005, *Toolkit for International Consultants Involved in Implementation of Public Administration Reform in the Russian Federation*, third edition, July (Russia: DFID/WB Donor Secretariat).

Diamond, J., 2003, "From Program to Performance Budgeting: The Challenge for Emerging Market Economies," IMF Working Paper, June (Washington: IMF).

——, 2004a, "Establishing a Performance Management Framework for Government," IMF Working Paper, April (Washington: IMF).

——, 2004b, "The Institutional Basis of Budget Reform," IMF Working Paper, April (Washington: IMF).

GAO, 2002, *Performance Budgeting, Opportunities and Challenges*, GAO-02–1106T (Washington: Government Printing Office).

22 The Experience of Bogota

Israel Fainboim Yaker

During the decade 1993–2003, the city of Bogota made significant progress in many areas. Civic culture strengthened. The coverage of core social and public utility services expanded and their quality rose, improving poverty indices based on the coverage of these services. Crime rates declined. The existing transport system is being replaced by a faster and more efficient system based on articulated buses circulating on exclusive lanes. Schools and libraries were built with high-quality infrastructure in the poorest areas of the city. Public spaces were reclaimed and recreational areas expanded with the construction of parks.

This progress has been impressive especially because it occurred in a context of rapid population growth, which created pressure to provide infrastructure and public utilities in the city. Population growth was greater in Bogota than in other Colombian cities because of the internal migration of people displaced by violence or attracted by the services offered.

These developments have been made sustainable by the strategy of financing the city's expenditure needs through an increasing tax effort and by ensuring efficient and transparent use of public funds. Improvements in the provision of services resulted from a process of modernization of the public sector that involved the restructuring of some agencies (particularly the electricity company) and the introduction of a number of market-based governance elements (particularly concession contracts). Within this process, and to improve public management, increase transparency and accountability, and strengthen the city's finances still further, in 2000 the city began to develop a new budgetary system based on a performance budget,[1] linked to a medium-term expenditure framework (MTEF) and supported by an activity-based costing system.

The recent progress and the fact that Bogota has pioneered the development of these new budgetary instruments in Colombia and in Latin America can be attributed largely to the political and institutional changes made in the second half of the 1980s and the early 1990s, which included the introduction of democratic elections for Mayors, making it possible for mayorships to be won by candidates who were independent of the traditional parties and untainted by the cronyism practices of the past, and the approval of an Organic Statute for the city, which abolished the co-administration of its entities by the city council and the latter's participation in procurement decisions and treasury management, thereby substantially reducing corruption.

The experience of Bogota with performance budgeting is relevant for at least three reasons. First, the deepening of decentralization and the increasing transfer of competencies and resources in Colombia over the last decade, as occurred in many other countries, mean that it is the local authorities rather than the national government that have the responsibility for the provision of the most important social and public services, and therefore it is they that should be held accountable for these services and not the national government; and a performance budget is the best instrument that can be used by them for accountability purposes. Second, the experience of Bogota shows that even the cities in developing countries can implement performance budgets without undue difficulties. Finally, the planning and budgeting institutions in Bogota are very similar to those of many Latin American countries, therefore the changes made can be used as a reference for other countries in the region.

This chapter describes the process of implementing a performance budget in Bogota. It begins by explaining the reasons and motivations for introducing this instrument in the city. It goes on to describe the activities carried out to implement this tool, and identifies the obstacles encountered and presents the results obtained. The last section provides some conclusions and recommendations, suggesting, among other things, possible ways of ensuring the permanency of the instrument. This latter point is important because although the city made considerable progress in implementing a performance budget between 2000 and 2003, the use of this instrument became a mere formality and for all practical purposes came to a halt in 2004 following the change in government—a risk faced by all reforms that are not embedded in the country's legal framework. Before describing the implementation process, basic information on the city is provided to give the reader at least a general idea of the setting in which the process has unfolded.

Bogota's background

Bogota is Colombia's biggest city, with a population of 7 million, which makes it larger than at least six Latin American countries; its share of Colombia's population is 18 percent. It had a per capita income in 2004 ($ 2,700) 30 percent larger than that for the nation ($ 1,900). It is "the country's major financial center, the largest industrial city and the center of culture" (Gilbert and Davila, 2002, p. 29).

The city's administration comprises 64 institutions and 53,000 civil servants. It has the responsibility for the provision of the most important social and urban services (water, sanitation, electricity, sewerage, transport, road maintenance and construction, education, health, housing, social assistance, street lighting, and so on) and competes in the provision of telecommunications services.

As it is also a capital district, it receives both departmental and municipal revenues. Its main revenue sources are the industry and commerce tax (a business tax levied on gross revenues), the property tax, and the gasoline surcharge, which between them account for over 90 percent of the city's tax revenues. The city's budget for 2006 amounts to roughly $2.4 billion.

Political context

Up until 1988, the capital was different from other cities in Colombia in that the Mayor was appointed by the President; in the other cities, he/she was appointed by the Governor, who in turn was appointed by the President of the Republic (Gilbert and Davila, 2002, pp. 32–3). The President usually appointed Mayors who shared his political affiliation. With the constitutional reform of 1986, all the Mayors are now democratically elected; the first of these elections took place in 1988. The system of democratically elected Mayors has resulted in the election of candidates that are independent of the traditional parties. Of the seven Mayors elected since that year, only two have been from the President's party (Gilbert and Davila, 2002, p. 33). This has led to periodic conflicts with the national government and to the city's dependence "on the goodwill of the president and the finance minister when it came to finding money for major projects" (Gilbert and Davila, 2002, p. 45).

The Mayor's term of office was initially set at two years, but the constitutional reform of 1991 increased it to three and a new reform in 2004 further raised it to four—the same term as the President. The benefit is that it increases the authority of the Mayor and makes longer-term planning possible. The legislation allows the Mayor to be reelected, but not immediately, which gives rise to changes every four years in the management positions of institutions, limits policy continuity, and prohibits timely rewards to Mayors who have had a successful administration. Since the introduction of democratic elections, one of the Mayors (Antanas Mockus) has been re-elected.

The election of independent Mayors has also resulted in conflicts with the city council. The council has been democratically elected since 1974 (Gilbert and Davila, 2002, p. 33) and its term is the same as that of the Mayor. The legislation establishes that the number of council members must increase in proportion with the population, as a result of which the number has grown from 20 in 1972 to 42 in 2004. The council is very fragmented politically, which makes it very difficult to have dialogue to approve projects submitted by the administration, which must be sanctioned by practically every council member.

Although the council has always been dominated by traditional parties, and predominantly by the Liberal Party, the councils have no particular party line and are composed of various factions which, in many cases, are connected to individual council members; over time, the number of organizations represented on the council has increased, particularly religious organizations and movements with short political lifespans.

According to Gilbert and Davila,

> given the fragmented nature of party politics in Colombia, and particularly the lack of party discipline, it is in the interest of many councilors to give the mayor a hard time. Few councilors can be relied upon to support the mayor; practically

> every vote has to be won. How that vote is to be won is a real problem insofar as it has frequently required the granting of favors. The mayor is expected to help secure public contracts, to direct public works projects to selected barrios, and to find jobs to councilors' friends and allies. (2002, pp. 43–4)

This practice has caused serious conflicts between the executive and the council, which were particularly acute during the administrations of Mayor Antanas Mockus, who was opposed to any type of agreement that involved trading favors between the administration and the council for the approval of draft arrangements.

Up until 1993 the council members also sat on the boards of enterprises and district institutions, and participated in decision-making on hiring and cash management in the city. The Organic Statute of the city (Decree 1421 of 1993), issued by the central government in compliance with and obligation established in the 1991 Constitution, changed that situation and established a clear separation of functions and powers between the district executive and the council. The statute abolished the co-administration of its entities by the city council and the latter's participation in procurement decisions and treasury management, thereby substantially reducing opportunities for corruption.[2] It also initially afforded the city greater administrative, tax, and budgetary autonomy than other municipalities in Colombia and granted the executive the power to change the internal structure of institutions without needing approval from the council.

The relationship between the city administration and the national Congress has not been good. Several city administrations have had to make enormous efforts to have members of Congress defend their interests. This is partly due to the fact that their interests are under-represented in the Congress. Although the city has become a separate electoral area since 1991, allowing it to send its own representative to Congress, the number of representatives that it can elect is very small in proportion to its population. The majority of the Congress is opposed to the interests of the capital, using anti-centralist arguments, despite the fact that many senators (elected at the national level) come to office predominantly on the basis of votes from the city.

In terms of intergovernmental transfers, Bogota has received per capita (or per poor inhabitant) much less than other cities. It was only in 1996 that the Congress accepted the results of the 1993 population census, which improved the population's situation with respect to transfers.

The difficult relationship between the National Executive, Congress, and the council has motivated the trend to have the city increase its self-financing capacity and to cease being dependent on decisions from those agencies to finance its plans and programs.

Despite Mayors' short terms in office and the impossibility of immediate re-election, one of the factors that explain the improvements in the quality of life in the city in the 1990s and 2000s is the maintenance of a certain degree of continuity in policies and long-term targets across administrations. According to Gilbert and Davila (2002), the quality of city government "improved during the 1990s as a succession of mayors built on the achievements of their predecessors and made genuine improvements to the quality of urban management." This has been because Mayors have tended to agree on the appropriate solutions to the challenges facing the city, and also because they have agreed that these responses must be medium term.

Planning, budgeting, and evaluation cycle at the sub-national level

Performance budgeting was not developed in Bogota in a vacuum, but drew on processes and instruments already established in the city, by integrating and strengthening those processes most useful for performance-based management and budgeting. These processes and instruments, which are largely the same as those used by the national government, include a Development Plan, a Multi-year Financial Plan, a Multi-year Investment Program (MIP), and an annual investments work plan (POAI), together with an action plan and the development of strategic plans by individual institutions. One major difference with the national government is a requirement that a document containing the government program must be prepared.

As at the central government level, the district budget is essentially based on the city's Development Plan (PD). Unlike the national approach, the PD must be based not only on the multi-year financial plan but also on the Government Program. The Government Program is the document that each of the mayoral candidates presents to the public as a political platform for the elections. The program has to be prepared by identifying the city's main needs and proposed solutions. The elected candidate must set out in the Development Plan the objectives and instruments proposed in the Government Program. When the citizens vote for a candidate, they vote for a Government Program and have the right, granted by the Constitution and the law, to demand that the Mayor-elect acquit this program.[3]

The Constitution incorporated an additional mechanism of democratic political accountability, the recall of mandate in the event of non-fulfillment of the Government Program,[4] which strengthens the traditional tool of elections and provides incentives to an administration to produce results. Although a recall is hard to achieve because the requirements are very demanding,[5] its mere existence forces administrations to prepare realistic Government Programs (and as a consequence, realistic development plans) that they can fulfill.

The link between the Development Plan and the agencies' responsibilities with regard to specific targets is provided by strategic plans that define the entity's mission and vision, and establish its long-term objectives. Their preparation is not compulsory in Colombia, but they have long been prepared in most public entities and are a useful tool for public managers. The strategic plans are the basic instrument of the entities for preparing their annual budgets.

The budget process in Bogota (see Box 22.1) is a two-stage and centralized one in which the agency responsible for finance—the Finance Secretariat—prepares the Annual Financial Plan, determines the aggregate expenditure ceilings for each of the agencies, and submits the budget proposal to the council. It is difficult for the council to amend the draft budget, because any proposal to amend the budget, or any *Proyecto de Acuerdo* (regulations issued by the local council) that involves additional spending, requires prior authorization by the government for its approval. The executing units also have very little leeway to change their budget during its execution.

Box 22.1 The budgetary process in Bogota

The budgetary process begins with the Mayor defining the budget policy guidelines, which are notified to line agencies by April 1 of each year. These guidelines are established after consultation with the District Economic and Fiscal Policy Council (CONFIS) and define the objectives, targets, and parameters to be considered in drafting the budget for the next fiscal year.

The Budget Directorate of the Finance Secretariat (SH) prepares central government revenue forecasts for the following fiscal year, in coordination with the Tax, Treasury, and Economic Research Directorates of the SH; and the forecasts for public establishments to generate their own revenue are revised. The expenditure initially forecast is the result of working group discussions between the Finance Secretariat, the District Planning Administrative Department (DAPD) and the various line agencies, in a forum created for that purpose called a "functional committee."

On the basis of these exercises, the SH adjusts the Financial Plan (PF) and prepares an annual version of the plan, which it presents to CONFIS for consideration. Based on the annual PF, the SH defines and reports overall expenditure quotas for each entity, for functional expenses and investment. Each entity prepares an Annual Operational Investment Plan (POAI) based on the assigned quotas and the working group discussions and submits it to the DAPD so that the projects can be recorded in the Programs and Projects Databank, and produces and submits its preliminary draft budgets to the SH and the DAPD.

The preliminary drafts are finally discussed with the SH and the DAPD in the "functional committee" and, when an agreement is reached, the preliminary draft POAI is prepared, followed by the preliminary draft budget, which must be approved by CONFIS. The latter may amend the drafts to provide a final draft budget, which is sent to the city council. Since 2000, the performance budget has been included as an annex to this document. In 2003, the draft also included information on contingent liabilities and medium-term expenditure framework exercises for various sectors.

The draft must be submitted to the city council at the beginning of November for review and approval. The council has until December 31 to approve it. The council may only increase aggregate projected revenue and/or expenditure with the agreement of the Finance Secretary. It is also restricted in its power to reduce or delete individual items in the expenditure budget. If the council does not forward the budget by December 31, the government draft prevails, including any amendments approved during council debates. If the draft is rejected, the current budget prevails. If the council approves the budget but the Mayor objects to it on the grounds that it is illegal or unconstitutional, the government must refer the budget to the administrative tribunal of Cundinamarca for judgment.

Budget appropriations may be changed by the administration during the budget execution stage by means of budget transfers, additional credits or reductions, postponements or cancellations of previously approved appropriations. Budget transfers within an aggregate set aside for investment, operations or debt service may only be executed with the prior endorsement of the Budget Directorate (and the DAPD if the transfer affects investment items). In the event that the transfer involves a change in the aggregate amounts initially authorized, it must be submitted to the council for approval. Increases in appropriations must also be approved by the council.

Motivation for the move to performance budgeting

The performance budget (PB) was introduced in the city as an initiative of the administration and not as the result of any legal obligation to do so, and the motivation for its adoption arose from the government and not from the legislature. There is no legal obligation in Colombia to adopt performance budgeting at the national or local levels, unlike, for example, the legal requirement supporting the medium-term fiscal framework. In fact the performance budget in Bogota has been presented to the city council alongside the traditional budget project, and the latter is still the document that the council is legally required to approve.

Basically there were three reasons for Bogota to move to a performance budget: the first was to increase the transparency and efficiency of the use of public funds, and to hold the government more accountable for its results. Prior to 2000, very few public entities produced periodic reports on the outcome of its programs, but new programs and new expenditures continued to be executed without considering how the existing programs had performed. Inefficiency and waste of resources were rife, and widespread political corruption and cronyism had caused politics to lose credibility.

The aim was to restore confidence in the government and increase its legitimacy through transparent and efficient management. The administration of Mayor Mockus (2001–03), during which the PB was consolidated, considered public resources to be sacred; the public officials held them in trust, had to answer for them, report on their use, and use them efficiently. Accountability and honesty in government were central to his program;[6] and one of the main objectives of his administration was to improve probity in the use of resources. It was thought that the PB, which uses language that is accessible to the public, would facilitate accountability and promote public debate and participation in discussions on the budget and in monitoring and control of its execution.

The second motive for implementing a performance budget in the city was to reorient the public debate on the budget, by curtailing the endless discussions on line-items between the administration and the municipal council and refocusing it on the outcomes and outputs it was proposed to obtain with the budget. This sought to eliminate or at least restrict the "micro-management" intentions by the council, through lengthy discussions on investments, general expenses, wages, and contracts of each public entity. The belief by the administration that the presentation of the budget frames the public debate was a key factor underlying this decision.

Similarly, the PB was intended to discourage ad hoc budget reform proposals that would favor the interests of individuals or special interest groups by subjecting all expenditure proposals to the test of how they contribute to achieving any public objective established in the government program and in the PD.

Finally, the third factor that accounts for the introduction of the PB in the city was the involvement of former staff and consultants of the national government who played a key role in diagnosing existing problems in the budget process in Bogota, and implementing reforms. This group of technocrats, which had a shared vision of the reforms needed in the budget process, found that Bogota was fertile ground for applying their knowledge, since the matter was not moving forward at the national level.

Information base for performance budgeting

Information systems

In 1999 work began on development of an integrated financial management system in the city developed in-house with the support of a small group of external experts. The project was developed in modules, and in 2003 the key modules (budget, accounting, and treasury) were already in place.

Alongside this, in 2001 a performance information system was designed, that complemented the budget information module (PREDIS) of the financial management information system. This system records information on outputs and outcomes and their costs. Special care was taken in its design to ensure that expenditure data prepared on the basis of an economic classification more or less consistent with the *Government Finance Statistics Manual* (*GFSM*) *1986* would be used to produce information by objectives and programs. As no functional classification of expenditure has been implemented in Bogota, the accounts that were structured by institutional and economic classification had to be reorganized by objective.

At the same time, a number of information systems were being developed and used in the sector, which produced periodic information on outputs and outcomes to feed the performance information system developed by the Finance Secretariat.[7]

Selection of performance indicators

The selection of indicators by public entities for the performance budget was based fundamentally on the indicators of the Development Plan. The Development Plan of the Mockus administration (2001–03) included 81 specific objectives, of which:

- 41 corresponded to outcomes or impacts by individual entities, including citizens' perception of those benefits among them
- 25 involved the provision of goods and services (outputs) by individual entities
- 15 involved the provision of outputs by more than one agency.[8]

The task of selecting the indicators was facilitated by the fact that the Development Plan largely followed the recommendation that "key priorities should be measurable, achievable, outcome-oriented, and have defined time horizons."

Although the indicators selected by the entities for their performance budgets covered 60 percent of the plan's targets (48 indicators included in the PD), their measurement required a much larger number of indicators, because they were defined in aggregate form in the Development Plan.[9]

The main reasons why the selection of outputs predominated in Bogota were as follows:

- For some areas it was very difficult to define the outcome indicators. A clear example of this problem arose in connection with the *Citizenship Culture* priority, whose outcomes are very difficult (or impossible) to quantify.
- Some outcomes take more time to achieve than the three-year term of office. It was practically impossible to commit to the achievement of them in such a short time span. Output indicators can be used to check targets annually.

Efforts were made to specify relatively few outcomes and outputs for each entity, although this objective has not been fully achieved. The performance budget programmed for 2004 included 102 outcomes (objectives) and 230 outputs, which amounted to an average of 14 indicators per entity. Four to five indicators per program, defined for the most important programs, would have been sufficient.

The indicators were selected on the basis of characteristics widely recognized in the literature as appropriate (Hatry, 1999; Government of Alberta, 2000), such as meaningfulness, reliability, timeliness, and comprehensiveness.

Baselines and benchmarks

Baselines were established for 2000, and annual targets were set for the period 2001–04. Benchmarks often depended on the sector and program in question. In education, the results of academic tests were compared between public and private schools. Also, the cost of providing basic education services for a child was compared with the cost resulting from a concession contract. In the case of health services, benchmarking was performed by comparing the financial results of the 11 public hospitals as well as some non-financial performance indicators. In the case of security (or crime rate) indicators such as the homicide rate, comparisons were made with the country's other large capital cities and with the nation as a whole.

Measurement of indicators

Indicators were measured almost entirely by the agencies. In some areas surveys were used to obtain information on public perceptions of the effects or to quantify them; this happened particularly with regard to the *Citizenship Culture* and *Admirable Public Management* priorities. The quality of the indicators used and of their measurement improved steadily during the government term. The agencies provided regular feedback with comments on the data recorded, thereby making improvements possible. However, there was no external auditing of the quality of them.

Adoption of ABC cost accounting for measuring efficiency and effectiveness

There are two ways in which a government can implement cost accounting (Kelly and Rivenbark, 2003):

- develop an independent costing system, and reconcile it regularly with the existing integrated financial information system (IFMS) to ensure its accuracy. The advantage of this alternative is its flexibility in identifying the costs of service functions separately. Its disadvantage is that it takes time and uses resources to keep the system

- adopt program-based costing, with accounts structured around programs. This makes it possible to monitor direct costs permanently with the IFMS. The total cost of each program can be calculated by distributing support services data from the IFMS among programs, using a standard methodology that includes indirect costs and depreciation of the capital assets of the respective program.

Following an investigation of existing costing models in national public sector bodies, and also in other countries, it was decided to adopt the first strategy and develop an activity-based costing (ABC) system; and to implement it initially among secretariats and decentralized bodies in 20 district entities, for later extension to the remaining entities. It is worth mentioning that there is no regulation requiring public bodies, either at the national or at the local governments' level, to produce cost accounting information.

The ABC system was chosen, among other reasons, because it was considered as the method that best allocates indirect costs (overhead) among products and because it provides data for cost management, making it possible to identify inefficient areas and activities. ABC provides a clearer picture of the total cost of a process than other costing methods.

Also, standard accounting does not allow for reporting on the costs of processes that traverse the boundaries of an organization's various departments and therefore it has shortcomings for decision-making. Standard accounting allows for costs to be determined only in terms of vertical organizational structures, whereas ABC permits cross-cutting costing procedures. This is because in the first case the information is structured for the collection of data on transactions by departments.

It is worth noting that the resistance faced for adopting ABC by the private sector, because it requires great detail and much more work than other costing methods, has diminished over time as ever-more efficient information technologies have become available. It should be mentioned that Bogota has an accrual accounting system, which facilitated the implementation of ABC, because ABC basically translates information from financial statements into cost data (Cokins, 2000).

As a result of actions taken in the selected pilot entities,[10] the costing model was defined for 16 entities, structured as follows:

- *Definition of resources*. Accounts were analyzed and resources defined on the basis thereof. Standardization of resources and their allocation to activities allowed for a cross-cutting analysis of their use.
- *Graphical model of activities*. This made it possible to group together the different tasks undertaken by the public entities to achieve the objectives and fulfill the mission of each organization. Roughly 2,500 activities were defined, and specifications of the support activities of the different entities were standardized, thereby allowing for analysis not only at the entity level, but also at the sectoral and district levels.
- *Cost objects*. The outputs, goods, and services to be costed were defined.
- *Inductors*. Inductors, or criteria for distributing resources to activities, were defined.

The ABC system was put into operation in 20 entities by December 2003. Between 2001 and 2003 a simplified costing method was used, which implied the definition of "cost centers" for allocating costs to products. No comparison of the accuracy of the two methods was made, but the cost of implementing the simplified methodology was much lower.

Development of a performance evaluation methodology[11]

Although performance evaluation is the last stage in the cycle of public management, it must provide feedback for the budget planning, budget programming, and public policy execution processes, and provide information for reporting. Performance evaluation can yield the following benefits, among others:

- at the level of organizational units, it can enhance operating capacity (improving internal processes) by identifying the causes of the failure to achieve targets
- at the sectoral level, it can improve coordination among the agencies responsible for achieving shared objectives and defining public policy.

In the final months of 2003, a methodology for evaluating the results of the term was developed. The methodology was designed to determine not only whether or not the institutions achieved their intended objectives, but also to establish whether the outputs and objectives were well defined and coherent. Consequently, this was based on integrating the three levels of evaluation.

At the first level, the aim was to evaluate the strategic planning capacity of the institutions based on the consistency of the institutional mission with the organizational objectives defined by the institution and the consistency of those objectives with the outputs delivered. For that purpose:

- a consistency indicator was developed that identifies the number of objectives that did not contribute to the fulfillment of the mission, or whose contribution is unclear
- efforts were also made to determine whether the objectives are well defined, that is, whether they correspond to a benefit that the institution hopes to provide to a third party
- an index of the relevance of each indicator to the objective being measured was also constructed. Its purpose was to establish whether the index measures progress toward the objective rather than what the institution is doing to achieve such progress, that is, if it adequately covers in its definition the benefit produced. The indices for individual indicators were consolidated into a summary index of the relevance of each institution's performance indicators as a whole
- similar indicators were established for outputs, with the purpose of: (1) determining whether they are well defined, that is, whether they correspond to a good or service that the institution hopes to provide to a third party; (2) whether they adequately measure at the individual level the quantity, quality,

and/or timeliness of delivery of goods and services; (3) whether they do so as a group, in order to identify whether there are outputs whose delivery is not measures, or whether it is not clear what is being measured; and (4) whether the output is consistent with the objective.

Based on a simple average of these indicators, an overall rating of strategic planning by institutions was established.

At the second level, the intention was to evaluate to what extent the delivery of outputs (goods and services) had been achieved. For this purpose:

- an indicator of effective provision of outputs which compares planned targets with actual values was defined
- an indicator of changes in efficiency in the provision of outputs was also defined. It relates goods and services delivered to resources transferred and compares the performance of prior fiscal years. There was no proposal first to measure efficiency per se since the methodologies developed for rigorously obtaining information on output costs have not yet been applied.

At the third level, the aim was also to evaluate success in impacting the sectoral level (that is, achieving the objectives identified), by means of an analysis of the change in the institution's effectiveness. To do so, based on the evaluator's selection of the most important sectoral objectives, weighted effectiveness is compared using the weight of outputs as regards the achievement of objectives with the effectiveness of the weighted objectives based on the importance of their indicators.

The indicators being developed are easy to understand, and although they are not completely sound conceptually and reflect some of the subjectivity in their design, they are relevant and low cost in obtaining information and estimates. To quantify more rigorous indicators would have meant a much higher cost for information-gathering and estimation.

The evaluations draw on the information reported by the institutions for the performance budget. The ratings generated automatically through the performance evaluation sub-module designed for that purpose, which is connected to the budget module (PREDIS) of the Bogota financial information system. To be useful to the managers, the ratings must be accompanied by a qualitative analysis that seeks to identify the reasons for poor management performance.

To make the process more credible, two evaluations were to be produced: one by the institution itself (self-evaluation) and another by an external entity, more specifically the Finance Secretariat. The financial information system included an option for to self-evaluate, in addition to receiving the automatic rating it generates.

Along with the development of evaluation tools by the Finance Secretariat, the DAPD produced performance evaluations of the Development Plan using its own information system, the Development Plan Monitoring System. This is a reflection not only of the existence of two different evaluation processes in Bogota, but also of planning and budgeting.

Implementation steps

Before describing some key implementation steps of the performance budget it should be underscored that its introduction in Bogota received political support from the highest level of the administration, both from the Mayor and from the directors and managers of the various entities.

The District Finance Secretariat was in charge of implementing this instrument. The administration opted for a quicker full-scale implementation of the PB, due to the limited time available; a pilot or incremental approach increases the overall length of time required for implementation, and the Mayor's term in office was only three years.

Institutional diagnostic study

The implementation process began with a diagnostic study of existing institutional arrangements, and particularly of the rules of the budgetary process in force in the city, and their impact on fiscal sustainability, strategic prioritization of expenditure, and efficient resource use.

The diagnostic study was performed as part of the District Institutional Reform Mission, conducted by a team of consultants of the Finance Secretariat, the main objective of which was to provide a comprehensive overview of governance institutions in the city and propose a set of short- and long-term reforms to improve it.[12] This made it possible to focus the project from the outset on addressing the problems identified and overcoming potential obstacles to implementation of the desired budgeting system.

Identification of best practices

In designing the performance budget, studies were made of performance-based budgetary systems and governance models in Australia, New Zealand, the United Kingdom, Sweden, Canada, the United States, and some North American cities that use (or have used) performance budgets, such as Sunnyvale (California), Coral Springs (Florida), Austin (Texas), and Indianapolis (Indiana).

External technical assistance

The design of the instruments also benefited from technical assistance provided by some international experts. Malcolm Holmes, co-author of the World Bank's *Public Expenditure Handbook*, provided technical assistance in the design of the performance budget and, in conjunction with Joris van Dijk,[13] assisted the administration in developing the medium-term expenditure framework. Design of the ABC costing system received assistance and training from Paul Sharman.[14]

Creation of a special unit to design and implement new budget instruments

To coordinate and direct the process, a special unit composed of consultants was set up outside the Budget Directorate, attached directly to the Office of the Secretary of Finance, with responsibility for definition of an action plan and the design and operational testing of the PB, and training of staff. A consulting team reporting directly to the Accounting Director Office of the city (an office that depends on the Finance Secretariat) was also established to design the costing system.

Possibly one of the errors made in the process was not to integrate these units into the structure of the Finance Secretariat; the fact that it was composed of consultants generated some resistance from the staff, which hindered their assimilation of the system. Nonetheless, if this unit had been incorporated into the structure of the Secretariat, it would have been unable to hire qualified staff owing to salary restrictions.

Training

Part of the team of consultants was assigned to provide training and technical assistance to the entities. Each consultant was responsible for providing training and technical assistance to roughly six entities. Presentations were made, and workshops and meetings were held with staff from all entities, to disseminate the new concepts and encourage the development of planning exercises within them, thereby laying the foundations for annual programming of the performance budget.

Interagency coordination

As many outcomes were the responsibility of several agencies, achieving them required a coordinated effort. This was particularly important in the areas of mobility, public space, and social development. For that purpose, the administration organized coordination committees for each strategy of the Development Plan (the plan had nine strategies) and for each sector, chaired by the person with greatest responsibility for the outcome in question.

The Mayor held regular meetings with the objectives coordinator and the sectoral coordinator, "which made it possible for the actions to be seen from the two perspectives. These two different perspectives enhanced monitoring and the number of opportunities for coordination" (Mockus, 2004, p. 55). This was also important in a context in which public institutions are not properly grouped and ranked on the basis of sectoral structures that allow the public to clearly identify those responsible for performance.[15]

Results

Coverage of the performance budget

The performance budget was implemented as an information structure in all secretariats, administrative departments, and public establishments (that is, a total of 37 entities). Systemized information on costs, outputs, and outcomes for these entities is available for the period 2000–03.[16] Progress was expected to be made in 2004 and 2005 in the coverage of public enterprises, hospitals, and local district administrations. As mentioned above, ABC costing was put into operation in 20 entities in 2003. Although the performance budget was not implemented in all the city's entities, its adoption was always planned as a gradual process that would take a number of years to consolidate.

Monitoring and evaluation of outcomes and outputs

Information is published annually on performance and output in an annex to the budget documents. As mentioned earlier, only in 2003 was a performance evaluation methodology developed, and it cannot be considered a full program evaluation (for example, cost-benefit or cost-effectiveness evaluations),[17] although it was more than a mere analysis of indicators.

As indicated, this methodology includes a review of consistency of objectives with outputs; an analysis linking outputs an objectives to offer some information on expenditure effectiveness; a comparison between results planned and results obtained (efficacy); and a comparison between results obtained with a given budget in the respective year with those obtained in previous years, to offer some information on expenditure efficiency. The methodology has been applied in the environment, education, health, social welfare, and culture sectors, with the results reported (see Polania, 2004a; Moreno, 2004).

Use of performance information by government and council

Since year 2002, during the budget preparation stage allocation decisions were supported with performance information, resulting in some modifications, albeit minor, to resource allocations. Outcomes and outputs began to be analyzed and achievements used in the "functional committeees" as an input for feedback on decision-making. These committees are the mechanism through which the Finance Secretariat discusses with the corresponding directors each entity's expenditure quotas in the budget and its distribution between the different programs. The Secretariat's sectoral specialist, the director of the special unit for developing the performance budget and the directors of the public entity attended these meetings. Usually the Finance Secretary attended the meetings for those entities that have large budgets.

The most important programs of each institution were analyzed with some degree of detail in this scenario. If the institution could show that the failure to achieve intended outcomes was due to inadequate budget funding, more appropriations were sought for the program. However, if the sectoral specialist from the Finance Secretariat showed that the outcomes were poor due to improper program management, the resources per unit of output would not be changed and the discussion would focus on ways of improving program implementation. As the Finance Secretariat began to produce approximate information on the unit costs of outputs since 2000, it was not easy for the institutions to prove that they needed additional resources per unit of output to produce a predetermined level of goods and services.

Since 2000, performance budget documents began to be delivered annually to the council in addition to the required budget documents. These documents contained information on the mission, vision, strategies, and priorities, together with a list of outcomes and other outputs; information on achievements in the previous year (without comparing them against the targets of that year); projected targets for the current year and those programmed for the following one; and information on investment and operating costs for the current and following year, whenever that was easy to determine. However, the document did not identify or provide information on uncontrollable external factors that could affect outcomes.

The external audit entity (*Contraloria*) and the council used the information provided to debate budgetary issues and to exercise political oversight of commitments undertaken and the outputs and outcomes achieved by the city administration.[18] Since 2000, the budget discussion with the council has been increasingly centered on outputs and outcomes and less on inputs. This change in the way the budget is discussed was a very important step forward, since it was the first time in the history of Colombia that an institutional arrangement provided a mechanism whereby the inhabitants of the city and their political representatives could access information to evaluate mayoral performance.

Although the council continued to appropriate resources by agency and expenditure item, rather than by outputs or outcome targets, the information contained in the performance budget allowed for a more informed discussion of the budget and resulted in a number of minor changes in appropriations.

It should also be mentioned that in 2003 the council approved Agreement 67, which requires the administration to publish information on performance indicators. The Decision 67 initiative arose partly by contagion resulting from the use of performance budgeting by the administration, and partly also as a result of the influence of the *Bogota Como Vamos* project (described below). The indicators selected in the decision were developed with the unit responsible for the performance budget project in the city, although the council added a number of its own.[19]

The other key component of a performance budget is the flexibility to be given to managers in administering programs, in exchange for assuming responsibility for their outcomes. This doesn't exist in the city, because managers are free to reallocate resources only between "investment programs" and within them, provided the entities did not weaken their output (or, in some cases, outcome) commitments and conditioned to an authorization by the Finance Secretariat (or the DAPD in the case of capital expenditures). Furthermore, the city council approves the budget for the institutions and large items (total per institutions for investment, operations, and debt service),[20] which gives the administration greater flexibility in reallocating expenditure. The proposal for this, which was not implemented, was that as public managers produced better outcomes, the Finance Secretariat would allow them more flexibility in the use of resources.

Impacts on effectiveness and efficiency of service delivery

Although government provision of goods and services became considerably more effective and efficient between 2001 and 2003, it is hard to attribute the improvements to the use of performance budgeting. This is due to the fact that performance budgeting was introduced along with a large number of reforms aimed at improving governance and the provision of services to citizens, which jointly can be classified as "market-based governance" mechanisms. These included the liquidation of a number of public agencies that were no longer providing useful services to citizens; partial privatization of electric power and telecommunications firms; restructuring of entities through radical staff downsizing; and the introduction of concession mechanisms for the provision of many services.[21] In several cases these mechanisms included the adoption of performance contracts (water supply, park maintenance, education services, transport).

Effects on transparency and accountability

Results data (outputs and outcomes) were collected in many cases on a monthly basis; reports to citizens were provided once a year and annual accountability meetings were held in 2002 and 2003 (reports were also made to the council in budget documents, which are public). In 2002 and 2003, annual reports on the results of PB management were produced, and two exercises of citizenry accountability were performed on the results obtained. A standard alternative was thus offered for reporting the administration's performance to the council and the citizens. Formerly, each entity presented individual outcome reports, which usually entailed a numerical-legal analysis of public expenditure, without a major benchmark in terms of outputs delivered and the benefits for the city.

Citizens were able to ascertain the approximate cost of most goods and services provided by the administration. Moreover, in the discussion of priorities, these costs have become units of measurement for the existing trade-offs, such as: how many school places would be sacrificed if it were decided to construct a pedestrian crossing?

Box 22.2 *The Bogota Como Vamos* project: an important accountability mechanism

The *Bogota Como Vamos* project has been promoted since 1998 by *Casa Editorial El Tiempo* (the country's largest circulation daily newspaper), Fundación Corona (a non-governmental organization), and the Bogota Chamber of Commerce, associated with the strongest private sector professional association in the city. It aims to measure changes in the levels of quality of life and well-being in Bogota, to provide citizens with basic information to evaluate governance, and to promote efficiency and transparency in district administration. The project evaluates the fulfillment of each administration's Development Plan, analyzing changes in people's access to core services and the level of citizen satisfaction through indicators of the coverage and quality of services, and citizens' perception towards them.

There are 12 areas of evaluation: education, health, highway mobility, public space, public finances, environment, governance, security, public utilities, housing, citizen responsibility, and economic development. Indicators for each area were defined on the basis of discussions with the administration, and are measured annually. Most of the information is provided by the city. Each administration can include new indicators in the evaluation, but cannot remove the existing ones. On a complementary basis, the project gathers monthly data on 75 variables, in a process known as the *Bogotanometro*.

Also, to gauge citizens' perception on a wide variety of issues, it conducts an annual survey, interviewing no less that 1,500 citizens. The survey asks about: the climate of opinion (general climate, economic climate, food situation); sectoral aspects (health, education, childhood issues, domestic services, housing, and so on); general aspects (citizen responsibility, mobility, environment); and government aspects (public administration, and so on). Each evaluation is debated by public officials, and the results are disseminated through a variety of communications media.

It should also be stressed that Bogota is subject to external monitoring of the outcomes of the Development Plan, undertaken by the *Bogota How Are We Doing* (*Bogota Como Vamos*) project (see Box 22.2). This has made a significant positive contribution to improving the quality of public debate, providing annual data on the outcomes achieved by the development plan, and discussing them publicly. The information collected by the project comes from the public agencies, and is complemented with survey data.

Conclusion

Although the district has made a great effort to implement a performance budget, much hard work is still needed for its consolidation. The performance budget adopted by the city worked well as an information structure and therefore as an instrument for political control and citizen's participation. However, its role as a tool for expenditure allocation was more limited, as was the use of the performance information as a managerial tool.

The budget cycle must go beyond a list of performance commitments annexed to the budget. The process of allocating resources must be based on how enforceable and sustainable such commitments are. The budget now includes information on performance, yet decisions are not being systematically taken on that basis, nor are the medium-term implications of the various programs being systematically considered, despite the fact that this activity is a key underpinning of the performance budget.

The following additional steps are desirable to create the conditions for consolidating the performance orientation of the public resource management cycle:

Step 1. It is advisable for Bogota to institutionalize a high-level (cabinet) forum for open, collegial procedures that would evaluate the various policy options and have them compete for resources, within the framework of medium-term restrictions. This forum would be in charge of ensuring that the policies are enforced and feedback is given on their design (or for developing alternative policies), based on performance. Sectoral expenditure directors and the authorities responsible for discipline and guidance in government management should have seats in the forum to make the process of resource allocation an open discussion, which would legitimize the policies to be developed within the administration, and would help reconcile top-down restrictions (political priorities and availability of resources in the medium term) with bottom-up restrictions (resource needs in the short and medium term by the different sectors of government to maintain current policies or introduce new ones).

Step 2. Another point that merits attention in the future is the importance of broadening the vision of the budget to a multi-year format. To achieve this, there must be continuity in the implementation of the medium-term expenditure framework, not only as a tool for information on future spending, but as a policy-making process that requires agreements among public managers on the direction of policies and, consequently, expenditure trends.

To the extent that Bogota still does not regularly use comprehensive expenditure categories at the policy and program level, it is not clear how institutions are linked to develop them and whether policy performance is enforceable. The preparation of Sectoral Strategic Plans as building blocks of the medium-term expenditure framework will make it possible to consolidate credible medium-term contracts to allocate public resources to strategic priorities and enforce the respective outcomes. With these plans, objectives common to several entities could be coordinated on the basis of these policies and inter-institutional work encouraged.

The sectoral focus would provide a more strategic approach to the budget, creating a better environment for its formulation. It will also reduce pressure on public spending, since the formulation of sectoral plans would increase the possibility of transferring resources within the sector, promoting their internal reallocation. In a context of tight resources restrictions, additional amounts for new policies will have to be sought within the sector by promoting program savings. The Sectoral Plans and the medium-term expenditure framework should gradually replace the Development Plan as the medium-term reference framework for annual budget decisions.

Step 3. The annual budget process should include: (a) a definition and/or review of sectoral policies, with a view to reaching an agreement at the highest level on the amounts to be allocated to each policy; (b) an initial definition of quotas, based on which meetings would be held (task forces) focusing on analysis and establishing performance commitments; and (c) a performance analysis as a reference for final discussions on budget distribution.

Step 4. The United Nations functional classification of expenditure (COFOG) should be adopted as a bridge between the budget information by line-item and budget performance data. This classification should have the force of law within the administration.[22]

Step 5. One key institutional aspect is the importance of creating the organizational conditions necessary for formally implementing the new budget rules within the political/administrative structure of the district. On this point, the problems with the current organizational structure are well known, namely too many institutions operating within an inflexible institutional structure, with no connection to sectoral structures to which one can delegate and demand accountability for performance. As a result, in each administration, as mentioned earlier, informal coordination mechanisms arise that do not have sustainability over time.

Step 6. The new budget instruments (medium-term expenditure framework and performance budget) should be given a firm legal basis.[23] This would guarantee its permanency across changes of government.[24]

Step 7. Line agencies should be given more autonomy over the management of their resources in exchange for accountability for outcomes. Ex-ante control imposed by the District Finance Secretariat and the District Planning Administrative Department on internal transfers of large investment and operating items should therefore be lifted, provided that these entities do not dilute their commitment to outcomes. This increased flexibility could be granted gradually and selectively to those institutions that demonstrate better-defined objectives and outputs and greater commitment to outcomes with the resources available.

Step 8. Finally, without changing the civil service system, the use of the performance information as a managerial tool will have limited impact. The civil service system seriously restricts the introduction of individual incentives. Also, civil servants are generally unskilled and hold their posts through political recommendation. The related legislation, which is national, is at a stalemate and staff have been unable to be promoted on the basis of performance. Other incentives to achieve results relate to public recognition and they were used considerably by Mayor Mockus's administration.

Notes

1. It should be noted that the new budget model was called a "results-oriented budget" not a "performance budget," but the latter designation will be used in this chapter to refer to the new instrument the city has adopted.
2. Also, the 1991 Constitution prohibited the system of transfers or "*auxilios*," whereby a small portion of the budget is distributed among the council members (or, at the national level, among legislators) for them to use the resources supposedly for projects in their communities.
3. Article 259 of the 1991 Constitution introduced the concept of "programmatic vote" in elections for Mayors and Governors (regulated by the Law 131 of 1994), which means that voters electing candidates to such posts mandate the elected candidate to implement the Government Program that he or she presented when registering as a candidate.
4. Articles 40 and 103 of the Political Constitution.
5. This mechanism can be invoked when at least one year of the term of office has elapsed, following a call for popular vote by at least 40 percent of the total votes obtained by the elected candidate. Recall can occur if it is approved by an absolute majority of citizens participating in the vote, provided the number of votes is at least 55 percent of those registered when the candidate was elected.
6. His popularity came from the fact that he did not represent any of the parties and from his record of honesty.
7. One of these is the SUIVD (Unified System of Information on Violence and Delinquency) (<www.suivd.gov.co>), operated by the Government Secretariat and drawing data from the Metropolitan Police and the Forensic Medicine Institute. The other is the information system operated by the District Culture and Tourism Institute.
8. Some analysts have argued that an organization should use both output and outcome indicators, and even input indicators, on the grounds that the various users of performance information (politically elected officials, managers, citizens, legislators) require different indicators.
9. For example, one of the targets was "to achieve useful inoculation coverages (95 percent for polio and measles, and 85 percent for diphtheria, tetanus, whooping cough, haemophylus influenza, hepatitis B, rubella, and tuberculosis)." As a specific measurement was required for each type of vaccination, this target alone required nine indicators.
10. These were public entities from the central and decentralized sectors of the Capital District, including an industrial and commercial enterprise (*Metrovivienda*) and a state social enterprise.
11. This section is based on Polania (2004b).
12. The Mission studies were supported by a loan provided by the Inter-American Development Bank (IADB).

13. Consultant in macroeconomics and public finance for the Division of Macroeconomic and Sector Policies of ECORYS, Netherlands.
14. President, Focused Management Inc.
15. The Mockus administration proposed to the city council on several occasions that they adapt the city's institutional structure, grouping it into sectors and establishing a hierarchy of relationships between the institutions in each sector, but the council never approved the proposals.
16. This can be consulted directly on the internet at the Finance Secretariat website (<www.shd.gov.co/PI>).
17. Note that "outcome measures can identify trends and developments that need attention, but a full program evaluation is needed to establish whether the cause of poor performance...has anything to do with its financing" (Joyce, 1999).
18. The external audit entities in Colombia, as in most other countries, are required to examine not only the legality of operations but also the economy, efficiency, and effectiveness of the provision of goods and services.
19. Currently (2006), although the information requirements of the Agreement are fulfilled, its presentation has become a mere formality.
20. It should be noted that the existing flexibility diminishes at the national level because Congress has the power to approve the budget up to the investment program level.
21. Among the services concessioned to the private sector were: education, street cleaning and refuse collection, mass transportation (*Transmilenio*), the client services activities related to water and sewerage services, management of the Tibitoc water treatment plant, the sanitary landfill, parking lots, cemeteries, gas, lotteries/betting, street lighting, issuing vehicle number plates and administering mechanical checks on buses and trucks, citizen information services and payment of utilities' bills (CADEs), and park maintenance.
22. It could be part of the Budget Settlement Decree approved by the Mayor upon completion of the budget discussion in the council.
23. This requires changes in the national legislation.
24. This is a necessary but not a sufficient condition for a successful adoption of a performance budget. It is the use that the different stakeholders (legislature, citizens, civil servants) give to these instruments that will determine its consolidation as a governance tool.

References

Cokins, G., 2000, "Overcoming the Obstacles to Implementing Activity Based Costing," *Bank Accounting and Finance*, Vol. 14(1).

Gilbert, A., and J. Davila, 2002, "Bogotá: Progress Within a Hostile Environment," in *Capital City Politics in Latin America: Democratization and Empowerment*, ed. D.J. Myers and H.A. Dietz (Boulder: Lynne Riener Publishers).

Government of Alberta, 2000, *Results-Oriented Government. A Guide to Strategic Planning and Performance Measurement in the Public Sector,* <www.finance.gov.ab.ca/publications>, accessed July 2006.

Hatry, H.P., 1999, "What Type of Performance Information Should be Tracked," in *Quicker, Better, Cheaper? Managing Performance in American Government*, ed. D.W. Forsythe (New York: Nelson A. Rockefeller Institute of Government), ch. 2.

Joyce, P.G., 1999, "Performance-Based Budgeting," in *Handbook of Government Budgeting*, ed. R. Meyers (San Francisco: Jossey-Bass), ch. 24.

Kelly, J.M., and W.C. Rivenbark, 2003, *Performance Budgeting for State and Local Governments* (Armonk, NY: M.E. Sharpe).

Mockus, A., 2004, "Modernizacion del presupuesto, evaluación y calidad del gasto publico," in *¿Por qué evaluar el gasto publico? Experiencias internacionales y el caso Colombiano* (Bogotá: BID, World Bank, and DNP).

Moreno, F., 2004, "Aplicación de la propuesta para evaluar la gestión pública. Sectores: educación, cultura, bienestar social y salud." Mimeo, Secretaría de Hacienda de Bogotá, January.

Polania, D.F., 2004a, "Evaluación de la gestión pública en el sector medio ambiente." Mimeo, Secretaría de Hacienda de Bogotá, January.

——, 2004b, "Lineamientos y propuesta procedimental para la evaluación de la gestión pública en el Distrito Capital." Mimeo, Secretaría de Hacienda de Bogotá, January.

23
Performance and Budgeting Under the Separation of Powers

Philip G. Joyce[1]

Many nations are attempting to change their budget processes to focus more on the connection between resources and results, rather than focusing budget decisions solely on inputs or activities of government. In this context, the role of the legislature in budget reform can be important, particularly in those countries where the legislature plays a significant independent role in resource allocation. This chapter focuses on three key obstacles to performance-oriented budget reform in these countries; namely, that:

- the fragmentation of power that is characteristic of independent legislatures often leads to ambiguous or conflicting policy objectives
- legislatures often base decisions on information that has little to do with overall performance, relying instead on either input data or on anecdotal information
- legislatures frequently do not conduct detailed programmatic oversight.

Against this background, the chapter considers changes that may promote more attention by legislatures to performance.

Government programs and institutions exist to further societal ends. Many government budget processes, however, have focused on inputs—resources required—or outputs—the work performed—as if they were the end products of government. Increasingly, in countries throughout the world, this trend has been countered through the establishment of systems that attempt to connect the resources used with the effects that those resources bring about. This type of a system is part of an overall reform movement in which decisions within government—by elected officials and government employees—are informed by considering the performance implications of those decisions. Governments with budgeting systems in which performance information is used apply many analytical tools—including cost allocation, performance measurement, and evaluation—in the process of allocating and managing resources.

Multiple positive effects can occur as a result of making explicit linkages between results information and the allocation of resources. First, such a linkage fosters a more efficient use of government resources, since questions about the success of government activities are tied to the allocation of resources. Second, a performance-focused budget system can help demonstrate to key stakeholders—who fund government activities and/or receive public services—that they are receiving "value for money." Third, when either additions or deletions from the government budget need to be made, these can be targeted in a way that government performance is optimized. Government resources are scarce; therefore the way in which these resources are allocated is crucial to maintaining some degree of domestic consensus and reaching societal objectives.

The challenge of ensuring effective use of scarce resources has led to a number of specific past and current reforms, designed to more closely link performance data to the allocation and management of resources. In the US, these reform efforts date back more than 50 years, and include such reforms as program budgeting (and its federal manifestation, the Planning, Programming, and Budgeting System—PPBS), zero-base budgeting, and management by objectives (see Schick, 1966; Harkin, 1982). More recently, all three levels of government (federal, state, and local) have been engaged in renewed efforts to establish closer linkages between performance evidence and the budget. At the federal level, the main impetus was the passage of the 1993 Government Performance and Results Act (GPRA), requiring strategic plans and performance measures for all federal agencies. The Bush administration has carried that reform a step further, moving beyond the production of data, to emphasizing the use of performance information in the budget process (see Joyce, 2004). Some US state governments—most notably Washington, Virginia, Utah, Michigan, Louisiana, and Texas—have progressed even further than the federal government in the use of performance information for budgeting and management.[2] Local government experiences are harder to summarize (there are approximately 88,000 local governments in the US), but organizations such as the International City/County Management Association have been encouraging their member governments to focus more explicitly on focusing upon and assessing performance.

Similar reforms are being pursued in both developed and developing countries all over the world. Many OECD countries have attempted to reform their budget processes to incorporate performance measurements. Four countries in particular are frequently mentioned as being at the forefront of public budget reform efforts: Australia, Canada, the UK, and New Zealand (Premchand, 1999). In addition to developed countries, however, developing countries have also been pursuing these reform efforts, supported by international institutions such as the World Bank and the International Monetary Fund. In the interest of space, the experience of these countries will not be reviewed in detail here, but all of them have in common an emphasis on: planning; measuring results; and using performance information to allocate resources.

What is the role of the legislature in budgeting?

The type of governmental budget system will affect substantially the manner in which the legislature deals with the budget. Depending on the country, the legislature may play a crucial role in determining the level of funding for public agencies and programs. In some nations, however, the legislature is, in effect, an extension of "the government" or plays a role of providing a check on what the government or governing coalition does. Still others occupy some middle ground between these two extremes.

Pelizzo and Stapenhurst, in a recent World Bank Institute paper, characterized governmental systems of 48 different countries as presidential, semi-presidential, or parliamentary (see Table 23.1). Presidential systems, which include countries such as the United States, Indonesia, Brazil, and Chad, generally have an independently elected chief executive and legislature. In the parliamentary systems, which include the Westminster-style countries (such as the UK, Canada, Australia, and New Zealand) in addition to countries such as Germany, Turkey, and the Czech Republic, the party (or parties) in control of the parliament are actually in charge of the executive. These countries normally have a Prime Minister, who is the head of the executive and a member of parliament. The semi-presidential systems, such as France, Romania, and Niger, represent some hybrid of these two forms. In these instances, there is frequently both a Prime Minister *and* a President who has some independent constitutional authority (Pelizzo and Stapenhurst, 2004).

While governments in any of these types of systems may attempt to adopt a more performance-oriented budget process, legislative support is not equally important in each country. The countries of primary interest in this chapter, therefore, are those in which the legislature exercises independent control over the budget. While it is tempting to assume that this sort of legislative independence operates on a continuum where presidential systems are at one end (with substantial legislative control) and parliamentary systems are on the other (with virtually none), research into legislative budgetary power suggests otherwise. Another recent study, by Lienert, in attempting to characterize legislatures in terms of the level of control that they exercise over the budget, divided governments into five separate forms—presidential, semi-presidential, parliamentary republics, non-Westminster parliamentary systems, and Westminster parliamentary systems. It then characterized the separation of powers among these countries. At the two extremes, the results were not surprising. The presidential systems had the most substantial separation of powers between the branches, while the Westminster systems had none. There was virtually no difference, however, between the other three cases—each had similar degrees of legislative/executive separation (Lienert, 2005).

The Lienert study goes a step further, however, in attempting to characterize these countries in terms of the separation of *budgetary* powers. The study looks at several factors in determining the extent of legislative separation, the most important of which is the extent of formal power to make changes in the budget. Significantly, this analysis finds no consistent relationship between the extent of political separation of the executive and extent of budgetary power exercised. The presidential systems

Table 23.1 Form of government and number of parliamentary oversight tools

	No. parliamentary oversight tools			
Form of government	*4*	*5*	*6*	*7*
Presidential	Côte d'Ivoire Kazakhstan	Nicaragua Palau	Benin Brazil Cyprus Guinea Korea Chad Tunisia	Costa Rica Indonesia
Parliamentary	Liechtenstein	Australia Turkey	Canada Germany Guinea Bissau Jamaica Luxembourg United Kingdom	Austria Belgium Croatia Czech Republic Estonia Greece Hungary Japan Lithuania Spain Sweden
Semi-presidential	Angola Armenia Rwanda	Cameroon Senegal Yemen	Niger Togo Yugoslavia	France Gabon Madagascar Mali Romania
Other			Switzerland	

Source: Pelizzo and Stapenhurst (2004, Table 5, p. 6).

and the Westminster systems still prove the extreme cases, but the study finds that (for example) the average non-Westminster monarchy has a greater degree of independent legislative budget power than a typical semi-presidential system. It concludes, not surprisingly, that the form of government doesn't necessarily matter, but rather a series of country-specific characteristics. The study summarizes factors influencing legislative budget independence as follows:

- *Political factors*. If there are fewer strong parties in the legislature, or if the government results from a parliamentary minority, there tends to be more legislative power exercised. This is also true of presidential systems with many political parties, or countries with bicameral legislatures.
- *Constitutional and legal limitations on executive budgetary power*. In many countries, legislatures have formally limited executive power, usually in response to a perceived excessive exercise of power by the executive. In parliamentary systems, laws tend to explicitly enhance the power of the executive. Alternatively, constitutional changes may specifically curb or enhance the legislature's budget power. Further, laws may create greater staffing capacity in the legislature, or may affect the level of debate on the budget.

- *Non-legal constraints*. In some countries, there is a practical requirement to gain agreement among many different political parties prior to the enactment of the budget. This happens, for example, in countries ruled by coalition governments. Country-specific cultural (for example, a history of a strong monarchy) or political (for example, the existence of legislative term limits) realities may also impose idiosyncratic constraints.

Despite these elaborations on the typology, the study confirms the presumed strong distinction between the presidential and Westminster-style systems. On a scale of 0 to 10 (with 0 representing the weakest independent legislative budget power and 10 representing the strongest) New Zealand, Ireland, and Greece (0) have the weakest legislatures, with Sweden (9) and the United States (10) occupying the other end of the continuum among the 28 countries studied. The other Westminster countries—Australia, Canada, and the UK—all prove weak in terms of legislative independence. Most countries occupy a middle ground, with "budgetary independence" scores between 4 and 7—these include Argentina, Bolivia, Hungary, Italy, and Japan.[3] (See Table 23.2 for a full listing of these countries according to legislative budgetary powers.)

These findings are significant because, while the level of independent budgetary powers varies quite a bit, in the majority of non-Westminster countries it is reasonable to think in terms of some "separation of powers" between the branches. Where such a separation exists, it is appropriate to consider what effect that separation has on various aspects of budgeting and management. For the purposes of this review, this means considering what effect the separation of powers would have on the movement of countries toward a performance-informed budgetary process.

The observations that follow in this chapter, therefore, apply most specifically to those governments where the legislative branch exercises substantial independent control over the budget. In these countries, the legislature has a particularly important role to play in establishing the environment for government performance, making decisions concerning how resources are allocated, and providing important follow-up that attempts to ensure that agreed-upon performance levels have been achieved. For this reason, it is important to understand precisely the manner in which these legislatures can contribute to (or detract from) performance, and how interested parties can think about the necessary incentives for these legislatures to better enable the effective use of scarce resources.

It is also worth noting that the choice of a political system in which the legislature has more independent budgetary power is just that—a choice, made for specific reasons and with political ramifications. While it may be much easier to set clear direction and unified policy for a political system without such a separation, that does not necessarily mean that the likely greater efficiency and clarity in policy is worth the price that might be paid in a given country. Many nations (for reasons of history, culture, or political theory) consciously choose messier power-sharing arrangements over arrangements in which direction for the government is set (at least at a given point in time) by one coalition or party. While it would be, in one sense, easier to operate in a system that encouraged greater goal clarity, that

Table 23.2 Indices for the legislature's budget authority in 28 countries

	Type of government	*1. Medium-term framework*	*2. Amendment powers*	*3. Time for scrutiny of budget*	*4. Technical support of legislature*	*5. Restrictions during execution*	*Total index*
Argentina	Presidential	0	2	1	0	1	4
Australia	Westminster	0	1	0	0	0	1
Austria	Semi-presidential	0	3	1	0	2	6
Belgium	Parlia. monarchy	0	3	1	0	0	4
Bolivia	Presidential	0	3	1	0	1	5
Canada	Westminster	0	0	0	1	0	1
Denmark	Parlia. monarchy	0	3	1	0	1	5
Finland	Semi-presidential	0	3	1	0	2	6
France	Semi-presidential	0	2	1	0	1	4
Germany	Parlia. republic	0	3	1	0	0	4
Greece	Semi-presidential	0	0	0	0	0	0
Hungary	Semi-presidential	0	3	1	0	2	6
Iceland	Parlia. republic	0	3	1	0	2	6
Indonesia	Presidential	0	2	2	1	1	6
Ireland	Semi-presidential	0	0	0	0	0	0
Italy	Parlia. republic	2	3	1	0	1	7
Japan	Parlia. monarchy	0	3	1	1	2	7
Korea	Semi-presidential	0	0	1	2	1	4
Mexico	Presidential	0	1	0	2	0	3
Netherlands	Parlia. monarchy	0	3	1	1	1	6
New Zealand	Westminster	0	0	0	0	0	0
Norway	Parlia. monarchy	0	3	1	0	2	6
Portugal	Semi-presidential	1	3	1	0	0	5
Spain	Parlia. monarchy	0	1	1	0	1	3
Sweden	Parlia. monarchy	1	3	1	1	2	9
Turkey	Parlia. monarchy	0	1	1	0	1	3
United Kingdom	Westminster	0	0	0	0	1	1
United States	Presidential	1	3	2	2	2	10

Source: Lienert (2005, Table 2, p. 23).

does not mean that the benefit of making such a change would be worth the cost. The purpose of this chapter, therefore, is not to argue that political systems with concentrated power are "better" than those with separated powers, but rather to identify the ways in which independent legislatures often impede results-oriented budgeting. The assumption is that understanding these limitations, and the reasons for them, can assist in devising solutions, as appropriate, for the challenges created by separated executive and legislative power.

One other contextual observation seems in order. Most public budget processes in countries with independent legislatures have clear (if not always smoothly functioning) stages of the budget process, any of which can be affected by the separation of powers (see Lee et al., 2004, ch. 3):

- budget preparation, as agencies or ministries develop internal budget allocations and requests that are eventually (after some give and mostly take) integrated into a proposed (or recommended) budget

- budget approval, at which point the budget proposal is acted on and officially approved by the relevant governing body (a parliament, or a state legislative body)
- budget execution, as agencies/ministries implement the budget, within the constraints established in the budget law(s)
- audit and evaluation, as agencies/ministries and auditors/evaluators decide (after the fact) what the effects (financial and performance) of budgetary activities have been.

If a given budget process is to become more informed by performance data, two factors must be considered simultaneously at each stage of the budgeting cycle. The first is the availability of appropriate information—on strategic direction, results, and costs—in order to make budgeting more results-focused. The second is the actual use of that information to make decisions (Hilton and Joyce, 2003; Joyce, 2004).

It is important that these questions be asked throughout the budget process, since there are multiple decisions at many stages of that process that can be illuminated by performance information. Often the focus is only on decisions that are made by the Ministry of Finance or the Budget Office, and on approval of the budget by the legislature, as if these are the only places where "budgeting" occurs. This encourages an overly narrow view of the budget process. It, for example, ignores the substantial discretion that ministries may have in allocating and managing resources in the budget execution stage, or the important role played by performance auditors in the evaluation stage. Decisions made at these stages are also about budgeting, in the sense that they directly or indirectly affect the allocation of resources. Thus, they are important to focus on in our understanding of how performance is affected by the budget.

A full review of all of the ways that performance information can be produced and used at each of these stages is beyond the scope of this chapter.[4] For our current purposes, the important thing is to understand that the legislature—in different ways and to varying degrees—can affect the level of effective integration of performance information at all stages of the budget, not just at the point of approval. That is, the legislature's orientation towards the budget affects the preparation of the budget in the executive branch, the implementation of programs, and the evaluation of government activity after the fact. The next section of this chapter will outline the ways in which legislatures can particularly impede development of a performance-oriented budget process.

Greatest obstacles legislatures create for performance-informed budgeting

There are many ways in which legislatures can promote or impede the ability of their respective governments to emphasize performance. The most important of these fall into three categories. First, laws passed by legislatures are frequently quite unclear in setting overall goals and direction for programs, leaving ministries and program managers in a position of having to establish objectives, and strategies for achieving them, without clear direction on goals and priorities. Second, legislatures often base budget decisions on information that has little if anything to do with overall performance. They may instead focus on anecdotal information, or information with limited relevance to results (for example, the distribution of inputs). Third, legislatures often fail to engage in oversight designed to focus on performance in a comprehensive way, choosing instead to either ignore the oversight function entirely or to focus attention on reacting only to allegations of wrongdoing.

In addition to these three obstacles, of course, one way that legislative bodies can impede performance is through the excessive use of budget controls. Substituting accountability for the use of inputs for accountability for results can create counterproductive incentives. For example, the US Congress routinely prohibits federal agencies from closing particular facilities, or requires them to open new ones, without regard to the performance implications of these actions. It also frequently imposes personnel floors or ceilings on agencies that prevent these agencies from exercising flexibility in managing their human resources. These broader performance constraints are somewhat beyond the scope of this chapter, but should be kept in mind by governments thinking about the relationship between legislatures and the creation of an environment that is supportive of performance.

Establishing and promoting unclear policy objectives

The development of appropriate performance information, whether it is to be used for budgeting or any other purpose, implies that public entities need to know what they are supposed to accomplish. Malcolm Holmes, who was an architect of the Australian budget reforms, noted that a key condition for results-oriented management in government was "clarity of task and purpose" (Holmes, 1996). The desire for goal clarity as a precondition for effective performance is the reason that most governments that have embraced a greater performance orientation have started with some sort of strategic planning effort. Strategic planning enables decisions to be made that establish clear direction for government programs and ministries. This is often quite difficult to carry out in practice, particularly in countries with a horizontal and vertical diffusion of authority, responsibility, and political decision-making. It is relatively easier in parliamentary systems (especially, as noted, of the Westminster variety), where the majority party or coalition actually runs cabinet ministries.

Despite its difficulty, however, strategic planning is an important focus of budget reformers. It explicitly establishes the context in which performance and dollars can be linked. In order for any organization to evaluate either its performance, or its use of resources in pursuit of that performance, it must first know what it intends to do. Legislatures can impede the development of effective strategic planning, and the coincident establishment of policy direction, because of a tendency to send unclear and ambiguous—or even contradictory—signals concerning what agencies or programs are to accomplish.

Legislatures can produce vague and sometimes conflicting legislation for several reasons. Put simply, the process of establishing legislative coalitions may demand it. Further, legislatures may either: lack the expertise required to specify precise actions in advance and/or conclude that changing circumstances require that they delegate some power to executive agencies. On the first of these points, legislation is normally produced as a result of carefully crafted compromise. Making laws more explicit often has the effect of revealing clear winners and losers. While this may be desirable in one respect (it promotes transparency, for example), it may tend to make the law in question more difficult to pass. This is not a recent phenomenon. In 1949, Paul Appleby argued in *Policy and Administration* that public officials were necessarily involved in policy-making (rather than simply carrying out out policy in a more ministerial fashion) because legislatures tended to pass vague legislation. This leaves executive branch agencies to "fill in the details," meaning that the ends of government themselves are partially under the control of the bureaucracy.

This is realistic, largely because of the technical limitations of legislative bodies. Even where legislatures operate through relatively specialized committees, these committees and their staffs do not possess the level of expertise that resides in administrative agencies. Particularly in departments where laws require scientific or other technical judgment, the power to specify implementation details may be delegated to appointed officials. For environmental policy, for example, it may be essential to delegate the specifics of regulation to administrative agencies, since the expertise required to determine how to translate "clean air" into a specific permissible level of a given pollutant may only reside within the bureaucracy. This is not just a matter of expertise. Given the large scope of legislative activity, and the limited time and the relative small size of legislative staffs to assist in lawmaking, it is not surprising that laws are relatively vague. Finally, legislation must frequently permit flexibility, in order to be able to adapt efficiently to unforeseen circumstances.

As long as there is consistency between the intent of a law and administrative interpretation of that law, the delegation of power doesn't necessarily create constraints to establishment of objectives, and (subsequently) performance measures.[5] Often, however, vague laws and subsequent administrative interpretation yield legislative reactions to those interpretations. These reactions might be unified—that is, reflective of the legislature as a whole. More often, they are fragmented (generated from individuals or committees within the legislature). Legislative response can in turn create substantial ambiguity for the ministry or agency involved, because it is not clear whether the agency is to follow: (1) the law as written; (2) the law as interpreted by the administrative agency; or (3) the law as interpreted by the administrative agency and then reinterpreted by the legislature or some sub-set of the legislature. If it is truly not possible to develop performance measures independent of clear objectives, certainly the objective-setting process under the separation of powers can impede measurement of performance.

In an evaluation of the management effectiveness of US federal agencies conducted between 1997 and 2002, lack of goal clarity was identified as an issue in numerous agencies. These included the US Customs Service, which is buffeted between twin goals of promoting the efficient movement of goods into the country and preventing harmful substances from entry. Also included are agencies such as the Forest Service (conservation versus harvesting forests), the Federal Aviation Administration (promoting timeliness versus security), and the Immigration and

Naturalization Service (enforcement of immigration laws versus providing services to immigrants). In each of these cases, agencies are left in the position of having to deal with multiple (and often conflicting) goals, with little clear direction in terms of how to resolve the inevitable ambiguity created in the legislative process. Lack of goal clarity, and lack of clearly established priorities between goals, often makes it difficult to identify performance measures that can be used to evaluate progress (Ingraham et al., 2002, pp. 94–102). Notably, in reviewing lessons learned from reviewing management effectiveness at all levels of government in the US, Ingraham, Joyce, and Donahue identified four conditions under which management effectiveness could make the most difference in delivering results; one of these conditions was "clear purpose and mission" (Ingraham et al., 2002, pp. 123–4).[6] This is another way of saying that without a clear articulation of purpose, it is difficult to manage effectively.

Making ill-informed budget decisions

Even if agencies have clear objectives, this does not by itself guarantee that appropriate performance measures relevant to those objectives will follow. In addition to setting appropriate objectives, then, a related condition for performance-informed budgeting is the collection of appropriate performance and cost information, *and use* of that information in resource allocation and resource management decisions. This creates problems beyond the frequently-cited conceptual challenges of defining relevant indicators. Most public sector organizations reasonably resist being held accountable for outcomes, since they are influenced by so many factors that are beyond their control. Further, there are conceptual problems with measuring costs—many public organizations cannot track how much it costs to deliver an output, largely because of problems with allocating indirect costs (Anthony and Young, 1984). It is that much harder to go the next step to measuring outcomes.

Even if these problems related to producing performance and cost data could be overcome, however, legislatures frequently do not have incentives to demand appropriate performance and cost information when making decisions on funding for agencies or programs. There are several specific problems that inhibit linkages between performance and budgeting in this regard. Perhaps the most significant is that legislatures frequently see no observable connection between having—and acting on—information on results and the electoral benefits that may be paramount in their minds. This point is particularly salient in cases where legislators need to stand for election frequently. Political scientist Morris Fiorina, writing about the US Congress, argues that the members of that legislative body (and particularly the House of Representatives, who must stand for election every two years) have little incentive to spend their time in legislating (by this, he means engaging in lawmaking designed to promote national interests), and instead focus on more localized pursuits with more a more explicit short-term electoral connection. Fiorina highlights two such localized activities: casework, which represents efforts to intervene on behalf of constituents with administrative agencies; and "pork barreling," which represents efforts to bring resources home to individual legislative districts (Fiorina, 1989).

The latter activity—pork barreling—is antithetical to a broad performance orientation on the budget. The definition of policy success under pork barrel practice is decidedly input-focused, rather than focused on results. For example, the typical legislative press release targeting the delivery of local benefits will not discuss the broad policy outcomes to be achieved from the expenditure, but will normally present the expenditure as more or less an end in and of itself. In fact, in their book, *Perpetuating the Pork Barrel*, political scientists Robert Stein and Kenneth Bickers (1995) argue that "[a]t the heart of most policy subsystems is a set of government programs" and that these programs are "bundled together" in ways that address the preferences of the actors in the sub-system. These actors include interest groups and executive branch agencies (two-thirds of the traditional "iron triangle"), but also include legislators. For legislators, the key preference is re-election, and a key path to re-election is the delivery of benefits—usually defined as jobs and money—to the home district.

But, while apparently inefficient, pork barrel spending is not without its justification. A recent book on the practice of pork barrel spending in the US argued that, as much as pork barrel spending may be reviled (and it is certainly easy to criticize on a case-by-case basis), it has the positive effect of fostering coalitions to pass legislation that otherwise might not achieve a majority. To the extent that this legislation may deliver general, rather than particularistic, benefits, these benefits may be worth the cost of a little pork (Evans, 2004). Further, it may not actually represent that much money—informal estimates are that "pork" represents less than 1 percent of the US federal budget.

In terms of impediments to performance, there are less visible, but probably more important, problems than the direct attempts to focus attention on inputs. Among these are misconceptions concerning the appropriate ways to measure performance, or to understand its relationship to budgeted amounts. Unfortunately, many legislators may be inclined to either not use performance information at all, or to use it in ways that do not really relate to performance. This last problem has at least two manifestations. First, there is the simple, but incorrect, approach (allegedly embraced by some members of the US Congress) that argues that the way to use performance data for budgeting is to "simply" take money from those who fail to meet performance targets, and give more money to those who meet targets.[7] While this may sound good, it relies on heroic assumptions, one of them about the causal link between money and results. For many programs, we do not know whether the failure to achieve performance targets is an argument for more money (the program could not achieve its objectives because it was insufficiently funded) or less (it is an ill-conceived or badly managed program). In fact, for any program, sorting out the contribution of funding versus other factors requires a full understanding of the logical relationship between inputs, outputs, and outcomes, taking into account both internal and external factors that influence performance. Further, budget decisions are appropriately influenced by other (non-performance) concerns, such as relative public priorities, unmet needs, and equity concerns, to name three.

Second, there is the tendency to assume that anecdotal information is the same as performance information. It may be true that an extremely large number of anecdotes might equate to some overall sense of agency or program performance. Often, however, legislators rely on sporadic anecdotal information, or data limited in geographic scope. A legislative leader in a large US state once noted that he was sure that the state Department of Transportation was doing a bad job "because there are lots of potholes in my district." Without doubting the veracity of that statement, this piece of data by itself neither yields information about how the Department is performing overall, nor does it in any way indicate what level of resources would need to be provided in order to improve performance. In the US federal government, Kenneth Kizer (Undersecretary of the Department of Veterans Affairs in the first Clinton administration), decried what an article later called the "tyranny of anecdotes." In this case, individual stories about the health of military veterans prevented members of Congress from focusing on the big picture of veterans' health—rather than the more episodic and localized issues related to particular states and Congressional districts. Kizer argued that "[i]f you govern by anecdote, you're chasing your tail because you're continually chasing that one person. You can't judge the process if you're looking at a series of one" (Laurent, 2002).

Successful performance-informed budgeting occurs only when those involved in the budget process move beyond mere production of information to the *use* of information to make decisions about resource allocation and management. This can only occur if all budgetary actors have effective incentives (and resources) to collect and use information. In fact, the incentive question is probably the most important one on which to focus on in analyzing the extent to which performance information will actually be used as an input in the various stages of budget decision-making. Aaron Wildavsky, writing in 1969 about an earlier US reform, argued convincingly that legislators would not use performance data because it was supplied; rather it was crucial to focus on the demand for analysis. Giving legislators data that they do not want and they did not ask for is not an effective means toward getting those data used to make legislative decisions (Wildavsky, 1969).

Inadequately focusing oversight

As legislatures recognize the extent to which power to make specific policy out of vague legislative direction is delegated to administrative agencies, they often develop a greater focus on oversight. Development of an oversight orientation allows legislatures to couple the grant of substantive policy-making with the capacity to discover what the executive branch has done with that power. In the US, for example, the recognition that administrative agencies were involved in policy-making led to specific efforts on the part of the Congress to provide checks on federal agencies. This effort was characterized by specific legislative reactions to bureaucratic power (such as the Administrative Procedures Act and the Legislative Reorganization Act, both passed in 1946) as well as a more general orientation toward greater oversight (see Rosenbloom, 2000). In fact, the 1946 Legislative Reorganization Act directed Congressional committees to exercise "continuous watchfulness" of executive branch agencies (Aberbach, 1990).

In nations with strong independent legislatures, oversight represents the key tool that legislatures can use to maintain control over bureaucratic agencies. Problems discovered during the oversight process can be rectified through subsequent legislative, or other, action designed to influence bureaucratic behavior. Legislatures have responded to this need for increased oversight by establishing organizations designed to provide information to them on the operations of government programs. One of the reasons for the establishment and subsequent expansion of the mandate of the General Accounting Office (GAO, now the Government Accountability Office) in the US has been the desire on the part of the Congress for increased information on the operations of federal programs and agencies. Prior to around 1970, the GAO had mainly been responsible for conducting financial audits. It has moved substantially into more "programmatic" audits over the past 30 years. This also has been a trend at the state level. A recent review of "performance auditing" in the states cited 12 examples of particularly strong performance audit capabilities in US state governments.[8]

Outside the US, virtually all countries use some oversight tools in reviewing actions by the executive branch. Pelizzo and Stapenhurst found, in their survey of 84 countries, that all of them employed some oversight tools, ranging from hearings, to "question time," to employing an ombudsman. In fact, in their systematic review of the use of 7 different oversight tools, they found that roughly 80 percent of these countries (67 out of 84) used at least 5 of these 7 oversight tools (Pelizzo and Stapenhurst, 2004, pp. 3–5; esp. Table 3, p. 5) (see Table 23.1 for a listing of some of these countries and the extent of the use of oversight tools). Many countries have either independent auditors (elected or appointed) or legislative staff ministries designed to assist in the performance of the oversight function. An example of this is Russia's Audit Chamber, which employs more than 500 staff and conducted more than 3,000 investigations between 1995 and 2000. (Although it should be noted that the nature of the work of the Audit Chamber seems to be more "financial" and less "performance" related (Remington, 2004).) The Polish Chief Board of Supervision is another example of an audit agency that is under legislative control (Olson, 2004).

Capacity to perform oversight and even oversight quantity are important, but quality must also be considered. Having the capacity for oversight is not the same thing as having the will to perform oversight in a systematic fashion. Systematic oversight—the kind that attempts to discern whether programs or agencies are performing well on a comprehensive basis—occurs with substantially less frequency than more episodic forms of legislative review. This is chiefly because systematic oversight is time consuming, and does not carry with it the kind of rewards that are associated with other forms of legislative activity. Therefore much of this oversight tends to be episodic, and focused on specific instances of wrongdoing or perceived failure that may or may not be indicative of any general trend within the agency or program. In fact, the criticism of Congressional oversight historically is that this oversight has not been focused on the extent to which programs have achieved their objectives. Rather, oversight has been used to focus attention on politically sensitive or high-profile issues.

Political scientists Matthew McCubbins and Richard Schwartz, in an attempt to describe this phenomenon, differentiated between two types of oversight as practiced by the US Congress. The first, which they called "police patrol" oversight, occurs when the Congress (or specifically a Congressional committee) attempts to discern how an agency is performing through routine reviews initiated by the committee. That is, the committee (or the committee staff) initiates a review designed to bring any necessary issues to light. The second case, "fire alarm" oversight, occurs when committees respond to issues that are brought to their attention by interested parties, and then hold hearings designed to "get to the bottom" of problems that have been raised (McCubbins and Schwartz, 1984).

The McCubbins and Schwartz thesis is that fire alarm oversight is more cost-effective than police patrol because it enables committees to spend their attention on those issues worthy of their attention, without the cost of discovery. Thus, they can focus on those issues that carry with them the most political benefit, but rely on constituents, the media, and others to bring those issues to their attention. In a later comprehensive analysis of Congressional oversight, Joel Aberbach found that the police patrol approach actually dominated, in spite of McCubbins and Schwartz's arguments to the contrary. Aberbach (1990, pp. 98–100) argues, interestingly, that the method may have changed over time, in response to resource scarcity; that is, that when resources are scarce, Congress is more likely to be proactive in engaging in oversight, as a means to justify reductions in expenditures for programs that are found lacking.

This would seem to offer some ray of hope for performance-focused oversight, particularly when budgets are tighter. It seems appropriate to observe, however, that in neither of these approaches does oversight represent an effort to look at programs or agencies "from the ground up." Thus, while "police patrol" oversight may involve more comprehensive investigations than "fire alarm," it is still constrained by the questions that the committee—or legislature—wants to ask. If the committee does not want to ask "How is this agency performing overall?" then the oversight agenda will not reflect this kind of broad attention to performance. In fact, in surveys that Aberbach conducted of members of Congress and their staffs, both identified "evidence of malfeasance in administration: scandal" as the top factor explaining a decision to conduct oversight hearings (Aberbach, 1990, p. 110).

In the end, then, once again the problem is one of incentives. In order for detailed oversight to occur, someone must believe that the benefits (in this case, more detailed knowledge about performance) are worth the cost (in this case, precious legislator/staff time and resources). This matters because if legislative oversight attention to what is "right" and "wrong" is to contribute to possible legislative and policy changes, it is necessary that these reviews be as "performance-focused" as possible. If, as discussed above, legislation is more explicit about specifying expected performance, it will be far more likely that oversight will also focus on these performance issues. A benefit of more detailed oversight, in fact, is that it would communicate to agencies that performance is important to the legislature. This is rarely the case at present. The cold fact is that there are currently limited incentives for members of oversight committees—in most countries—to focus in detail on the performance of programs or ministries. Such oversight has few electoral benefits for legislators who must stand for election on relatively short cycles. More emphasis on oversight is unlikely to occur without substantial attention to the question of *why* the legislature would want to conduct that type of oversight.

Another issue affecting the quality of oversight is the availability of information for the legislature. Following the trend set by Australia, New Zealand, and other (primarily OECD) countries, the last 15 years have seen substantial legislative impetus for performance measurement in the US and, therefore, for a greater performance focus in audit and evaluation. The Chief Financial Officers Act, the Government Performance and Results Act, the Clinger-Cohen Act and other laws had in common the notion that policy-makers and the electorate alike should better understand the relationship between resource use and results. The present Bush administration's initiatives share this focus, perhaps particularly manifested in the Program Assessment Rating Tool. This system requires after-the-fact knowledge of performance and inputs in order to succeed. If performance reports are required of agencies, to the extent that gaps between expected and actual performance are highlighted, the reports themselves will be useful tools for future oversight planning.

How to support performance in systems with independent legislatures

The reader might be forgiven at this point for believing that constraints presented by a separation of legislative and executive powers are so great as to make the development of a more performance-oriented budget system very difficult, if not impossible, in these nations. This concluding section takes a different view, arguing that there are actions that might be taken to contribute to a greater performance orientation (or, at a minimum, not detract from such an orientation). In most cases, government is essentially incremental, therefore incremental changes can have non-trivial consequences. There are four separate kinds of actions that might be taken to contribute to better public sector performance in governments with independent legislatures:

1. establish a clear schedule for authorizing or reviewing programs
2. invest in production of performance data, and legislative capacity to package and review these data
3. increase transparency of legislative decision-making
4. recognize the performance implications of legislative constraints placed on executive branch agencies.

Establish a clear schedule for reauthorizing programs

Public programs, once created, have a tendency to live in perpetuity. Establishing some set schedule for review by the legislature may, at a minimum, encourage attention to issues of program design, implementation and therefore performance. Systematic conduct of reviews has the added advantage of permitting comprehensive rather than piecemeal analysis of a given program. Among the important questions that can be asked are:

- What are the program's current objectives?
- Have the purposes of the program been achieved? If not, through what means, and when, is achievement likely?
- What is the historical relationship between funds provided for the program or agency and the achievement of objectives?

Establishment of clear objectives, and systematic reauthorizations, for a program can go a long way in focusing the funding and oversight agenda around comprehensive performance questions, rather than more narrow parochial concerns. Another means of ensuring such review may be to identify a specific sunset for programs, such that on some predetermined schedule (for example, every five years) legislation needs to be passed in order to keep the program operating. It is worth noting, however, that sunset reviews have a rather checkered history. The main problem with sunset proposals is that they need to be taken seriously in order to work. That is, if legislative committees comply with the letter of the sunset review, but not the spirit, the end result may be to create a lot of work for the executive branch without the desired benefits associated with more detailed program review.[9]

Invest in production of performance data and legislative capacity to review programs

Related to the periodic review of programs, if legislatures express more interest in specific measures used to gauge performance, this will send signals to ministries that will in turn focus their efforts. In such cases, involving the legislature as a full partner in establishing performance measures in the first instance will go a long way toward a unified, consistent approach to performance. Involving legislative stakeholders and affected interests up front—developing agreed-upon measures—can assist in avoiding the temptation to treat reform as an entirely executive-focused activity. It is also important to pay attention to the manner in which performance is reported to the legislature. Performance information is most likely to engage legislatures if it meets two tests. First, it should provide the legislature (or individual legislators) with information that they consider useful. Second, a limited number of high-level measures should be reported to that level. Nothing discourages attention to performance measures like reporting a large number of very detailed measures to people who neither need nor can digest that volume of detail.

There are also legislative capacity issues to consider. Legislatures that develop an internal capacity to both review executive branch performance data provided, and to initiate performance reviews of their own, are more likely to engage in discussions concerning legislative affects on performance. Legislative bodies should consider development of performance audit capacity independent of the executive branch as one means of providing the legislature with the ability to initiate and check performance data. Another reason that attention to institutional capacity is important is that legislatures may tend, particularly in systems with a separation of budgetary powers, to distrust information coming from the executive branch. In this context, if a legislative branch agency is empowered to review and summarize data for the legislative branch, those data are more likely to be viewed as accurate, and are therefore more likely to be used.[10] Bourdeaux (2005, p. 16) argues that legislative use of performance information is in part related to "legislative staff capacity, legislator ability to assimilate information, and developing a culture of trust," and concludes that the development of an independent or legislative staff capacity to audit or summarize performance data may be crucial to promoting legislative use of those data. Here there is hopeful news. Schick (2002) notes that the general trend in many countries is toward more staffing capacity for legislatures, and more independent audit offices that legislatures can rely on for information on fiscal and programmatic performance.

Some have argued that movements to legislate performance contribute to the development of an agreed-upon set of performance measures. Many countries that have adopted performance budget reforms have done so in response to the passage of laws requiring strategic planning and performance measurement. Certainly, this is true in Australia, New Zealand, and the UK. In the US, the Government Performance and Results Act at the national level, and the myriad state laws mandating performance measurement, have provided an impetus for the development of better measures and have created a number of forums for discussion of the appropriate measures that should be used.[11]

Increase transparency of legislative deliberations

In the end, perhaps nothing can encourage attention to performance more than transparency. If legislatures are making budget decisions based exclusively on input or output concerns, or based on incremental changes from past practice, the opportunity cost associated with those decisions must be illuminated. In any resource allocation process, the opportunity to ask the question "compared to what?" must be preserved. Here the role of citizens, interest groups, and the media is important in publicizing legislative budgeting practices, and making transparent the cost of paths not taken. Practically, incentives to change these practices must be connected to things that legislators value: for example, how they are viewed by constituents, and likely success in re-election efforts. Sunshine tends to be the enemy of inefficient resource allocation, not because inefficiency is "wrong" in some normative sense, but because it is embarrassing in a political sense. This potential embarrassment can be the factor that leads to the kind of demand for performance data that Wildavsky suggested is so crucial to the use of more performance information by the legislative branch.

Understand importance of budget execution and constraints created by legislatures

As important as it is for legislatures to specify performance expectations, to support the development of appropriate performance measures, and to make decision processes transparent, it is also important that they understand the ways in which legislative practices may impede agencies in executing budgets in an effective manner. Legislated constraints have the intention of, or at least result in, compromised executive branch flexibility in implementation. Overly-specified line-items can make it difficult for an agency to effectively manage spending. For example, fixed lines for hiring personnel versus contracting can prevent agencies from determining which represents the more cost-effective method to achieve a given outcome. Legislative prohibitions against reducing staff at given locations or closing particular facilities—and their mirror image, mandates for a given staff level or a particular amount of expenditure in a given location—inhibit the ability of the agency to manage resources well.

There are perfectly legitimate reasons for legislatures to try and constrain executive activity. Holding bureaucracies accountable is an important function of legislatures, particularly given the substantial power that can be delegated to bureaucracy. It is also important, however, to recognize the negative consequences of control.

Conclusion

Decisions by countries to empower legislatures to make decisions about the budget can make it more difficult to implement budgetary reforms that rely on common understanding of what is to be accomplished, common standards for review of competing claims for resources, and commitment to understanding the effects of the implementation of programs. The independence of legislatures, however, should neither be used as an excuse for inaction nor as a justification for taking power away from the legislatures. Rather, it is crucial to understand the incentives present for these independent legislatures and promote reforms based on the particular needs of these elected bodies. It is tempting, and also potentially incorrect, to assume that the answer must be to weaken the legislature at the expense of the executive.

On this last point, a recent analysis of the 50 US states conducted by Bourdeaux finds support for an earlier argument in the literature suggesting that more powerful legislative bodies actually exercise more budgetary responsibility that weaker ones. The argument, in brief, is that having both a strong legislature and a strong Governor may promote responsibility, and that strong gubernatorial powers (such as the line-item veto) may promote irresponsible behavior on the part of elected legislative representatives, which seek to shift the burden of responsibility for budget outcomes to the Governor.[12] Bourdeaux's own research concludes that "given authority over the budget, legislators may be more interested in reforms that promote administrative efficiency and that this engagement may positively affect implementation across multiple dimensions" (Bourdeaux, 2006, p. 136). If this is true, then the problem of squaring performance-informed budgeting and the separation of powers is not insoluble, but demands creativity in devising tools and incentives that make it more likely that legislative action will promote, rather than impede, government performance.

Notes

1. The author wishes to thank Rita Hilton and Marc Robinson for helpful comments, and Nathaniel Taylor for research assistance.
2. The Government Performance Project is a joint academic/journalistic evaluation of management of the 50 state governments, funded by the Pew Charitable Trusts. For current results of this project, see <http://results.gpponline.org>.

3. There are numerous other presidential countries that were not included in this study. These include, for example, Brazil, Guinea, Chad, Tunisia, and the Côte d'Ivoire.
4. See Joyce (2004) for such a comprehensive review of performance and the budget at each stage of the budget process.
5. There might be problems of political legitimacy through providing the unelected bureaucracy with more power than some would be comfortable with, but that is a different story.
6. The other three were: flexibility to pursue agency or government purpose; where predictable action is valued for linking managerial action to performance; and where new leadership requires institutional strength and support for effective change.
7. Paul Posner, then of the US General Accounting Office, described this relationship as motivating some members of Congress, in a presentation before a conference on performance-based budgeting, Queenstown, Maryland, March 31, 2003.
8. The Government Performance Project, at <http:/results.gpponline.org>.
9. Aberbach (1990) discusses the rather limited prospects for sunset to make much difference in *Keeping a Watchful Eye* (particularly pp. 205–7).
10. Grizzle and Pettijohn, in discussing the state of Florida's experience with budget reform, note that "[t]he Florida legislature's organizational culture includes beliefs that agency staff cannot be trusted to do what is right." See Grizzle and Pettijohn (2002, p. 56).
11. On US state-level requirements, see Melkers and Willoughby (1998).
12. The earlier articles cited by Bourdeaux include Barrilleaux and Berkman (2003), and Abney and Lauth (1998).

References

Aberbach, J., 1990, *Keeping a Watchful Eye: The Politics of Congressional Oversight* (Washington: Brookings Institution).

Abney, G., and T. Lauth, 1998, "The End of Executive Dominance in State Appropriations," *Public Administration Review*, Vol. 58(5), pp. 388–94.

Anthony, R., and D. Young, 1984, *Management Control in Nonprofit Organizations*, third edition (Homewood, Ill.: Irwin Press).

Appleby, P., 1949, *Policy and Administration* (Tuscaloosa: University of Alabama Press).

Barrilleaux, C., and M. Berkman, 2003, "Do Governors Matter? Budgeting Rules and the Politics of State Policymaking," *Political Research Quarterly*, Vol. 56(4), pp. 409–17.

Bourdeaux, C., 2005, "Do Legislatures Matter in Budget Reform?" Paper presented at the conference of the Association for Budgeting and Financial Management, Washington, November 7.

——, 2006, "Do Legislatures Matter in Budget Reform?" *Public Budgeting and Finance*, Vol. 26(1) (Spring).

Evans, D., 2004, *Greasing the Wheels: Using Pork Barrel Projects to Build Majority Coalitions in Congress* (Cambridge: Cambridge University Press).

Fiorina, M., 1989, *Congress: Keystone of the Washington Establishment*, second edition (New Haven: Yale University Press).

Grizzle, G., and C. Pettijohn, 2002, "Implementing Performance-Based Program Budgeting: A System Dynamic Perspective," *Public Administration Review*, Vol. 62(1) (January/February), pp. 51–62.

Harkin, J.M., 1982, "Effectiveness Budgeting: The Limits of Budget Reform," *Policy Studies Review*, Vol. 2(3), pp. 112–26.

Hilton, R.M., and P.G. Joyce, 2003, "Performance Information and Budgeting in Historical and Comparative Perspective," in *Handbook of Public Administration*, ed. B.G. Peters and J. Pierre (London: Sage), pp. 402–12.

Holmes, M., 1996, "Budget Reform Experience from the Past 15 Years." Notes for a presentation to the South African Conference on Expenditure Budget Reform, Pretoria, South Africa, April 1–2.

Ingraham, P., P. Joyce, and A. Donohue, 2002, *Government Performance: Why Management Matters* (Baltimore: Johns Hopkins University Press).

Joyce, P., 2004, *Linking Performance and Budgeting: Opportunities in the Federal Budget Process* (Washington: IBM Center on the Business of Government).

Laurent, A., 2002, "The Tyranny of Anecdotes," *Government Executive* (March 1), pp. 36–9.

Lee, R., R. Johnson, and P. Joyce, 2004, *Public Budgeting System*, seventh edition (Boston: Jones and Bartlett).

Lienert, I., 2005, "Who Controls the Budget: The Legislature or the Executive?" *IMF Working Paper* (Washington: International Monetary Fund).

McCubbins, M., and T. Schwartz, 1984, "Congressional Oversight Overlooked: Police Patrols versus Fire Alarms," *American Journal of Political Science*, Vol. 28, pp. 721–48.

Melkers, J., and K. Willoughby, 1998, "The State of the States: Performance-Based Budgeting Requirements in 47 out of 50," *Public Administration Review*, Vol. 58(1), pp. 66–73.

Olson, D., 2004, "Administrative Review and Oversight: The Experience of Post-Communist Legislatures," in *Legislatures and Oversight*, ed. R. Pelizzo and R. Stapenhurst (Washington: World Bank).

Pelizzo, R., and R. Stapenhurst, 2004, "Introduction," in *Legislatures and Oversight* (Washington: World Bank), pp. 1–9.

Premchand, A., 1999, "Budgetary Management in the United States and in Australia, New Zealand, and the United Kingdom," in *Handbook of Government Budgeting*, ed. R. Meyers (San Francisco: Jossey-Bass), pp. 82–115.

Remington, T., 2004, "Separation of Powers and Legislative Oversight in Russia," in *Legislatures and Oversight*, ed. R. Pelizzo and R. Stapenhurst (Washington: World Bank).

Rosenbloom, D., 2000, *Building a Legislative-Centered Public Administration: Congress and the Administrative State, 1946–1999* (Tuscaloosa: University of Alabama Press).

Schick, A., 1966, "The Road to PPB: The Stages of Budget Reform," *Public Administration Review*, Vol. 26(4), pp. 243–58.

——, 2002, "Can National Legislatures Regain an Effective Voice in Budget Policy?" *OECD Journal on Budgeting* (Paris: OECD).

Stein, R., and K. Bickers, 1995, *Perpetuating the Pork Barrel* (Cambridge: Cambridge University Press).

Wildavsky, A., 1969, "Rescuing Policy Analysis from the PPBS," *Public Administration Review*, Vol. 29 (March/April), pp. 189–202.

24
Formula Funding in Ethiopian Higher Education[1]

Kate Ashcroft

This chapter briefly describes a funding formula which has been developed for Ethiopia's higher education institutions. It places this in the context of Ethiopia's history and development stage and the particular requirements of its higher education context. It is argued that such a formula is an important element in the reform of Ethiopia's civic society by providing:

- protection for institutional autonomy and academic free speech, while requiring accountability
- transparency of funding decisions and limiting the potential for government bias or control
- support for the move towards a more flexible, responsive, outcome-oriented, customer-focused public service.

For 2,000 years Ethiopia was a feudal society ruled by a series of absolute monarchs, briefly interrupted from time to time by civil wars and from 1936 to 1941 by the occupation by Italian fascists. In 1974, a revolution deposed the monarchy and instituted a hard-line communist government (the Derg) committed to extreme centralization, the imposition of "scientific socialism," and nationalization/collectivization. This regime was particularly brutal and caused the deaths and detention of many academics and other intellectuals. Eventually, in 1991 this oppressive dictatorship was overthrown by a coalition of liberation fronts, of which the Ethiopian People's Revolutionary Democratic Front (EPRDF) has gradually developed into a grouping resembling a coherent political party. The EPRDF held its first elections in 1995 and received an overwhelming majority of the vote (Pankhurst, 1998). After three elections, each more open and democratic than the last, in 2005 the ruling political party once again won the most seats in parliament, albeit with a greatly reduced majority and amidst some controversy about the fairness of the election.

The liberation front took over a country that was in a parlous economic and social state with a tradition of extreme centralization and authoritarianism, poor leadership and management capability, deadening bureaucracy, widespread food insecurity, and periodic famine. There was little industry or private enterprise, a limited transport and communication infrastructure, poor health and education, many harmful traditional practices, and large increases in population and widespread illiteracy. In addition, the new government was confronted with a long-running border dispute with the newly independent Eritrea, which erupted into war between 1998 and 2000.

Ethiopia has an estimated total population of 72.4 million with diverse languages, culture, and topography. Out of the total population of the country, 15 percent is urban and 85 percent is rural. The population is growing at a rate of 2.7 percent so ever-more children and young people will require education, including higher education. About 85 percent of the population earn their living from rain-fed agriculture which constitutes 52 percent of GDP. The country is one of the poorest in the world with average income below $100 per year.

In 2003/04 there were 13.95 million primary school-age (7–14) children, of which 9.54 million are enrolled in formal primary schools (57 percent male and 43 percent female). Enrollments in grades 1–12 rose at about 9 percent a year between 1992–93 and 2001–02. In 2003/04, the gross enrollment of girls and boys in the first cycle secondary education (7–10) was 15.9 percent and 28.2 percent respectively, with a total gross enrollment rate of 22.1 percent. The gross enrollment in the 10–12 grade pre-HEI (higher education institution) program stands at about 2.3 percent. Less than 2 percent of the age cohort is currently enrolled in post-secondary education. Government plans a ten-fold increase in public technical and vocational education and training (TVET) over four years at a capital cost of $210 million for the construction of 71 new TVET facilities and five colleges.

There has been considerable development within Ethiopia's higher education system. It has grown in the last decade, from two universities to eight in 2004, and will soon expand to 22 with the opening of 13 new higher education institutions and an open university. Higher education enrollment has expanded from 42,132 to 172,111 in 2004/05. However, Ethiopia's gross enrollment figure remains low by world standards, at 1.5 percent.

There is a shortage of university educated leaders and staff in teaching positions at the secondary and university level. The percentage of qualified teachers at secondary level grades 9–12 was only 44.4 percent in 2003/04. Pressure to expand secondary education is building as a rising percentage of the age cohort completes primary education.

Despite these difficulties, over a 13-year period the ruling party has moved Ethiopia from a centralized dictatorship to a federated state with much power devolved to the regions, supported by elected regional government. At the same time the federal government has slowly liberalized the economy and society, allowing a somewhat freer press and some denationalizing of various state-owned enterprises, starting to free the financial system from over-regulation, reforming various aspects of the legal system, and, in 2003, initiating widespread reform of the higher education system.

In 2003 the federal government introduced a Higher Education Proclamation (Federal Democratic Republic of Ethiopia, 2003), establishing wide-ranging reforms to the higher education system and set up key agencies to guide and oversee the sector, including the Higher Education Strategy Center, the so-called "Brain Center" set up to advise government of higher education strategy and policy, and the Higher Education Relevance and Quality Assurance Agency (HERQA) to undertake quality assessment at subject level and institutional accreditation.

The reforms introduce elements of a quasi-market in higher education: learners are sharing the costs of higher education, and therefore are moving into a more customer-like relationship with higher education institutions; private higher education is expanding fast; and there is a gradual move away from state funding of public higher educational institutions through the encouragement of income-generation activity. The reforms also enable a move from extreme centralization towards institutional autonomy and internal devolution of budgets.

The Vice Minister for Higher Education emphasizes the higher education sector's central role in increasing and diversifying knowledge and competitiveness in a global and knowledge-based market, as well as its role in the protection of democratic culture and society (Teshome, 2003). This role is facilitated by the rapid and substantial investment in higher education by the Ethiopian government, the World Bank, and other donors. Ethiopia requires a massification of its higher education system in order that its graduates might manage the processes of a civil society, oversee its economic and social development, and provide the professional class of teachers, business people, health workers, and so on.

Greater autonomy for HEIs has been achieved by various measures: a board no longer chaired by the Minister of Education; more powers given to HEI Boards and institutions to hire, reward, and manage of all categories of staff; HEIs given more independence to determine their internal organizational arrangements; the introduction of a funding formula and a block grant (Federal Democratic Republic of Ethiopia, 2002).

The World Bank (2004) notes that before the reforms the government routinely appointed university Presidents and Vice Presidents; all academic staff were civil servants managed by the Civil Service Commission rather than the HEI; line budgets were allocated centrally and increased incrementally irrespective of numbers of students or quality; additional income generated was deducted from budgets; and quality assurance was not an explicit concern.

International context

There are a variety of models for a funding formula across the world. These vary from the relatively simple to the highly complex. Funding through formulas is unusual in Africa. In most countries, separate negotiations take place for each public institution between the senior managers of the institution and the Ministry of Planning and Finance (Mozambique is an example). In others the system is so small (that is, only one HEI in Namibia or Malawi, for example) that a formula would make no sense.

The funding of public universities in Kenya is an example of a very simple method. Currently it is based on a unit cost. The current unit cost of $1,600 is comprised of tuition of $1,147 and catering, accommodation, and other costs that amount to $453. The method does not take into account differential costs of the various degree programs (INHEA, 2005).

Australia provides another example of a relatively simple system. The Australian government has recently moved from funding public higher education through block grants determined largely on a historical basis to a formula based on student places "delivered" each year within various discipline categories (ten in all). Each higher education provider receiving funds under the formula enters into a funding agreement with the government, specifying the number of places and the discipline mix that the Australian government will support. The agreement is negotiated annually in the context of each provider's mission and strategic direction for course provision and labor market needs. Unfilled places from providers that consistently under-enroll will be redistributed to other higher education providers according to Australian Government priorities. Over-recruitment to programs will be funded provided that this does not exceed 5 percent. These new arrangements are accompanied by partial fee deregulation to allow higher education providers to charge fees to the student contribution level to a maximum determined by the Australian government. Students can fund their contribution through an income contingent loan supplied by a government agency (Department of Education, Science and Training, 2004).

In the UK, a much more complex system was introduced, though it is currently being reviewed. The Higher Education Funding Council for England (HEFCE) uses formulas to determine how most funding is allocated between institutions. Although subject categories are relatively crude (subjects are grouped into only four categories for funding purposes), complexity is created by the number of additional variables that are included as "premiums" in the formula. These include student-related factors, course characteristics, institutional characteristics, and the volume and quality of research. The money is provided in the form of a "block grant" which institutions are free to spend according to their own priorities within broad guidelines. The HEFCE is explicit in its expectation that institutions should not model their internal allocations on its own funding method. After an HEFCE grant, tuition fees are usually the other major source of funding for teaching. In the late 1980s and early 1990s, the UK government sought to use various performance indicators as a way to establish an accountability relationship with higher education (for example, access as indicated by numbers of students from state schools, deprived areas and low-participation areas, and disabled students; employment rates; year 1 student drop-out rates). The HEFCE derived a range of measures for these, but no consensus emerged on what should be the key indicators and how (or whether) they should relate to funding.

The HEFCE funding formula takes into account the number of students, subject-related factors (four categories are assumed), level of study, student-related factors, and institution-related factors. The HEFCE operates a plus or minus 5 percent tolerance band, restricting year-to-year changes in the unit of funding to that amount. In addition, the HEFCE makes separate allocations to recognize the additional costs of recruiting and supporting students from disadvantaged and non-traditional backgrounds, and students with disabilities. The formula takes into account additional costs associated with students on long courses, part-time students, and students on two-year foundation degrees. In addition, the formula takes account of additional costs associated with institutional factors. These result in the premiums for operating in London (weighting), small institutions, and those with old and historic buildings (HEFCE, 2004).

Along with various other countries, both Australia and the UK also have formulaic mechanisms to reward the volume and quality of research output. Since these are not relevant to Ethiopia at the present time, they are not described here.

Not all funding formulas for higher education are designed to reward performance. It is useful to distinguish those that are based on input (the costs of providing a service—in this case education—irrespective of whether that service produces desirable results); those that are based on outputs (for example, complete courses of study) and those based on outcomes (for example, the numbers of graduates provided to society). Using the term "outcomes" in this way is unconventional in higher education circles, where outcomes are usually used to refer to student learning (skills, knowledge, and understanding acquired) and tangible benefits of such learning (for example, graduates employed in professional capacities). Numbers of students graduating or successfully completing each year are seen in academe as indicative of, but by no means the same as, an outcome. They are therefore a "proximate" outcome (as opposed to a high-level outcome such as a more productive workforce and faster economic growth). The link between high-level outcomes and the effects of actions by a higher education institution is impossible to measure accurately. However, the level of student graduations is probably a good approximation that is sufficiently measurable to be used for funding purposes.

Funding formulas across the world may be based on inputs or outcomes. For example, the Australian model is based on output (those students educated each year), but not outcome (that is, those successfully graduating). The HEFCE model mixes measures of input (for example, the additional costs of certain forms of building) and of outputs (students being taught) and outcome (students successfully completing each year). Elsewhere in the world these are models based almost entirely on inputs. For example, in the US the Massachusetts model is based on prescribed student–faculty ratios by discipline, faculty workload, required direct support staff, and other non-salary costs in relation to credit hours. It estimates the level of need for support services based on assumed expenditures per student by service area and the estimated need for the physical plant level based space–facilities ratios, square feet of campus buildings, acreage occupied by the campus, historic rates of utility consumption, and the current replacement value of equipment used to maintain and operate the physical plant.

South Africa has introduced more goal-oriented public funding of higher education institutions through a revised and simplified funding formula accompanied by an increase the proportion of available funds for earmarked funding (that is, the proportion of funds outside of the formula). Its formula is based on the planned (full-time equivalent, or FTE) enrollments in different fields and levels of study at each HEI. Like the UK system, funding rates per FTE student place vary according to which of the broad fields the subject falls into and the level of study, and is standard for all institutions. Unlike the UK, initially the government rejected inclusion of student completions and research publications in the funding grid. It accepted the need to improve institutional efficiency and effectiveness, but the apartheid legacies of existing institutions meant that this would disproportionately benefit some HEIs and disadvantage others (Department of Education, 1997). However, more recently, 14 percent of the funding from the formula relates to graduation rates and 6 percent to institutional factors (Ministry of Education, 2004). This has added complexity to the formula.

Not all higher education systems are funded using formulas, but it does seem to be becoming more common across the world. There are a variety of reasons for this. First, a formula enables transparency and objectivity in funding decisions and so is a useful means of protecting institutional autonomy—individual HEIs are less subject to the whim of government. Second, a formula enables governments to fund larger and more complex systems where individual negotiations with HEIs to determine their "needs" would be impractical. Third, formulas, when based on outputs or outcomes, can be a useful means of ensuring greater focus on the core mission of HEIs and accountability for the allocation of taxpayers' money (generally educating sufficient numbers of students, preferably to graduation).

Countries (or states) express their objectives with respect to the operation of a funding formula differently. For example, the South African aims include the achievement of:

- an appropriate balance between institutional autonomy and public accountability
- procedures that are simple, transparent, flexible, and fair, and which are capable of being managed within the available and foreseeable capability of the Department of Education and the institutional councils, managements, and academic leadership.

The HEFCE's aims are to:

- increase opportunities for students from all types of backgrounds to benefit from higher education
- maintain and enhance the quality of teaching and research
- encourage universities and colleges to work with business and the community
- support diversity
- encourage efficiency in the use of public funding
- provide stability in funding from year to year.

However, when one looks in detail at the expressed principles, certain themes emerge: a commitment to institutional responsibility, efficiency, transparency, and fairness, student access to higher education, and so on.

There have been some undesirable consequences of funding higher education through formulas that have emerged across the world. Since certain outcome measures are used as "proxies" of quality as well as quantity (for example, student graduation rates), and because these measures are imprecise in these terms, institutional behavior may be distorted. Examples of this include a tolerance of "grade inflation" as a means of ensuring high undergraduate pass rates in UK HEIs and "salami publishing" (publishing several papers from the same data) in those countries where the volume of research output is rewarded (for example, some states in the US). Most countries have instituted agencies responsible for checking quality as well as quantity to ensure that standards do not slip: for instance, in the UK the Quality Assurance Agency checks the quality of taught programs and the research assessment exercise uses peer review panels to check the volume and national and international standing claimed for research output.

In addition, governments often put in place regulatory and other mechanisms to ensure that institutional behavior conforms to certain standards and practices: for example, student learning outcomes that must be included in programs in each subject; codes of conduct; student appeals processes and systems; published performance indicators, and league tables, as well as intake targets to particular programs. They often earmark funds in addition to those within the formula to incentivize HEIs to pursue particular government objectives such as increased access for disadvantaged groups or industry linkages.

Origins of the funding formula

Until 2005, HEIs were funded through a line budget, negotiated annually with the government. This meant that each HEI had to make a case based on need for an enlarged budget (an input model of funding), and this case might be accepted in whole or part by the government. HEIs were not free to vire between budget heads, even within the revenue account, and neither were they allowed a contingency fund. Therefore it was in their interests to overstate their needs in order to ensure that unexpected costs in any line would be covered.

Prior to 2003 the situation was even more constrained, with HEI staff being technically civil servants, employed by the state: the decision to employ a new member of staff or to replace an existing one, along with their terms and conditions, had to be approved by the Ministry of Education and fit within the Civil Service Commission structure. This ensured a very close relationship with the Ministry of Education, amounting to control and surveillance. In effect, HEIs were financed much as if they were core government departments.

It was also the case that different HEIs appeared to achieve very different rates of productivity, with some seemingly very much more expensive in terms of costs per student than others. However, there was no way of knowing whether these apparent inefficiencies were the result of the subject mix or levels of study within the various HEIs, or whether some were indeed delivering comparatively poor value for money.

There was a lack of focus on efficiency—it was not in any HEI's interest to seek economies: any end-of-year surplus could not be rolled over to the next year, and any apparent efficiencies would be assumed in the next year's budget. It was in the HEI's interests to spend up to the limit of every line in the budget and so to make the case for a larger allocation in the following year. Often there was a scramble to spend any remaining funds just before the end of the financial year. There was also a lack of focus on effectiveness—for example, there existed no penalty for high drop-out rates of students from programs. Indeed, a cynical HEI manager might welcome a high level of drop-out early in the year, since this would reduce the total costs of teaching.

A funding formula was seen as desirable by government as a means of encouraging greater efficiency and a greater focus on outcomes. It was welcomed by HEI managers as a means of enabling more rational decision-making and preventing unnecessary interference by government in institutional affairs. In addition, it was seen as essential for the block grant and a means to enable HEIs to reflect institutional performance objectives in the objectives and rewards for their staff. HEI managers, perhaps rightly, have been slow to introduce financial incentives for better-performing staff: such incentives can, and often do, have unintended consequences, especially for the morale and performance of the majority of (perfectly satisfactory staff) who do not receive the incentives. Rather, HEI leaders see the funding formula and the associated block grant as enabling better management and providing greater rewards for staff through devolved decision-making and the satisfactions of greater autonomy and reduced bureaucracy.

The Higher Education Proclamation (No. 351/2003) determined that there would be a funding formula for higher education and created the obligation to:

- decide on its form
- devise rules for its operation
- devise the transitional arrangements for its introduction.

At the time that the government chose the author to lead this development, she was Acting Director of the Higher Education Strategy Center (the leading strategy and policy development body for higher education in Ethiopia) and had just completed chairing the National Committee of Enquiry that had resulted in the *Report of the Higher Education Strategy Overhaul Committee of Inquiry into Governance, Leadership and Management in Ethiopia's Higher Education System* (Ashcroft, 2004).

During the early part of 2004, the author (with others) visited 13 higher education institutions: all six of the Ethiopian public universities funded through the Ministry of Education; one of the institutions that became a university during 2004; one that was upgraded in 2005; four of the private institutions that aspired to university status; and one higher education institution funded by a ministry other than the Ministry of Education. During the visits to public sector institutions under the Ministry of Education, a series of meetings was conducted with groups of senior managers, academic staff, and students. In all but one of the visits meetings were held with a group of administrative managers, and in all but two a tour of the site, which included the library, IT facilities, student facilities, a typical classroom, a typical laboratory, and other facilities, was organized. Where the institution was a multi-campus operation, these tours generally included visits to more than one site. In all institutions except two, individual meetings with the librarian, a science instructor, and the IT center manager took place.

In the visits to the institutions not funded by the Ministry of Education, a scheduled meeting took place with senior managers in three of the institutions and with middle managers in two of them. A tour of the site was given in three of them.

The author's knowledge and experience of the UK higher education system was used in developing the funding formula: she had worked as a senior executive and middle manager in four public sector higher education institutions, chaired a national university forum, and been a member of a variety of government working parties. In addition, she drew on her work as a member of the senior management team of the Higher Education Funding Council for England.

This combination of fairly extensive and in-depth knowledge of the Ethiopian higher education context and direct experience of the operation of a higher education funding system from the point of view of both the funder and of the recipient of funding (albeit in a northern context) proved essential to developing a workable funding formula for Ethiopia.

In developing the funding formula, it was decided that it would be undesirable to "import" a model from abroad wholesale, and, equally, it would be important to inform the development by direct experience of operating within a context that uses such a formula. Direct experience and knowledge of the higher education context, its mission, and the type of people and systems that it employs proved to be indispensable. The maintenance of particular values and principles are essential to higher education. It would be inappropriate to adapt a formula for the funding of (say) the police service to the higher education context—higher education by its very nature is staffed by professionals who value their autonomy highly and who must work in a context of high trust if they are to undertake the necessary research and curriculum innovation. This requires a "light touch" formula with the minimum of policy drivers if it is to create the environment necessary for innovative thinking and action.

The team developing Ethiopia's funding formula was very small: one administrator, one statistician, and the author. The first two members of the team had no higher education management experience: one had operated within a funding formula context abroad as a senior manager in a police force, and the other worked as an instructor within an Ethiopian university.

For this reason, the team relied heavily on appropriate models developed by others. The most useful were found to be a study undertaken by the Ministry of Education in Ethiopia and the World Bank (Merisotis, 2003) and experience in other parts of the world of introducing similar funding formulas, particularly the HEFCE.

As the model developed it was subjected to statistical modeling and refinement and presented for further comment to the Minister and Vice Minister responsible for higher education, Ministry of Education and Ministry of Finance and Economic Development staff, and senior managers of HEIs across Ethiopia. Their feedback was incorporated as appropriate.

Values informing the funding formula

There were three overriding values that informed all of the work on the funding formula.

Value 1: The formula should support institutional autonomy while providing appropriate accountability.

The introduction of a block grant based on a formula taking account of the output of graduates in various subjects is supportive of autonomy and accountability: it enables HEIs to make their own financial decisions, provides a public, objective, and transparent basis for funding, and therefore eliminates the fear of government penalties if HEI staff do not toe the party line, while providing accountability by making funding dependent on the achievement of outcomes.

In democratic countries, universities are one of the pillars that support freedom, alongside an elected government, a free press, and an impartial judiciary. It is no coincidence that academics are among the first to suffer in a dictatorship. Universities are one of the more important sources of new ideas, of new ways of conceptualizing work and society, and of the articulation of dissident opinions. Many of the notions stemming from the universities will be unacceptable to government (at least initially), but they are essential to providing the checks and balances on government power. Universities can only fulfill their democratic functions if there will be no penalty for expressing unpopular or novel ideas. A funding formula, by providing a public and objective measure of the funding for each HEI based on outcomes, takes away the fear of financial penalty for anything but underperformance. In an emerging and fragile democracy such as Ethiopia, this protection is critical.

Value 2: The formula should reward performance and outcome in a fair and consistent way.

The funding formula is also a tool for rewarding performance. Until the funding formula and its associated block grant are introduced, HEIs must negotiate line budgets with government. A line budget has the disadvantage that it focuses on activities, input, and processes, rather than outcomes and outputs. A formula based on (say) student graduation rewards those HEIs that positively respond to the call for expansion and that teach students well so that they do not drop out. Any funding formula may have unintended consequences. It is important to anticipate these as far as possible. One consequence of a formula that rewards throughput (student graduations) is that HEIs might be tempted to pass students who have not achieved the necessary standard. Another is that the student experience may be eroded in the pursuit of quantity. In other words, there is a danger that the quality and standards of the education provided may be compromised. Most governments that have used targets or performance-related funding have also put in place a mechanism to check quality. Such a formula was not a realistic proposition in Ethiopia until the establishment of the HERQA, which could provide assurance that each HEI's outcome standards were appropriate. The HERQA is presently developing methods and criteria to check that institutional processes are adequate to ensure standards and that the quality of teaching and learning practices and facilities are appropriate. If it fails to bring sufficient rigor to its task, there is a real danger that slackness rather than real performance may (at least in some instances) be rewarded.

Funding formulas like all other methods of funding can encourage undesirable behavioral consequences. They must use data that are relatively simple to measure. These cannot represent the full range of desirable institutional behavior. This may lead to a focus only on these factors and not on others (such as the qualitative elements of instructional behavior and student learning) that are equally desirable. In addition, no matter how sophisticated the formula, the values within it cannot be precise in all circumstances. Even if it is possible to measure exactly the average cost of (say) educating an undergraduate student in psychology to graduation, there will be some courses that contain more laboratory work than others and so are expensive, but nonetheless useful in that they turn out the kind of graduate that will be needed to fill (say) research posts. This means that the reward of all desirable outcomes is an unobtainable goal, but it should not be taken to imply that the reward of some important aspects of performance is not worthwhile.

It was decided that the education and graduation of students is the main job of HEIs in the Ethiopian context. Research and other outputs are less important to the country's development than the supply of trained personnel. For this reason it was decided to base the funding formula on the number of students successfully completing each year of study. At this stage, taking account of quality indicators (for example, graduate employment) would depend upon data that were completely unavailable. It was therefore decided to leave quality issues out of the funding equation and to rely on the newly established HERQA to ensure that desirable qualitative outcomes are achieved.

The funding formula does not need to include a process by which the government can control enrollments. At present students are centrally assigned to HEIs by the Ministry of Education, and therefore HEIs have no control over their intakes. At a later stage, it is likely that the assignment of students to programs will be devolved to HEIs, and so rules governing the formula will need to be adjusted to take account of intake targets as well student completions.

Value 3: The funding formula should encourage efficiency and effectiveness in the system.

The funding formula is a tool to create a more efficient and effective higher education system. Until 2005, HEIs bid for their funds on the basis of "need" and historic funding. They could not keep any element of funding that was unspent at the end of the financial year. This provided incentives for HEI managers to emphasize short-term financial planning, to neglect maintenance, to bid for the maximum number of staff they felt would be acceptable rather than seeking staff economies, to bid for large capital goods such as cars without examining the intensity of the use of assets already owned, and so on.

The current allocation funds HEIs in the form of a line budget. This creates the incentive to overstate funding needs in each line in order to provide a margin of safety should there be unplanned demands on the budget. It is also difficult to obtain additional money during the financial year so again HEIs are encouraged to bid for as much as possible at the start of the year. All of this contributes to inflexible financial management.

Income generation is formally encouraged, but any income generated tends to be assumed for the following year and subtracted from the amount allocated to the HEI. This is a strong disincentive to entrepreneurial activity: the HEI carries all the risks with few of the benefits.

These problems with the centralized funding system make it likely that a funding formula will encourage HEI managers to become more outcome-oriented, to act with prudence, to increase efficiency and effectiveness, to plan investment, and to assess the relative costs and benefits of various forms of action and give HEIs the flexibility to respond to changes in demand and to opportunities.

The funding formula is also essential to enable the ministry to manage the expansion of the system. The government could negotiate detailed line budgets with the management of each HEI, monitor line by line the HEI's spending, and approve each staff appointment against the budget when there was only a handful of HEIs to deal with. Once the number of HEIs increased, this process became unmanageable. A formulaic system of funding allocation became essential to allow freedom to HEIs to determine their own spending within the funds allocated, with accountability through financial and quality audit systems.

Principles underpinning the funding formula

These overriding values are reflected in the ways that the principles below are actualized. Some of these principles proved more difficult than others to operate in practice. Each of them is discussed in some detail below.

Principle 1: The formula should be based on a unit (base) price which reflects the costs of teaching within the subjects and includes weightings to reflect subjects that are more expensive to deliver and other additional expenses.

Since it is important that HEIs graduate students in a variety of subjects and not just in those that are cheaper to teach, the model has to reward graduation in different subjects at different levels. It is not possible to assess accurately the actual costs of subject teaching within Ethiopia. There was a limited amount of research done by the World Bank and the Ministry of Education in 2003, but the data provided by HEIs suffer from problems of validity and incompleteness, and few HEIs took advantage of the opportunity to comment upon the provisional results.

The author therefore requested each public sector HEI to provide detailed data on the costs per student of teaching in various undergraduate and postgraduate subjects and the level of funding for research. A one-day workshop was held for the Administrative Vice Presidents and Heads of Finance of the HEIs to outline why the data were needed, to present the format for recording the data, and to answer questions and queries with respect to the data collection instrument and any other matters. Representatives from all but one of the HEIs attended. Despite this good attendance, only four HEIs responded by sending data and of these only one presented complete data. The problem is that HEIs allocate their funding according to categories of spending (that is, according to the "lines" within the budget determined by government), and not to cost centers. There is little devolution to departments, and so budgets and all but minor spending tends to be approved centrally. They know what was spent on (say) stationery across the institution, but have few records of what was spent in total by any particular department.

The approach has to be one where funding is allocated in a fair and transparent way, with no institutional "favorites." This implies that benchmarking of costs must be undertaken. In a small system such as Ethiopia all the HEIs could be "benchmarking partners," but the benchmarking data remain chronically weak. Given this weakness of the data, a decision had to be made as to whether to delay the development of the formula for one year to allow HEIs to collect better data. However, although HEIs had been asked to provide similar data in 2003, that provided in 2004 showed no improvement. HEI managers had known for a year that the funding formula was to be introduced and the data that would be needed to support it. HEIs had not managed to create systems to collect necessary data in the intervening period. After consultation it was felt that the HEIs will only start to collect data department by department when the funding formula is introduced and they need to know and control such costs. While a line budget is in existence, they will continue to collect and analyze data line by line. Therefore it was agreed with the HEI Presidents and the Vice Minister for Higher Education not to delay the development of the formula.

Data for the relative costs for masters and doctoral programs were particularly weak: these courses had been subsidized from the undergraduate program to an unknowable extent. In developing advice to the government about the weightings for Masters and doctoral programs, the author therefore took experience from elsewhere in the world and the anecdotal accounts of the higher costs of Masters programs in Ethiopia (the need to concentrate expatriate staff in these programs, the need for small class size, and so on) to come up with a recommended weighting.

Ethiopian higher education institutions declared remarkably low levels of spending on research and consultancy. If these data are a true reflection of the actual level of spending, they represent an undesirably small proportion of institutional budgets. Little attempt has been made by HEIs to separate costs for research and consultancy from those for teaching and learning and it is likely that some costs (especially overheads) have been grossly underestimated. In addition, the level of research activity as revealed by the rate of publication is startlingly low. This is evidence that Ethiopian HEIs are not undertaking the scale of research either to inform policy and practice, or to develop as the economic engines and income generators that the country needs. A level of funding for research and consultancy was therefore recommended higher than that suggested by the data, to allow HEIs to start in a small way to undertake research that could be the basis for consultancy and knowledge transfer of the kind that generates substantial economic activity in most modern HEI systems.

The estimated costs were a less than ideal model on which to base the formula; however, they represented the best information available at the time. The data will need to be tested and improved by empirical tracking of costs over time. HEIs and the Ministry of Education will need to develop systems to routinely collect actual delivery costs, including indirect costs such as maintenance and equipment costs, HEI management and administration, student services, and so on. Even so, the pattern of costs might reflect resource availability rather than desirable levels of spending.

Principle 2: The funding formula should be as simple as possible, with relatively few variables.

There have been difficulties found with complex funding formulas in other countries from the point of view of rewarding performance: the opportunities for game playing by HEIs are great and some factors that may be rewarded relate to increased input costs not desirable outcomes. In addition, increased complexity increases the accountability burden and requires increasingly sophisticated management information systems of the kind that do not exist even in embryo form in Ethiopia.

Reviews of the operation of funding formulas tend to increase complexity. For example, in its recent review of the funding formula in England, the HEFCE (2005) describes the current formula funding method as an attempt to resolve tensions, and sometimes conflicting objectives: seeking to reflect government priorities and giving institutions scope for discretionary actions. Many of the issues which HEIs identified during the review could only be resolved by a much more finely grained formula funding method, which would increase the burden on both the sector and the funding council. In addition, the HEFCE has concluded that more detail in the formula funding method would provide less flexibility for institutions to manage their allocations and changes in the numerous premiums and price groups reduce predictability and created difficulties for some HEIs.

In seeking to develop a funding formula for Ethiopia, it was decided that simplicity should be a guiding principle, first as a matter of pragmatics (there are simply no data to support a more complex formula) and second, those systems with simpler formulas do not seem to be less efficient than those with complex ones. There is no doubt that complex formulae create an accountability burden on institutions, and in the Ethiopian context, HEI managers have insufficient systems and management capacity to manage such complexity. In addition, the complexity of some systems (such as in the UK) undoubtedly favors certain HEIs (while disadvantaging others), but it is uncertain that the inclusion of many of the variables benefits the country as a whole: it is not clear why the taxpayer should pay more for students in specialist colleges or those educated in London, since there is no evidence that the graduates disproportionately benefit the economy or society.

On the other hand, there are some variables that are unavoidable in any formula that rewards performance. Some allowance must be made for the different costs of teaching students in different subjects to graduation. This can be approached in two ways:

1. looking at the actual costs of different subjects and developing a formula that reflects each of these
2. looking at the average costs associated with different forms of delivery (for instance, classroom-based courses, laboratory-based courses, courses that include significant clinical elements) and developing a formula that reflects each of these.

The problem with the first of these approaches is that the formula would end up with a large number of individual categories (one for each subject or broad group of subjects) and that new weightings will need to be devised for any new subject introduced into the curriculum. The advantage is that the cost of teaching each individual subject is likely to be reflected more accurately in the formula than with the second approach. In Ethiopia, the data are insufficient to support this model and therefore this model was not recommended.

The problem with the second approach is that the weighting for each category would reflect only very approximately the actual costs of teaching any particular subject. The advantage is that it requires relatively fewer categories (subjects can be arranged into a few academic discipline clusters according to the features of their delivery) and therefore would be much simpler to administer and new subjects could be easily allocated to a particular weighting band according to the main teaching approaches within the subject. Allowance could also be made for the higher costs associated with Masters and PhD programs compared with undergraduate programs. Despite its problems, this was the approach that was recommended in the Ethiopian context. However, it must be recognized that, since prices will be at best approximate, some HEIs will be tempted to shift the mix of the programs they offer towards those where they make a "profit." The protection against this in the Ethiopian system is the central allocation of student intakes that makes such "game playing" difficult. If (as expected) in the near future the government devolves student admissions to HEIs, this system will need to be replaced by a contractual relationship whereby each HEI agrees to achieve student targets within different subject programs.

Principle 3: The formula should be based on rough costings and will not be accurate with respect to the actual costs of teaching any or all subjects with any or all HEIs.

The reward for student outcome is intended to operate at institutional level. This means that the reward has to be commensurate to the outcome of an HEI as a whole, and not necessarily fair in terms of any particular subject department (it is up to the HEI to distribute its resources between departments fairly). This means that the costing on which rewards are to be based can be quite rough and ready, provided they are broadly appropriate. In the proposal, each student within each of the subjects within an HEI will be funded according to one of seven "price groups," as shown in Table 24.1.

Table 24.1 Funding formula price groups

	Group 1, least expensive subjects (classroom-based subjects)	*Group 2, intermediate subjects (those requiring more than 30% supported placement or laboratory work)*	*Group 3, more expensive subjects (dentistry, veterinary science, and clinical medicine)*
Undergraduate	Price Group A Least expensive, anchored at 1	Price Group B Intermediate	Price Group C Intermediate
Masters	Price Group D Intermediate	Price Group E Intermediate	Not applicable
PhD, MD, etc.	Price Group F Intermediate	Price Group G Most expensive	Not applicable

The choice of only three subject groupings for funding purposes is rather more crude than is common in the rest of the world (the UK and South Africa use four and Australia uses ten), but the use of three "levels" (undergraduate, Masters, and PhD/MD) is fairly conventional. However, all formulas group subjects into categories and therefore in all systems the actual costs of teaching any student may be lower or higher than the average for that weighting band. The assumption was that an individual HEI will find that the formula benefits it with respect to the teaching costs associated with graduating students for some subjects but disadvantages it with respect to the costs within other subjects. Thus, it is likely, though not certain, that the overall effect will be broadly neutral. As stated above, such approximation may encourage profit-maximizing and loss-minimizing behavior unless government either allocates student intakes or sets intake targets at program level. If it is found that the advantages of such a crude categorization of subjects are outweighed by the disadvantages (though this is by no means certain), Ethiopia may decide to develop more precise categories as data become available.

The approximate nature of weightings within the formula compared with actual costs for any particular subject implies that HEIs should not slavishly follow the formula funding when allocating funding to subject departments internally, but rather use it as a rough guide. It also requires that the funds should be allocated in the form of a block grant and HEI managers and boards should be free to allocate them as they see fit, provided that such allocations are transparent and conform to principles of probity and sound financial management.

Principle 4: The formula should be designed to cover all institutional costs except for a limited number of specific items, which should be funded separately.

The reward to an institution from the funding formula is intended to cover a range of indirect costs. Thus the HEI could allocate the budget derived from the funding formula to cover matters such as administrative costs, heating, lighting and utilities, student services, maintenance, repairs, equipment, library, ICT, and other overheads, as well as faculty expenses. This creates an incentive to reduce the subsidy for items unrelated to the academic mission of the HEI such as students' food and lodging, since the HEI will then be able to allocate more resources to its core business.

The proposal for a funding formula therefore is not dependent on activity-based costing, except so far as teaching students to graduation could be seen as "activity." It places the responsibility for activity-based costing with institutions themselves: they will have to develop their own budgetary allocations to departments with very different functions, including assumptions about indirect costs. In doing this they will determine not only what the costs *are*, but also what they *should be*. This will encourage targeted action on aspects such as the ratio of administrative staff to academic staff: at the moment this ratio (2:1) is very high.

It is important that the values within the formula should not be adjusted to take account of the income generation activity of an institution (that is they would not be adjusted downwards as HEIs develop alternative forms of income). Such additional income could be used to add value or quality to the basic provision by government or to invest in areas of excellence for the future. Thus income generation (except for income from the national system of cost sharing with students) would not affect the funds provided to an HEI by government. This requires that HEIs can hold over any unspent budget to the following year.

In addition, if the formula is to be simple and manageable, a separate system remains necessary for the allocation of funding to run university hospitals, for research and consultancy, for major capital works, for incentives to achieve various government policy objectives, and for funds to support the establishment and initial support for new higher education institutions. In the medium term, a fair and competitive system will be needed to reward relevant and high-quality research and income generation through consultancy. This would provide the incentive to ensure that HEIs develop the kind of research culture and profile that is necessary for income generation through knowledge transfer.

In the short term, one option is for the funding for research and consultancy to come from a premium on the base price of a research student. This has the advantage of simplicity, but it was not recommended as a model, since it relies on the assumption that the number of research students has a linear relationship to the volume and quality of research and consultancy occurring in an HEI. This is highly doubtful: as the numbers of Masters and PhD students increase in a particular university, it might receive additional funding that was not justified by the levels of research produced. Such a system might also encourage an HEI to recruit more research students than it could realistically resource or accommodate.

Another model is to estimate the desirable level of funding for research infrastructure that could "kick-start" the level of research activity and publication for HEIs to develop as significant producers of income from knowledge generation and transfer, and as sources of policy advice and evaluation, and to allocate this to HEIs as a lump sum. This has the advantage of simplicity, but it has the disadvantage that there is no guarantee that it would be used appropriately. The way chosen to ameliorate this disadvantage was to require each HEI to develop a satisfactory strategic plan to develop research capacity and an action plan to spend the funds allocated.

Principle 5: In the initial stages, the formula should be based on those data that are presently available.

The formula might have been driven by rewarding or penalizing all sorts of variables: those students who enter; those who fail to complete each year successfully, and those who graduate; the type of student (for example, sex, regional origin, disability, entry qualifications) and the additional costs of teaching them; and institutional characteristics such as size and location. Experience elsewhere suggests that the advantages of a complex funding formula are not great and that such complexity encourages "game playing" by institutions to maximize their funding by reclassifying activity to profitable categories. A more complex formula might lead to a more accurate allocation of the funds for teaching with respect to actual costs, but it is likely that each premium is an inaccurate refection of costs in the case of any one HEI. Where there are many variables in the formula, most institutions will benefit from some premiums but not others. Since the total "pot" of funding for higher education is unlikely to increase with the number of premiums, the effect on the funding of most HEIs is probably broadly neutral.

In Ethiopia, many of these data were not easily available. The number of students enrolled was easily obtained from HEI registries and checked by the Ministry of Education against those allocated to HEIs by subject. However, it is intended that the formula should reward performance and so the allocation is to be based on the numbers of students graduating and successfully completing each year, rather than on those entering. These data can also be easily obtainable from registries and can be audited by the HERQA during accreditation visits. This should eliminate any incentive for HEIs to pass students not reaching required standards.

Non-completion rates could have been dealt with either by funding "drop-out" students for half of any year, or by not funding them at all. Since funding students for half of any year they fail to complete successfully would be paid for by reducing the funding for other students (the total "funding pot" being finite), the effect on the total funding for the average HEI would be broadly neutral whichever system was used. Eliminating all funding for students who fail to successfully complete the year has the advantage of simplicity and fits with the notion of rewarding outcomes. This was chosen as the method of calculation.

Principle 6: Incentives for different activities should be funded through a top-slicing of the funds available for learning and teaching, rather than through the formula itself.

All governments wish to influence the direction of higher education, and indeed, as representatives of the society at large, government has the right to do so, provided this right does not conflict with other rights such as academic freedom. It was decided that government should exercise this right through the operation of a top-slice of 10 percent of the overall higher education allocated to HEIs on the basis of their contribution to government priorities. At the present time these priorities include access for disadvantaged students and improving graduation rates. It was decided that the top slice will become an incentive fund outside the formula.

The World Bank's analysis of the proposed funding formula supported the idea that incentives for various forms of activity should not be included in the funding formula:

> *Non-base funding* comes in addition to the funding provided through the base formula. This type of funding is usually a pool or pools of resources directed to specific purposes, and is therefore somewhat better suited to steering. It also offers more flexibility than base formula funding and can be adapted to address new needs and goals. There are several different types of non-base funding approaches. These include earmarked funding, which is funding dedicated or earmarked for a specific program, mini-formulas, which use an algorithm separate from the base formula to determine how funding is allocated to institutions, and other approaches that are on top of the base formula. In the compass analogy, these non-base funding approaches can often be more precise in targeting coordinates. (Merisotis, 2003)

A system of top-slicing has the additional advantage that incentives can reflect changing national and government priorities (for instance, the support of disadvantaged students and the maintenance of community-based programs) without disrupting the main formula.

The World Bank suggests that HEIs should be rewarded for surpassing previous performance:

> Such steering mechanisms tend to work best when they use the baseline performance of an individual institution as the starting point for determining the amount of funding provided. In other words, the pool of resources does not reward those who are already advantaged—it rewards attainment of policy goals in relation to where that individual institution was previously. (Merisotis, 2003)

The problem with this approach in the Ethiopian context is that HEIs are not responsible for the allocation of students and therefore have very limited control over the admission of students from disadvantaged groups, whilst carrying the additional costs that their proper support necessitates. In addition, HEIs have made markedly different amounts of targeted effort to support disadvantaged students. A system which requires HEIs to surpass their previous best would disadvantage those who have good systems already in place.

Another method of allocating incentive funding—used, for example, in the UK—is to set aside funds to be allocated by a competitive bidding process in which each HEI bases its bid on a strategic plan for the utilization of funds and/or past performance in that area. Such a system would require expert staff and expensive and sophisticated assessment systems that do not yet exist in the Ministry of Education. Given the relatively small amount to be devoted to incentive funding, and given that the intention of the new system is to reward performance and outcome, it is not clear that it would have substantial advantages over a simpler system.

It was therefore proposed that 10 percent of the funding available for higher education should be top-sliced to create an "incentive fund" and allocated formulaically (per head) to compensate HEIs for the additional costs of teaching and supporting disadvantaged students, and to reward better-than-average graduation rates for disadvantaged students and students in each price group. This top-slice arrangement allows the government some leeway and to change the criteria in the future if it wishes.

Principle 7: As far as possible, individual HEIs should not be destabilized by the way the formula funding is introduced.

A key issue raised by outcome funding is the funding risk created for the HEIs, since they are not entirely in control of their outcomes: in this case, students' successful completions of each year and final-year graduations. In part these depend upon factors such as the quality of intake that are determined by government rather than by the institution itself. For example, the Ministry of Education is planning to open 13 new HEIs in the country at the same time as incentives are planned for the expansion of the private sector. If, at the same time, more disadvantaged students are admitted, there is a strong possibility that factors outside of the control of the HEIs will lead to lower graduation rates and more failure at the end of each year of study. Provided that there are not systematic differences between the intakes of different universities, and all are affected to the same extent, and provided that none decides to compensate by lowering examination standards, the net effect on each may not be great, but these provisos do create risk. This risk implies that there must be measures put in place to protect HEIs from the effects of the funding formula and to allow them time to adjust to different levels of funding.

A preliminary analysis of the data produced by the World Bank and Ministry of Education indicates a large variation in the levels of funding per student received by different HEIs within Ethiopia. HEIs could be destabilized or experience unearned windfall profits by the precipitous introduction of a formula. The draft formula was tested and adjusted in the light of historical funding allocations to HEIs in Ethiopia, but it is clear that it should be further reviewed as data became more accurate. Thus, a precipitous introduction of the formula with no safety net could unfairly penalize certain HEIs. In addition, HEIs need time to adapt their costs to any changes in income caused by the introduction of the funding formula. Therefore, it is desirable that, where the historical funding for an HEI implies a unit price markedly different from that which it would receive through the formula, the funding the HEI actually receives should gradually be adjusted over a number of years until it conforms to the formula.

The World Bank analysis suggests that one way of ensuring that HEIs are not destabilized is to use a three-year rolling average of their student numbers within the formula.

> To ensure that there is not a "drop off the cliff" phenomenon that results from annual fluctuations, the formula instead could use a simple three-year actual

> rolling average. The three-year rolling average would be based on an average of each of the three factors for the three years prior to the current year. For example, to calculate the number of diploma and degree program graduates for 2004, the numbers from 2002, 2001, and 2000 would be averaged. This would help to promote system stability as it continues to transition and transform. (Merisotis, 2003)

The problem with this approach is that, in a context of extremely rapidly expanding student numbers, those institutions that had responded positively to the call for rapid expansion would be disadvantaged.

It was therefore proposed that there should be a transitional period to enable HEIs to adjust to the effects of the formula on their funding. In each year the average unit funding an HEI receives for each student through the funding formula will not vary by more than plus or minus 5 percent over that in the previous year, plus an adjustment (determined each year by the government) for inflation and other factors.

Next steps

It is recognized that as Ethiopia's system becomes more sophisticated and allows additional different modes of study, and as more data become readily available, a more sophisticated formula may be needed. In the introduction of any new system there will be teething problems and adjustments will the needed. In addition, HEIs will need considerable guidance and training in its operation.

It is therefore proposed that a full review and evaluation of the operation of the formula should be undertaken after the first and second year of operation and necessary adjustments should be made to the weightings and some of the rules governing the formula's operation. This review should take particular account of the fact that the data for the costs of postgraduate courses were especially weak and therefore the weightings were in large part based on anecdotal evidence.

Conclusion

As the development of the formula progressed and discussion occurred it became clear that its introduction offered very real advantages over the previous system. HEI managers supported its introduction and saw it as a prerequisite for the block grant, which in turn offered them a number of efficiencies. In particular they saw the formula as an important protection for HEI autonomy.

The Ministry of Education supported the introduction for various pragmatic reasons (for example, it was a prerequisite for World Bank support and the fact that as the sector expands the ministry can no longer monitor all the various line budgets and so has to delegate this responsibility to the HEIs themselves) but also for other more idealistic reasons such as enabling transparency of funding decisions and encouraging the delegation of budgets which is seen as an essential element of HEI good management. The government is committed to developing more customer-centered and outcome-oriented public services, to HEIs being funded for outcome not on the basis of history, and to develop a more responsible approach to students, who should be seen as income earning rather than as expenses.

Historical funding allocation provides an incentive to maximize expenditure and gives no incentive for generating income—it is agreed that this should cease and HEIs become more cost conscious and make more rational choices as to priorities as they exercise the freedom to allocate internal budgets. In turn it seems likely that this will result in better forward planning and the ability to respond more quickly to changing priorities and to offer more attractive salaries for instructors in "hard to recruit" subjects such as ICT. In short, the formula funding and the associated block grant provides incentives for cost saving and income generation by HEIs (underspending and income are not clawed back). On the other hand, HEIs must act responsibly and develop financial systems: they cannot turn to government to bail out unexpected expenses, and therefore must generate surpluses and carry these over from year to year.

It will be found that some HEIs generate higher than average teaching costs. They will have to instigate efficiencies, some of which may be painful and may affect quality in the short term: for example, increasing class size and closing courses that recruit too few students. Others may be more desirable, such as changing teaching and learning methods to reduce class contact time, and a more intensive use of resources and targeting administrative costs, so that a higher proportion of spending goes on the academic mission.

In any case, HEIs will need to rapidly develop systems and processes that are largely absent at the moment. These include mechanisms for making rational decisions about matters such as the amounts to be spent on different activities, staff incentive schemes, and investment in the future. They will be able to target reductions in certain expenditures and increase others. Some may start to undertake asset audits. Importantly, they will need the Management Information System to monitor cost commitments and outgoings, accurately track students, and record the costs of each kind of activity. Preparation for the change should include budget monitoring training for all budget holders so that all managers can read and monitor accounts and marketing systems to attract fee-paying students and consultancy. Each of these requirements is a step change from the present position. In total, the formula forces a modernization of the entire system that could move it in the direction of better governance and management.

The most important benefit of the funding formula may be that it directs institutional attention to the achievement of outcomes that the country needs (more trained personnel). In the longer term the formula may take account of outcomes such as graduate employment, HERQA quality assessments and research volume, quality, and relevance.

In summary, the benefits to HEIs are potentially great, but so are the risks. If managers do not rise to the challenge of devolved budgets, good budget planning and monitoring and more strategic planning for the future, HEIs may end up with resources badly utilized, unmanageable bureaucracy, and crisis management. HEIs may be tempted to "game play" and undesirable institutional behavior may be encouraged.

The government too must develop its infrastructure to allocate its funding according to the formula. So far it has failed to do so. The introduction of the formula was planned for July 2005 but has been delayed for more than a year.

It seems likely that the potential benefits of a funding formula depend upon it being designed to suit the context (the country and the sector) and being informed by best practice from across the world. This implies that consultants from abroad working on such a design will need experience of the sector and knowledge of funding formulas and how they work, but they will also need to spend time in the country, not just enquiring into the financial context, but developing an in-depth understanding of the management; values; and historical, sociopolitical, and cultural contexts in which the formula will operate. Even with such knowledge, they will need to consult often and widely so that unintended consequences of different approaches can be understood and so that the benefits of the change can be maximized.

Note

1. The full document, *The Introduction of a Funding Formula for Teaching and Learning in Higher Education Institutions in Ethiopia,* can be found on <www.higher.edu.et>.

References

Ashcroft, K. (Chair), 2004, *Report of the Higher Education Strategy Overhaul Committee of Inquiry into Governance, Leadership and Management in Ethiopia's Higher Education System* (Addis Ababa: Ministry of Education).

Department of Education, 1997, *A Programme for Higher Education Transformation White Paper on Higher Education* (Pretoria: South African Department of Education).

Department of Education, Science and Training, 2004, *Fact Sheet: Commonwealth Grant Scheme—Commonwealth Course Contributions* (Canberra: Australian Department of Education, Science and Training).

Federal Democratic Republic of Ethiopia, 2002, *Education Sector Development Program II (ESDP II)* (Addis Ababa: Ministry of Education).

——, 2003, *Proclamation No. 351/2003: Higher Education Proclamation* (Addis Ababa: Federal Democratic Republic of Ethiopia).

HEFCE, 2004, *How the HEFCE Allocates its Funds* (Bristol: Higher Education Funding Council for England).

——, 2005, *Review of the Funding Method for Teaching Aims of the New Method and Progress of the Review* (Bristol: Higher Education Funding Council for England).

INHEA, 2005, *Higher Education Country Profiles.* International Network for Higher Education in Africa, <www.bc.edu./bc_org/asp/soe/cihe/inhea/profiles.htm>.

Ministry of Education, 2004, *A New Funding Framework: How Government Grants are Allocated to Public Higher Education Institutions* (Pretoria: South African Ministry of Education).

Merisotis, J.P., 2003, *Higher Education Funding in Ethiopia: An Assessment and Guidance for Next Steps.* The World Bank Africa Technical Families UPI No. 00000258377, August.

Pankhurst, R., 1998, *The Ethiopians: A History (Peoples in Africa)* (Oxford: Blackwell).

Teshome, Y., 2003, "Transformations in Higher Education: Experiences with Reform and Expansion in Ethiopian Higher Education System." Keynote paper at conference "Improving Tertiary Education in Sub-Sahara Africa: Things That Work," Accra, Ghana.

World Bank, 2004, *Higher Education Development for Ethiopia: Pursuing the Vision* (Washington: World Bank).

25
Wage Spending Flexibility in Low-Income Countries[1]

Matt Davies, Marijn Verhoeven, and Victoria Gunnarsson

A fundamental characteristic of performance budgeting is the shift from input control toward accountability for results. There are many types of performance budgeting with much variation in their complexity and ambition (see Chapter 1). All, however, carry with them a presumption that those in charge of policy implementation at the disaggregated micro level—primarily, managers of government departments and agencies—are held to account for what they are achieving rather than for remaining within prescribed input limits. The basic idea is that such managers understand better than decision-makers at the central level how to organize their inputs to achieve specific objectives. In contrast, centralized control of budgets at the line-item level is believed to stifle innovation at the micro level, move incentives toward spending rather than economy, and dilute the focus on policy objectives (Roberts, 2003).

Human resources are a key input for government output, and effective performance budgeting includes devolving employment and compensation decisions to managers at the micro level. They need to be able to trade-off labor inputs against other inputs, and to vary the type of labor and its compensation to be able to efficiently produce those outputs that contribute most to policy objectives.

Thus, effective performance budgeting requires flexibility in the use of human and other resources at the micro level. In particular, such micro-flexibility is important for the efficiency and effectiveness of spending because it: (1) facilitates a more efficient mix of labor and non-labor inputs, thereby contributing to technical efficiency; (2) permits the reallocation of human resources between different programs and purposes to yield a more optimal mix of outputs, thereby contributing to allocative efficiency; and (3) permits remuneration and employment practices which motivate government employees more effectively.

In low-income countries (LICs), employment and compensation decisions are often made separately from other input decisions, and are typically highly centralized. Non-wage inputs are determined through the budget process (in a number of cases, the decision-making on capital spending is also different from that on current spending). But it is typical for decisions on hiring, firing, transfers, promotions, and compensation to be decided by a central ministry or high-level commission (see below). Stringent procedures for such human resource decisions often not only apply to central government agencies, but sub-national governments and autonomous entities as well. As a result, overall discretion for decision-making in the human resource area is often limited for managers of departments and agencies in government.

It is not obvious that wage spending in LICs is sufficiently flexible to ensure that performance budgeting is effective. Inflexibilities at the micro level can be a major obstacle for effective performance budgeting in LICs. In particular, three forms of such inflexibilities often exist in the public sector: (1) the lack of capacity to terminate employment (and sometimes also to hire new employees—for instance, in the case of a hiring freeze or centralized decision-making on hiring); (2) the inability to transfer government workers between agencies or between programs and activities; and (3) rigidities in the compensation structure and level.

Such spending inflexibilities at the micro level may also jeopardize government control of overall wage spending. Lack of control over the wage bill poses a serious challenge for maintaining overall aggregate budget flexibility, macroeconomic stability, and fiscal sustainability (see, for example, Maguire, 1993). In addition, inflexibilities in public sector employment and pay policy can have adverse macroeconomic implications through their impact on private sector labor supply and wage levels.

Achieving and retaining control of the wage bill is critical, and has been the dominant concern in many LICs. The concern about wage bills stems from the perception that in countries with weak fiscal discipline and governance structures, the wage bill is easily expanded during economic good times and in response to political pressures, but much harder to bring down during periods of economic adversity (Fedelino et al., 2006). The downward stickiness of nominal wages in the public sector and the lack of instruments for downsizing the public payroll contribute to the perception that increases in the government wage bill are unlikely to be reversed. Therefore, frequently a distinction is made between decision-making on non-wage recurrent spending and wage spending. Changing the composition of non-wage recurrent spending is typically seen to have a limited permanent impact on overall spending levels,[2] while decisions to increase employment and compensation, even within a fixed budget constraint, are seen to enhance long-term spending pressures.

This chapter seeks to better understand the relationship between wage bill control, the flexbility of wage spending, and options for moving toward performance budgeting in LICs. We first review the relevant literature on the size and determinants of the wage bill. Although economic theory suggests that wage bills as a share of gross domestic product (GDP) tend to rise over time, empirical studies do not find evidence for this. We then look at data for 1990–2000 for 37 LICs with IMF-supported programs to increase our understanding of the degree of wage spending inflexibility in countries undergoing fiscal adjustment. Our empirical analysis confirms that countries have typically managed to exert control over the size of the wage bill over time. But we also find evidence that the wage bill is less flexible than other spending categories, particularly in the short run. The chapter then reviews how institutional processes contribute to spending inflexibilities. In particular, we investigate institutional constraints to various forms of wage spending flexibility and how these can facilitate or frustrate attempts to improve civil service performance and the implementation of performance budgeting.

The chapter draws tentative conclusions on how wage spending inflexibilities at the micro level can be removed to support a move to performance budgeting and greater control of the overall wage bill in LICs. It reviews evidence from LICs and OECD countries on the success of civil service reform and performance budgeting and how the two processes interact. Given this experience, it concludes that a number of mechanisms used to increase wage spending flexibility at the spending agency level in OECD countries could aid control of the wage bill as well as support efforts to improve the performance of the civil service in LICs. However, given the constrained institutional and volatile political environments found in many LICs, we advocate a gradual approach to decentralization of civil service management.

Determinants of the wage bill—theory and analysis in the literature

Early literature on wage bill determinants focused on long-term trends, and concluded that the government wage bill was likely to grow as a proportion of national income over time. The first articulation of this was by Wagner in the nineteenth century. He postulated that economic development would lead to a rising share of public expenditure due to the increase in the demand for, and relative cost of, public administration and regulation in a more developed economy. This basic notion was rephrased by Baumol (1967), who focused on public sector productivity. He suggested that while labor productivity in the goods-producing sector would tend to increase, productivity in the public sector (and the services sector in general) would tend to lag due to the labor-intensive nature of services and the limited options for labor productivity enhancement in such service activities as education (where Baumol refers to limits to reasonable class sizes and student–teacher ratios as key factors constraining labor productivity improvements). This would imply that in order for the government to maintain a given level of services per person and as wages rise reflecting productivity increases in the goods-producing sector, its wage bill must grow as a share of national income.[3]

Average wage bill spending as a share of GDP is lower in LICs than more developed countries. Table 25.1 shows that LICs, on average, have a wage bill of 4.8 percent of GDP, which is about 1 percentage point of GDP below average levels prevailing in middle-income countries (MICs) and high-income countries (HICs). However, measured as a share of overall government expenditure, the government wage bill is higher in LICs than in MICs and HICs. Also, in countries where the level of development is higher, the relative government wage tends to be lower while public employment is higher. But the large variation in regional averages suggests that these stylized facts obscure large differences in country experiences. Also, care needs to be taken in interpreting this empirical information because of data problems (Box 25.1).

Table 25.1 Government wages and salaries, 2000[a]

	Wages and salaries as % of GDP	*Wages and salaries as % of government expenditure*	*Average wage to per capita GDP ratio*	*Public employment as % of total population*
Asia and the Pacific	4.8	25.3	2.4	4.6
Europe	4.7	15.9	3.8	10.3
Western Hemisphere	5.4	28.5	1.9	4.4
Middle East and Central Asia	10.2	37.6	2.0	...
Sub-Saharan Africa	7.1	33.7	3.9	2.4
Low-income countries	4.8	27.1	3.9	2.3
Middle-income countries	6.0	25.8	3.6	6.7
High-income countries	5.7	20.1	1.3	8.5

[a] For 2000 or most recent year available. Most data cover the general government. Public employment numbers cover public enterprises as well as the general government.

Sources: IMF World Economic Outlook database; IMF Government Finance Statistics database; World Bank Administrative and Civil Service Reform database; World Bank World Development Indicators database; ILO LABORSTA database.

Box 25.1 Data issues

Empirical analysis of government employment and wage levels is hampered by the lack of availability of consistent data between countries. Reliability of government employment statistics is an issue in many LICs. Where data are reliable, important definitional questions can arise. Countries differ in what they consider to be government employment, and therefore the same terminology is often used to refer to different categories. For example, some countries include teachers and health workers in the civil service, while others do not. Some countries consider local government employees paid from the central budget as local government staff, whereas others designate these as central government staff. International comparisons of government data on government wage levels are still more complicated because of the role of allowances and the presence of in-kind benefits, which are not consistently included in wage statistics.

However, the literature provides little empirical evidence that in LICs wage bills tend to increase as a share of GDP over time.[4] In fact, partial data suggest that ratios of wage bills to GDP in LICs have remained broadly stable, or even declined, on average in recent decades. For example, Lienert and Modi (1997) show for 32 LICs in sub-Saharan Africa that, despite some large movements in individual countries, average wage bills declined by 1 percentage point of GDP to 6 percent of GDP during 1986–96, mainly driven by a decline in average real government wages. They also find that the government employment trends in sub-Saharan Africa were mixed. While a number of countries contracted government employment sharply, often in conjunction with real wage increases, an equal number moved in the opposite direction. In another example, Kraay and van Rijckeghem (1995) do not find a statistically significant time trend for the ratio of wage spending to GDP in a sample of 34 LICs during 1972–92. Finally, our data for a sample of 37 LICs that undertook macroeconomic reform show a decline in average wage spending from 7.2 percent of GDP in 1990 to 6.0 percent in 2000 (see below).

Kraay and van Rijckeghem (1995) find that wage bills in LICs are affected by a variety of factors. For a sample of 34 LICs, they consider a range of explanatory variables, covering macroeconomic conditions, fiscal pressures, labor supply and quality, demand for public services, and external pressures, and find the following statistically significant relationships:

- *Employment.* The variable with the strongest (negative) effect on employment appears to be the presence of an IMF-supported adjustment program. Other variables with a positive, albeit small, effect are revenue effort and the real effective exchange rate. Urbanization and foreign financing also have a positive effect. Secondary school enrollment has a small negative effect as does population size, suggesting increasing returns to scale of a larger population.[5]
- *Real wages.* Real government wages decline with real per capita GDP, presumably because the shortage of skills employed in government falls with economic development. In addition, real wages increase with revenue and decline with debt. IMF-supported structural adjustment programs have no significant impact on wages, but IMF-supported stabilization programs do have a significant negative impact.[6] Real wages decrease with secondary school enrollment (because of its impact on the relative scarcity of skills employed by the government). The real effective exchange rate has a negative effect on real wages expressed in purchasing power parity (PPP) dollars, but not on real wages relative to GDP per capita.
- *Overall wage bill.* The statistical relationship between real GDP per capita and wage spending as a share of GDP is negative, consistent with the impact on real government wages. In addition, secondary school enrollment has a negative effect, as the adverse impact on wages outweighs the associated increase in employment. Revenue effort and foreign financing both have a positive impact, mainly through allowing extra employment. The presence of an IMF-supported structural adjustment program has an overall negative effect, stemming from reductions in employment.

Despite the observed relative stability in average wage bills in LICs over the longer term, countries may find it difficult to contain wage spending at sustainable levels. Many LICs face an urgent need to enhance public service delivery, including meeting the Millennium Development Goals, and need to achieve this within a sustainable fiscal framework. Fedelino et al. (2006) discuss how undue increases in wage spending can jeopardize the achievement of macroeconomic objectives, and that in such cases IMF-supported programs have included conditionality on the size of wage bills. Such conditionality, often in the form of ceilings on the size of the wage bill, were included in as much as half of the 42 LICs with arrangements under the IMF's Poverty Reduction and Growth Facility between 2003 and 2005.[7] Fedelino et al. emphasize that wage bill ceilings provide only a short-term fix and ultimately need to be supplanted by civil service reform, and caution that countries may seek to meet wage bill conditionality (or targets for wage spending unrelated to IMF-supported programs) with short-term measures, which may lock in inappropriate civil service structures that are both unsustainable and costly in terms of economic efficiency. In the next section, we will explore wage bill flexibility in LICs in more detail, and particularly what can be inferred from the more short-run developments in wage bills about the cost of maintaining control over the wage bill through wage bill ceilings and other measures.

Wage spending flexibility—empirical analysis

This section examines how wage bills have been kept under control in LICs, in particular during periods of fiscal adjustment. The analysis up until now has revealed little about the relative movements of wage bills and overall expenditures. Inflexibilities in the wage bill may, in fact, be relative to other expenditure categories, especially in the short term. This would be particularly important in LICs undergoing periodic fiscal adjustment, and the analysis in this chapter focuses on this group of countries. If the wage bill is not flexible in the short term, other spending will have to bear the brunt of budget cuts. This could have a significant impact on public sector performance and economic growth. Our empirical analysis employs an explicit strategy. To test for the presence of inflexibilities during a fiscal adjustment process the analysis below looks at two areas to assess wage bill inflexibility: (1) the relative share of wages in primary expenditures and GDP in the longer term;[8] and (2) the short-run responsiveness of wages to movements in annual levels of primary expenditure.[9] Box 25.2 describes the dataset used for the analysis.

Flexibility in the trend of wage spending

Over the period 1990–2000, average wage spending decreased both as a share of GDP and of primary expenditures (Table 25.2). Average wage spending declined from 7.2 percent of GDP in 1990 to 6.0 percent in 2000.[10] In part, the decrease in wage spending reflects the decline of the average fiscal balance by around 3.2 percent of GDP, with average primary expenditures falling by 5.0 percentage points of GDP. But wage expenditure, on average, declined by more than primary spending, and the share of wages in primary spending was reduced from an average of 28.6 percent of primary spending in 1990 to 25.9 percent in 2000.

The government wage bill was reduced most in countries that in 1990 had a relatively high level of wage spending (Figure 25.1). At the same time, countries with a relatively low initial level of wage spending increased their wage bills on average. This convergence of initial outliers to the middle also explains the reduced dispersion in wage spending across countries (Table 25.2 shows that the standard deviation of wages as a percentage of GDP decreased from 15.8 to 11.3 during 1990–2000, and from 13.7 to 7.7 as a proportion of primary expenditures). For

Box 25.2 The dataset

This chapter considers wage bill data for 1990–2000 in a sample of 37 LICs that undertook macroeconomic reform in the context of an IMF-supported program.[a] We use a database constructed by Gupta et al. (2002) that draws from the World Economic Outlook (WEO) and other IMF databases to obtain macroeconomic and fiscal data for 37 LICs which received a concessional loan from the IMF in the 1990s. The fiscal data are measured on a cash basis and at the general government level (except for Lesotho and Yemen, where the data cover only the central government).

By using a dataset for LICs that undertook macroeconomic reform, our analysis is focusing on cases where there was a likely need for spending flexibility. In other words, the analysis is considering cases where the flexibility of government spending in general, and of wage spending in particular, may be an issue. Moreover, by focusing on the whole period for 1990–2000 and not just the years where an adjustment program was in place, the database contains episodes of both fiscal consolidation and expansion.

The strength of the database is in providing comparable macro-fiscal variables across a wide range of LICs. Nevertheless, the analysis remains vulnerable to unobserved changes in the coverage of the wage bill and other fiscal variables. For that reason, large movements in wage-related variables within the dataset are investigated and described following the main empirical analysis.

[a] Albania, Armenia, Benin, Bolivia, Burkina Faso, Cambodia, Cameroon, Central African Republic, Chad, Djibouti, Ethiopa, The Gambia, Georgia, Ghana, Guinea, Guinea-Bissau, Guyana, Honduras, Kenya, Kyrgyz Republic, Laos, Lesotho, Macedonia (FYR), Madagascar, Malawi, Mali, Mauritania, Mozambique, Nicaragua, Niger, Rwanda, Senegal, São Tomé and Príncipe, Tajikistan, Tanzania, Yemen, and Zambia.

example, wage spending in Benin dropped from 50.9 percent of primary spending in 1990, which was almost double the sample average, to 26.1 percent in 2000, which was just 0.1 percentage point above the sample average. Tanzania, on the other hand, increased its wage expenditures from 3.7 percent of GDP in 1990, or about half of the sample average, to 4.5 percent by 2000, while the sample average fell over the same period.

For the countries that started with high wage expenditures, the motivation for reducing wage spending as a share of GDP and primary expenditure is likely to have been to protect macroeconomic stability and fiscal sustainability (see Fedelino et al., 2006).[11] In those countries, the wage bill absorbed such a large proportion of expenditure that vital growth and productivity enhancing expenditures were being squeezed out. For the countries with a low initial level of wage spending, the upward adjustment of wages is likely to have been aimed at expanding public service delivery and enhancing motivation, recruitment, and retention.

However, in countries where primary spending contracted during the 1990s, wage spending was not reduced in line with overall spending trends, although it declined as a share of GDP. In these countries (fiscal contraction countries), the average wage share in primary expenditure was volatile in the early 1990s, to stabilize at around 27 percent in the second half of the decade. This was still well above the initial level of 24 percent of primary spending, implying that non-wage spending was cut by more than overall primary spending. However, these averages obscure important country differences; wages actually fell as a share of primary spending

Table 25.2 Summary statistics, 1990 and 2000[a]

Country group	*Variable*	*Wage bill as % of primary expenditures 1990*	*2000*	*Wage bill as % of GDP 1990*	*2000*	*Primary expenditures as % of GDP 1990*	*2000*	*Budget balance as % of GDP 1990*	*2000*
All	Mean	28.6	25.9	7.2	6.0	29.2	24.3	–7.6	–4.4
	Maximum	63.4	43.8	20.3	14.9	84.3	65.7	–0.4	2.9
	Minimum	7.4	12.5	0.8	2.7	13.8	12.1	–42.2	–14.2
	Standard deviation	13.7	7.7	3.7	2.8	15.8	11.3	9.0	3.7
Lowest wage shares	Mean	10.1	19.1	5.1	6.1	50.4	32.2	–16.6	–7.3
	Maximum	12.2	30.1	9.0	10.7	84.3	58.4	–2.7	–4.1
	Minimum	7.4	12.5	0.8	2.9	26.0	18.1	–42.2	–14.2
	Standard deviation	1.8	6.2	2.9	2.9	23.2	14.4	18.7	3.7
Mid-sized wage shares	Mean	26.7	25.7	6.3	5.6	25.4	22.6	–5.9	–4.0
	Maximum	41.1	43.8	10.6	14.6	57.2	65.7	–0.4	2.9
	Minimum	18.2	13.5	2.0	2.7	13.8	12.1	–19.9	–11.5
	Standard deviation	6.0	7.1	2.0	2.4	10.2	11.1	4.4	3.3
Highest wage shares	Mean	51.2	32.0	12.2	7.7	23.7	23.2	–5.5	–3.1
	Maximum	63.4	42.6	20.3	14.9	41.8	35.0	–0.5	1.3
	Minimum	43.8	23.8	8.0	4.8	15.8	16.2	–7.6	–9.7
	Standard deviation	5.9	6.8	5.0	3.6	9.3	6.6	2.8	4.2
Fiscal contraction	Mean	23.7	26.7	7.1	5.8	34.2	22.5	–8.6	–4.2
	Maximum	51.0	43.8	20.3	14.9	84.3	58.4	–0.4	2.9
	Minimum	7.4	12.5	0.8	2.9	13.8	12.1	–42.2	–14.2
	Standard deviation	11.9	9.0	3.9	2.7	17.8	10.2	10.5	4.0
Fiscal expansion	Mean	36.8	24.4	7.4	6.4	20.4	27.1	–5.8	–4.8
	Maximum	63.4	38.8	17.8	14.6	28.1	65.7	–0.5	–0.2
	Minimum	21.7	13.5	2.0	2.7	15.5	16.8	–19.9	–11.5
	Standard deviation	12.9	7.3	3.6	3.0	4.2	12.6	5.1	3.1

[a] 1990 or earliest year available.

in 8 out of 23 contractionary countries. At the same time, countries which boosted primary expenditure over the decade (fiscal expansion countries) saw the share of primary spending devoted to wage spending fall, from about 36 percent in the early 1990s to 24 percent in 2000, while wage spending as a share of GDP did not show a clear trend.

This analysis of spending trends over the 1990s suggests that LICs in our sample managed to adjust wage spending, especially when the initial wage bill was relatively high and when seeking to reduce overall spending levels. On average, countries that contracted their primary spending between 1990 and 2000 also brought down wage spending as a share of GDP, but still saw wage spending as a share of primary spending rise. This implies that non-wage spending has had to adjust more, and may be an indication of the relative inflexibility of wage spending. It may also reflect optimal policy choices—for example, the long-term cost of losing government workers with scarce skills may outweigh the short-term benefits from cutting them from the government payroll. The next two sections look more closely at disaggregated data which underpins the trends in sample and group averages that we have considered until now.

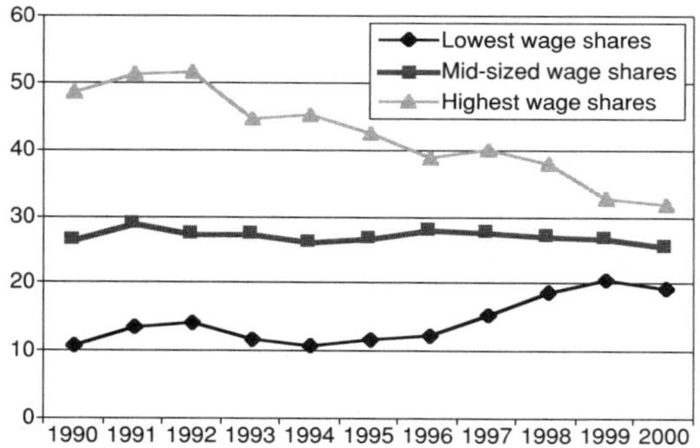

Figure 25.1(a) Wage bill as a percentage of primary expenditures by size of 1990–92 wage share of primary expenditures[a]

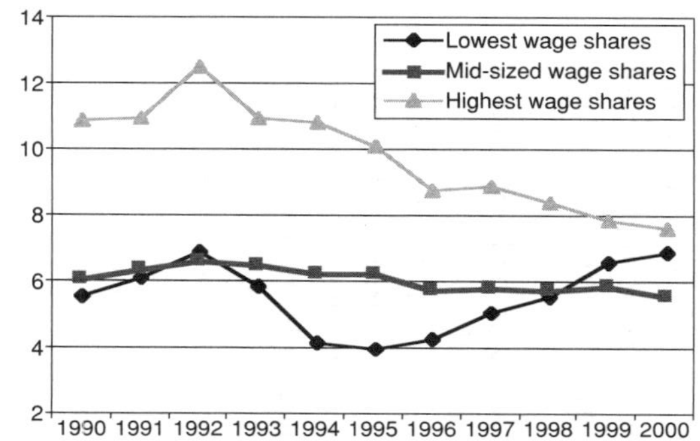

Figure 25.1(b) Wage bill as a percentage of GDP by size of 1990–92 wage share of primary expenditures[a]

[a] The sample was disaggregated into three groups (lowest, mid-sized, and highest) based on wage spending as a percentage of primary expenditures at the beginning of the period (1990–92). The lowest group includes the group of countries with wage spending as a percentage of primary expenditures less than one standard deviation below the sample mean in 1990–92 (Armenia, Guyana, Mozambique, and São Tomé and Príncipe). The highest group includes the countries with wage spending as a percentage of primary expenditures above one standard deviation above the mean in 1990–92 (Benin, Cameroon, Djibouti, Honduras, Kyrgyz Republic, Senegal, and Yemen). The remaining countries in our sample are in the mid-sized group (except for Georgia, Guinea-Bissau, and Rwanda, which are excluded from the figures because of data inconsistencies).

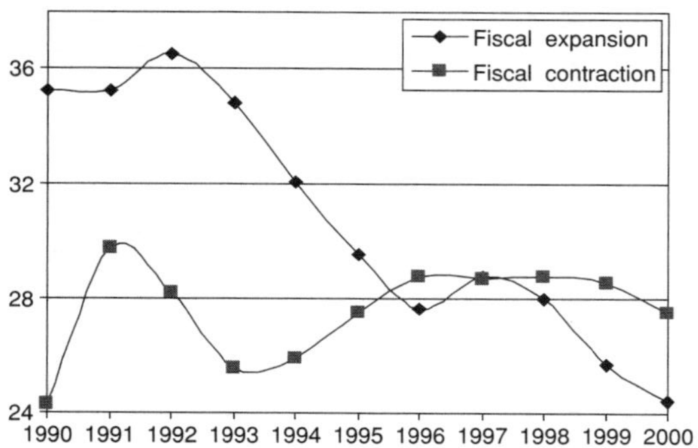

Figure 25.1(c) Wage bill as a percentage of primary expenditures by direction of trend in primary expenditures[b]

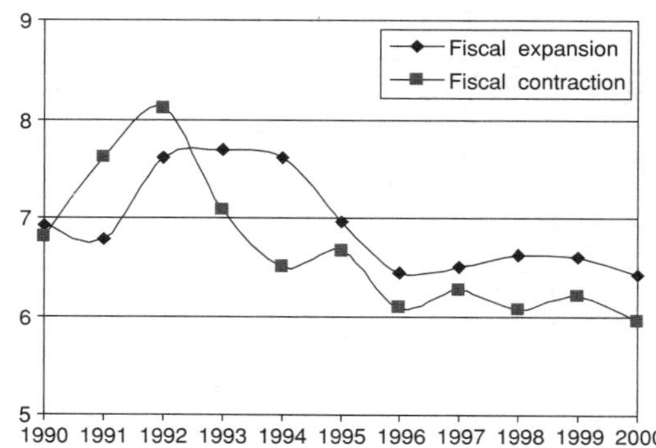

Figure 25.1(d) Wage bill as a percentage of GDP by direction of trend in primary expenditures[b]

[b] Fifteen "fiscal expansion" countries had a higher level of primary spending as a share of GDP in 2000 than in 1990 (Benin, Bolivia, Burkina Faso, Cambodia, Ethiopia, Ghana, Honduras, Laos, Lesotho, Malawi, Mali, Nicaragua, Senegal, Tanzania, and Yemen). In the 23 remaining "fiscal contraction" countries, primary expenditure declined over the same time period.

Short-term responsiveness of the wage bill to primary expenditure

The short-term responsiveness of wage expenditure to primary spending can be assessed from correlations and elasticities. This section considers several indicators of responsiveness. First, the share of countries with a large correlation between annual changes in the wage bill (and other spending components) and annual changes in primary spending indicates how close the short-term co-movement is between the wage bill and primary expenditures. Second, to understand the proportional relationship between wages and spending, the elasticity of wage spending to primary spending reveals the size of the annual change in the wage bill in relation to the annual change in primary spending.

Annual movements in the wage bill as a share of GDP are positively correlated with movements in primary expenditures (Table 25.3). In half of the countries, the wage bill in percentage of GDP moves positively with changes in primary expenditures as a percentage of GDP. But, in 56 percent of the countries, there is a negative relationship between wage spending as a percentage of primary expenditure and primary spending as a share of GDP. This indicates that, as primary expenditure increases or decreases, wages tend to move in the same direction but not in a proportional amount. Table 25.3 also shows that movements in other expenditure components, such as capital expenditures and goods and services, are more strongly correlated to movements in expenditures than are movements in the wage bill.

The pair-wise correlations also show that countries which fiscally contracted during the 1990s reduced their wage bills as a share of GDP, but not in equal proportion to the decline in primary spending. The correlation between the wage bill as a percentage of GDP and primary spending is strong and positive in more than half of the countries, while it is negative and strong between the wage bill as a share of primary spending, and primary expenditure is negative and strong also in more than half of the countries. Furthermore, in only 39 percent of the countries do expansionary fiscal conditions have a large positive impact on the wage bill as a share of GDP, while in 23 percent of the expansionary countries there was a strong negative impact on the wage bill as a percentage of GDP. Hence, in 54 percent of the expansionary countries, the share of primary expenditures composed by wages was strongly reduced as primary expenditures grew. These results are consistent with the earlier findings on average spending trends. The relationship between wage spending and other macro-fiscal variables, such as GDP growth, total revenue and the budget balance, is similar to that of the wage bill and primary expenditures, although slightly weaker.

The elasticity of the wage bill to changes in total primary expenditures and total revenue is smaller than for other expenditure aggregates (Table 25.4). The average elasticity of the wage bill to primary spending is 0.51 (that is, a 1 percent increase/decrease in primary spending is associated with an increase/decrease in the wage bill of 0.51 percent) while the elasticities of capital spending and spending on other goods and services to primary expenditure are 0.92 and 0.68, respectively. The elasticity of spending on transfers and subsidies is 1.07, which means it is more than proportionally responsive to movements in overall primary spending. The results are robust to dividing the sample based on trends in primary spending

Table 25.3 Percentage of countries with strong pair-wise correlations, 1990–2000[a]

Group[b]		*Primary expenditures*		*GDP per capita growth*		*Total revenue*		*Budget balance*	
		Positive	*Negative*	*Positive*	*Negative*	*Positive*	*Negative*	*Positive*	*Negative*
All	Wage bill	50.0	8.3	5.6	19.4	30.6	11.1	2.8	50.0
	Wage bill (% of prim. exp.)	2.8	55.6	8.3	22.2	13.9	47.2	22.2	11.1
	Capital expenditures	80.6	0.0	22.2	11.1	38.9	2.8	5.6	22.2
	Transfers and subsidies	38.9	2.8	13.9	19.4	38.9	8.3	8.3	16.7
	Goods and services	56.3	0.0	18.8	6.3	28.1	12.5	9.4	31.3
Fiscal contraction	Wage bill	56.5	0.0	8.7	21.7	43.5	8.7	4.3	39.1
	Wage bill (% of prim. exp.)	4.3	56.5	13.0	13.0	21.7	52.2	30.4	4.3
	Capital expenditures	73.9	0.0	13.0	17.4	43.5	4.3	4.3	30.4
	Transfers and subsidies	39.1	4.3	8.7	21.7	26.1	8.7	0.0	26.1
	Goods and services	59.1	0.0	27.3	9.1	36.4	9.1	4.5	31.8
Fiscal expansion	Wage bill	38.5	23.1	0.0	30.8	7.7	15.4	0.0	69.2
	Wage bill (% of prim. exp.)	0.0	53.8	0.0	38.5	0.0	38.5	7.7	30.8
	Capital expenditures	90.9	0.0	36.4	0.0	45.5	0.0	0.0	9.1
	Transfers and subsidies	0.0	38.5	30.8	7.7	61.5	7.7	23.1	7.7
	Goods and services	50.0	0.0	10.0	0.0	0.0	10.0	20.0	30.0

[a] Correlation coefficients were calculated on a country-by-country basis. Countries with strong pair-wise correlations are defined as countries where the correlation in the variable pair during 1990–2000 is 0.5 or above, and which are also statistically significant at the 5 percent confidence level. If the correlation coefficient is larger than 0.5, the country is added to the "positive" column, while it is added to the "negative" column if the correlation coefficient is smaller than –0.5. Variables are measured in percentage of GDP, unless indicated otherwise.

[b] The country groups are defined as in Figures 25.1(c) and (d).

over the period, which implies that the size of the average response to an increase and decline in primary spending is symmetric. Moreover, although wage bills are somewhat responsive to changes in revenue, spending on transfers and subsidies as well as goods and services are more flexible to revenue changes.

Table 25.4 Elasticities of government spending, 1990–2000[a]

Group[b]		*Primary expenditures*	*GDP per capita growth*	*Total revenue*	*Budget balance*
All	Wage bill	0.51	–0.07	0.57	0.07
	Wage bill (% of prim. exp.)	–0.49	–0.11	–0.00	–0.06
	Capital expenditures	0.92	0.03	0.21	0.12
	Transfers and subsidies	1.07	0.10	1.03	0.33
	Goods and services	0.68	0.10	0.69	0.17
Fiscal contraction	Wage bill	0.49	–0.06	0.54	–0.01
	Wage bill (% of prim. exp.)	–0.51	–0.10	–0.03	–0.10
	Capital expenditures	0.94	0.04	0.03	0.03
	Transfers and subsidies	1.10	0.19	1.04	0.32
	Goods and services	0.59	0.13	0.71	0.15
Fiscal expansion	Wage bill	0.59	–0.08	0.62	0.25
	Wage bill (% of prim. exp.)	–0.41	–0.09	0.00	–0.00
	Capital expenditures	0.94	0.03	0.70	0.31
	Transfers and subsidies	0.92	–0.14	1.07	0.26
	Goods and services	1.14	–0.00	0.82	0.85

[a] Elasticities are not calculated on a country-by-country basis but on the pooled panel of countries. The elasticity is defined as the regression coefficient from a single regression of each variable pair in logs. Variables are measured in percentage of GDP, unless indicated otherwise.
[b] The country groups are defined as in Figures 25.1(c) and (d).

Conclusions from the empirical analysis

The empirical analysis of 37 LICs that undertook macroeconomic reform during the 1990s under IMF-supported programs yields the following key findings:

- *Wage spending trends have, by and large, supported fiscal adjustment.* In our sample of countries, wage expenditure as a share of GDP tends to go down during periods of fiscal contraction, and particularly when wage spending is initially high. The response of wage spending to a fiscal expansion is more ambiguous—wage spending as a share of GDP actually fell on average in the group of countries where primary expenditure increased during 1990–2000, and in 23 percent of the sample countries the wage bill-to-GDP ratio declined signicantly in years in which the share of primary spending in GDP rose.
- *At the same time, there is evidence of some wage bill inflexibility, at least in the short term.* Wage bills tend to be less volatile than other components of primary expenditures and less correlated with and elastic to annual movements in primary expenditure. Wage bills across the sample were as flexible—as measured by the coefficient of variation—as primary expenditure over the entire period. Nevertheless, the elasticity of wage spending to changes in primary expenditures

is smaller than that of other expenditure items, in particular capital spending and goods and services, suggesting that in the short term the wage bill may be less easy to adjust than other expenditure components.[12]

Such wage spending inflexibility may, in part, reflect national wage and employment policies. In situations where fiscal consolidation is needed, the cost of adjusting other spending components may be smaller, as reducing wage spending during downturns may result in the loss of highly skilled workers which were attracted and trained at high cost to the government. Similarly, quickly expanding wage spending by stepping up hiring or granting large wage increases during upswings may be difficult to undo later, and thereby jeopardize fiscal sustainability, while perhaps not yielding significant pay-offs in terms of better public service delivery.

However, the short-term inflexibility of wage spending also reflects institutional arrangements in many LICs. The next section examines how such arrangements can promote inflexibilities in wage spending at the micro level. A key question concerns the institutions and institutional processes that contribute to inflexibilities in wage expenditure, and the extent to which they are amenable to reform. In particular, what would be needed to establish an appropriate institutional environment for performance budgeting?

Institutions, wage spending flexibility, and performance budgeting

Government decision-making on wages and employment is the product of political and bureaucratic institutions and processes. These affect the wage bill through their impact on aggregate employment and wage policies, while also affecting the skill composition and motivation of the government workforce, and thereby its performance. An examination of these institutions and how they can affect wage bill flexibility and civil service performance is key for understanding how and where performance budgeting can drive changes in input composition and performance.

Although institutions differ in each country, and are often markedly different between regions, a number of typical institutions that particularly influence the flexibility of wage spending can be identified. Following Kiragu et al. (2004), we analyze relevant institutions and processes in four groups: administrative, political, trade union, and donor institutions.

Administrative institutions and processes

Centralized personnel management agencies and processes

Most governments have a department or agency dedicated to personnel management issues. These often were established in an effort to limit political influence on the civil service, and can be important in curbing the effects of corruption in government departments and agencies. In some countries these centralized agencies for personnel management may be part of the mainstream architecture of government (for example, in Tanzania); in others they may be semi-independent (for example, in South Asian countries such as Sri Lanka and Pakistan). Whichever model is chosen, these institutions are often responsible for administering a highly regulated set of positions, job classifications, and grading and promotion criteria that individual departments are unable to change without the approval of the central agency. These can introduce inflexibilities in a number of different ways:

- Promotions based on seniority rather than merit place a natural upward pressure on the wage bill and provide a disincentive to performance. They are more likely to be relied on where the central agency regulates promotion decisions, perhaps because the central agency is more distant from performance. To the extent that promotions become automatic, these systems build an autonomous buoyancy into the wage bill.
- Management of the number of established posts, which is often immune to change, especially in a downward direction. In some regions the overall number of established posts also has sub-ceilings for particular cadres that over time become entitlements for particular specializations. These cadre systems (for example, in South Asia and Ethiopia) may be based on previous models of government and, if they are not amenable to change, can inhibit the ability of institutions to adapt to changing functions or the nature of demand.
- Central hiring and firing regulations, in particular where civil servants have de facto tenure, can prevent reductions (or increases) in the government labor force in response to changing demand conditions or budgetary pressures. Williamson (2003) notes that these regulations in Uganda have prevented institutions attempting to implement performance budgeting from varying the skill mix.

Nationwide pay scales and settlements

It is widespread practice for public service pay to be set according to a single pay scale, differentiated by grade that covers the entire civil service or a specific cadre within it. When wage increases are granted—often annually, but not always in the context of the annual budget—they affect the whole scale, often without differentiation by grade. Wage increases may be formally linked to external indicators, such as consumer price inflation or earnings in the private sector. It may also be the result of a central collective bargaining agreement (see below on trade unions) or be an entirely discretionary decision by the government (see below on political institutions). In many systems civil servants are entitled to service-related increments in addition to the global increase in pay scales. The main issues to consider in connection with wage spending flexibility include the following:

- Comprehensive pay scales in principle enable governments to exercise control over the overall wage bill, in particular where pay increases are a discretionary policy decision. Although political factors may not allow for this opportunity to be grasped, there is evidence from OECD countries in the 1980s that centralized systems are more successful at controlling wage bills (Meurs, 1993). Lienert and Modi (1997) note that in countries of the CFA franc zone in the mid-1990s, macroeconomic affordability of the wage bill was achieved by granting limited across-the-board nominal wage increases in the face of high inflation.

- However, to the extent that this control is not, or cannot, be exercised (for example, where scale revisions are tied to an external indicator not under the control of the authorities), the broad applicability of the scales can exacerbate the fiscal pressure from the wage bill. For instance, in Tanzania, central wage settlements have caused other inputs to be squeezed out, particularly in labor-intensive sectors.
- Where service-related increments are part of the system, these can contribute to the buoyancy of the wage bill, which can be problematic if fiscal contraction is required in an economic downturn.
- The key problem of systems with nationwide pay scales and settlements is that they restrict managerial and labor market flexibility. Managers are rendered unable to reward good performance with pay and to vary wage rates according to local or sectoral market conditions (Meurs, 1993, reports the same finding in the context of OECD countries).

Fragmented remuneration

In many countries the basic salary of a civil servant is a relatively minor proportion of their overall remuneration. Complex systems of allowances and entitlements in cash (hardship, task-based, and cost-of-living allowances), in kind (free transportation and housing), and of an intangible nature (status, job security, and access to power and rent-seeking opportunities) significantly increase compensation over the basic wage. For instance, Indonesia operates a system of allowances for each department, funded from the development budget, based on the number of projects the department implements, which raise salaries by almost 100 percent (Manning, 2000). These allowances make pay policy harder to manage, and raise a number of issues in relation to wage spending flexibility:

- The total value of allowances may be unknown, both in cash terms to the budget and in terms of relative importance in the total remuneration of government employees. As such they are unlikely to be subject to the same degree of monitoring and control as wages.
- The allowances may be outside of the scope of pay revisions and negotiations, and contain explicit or implicit indexation (for example, a cost-of-living allowance directly indexed to a price index was recently proposed in Sri Lanka). The provision of housing, which is a widespread benefit for senior civil servants in LICs, is an example of an in-kind allowance that is implicitly indexed to an external variable. While this may not have a large short-term cash impact on the budget, it does have an opportunity cost and can significantly impact public-private sector wage differentials with a consequent impact on recruitment, turnover and, ultimately, performance.
- To the extent that they are valuable to employees and differentiated between departments and agencies—as in the case of Indonesia—they can be an obstacle for the mobility of labor within the public sector and compromise

the ability of agencies with lower allowances to attract adequately skilled staff. This is particularly damaging where the distribution of allowances is at odds with the government priorities because it reflects, for example, the scope for the ministry or agency to generate own revenues to fund allowances for its workers.

- If funding for salary top-ups is time limited it can have implications for the human capital of an agency as experienced and talented staff leave as allowance top-ups disappear. In Nicaragua, this has also resulted in an upward pressure on the aggregate wage bill because a rigid labor code enforces the continuation of these allowances after the funding source has disappeared.
- The formal wage bill in the government accounts may not accurately reflect total personnel-related costs. Pay decisions may also affect other line-items of the budget—for instance, public sector pensions that may be linked, formally or informally, to the public sector pay scales. Wage bills may also be hidden in current transfers to public sector agencies. In Nicaragua it is estimated that almost half of the wage bill is reported in non-wage budget items.

Political institutions and processes

All the components of the wage bill have great political significance, particularly in LICs. Public sector employment is a highly visible policy instrument and often an important tool of political patronage. Similarly, wage policy can be a valuable political tool particularly where the public sector is large or acts as a social safety net. At the extreme, for instance in Honduras (World Bank, 2002), the legislature has complete control over public sector wage setting and negotiations. In most countries the wage bill is the result of a balance between political and technical considerations. The main mechanisms through which political institutions affect the flexibility of wage expenditure are as follows:

- *Pay increases linked to the electoral cycle.* The nationwide pay scales and settlement process described above provide a very visible mechanism for ruling political parties to provide pay increases to a large and politically influential group (see below on trade unions). As such they can result in large movements in the wage bill that may work against sound macroeconomic policy.
- *Political preferences for wage compression.* Katz and Krueger (1993) note for OECD countries that the political motivations on pay tend to lead to greater wage compression than technical considerations would recommend. The political debate in many countries is both against excessively high wages and for "fair" wages to the lower-paid. A widening of the differential may under such circumstances not be politically expedient, irrespective of technical considerations. This is borne out by the evidence across sub-Saharan Africa, where, despite wage compression being an acknowledged constraint to improved civil service performance, compression ratios generally remained stagnant or deteriorated through the 1990s (Kiragu et al., 2004; Stevens and Teggemann, 2004).

- *Political- and electoral-based hiring*. In varying degrees, patronage affects employment policies in many LICs. The skill set of workers hired for patronage reasons tends to be inconsistent with the needs of the government, and successive rounds of patronage-driven hiring as governments change can drive up government employment and the wage bill over time, as it may be hard to reverse hiring by previous governments. In addition, in some countries (for example, Yemen; see World Bank, 2002), the government has acted as an employer of last resort by absorbing redundant workers from public enterprises, army retirees, or recent university graduates. Employing workers in order to meet short-term political aims reduces the funds available for more productive expenditure. It also complicates the management of public agencies.

Trade unions

Powerful and large public sector unions can also contribute to wage spending inflexibility. Trade unions exist to serve the interests of their current members and thus have a vested interest to resist any reform that would reduce the size, job security, or real wage level of the civil service. In many countries they are also a very powerful political force and thus have substantial negotiating power. Kiragu et al. (2004) show that in three countries with strong trade unions (Benin, Burkina Faso, and Zambia), such unions have been a force against pay restraint and modernization of compensation determination frameworks. Stevens and Teggemann (2004) note that Zambia's political context, including the lack of willingness to take on the trade unions, was a particular source of failure in the civil service reform program.

Trade unions typically support wage compression. As the bulk of their members hold relatively low-paying positions, their negotiating strategy is typically to maximize the average wage through increases at the lower end rather than substantial increases for the much smaller number of senior managers (Katz and Krueger, 1993). This observation is borne out in the analysis of Kiragu et al. (2004), which shows that in countries with strong trade unions, wage compression either stayed high or increased. Countries with weak trade unions, on the other hand, achieved periods of salary decompression (although this result was not found over the entire period).

Donor community

The donor community can have a significant impact on the wage bill in LICs. Its influence is felt in two main ways:

- *Advocacy*. In many LICs the donor community is a forceful voice in favor of civil service reform. It supports it through a mixture of advocacy, financial assistance, and program conditionality. The donors can be a valuable ally for a government that wants to implement public sector reforms in the face of political or trade union opposition. For instance, in Burkina Faso, a 1998 law on public administration reform was passed despite strong union opposition, largely through the support and urging of the donor community. In this sense the donors are a significant, although far from dominant, force for flexibility in the wage bill (see World Bank, 2002, for a review of the effectiveness of conditionality on civil service reform; Fedelino et al., 2006, for a review of wage bill ceilings in IMF-supported programs).

- *Project-based employment and pay.* Donors also affect the wage bill through the projects they fund. The primary channel is through the use of salary top-ups and other project-related cash and in-kind allowances (see above on administrative institutions and processes). Another channel is through the additional contractual employment that donor projects may create in government departments. These contractuals are not formally part of the established strength of the civil service and their remuneration is generally not part of the government wage bill (the costs are normally to be found in the investment budget). However, typically these contractual workers are converted into civil servants once the project expires, thereby contributing to the size of the government payroll (for example, in Bangladesh). And the contractuals hired for foreign-funded projects may not have the skill mix needed most by government, in which case it also contributes to the mismatch between worker skills and government needs.

Implications for performance budgeting and civil service reform in LICs

The previous section has described how the nature and quality of the administrative and political institutions that have to manage the process in LICs often work against the flexibility that is required for control of the overall level of wage spending, performance budgeting, and other reforms aimed at enhanced government performance (see also Box 25.3). It also showed that the institutional arrangements, and in particular centralization of employment and wage decisions, have allowed governments to exercise control over overall wage spending. This section reviews the approaches taken in both OECD countries and LICs to civil service reform and performance budgeting, while retaining control of the overall wage bill.

The experience of OECD countries shows that strengthening managerial flexibility can be consistent with macroeconomic control of the wage bill. In fact, it has typically been severe macroeconomic pressure and concerns about the size of the wage bill that have prompted governments to tackle the difficult political issue of civil service size, cost, and performance. As a result, periods of fiscal stress in OECD countries are generally well correlated with public sector reform programs,[13] often alongside or directly linked to performance budgeting reform. In the area of employment and wages, such reforms have focused on remuneration. Although individual country institutions differed widely, Marsden (1993) notes a number of commonalities in the approaches to public sector pay. The reforms sought to reduce indexation, include greater sensitivity to local labor market conditions, adapt pay systems to new management methods (for example, performance budgeting), and move towards performance-related pay (OECD, 1993, 1995). The mechanisms that are potentially relevant to LICs for increasing the wage bill and managerial flexibility include the following:

- *Delegated pay bargaining.* Although the precise model and the level of delegation varies, the movement away from civil service-wide pay scales and pay agreements has been one of the fundamental changes observed in the OECD countries. One example is the one-line running cost budgets used in the UK. These cover both labor and other goods and services used in the administration of public services. This mechanism allows savings on non-wage inputs to fund necessary enhancements of the wage bill or vice versa. It is, however, only meaningful with delegated pay bargaining. There is some evidence from the UK (Marsden, 1993) that the dispersion of public sector pay has gone up with increased autonomy.
- *Different rates of pay and pay adjustment for different groups and locations.* This, in effect, is a more nuanced set of pay scales so that remuneration is more closely linked to either regional or occupational labor markets. While it was attempted in a number of OECD countries (notably by the US federal government), it was not as widespread or as successful as was expected (Marsden, 1993). One reason was the perceived problems in withdrawing location and other specific pay enhancements. It was feared that withdrawal would lead to reduced labor mobility while retention would undermine control over the wage bill.
- *Performance-related pay.* This was adopted for four main reasons: as a complement to management change; as a symbol of organizational change; as a motivator;

Box 25.3 Nicaragua (2000–05)—institutions and wage spending

Wage setting in Nicaragua is complex and fragmented. Before 2003, the determination of wages in public institutions was entirely discretionary, and mainly determined at the spending agency level. A 2003 civil service law created a centralized pay scale based on job complexity. However, this pay scale does not apply to specialist sectors (such as health and education employees) and covers only 20 percent of central government employment. The specialist groups have separate negotiated wage settlements.

Arrangements regarding decentralized entities reduce control and transparency, and are a source of wage inflation. Wage bills in these institutions (for example, schools) are recorded as current transfers and are not included in the government's wage bill. Decentralized entities set their own compensation levels with no reference to the ministry of finance. Their wage levels are twice that of the rest of the civil service and have seen the largest wage increases in recent years.

The legislature can, and does, override executive wage policy after its own negotiations with public sector trade unions. Direct wage negotiations between the strong public sector groups excluded from the civil service law and the assembly have resulted in large, unplanned wage increases.

A rigid labor code constrains flexibility. The code treats all benefits that have been granted as an acquired right of beneficiaries and also contains provisions that constrain the ability of the public sector to reduce employment. These provisions have caused particular problems with respect to donor projects where salary supplementation and project-based employment is forced to continue beyond the expiry of projects.

The result has been upward pressure on the total wage bill. Between 2000 and 2005, the formal wage bill remained around 4 percent of GDP, but total compensation of public employees increased from 7.5 percent to 8.5 percent of GDP. Over the same period, public sector wages increased by 34 percent while average wages in the formal private sector dropped by 6 percent.

> and to increase pay flexibility by breaking the link between length of service and pay level. But to be successful, performance-related pay needs to extend beyond annual pay increases. Policies and controls on advancement need to be linked to performance rather than seniority, and in order to resolve the tension with wage bill flexibility, performance-related pay should not be incorporated into base pay. However, these conditions have rarely been met. By the end of the 1990s most OECD countries had some form of performance-related pay, but few actually had an extensive system (OECD, 2005). Many systems focus only on senior civil servants, in order to minimize the costs of implementation and maximize the value for money of substantial performance rewards. In cases where more junior staff are included in the performance-related pay system, they tend to have more modest incentives.

The constrained institutional capacity and the sometimes volatile political environment add complexity to performance-based civil service reform in LICs. Even in the OECD countries, with their more sophisticated and effective institutions, there has been a tendency to overrate the potential of performance-based approaches to change behavior and culture (OECD, 2005). Reforms aimed at increasing managerial flexibility, as described above, need to be balanced with adequate control. This requires strong central management and coordination, and often a continuation of direct centralized control over at least some wage and employment decisions. Against this background, there are a number of questions that need to be addressed in LICs before undertaking a reform program along the lines pursued by OECD countries:

- *To what extent is a national public service with smooth mobility between agencies required or desired?* The greater the degree of differentiation in pay scales and job ratings, and the greater the level of delegated pay setting, the less meaningful becomes the notion of a national public service.
- *To what extent is pay competition between government agencies desirable?* Unconstrained competition between agencies for the best staff is unlikely to result in an optimal distribution of labor from the viewpoint of the government. Therefore, careful regulation of a system of delegated pay bargaining is essential (see World Bank, 2002).
- *What mechanisms will be available for the center to influence and control the wage bill at both the aggregate and the agency level?* The wage bill remains a key macroeconomic and structural variable over which the central agencies cannot abandon their control, even with delegated wage setting. Any such system needs to recognize that, and retain central powers of oversight and, when necessary, intervention in agency level policies and agreements.
- *Will selective labor market-related pay rises put upward pressure on the aggregate wage bill?* Revising pay scales for particular high-profile groups—for instance, nurses or teachers—appears a sensible way to improve the competitiveness of key public sector wages in a situation where resources are limited. However, there is a possibility, particularly where public sector unions are strong and

the government is politically vulnerable, that this will create a benchmark for the rest of the public service to follow in subsequent pay negotiations.

- *Will the introduction of more discretion and differentiation in pay increase patronage and corruption in the public service?* Care needs to be taken to align the incentives and sanctions for performance with the level of delegation of pay setting and advancement decisions. In the highly politicized environment that many LIC civil services operate in, it is quite possible that well-intentioned pay reforms can serve to decrease rather than increase the productivity of the public service by increasing the scope for politically motivated, rather than efficiency motivated, decisions on pay and promotion.

Civil service reform in LICs has tended to tackle the different types of flexibility in sequence. Attempts at civil service reform in LICs can be separated into first and second generation reforms (see Stevens and Teggemann, 2004; Lienert and Modi, 1997). First generation reforms, which were often components of the structural adjustment programs of the late 1980s and early 1990s, focused almost exclusively on the macro-fiscal objective of controlling the wage bill. The main techniques employed were retrenchment, civil service censuses, and removal of ghost workers from the payroll. The focus on macroeconomic stabilization meant that real wages, despite their fall over the previous decades, were often further decreased. By contrast, second generation reforms focus more on a differentiated approach to pay, in particular concentrating on wage decompression; reform of government functions and machinery; and improving performance and incorporating other areas of public sector reform, notably public finance management systems. Although success has been achieved in individual cases (Box 25.4), overall progress with these reforms has been modest.

In practice, the process of civil service reform in LICs has not extended to performance budgeting. Roberts (2003) assesses seven country case studies of the implementation of performance budgeting in LICs. He notes that in practice, decision-making flexibility has been very limited below ministerial levels, and thus the ability for managers to vary inputs, including labor inputs, did not materialize. For instance: non-wage resource envelopes at the agency level were squeezed by central pay agreements in Tanzania (Ronsholt et al., 2003); central hiring and firing regulations inhibited changing the skill mix in Uganda (Williamson, 2003); also in Uganda, low real wages led to only partial employment of the strongest performers (Williamson, 2003);[14] and in all seven countries of the sample, pay and promotion mechanisms did not provide the ability to reward good performers (Roberts, 2003).

But this does not mean that implementing performance budgeting models in LICs is a futile task. However, realism is required as to the extent of changes in the level and quality of outputs and outcomes that can be achieved through performance budgeting where significant wage spending inflexibilities exist. But by providing a framework for improving accountability and incentives, improving the flexibility and quality of wage and employment policies would have its own benefits, as well as establishing critical requirements for the introduction of performance budgeting

Box 25.4 Tanzania (1999–2004)—signs of success

The civil service department (CSD) and the public service commission (PSC) administer a traditional national civil service system with national pay scales. In agencies where measures to monitor and improve performance within a hard budget constraint have been established, measures to move away from the centralized pay and employment environment have been encouraged.

The flexibility of national pay scales has been increased by an experimental salary enhancement scheme. Donors are funding a salary top-up scheme to reward strong performers in key positions, with salary enhancements of up to 25 percent. This level of top-up was designed to be fiscally affordable when donor funding expires. However, implementation of the system was slower than envisaged, and government contributions have been slow to materialize.

Executive agencies have been freed from central personnel policies. Agencies with substantial own revenues have been granted executive agency status. There are 19 of these agencies that, on the basis of a three-year plan with clear performance indicators and audit and accountability standards, are released from normal personnel and budgetary procedures. This includes the ability to set their own wage levels and employment policies.

Administrative reforms have provided cost savings to finance the process. A computerized integrated personnel and payroll system was established in 2000. This has delivered substantial cost savings by identifying ghost workers and duplicate salaries, and preventing fraud. The sound records management provided by this system has also underpinned the salary enhancement scheme.

The political environment has been favorable. The stable and relatively non-competitive political environment with weak trade unions provided ample space for the political level to provide the strong backing required for effective civil service reform. The recent advent of a somewhat more competitive political environment and stronger trade unions has created new issues, in particular an increase in allowances which placed upward pressure on the wage bill.

The wide-ranging public sector reform program provides indications of the type of mechanisms that may be useful in increasing wage-bill flexibility alongside performance budgeting. This has been achieved without creating undue macro-fiscal pressure. In fact, Tanzania has had some success in raising real wage levels and improving incentives while keeping the wage bill stable at around 4 percent of GDP (although further real wage increases planned for coming years are expected to put an upward pressure on the wage bill).

in the future. There are a number of civil service reform mechanisms that have the potential for allowing managers more flexibility within a performance budgeting environment without placing unacceptable risks to macroeconomic control. These include: salary top-ups; delegation of promotion decisions within a rigid grade structure (to avoid unintended upward drift in average salaries); and selective pay scale revisions that reflect Poverty Reduction Strategy Paper priorities and respond to external labor market pressures.

The prevailing political and institutional environment will clearly condition the extent to which the type of mechanisms utilized by OECD countries can be adopted in LICs. Even in the OECD, "modernization depends on context" (OECD, 2005) and a particular mechanism is not readily transferable between different countries. Reforms that increase the flexibility of pay determination heighten the risk of reduced control of the overall level of the wage bill, particularly if the central agencies are not strong enough or politically empowered to enforce crucial elements of the overall package. At the microeconomic level, increasing managerial flexibility in the absence of an effective accountability, incentives, and control package run the risk of intensifying existing problems of political patronage and interference in the civil service. Widespread delegated pay bargaining or running cost budgets are therefore unlikely to be a viable solution to resolving wage inflexibilities in most LICs.

Future attempts at civil service reform in LICs need to draw heavily on the lessons learned from second generation reforms. These lessons are relevant, both for control of the aggregate wage bill and improving performance and flexibility at an agency level:

- *A favorable political environment is the most important prerequisite for civil service reform* (Stevens and Teggemann, 2004). The government needs political space to push through reforms that will inevitably be unpopular in some quarters. Attempting to embark on a substantial reform program in a volatile political climate or with a fragile administration is likely to end in disappointment.
- *Establishment of a strong information base should precede the design of reforms.* An accurate and comprehensive measure of the wage bill and its components is a vital starting point for any program of reform. The measure of the wage bill should include all labor-related costs including base salary, top-ups, allowances, pensions, and costs of contractual labor. Other information should include the composition of the civil service by employment status, grade, occupation, and age. Without this basic information it is impossible to know how structural reforms may affect the ultimate wage bill. Information on private sector remuneration is also important in order to be able to judge the effect that reforms may have on the competitiveness of government wages.
- *A realistic assessment of the institutional context is vital.* It is crucial that the reform program components are appropriate, technically sound, and well-sequenced (Stevens and Teggemann, 2004). Attempting to reform the wage bill without addressing the institutional processes that underlie it is likely to result in failure. In particular, it is unlikely that a move toward fixed-term contracts and performance-based pay will be feasible or productive in the institutional context of most LICs (World Bank, 2002). Institutional processes that, for example, promote wage increases for selected groups of civil servants that spill over into wage demands by other groups need to be considered up front, rather than being dealt with as a complication during the reform process.
- *A reform program needs to be set in a realistic and funded medium-term framework.* Budget constraints for the wage bill, including proposed increases to salary scales or top-ups, need to be realistic in both the short and medium term and have identified financing.
- *Appropriate administrative structures for the management of the public service are crucial, and dismantling centralized institutions for the management of wage and personnel policy may not be feasible in the short term.* Institutional structures

are important and need to be embedded in the core public service (Stevens and Teggemann, 2004). In some African countries (for example, Uganda) this has meant a return to a centralized and semi-independent civil service commission after they were abolished. This has helped to embed the new system and provide a bulwark against political interference in public sector personnel decisions.

- *Implementing performance management systems may not be the most effective means of improving performance.* A World Bank (2003) study of three transition countries (Slovak Republic, Romania, and Kyrgyz Republic) and their differing levels of development and public administration legacies found that meritocracy was the only consistent influence on overall public sector performance. This was particularly so in the two more advanced countries. It also found that a well-functioning system of administrative procedures was crucial in laying the framework for meritocracy. In contrast, the implementation of performance management systems was found to be irrelevant to civil service performance, particularly in the absence of a well-functioning and meritocratic administrative framework.

Notes

1. We gratefully acknowledge invaluable comments from Marc Robinson and participants at the Seminar on Performance Budgeting held at IMF Headquarters (Washington, DC), December 5–7, 2005. All remaining errors, of course, are ours.
2. Although this is not necessarily the case—a reduction in maintenance spending may increase the need for maintenance and investment spending in the future.
3. Kraay and van Rijckeghem (1995) note the role of self-interested public sector employees in long-term wage bill trends. They develop an insider-outsider model of wage negotiation which suggests that public sector employees have the incentive to restrict the growth in employment to ensure that their wage increases and rents are maximized.
4. However, based on a comprehensive cross-country empirical analysis including developed as well as developing countries, Schiavo-Campo et al. (1997) find evidence of a positive relationship between government employment and GDP levels. They also find an association between high wage levels and low levels of government employment, and weak support for positive correlations between deficits and employment.
5. Schiavo-Campo et al. (1997), using slightly different techniques, found a negative relationship between wages and employment and weak support for positive correlations between deficits and employment.
6. Kraay and van Rijckeghem (1995) considered the situation in the mid-1990s, when structural adjustment programs supported by the IMF's Structural Adjustment and Enhanced Structural Adjustment Facilities (SAF and ESAF) focused on medium-term measures aimed at structural reforms, including civil service reforms. IMF-supported stabilization (Stand-By) arrangements generally are of a short duration, and their policy instruments are limited to those that are macroeconomic in nature.
7. Fedelino et al. (2006) also conclude that there is no evidence that such wage bill ceilings have limited government wage spending when donors have made additional resources available.
8. Primary expenditure excludes interest spending, the major item of non-discretionary expenditure in most countries. This allows the analysis to focus on items of expenditure where there is at least some discretion for the government in setting expenditure levels in response to changing macro-fiscal circumstances

9. A similar strategy for assessing the flexibiliy of spending is employed by Mattina and Gunnarsson (forthcoming).
10. But, over the whole sample, changes in the average wage bill over the period are not statistically different from zero at the 5 percent significance level.
11. The convergence of outliers to the middle we observe in our dataset resembles mean reversal, the stochastic process in which outliers tend to return to a common population mean. This suggests that the convergence in wage spending in our sample may be the result of a statistical phenomenon and not deliberate policy choices. However, the key assumption for the observed data trends to be driven by mean reversal is that wage spending across countries would have a common, or "natural," mean and that movements around this mean could be represented as a stochastic process. This key assumption seems obviously not to be met in this case.
12. Shortcomings of the dataset prevent a substantive analysis of whether movements in wage bills are driven by employment or wage changes. The dataset used for this study does not include wage level and employment data. However, findings from the literature suggest that countries have made adjustments to real wage levels to keep the wage bill under control (for example, by letting nominal wage increases lag behind inflation—see Lienert and Modi, 1997). Our sample provides some support for the conjecture that inflation and wage bill adjustment are linked. The correlation between annual consumer price inflation rates and the change in the wage bill as a share of GDP is –0.17 and that between inflation and the wage bill as a share of primary spending is –0.13. Both correlations are statistically significant at the 10 percent confidence level.
13. A striking example is the wide-ranging public sector reforms in New Zealand in the late 1980s, which in many ways led the way for the implementation of performance budgeting in OECD and other countries. The impetus for these reforms stemmed from a significant fiscal crisis that required major reforms both in the level of fiscal balances and the effectiveness with which public resources were utilized.
14. This is despite Uganda achieving one of the most drastic wage decompressions in sub-Saharan Africa. See Kiragu et al. (2004).

References

Baumol, W.J., 1967, "Macroeconomics of Unbalanced Growth: The Anatomy of Urban Crisis," *American Economic Review*, Vol. 57(3), pp. 415–26.

Fedelino, A., G. Schwartz, and M. Verhoeven, 2006, "Aid Scaling Up: Do Wage Bill Ceilings Stand in the Way?" *IMF Working Paper* 06/106 (Washington: International Monetary Fund).

Gupta, S., B. Clements, E. Baldacci, and C. Mulas-Granados, 2002, "Expenditure Composition, Fiscal Adjustment, and Growth in Low-Income Countries," *IMF Working Paper* 02/77 (Washington: International Monetary Fund).

Katz, L., and A. Krueger, 1993, "Public Sector Pay Flexibility: Labor Market and Budgetary Considerations," in *Pay Flexibility in the Public Sector*, OECD Public Management Studies (Paris: OECD).

Kiragu, K., M. Rwekaza, and M. Denyse, 2004, "Reforming Pay Policy: Techniques, Sequencing and Policies," in *Building State Capacity in Africa: New Approaches, Emerging Lessons*, ed. B. Levy and S. Kpundeh (Washington: World Bank).

Kraay, A., and C. van Rijckeghem, 1995, "Employment and Wages in the Public Sector—A Cross Country Study," *IMF Working Paper* 95/70 (Washington: International Monetary Fund).

Lienert, I., and J. Modi, 1997, "A Decade of Civil Service Reform in Sub-Saharan Africa," *IMF Working Paper* 97/179 (Washington: International Monetary Fund).

Maguire, M., 1993, "Pay Flexibility in the Public Sector—An Overview," in *Pay Flexibility in the Public Sector*, OECD Public Management Studies (Paris: OECD).

Manning, C., 2000, "Labor Market Adjustment to Indonesia's Economic Crisis: Context, Trends and Implications," *Bulletin of Indonesian Economic Studies*, Vol. 36(1), pp. 105–36.

Marsden, D., 1993, "Reforming Public Sector Pay," in *Pay Flexibility in the Public Sector*, OECD Public Management Studies (Paris: OECD).

Mattina, T., and V. Gunnarsson, forthcoming, "Budget Rigidity and Expenditure Efficiency in Slovenia," *IMF Working Paper* (Washington: International Monetary Fund).

Meurs, D., 1993, "The Rationale for, and Implications of, Centralized Pay Determination Systems in the Public Sector," in *Pay Flexibility in the Public Sector,* OECD Public Management Studies (Paris: OECD).

OECD, 1993, *Private Pay for Public Work: Performance Related Pay for Public Sector Managers* (Paris: OECD).

——, 1995, *Performance-Related Pay Policies for Government Employees* (Paris: OECD).

——, 2005, *Modernising Government: The Way Forward* (Paris: OECD).

Roberts, J., 2003, "Managing Public Expenditure for Development Results and Poverty Reduction," *ODI Working Paper* 203 (London: Overseas Development Institute).

Ronsholt, F., with R. Mushi, B. Shallanda, and P. Assey, 2003, "Results-Orientated Expenditure Management Country Study—Tanzania," *ODI Working Paper* 204 (London: Overseas Development Institute).

Schiavo-Campo, S., G. de Tommaso, and A. Mukherkee, 1997, "Government Employment and Pay: A Global and Regional Perspective," *World Bank Policy Research Paper* 1771 (Washington: World Bank).

Stevens, M., and S. Teggemann, 2004, "Comparative Experience with Public Sector Reform in Ghana, Uganda and Tanzania," in *Building State Capacity in Africa: New Approaches, Emerging Lessons*, ed. B. Levy and S. Kpundeh (Washington: World Bank).

Williamson, T., 2003, "Targets and Results in Public Sector Management: Uganda Case Study," *ODI Working Paper* 205 (London: Overseas Development Institute).

World Bank, 2002, *Civil Service Reform: Strengthening World Bank and IMF Collaboration* (Washington: World Bank).

——, 2003, PREM Unit, European and Central Asia Region, 2003, *Understanding Public Sector Performance in Transition Countries—An Empirical Contribution* (Washington: World Bank).

Index

Compiled by Sue Carlton